CANADA

A Celebration of our Heritage

J.M.S. Careless

"Partners in Progress" – P.J. Koene

CANADA:
A Celebration of Our Heritage

Published by:
Heritage Publishing House
7160 Baywood Court
Mississauga, Ontario, Canada
L5N 5N6

Layout and Graphic Design by:
Koene Corrales Enterprises

Canadian Cataloguing in Publication Data

Careless, J. M. S., 1919-
    Canada : a celebration of our heritage

Includes index.
ISBN 1-895598-04-4 (tv. 1)
ISBN 1-895598-05-2 (v. 1 : deluxe ed.)

1. Canada - History.   I. Title.

FC164.C26 1994   971   C94-932419-1
F1026.C26 1994

Library of Congress Catalog Number: 94-079470

U.S. mailing address:
352 Finch Court
Big Rapids, MI 49307

Printed and bound in Canada

Overleaf. *Canada's motto "A mari usque ad mare" ("From sea unto sea") was taken from the Judeo-Christian Scripture's Psalm 72:8, which reads, "He [God] shall have dominion also from sea to sea, and from the river unto the ends of the earth." These highly suitable words for a Canadian union were put forward by Samuel Leonard Tilley of New Brunswick in discussions of that union: to be adopted at its outset in 1867. The Arms of the Dominion of Canada were set forth in 1921 by a committee of senior government officials and the College of Arms in Britain, there to be approved and proclaimed by King George V, on November 21, 1921. The three lions in the crest are symbols of England, first used as early as 1198, while the single lion inside the frame is Scottish, and dates before 1285. The Irish harp was adopted about 1541 for the Kingdom of Ireland by King Henry VIII. The fleurs-de-lis were a badge used by the Kings of France since the 12th century. And the maple leaf itself was called the "emblem of Canada" as early as 1805 by* the Quebec Gazette. *It received official status as such in 1868 from Queen Victoria.*

Table of Contents

About the Author

James Maurice Stockford Careless was born in Toronto on February 17, 1919. He earned his B.A. in 1940 from the University of Toronto, and his M.A. in 1941 and Ph.D. in 1950 from Harvard University. He served at the Canadian Naval Headquarters in Ottawa from 1942-43, and the Department of External Affairs from 1943-45 (including voyages to Spain and Sweden in the diplomatic ship "Gripsholm," in 1944, exchanging Allied and German prisoners of war).

He was appointed a Lecturer (History) at the University of Toronto in 1945, Assistant Professor 1949, Associate Professor 1954, Professor 1959 (Chairman of History

James Maurice Stockford Careless, Ph.D., O.C.

Department, 1959-67), and University Professor in 1977. He held the Rockefeller award (to Cambridge University) 1955-56, Carnegie award (to Australian Universities) 1958, visiting Professorship, University of Victoria 1968-69, Senior Research Fellowship, Australian National University, Canberra, 1978. He was appointed University Professor Emeritus, 1984, Senior Fellow Emeritus, Massey College, 1985, Senior Research Associate, Victoria College, 1987, Donald Creighton Lecturer, University of Toronto, 1987.

Careless is the author, or co-author, of numerous works, including *Canada, A Story of Challenge* (1953; Japanese Edition, 1978; latest Edition, 1986), *Brown of the Globe* (2 volumes 1959, 1963), *Union of the Canadas* (1967), *Colonists and Canadians* (1971), *Rise of Cities in Canada* (1978), *PreConfederation Premiers* (1980), *Toronto to 1918* (1984), *Frontier and Metropolis* (1989), *Careless at Work* (1990), and *ONTARIO: A Celebration of Our Heritage* (1991, 1992, 1993). He has published many articles and reviews, in both scholarly and popular journals, and essays in collective volumes.

His numerous distinctions include: Governor General's Award for 1954 and 1964; University of British

Columbia Medal for Biography 1960; Tyrrell Medal, Royal Society of Canada 1962; Cruikshank Medal, Ontario Historical Society 1967; City of Toronto Awards, 1984 and 1985; Doctor of Laws or Letters, Laurentian University 1979, Memorial University 1981, University of Victoria, 1982, Royal Roads, 1983, McMaster, 1983, U.N.B., 1984, Calgary, 1986. He has served as President of the Canadian Historical Association in 1968-69, Fellow Royal Society of Canada since 1962, Chairman Historic Sites and Monuments Board of Canada 1980-85. He was awarded Officer of the Order of Canada, 1981, Order of Ontario, 1987, National Heritage Award, 1987.

His many public services include: Director of the Ontario Heritage Foundation 1975-81 (member of preceding Ontario Historic Sites Board 1954-75); Trustee, Ontario Science Centre 1965-73; Trustee, Ontario Historical Studies Series since 1975; Member, Ontario Commission on Post-Secondary Education, 1969-73; Member, Historic Sites and Monuments Board, 1972-85. He also served as Chairman of the Multicultural History Society of Ontario from 1978-88; co-editor, Canadian Historical Review 1948-58; advisor, National Film Board historical series 1961-66; consultant, National Museum of Man urban historical series 1976-82; and variously of numbers of CBC and TVO radio or television scripts. He also served as Chairman of the Ontario Historical Studies Series since 1982.

J.M.S. Careless has travelled and lectured in Canada, United States, Great Britain, Australia, India, and Japan. He has served as the Canadian editor for the *Book of Knowledge*, and participated in varied radio and television programs, as well as maintaining a major concern with teaching and writing Canadian History.

Foreword

Canadians have traditionally worn their patriotism in muted tones, rarely daring to offer any bright display attesting to their pride of country. We may, therefore, well wonder if the pages of Canadian history are as bereft of heroes as our November landscapes are of colour. Is it really that we have so few heroes to stir our patriotic fervour or is it, rather, that our heroes are traditionally unsung? *Canada: A Celebration of our Heritage* offers a rich panorama of the often forgotten people and circumstances that have shaped our nation.

If we were to consider the men and women who created a thriving, multihued nation from a geography so physically challenging that the very act of survival was an accomplishment in itself, we would quickly discover a kaleidoscope of fascinating individuals. However, it is not only to the past that we must look in seeking those who have had a major imprint on the social, cultural and political fabric of our land, but also to the present and future. As the distinguished Canadian historian, Donald Creighton commented, "Heroism is not a memory of the past. It is the virtue by which a nation can preserve its identity and fulfill its destiny." Canada continues to offer the world Nobel Prize laureates and internationally renowned experts, as well as world-class athletes and performers. It rejoices when its space arm flies as an inherent part of an American spaceship and when its expertise in telecommunications is sought around the world. It takes pride when its authors are read and its artists recognized around the world.

In 1974, the Montreal novelist, Hugh MacLennan

**His Excellency The Right Honourable
Ramon John Hnatyshyn
Governor General of Canada, 1990-1995**

remarked: "Ours is not the only nation which has outtravelled its own soul and now is forced to search frantically for a new identity. No wonder, for so many, the past Canadian experience has become not so much a forgotten thing as an unknown thing." In recognizing Canada's 125th anniversary in 1992, Canadians continued their journey of self-discovery along the challenging path of national identity by giving expression to the sense of pride which they had slowly but gradually nurtured over the years through the celebration of their country's historic milestones. We have also learned to cherish the majestic images of our geography, have learned to enjoy the vigour of our traditions and have learned to appreciate the rich tapestry of people and events that have enriched our heritage.

Canada, with its own variegated history, has traced a unique record of its progress as a state. As we turn the pages of *Canada: A Celebration of our Heritage*, let us move on to the next exciting chapter in our history, keeping in mind that there are many untapped resources, both human and natural, which are yet to be explored to their full potential. Sir Wilfrid Laurier declared that the twentieth century belonged to Canada: his bold prediction will be carried forward to the first century of the next millennium.

Ramon John Hnatyshyn

Chapter One
The Giant Land

Heritage and History

Many heritages would join in shaping Canada's history, in all its sweep and rich variety. There were the age-old legacies of its native peoples, Indian or Inuit; the major bequests laid down by transatlantic newcomers from Britain or France, who first began arriving close on five centuries ago; the valuable endowments brought by later arrivals from other parts of Europe or America; and most recently, from still more distant areas spread far around the globe. Nor were these ethnic contributions all. Distinctive political, social and cultural traditions themselves emerged within the rising Canadian national domain in North America. No less distinctive economic activities and interests developed in each of the great regions which together formed a country more than half the continent in size. And yet, behind these growing national or regional patterns — and beyond all the other human inheritances that shared in making Canada — one further moulding factor was ceaselessly at work: the natural heritage bestowed by the giant land itself, by the vast Canadian environment.

That environmental heritage most strikingly appeared in the grandeur of soaring mountains, the majestic thrust of waterways, or in the huge expanses of territory which stretched from the same latitude as the northern border of California to icebound islands edging polar seas. That natural inheritance appeared as well in the stored-up wealth of soil, mineral and energy resources, in abundant plant, forest, and animal life, not to mention teeming fisheries off both the Atlantic and Pacific coasts. But the forces of the Canadian environment were equally displayed in massive geographical barriers across the land, in stiff restraints of climate, and over all, in stern limits set on human dealings with a difficult physical world. For now the main point is, however, that meeting the challenges of the land to gain its bounties composed a basic theme that would run right through Canadian history, in every region of the country. This was as true for Inuit hunting families ranging primeval Arctic wilds as for seventeenth-century English fishermen settling into rugged Newfoundland; for

Overleaf. The Canadian Landmass. *As photographed by satellite from space, and showing its chief natural outlines, vegetation cover and huge, continental scope.*
Atlantic Lighthouse. *Towers of this kind would come to guard Canada's Atlantic coasts, marking their cliffs and rocks, which often screened safe inlets and good harbours. The particular tower displayed is of a nineteenth-century lighthouse station at Forteau, on the Labrador coast.*

early French fur-traders probing up the long St. Lawrence-Great Lakes water system as for Ukrainian immigrants of the young twentieth century carving out farms on open western plains. It was just as true for miners, ranchers and loggers who penetrated the far west mountain region and steep Pacific slopes. Over all, Canada's varied human elements from different backgrounds constantly had to adapt and respond to the demanding problems of environment. That, indeed, is rooted in Canadian experience. We simply need to be reminded of it by history — once again today.

Accordingly, the course of that history can best be introduced here, at the start, by looking at each of the great Canadian regions in which it grew, surveying them in turn from the Atlantic to the Pacific. Archaeology does indicate that the original native peoples of Canada (or rather, their remote ancestors) came the other way: crossing from Asia to Alaska perhaps more than ten thousand years ago, during the last ice age, when a land bridge extended between Siberia and Alaska. Over more thousands of years they spread on into the Americas. And as the enormous ice sheets melted, their hunting cultures occupied the Canadian land-mass from Arctic to Atlantic. The archaeological record of this oldest human heritage in Canada now lies in the ground, while the present native peoples form living testimony to the prehistoric past. And yet the Canada we know today is crucially a historic product of the far later arrival of Europeans around 1500 A.D., to start their own advance westward across the continent. More than that, these European venturers brought the art of writing as we know it, and thus recorded history, for better or worse to replace vague ages of prehistoric time. And so our own opening survey of Canada's environmental heritage in history will start, as did the intruders from Europe, with the Atlantic region; and then move west from there.

The Main Physical Divisions of Canada (as shown on a map drawn before 1949). *The titles shown on the map are listed with alternatives, also widely employed.*

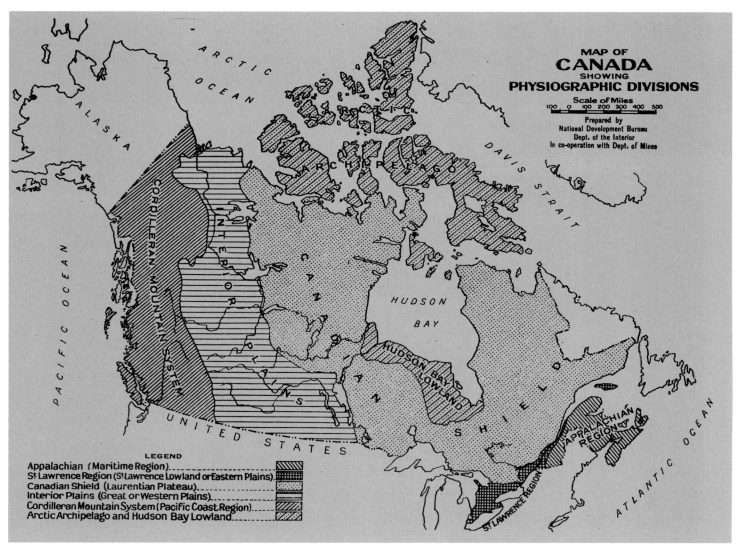

Aspects of the Giant Land.
1. *Eastern Approaches*
2. *Autumn Inlands*
3. *River Highway*
4. *Shield Country*
5. *Native Inhabitants — Woods*
6. *Native Inhabitants — Waterside*
7. *Polar Bears on Hudson Bay*
8. *Forest North*
9. *Cordilleran Mountains*
10. *Great Western Plains*
11. *West Coast Rain-Forest*
12. *National Emblem*

3

1

4

2

5

6

7

8

9

10

11

12

Environment and Canadian Regions

In terms of history, Atlantic Canada would come to include the coastal or Maritime provinces of Nova Scotia, New Brunswick and little Prince Edward Island, along with the big sea-isle of Newfoundland that lay across the ocean approaches to the mainland. In environmental terms instead, this was a region of ancient, worn-down mountains, lined with valleys which the sea had penetrated deeply, past jutting headlands into sheltered coves and harbours. Inland, the valleys were hemmed by high rock ridges, rough, hard terrain that in New Brunswick rose northward to the crests of the Appalachian ranges, a formidable barrier between the Atlantic region and the rest of Canada beyond. But seaward, the open waters gave ready access all around the shores, or carried Maritime and Newfoundland ships to Old or New England, to the Caribbean and the Mediterranean as well. The chief cities of the region were seaports first and foremost: St. John's, closest to Europe on the eastern edge of Newfoundland, Halifax, the main naval base fronting Nova Scotia, or busy, ship-building Saint John on New Brunswick's southern shore. Moreover, prolific fishing grounds along the coastline, extending far out into the Atlantic off Newfoundland, supplied a basic livelihood for the hardy peoples who developed in this sea-domain. Saltwater and safe harbours, fishing and ocean commerce, would enter vitally into the Canadian Atlantic heritage.

Nevertheless, the land, too, offered its returns. Aside from pockets of good agricultural soils scattered through it, there was the long and lovely Annapolis Valley of western Nova Scotia, where thriving farms stretched far along the slopes of the North and South Mountains that guarded it on either side. Or there were the fertile "intervales" that bordered the Saint John, Atlantic Canada's greatest river, which rose in the Appalachian highlands, flowed down the western side of New Brunswick through picture-perfect country, and emptied into the Bay of Fundy by the city of Saint John. Above all, there was Prince Edward Island, the "million-acre farm": a pastoral isle of gentle hills, lush green fields, red soil and sandy shores, set like a gem amid the blue Gulf of St. Lawrence.

It was still the case that a good deal of the Atlantic territory would not favour agriculture. Given the frequently thin soils and cool, damp oceanic climate, farmsteads in the region — especially in Newfoundland — were often limited to root or fodder crops and pastures; largely serving just to supplement fishing and other pursuits. Yet there were also mineral riches within the land which would be tapped in Nova Scotian coalfields, particularly on Cape Breton Island, iron and copper ores in Newfoundland, or coal and base metals in New Brunswick. Much more extensive activities, however, were to arise in lumbering: through cutting timber or pulpwood from the vast evergreen forests that covered so much of this Atlantic area.

The cutting of trees that had taken centuries to grow, even in a moist, cool climate, often left only scrubby bush behind them. A resource which indeed looked inexhaustible for many years proved, ultimately, not to be so. Yet

1. St. John's, Newfoundland. *This print from around 1879 shows neither the early times of shipping at this harbour, used by European fishermen from the opening 1500s, nor its present, built-up cityscape. Still, it does convey some lasting features of the historic Atlantic port; such as the steep cliff-face along its one side, allowing only a fringe of wharfs and buildings, while on the other, there is much wider space for docks and the town itself, which then rises up the nearby hillslopes. At the right-hand bottom corner of the picture is Signal Hill, facing out to sea and topped by the flags of a ship-signalling station. And vessels are seen proceeding out the harbour gateway to the open ocean.*

2. Low Tide on Fundy. *This early photograph of the 1860s shows the effect of Atlantic tides on the long, shallow, and relatively narrow Bay of Fundy. A rising tide rushes high up the funnel of the Bay. A falling tide sinks no less fast and far — leaving small craft stranded near the shore until the tide turns round again.*

1

2

1

2

3

4

1. Inland Countryside behind Halifax. *This painting, done about 1810, looks northward over rolling country toward Bedford Basin, a broad sheet of water behind Halifax harbour, where ships could anchor in numbers — and where great convoys might be marshalled for naval escort overseas, from the Napoleonic wars to the Second World War.*

2. Entry from the Bay of Fundy to Saint John, New Brunswick. *Here a watercolour of 1835 depicts two sailing ships — British and American, come to trade at the busy port — while Partridge Island looms in the background. This island, which received Saint John's first lighthouse in 1791, would also become a landing place and hospital for streams of poor Irish immigrants in the late 1840s, many of whom died here of cholera or typhus, during a bitterly dark time in transatlantic migration.*

3. Haying Scene near St. John, New Brunswick. View of Retreat Farm at Windsor, Nova Scotia. *Windsor, a thriving port off the Minas Basin at the head of Fundy, was a fairly early English-speaking Nova Scotian settlement (1764), though Acadian French colonists had dwelt here from 1684. The surrounding countryside is well illustrated by this pastoral scene, drawn in 1839.*

4. View of Retreat Farm at Windsor, Nova Scotia. *Windsor, a thriving port off the Minas Basin at the head of Fundy, was a fairly early English-speaking Nova Scotian settlement (1764), though Acadian French colonists had dwelt here from 1684. The surrounding countryside is well illustrated by this pastoral scene, drawn in 1839.*

5. Sunny Side Stock Farm, Prince Edward Island. *The picture presents a successful farming venture of the 1870s on the fertile garden lands of this favoured Maritime isle.*

"SUNNY SIDE STOCK FARM" RES. OF ROBT FITZSIMONS, LONG RIVER, NEW LONDON, LOT 20, P.E.I.

ROBT. FITZSIMONS ESQ.

5

lumbering would nevertheless long flourish in Atlantic Canada, and especially in New Brunswick. In Newfoundland, the shore forests were fairly early cut off for fuel, shelter and ship-building, while the interior of the island proved difficult of access, thanks to its steep rock barrens, and tangled, marshy lowlands. Nova Scotia — with no wide inlands — also saw more limited lumbering activities. But in New Brunswick, spreading well northward to the Appalachian barrier, there were broad pine forests of superb height and prime value: made accessible to lumbermen by major waterways like the Saint John or Mirimichi that carried the big timber out for export overseas. And so Atlantic Canada, because of its environment, also built a celebrated lumber heritage; from Paul Bunyan, the giant woodsman hero of lumber-camp legends, to the very real mills, ships and business fortunes that appeared around the coasts.

So much for the Atlantic lands — if hardly sufficient still. Beyond them, on the other side of the Appalachian barrier, the great St. Lawrence River stretched from the Gulf of St. Lawrence westward into the very core of the continent. Along the farspread lower river, its shores were but distant lines seen across the surging waters. Yet by the time the site of the present city of Quebec was reached (already well upstream) the shores were closing in; though still wide apart by the standards of more usually "big" rivers. From here, from Quebec to the site of Montreal, the St. Lawrence flowed in mid-course through broadly fertile countrysides that rolled down to its banks: the heartland of rural French Canada to be, and of the future, powerful province of Quebec. Then above Montreal, where the Ottawa plunged down from the northwest to join the main river, the upper St. Lawrence took its own way west, past foaming rapids and rocky islets until it came to Lake Ontario, and the start of the whole magnificent chain of the Great Lakes.

The river itself here ended, in what would ultimately become the province of Ontario. Yet the great water highway ran right on: through Lakes Ontario, Erie and St. Clair, across the Upper Lakes, Huron and Superior, to cease at last just west of the head of mighty Lake Superior. At that limit, however, other nearby streams opened further routes onward to west and north; even across the wide interior plains and into the Rocky Mountains. In sum, this all-important St. Lawrence-Great Lakes pathway of communications offered a trunkline that could link much of the giant Canadian land-mass together — beginning with transport by canoes, moving on to sailing craft and steamboats, then to railroads and automotive highways. Here was a fundamental gift of the environment that all but destined Canada to become a vast nation.

Around this key St. Lawrence artery lay one of the most significant natural regions in Canada: the St. Lawrence Lowlands. This long reach of favoured territory, favoured in soil, climate and location, extended in a fairly narrow band for some 1,500 km., from the vicinity of Quebec City to the southwestern tip of the present province of Ontario along the Detroit River and Lake St. Clair. Thus

1. Cape Breton Coal Mine. *The photograph dates from the 1900s at Inverness. But coal workings on this rugged Nova Scotian island had developed long before.*

2. Falls in the St. John River. *A violent stretch of torrent, portraying the great streams that early carried down much of New Brunswick's lumber for export overseas.*

1

2

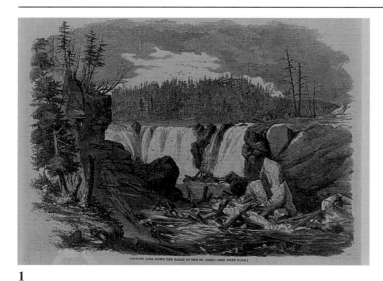

1

2

3

1. Driving Logs past the Falls of the St. John. *A graphic engraving of the 1850s, showing the dangerous work of "river-drivers."*

2. Lumber Rafts at the Junction of the St. Lawrence and Ottawa, early 1840s. *The growth of lumbering in Central Canada, along the Ottawa in particular, soon came to rival that enterprise in Atlantic Canada, principally based in New Brunswick. This picture is just one in a series of celebrated engravings by W.M. Bartlett, published in* Canadian Scenery, *1842.*

3. The St. Lawrence Ice-Bridge at Quebec, 1831. *When winter froze the great river between Quebec City and Lévis on the south shore, the "bridge" thus formed invited popular activity.*

4. Curling on the St. Lawrence in 1855. *A Scottish-derived but increasingly Canadian winter sport, here played on river ice in front of the leading commercial city, Montreal.*

5. Niagara Falls, by James Erskine, about 1784. *Here the swirling outflow from Lake Erie and the Upper Great Lakes crashes over the Falls to reach Lake Ontario. Niagara ("thunder of water") was not just a mighty transport barrier where Indian canoes had to portage, and ship canals be built in later days. It also became a main crossroads on inland communications, an area of rich farmlands in a rising Ontario; and it would provide a commanding source of hydro-electric power, besides, for industrial Ontario of the twentieth century.*

6. Pioneer Farm Clearing in Upper Canada, 1830s. *This frontier farm lay in the mild and fertile reaches of southwestern Ontario, within the broad Great-Lakes peninsula that stretch between Lakes Erie and Huron. Decidious native hardwood forests of the area enclose the whole scene.*

4

5

6

1. Toronto, Ontario Focus. *Founded in 1793 as the village of York, it grew as capital of the province of Upper Canada (later Ontario), and by the 1850s was second only to Montreal as a chief Canadian city. By the date of this picture (1854) Toronto was already on the verge, as well, of major railway and industrial development.*

2. London, in the Ontario Peninsula. *Seen here in the 1850s, the emerging town located on the Thames River would steadily flourish as a market and service centre for the prosperous agricultural community all around it.*

3. Mount McKay at the tip of Lake Superior, 1866. *This looming height above the Kaministiquia River, where Fort William arose as a major fur-trade headquarters after 1803, effectively marked the transport shift from the long St. Lawrence-Great Lakes water highway to smaller inland rivers which penetrate onward into the western interior of North America.*

4. Swampy Areas in the Precambrian Shield. *Along with sweeping granite crests and thick evergreen forests, the Shield region is also full of low-lying swamps or muskegs, often troublesome obstacles to transport — not to mention the bush flies and mosquitos that can accompany them.*

this strip would come to hold the most populous and closely developed parts of central Canada — Southern Quebec and Southern Ontario. Its tall stands of oaks, elms, maples and other deciduous trees early led to prosperous lumbering. Its ample rainfall and mild climate (by Canadian standards, but notably so in the "sun parlour" districts from the Niagara Peninsula on westward above Lake Erie) fostered high-value farming on the region's generally good soils. And the close presence of the St. Lawrence-Great Lakes water highway gave it effective access to outside markets and supplies. As a result, the St. Lawrence Valley and inter-lake plain produced solidly thriving farms and rural businesses; and, over time, populous, large cities like Quebec, Montreal and Ottawa, Toronto, Hamilton or London, along with major concentrations of industry and wealth. Compared with the total vastness of Canada beyond, this was a rather limited territory. Yet thanks especially to environmental factors, the St. Lawrence Lowlands would emerge in history as the country's most powerful and centrally dominant area.

Nevertheless, to northward — beyond well-groomed farmlands that would raise peaches, grapes and corn, as well as apples, grain or dairy herds — past quiet, tree-shaded towns of stone or brick, or crowded cities pulsing with factories and traffic — there was and is a far, far wider realm of outthrust ancient rock, high, rolling ridges and dense evergreen forest, of dark muskeg swamps and countless lonely lakes: the Precambrian Shield. Here is an enormous natural region immeasurably older than the last ice age, which covers most of the province of Quebec above the St. Lawrence Valley right from the Atlantic coasts of Labrador to Hudson and James Bays, extends onward through Northern Ontario and spans the upper half of Manitoba as well. Across Northern Ontario and into Manitoba, the Hudson Bay Lowlands edge the north side of this Precambrian mass. They are clothed in woods and bush much like the Shield country, but are generally low and flat, without great rocky outcrops. Then the Shield itself sweeps on to west and north beyond Manitoba, curving up towards the Arctic Ocean. The whole Precambrian region is hence much bigger than the

1

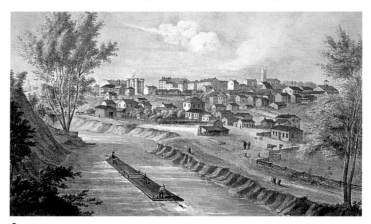

2

3

4

two big provinces of Quebec and Ontario, although it forms by far the largest part of each of them.

And the Precambrian Shield would prove vital in moulding Canada. Its abundance of fur-bearing animals, particularly the beaver, strongly shaped the historic fur-trade: a collaboration of native peoples and European venturers which would span the continent to Arctic and Pacific. The Shield's mineral riches (in gold, silver, copper, nickel, uranium and much more) would give this rugged land still greater value; as would its water wealth of lakes, streams and hydro-electric potential. Moreover, its forest resources in all kinds of lumber, and in pulpwood used for paper-making, were to gain international importance in Canadian trade. But still further, the dramatic brilliance of the Precambrian landscape — of towering granite bluffs, deep forests glinting under sun or snow, of racing waters, quiet lakes and sparkling air — would inspire a whole succession of artists, authors and nationalists, who found the very essence of Canada in this True North strong and free.

In more specific ways, the Shield country of both Quebec and Ontario played a major role in their own historic development within Canada. Indeed, it made each province a virtual empire with its own great northern resource-domain to exploit. Hence, out of this North Country and down to the dominating St. Lawrence Lowlands, flowed fur, timber and pulp supplies; precious or base metals, electric power and still more. In return, whether as fair exchange or not, the North got investment capital, markets and technology, settlers, expertise and infrastructure. Consequently, in Northern Quebec big pulpwood and metal complexes appeared from Lac St. Jean and Chicoutimi (up the broad Saguenay well east of Quebec City) to Noranda-Rouyn on the Quebec-Ontario margins, where gold-copper mines would long bulk large. In Northern Ontario, aside from silver and gold finds near the Quebec border, mining centres spread west to the Sudbury Basin, a focus of world-ranking nickel production; to iron mines that fed the steel mills at Sault Ste. Marie on the Upper Lakes transport system, and to further iron fields or other mineral workings north and west of Lake Superior. Moreover, the Ottawa Valley also developed as a major route into the tremendous pine and spruce, birch and hemlock stands across the Shield; while in general terms, the forest and mineral heritages of both Quebec and Ontario would play a large part in making them the leading provinces they were to become in Canada, on down to the present day.

All this can only sketch the regional environment of Central Canada — occupied by two provinces, Quebec and Ontario, that shared much the same basic geography, but would be shaped in history by different French or English-speaking heritages. It is time, however, to move our survey further

1. Young Birch Woods. *Paper birch, much-used by native peoples for covering canoes, grew widely across the Shield. Indeed, proliferating birches often spread as well on abandoned bush farms in the north, which were unsuccessful settlers' efforts to raise field crops on too-thin soils.*

2. Thunder Cape on Lake Superior, 1867. *A towering outthrust of Shield rock, it stands at Thunder Bay, where the town of Port Arthur developed from the 1870s. A century later, that town was to be combined with neighbouring, older, Fort William in the single Lakehead city of Thunder Bay.*

3. Buttonwood Tree (Sycamore) near Chatham, 1840. *The largest kind of southern Canadian hardwood, depicted in warm peninsula-Ontario surroundings, thus suggests how far that area reaches southward into the continental core of North America.*

1

2   3

westward, to the Great Plains region of Canada, popularly termed "the Prairies." Layered deep in fertile soil, once the bed of ancient seas, this huge plains territory stretches northward from the American border between the Shield and the Rocky Mountains, across the "Prairie" provinces of Manitoba, Saskatchewan and Alberta, and on through the North West Territories to the Arctic tundra. But here was no monotonous, unvaried, flat expanse. In the south lay actual prairie, a treeless grassland widely suitable for raising cereals like wheat; sometimes level, but very often boldly rolling country. In southwestern Saskatchewan the prairies thus rose into the high and beautiful Cypress Hills; in western Alberta, their grassy foothills climbed up towards the Rockies, offering open range for thousands of head of cattle; while east on the Manitoba plains they edged broad waters like shimmering Lake Winnipeg. And north of flowery prairie meadows spread the parklands belt, with its sheltering groves of trees to invite farm settlement. Beyond again, were full northern forests of evergreens, finally ending in subarctic bush and tundra. In truth, the Great Plains offered plentiful variety.

Yet some things were present there throughout. There was a sense of unlimited space, where crystal-clear horizons reached to the very curve of the globe; an awareness of sky, enormously arching, that foretold sun or storm, frost or blizzard, to hunting Indians or pioneering farmers alike exposed to a natural immensity beyond control. And there was distance and isolation, to draw small human beings together in common efforts amid the awesome sweep of plains. Here, then, was another Canada, too little perceived by those beyond it; but perhaps also leading those within it not to look very much outside.

The plains country could be harsh in climate, for all its deep fertility. Hot summers, at times with scorching months of drought, or bitter, windswept winters, might gravely damage western farm crops; while distance from export markets could impose costs and uncertainties on even bumper harvests. Nonetheless, this mid-continental land became and remained a world wheat granary, where a host of little grain-elevator hamlets served farmers and collected

1. Driving Lumber in Northern Quebec. *A typical Shield activity, whether for building lumber or pulp-wood — which here shows lumberjacks working at the start of a river drive.*

2. Hard-Rock Mining Underground. *A diamond drill in the highly productive Hollinger gold mine at Porcupine in Northern Ontario, which began its long-lasting output back before the First World War.*

3. Northern Reaches of the Shield. *This 1899 photograph of Quebec's Subarctic coasts on Hudson Bay, reveals the basic rock-mass of the Precambrian region, without any cloaking forests. And its grim, bleak grandeur is not at all relieved by the single sailing ship, or the few human places visible on land.*

4. Snow Scene on Hudson Bay, Quebec Coast. *Except to note the man on the big "snow-dune," no comment seems necessary here!*

1

2

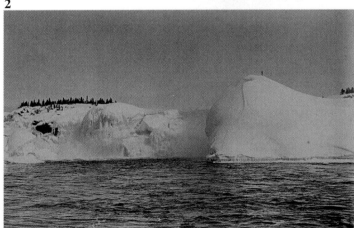

3

4

1

2

1. Winnipeg, Portage and Main in 1872. *This main downtown intersection today is dominated by skyscrapers in the modern Manitoba metropolis. But here the famous crossroads are seen one year before Winnipeg, booming with new prairie settlement, became a city — more in hope than in reality, that far.*

2. A Manitoba Farmstead. *Portraying the prairie home of established grain-farming settlers, who (from the dress shown) most likely stemmed from the waves of European migrants who came into the Plains through the late nineteenth into the early twentieth century.*

3. Prairie Grain Elevator. *These were the towers of the wheat-farming West which went up at collecting-points along railway lines, to store the golden harvests of the Plains for shipment on to eastern and overseas markets.*

4. Lake Winnipeg Shore, by Peter Rindisbacher. *A Swiss-born painter, he spent five years in the young Red River Colony on the Western Plains, arriving there in 1821 to make one of the earliest pictorial records of the country west of the Great Lakes in future Canada.*

5. Crossing Saskatchewan Plains in Winter. *This illustration from W.F. Butler's* Great Lone Land, *1881, makes all too evident what travel by cart-trail could be like on the open prairies, at least amid the rage of blizzards.*

6. Regina, 1884. *A new Plains town, rising with the first Canadian transcontinental railway, the Canadian Pacific, then building across the prairies westward: a town to be the capital of the farming province of Saskatchewan erected in 1905.*

3

4

5

6

their prairie gold to forward to market. In modern eras it has been chiefly linked to outside supplies and markets by the transcontinental railway lines, though automotive highways now play their part. But far earlier, in aboriginal ages and through fur-trading days, main water routes were vital: like the Saskatchewan River, whose long North and South Branches cross the plains from the Rockies and ultimately feed into Hudson Bay; or the mighty Mackenzie, the longest river in North America after the Mississippi, which stems from tributaries in northern Alberta, then runs northward from Great Slave Lake across the North West Territories to empty through the wide Mackenzie delta into the Arctic Ocean. Riverways and open prairies hence made the Great Plains widely traversable; whether for their original native peoples or the European newcomers who followed them.

In time, the course of history enlarged the region's economic activities. Wheat-farming would unquestionably remain basic, from southern Manitoba to the Peace River country of northern Alberta; though crops like sugar beets and canola (used considerably for its edible oil) also brought more diversity to agriculture. Cattle-ranching, besides, flourished from the Alberta foothills back into Saskatchewan; while lumbering advanced in more northern forest areas, and even commercial fishing was far from insignificant in major freshwaters like Lake Winnipeg. Above all, however, large-scale mining activities developed as well. The plains assuredly would yield great quantities of oil and natural gas (especially but by no means exclusively in Alberta), of potash and uranium in Saskatchewan, and metal ores notably in Manitoba. Furthermore, manufacturing and service industries grew also in major cities of the region. Among these are Winnipeg, Manitoba's transport gateway to the Plains West; Regina and Saskatoon, the top commercial centres in Saskatchewan; Edmonton, Alberta's key to the wide North above it; and Calgary, chief focus of the foothills, initially of the cattle trade, but now of the high financial world of Canadian oil. Together such leading cities express the present drive and power of the Prairie provinces, grown far from their pioneer beginnings. Beyond that, these urban places still mark the geography and history of the Great Plains, which always loom so tellingly around them.

West of the Plains, the mountainous Cordilleran region extends to the Pacific. The Cordilleras, enormous chains of mountains, march up the whole western side of the Americas: from the bottom of South America along the colossal Andes to Central America and Mexico, on across the western United States to Canada, and then north through the province of British Columbia and

View of the Rocky Mountains, 1887.
The work of Lucius O'Brien, a leading Ontario artist who was sponsored by the C.P.R. to record the majesty of landscape along its newly opened transwestern line.

the Yukon Territory to end at last near the Arctic shores of Yukon and Alaska. In Canada, the heights of the Rocky Mountains (the easternmost and loftiest of the North American ranges) form both the continental divide between Atlantic- and Pacific-flowing waters, and the boundary line between Alberta and British Columbia. Beyond these snow-crowned mountains, and within British Columbia, lies the low Rocky Mountain Trench — a slash of wide open valley that reaches from below the Montana border nearly up to the Yukon, and provides streambeds for giant westward-flowing rivers. Chief of these are the Columbia, whose long, curving course finally takes it out to the Pacific through the American State of Washington; and the turbulent Fraser, which turns north, then west, to break through further mountain ranges and reach the British Columbian coast. But beyond the Rocky Mountain Trench, the further ranges westward include the Selkirks, the Purcells and the Cariboo. Then comes the high Interior Plateau of central British Columbia, broad, dry uplands sometimes wooded, but widely supplying good ranching country. Beyond again, other towering peaks rise in the Coast Mountains that edge the Pacific shores of British Columbia. Even this is not the total. On Vancouver Island, the big forested isle just off the mainland, more mountains climb; as they do in the faraway and lovely Queen Charlotte Islands farther northward up the Pacific coastline.

The rugged Pacific Coast, a domain of giant trees, spectacular fiords and rich fishing grounds, is virtually a natural region in itself. Here prevailing winds off the Pacific shed their rain clouds on the coastal mountain slopes, to support a

1. Ranch in the Rockies. *Painted by Edward Roper a few years later, it focuses on a more human setting, with the great mountains as a background.*
2. Gold Miners in the Cariboo. *The gold rush of the 1860s to the Cariboo country further westward helped open interior British Columbia to mining settlement; as even this crude, canyon-wall miners' shack can indicate.*
3. Cochrane in the Southern Alberta Foothills. *Here, along the western side of Alberta, the Plains rise up towards the Rocky Mountains, and here cattle-raising on the rolling grasslands would widely take over from wheat-growing.*
4. Columbia River Canyon near Revelstoke, B.C. *This photograph of the long Columbia, which flows out of the Rocky Mountain Trench to reach the Pacific, conveys something of the ever-challenging Cordilleran country — just beyond its easternmost range, the Rockies, but with more huge barrier ranges still ahead.*

1

2

3

4

1. Coastal Rain-Forest. *The moist, mild Pacific Coast produced masses of great trees — here seen with a 1920s lumberman (West Coast, "logger") who apparently aims at taking them down.*

2. The Cariboo Road *was a spectacular wagon route built along the Fraser River into the ranges, to supply the "gold diggings" from the West Coast of British Columbia: a costly effort, but vital in itself.*

3. Camping-Ground at Dawson, Yukon, in the Klondike Rush of 1898. *There were many further gold finds in the Cordilleran Mountain region, from the Fraser and Cariboo far northward to the Yukon wilds above B.C. Some proved just "flashes in the pan" (like the show of gold-colour in miners' washing-pans). Others brought big new rushes, such as this scramble to the Klondike district in the Yukon — to fill in Far Western settlement still further.*

1

temperate rainforest of monumental Douglas firs, western cedars and other luxuriant growths. On southern Vancouver Island in particular — set in a sun pocket behind the Island range — British Columbia's capital, Victoria, enjoys the earliest springtimes in Canada, with a profusion of flowers that lasts practically around the year. On the nearby mainland, the West Coast business metropolis of Vancouver has much the same mild climate, if somewhat wetter, amid its own surrounding bowl of mountains. But inland, past the fertile Fraser delta and Lower Mainland area that centres on Vancouver, the steep mountain country of snowfields, crags and high plateaus presents a much harsher, colder terrain. Hence travel across the Cordilleran region has always involved formidable difficulties and exacting transport costs.

Mountain rivers could be too violent to navigate. Indian bands and fur-traders' pack trains then picked their way instead along narrow canyon trails, and climbed overland through high passes that might well become blocked by winter snows. The transcontinental railways that came later still had to deal with steep gradients and high running costs (thus the "mountain differential" on their rates); not to mention expensive tunnelling and massive snow-sheds to ward off avalanches. And still later, trunk highways might no less be swept and blocked by snowfalls — as from time to time they have been. Travel north-south, along valleys between the ranges, could be relatively easy by comparison. But east-west linkages were something else: which inevitably had a major impact through Canadian history, not only on problems of binding a whole transcontinental union together, but on the relative separation of the Far West behind its mountain ramparts.

Still, the valleylands between the ranges were often warmly sheltered and well-watered; while irrigation from mountain streams above could spread croplands further up high, semi-arid slopes. This was certainly the case in the Okanagan districts of the interior, where grapes, peaches, apples and other fruit would most successfully be cultivated. And so, although the Cordilleran region, over all, could not become a major agricultural area like the Great Plains, it did develop remarkably productive farming, often specialized and of high worth. As well as farming, of course, widespread ranching grew across the interior uplands from early years of settlement. But mining would prove still more historically important — in launching both British Columbia and the Yukon as organized territories. Gold strikes up the Fraser River, then on into the Cariboo country, led to the very creation of the province of British Columbia in the mid-nineteenth century; while the world-famed Klondike gold rush northward late in the century brought the Yukon Territory into being. Major gold finds in time subsided (though there were others right across the region), while less dramatic mining activities took on increasing and more enduring weight: from silver-lead mines and coal fields in the British Columbian interior to copper in the Yukon. Particularly, the great smelters at Trail near the inland American border, and the

2

3

lead-zinc-silver deposits at Kimberley in the Kootenay mountains of the south-east, attained world-wide significance. Cordilleran rock was mineral-rich. Hence the region's history was constantly to be related to its mining heritage.

That history would equally relate to Far Western logging: a west-coast term that came effectively to replace "lumbering" throughout the region. Logging within the interior, in long, forested valleys or in various wooded upland areas, would prove very far from negligible, well up to Prince George, B.C. Yet logging in the great coastal rain forests bulked a good deal larger. Here the mammoth trees were cut and dropped into ocean fiords, for shipping by tug-drawn rafts to coastal or island mills. But the early years of hauling the timber down to waterline by oxen led on to steam "donkey-engines," or to logging railways that took out still more of the giant wood. Today heavy trucks on logging roads handle the task. Still, it all adds up to another West Coast use of costly (if crucial) means of transport to carry its resources out to world markets far beyond. Fishing, too, especially for salmon in bountiful coastal waters, further came to serve world markets. The can of "B.C. Salmon" would become well known from Europe to Australia.

Apart from West Coast mining, logging and fishing, sizeable processing and industrial activities also developed across the area, most fully in Vancouver. Wood-working plants and lumber mills, fish canneries, shipyards and other factory enterprises, would appear from Vancouver or Victoria to Prince Rupert on the Skeena, well north along the Pacific coast. But the chief transport, commercial and investment services within this wealthy region — pushing its interests well eastward into the Prairies — centred in Vancouver's skyscrapers

1. Victoria, Island Gate to the British Columbia Mainland, 1879. *Venturers into young British Columbia largely arrived by sea; and especially through this growing town on Vancouver Island, which developed out of a fur-trade Fort Victoria founded in 1843. Victoria rose particularly in gold-rush days from the 1850s; but it also became capital of British Columbia, and thrived as well on shipping, logging and fishing. Still further, set as it is in a southern sun-pocket of beautiful Vancouver Island, Victoria enjoys one of the mildest climates in Canada, and over the years would decidedly benefit from tourism.*
2. Early Logging with Oxen on Vancouver Island. *The picture displays both the size of West Coast logs and the hard way of shifting them down to water, just with ox-teams.*
3. Steam-Logging — A Better Way. *Here is later technology: a train-load of hefty Douglas firs (52 cars), to be towed away from the waterside in log rafts, by steam tugs heading to mills along the Pacific coast.*

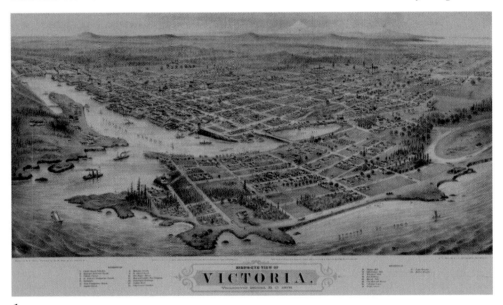

1

2

3

and its busy port. Here, indeed, is now the fastest-growing area of Canada, as its links across the Pacific to Asia expand steadily. Altogether, in what must remain an incomplete examination of the Canadian Far West, this is a region to wonder at: of dazzling white snow lines and shadowed green forests, of blossoming valleys, turquoise mountain lakes, and high, brown uplands — a land of natural splendour, yet also of vibrant human achievement.

The Arctic lands, which form a final quarter of all Canadian territory, have their own splendour and severity. They lie north of the treeline in a realm of permafrost, where the sub-surface ground stays constantly frozen; yet where thick mats of tundra vegetation — mosses, flowering plants and shrubs like dwarf willows and birch — extend in every direction, interspersed with shallow pools and lichen-crusted bedrock. This treeless tundra, low and wind-scoured, has in part been termed the Barren Lands; though no name could be more inadequate. True, its season of growth following the grim severity of winter is both rapid and short. But then radiant flowers of every colour explode across the tundra, where bird, animal (and insect) life grow equally exuberant, and where trickling waters, a brilliant sun of twenty-four hours' duration, and cool, fragrant breezes make the Arctic summer utterly worth waiting for. Furthermore, even in the long, black winters, when ripples of hard snow encase the land itself, the plentiful life of the neighbouring seas, in fish or seals and other marine animals, has effectively supported a sturdy native population; one that knew the icy wilderness for its food-rich offerings as well as its bleak rigours.

1. Arctic "Island of Ice." *The iceberg shown was painted by John Ross in July, 1818, when in command of a Royal Naval expedition to seek a navigable North West Passage to Asia. This, Ross's first attempt, took him north from the Atlantic into unknown waters up between Greenland and Baffin Island. On his second venture, he penetrated Lancaster Sound westward above Baffin in the High Arctic; but there his ship was ice-bound through four years, until at last he escaped home.*

2. Vancouver, Continental Terminus. *Vancouver appeared later than Victoria, after the C.P.R. tracks from the east had reached its splendid harbour by 1886 to meet Pacific shipping. This photograph of the port city in the 1920s, with a mountain backdrop beyond its rising skyscrapers, helps suggest the future metropolis of Pacific Canada.*

3. Fishing Fleet off the B.C. Coast. *Salmon fishing and canning became major enterprises along Canada's West Coast of rugged islets and mountain fiords; but especially around entries to its great rivers, like the Fraser, Skeena and Nass.*

1

2

3

This Arctic North in Canadian heritage (really comprising several related natural regions) extends from Ungava, at the northern tip of Quebec, across the wide shorelands surrounding Hudson Bay and on westward along the northern continental seacoasts to the borders of Alaska. But well above these mainland Arctic or Subarctic areas lie the huge islands of the Arctic Archipelago, which makes the closest Canadian approach to the North Pole. In the east, past neighbouring Greenland, there is Baffin Island, Canada's largest island and the fifth largest in the world; spectacular in its high rim of Precambrian mountains and giant ice-fields, looming over gravel slopes and tundra at the cadmium, zinc and lead mines of Nanisivik. Beyond and above Baffin, Ellesmere Island carries Canada's northern limits to some 7,000 kilometres from the Pole. No less spectacular in mountains, it is edged by deep-cut fiords or permanent ice-shelves, and is largely a polar desert in itself. Yet even Ellesmere holds modern polar stations like Eureka and Alert, a lasting Inuit community, and evidences of human occupation dating back 4,000 years. West and south of Ellesmere, other large islands of rock and tundra spread through ice-choked waters to the Beaufort Sea off Yukon and Alaska. Here along the Beaufort there are no more great islands; but here as well, a past century of whaling has now been overtaken by modern drilling for oil from man-made islets set in shallows near the mainland; not to mention projected natural-gas pipelines to run southward from the shores.

Plentiful in whales or caribou, walrus or musk ox, foxes, hares or ptarmigan, the stark domain of the North was never simple or the same. It was desolate, but strikingly rich and beautiful; overpowering in harsh dangers, yet delicately fragile in life-balances: truly a land of constant contradiction. In any event, the Arctic lands had known prehistoric humankind for thousands of years before historic man first entered there from Europe. And with the rise of the fur trade, European invaders indeed opened their own way into the midst of the American continent

1. Return of the Sun to Discovery Harbour, 1876. *This scene of a spring sunrise, after total winter darkness, comes at Ellesmere Island, Canada's northernmost territory, that borders the permanently frozen Polar ice-cap.*
2. A Young Male Walrus. *Seal-like, but much larger, walrus are found chiefly on eastern Arctic shores.*
3. Muskox on Devon Island. *These large-horned, shaggy rangers of the northern tundra instinctively form tight defensive groups against attackers — effective enough for meeting wolves, much less so against men.*
4. Seal-Hunting by Inuit. *Here Arctic natives wait and listen at seal-holes on the ice, as portrayed by Captain G. Lyon during another naval search for the North West Passage led by in 1821-23 by William Parry, formerly with Ross.*

1

2

3

4

from these northern expanses. The cold inland ocean of Hudson Bay could be reached by ships sailing from the Atlantic. In the later seventeenth century, fur-traders of the English Hudson's Bay Company became established on the margins of the Bay, spreading European contacts westward and southwestward — inland from the northern seacoasts of future Ontario or Manitoba-to-be. As a result, the North would long provide a seaway into the Canadian interior, which thus was entered not only from the east, but from northern coastal bases also. To summarize, the Arctic Northlands did not just recently come into Canadian growth in terms of their oil, natural gas and mineral wealth, but actually run far back into history, and in prehistory, a great deal further. The last and remotest of Canada's regions is in many ways among its first as well.

These, then, comprise the six main historic regions in Canada's past experience and present life, all of them deeply shaped by the physical forms and conditions of the land itself: the largely tundra world of the Arctic and Subarctic North, the Atlantic East, Southern Quebec and Ontario in Central Canada, the Shield Country, the Plains West, and the Cordilleran Far West. Unquestionably, all six of the great segments were based on natural regions; but on such regions as grouped or interrelated by human history. And so the whole Canadian community would grow within these regional historic units, and within their member-provinces, in a process which continually revealed the magnitude of the environmental heritage they held.

1. Seal-Hunting by Sailing Steamer, 1880s. *This sort of vessel carrying many hunters (seen here amid the ice-fields) spread north from Newfoundland-Labrador areas. And ships like these would reach across the Arctic, notably to carry whaling, as well, both to Canada's northwestern coasts and Alaskan waters still further west.*
2. Iceberg, Ship and Walrus in Hudson Strait, 1840s.
3. Aurora Borealis, with seal in foreground.

1

2

3

The Limits of the Land

One must always recall that this huge inheritance was not just a ready store of wealth open for the taking, of unbounded resources leading to inevitable "progress." The limits of Canada's environment were real and unrelenting. Human mischance or mistake could bring disaster; the best of plans and efforts might be tossed aside by incalculable physical forces; and the misuse of natural bounties, through ignorance, waste or simply human greed, in the long run could cost dearly — even to the very ruin of environment. There is room here for only a few illustrations, among which aspects of climate must stand out. Above all, there are the limits set by cold, in a country that would be called "The Lady of the Snows."

The Arctic Northlands, of course, present the most striking example: one quarter of Canada that generally cannot grow trees, not to mention arable crops; that is shrouded in snow and ice for most of the year, and is underlain by permafrost: which, if melted, can cause buildings or pipelines to shift and subside in soft mud. This is not to say that such largely technical problems cannot be met (at costs), or that the North does not have wider values beyond providing brief tundra pastures for herds of caribou. Yet the limitations of Canadian climate are also apparent elsewhere. They are very evident in high, bleak Cordilleran country where glaciers still persist, or in many western ranching areas swept by winter blizzards. Certainly sub-zero cold also pervades a wintry Precambrian Shield and touches East Coast lands. And even in the more moderate St. Lawrence Lowlands, frosts and heavy winter snowfalls may cause serious crop damage from time to time. Yet most vulnerable, in a sense — because it so strongly relies on agriculture — is the Plains West with its vast, fertile grainfields. Not only may early frosts wither ripening crops, but sleet, hail or drought can also do broad harm. In any case, crop insurance and government aid to stricken western farmers form parts of the realities of Plains life: bound in by a climate that can be hot enough, cool enough, rainy enough, and dry enough — but all too often, not enough at the right time.

The restrictions of climate appear in other ways besides. Indeed, Canada's temperature range, even in its milder regions, imposes a constant annual expense for heating or insulating homes and workplaces beyond what is required in the more southerly United States, let alone in warmer climes elsewhere. These higher costs of heat energy (and of lighting, too, for the longer northern dark of winter) inevitably load heavier charges on the work and products of Canadians as compared with many foreign competitors. So do the greater expenses of keeping

British Columbia's Emblem — the Dogwood. *A reminder that hard country crowned with snowy peaks may not be always chill and bleak, for fragrant dogwood blossoms also grace the warmer lands of Canada's Pacific realm.*

highways and railways open through repeated snows, dealing yearly with ice-bound city streets, or even with rust and weather damage to vehicles and routes. Without doubt, King Winter (who came as a shock to many earlier European settlers in Canada) still sets his burdens and his sharp constraints upon the country — however one may revel in crisp ski-holidays under bright winter sun and sparkling skies. Climate limits Canada, moreover, in the very range of crops it can produce; which may result in close dependence on a relative few great staples. Traditionally, we have grown huge quantities of wheat, but far less corn than on warmer American farmlands — aside from no cotton, oranges or sugar cane! Over all, in consequence, we have known world standing in yields of grain, wood, and many minerals; but our climate has imposed a narrower base on agricultural products generally, and has plainly weighed on transport and manufacturing economies as well.

Limits of resources are quite as evident as restraints of climate; although it is no less clear that Arctic, Shield or Cordilleran country can still be immensely productive, for all their lacks in farmland. But natural resources are not infinite, even in Canada; not even so-called renewable kinds like forest or water wealth. As for the unrenewable sorts, few people should still need to be told that mines do finally run out, or soils lose fertility — especially thin, abused or neglected soils. Yet it remains surprising how many Canadians have believed that their mine, their livelihood, their very town and factory, would never fail (at least not in *their* time), or that their own farms would go on forever, whatever the mounting signs of worn-out land. Human wishes and failings, or simple indifference, no doubt have entered here. But so also did a great myth, dating virtually from European settlement, that Canada's land resources truly were unending, and there was always more good country somewhere out there — a factor, indeed, in the historic westward frontier movement across North America. Yet European minds, dazzled by sheer space and the range of resource discoveries, took very long to accept that even a wilderness continent might eventually run short of new bonanzas. Perhaps only in the last few decades have the Canadian public come increasingly to recognize that there is no limitless bailing-out, no more "endless" forests or "inexhaustible" wealth always waiting in the ground — and that, as Mark Twain did note long ago, they aren't making any more land. At any rate, the limits to non-renewable resources have but lately been marked by Canadians, despite many bitter consequences through past history.

But what of forests, freshwaters, or at least well-tended soils — are such

Horseshoe Bend Dam. *This major dam at Bassano in Alberta has achieved much by irrigating drylands in southern districts of the province into abundant production. Yet the long-range damages done to the environment by such large-scale works are widely under consideration today.*

resources as these not renewable? Possibly, with proper understanding, care and support; though failure to watch the vital limits can spell destruction, too. Forests in particular do not quickly or easily recover from lumbering, even with re-planting, all too often done inadequately. Furthermore, clear-cutting, total tree-removal, may seem economic to lumber corporations with an eye to maximizing profits and dividends; but it can disrupt the whole complex ecology of the woodlands. And reforesting with just a few chosen species for future cutting, widely produces an unvaried forest weak against a host of rival natural forces. In fact, from Ontario to British Columbia clear-cutting has brought intense controversy over its waste, ugliness, and lasting damage. In terms of short-range enterprise, clear-cutting may seem an instance of efficient, cost-saving technology. But technology, a powerful servant, can prove a ruthless long-run master.

Another instance may lie in dragger fishing off Newfoundland — clear-cutting at sea — by big ships drawing deep nets which literally clean off the North Atlantic ocean shelves, taking not just mature cod but fish too young to have spawned, and other species just to be thrown away, thus reducing the future fish supply as well as ripping up the feeding bottoms. In brief, cost-effective(?) technology here despoils the future for quick, immediate gains. This is the sort of problem, also, which afflicts the use of supposedly unlimited freshwaters inland. Dams may be built to supply hydro-electric power or provide waters to irrigate dry lands for crops. The technology here seems surely positive in purpose. And yet, the frequent destruction of life-bearing wetlands in the process, the flooding of other useful areas, or the constant irrigation of soils so that over the years they actually build up killing salts from the evaporation of the water brought in, further show how very often we do not realize the continuing presence of environmental limits — which may only be transgressed at peril.

Finally, there are other damages through which we constantly restrict the natural wealth of the environment: the dangerous pollution of freshwater sources by industrial and human wastes, the garbage land-fills piled up in countrysides, the tree-killing acid rain that spreads from big mining smelters or many factory stacks, and the toxic fumes that collect above our urban centres from their mass concentrations of cars and buildings. None of this is pleasant. All of it is grave — and amounts to deadly constraints which we ourselves have set upon the Canadian land, to affect our whole heritage and history. But here we must leave the enduring question of physical limits, to turn to the original human inhabitants of Canada: who showed much keener awareness of the natural environment, and did much less harm to it, both through their ways of life and far less powerful technology. Accordingly, we move from the fundamental inheritance of the giant land to its first occupying peoples, the Indians and the Inuit.

Garbage Dump on the Toronto Waterfront in 1922. *Back then, all sorts of refuse was constantly being dumped along main waterways at many a Canadian city and town — heedlessly, too, as if "Nature" somehow would swallow it all up, without harm. By now we know a good deal better; but still face unsolved problems over what to do with all our junk, waste and pollution, particularly as produced at Canada's major population centres. Beyond that, a lot of smaller places no less raise anxious problems of disposal, especially if they have dangerous waste-products to deal with: all of which threaten the environment, the natural world we live by.*

500 B.C. Dorset Inuit culture emerging

1000 A.D. Thule Inuit culture moving eastward from Alaska

1000s Norsemen in Newfoundland (Nfld.)

1480s English probably now fishing off Nfld.

1492 Columbus reaches the West Indies, for Spain

1497 Cabot lands in North America, in English ship

1500s Iroquois Five Nations confederacy takes shape within the continent

Europeans increasingly fishing off Atlantic shores

1534 Jacques Cartier sails to Gulf of St. Lawrence; claims the lands for France

1535 Cartier sails up St. Lawrence, the "River of Canada"

1550s Basques whaling along Labrador coasts

1576 Martin Frobisher reaches up to Baffin Island in Arctic waters

1583 Sir Humphrey Gilbert proclaims England's title in Nfld.

1603 Samuel de Champlain visits St. Lawrence

1604 Sieur de Monts forms company to trade and colonize in Acadia, Canada, and "other places in New France" (N.F.)

1605 De Monts establishes Port Royal in Acadia

1608 Champlain founds Quebec on the St. Lawrence as French base in Canada

1609 Champlain and Indian allies travel to Lake Champlain; fight with Mohawks

1610 John Guy establishes an English colony on Conception Bay, Nfld.

1610-11 Henry Hudson winters on James Bay

1613 Champlain goes up Ottawa River English seize control of Port Royal from French

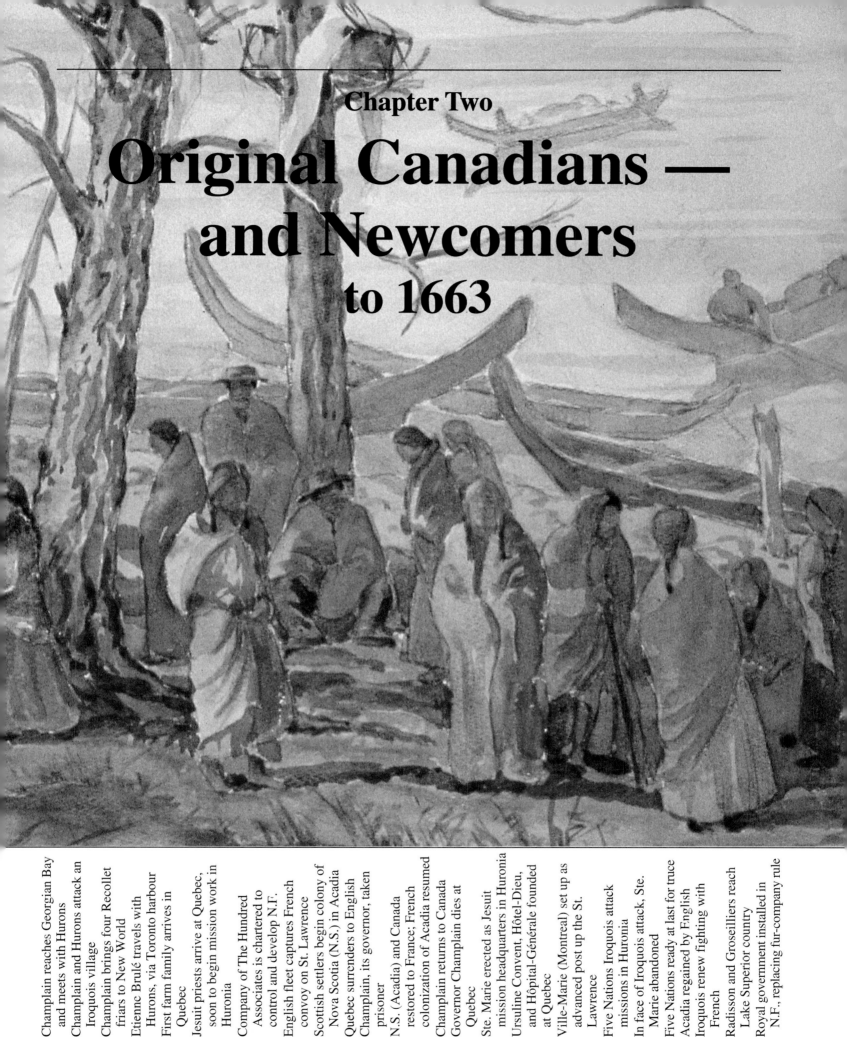

Original Canadians —
and Newcomers
to 1663

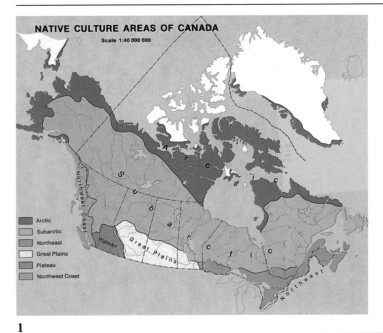

1

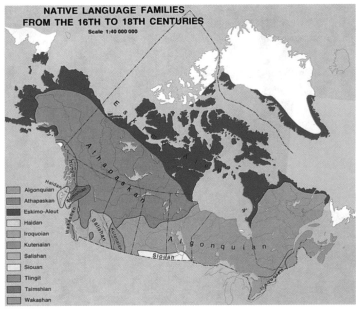

2

3

4

Timeline. *The timelines represent the time spanned by each chapter and the events which occurred in them. The amount of space between entries in the timeline is not always proportional to the number of years spanned.*

Overleaf. Arriving for Tree Burial, by Canoe. *Water colour of an Indian ceremony in British Columbia, painted by Joanna Wilson about 1919-20.*

1., 2. Native Cultural and Language Groupings.

3. Montagnais-Naskopi Lodges on the St. Lawrence near Sept-Iles, c. 1863. *This Lower St. Lawrence scene shows both wigwams and a European-style church building.*

4. Malecites in New Brunswick, c. 1837. *Spearing Atlantic salmon by torchlight, on the Nashwaak River.*

5. Indian Hunter Calling. *Engraved from the work of Cornelius Krieghoff, the brilliantly perceptive Dutch artist who lived in Quebec and Montreal from the 1840s to the 1860s, who here envisaged the native Indian of eastern Canada — romantically but by no means unrealistically.*

5

Aboriginal Society and Culture

Canada's native peoples may have begun as immigrants from Asia in the far-distant past. But their presence in North America over thousands of years certainly justifies considering their society and culture to be native or aboriginal. Ancient artifacts recovered by archaeology, traditions, legends and customs as traced by anthropology, can reveal a good deal about the evolution of these peoples throughout eons of prehistory. Still, our own concern is history. And so, while by no means disregarding the findings of archaeology and anthropology for either the prehistoric or historic periods, we will look at the first Canadians at about the time they were to enter into written historical record, with the arrival of newcomers from Europe. We will observe them on the eve, so to speak, in a broad survey of the main native cultural groupings across the territories of Canada-to-be; once again taking our course from east to west and north.

In Newfoundland, then, there were the Beothuks, a small group of coastal dwellers who largely lived by fishing and seal-hunting. Yet all too little is known about them; driven inland or brutally slaughtered by invading European fishermen from about 1500 on, and brought to extinction before the 1830s. It is said that the Beothuks' liberal use of red ochre, a pigment made from hematite (iron ore) with which they stained their bodies, led to the name "Red" Indian that would be applied across North America: a sad sort of bequest from a vanished native people. On the Atlantic mainland, however, the more numerous Micmacs endured. Behind the Micmacs were the Malecites in what is now New Brunswick; both tribes being Algonquians in language.

In fact, Algonquian-speakers formed one of the largest linguistic families or groupings throughout aboriginal Canada, reaching from the eastern woodlands north to the Subarctic and west into the Great Plains. In this truly extended family, the Blackfoot of the Alberta prairies might have nothing much in common with the Micmac in Nova Scotia other than language forms. Still, the Algonquian peoples in general were migratory hunters, fishers and gatherers, though some of them might practice a little corn-growing and garden-tending in more southern areas. Outside the Atlantic region, the main Algonquian-speaking tribes included the Montagnais-Naskopi, north of the St. Lawrence in the Shield country of eastern Quebec; the Algonquins (the tribe-name lacks the "a") located around the Ottawa, and the Nipissings beyond them; the Odawas (Ottawas) of Lake Huron, and the Ojibwas (Chippewas) above Lake Superior. Still further,

1. Micmacs near Halifax, 1808. *One should have in mind that even by this date the Micmac Algonquians had been in contact with Europeans for something like two centuries. And so along with the bark canoe and wigwam, there are guns here, a European-style hat (feather-decorated) on a man, and cloth dresses on the women.*

2. Shanawdithit, Last-Known Beothuk in Newfoundland. *In 1823, she and her mother and sister were captured in the woods at the point of starvation, and were brought to St. John's. There, the latter two women soon died of tuberculosis; but Shanawdithit was taken into a household, learned English, and gave invaluable information on Beothuk life and customs — until she, too, was killed in 1829 by tuberculosis, a white man's disease that had ravaged her own people.*

1

2

there were the Algonquian-speaking Cree, a farspread tribal family in itself, comprising the Swampy Cree along the shores of James and Hudson Bay, the Woods Cree northwest through Manitoba and Saskatchewan, and the Plains Cree from Saskatchewan across Alberta territory.

Algonquian tribes, however, were largely just units of common ancestry, beliefs and practices, without commanding authority. The real working unit within them was the band: a much smaller community of families which ranged over its own recognized territory throughout the year, guided by shamans, the spiritual leaders, as well as by its chief, frequently a noted hunter at the head. During the winter, the band broke up into member-families, to carry on the hunt for very survival in the snowy wilds, tracking deer, elk, moose and other game. In warmer seasons the band came back together; to fish at well-established river or lake locations, to gather berries, wild rice and other plants, and to continue hunting, whether for birds or beaver, rabbits or bear. The canoe — especially the elegant, efficient birch-bark canoe made where white-skinned paper birch grew — the snare, the bow-and-arrow and the flint knife, or woven, portable basketry and light, bark-covered wigwams: all these were prime and necessary features of Algonquian migratory culture, in which free movement across rock and forest was an inherent part of life itself.

Much more limited in range of territory, yet far more concentrated and strongly organized, was the next linguistic family, the Iroquoians. They mainly occupied the St. Lawrence Lowlands-Lower Great Lakes region in Canada, a narrow southern confine compared to the vast areas beyond it known to Algonquians and other language groups; but a considerably favoured region, as we have seen, which could support a sizeable native population in itself. The Iroquoians, moreover, had basically taken to corn-culture, growing beans and squash besides; so that, long before the historic period began, hunting and fishing had become only supplementary for this largely-settled people, dwelling in substantial villages that might hold well over a thousand inhabitants each. Surrounding garden lands cleared from the forests provided a food supply that could be stored each year; so that, barring natural calamities, the Iroquoian gardeners were released from the winter shortages that continually threatened the roaming Algonquian hunters. This greater security and stability thereby enabled the village-dwellers to organize far more effective tribal authority. Furthermore, their organization and authority promoted power — which might lead on to war. In any event, the Iroquoians could and did conduct purposeful inter-tribal warfare, in conflicts largely beyond any clashes of small Algonquian bands.

With the rise of power and fighting prowess among Iroquoian tribes, their villages came to be defended by encircling log palisades, sometimes in three rings, surmounted by platforms for bowmen and stone hurlers. Inside the palisades, the inhabitants lived in large bark-covered longhouses, each holding ten to thirty related families, while apartment quarters and fireplaces were allotted to every family. Relationships came through the female line; a married

1. Ojibwas fishing near Sault Ste. Marie, 1869. *The Ojibwa were, and remain today, a sizeable Algonquian tribe in Northern Ontario.*

2. Cree Indians on Hudson Bay, 1817. *A rather doubtful picture (given the seeming palm-tree); but at least the leadsman has his pipe. Portrayed and published in England, such early illustrations often showed what might interestingly be, rather than what actually was.*

1

2

man moved into his wife's longhouse; and senior family-matrons elected the tribal chiefs, who were men, but who could be removed if these elder headwomen so required. Women, furthermore, planted the crops and tended the gardens, which freed the men for war as well as for hunting or trading, yet also gave the women a central economic role to add to their social and political importance. In a real sense, Iroquoian society and culture showed aspects of both democracy and feminism. How "primitive" was the heritage of people such as these in Canada?

The Iroquoians dwelt on both sides of the Lower Great Lakes, however; particularly in what would become the American state of New York, as well as north above those lakes in "Canadian" territory of the future. There was thus much interflow between tribes across a non-existent border, and many contacts, including hostile ones, between the Iroquoians north or south of Lake Ontario. The most powerfully organized tribes, indeed, were centred to the south in the area of modern up-state New York. These were the Five Nations of the Iroquois (as Europeans would come to know them), who stretched west from the Hudson River through the Finger Lake country to the Niagara Peninsula. From east to west they consisted of the Mohawks on the upper Hudson, and in order, the Oneidas, the Onondagas, the Cayugas, and the Senecas on toward Niagara — the last of whom at times located villages on the "Canadian" side of Lake Ontario as well. The Five Nations Iroquois moreover had formed a league or confederacy around the 1500s, which kept them at peace with one another under a grand

1. Part of Reconstructed Huron-Iroquoian Village near Midland, Ontario. *This well-documented modern re-creation of the Huron and French mission base at Ste. Marie, on Georgian Bay, does show the real look of Iroquoian village walls, and the arched longhouses within them.*
2. The Iroquoians — a Palisaded Village. *This "Indian Fort," set forth on a published 1720 map of French America, is certainly a European guess at the real thing. What it amounts to is a fairly well-based but poorly-drawn interpretation of an Iroquoian farming village (ignore the palm tree). There are the bark-covered longhouses as communal family dwellings, and some evidence of the crop fields beyond. And the surrounding village palisade is there, if probably shown too widely spaced. Still, Iroquoian stockades of tall poles were not originally intended to give close protection against white musket-fire, but to keep native attackers out, while defending bowmen shot back from platforms along the palisade.*
3. Iroquois Council Fire within a Longhouse. *A nineteenth-century imaginary rendition (again for publishing purposes) of a council meeting between Iroquois leaders and European venturers of the 1600s. Yet the setting once more conveys some facts — the rough interior, the central fire, the big tree-trunks that support the longhouse roof.*

1

2

3

council of fifty chosen federal chiefs, and united them against any outside enemies. The Iroquois League thus emerged as a military force to be reckoned with; not only by neighbouring Indian tribes, but by Europeans, too, when they arrived. In fact, this Iroquois Confederacy became the one native power to be feared (and rightly so) by incoming Europeans for a century and more after 1600. Still, Iroquois strength did not just stem from skill in the swift raids of forest warfare. It also came from skill in diplomacy and debate, and from the high, determined morale of a well-knit people who decided their own affairs.

North of the Five Nations, the main Iroquoian peoples dwelling in Canada were the St. Lawrence Iroquois, whose villages were there at the sites of Quebec and Montreal when the first French ship came up the great river in 1535; the numerous Attiwandirons, who spread westward from the head of Lake Ontario towards the Detroit River; and the Hurons, centred on the fertile Georgian Bay shores south of Lake Huron, but who extended their sway down to the harbour of Toronto on Lake Ontario. The Hurons in many respects were the strongest rivals to the Five Nations Iroquois. They were flourishing and populous in their own large villages set in parklike cornfields. They traded actively with Algonquian tribes east, west and north, exchanging garden products for skins, furs, fish and game. They also had their own Huron Confederacy of five tribes, formed in part as a defensive alliance against the weight of the Iroquois League. But the Hurons' Confederacy would prove less well co-ordinated — and perhaps the Europeans' early presence in their midst lessened their own resolve, as well as bringing white men's diseases that gravely weakened them. At any rate, the Hurons were to fail and disappear — which is a story for the telling later.

Moving further west in Canada beyond the Iroquoians, we have already noted the Algonquian tribes that lived along the Upper Great Lakes or through the Precambrian Shield country into Manitoba and beyond. Yet the Great Plains region which here opened out contained another distinct type of aboriginal society, even though there was a good deal of linguistic variety within it. It included Algonquian-speakers, of course, like the already-mentioned Plains Cree or Blackfoot; but it also held the Assiniboine and the Sioux (or Dakota) of southern prairie areas, and the Stoneys in the foothills of the Rockies, all of whom belonged, in language, to a wider Siouan family that reached well down into the American Plains West. And there were the Sarcee in country around a future Calgary. The last-named spoke the Athapascan tongue generally associated with vast areas northward into the Subarctic; though they evidently

1. Deer Hunt by the Hurons. *A clearly European seventeenth-century picture of natives running deer in Georgian Bay "wilds," with neatly-built fences, too! Yet the event itself was originally described by the French explorer, Champlain. And if this stylized view (produced for the accounts of his travels published in Paris in 1632) was not that accurate, it did indicate the Hurons' well-organized group-hunting methods.*

2. Plains Indians — the Blackfoot. *These Algonquian-speakers who ranged the Western plains from mid-Saskatchewan to the Alberta foothills are seen here with two characteristic features of their nomadic hunting life as it developed on the open prairie: the horse and the travois, which, though wheelless, could transport te-pees, food and family goods across the open grasslands.*

1

2

had moved south in prehistoric time, and had adopted Plains culture.

That culture was essentially dependent on the buffalo: the North American bison, whose great herds had roamed mid-continental grasslands since time immemorial. The buffalo amply fed the Plains Indians; provided them with warm clothing and thick robes against sub-zero winters; furnished skins to cover their tepees, bones for their tools and sinews for their bowstrings or snares. In sum, the buffalo supplied a whole vigorous Indian economy of the Plains. Yet the tribes who lived by it had had to hunt the buffalo on foot; since the horse, once native to America, had died out there thousands of years before; not to be re-introduced until the Spaniards brought it with them from Europe in the 1500s. Only the dog carried some share of family baggage, as the Plains tribes roamed across the prairies following the buffalo herds. Mass kills were made effectively at "buffalo jumps." Here a herd was stampeded over a steep prairie decline, funnelled to it by pre-placed stones and brushwood, and by Indians shouting from either flank, until the broken animals left lying at the bottom could readily be slain. But hunting down single beasts by foot, crawling in to kill with bow and spear, was a process of endless craft and patience — until the horse arrived, to revolutionize Plains Indian life.

Horses that strayed from Spanish-held lands in Mexico in time led to wild

1. Cree or Assiniboine Tepees in Alberta, 1848. *Painted in the foothills at Rocky Mountain House (a jumping-off point for the high country to westward), this was the work of one of Canada's most distinguished artists, Paul Kane of Toronto, who turned to portraying the life of the Western Indians. From 1846 to 1848 Kane canoed, snowshoed or rode thousands of miles from Fort Garry (Winnipeg) to Victoria and back, returning with 700 most valuable sketches of some 80 tribes.*
2. Buffalo Hunt by Plains Indians. *This painting by George Catlin, noted early portrayer of the Plains in the United States, shows mounted Indians hunting prairie bison, as they would do in British territory to the north. Moreover, it was actually an exhibition of some of Catlin's pictures which inspired Paul Kane to go West and do likewise, north of the border.*
3. Drying Saskatoon Berries. *The sweet, fleshy berries of the Saskatoon plant grew from northwestern Ontario across British Columbia. Among Plains Indians, they were especially gathered to be used as a component of pemmican, a long-keeping and easily carried foodstuff made basically from dried and pounded buffalo meat. This high-protein source helped the roaming Plains Indians to survive when winter blizzards closed in, or buffalo herds did not appear.*

1

2

3

herds that flourished freely on the grassy prairies of mid-America; and the native peoples of that world increasingly learned to catch, tame and ride them. Hence by 1730 or so, tribes in the Canadian Plains West were tending and riding their own stock of horses. The results appeared in vastly increased mobility and warlike power for Plains Indian society. Its members still lived by the buffalo; but they had far more ability to get it, far more security of food supply. Consequently, the native tribes of the region built up a distinctive horse-based culture and society, confident in peace or war, with their own strong sense of freedom on the open land, and led by chiefs approved by councils of the elders.

In the high Cordilleran ranges that climbed west of the plains, native life was understandably focused within mountain valleys or on the upland Central Plateau of British Columbia. Here in areas between the Rockies and the Pacific slopes, the Plateau peoples included the Kootenays to the east, and the Interior Salish to the west, while Athapascan-speaking tribes ranged on northward. Yet these were fairly small groupings in an often difficult terrain: societies of non-agricultural and semi-nomadic hunters who also depended considerably on salmon taken from the mountain rivers, especially on towards the coast. Very much more numerous, organized and influential, however, were the aboriginal peoples still further west, on Canada's Pacific or Northwest Coast.

Given its mild climate and plentiful resources of both land and sea, it is none too surprising that the Pacific shore would produce the most thickly populated and complexly developed societies to emerge in native Canada. Their richness even appeared in language diversity, for here there was not one or even a dominant linguistic family. In the north, edging Yukon and Alaska, were Tlingit

1. A Buffalo Jump, 1867. *The picture by Alfred Miller tells graphically how Plains tribes drove buffalo to death over chosen sharp drops or rifts in the prairies, to create a massive meat-supply at the bottom.*
2. Stoneys at Banff in 1906. *These Indians, like the area itself, stood where the outlying Cordilleran ranges climbed above the plains.*
3. Indian Salmon Weir on the Cowichan River, 1866. *This fishing site (with dugout canoe at hand) was typical of native food systems in a coastal area richly supplied with Pacific salmon.*

1

2

3

1. Indians of the Pacific Coast. *Wakeshan (Nootka) Indians of northern Vancouver Island, wearing close-woven bark-fibre hats, good for the rainy coastal climate.*
2. Kwakiutl House and Totem Pole on Vancouver Island. *A Wakeshan -language people, the Kwakiutls inhabited large, planked communal houses, with carved totem poles outside symbolizing their clans. This living pattern was found widely along the prosperous Northwest coast.*
3. Tribal Shaman ("Medicine Man") at Kitwanga, 1915. *Here up the Skeena near the coast, we see a native figure of much authority, poorly described by the often-derogatory white term, "medicine man." He is a healer; yet of both body and mind, whether through native herbal lore or psychology and belief. He is, as well, a spiritual guide, seer, and knower of timeless rituals.*

1

2

3

speakers; the Haidan tongue was found in the Queen Charlottes, the little-related Tsimshian language group on the adjacent mainland. Further south, there were the Nootka and Nitinat on Vancouver Island, along with mainland elements of their own linguistic Wakeshan group. Below these again, on island and main, were Coast Salishan speakers. Altogether it added up to nineteen mutually unintelligible native languages spoken on the British Columbian coasts alone.

These early linguistic differences might scarcely seem to matter in the history of Canada — yet for a country later to be split by language, they might suggest some enduring problems of heritage. More significant for now, however, are the major tribes to be seen within this West Coast language diversity: since they lived much the same kind of lives in their Far West setting, although with some specialties of their own. The Haida of the Charlottes, the Tsimshians on the Skeena, the Bella Coola south of them, or the Kwakiutl, Comax, and other peoples down to the lower shores of Vancouver Island, all present a similar story of life in great wooden village-houses set beside a generous sea. Salmon, fresh or dried, taken in the annual salmon runs, formed a staple of diet; but shell fish and other fish were available in plenty. Seals, porpoises — and whales harpooned by Haida or Nootka — added to that plenty, as did berries and edible plants on land, or land animals from deer and elk to bear and mountain goat: all to provide for a securely stable and well-developed West Coast native society. The great trees of the rain forest, moreover, furnished the peoples with excellent timber, which they split into long planks (using just stone tools with remarkable skill) to erect their big communal dwellings. The massive tree trunks that made the supporting house-posts were carved with the same skill to display clan crests or totems, from which developed the lofty totem pole, still more elaborately carved and painted with the symbols of the whole genealogical past of tribal clans.

The wood-working abilities of West Coast craftsmen were no less displayed in bowls, dishes or painted chests; but especially in their dugout canoes. These long, sea-going craft (from which whales were taken in open waters) were shaped from thick cedar trunks, yet were so carefully hewed and chiselled out that the heavy mass of wood was pared down to sturdy yet slim and graceful vessels that often carried sail. But if wood-working, or carving, was man's work, so weaving was the woman's: producing cloaks and blankets finely crafted from cedar bark and mountain-goat wool, large rush mats to line the houses for warmth, broad-trimmed bark hats closely woven to keep out the frequent rains, baskets of spruce-root, fish nets of spun twine, and still more. In view of this

1. A Woven Cedar Costume at Quatsino, Vancouver Island, 1920. *This is an admirable example of the West Coast Indian ability to produce skilfully made artifacts for a far-from-simple native culture — from hat, dress and necklace to cedar-string basket.*
2. A Kwakiutl Potlatch, by Joanna Wilson, c. 1919-20. *The Potlatch, a ceremony of feast and gift which demonstrated high status, here is displayed by all the finery of a chief and his wife: further evidence, as well, of affluent and class-graded Pacific Coast native society.*

1

2

richly-productive society, it is not too surprising that it came to show class differentiation. While clan and kinfolk bonds joined the dwellers within each village house, the ownership of real property — of house sites, berry patches, fishing and sealing places — led to some elements amassing wealth. There hence were upper and lower levels within this tribal society, though each village itself stayed relatively independent. And at the very bottom level were slaves, captured in war or purchased, who did the most menial tasks. Furthermore, in a social confirmation of rank and power, wealthy, honoured persons held potlatches, great ceremonial feasts at which they liberally distributed gifts in testimony to their standing. Solid, self-assured and prosperous, the peoples of the Pacific Coast lived with potlatches and high ceremonies that did indeed display how well endowed they were.

Turning north and inland, we enter the harder, far less endowed native worlds of the Subarctic and Arctic. While Algonquians occupied the eastern Subarctic areas across the Shield, chiefly Montagnais and Cree, the western Subarctic was the province of another major language family, the Athapascan, whose members widely called themselves the Dene (de-nay), in that tongue meaning "the people." These western Athapascans covered an immense territory; but lived in small, scattered bands of hunters ranging through the northern forests. Like the Algonquians, whose life was not dissimilar, the band was much more the daily reality than the tribe. Yet there still were tribal differences and diversity, because the Subarctic expanses varied widely in themselves, from

1

2

1. Dance of the Kutchin Indians, 1851. *An Athapascan Subarctic people of the Yukon and Lower Mackenzie Valleys, they are shown dancing the Kutcha-Kutchi — truly.*
2. Chipewyans Preparing a Moose Hide, 1918. *Seen in northern Alberta near Waterways, these widespread Athapascans ranged well up to the Yellowknife area in the North West Territories, and northeastward across the Subarctic Barrens towards Hudson Bay.*

mountain uplands in the Yukon to valley plains along the great Mackenzie river system, or to tundra country eastward on to Hudson Bay. Thus the Tutchone people in the Yukon, inhabiting the northern extension of British Columbia's Central Plateau, often depended on salmon fishing as well as on seeking moose or caribou. The Sekani hunted moose and mountain sheep on the Rockies' slopes, but were excluded by their enemies from the buffalo on the plains below. The Slaveys lived by lakes and streams from the Hay River and Slave River north to Great Bear Lake, taking fish, berries, small game and moose, in a culture of little winter groups and bigger summer bands, again considerably like the Algonquians. And the Chipewyans, most numerous of the northern Athapascan peoples, held the Subarctic forest fringe east to the Coppermine River and the tundra Barren Lands beyond, which they roamed in pursuit of caribou. For the Chipewyan, life was regularly built about following the annual migration of great caribou herds, from their winter shelter in the forest to summer pastures on the open barrens.

The final aboriginal Canadians to be surveyed are the Inuit, the Eskimo-Aleut-speaking peoples of the Arctic. Never large in numbers — not surprising, considering the nature of their territory — their very survival expressed their own high resourcefulness and adaptability. They formed but a single language group, one related to Siberian peoples but not to any Amerindian ones; which suggests that the Inuit migrated from Asia later than the Indians (who moved on southward) and instead adjusted to the Arctic as their own permanent home. There the earlier Dorset Inuit culture emerged around 500 B.C., and it produced the soapstone lamp, the igloo and the dog sled. Yet the later Thule culture, that came eastward from Alaska around 1000 A.D., brought more advanced sea-hunting techniques and included whale-catching. By about 1400,

1. Labrador Eskimo in a Kayak, c. 1821. *This early work by Peter Rindisbacher uses the name "Eskimo" long given in French or English to the Inuit, while also identifying their Labrador tribal group. In any case, the portrait is "drawn from nature," and depicts the all-important sealskin boat of these far northern coastal-dwellers.*
2. Inuit Dog Sled On Shore. *Photographed in the 1940s in the Padlei district of the North West Territories — inland from the western edge of Hudson Bay, where some scattered, scrubby trees do exist.*

1

2

accordingly, a Thule Inuit population had spread — if thinly — all around Arctic Canada north of the treeline, and from Alaska to the shores of Greenland.

These, then, were the Inuit by the opening of the historic age in Canada. They now existed in major tribal groups: the Labrador, Baffin Island, Netsilik (Seal), Caribou and the Copper Inuit among them. For such nomadic hunter-gatherers, however, the band once more was the operative unit, consisting of a few interrelated families, though coming together in larger regional bands in winter, as at sealing camps. The leader of a family band was usually its oldest active huntsman; but despite the seeming looseness of authority, the family ties were strongly binding, while close co-operation and sharing among band households were hallmarks of the Inuits' society. In summer they lived in sealskin tents, as they hunted caribou, fished or gathered berries. In winter they built their igloos — a brilliant instance of dome-construction with materials readily at hand — and they used another first-rate technological invention, the skin kayak, to take seals and other sea-mammals amid the icefields themselves.

The keen ingenuity of the Inuit appeared in the use of their few (if ample) resources. Bones substituted for wood in construction, though driftwood might sometimes be employed. Tools and weapons were edged with native copper: the Inuit found metal, where any was available, far better than stone. Seal oil fed their lamps. Sealskin, left haired, made winter boots; hairless, waterproof summer ones; while caribou fur supplied warm winter parkas. Insulated also against cold by energy-rich animal foods — particularly seal meat or whale blubber — the Inuit in a wide variety of ways successfully responded to the fiercest challenges of the Canadian land. Yet they still had time for creative art, for delicately rendered carvings in whalebone or walrus ivory, or else for story-telling, singing, drumming, or string games of dexterity and memory. This tough, cheerful people of the Arctic really built up the most distinctive native heritage in Canada.

1

1. Sled Teams in the Coppermine Region, N.W.T. *A compelling picture of Arctic winter travel, it was taken about 1949 by Richard Harrington, photographer of the Canadian North.*
2. Copper Inuits' Summer Tent, July, 1915. *Covered with caribou skins, it stands on open land, but beside still-frozen water.*
3. Summer Camp at White Bay, N.W.T. *This later scene (1951) presents an Inuit woman sewing sealskins pegged out to dry on slopes above the shores.*

2

3

The Native Canadian Heritage

The legacies from all the original Canadian peoples certainly did not end when Europeans arrived. For one thing, it was the skills and lore of native inhabitants which virtually enabled the new arrivals to survive a daunting wild environment. The first Canadians provided them with knowledge of the canoe, that invaluable means of forest travel, the toboggan and the snowshoe for winter, the dog team for the Subarctic and Arctic. They also instructed early European venturers inland (the clumsiest, most ignorant of idiots in native eyes) how to live off the country and follow its paths — through what was anything but a trackless wilderness to aborigines. In fact, they taught the newcomers basic geography. The old Euro-centric idea of "discovery," of white explorers from Europe finding an unknown America, ignores the essential truth that the native peoples already knew where things were, and thus led their wide-eyed visitors (perhaps with either tolerance or some disdain) into expanses which the transatlantic tourists would later blatantly claim for themselves. But there were a host of further native bequests: from the Iroquoians' "Indian" corn and tobacco to the pemmican of Plains tribes: a nutritious mixture of dried buffalo meat pounded with berries and fat which became a basic staple for the western fur traders. Or there was Far West smoked salmon, eastern Algonquian maple syrup and wild rice. Furthermore, the wearing of moccasins or parkas onward to today, the playing of lacrosse derived from St. Lawrence Valley tribes, or the running of kayaks down turbulent streams, demonstrate just a few other varied inheritances from the native past. But more noteworthy still, are the artistic endowments that have stemmed from the first Canadians.

Those that came from the Inuit have already been touched on; although not enough to express the continued widening and deepening of their arts right to the present; wherein carving in soapstone and other materials, work in printmaking and other graphic forms, have now brought them world regard. Similarly, the artistry of the West Coast tribes has been mentioned; yet not enough to indicate that it, too, would win world recognition — in wood-carving from totem poles and masks to mythic statues; in works of argillite, a soft black slate, or bold, bright symbolic paintings done on wood. Moreover, Plains art set out its own symbolic paintings on the hides of prairie tepees, while the Iroquoians bequeathed a long tradition of handsomely decorated pottery and superbly carved tobacco pipes: since tobacco held a ritual significance when smoked at native ceremonial or sacred occasions. And the Algonquians not only produced intricate embroidered designs in porcupine quills (or later, beads) to adorn their basket work or deerskin garments; but in modern years have also created outstanding paintings, by artists who combine contemporary techniques with images of their age-old legends and spiritual beliefs.

In truth, we must not omit the spiritual reach of native heritage in general. Christianity would enter and spread with the Europeans, but it never eliminated the aboriginal patterns of religious belief, some of which would revive and renew their inheritance among native Canadians within more recent time. It is difficult to generalize fairly. Still, it may broadly be said that aboriginal faiths held powerful creation-myths, believed in supernatural beings to be honoured and supplicated with rituals and ceremonies, and had a sense of afterlife in a realm of the dead, which human agents might contact in order to re-unite with loved ones.

1. Building a Birchbark Canoe, *c. 1900, most probably by Indians of the Lower St. Lawrence.*

2. Toboggan and Snowshoes of the Eastern Algonquians. *A native family travelling in the Quebec winter, painted c. 1860.*

3. Caughnawaga Mohawks, Lacrosse Champions of Canada, 1869. *This Mohawk Iroquoian community on the St. Lawrence later produced another, more surprising set of skilled performers: "high-steel" construction men, who worked in teams on lofty New York skyscrapers like the Empire State and United Nations Buildings during the twentieth century.*

4. Iroquoian Cradle Board. *Used for carrying infants, it shows Iroquois floral artistry in its decoration.*

5. Assiniboine Knife Sheath and Bag. *Illustrating the finely-beaded work of this Plains people.*

1

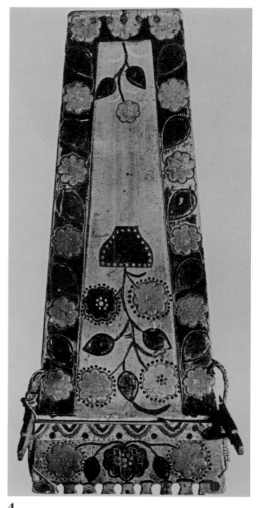

4

2

3

5

1. Haida Totem Pole. *This splendid traditional example of Northwest Coast art and carving was removed from the Queen Charlottes to stand at Prince Rupert on the mainland.*
2. Copper and Iron Fish Hooks of the Naskopi, c. 1863. *The sizeable hooks (for large St. Lawrence River fish?) show good use of European-derived metals by native adaptors.*
3. Cree Artifacts from Ruperts Land-Manitoba. *Sketched in 1858, they include saddle, whip and stirrup, and "sacred or medicine" drums.*

Moreover, spirits or souls resided in all living things, notably animals; and there was a senior Great Spirit-force of power and mystery, whether Orenda to Iroquoians, Kitchi Manitou to Algonquians, or Wakan Tanka to Plains tribes. To reach and deal with spiritual forces, shamans (however named) were crucially present throughout native society from Algonquian to Inuit, West Coast to Iroquoian. They were medical healers as well as omen-diviners, teachers as well as masters of ritual. But such necessary oversimplifications as these can by no means cover the many manifestations of native spirituality: from the Shaking Tent prophecies among Algonquians, the Huron Feast of the Dead, the Iroquois False Face Society that effected healing while wearing masks, to the Guardian-Spirit Quests of West Coast tribes; the great Sun Dance ceremonies on the Plains, or rituals for the sea-goddess Sedna among the Inuit. Religious culture was an integral part of native identity. Both thrived or weakened together.

Still, identity also needs numbers to keep it thriving. It is estimated that there were probably over one million native inhabitants across Canada when Europeans first arrived. And just some thousands of the latter would enter, for long years thereafter. Yet by 1867, when a Canadian federal nation-state came into being, there were around three and a half million people in Canada — of whom merely some 125,000 were of native blood. The aboriginal groups had not only failed to keep pace relative to total growth, but had most absolutely declined. What had happened? There were many reasons: repeated losses due to war, pillage and famine; the dispersal of whole tribes by victors, the European occupation of vital lands or resources, and a grim failure of confidence within the native cultures themselves that could not easily adjust to the strangeness — and power — of European ways. Moreover, there was alcohol, unknown to Indian or Inuit, yet peddled to them by the newcomers; a seeming escape from pain and loss which proved numbing, degrading and terribly destructive in its long-term results. No less disastrous in their effects, however, were the great sicknesses that also came with the intruders from overseas.

In days before all knowledge of germs or viruses, the entering Europeans were unaware that they might be carrying diseases, with which they had lived for centuries, to native Americans who lacked any immunity to them. Thus in North America, smallpox, dysentery, diphtheria, influenza, could destroy in many thousands, and even measles became a wholesale killer. The fact is, that while the Old World of Europe, Asia and Africa had continually experienced but survived the recurrent epidemics that had moved across it, along with people and trade, the New World of the Americas had been insulated by the surrounding oceans, ever since the ancient land-bridge to Asia had sunk beneath the waves. That is, until venturers from Europe learned to cross the Atlantic — and over time thus spread infections that could reduce populous aboriginal societies to near-demoralized remnants. It was not at all foreseen or understood. Yet in

1

2

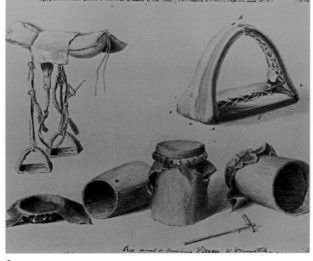

3

1. Painted Blackfoot Tepee, with typical symbols.
2. Haida Carvings in Argilite. *A soft slate which now is producing native works much in demand in world art markets.*
3. West Coast Winter Dance, 1914. *Two mythical birds are here represented by carved masks, Kotsuis and Hohhug.*

1

2

3

Canada the sweep of deaths due to disease, whether among seventeenth-century Hurons or nineteenth-century Inuit, added a terrible postscript to native heritage: one that appeared in the drastic decline of aboriginal populations down to 1867; and even till the 1920s, when at last it stopped, thanks largely to the growing effects of both natural and medical immunization.

Accordingly, disease amounts to a major factor in the obvious failure of the original Canadians to hold their territories across the continent against the transatlantic newcomers. But it is no less true that they faced great forces ranged against them, in a Europe already closely populated and complexly developed, even when Christopher Columbus sailing from Spain made his first landings in America's West Indies during the 1490s. It neither demeans the native cultures as "savagery," nor overpraises "civilization" in western European countries of that day, to note that the latter proved unquestionably stronger (not better) in the long run: through being far more widely organized in powerful political states, through having achieved much fuller economic development, and through having built up a cultural body of written knowledge, scientific learning and technical practices unknown to native Canadians by the time of European entry. More specifically, too, the Europeans had produced a potent metal technology, whether for utensils, tools and implements, guns and cannon, or even iron nails; while native Americans had not discovered how to smelt metals from ores, though they might use natural outcrops of copper or gold. Hence they had remained essentially in the stone age.

Emphatically, however, "stone age" again does not imply merely primitive existence in a pre-Columbian America: not when Inca civilization in Peru then could engineer huge works in stone, composed of perfectly fitted giant blocks, or craft delicate designs in gold jewellery; not when the Mayas of Central America erected splendidly carved and painted temple-pyramids, and excelled in astronomy and mathematics. And not when the Aztecs of Mexico constructed a rich and complex urban-centred empire, until it was overthrown by Spanish conquerors in the 1500s. Moreover, the evidence is there that native societies in Canada were still growing along their own cultural paths — certainly including the rising Iroquois and Huron confederacies — until the intervention of European power changed those paths forever. But that in no way meant that the legacies of the first Canadians would lose their significance, down to the present or even into the future. For there was a final, fundamental bequest they made: a keen awareness of environmental heritage, a ruling concern for the land and its

1. A West Coast Canoe from One Cedar Trunk. *Hewed by native workers at Mission, up the Fraser River near Vancouver, in the early twentieth century.*
2. Building An Igloo. *A set of photographs from the early 1920s, which together display the construction of this long-vital piece of Arctic housing.*

1

1. THE BLOCKS ARE CUT.
3. THE FIRST TIER COMPLETE.

2. THE FIRST BLOCK IS SET ON EDGE.
4. THE BEGINNING OF THE SECOND TIER.

5. THE THIRD TIER.
7. THE LAST BLOCK.

6. THE ROOF.
8. THE CAMP READY FOR THE NIGHT.

2

offerings, which all later Canadians should take earnestly to heart.

The first Canadian peoples lived in keeping with nature and its balances, respecting the life-giving plants and animals it supplied; not treating it as something alien to be mastered and exploited, as incoming Europeans would all too often do. The original inhabitants were by no means nobly super-human. It is of little value to move from old stereotypes of heroic settlers and vicious redmen to new ones of vicious pioneers and heroic natives. Plainly the facts, like human beings, are mixed. Besides, the aboriginal tribes did alter pristine nature, whether by clearing cornfields or burning off prairies to run buffalo. They might well have wrought more changes, if they had had the technological capacities. Nonetheless, it remains true that through religious beliefs as well as cultural patterns, the original Canadians deeply revered the natural world and its creatures, and sought by deed and faith to sustain them. Their reasons, of course, were practical as well as spiritual. But all the same, their heritage first taught the conserving of Canada's environment — a teaching far more urgent today, and one which we have only started to take into due account. So much, then, has stemmed from the country's native peoples. But now it is time to look at those who came after, bringing vast new consequences to the whole environment: the Europeans who crossed the Atlantic in the wake of the first voyage of Christopher Columbus to America in 1492.

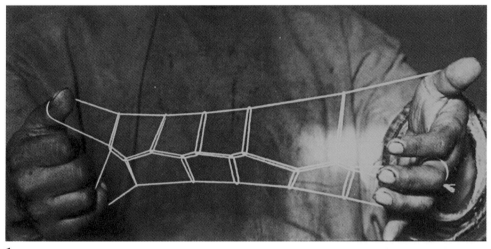

1

1. An Inuit String Game. *One of many, here shown among occupants of the Padlei country, N.W.T.*
2. Nunivak, Master of Arctic Ivory, 1927. *Carving a walrus tusk, in days before Inuit art became so widely regarded in Canada and beyond.*
3. Inuit Spiritual Forces. *Two works by native artists presented on Canadian postage stamps: a print of Return of the Sun, by Kinojouak, and the Sea-Godess, Sedna, sculpted by Kiawak.*

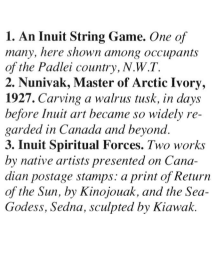

2

3

Atlantic Adventurers — and Fish and Fur

And yet, several centuries before Columbus first came upon America, the Norsemen had already reached Labrador and Newfoundland. Norsemen, Viking sea-rovers and traders from Scandinavia, had been the leading mariners of early medieval Europe. Navigating without a compass, they sailed and rowed their open longships to Ireland and Normandy, or down into the Mediterranean. In northern waters, they voyaged west to colonize Iceland. From there in 985-6 A.D., Eric the Red pushed on further to plant settlements in Greenland. Around 1000, Leif Ericsson (i.e. Eric's son) then acted on a report of lands seen southward by a Viking trader blown off course. According to old tradition, recorded in Iceland, Leif sailed from Greenland past Baffin Island and down the Labrador coast to land at wooded "Vinland," an uncertain place, but probably in Newfoundland. At any rate, he wintered here, gathering grapes (berries?), cutting vines to be used as fasteners in ship-building, and collecting timber needed in a treeless Greenland. Later Norse expeditions then tried to colonize Vinland; but armed clashes with native "skraelings" ("barbarians," probably Inuit, since they used skin boats) discouraged these attempts. While Norsemen still returned to trade for wood with the skraelings, they no longer tried to settle — although their trading contacts with natives would evidently spread from Greenland west to Ellesmere and Baffin Islands, perhaps into Hudson Bay, as well.

Vinland itself disappeared into the mists of time, whether it lay in Newfoundland or around Cape Cod, or even further south, as some have held. What we do know of it comes from the great Norse sagas, epic tales recited (and freely ornamented) for folk-audiences long before being written down. But that the Norsemen did enter the New World, and specifically came to Newfoundland, has now been strikingly confirmed by archaeology: through the discovery in the 1960s of an actual Norse base of the mid-eleventh century at L'Anse aux Meadows on the northern tip of the island. This one generally-accepted Norse site in America — now declared a United Nations world historic site — has been carefully excavated to reveal eight sod-walled buildings and workshops. These in turn have disclosed traces of iron-working and carpentry along with a man's bronze cloak pin and a woman's spindle for making yarn. It all suggests that this oldest known European settlement in North America was an actual colonial community, although it was evidently not occupied for long.

Still, the Norse presence in America did not lead to lasting European penetration. It was too soon. Medieval Europe did not yet have the concern or capacity for transatlantic expansion. Moreover, Norse settlements in Greenland withered in the later Middle Ages, as a colder cycle of climate (sometimes termed the Little Ice Age) began to fill northern seaways with dangerous ice floes, and to chill the Greenland shore pastures themselves. Although the folk memory of lands across the ocean remained in Norse heritage, the mass of

Norse Settlement in Newfoundland. *Excavated at L'Anse aux Meadows in the 1960s, and now restored, this Viking base dating to the mid-1000s provides material evidence that Norsemen did indeed settle in North America.*

1

3

4

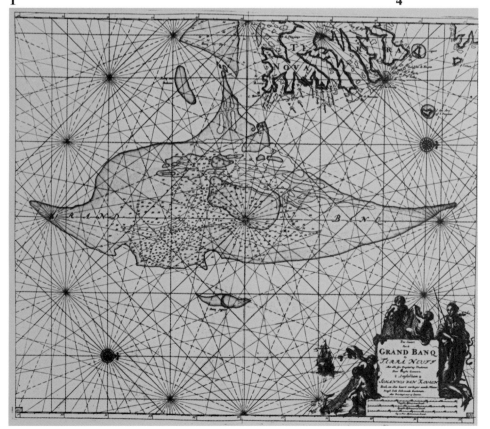

2

1. Inside a Sod Hut at L'Anse aux Meadows. *Here a reconstructed Norse dwelling vividly conveys how these early European forerunners lived and worked in America before 1100 A.D.*

2. The Grand Banks. *From a Dutch map of the 1680s. To view the map as we would today, it should be turned to place the coast of Newfoundland at its upper left-hand side. That then makes sense of the outline of the great island's eastern Avalon Peninsula, and puts the immense Banks properly out eastward in the Atlantic, with their narrow "nose and tail" extending to north and south along the map.*

3. Cabot on the Newfoundland Coast. *As imagined for a Newfoundland stamp of 1947: the 450th Anniversary of his voyage.*

4. John Cabot, European Discoverer, of the 1490s. *We really know little about Cabot: where and when he was born, or died; what shore he actually reached in North America, or what he looked like. What we do know, is that his voyage of 1497 opened up Newfoundland and its great adjacent fisheries to lasting European penetration — a most significant fact, in any case, for Canada's heritage.*

Europe paid no heed. It took other times, people and interests to turn attention westward, centuries later, when Christopher Columbus set sail.

By then, by the 1490s, the peoples of Western Europe had entered the vigorous new era of the Renaissance: an era of emerging nation-states and their powerful rulers, of burgeoning cities and commercial enterprise; of bold advances in learning, and eager, assertive desires to reach out and to know. Furthermore, there had been major improvements in ship design and navigation which brought sturdier, sea-keeping ships able to make some headway against adverse winds, along with the compass and other instruments, and ever-better charts. Then the development of gunpowder led both to shipboard cannon and individual fire-arms. Finally, there was the search for new trade routes by sea to India and China, since Turkish military power had been thrown across the old land routes from Asia into Europe. The interests and capacities, the times and the people, had all appeared — to open Europe's Age of Discovery.

The Portuguese, sailing down past Africa, had got to the Cape of Good Hope by 1488, as they sought a southeast passage to India. In 1492, Columbus in the royal service of Spain instead sailed westward into the Atlantic to reach the Orient. No one of any learning then doubted that the world was round. The real issue was, how large was it; and the critics of Christopher Columbus were not so wrong in holding that it was far bigger than he thought, making such a voyage impracticable. But through one of history's grandest human errors, Columbus ran into the unknown Americas halfway around — although till his death he went on believing that he had reached Asia. In any event, this new and unexpected American land-mass, which would bring Spain a great overseas empire, inspired further attempts to get beyond it, and so find a northwest passage onward to the spices, silks and riches of the East. Thus came the voyage of John Cabot in 1497, commanding an English ship from Bristol, authorized, if not financed, by King Henry VII of England.

Cabot, or Giovanni Caboto, was of Italian birth as was that other master navigator, Cristofero Colombo. But he sought to discover a shorter northern route to Asia by direct voyage west from England, not by Columbus's long swing south through warmer waters. Cabot, too, did not get to Asia. Instead he made the first recorded landfall on the northeastern coasts of North America since the days of the Norsemen. His actual landing-point remains debatable, whether on Newfoundland, Cape Breton Island or Labrador. Yet there is no question that he sailed along the shorelines, and on his return was awarded £10 by a lavish King

The English Dry Fishery in Newfoundland. *This seventeenth-century picture gives a compressed version of the highly important dry-fishing process. It leaves out a lot of Atlantic coastal waters, where the visiting fishing ship would not be located so conveniently close for hauling in the cod! Nevertheless, it is informative on structures and techniques: such as the landing stage where lie the fishermen's dories, which do most of the offshore catching by line; the cleaning and splitting operations carried on in the shed upon the stage; and the laying-out of the split cod on "flakes" for drying, after which it can be taken overseas.*

Henry for finding "the new Isle." Indeed, he gave England claim to this New Found Land. No less significant, in his voyaging Cabot also came upon the Grand Banks off Newfoundland, and took back word that the sea here was so thick with fish they could even be taken up in baskets. And thereby he proclaimed to Europe the enormous fishing wealth available across the North Atlantic.

It well may be that Cabot's ship was not the first European craft to discover the Newfoundland fisheries. Fish (mainly salted for keeping) had long been a basic foodstuff in western Europe, notably the big, fleshy cod. With mounting European population, especially in fast-growing towns, the demand for cod had steadily risen; so that vessels from Atlantic ports not only sailed north to fishing grounds off Iceland, but probed west as well in search of new grounds to harvest. And thanks to better ships and seamanship, they now might venture right to the Newfoundland banks. At any rate, it does appear that seamen from Bristol, a leading West of England port, were already in those waters during the 1480s, while the Portuguese were also thrusting expeditions westward. Moreover, Cabot's own voyage was funded by Bristol merchants looking to more Atlantic trade. But through his journey, what had been but a rumoured fishing area (why tell competitors?) now was officially reported across Europe as being so full of cod "they sumtymes stayed our shippes." And so, from about 1500, fishermen began crossing the open ocean to Newfoundland in ever-growing numbers; not just from England or Portugal, but from the Atlantic ports of France and Spain as well.

Over the next half century and more, visiting fishing ships came increasingly to know harbours on Newfoundland coasts, as they sought shelter for repairs, or for fresh water, deer and other game to vary scanty shipboard diet. Moreover, English ships in particular set up regular fishing stations on shore, because they practiced the "dry" fishery. The "green" fishery took back quickly gutted, heavily salted cod to Europe; and salt was readily available in warm southern European countries, where it was made by evaporating large pools of seawater on sunny beaches. But in cooler, damper lands like England, salt had to be imported and was expensive. Dry fishing, however — in which split cod, only lightly salted, was dried on wooden racks or "flakes" on shore — was not only salt-saving, but produced a good and lasting product, even for tropical markets, and was far more economical to transport, lacking any bulky water content. In fact, dry cod was one of the first, efficient, dehydrated mass-foods. Hence permanent English fishing stations came to flourish, concentrating strongly in the eastern Avalon Peninsula of Newfoundland — to be called the English Shore — while French stations scattered more thinly westward along the coasts, and Portuguese or Spanish, summer visitors in the green fishery, scarcely established themselves on land.

The results grew plain well before the sixteenth century had ended. In 1583, Sir Humphrey Gilbert came to the roomy, deeply sheltered harbour of St. John's — the chief Avalon place of arrival and departure for fishing ships from Europe

A French Fishing Station in Newfoundland. *Here is a considerably later enterprise (1844) on western island shores which then still remained open to fishermen from France. Yet basically, the fishing stage and cleaning shed are still present, with drying racks beyond them — even though the French had long stayed more with the wet or "green" fishery than the dry.*

— and there with full ceremony proclaimed England's title in Newfoundland, before some thirty-six vessels in port, French, Spanish and Portuguese as well as English. Five years later, England's defeat of the mighty Spanish Armada heralded a long decline in the sea power of Spain, which by then had taken over Portugal. By then, too, the French, who had become increasingly active in both the dry and green fisheries, had got to mainland shores beyond Newfoundland — to shape a whole new age in Canada's history. But that really went back to the 1530s and the voyages of Jacques Cartier a sea-captain from Saint-Malo on the Atlantic coast of France who had been commissioned by King Francis I to seek riches of gold and silver such as Spain had found in America, and to unlock the long hoped-for Northwest Passage to Asia.

In 1534, Cartier had reached the Labrador approaches to the Strait of Belle Isle, an area already known to French fishermen. He sailed on through the Strait into the Gulf of St. Lawrence, coursing around its shorelines. And in the Gulf, at the Bay of Chaleur, something highly significant took place. Micmac Indians arrived on shore from a fleet of canoes, and with much shouting held up furs on sticks, beckoning to Cartier's ship. He sent two men ashore, who in return for furs offered the natives knives, ironware and a "red cap" for the chief. This certainly was not the first fur-trading encounter. No doubt, the Indians had previously bartered with visiting fishermen, bringing them not just deer and game in exchange for white men's hatchets, kettles and trinkets, but glossy furs and beaver robes, which could be sold in Europe more profitably than fish. Nevertheless, this exchange recorded here by Cartier did mark a developing fur trade between native inhabitants and Europeans newcomers. It was to mould Canadian history and heritage through ages yet to come. For beyond fish, which had brought Europeans across to Canada's coasts, fur would lead them right on into the continent.

On the Gaspé Peninsula, Cartier erected a tall, wooden cross, claiming the lands for France; but he did not enter the St. Lawrence River, that broad waterway thrusting onward into North America. He returned in 1535, however, with three ships, and sailed up the great river to the Iroquoian village of Stadacona, where the city of Quebec now stands. The Indians who welcomed him there referred to their village as "Kanata," an Iroquoian word meaning village or settlement. Yet Cartier took the term to apply to the surrounding country as well, calling that "Canada," and the St. Lawrence that flowed through

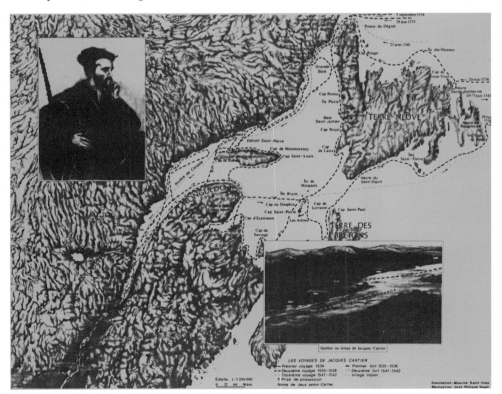

Jacques Cartier, Who Unlocked a St. Lawrence Empire to France. *The sixteenth-century sea-captain from St. Malo celebrated by this map of his historic voyages, opened the way for New France; and for the enduring French-Canadian heritage that followed.*

it the "River of Canada." From Stadacona, the French then voyaged on up-river to Hochelaga at the site of present Montreal, another large St. Lawrence Iroquoian village set in cornfields. Here tumbling rapids barred their ships from going further; and Cartier climbed Mont Royal, to see the river stretching on westward into distant forests.

After a harsh winter back at Stadacona — terrible to the unprepared French — Jacques Cartier returned to Saint-Malo in mid-1536: without real gold or silver, yet with knowledge of a mighty waterway that could be the key to France's empire in America. Accordingly, it was decided to plant a French colony in this new land of Canada, from which explorations to find gold and a Northwest Passage could continue. Various delays still held the project back till 1541, when 150 colonists came out with Cartier, to settle at Cape Rouge near Stadacona. Another killing winter followed. Cartier left with the survivors before the Sieur de Roberval, the official leader of the colony, finally arrived with still more settlers — many of whom would also die at Cape Rouge, in ruinous French ignorance of the North American land environment. Consequently, Roberval and the remaining colonists would go back to France. There were no gold mines to support a colony, no passage to the Orient. And the rise of Catholic-Protestant civil warfare within France itself soon left little margin for more colonial adventures from the 1540s.

All the same, fishing and fur-trading persisted. By mid-century, the Basques, both Spanish and French in background, had built up whaling at points along the Labrador coasts. Whalers, fishermen, and increasingly venturers who came to trade, spread into the Lower St. Lawrence, where Tadoussac at the mouth of the Saguenay particularly became a place of summer meetings between the trading ships and the Indians who gathered there with furs. The latter were mainly Montagnais, Algonquians from the St. Lawrence north shore; though in time other tribes up-river also sent pelts down to Tadoussac. Moreover, since beaver fur made excellent rain-resistant felt hats, and hats such as these grew fashionable in Europe during the later sixteenth century, the demand for plentiful Canadian

1. A Lasting Market for Canadian Fur — the Beaver Hat. *Unfortunately, this expressive drawing does not go back quite far enough, to the late sixteenth and early seventeenth centuries, when fashionable broad-brimmed, fur-felt hats first raised demands for large quantities of beaver pelts.*

2. Cartier Sails up the St. Lawrence to Stadacona, 1535. *Here his little fleet is met by Indians from the Iroquois village of Stadacona, which lies by the heights and narrows where a capital city, Quebec, will one day arise.*

3. Whaling off Atlantic Shores. *Another exaggerated version of the new American scene; but still showing major whaling operations, in which Basques from Spain were active along the Labrador coast, from the 1550s at least.*

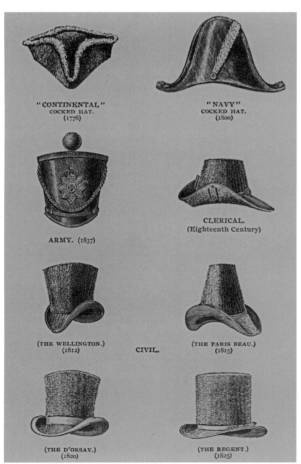

1

2

3

beaver rose in consequence. In fact, the beaver hat, broad-brimmed or narrow, then in later three-cornered or top-hat form, would reign through varying European styles for centuries ahead, in female as well as male versions.

At the other end of the trade, the Indian demands for European goods no less enlarged: for iron axes and edge-tools much better than stone, or iron traps to replace root-and-sinew snares; for fireproof metal kettles instead of woven baskets or breakable pottery; for manufactured cloth and blankets instead of animal skins, or glittering glass beads instead of shell or quill-work decorations. Furthermore, the Indians in direct contact with Europeans might pass trade goods on to tribes behind them, to gain more furs to barter with the white arrivals. These "middlemen" native groups could thus become important agents in the fur commerce, spreading awareness and desires for trade to inland peoples, even before the latter had actually seen a European. And so the fur trade developed as a crucial, mutual link between native societies and the newcomers. But in the process it would disrupt the former and emplace the latter firmly on Canadian soil.

1

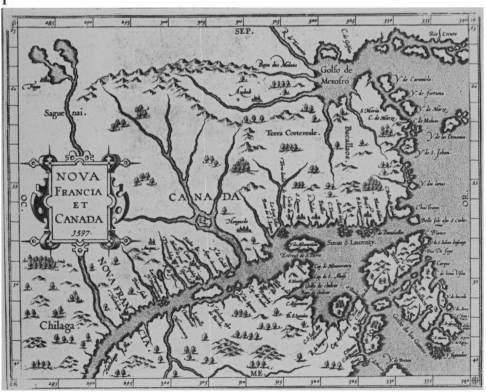

2

1. Cartier Claims Canada for France at Gaspé, 1534. *The arms and banner of France are there. The Indians with chiefs in Prairie-style feathered war-bonnets are less convincing, in this Montreal newspaper rendition done in 1908.*
2. Canada and New France, 1597. *A dubious map, showing Newfoundland divided into islets and a mainland where "New France" lies west from "Canada," it does reveal how indefinite still were names and European knowledge of the transatlantic territories before 1600.*

29 Jany 1611 Last Sondaye the Lord Archbyshopp was sworn a pryvye Consellor af Greenewych.

Last Sondaye heere aryved the Landgrave of Hessens eldest Sonne of 17 years age attended with 26 persons, and is to get in a Duch Ghest house in Lombard street. His chief gentleman and I had some conference, wherein he glanced at an entent of a mach with the Lady Elizabeth, "marry" he sayd that his Lords comeing was to see his Kingdom and to salute the (?bride) and princess.

The last weeke at Norwych upon a Soleme show daye in choosing their (?mayor) through a great crowd wch overthrew a scaffold there were 32 persons slayne and many hurt som were verye good accompt.

Last Tewsdaye at a Virgynya Court the Lord La Warre in person made his apollogye to the whole assemblye, saying allso that so soon as he could recover health he would be as willing to return to virgynya as any man.

The State & hope of the Bermudas was there fully dyscust and concluded to send a colony thither, the place so opulent, fertile and pleasant that all men now willing to go thither.

Mr. Guye of Bristow who the last yeare very discretely, honestly and providentlye wth a shipp and 30 honest persons well accomodated with all necessaryes as well quick creatures as other wayes, viz: Ducks, Geese, Henns, Conneyes, Goats, Swyne and Kyne, according to the terms of his Letters patient went to the Newfoundland, where he very orderly hath seated hymself, buylded a convenyent house, increased all sorts of his creatures, kyld many sorts of wyld beasts as Deere, Wolves, Foxes, and black foxes some of the skynns and other things he hath sent over for Testymony, and hath wrytten unto the rest of the adventurers his good estate, his farther dyscovery of the Countrey even in the winter season, when his people have healthfully endured the sharpest could, and that he hath all things yet for one yeares sustenance—The next Michaellmas he will com over in pson and prepare for further plantacon in that Contynent, whereunto all men are very forward to put in theyre moneyes, by reason this plantacon is very honest peacefull and hopefull, and very lykelye to be profytable.

Colonization, Cultural Change and Indian Conflict

As yet, however, in the years before 1600, no permanent European settlements had been made within the future bounds of Canada. True, in Newfoundland, especially along the English Avalon shore, there were fixed dry-fishing stations on land. But these were occupied by visiting transatlantic fishermen only over the summer months; although, in time, some "winterers" did stay on, to look after the docks, sheds and drying racks, and ready them for another season. Still, this was hardly effective colonization. Then around 1600, things rapidly began to change.

France recovered from its destructive period of religious wars under a strong, uniting monarch, Henry IV. Expansive business interests in the vigorous French nation-state now sought anew to build colonial property in America: through gaining royal charters that granted them monopoly rights to trade, lands and government in French claims overseas. In the prosperous, sea-minded England of Queen Elizabeth, and then of James I, enterprising merchant-capitalists took up similar designs. The upshot was a mounting series of new colonial ventures; for example, the chartered colony of some forty English settlers established in 1610 by John Guy, Bristol merchant, on Conception Bay in Newfoundland, or the successful founding of English Virginia by the well-heeled London Company at Jamestown in 1607. And as well, there was the very substantial group formed by the Sieur de Monts in France in 1604, which held a chartered monopoly of trade and settlement for "Acadia, Canada and other places in New France" — Acadia being the name which the French by now had given to the Atlantic mainland region beyond Newfoundland. De Monts set out to plant a colonial base within this broad monopoly grant. With him went Samuel de Champlain, royal geographer to Henry IV, an experienced soldier and seaman who had already visited the St. Lawrence in 1603. New France was about to grow.

The first efforts came in Acadia, where in 1605 de Monts established the little settlement of Port Royal on the Nova Scotian shores of the Bay of Fundy. Wooden houses that held forty people were built, enclosing a small courtyard. Fields and gardens were cleared; Indians came to trade furs. Yet Port Royal's success was definitely qualified, for its returns did not meet the costs: above all, of unlawful trading by monopoly-breakers ("interlopers"), who drained off furs along an open seacoast impossible to control. Thus de Monts, advised by Champlain, resolved to move his company's base to the St. Lawrence; a region much further from the ocean, but where the flow of furs down one great continental river would be both larger and easier to tend. Port Royal was abandoned, though later re-occupied and recurrently fought over. But the main thrust of French colonial ventures henceforth lay with the St. Lawrence — and with Champlain, who went there in 1608, as the company's "lieutenant in the country of New France."

He moved well above Tadoussac to establish a new monopoly trading base at Quebec, where the Iroquoian village of Stadacona had stood. Here furs could be intercepted before they got down to Tadoussac; narrows in the river would make checking interlopers more feasible; and the rugged heights of Cape Diamond above the stream could back and secure a post set by the water's edge. And so Champlain built a habitation at Quebec in 1608 for himself and twenty-seven companions, again composed of wooden houses linked in a courtyard, but with a

News on John Guy's English Colony in Newfoundland, 1611. *This printed sheet, an ancestor of newspapers soon to spread in Europe, covers other reports out of London; but particularly notes the founding by "Mr. Guye of Bristol" of an English settlement on the Avalon Peninsula.*

surrounding palisade, a moat, drawbridge and small cannon: a little fortress for any troubles ahead.

Stadacona and the other St. Lawrence Iroquoian villages once known to Cartier had gone. Why had they vanished? In part, it seems, because of the disrupting changes brought to native cultures by the fur trade. The French had been trading with Micmacs, Montagnais and other Algonquian hunting peoples well before they got up to the St. Lawrence villages of Iroquoian corn-growers, who were not major fur-hunters in themselves. Consequently, the Montagnais and their neighbours had acquired a superiority in white men's goods, in iron weapons and tools, enabling them to displace the Iroquoians from the vital St. Lawrence Valley trade route, and to make their deserted lands a hunting domain. No one can precisely give the details, but the spreading swirl of change would also affect the Five Nations Iroquois south and west of the St. Lawrence area, perhaps leading them to shape their own defensive League or Confederacy. In any case, the French increasingly became tied in with tribal alliances, native raids and war, as they sought to advance their fur-trade interests from a permanent base at Quebec. In 1609 Champlain and two other Frenchmen thus went with some sixty Indian allies, mainly Montagnais, south into the Iroquois country of the Mohawks, following the Richelieu River from the St. Lawrence to what would be named Lake Champlain. There they met and fought with a band of the formidable Mohawks; but shots from French guns killed three and scattered the rest of their opponents. It was a brief, unintended start to bloody cycles of French-Iroquois warfare — arising primarily out of the fur trade.

In repeated efforts to enlarge that trade, Champlain also made other expeditions inland, to develop relations with still more distant tribes who could send furs to Quebec. In 1613 he travelled up the Ottawa River from the St. Lawrence through the country of his trading allies, the Algonquin tribe, thereby opening a great Ottawa highway westward to French use. Two years later, Champlain undertook a still longer journey to the Huron country, paddling up the Ottawa again, and continuing via Lake Nipissing and the French River to Georgian Bay on Lake Huron. The "freshwater sea," he called it, as in July, 1615, the French first looked upon the Great Lakes. From here Champlain's party canoed to the foot of Georgian Bay, to the fertile, well-cultivated and populous lands of the Hurons: village-dwelling agriculturalists like their Iroquoian relatives — but long-term rivals — the Five Nations Iroquois south across Lake Ontario. The Huron Confederacy of four tribes was already sending furs down to Quebec, via the Ottawa and Algonquin allies along the way. And thanks to the Hurons' settled position at the heart of the Great Lakes basin, their well-established trading ties with hunting peoples to north and west, plus their own considerable strength, they were eminently fitted to become the key middlemen in the French fur trade — that is, in collecting furs from Great Lakes tribes to forward on to Quebec.

Still, the Hurons wanted not only trade goods from a French alliance, but armed support against their Five Nations enemies. Hence Champlain was soon committed to lead them in an attack on the Iroquois below Lake Ontario. In October, 1615, his army of Hurons, and some Algonquins, came upon a strongly fortified Iroquois village at the eastern end of that lake. A hasty, premature Indian attack failed, and deliberate, European-style siege warfare did not suit impatient Hurons. They retreated, carrying Champlain in a basket since he had been

1. Sieur de Monts, Colonizer of Acadia. *A trading entrepreneur created Lieutenant-General of New France, de Monts had made earlier voyages to America before organizing his chartered fur-trading company in 1604, and travelling out himself that year to plant a colony in Acadia. After a disastrous winter on isolated Ile Ste. Croix, near the entrance to the Bay of Fundy, de Monts moved his little settlement to better-located Port Royal, further up the Bay.*

2. Samuel de Champlain, Real Founder of New France. *Geographer, fur trader and colony-builder, Champlain himself had sailed to America in 1603, visiting the St. Lawrence. Thereafter, he went with de Monts to Acadia, pursuing coastal explorations; but more crucially, he led de Monts to shift his operations to the St. Lawrence. There in 1608, Champlain's founding of Quebec as the French company's new base truly began the mainstream heritage of French Canada.*

1

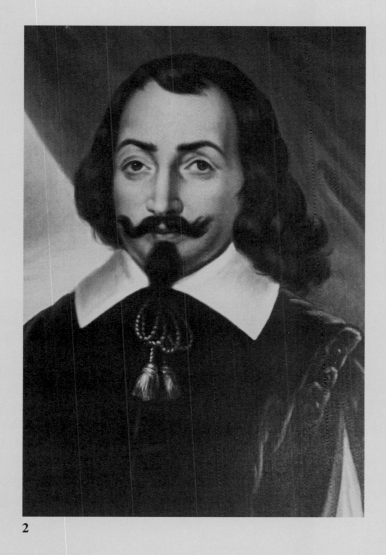

2

wounded by an arrow in the knee. Back in Huronia, he recovered over the winter, and visited the Petuns and Ottawas in the western, inter-lake peninsula of future Southern Ontario before returning to Quebec in 1616. The flow of fur from Hurons to French successfully went forward. But the former had lost some of their trust in all-conquering Europeans, while the Five Nations Iroquois felt new, resentful, confidence in themselves. Accordingly, to strengthen French political and cultural influences, Christian missionaries were sent into the Huron country.

It must be stressed that this did not mean some darkly cynical design behind the attempt to Christianize — and "civilize" — the Huron tribes. In the aftermath of great religious changes in Europe, where the Protestant Reformation had been followed by the Catholic Counter-Reformation, a Catholic France (or a Protestant England) was full of warmly zealous convictions, which often identified the aims of the true faith with that nation's political and economic purposes. Champlain, himself an ardent Catholic, wanted to send missionaries to the Hurons not just to Frenchify them or make them safe allies in the fur trade, but to lead them to Christian knowledge and salvation. He had already brought four Recollet friars out from France in 1615, one of whom, Father Le Caron, was in Huronia during Champlain's stay there. But the task was too great for the relatively small and weak Recollet community. And so the powerful Jesuit Order was called upon, highly trained and disciplined, and already serving the cause of Roman Catholicism in missions around the world. In 1625 three Jesuits arrived at Quebec, to begin a long Canadian heritage for their order — of courage, suffering, faith and devoted service. Among them was the outstanding Father Jean de Brébeuf, who began his work in Huronia the next year.

Meanwhile, the French settlement at Quebec had grown slowly, but significantly. By 1628, twenty years after its founding, the original fur-trade base of twenty-eight men was a village and the capital of New France, with around seventy inhabitants, including women and children; for some families now were settled there. Still, the bulk of Quebec's small French population were traders and storekeepers, workmen and dockhands, with soldiers, seamen and some clerics added. The first farmer, Louis Hébert (also an apothecary or pharmacist), had only arrived in 1617, to raise crops on the heights of Cape Diamond above Quebec. The settled colony could scarcely yet feed itself, being still dependent on the supply ships from France that took furs back overseas with them. As a result, when a minor war between England and France briefly erupted in Europe, an English fleet entered the St. Lawrence, captured a heavy-laden French convoy in 1628, and so compelled a starving Quebec to surrender by the next summer.

Champlain, its governor, was sent to England as a prisoner. But the fact that hostilities had already officially ended in Europe when Quebec was taken, led to its return to France in 1632. Then its former governor resumed his post, under the Company of The Hundred Associates, now the holders of the Canadian fur-trade

Champlain First Fights the Iroquois (Mohawks) in 1609. *This encounter, well west and south of Quebec on future Lake Champlain, was hardly more than a forest skirmish. But it brought the French and their fur trade into the strife between their own Indian tribal suppliers and the powerful Five Nations Iroquois. The scene, as shown, again is stylized, displaying rowboats rather than canoes, and a temporary Iroquois stockade under attack which would scarcely keep out a large poodle. Still, it represents a telling moment in French Canada's early history.*

monopoly. Actually, there had been several changes in the monopoly holders since Sieur de Monts' initial grant. Indeed, the creation in 1627 of a much more powerful chartered body, the Hundred Associates, had promised well — until the English war and the seizure of the Associates' first major convoy. Though restored in control, once New France was handed back, the company never fully recovered from this sizeable loss. Its later efforts to build the French colony were only limited. Nevertheless, more colonists, including farmers, did arrive. Trois Rivières was established as a settlement up-river; and by Champlain's death in 1635, there were about two hundred French in the vastness of the St. Lawrence holdings: remarkably few, yet an enduring base for a monumental French-Canadian heritage.

In any case, new problems were looming far in the wilderness interior. Here Jesuit missions spread in Huronia over the 1630s. By 1639, in fact, Father Jerome Lalement was erecting a self-sufficient mission headquarters at Ste. Marie on Georgian Bay near present-day Midland, the first European-built community in inland North America: with farm fields, stone bastions for its defending soldiers and a log chapel, hospital and workshop, together with a palisaded Indian village to house converts. All the same, the Hurons, like other native peoples, seemed to be more interested in immediate material benefits from trade goods than in future Christian salvation; while their own spiritual leaders, the shamans, were implacably hostile to the black-robed Jesuit "sorcerers." And so the efforts of the missionaries were not just discouraging, but hazardous. Then came the mounting impacts of European diseases in crowded Huron longhouses. The death rate was appalling: a Huron population of around 25,000 was nearly cut in half. The French, unknowing carriers, were hotly accused of evil magic. But the natives also came to feel that their own ancestral culture had failed them. Conversions mounted, as a sorely weakened, demoralized Huron people sought both help and hope: even as their Iroquois enemies moved to a decisive phase of conflict.

The Iroquois Five Nations had faced cultural change themselves, again associated with the fur trade, that crucial yet destabilizing tie between native and newcomer. They equally desired trade goods; but the French at Quebec were distant, and were allied with foes of the Iroquois — as the fight of 1609 on Lake Champlain had made sharply clear. Still, in the same year the Dutch arrived on the Hudson, and by 1624 had established New Amsterdam (later New York) at

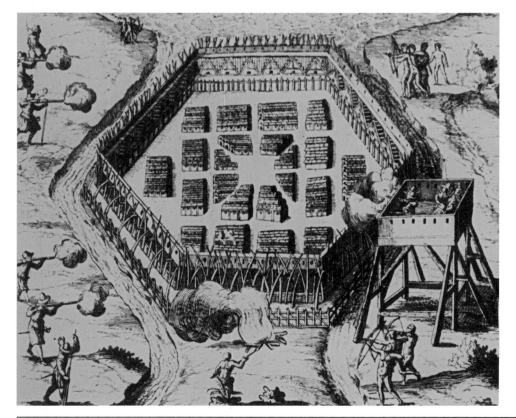

French, Hurons and Allies Attack Iroquois (Onondaga) Village on Lake Ontario, 1615. *The picture of this unsuccessful assault once more is thoroughly formalized — note the neat palisade and village layout, and even the French siege-tower more reminiscent of storming massive castles in Europe.*

1

2

1. Jesuit Fathers Arrive at Quebec, 1625. *Aboard ship off the little capital of New France, they are greeted by the Recollets — in a painting by C.W. Jefferys, one of Canada's most accurate historical artists.*

2. The English Capture Quebec, 1629. *As published in Holland in 1698, this is another overdone European version of the taking of the small French post at Quebec by a minor English expedition. Still, although the grand fortress towers depicted, and the proud city behind them, are far from authentic, the picture does mark a considerably significant event: the transfer of Canada to English control — even if that transfer proved very temporary, and would not be effected lastingly for 130 years more.*

3

3. French Jesuits in the Huron Country: Jean de Brébeuf. *One of the greatest of the Jesuit missionaries, he served in Huronia, 1626-39; and again in 1633-49, when he was tortured and put to death by Iroquois raiders at the mission of St. Ignace.*

4. Hurons Defending Mission Village. *This scene at St. Louis in 1648, shows that Huron warriors fought bitterly against their old Five Nations enemies. But they failed to save this or other centres, demoralized and weakened by diseases as they were.*

4

that river's Atlantic entrance. The Iroquois hence gained access to Dutch trade supplies, including muskets. In time, moreover, the rise of New England, where the strong English Puritan colony of Massachusetts Bay was founded in 1629, would offer another, if farther, source of valuable goods. In time, as well, the Five Nations grew thoroughly dependent on the traps, hatchets and guns of the Europeans. But not being primarily hunters themselves, the Iroquois like the Hurons also became middlemen, trading furs from other tribes. They sought to check the flow of pelts out to the St. Lawrence, to turn it down to their own villages instead, and on to the Dutch on the Hudson, where the English later took over. The Huron-Algonquin-French trade system proved too firmly entrenched, however. Consequently, traditional native rivalries of Huron and Iroquois swelled to a far more deadly struggle between committed fur-trade middlemen — in which, for very economic survival, one side had to demolish the other. And the Iroquois had escaped much of the terrible Huron losses from disease; most likely because they did not have white men regularly living in their midst. They were also politically well organized; their own morale was high; while by the later 1640s they held a massive lead in guns. All this spelled ruin for the Hurons, whom they sweepingly attacked; while the few or far-off French could do little.

In 1648 Iroquois raiders fell on the mission village of St. Joseph in Huronia, slaying the Jesuit Father Daniel and bearing away hundreds of prisoners. The same year St. Ignace and St. Louis were destroyed by an Iroquois army of 1,200, and Fathers Brébeuf and Lalement taken off to slow deaths by torture. The broken Hurons could make no effective stand. To prevent more bloodshed, the Jesuits themselves abandoned and burned their prized showpiece, the big central mission of Ste. Marie. The next year saw the survivors of the grand Jesuit experiment reach Quebec: just some sixty French, including soldiers who had come too late, and around 300 Christian Hurons, whose descendants would live on in settlements outside Quebec. The Hurons as a people had disappeared; though they had not actually been wiped out. Native warfare was seldom as ruthless as European conflicts could be. The defeated elements had been shattered and dispersed, some to flee east to shelter with the French, others west across the Great Lakes to tribes there, while still others would be incorporated in the Iroquois nations, as was the custom among the native peoples, especially in regard to women and children.

Nonetheless, Huronia had been effectively removed. The victorious Iroquois drove on to clear the inlands of any other rivals. The Petuns, Attiwandirons and Nipissings were scattered, leaving Southern Ontario virtually an empty hunting ground. Meanwhile, the Five Nations, having blocked the fur trade to the French, next struck directly at them. In 1650 Iroquois war parties came within a few miles of Quebec. And Montreal, then the advanced post of Ville Marie set up in

Ste. Marie Among the Hurons. *Here on river banks near Georgian Bay, one now can visit the careful reconstruction of the French Jesuits' main base in Huronia, built originally about 1639.*

1642 as a French mission and hospital base for Indians, was particularly embattled on the front line. But by 1653 the Five Nations were ready to cease fighting. In part, they had achieved their purpose of eliminating fur competitors; in part, they were worn down themselves, yet had not really cracked New France; and in part, they were under heavy attack from another people, the Eries, on their west. Accordingly, a breathing-space rather than a peace ensued. But during it, the fur trade — that be-all of New France — was able to revive after famine years of blockade. Moreover, since the native middleman trading system had now been virtually erased, the French themselves had to travel inland to western tribes for furs. And so the *coureurs-de-bois* took over.

These roamers of the woods had had their beginnings in Champlain's "young men" sent out to live with native peoples and learn their languages and customs. Among them was Etienne Brulé, who in 1615 had gone with Hurons south from Georgian Bay to Toronto harbour on Lake Ontario, thus probably becoming the first European to travel the Toronto Passage between the Upper and Lower Great Lakes, as well as (later) to be the first newcomer to enter Lake Superior. And by the 1650s, Brulé and others like him had found their heirs in French traders and trappers who knew the wilds about as well as the Indians: daring individualists, often self-seeking and fiercely unrestrained, who gloried in forest freedom and adventure. This breed of wilderness French included men like Pierre Radisson and Médard Chouart des Groseilliers, who traced northern routes above areas of Iroquois domination to reach new fur sources along the Upper Great Lakes. Radisson and Groseilliers visited the country around Lake Superior in 1659; and the next year returned to Quebec with a large fur cargo. Still, such temporary successes could not basically alter the problems of a weak, beleaguered French colony facing real prospects of economic collapse. In fact, the Iroquois Five Nations had returned to war again in 1658, cutting off trade and harrying French settlements afresh.

In these circumstances, the ruling French Company of Hundred Associates could do little; even though its trading operations had now been transferred to a select business group within Canada itself. But amid conflict and sharp doubt, the Jesuits still stood out as vital patrons and supporters of the distressed colony: wealthy and powerful in Europe and especially influential in New France, where the Jesuit Superior now stood second only to the company governor at Quebec. The staunch Catholic Jesuit presence there, through these harrowing times, would leave lasting heritage impressions on French Canada.

But by 1661 things were changing dramatically once more. A young monarch, Louis XIV, had taken full control of a rich and formidable French state, free now from wars at home, and able to pursue grand designs abroad, under its ambitious and absolute new ruler, Louis, to be called the "Sun King." Through the invaluable services of his colonial minister, Jean Colbert, the King worked diligently to remake and extend the French empire. Thus in 1663, an impotent company rule in New France was replaced by strong royal government, operating directly under the crown and its officials, while effective military action against the Iroquois was soon to follow. A new era for the French in Canada was under way, to last for virtually a century ahead. And as for the native Canadians themselves, they now faced not just passing Norse contacts or uncertain English and French venturings from overseas, but large and steadily-growing European communities on Canadian soil — as the white newcomers increasingly became settled, rooted inhabitants of America.

1. Ville-Marie (Montreal) in 1642. *The beginnings of a great city, established originally as an Indian mission and haven. It was to become a control point for inland transport and the fur trade, to and from the western wilds beyond.*

2. The Combat at the Long Sault, 1660. *A desperate struggle in the renewed French-Iroquois conflict. Here on the Lower Ottawa not far above Montreal, seventeen French and some forty Indian allies had sought to ambush Iroquois fur-seekers returning down the Ottawa. But the French-led group under Adam Dollard des Ormeaux was itself out-ambushed at this derelict palisade by well over 400 Iroquois. The French side was overwhelmed, though they killed many foes. Religious and nationalistic Canadien writers would come to hail their valiant resistance as saving New France. Later historians were not so sure that the Iroquois did not think that they had won the battle. In any case, whether a French moral victory or not, the Long Sault was to enter deeply into French-Canadian tradition as an episode of heroism.*

1

2

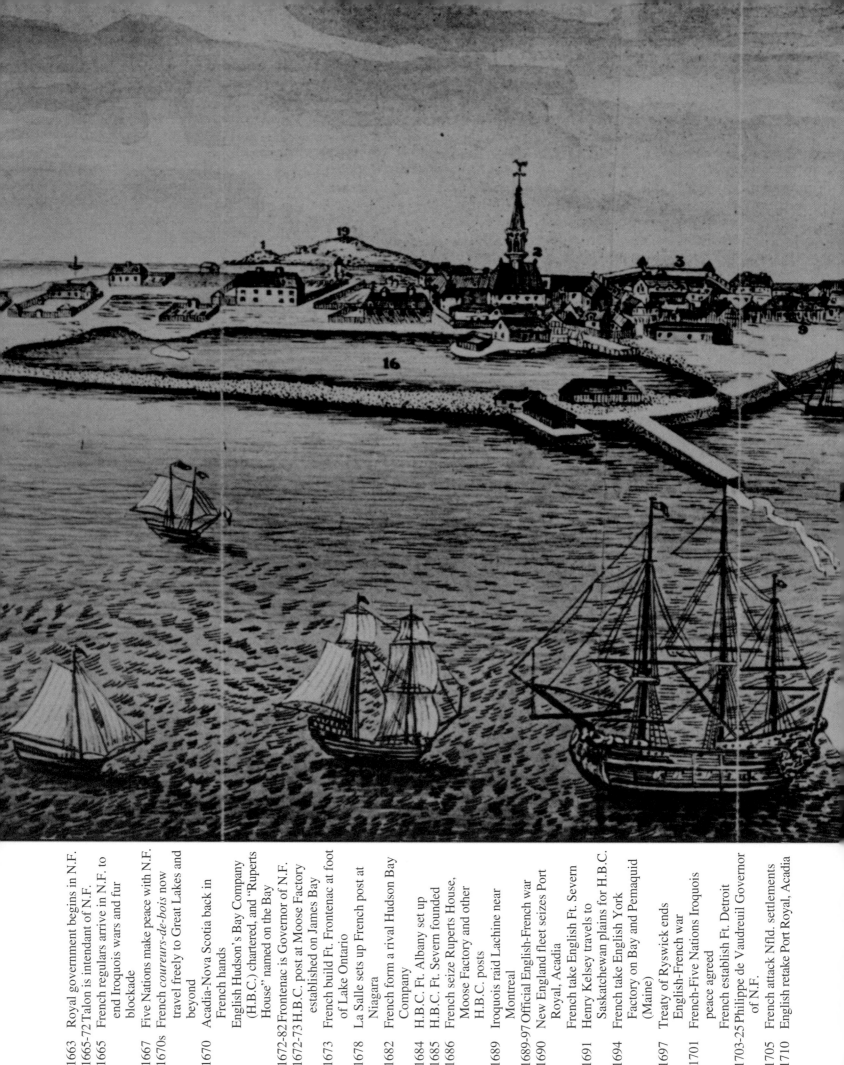

1663   Royal government begins in N.F.
1665-72 Talon is intendant of N.F.
1665   French regulars arrive in N.F. to end Iroquois wars and fur blockade
1667   Five Nations make peace with N.F.
1670s French *coureurs-de-bois* now travel freely to Great Lakes and beyond
1670   Acadia-Nova Scotia back in French hands
       English Hudson's Bay Company (H.B.C.) chartered, and "Ruperts House" named on the Bay
1672-82 Frontenac is Governor of N.F.
1672-73 H.B.C. post at Moose Factory established on James Bay
1673   French build Ft. Frontenac at foot of Lake Ontario
1678   La Salle sets up French post at Niagara
1682   French form a rival Hudson Bay Company
1684   H.B.C. Ft. Albany set up
1685   H.B.C. Ft. Severn founded
1686   French seize Ruperts House, Moose Factory and other H.B.C. posts
1689   Iroquois raid Lachine near Montreal
1689-97 Official English-French war
1690   New England fleet seizes Port Royal, Acadia
       French take English Ft. Severn
1691   Henry Kelsey travels to Saskatchewan plains for H.B.C.
1694   French take English York Factory on Bay and Pemaquid (Maine)
1697   Treaty of Ryswick ends English-French war
1701   French-Five Nations Iroquois peace agreed
       French establish Ft. Detroit
1703-25 Philippe de Vaudreuil Governor of N.F.
1705   French attack Nfld. settlements
1710   English retake Port Royal, Acadia

Chapter Three
A Century of New France 1663 — 1763

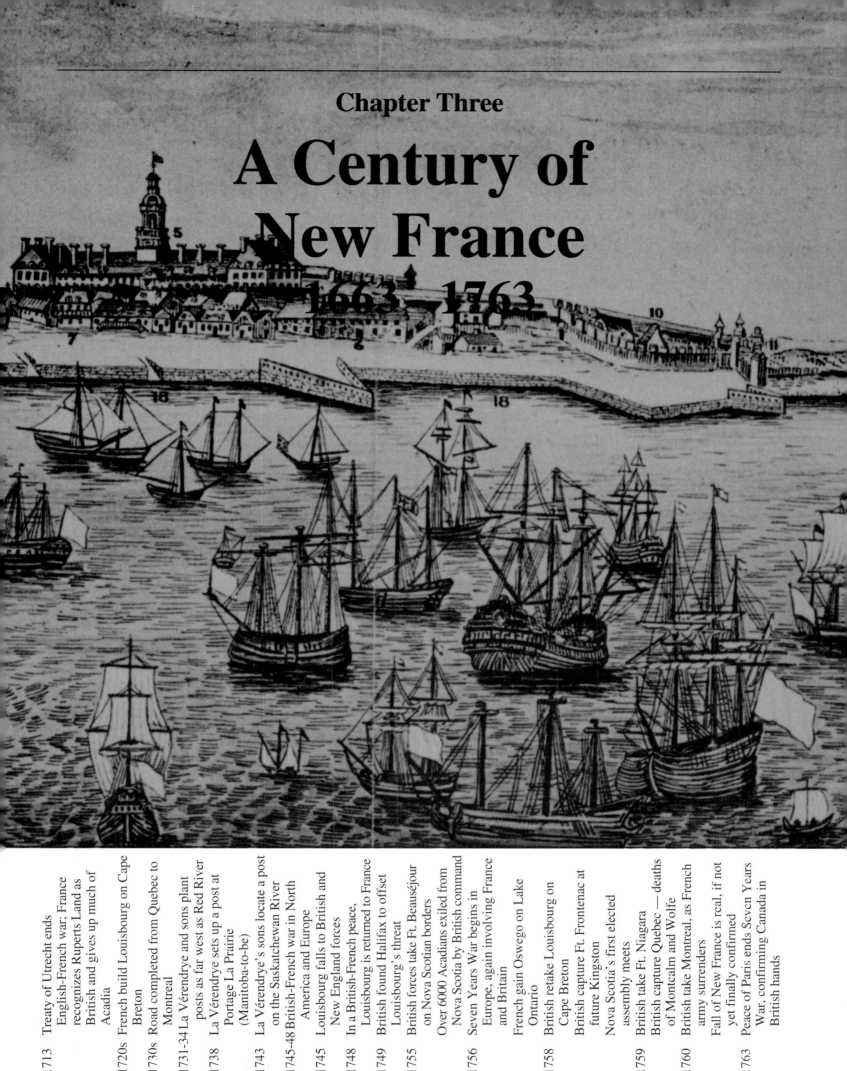

Colonial Growth, Imperial Expansion

By the early 1660s, the colonists of New France numbered less than 3,000 after half a century of occupation; though already over half of them were Canadian-born. Near-empty Acadia was not even in French possession at that time. Claimed as well by England, this Atlantic coastal area had repeatedly changed hands. The French had been driven out of a revived Port Royal in 1613. Instead, Scottish settlers had begun their own colony of Nova Scotia there in 1628, only to see the whole territory restored to France in 1632. Then, after short years of renewed French colonization, Acadia-Nova Scotia had again been taken over by English power in 1654; to be held until France came back once more in 1670 — which by no means put an end to Acadia's shifts. Meanwhile, in English Newfoundland, "planters" (colonists) largely brought out in the 1630s and 40s had in the main become permanent resident fishermen; though probably were still under a thousand by the 1660s. Of course, by then there were many more thousands of English colonists on the North American seaboard, from New England to Virginia. Yet in all the Canadian territories of the future there were only the mentioned few handfuls of European settlers. Within New France, however, this was about to change.

The new royal government established for that colony in 1663 sought vigorously to promote settlement, economic development and military security, closely guided and supported by the weighty central bureaucracy of Louis XIV's absolute French state. This new governing system, which would last to the end of French rule in Canada, had at its core a Sovereign or Superior Council, directly appointed by the crown and headed by three top officials, the governor, intendant and bishop. The governor, particularly concerned with military and external affairs, was nominally foremost; and in wartime, or in Indian diplomacy and the fur trade, he well would be. Yet the intendant, who broadly dealt with internal administration, especially in regard to settlement, land, law, and economic policies, could loom large indeed. And the bishop did not just lead the powerful, established Catholic Church within the colony, but, as a high officer of the ruling Council, could be influential in social, judicial and other matters brought before it.

Personal factors also had their effects, as witnessed by the career of François de Laval, first bishop of Quebec. The Jesuits' own candidate for that post, and named to it by both Pope and King, the forceful Laval not only complemented the Jesuit's own strivings by shaping an active, resident clergy for the people of New France, but also by maintaining a strong religious presence within the colony's ruling Council. In that Council's early years, he clashed with Quebec's first royal governor, the Chevalier de Mésy, whose personal piety still did not make him subservient enough to an authoritative bishop; though Mésy did do some useful work in getting the new government system into operation. More significant, however, was Jean-Baptiste Talon, intendant in New France between 1665 and 1672. A first-rate servant of an outstanding master, the minister Jean Colbert in Paris, Talon was critically important in the first decade of New France under royal government — which put that colony decisively on a path to lasting community growth.

Yet essential to that growth was the ending of the Iroquois' fur blockade, and their raiding onslaughts on the colony. In 1665, more than a thousand of the king's regular troops arrived from France to carry the war home to the enemy's

Overleaf. Louisbourg in 1731. *The French empire's great Atlantic fortress on Cape Breton was well established by that date; as is indicated by this view of its commanding citadel where Louisbourg's governor dwelt, with a substantial trading town in front of it.*

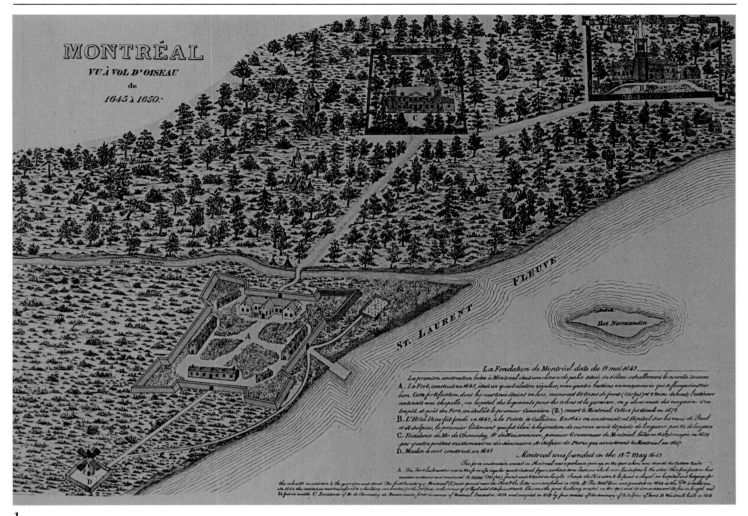

1. Montreal Around Mid-Century. *Shown for 1649-50, this sketch would already be bit out-of-date by the early 60s, though not seriously that far — Montreal's trading growth was largely to follow. In any event, the little mission "outpost" here displays its basic Fort by the river, and the Hotel-Dieu of the Church.*

2. Eastern Canada from a Map of 1662. *The map perhaps tells more about what still was not definitely known to Europeans, than what was.*

TERRITORIAL EVOL

☐	ENGLISH
☐	FRENCH
☐	SPANISH
☒	DISPUTED

1667

First successful French settlements in North America Port Royal (1606) and Québec (1608). English settlement in Virginia begins (1606-07). French and English territorial claims overlap Acadia. Acadia is recognized as French possession by the Treaty of Breda (1667). A Royal Charter (1670) grants sole trading rights in Hudson Bay drainage basin to the Hudson's Bay Co.

☐	BRITISH
☐	FRENCH
☒	DISPUTED
☒	DISPUTED
☐	SPANISH

1713

By the Treaty of Utrecht, France cedes Nova Scotia (excluding Cape Breton Island) to Great Britain, relinquishes her interests in Newfoundland and recognizes British rights to Rupert's Land.

☐	BRITISH
☐	DANISH
☐	SPANISH

1763

By the Treaty of Paris (1763) eastern North America becomes British territory except St-Pierre and Miquelon Islands (France). British colonial governments for Quebec, Newfoundland (with Île d'Anticosti and Îles de la Madeleine), Nova Scotia (including present-day N.B. and P.E.I.). Hudson's Bay Co. still administers Rupert's Land. Louisiana is ceded to Spain by France.

☐	BRITISH
☐	DANISH
☐	SPANISH

1774

St. John's Island is separated from Nova Scotia (1769). The Quebec Act (1774) enlarges Quebec to include Labrador, Île d'Anticosti, Îles de la Madeleine, and Indian Country to the north and to the west and south to the Ohio and Mississippi rivers.

The United State by the Treaty of from the Atlantic Cape Breton Isl

☐	BRITISH
☐	AMERICAN
☐	DANISH
☐	RUSSIAN

1849

The Province of Canada is formed by uniting Upper and Lower Canada (1840). The international boundary from the Rocky Mountains to the Pacific is described by the Oregon Treaty (1846). The northern portion of the Oregon Territory is called New Caledonia, a name used by Simon Fraser in 1806. The Hudson's Bay Co. is granted Vancouver's Island to develop a colony (1849).

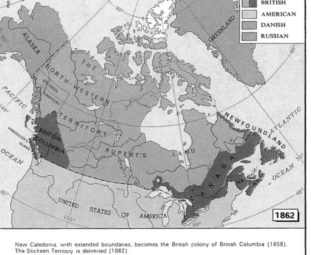

☐	BRITISH
☐	AMERICAN
☐	DANISH
☐	RUSSIAN

1862

New Caledonia, with extended boundaries, becomes the British colony of British Columbia (1858). The Stickeen Territory is delimited (1862).

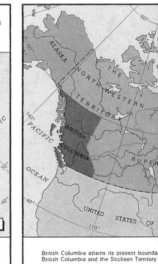

British Columbia attains its present bounda British Columbia and the Stickeen Territory

TION OF CANADA

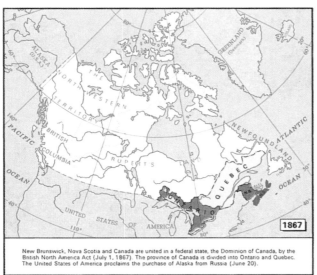

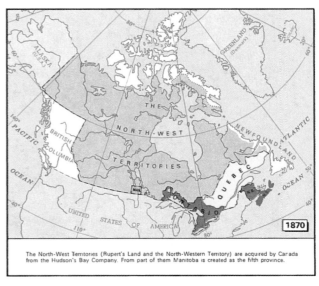

BRITISH
AMERICAN
DANISH
SPANISH

...ns independence from Britain ...S.A. boundaries are described Woods. New Brunswick and ...d from Nova Scotia (1784).

Following the Constitutional Act, Quebec is divided into Upper and Lower Canada (1791). Spain cedes Louisiana back to France (1800). U.S.A. purchases Louisiana (1803).

St. John's Island (Île St-Jean) is renamed Prince Edward Island (1798). Île d'Anticosti and the coast of Labrador from the St-Jean River to Hudson Strait are transferred from Lower Canada to Newfoundland by the Labrador Act (1809).

The international boundary is extended westward along the 49th parallel to the Rocky Mountains (1818). The Oregon Territory is occupied jointly by Britain and U.S.A. Reannexation: Cape Breton Island to Nova Scotia (1820); Île d'Anticosti and part of the coast of Labrador to Lower Canada (1825). Agreement between Russia and Britain on the description of Alaska boundary (1825).

...g of the colonies of Vancouver's Island. ...boundary along the 60th parallel.

New Brunswick, Nova Scotia and Canada are united in a federal state, the Dominion of Canada, by the British North America Act (July 1, 1867). The province of Canada is divided into Ontario and Quebec. The United States of America proclaims the purchase of Alaska from Russia (June 20).

The North-West Territories (Rupert's Land and the North-Western Territory) are acquired by Canada from the Hudson's Bay Company. From part of them Manitoba is created as the fifth province.

1

2

3

1. Bishop Laval Greets the Intendant Talon at Quebec. *The painting by Frank Craig conveys the coming of the powerful system of royal government to New France, with Jean Talon as intendant. An influential Catholic Church, headed by resolute Bishop Laval, here meets a new governor, De Tracy; but as well and more important, the vigorous intendant who will have charge of the colony's internal affairs.*

2. Jean Talon, Intendant, 1665-1672. *Talented and dedicated agent of the imperially-minded bureaucracy in Paris, this top administrator did a great deal to promote French colonization in Canada, to settle its farmland and encourage its trade and industry — backed, of course, by necessary support from the Crown's officialdom in France.*

3. Jean Colbert, Minister of French Empire. *Talon's master in Paris was the brilliant Colbert, Minister of Marine, who created a new French navy and built up the overseas empire, in accord with the grand ambitions of Louis XIV, absolute monarch of France.*

4. François de Laval-Montmorency. *A French priest educated by Jesuits, Laval was made a bishop in 1658, then named by the Pope to serve in New France. In 1674 he was given the actual title of Bishop of New France, and lived at Quebec till his death in 1708; though ill-health forced him in 1688 to yield his own strong sway to a successor.*

5. The Arrival of the French "Filles du Roi" at Quebec, 1667. *The sending out of these marriageable women by the French state (each supplied with a trousseau) was an effective part of the endeavours of Colbert and Talon to build up settlement in New France.*

4

5

lands. The next year, the seasoned Carignan-Salières regiment and a sizeable force of colonial militia marched into Mohawk country with drums beating, banners waving and guns massed, in a grand display of European armed strength. What proved even more effective, the French army razed Mohawk villages, burning their cornfields and food stores in a heavy blow to a settled Iroquois farming people. In 1667 the Five Nations sued for peace. Their power had been blunted, though not broken. But now developments already in hand within the French colony now could readily go forward.

Basic here was settlement. A new stream of immigrants arrived from France, state-assisted even to the provision of farm animals, seeds and implements. Intendant Talon also led the home authorities to agree to Carignan-Salières' officers and soldiers remaining as colonists. Those who chose to do so were granted lands along the Richelieu, thus forming a bulwark against future Iroquois attacks from the south. Furthermore, Colbert, with Talon's active support, sent 1,200 marriageable young women (the *filles du roi*, wards of the Crown) to this frontier colony, where in 1663 males had outnumbered females nearly two to one. Further still, Talon withdrew hunting or fur-trading privileges from bachelors, and provided money grants to young married men and fathers of large families. This indeed was supporting family values. By 1671, the intendant could happily report about 700 births to Colbert. During the first decade of royal government, in fact, population climbed to over 9,000. From then on, immigration fell away, largely due to declining government aid, as France became caught up in costly new wars in Europe. Nevertheless, the tradition of large French-Canadian families was now well set; and thereafter, a still-growing colony went on replacing over ninety percent of its people through natural birth, not immigration.

Settlement also meant land grants, to build a wider base for farming in New France. In this respect, the French seigneurial system of land-holding, already brought to the colony in its days of company rule, continued to set patterns for a rising countryside. Under this system long traditional in France, the crown granted large estates to chosen seigneurs, overlords, in return for duties of settlement and service. They in turn allotted individual farms to tenants — "habitants" in New France — who for their own part owed rents and services to their particular seigneur. Seigneurialism could be oppressive in a densely occupied Old France; but in New France where land was widely available, it was

The Seminary of Quebec, established, 1663. *An enduring institution founded by Laval, it suggests the new scale of emerging life in Quebec. In fact, this initial school for a Canadian priesthood led ultimately to French Canada's major Laval University in the mid-nineteenth century.*

far less so, and was the means of getting people on to farms. The seigneur or his agent dealt with arriving immigrants to invite them to splendid new land-holdings. (Developers have a long heritage of their own in Canada!) And so cleared farms spread out along the St. Lawrence shore, both eastward of Quebec and west towards Trois-Rivières. A rural, seigneurial French-Canadian society was thus taking shape, apart from the older fur-trade world.

Talon had much to do with supervising the whole process. Yet to carry out Colbert's instructions, he also fostered economic developments in more than farming settlement. The minister in Paris wanted essentially to broaden New France from a narrow reliance on furs; not only to make it much more self-supporting and less dependent on supplies from home, but also to enable it to provide supplies of its own — say, in grain or lumber — to France's plantation colonies down in the West Indies. Talon responded diligently. He strove to encourage lumbering, mining and shipbuilding, stressed domestic crafts, and even founded a Quebec brewery. His efforts were still hampered by the colony's relative lack of money, labour and internal demand. And Colbert's visions of an industrious, compactly integrated France overseas would effectively be denied by North American distances — and by the lure of the fur trade in itself. But while the colony was not to become solidly self-supporting, Talon's efforts and the growth of both agriculture and craftsmanship undoubtedly strengthened it: to make it a more substantial base for the expansion of French fur trade, which now was increasingly under way.

By the 1670s, the lifting of the hostile Iroquois barrier meant that the French could freely travel the Ottawa or Upper St. Lawrence rivers into the Great Lakes

1. La Salle, Key Agent in French Expansion. *Here this outstanding adventurer sits before a map of huge fur-trade domains to west and south, which he opened to French empire in the 1670s and 80s.*

2. The Comte de Frontenac. *Governor of New France, 1672-82 and 1689-98, Frontenac was an eager and even greedy expansionist, ever after fur-trade profits. Yet he carried the spread of New France far onward, through his support of audacious traders like La Salle.*

1

2

1

2

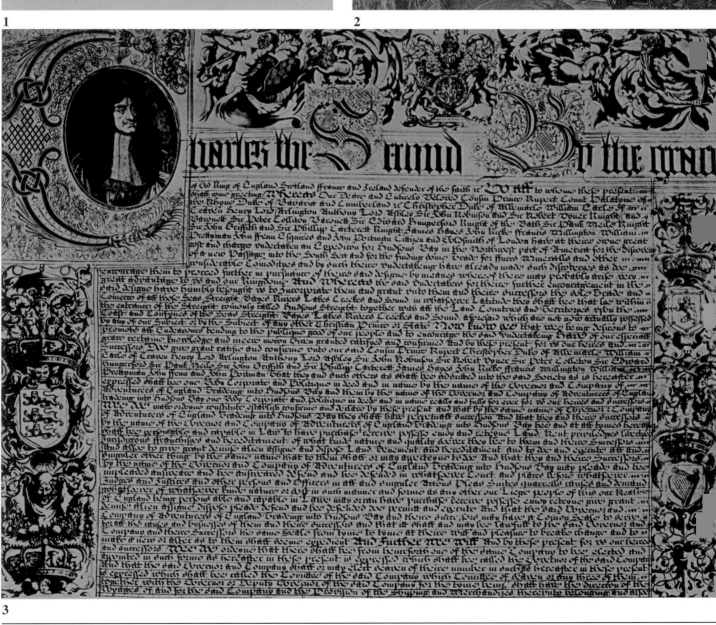

3

region, and to western furs beyond. Gone were the Huron middlemen, though the Ottawa tribes in some degree took on that role. But generally, the French themselves, as *coureurs-de-bois* and fur entrepreneurs, thrust their canoe routes northwest and southwest into the heart of the continent. They were enthusiastically backed by the Comte de Frontenac, Governor of New France from 1672 to 1682 — not just in order to expand French-Indian trade, but also to restore that governor's own debt-laden fortunes through fur profits. In 1673, an aggressive Frontenac established an advanced post where the Upper St. Lawrence met Lake Ontario at the future site of Kingston; and he granted this Fort Frontenac to one of his ablest fur-trade protegés, the Sieur de La Salle. From here, an ever-audacious La Salle went on to build a further post at Niagara in 1678; launched the first ship on the Upper Lakes, explored the Illinois country; and finally made his epic journey down the Mississippi, which took him southward to its mouth on the Gulf of Mexico in 1682. Consequently, La Salle enormously extended the French wilderness empire. Meanwhile, Daniel Greysolon du Lhut, *coureur-de-bois,* had reached Dakota (Sioux) territory beyond Lake Superior by 1679, and then established a fur post for the northwest, at Kaministiquia on the head of Lake Superior. Plainly, by the 1680s the French had spread their loosely-held fur domain over almost half a continent — to the considerable benefit both of Montreal, now the chief fur-trade headquarters, and Quebec, the key seaport and governing centre of New France.

Yet a rival English fur trade was advancing at the same time. It had long been growing along the inland margins of English seaboard settlements in America; and particularly along the Hudson River, where in 1664 England had seized the Dutch colony centred at New Amsterdam, which hence became New York. From the Hudson, English fur traders took up dealings with the Iroquois, and probed further inward along the forest frontiers of other English-American colonies. But much broader in long-range impact was a wholly new English fur trade that began about 1670, well to the north of New France, on the inland coasts of Hudson Bay and James Bay. It all stemmed back to earlier English searches for the Northwest Passage; right back to Martin Frobisher, who had voyaged north from the Atlantic and reached Baffin Island in 1576; and above all, to Henry Hudson, who in 1610 went west past Baffin to sail through the strait and into the giant Bay which now carries his name. Although he died there in 1611, after wintering on the shores of James Bay, Hudson had opened a navigable northern seaway from the Atlantic into the very core of Canada.

Years later, in 1659, the French *coureurs-de-bois* from the St. Lawrence, Radisson and Groseilliers, had found abundant high-quality beaver pelts in lands south of Hudson's Bay. But angered by the official seizure of these unlicensed furs on their return to Quebec in 1660, and then frustrated by failure to win their case in France, they instead took a bold proposal over to London in 1665: to use Henry Hudson's route into the great Bay already claimed by England, and tap by sea the wealth of fur within its surrounding territories. A trial voyage in 1668 from England to the Bay proved so successful that in 1670, the "Company of

1. Martin Frobisher, English Elizabethan Seaman. *A pioneer explorer of the Far Northern seas, as depicted on a modern postage stamp.*
2. The Last Voyage of Henry Hudson, 1611. *The English navigator who sailed into Hudson Bay was cast adrift by his own mutinous sailors, to die hopelessly with a few loyal supporters amid the icy waters he himself had revealed to Europeans.*
3. Charter of the Hudson's Bay Company 1670. *Granted by Charles II of England, it gave this new London-based company a fur monopoly and government rights in all the vast areas that drained into the great Bay uncovered by Hudson.*
4. Bay Company Post at Moose Factory. *Founded in 1673, but here shown much later, in 1854. "Factory" at first simply meant a base for traders.*

4

Gentlemen Adventurers trading into Hudson's Bay" was set up in London. Its charter from King Charles II gave it monopoly rights over fur trade, lands and government in all the territory that drained into Hudson Bay: a huge area whose extent was then unknown in Europe of the day, but one which actually reached from northern Quebec and Ontario of the future far west over the prairies to the Rockies, and northward deep into the Arctic. This enormous segment of Canada would form the basis of an English trading empire that spread across north and west; and existed, moreover, long before the final disappearance of New France in 1763. In short, any assumption that there was only a French Canada before that date is not true to our full Canadian northern heritage — not true from Labrador right out across the western plains.

Centrally active in forming the English Hudson's Bay Company of 1670 was the soldier Prince Rupert of Bavaria, Charles II's cousin. In recognition, the Company's chartered territory would be known as Rupert's Land; and its first post, set on the eastern (Quebec) coast of James Bay, was named Rupert's House in 1670. Moose Factory appeared by 1673 on the "Ontario" shore; Forts Albany and Severn in 1684 and 1685, farther along the northern Ontario coastline. By this time, however, the growth of Bay Company competition had come to worry the French, spreading as it did through territories which they considered to belong legally to New France. And so in 1682 a French Hudson Bay Company took shape in response — which soon would take to force, in order to drive the English from their posts around the Bay. Furthermore, far to the south, the Iroquois Confederacy was stirring again: increasingly alarmed by the fur trade flowing out of Great Lakes lands to the French on the St. Lawrence, but not to themselves and their English allies in the Province of New York based upon the Hudson. The French had never really been able to conciliate the powerful Five Nations, yet had rather tried to soothe and overawe them at the same time. Now, however, the rival interests were approaching open war over the inland fur trade.

On Hudson Bay in 1686, a French expedition sent north overland forcibly seized Ruperts House, Moose Factory and other English posts, along with fifty thousand prime beaver pelts. In the Great Lakes interior, the Iroquois erupted into Illinois country, an area once held by them but which was now tied into French fur commerce. French counter-blows in the interior proved ineffective, including a massive attack on the Senecas and Cayugas of the Five Nations in 1687. In their turn, the Iroquois descended on the village of Lachine outside Montreal in 1689, and killed many of its inhabitants. Yet French-Indian war and fur-traders' combat on Hudson Bay soon merged into a far wider struggle between France and England, in both Europe and America. In America, it would be fought in Acadia and Newfoundland as well on the St. Lawrence, the Bay, and in borderlands between New France and the colonies of New York or New England. Imperial expansion, both French and English, had brought the two colonial powers into major conflict within North America. It was really the opening round in a mighty contest for the continent.

Rival Fur Traders, Racing to an Indian Camp.

Contending Empires in War and Peace

The War of the League of Augsburg was declared in Europe in 1688; but neither its "official" name nor its European background need concern us here, when there are so many Canadian aspects to consider. In Newfoundland, for example, ships from the main French fishing and naval base at the island, Placentia on its southern coast, ravaged the English outport fishing settlements that had spread along the eastern Avalon shore; in 1696 briefly capturing St. John's itself, the leading English harbour. In Acadia, on the other hand, the French capital, Port Royal, was seized in 1690 by a fleet from New England — another shift in the control of the Acadian colony. French efforts in this quarter since the 1670s had sought in some degree to build up settlement, as in France's main St. Lawrence colony. Thus by the 1690s there were around 1,000 French settlers in Acadia, living chiefly near Port Royal along the Bay of Fundy: mostly farmers on lush tidal marshes, which they diked and drained, plus fishermen, seamen and still some fur traders dealing with the Micmacs. But this small coastal community had once more been neglected by French imperial interests looking to inland fur-trade expansion; while New Englanders from down the coast fished in its waters, supplied its settlers by shipboard, and adopted the view that Acadia should really be theirs. It is also true that Acadian and French privateers (effectively, licenced pirates) readily harassed New England ships and outlying settlements from time to time. At any rate, when open war began, Port Royal itself fell easily in 1690 to exasperated New England invaders. But the Acadian story was by no means over yet.

Meanwhile at Quebec, Frontenac, the pugnacious former Governor of New France, was back in command. Domineering, scheming and constantly quarrelling, he had been recalled to France in 1682, particularly because of an angry feud with Bishop Laval over trading brandy to the Indians. Laval and the Church had utterly condemned this ruinous trade. The Governor and his fur-trade allies had held that it was essential — better to have French brandy in demand than English rum. But after his recall, Frontenac's successors had not coped successfully with Iroquois power. Hence the old warrior was sent out again to New France in 1689, a very symbol of aggressive confidence. He needed all that confidence in 1690, when the New England fleet under Sir William Phips which had already taken Port Royal sailed up the St. Lawrence to a much bigger target, Quebec itself. Secure in fortifications high on Cape Diamond, Frontenac grandly told the English he would answer them from his cannons' mouths. And he did, while the ill-prepared, poorly-directed attackers battered uselessly away at the shores, until they withdrew in utter failure. Thereafter, the Governor was busy with sending forces southward to raid Iroquois lands or frontier hamlets in New York and New England; in campaigns that, though fiercely destructive, proved largely indecisive.

Far to the north there was another story. On Hudson Bay, the Montreal-born

French Victory Medal. *This commemorated the repulse of the English attack on Quebec in 1690.*

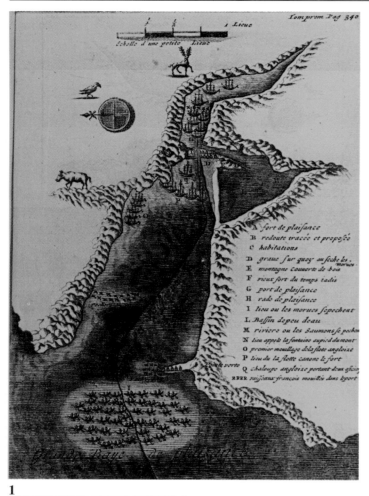

1

3

2

4

Sieur d'Iberville shaped a distinguished naval career: taking Fort Severn in 1690, capturing York Factory in 1694 — the new English headquarters near the mouth of the Nelson River — and then defeating a superior English fleet in the chill waters of the Bay. Iberville also sailed to Acadia in 1694, and took Pemaquid, chief English fort near the entry to the Bay of Fundy, which thus offset the French loss of Port Royal. To cap it all, there was his sweep along the Avalon Peninsula in Newfoundland and the capture of St. John's in 1696. And so the French had come out well by the war's end in 1697 — thanks notably to Iberville and other stalwarts like him.

In any event, heavy battling back in Europe had settled little, so that the Treaty of Ryswick in 1697 proved largely just a truce. Acadia was returned to France. York Factory was similarly to be restored to England — though in fact it was not; leaving the English only with Fort Albany on James Bay. The French-Iroquois war still continued. Old Frontenac himself grimly pursued it, carried in an armchair during a shattering attack on the Onondagas, until he died, worn out, in 1698. By then, however, the Iroquois Confederacy, abandoned by English allies now at peace with France, and devastated by both war and disease, were growing ready to stop fighting. Their own warrior force had been more than cut in half, to some 1,300 men, while French Canada's white population had climbed to around 13,000. The hard facts of numbers, if nothing else, directed the Five Nations to make peace in 1701. This leading native power could no longer hope in itself to overcome the ever-swelling French strength in Canada. Nevertheless, the Iroquois, still well-organized and resolute, would yet play a critical role in power balances between the French and English empires, each now contending for its own supremacy in North America.

In Europe, the interim truce between the major rivals only lasted to 1701. Then a new war, the War of Spanish Succession, began for reasons outside Canada, and went on till 1713. Within Canada itself, this second round of imperial conflict actually saw less widespread fighting, and the Iroquois largely stayed out of it. Still, Newfoundland settlements again were swept by French attacks in 1705, while St. John's fell once more in 1708. In Acadia, the English retook Port Royal in 1710: although their grand seaborne offensive on Quebec in 1711 failed disastrously without even getting near, after over-laden transport vessels foundered on reefs in the Gulf of St. Lawrence. The final outcome, however, was really settled by the decisive victories of England and its allies in Europe. There a much-battered and depleted France, overstretched by Louis XIV's visions of continental mastery, now had to accept hard peace terms. Accordingly, the Treaty of Utrecht of 1713 brought major gains in Britain's holdings in America.

Yet that word "Britain" first needs explaining. In 1707 England and Scotland had joined in the United Kingdom of Great Britain, so that henceforth there was a British empire under one British crown and parliament. And as for the gains that empire made in the Treaty of 1713, the Hudson Bay Territory — officially termed Ruperts Land — was now acknowledged by France to belong to Britain. So was all of Newfoundland, except for certain fishing and landing rights that France was granted on its western coasts; while Acadia was now definitely transferred to British hands as the Province of Nova Scotia. Plainly, the French-American empire had had to yield large and valuable possessions. All the same, it still was vast. New France yet spread out along the St. Lawrence to the

1. Placentia, French Base in Newfoundland. *Termed "Plaisance," on a French sketch depicting its fort and harbour at the end of the seventeenth century, the base obviously could draw a sizeable body of shipping.*

2. Sieur d'Iberville. *A brilliant leader, he not only won naval victories for France, and took English forts from Hudson Bay to Acadia and Newfoundland; he also discovered the mouth of the Mississippi by sea, established New Orleans upstream near there, and became the first Governor of Louisiana in 1704.*

3. Iberville Leads an Attack on an English Post.

4. Canadian Colonists on Snow Shoes, for Frontier Warfare.

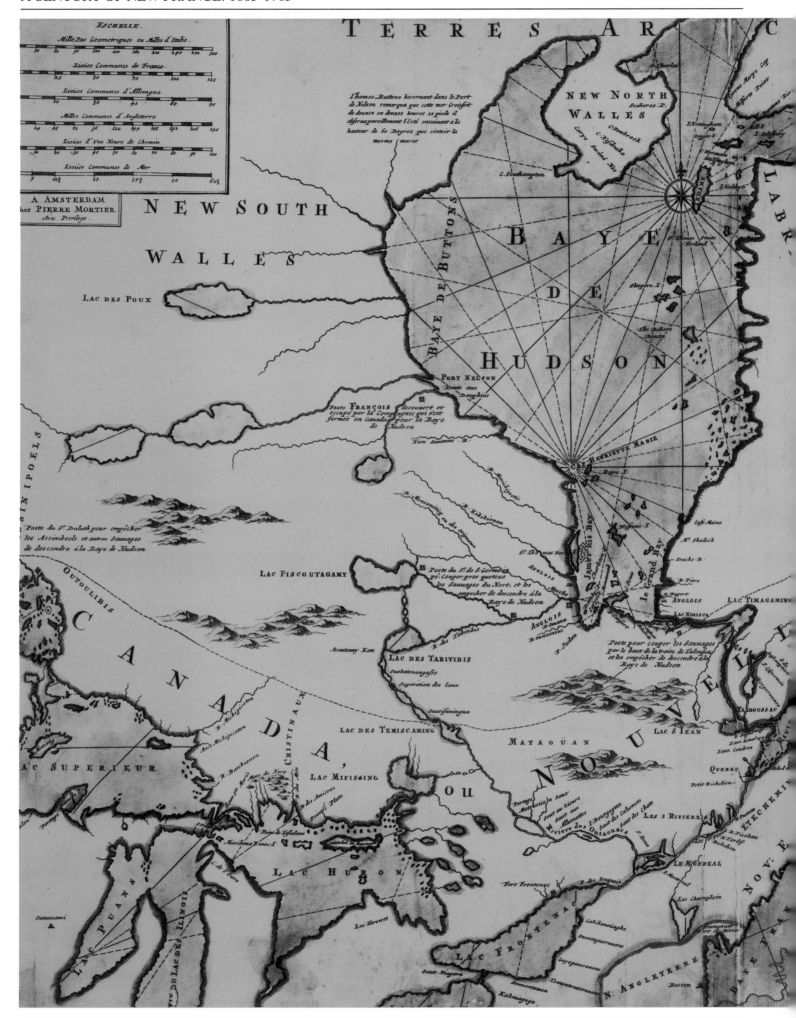

New France Prior to the Treaty of Utrecht. *The map here displays much of the French empire in America before Newfoundland and the Hudson Bay region were recognized as British territory, by the Treaty of 1713.*

Great Lakes and the northwest beyond; and was linked as well with the new wilderness French realm, to be known as Louisiana, that fronted south on the Gulf of Mexico but reached up the Mississippi and Ohio to the Great Lakes country. Here, then, was an enormous inland French domain behind the relatively narrow strip of British colonies along the Atlantic seaboard — and that interior domain of France would soon be pushing farther west again.

The official years of peace which followed the Treaty of 1713 were certainly not free from all armed violence; such as the two French wars with the Fox Indians in the Wisconsin country beyond Lake Michigan, in 1714-16 and 1728-33. But these conflicts stayed fairly localized, as did other raids or skirmishes, since both France and Britain really sought to maintain the general accord that had been achieved between them in Europe. Nevertheless, the two empires in America kept up their own competition, rivalry and defensive preparations. One good illustration lies in Nova Scotia-Acadia. Having had to abandon Placentia to a British Newfoundland, France began planning a new main fishing and naval base on Ile Royale, or Cape Breton; for that island and the neighbouring Ile Saint-Jean (later, Prince Edward Island) had not been ceded to Britain — only mainland Nova Scotia had. And the French still had a valuable North-Atlantic fishing fleet to harbour and protect, along with the need to defend the sea approaches to New France, now that Newfoundland itself no longer held French bases.

Hence the French imperial town of Louisbourg went up in the 1720s on a Cape Breton inlet facing the open Atlantic; not just as a fishing harbour and naval port (which it would be), but also as a massive stone fortress, to be the strongest citadel in North America. Lavish amounts were spent on its walls and defences, so that an exasperated King Louis XV asked if the streets were also being paved with gold. At any rate, by the 1740s, Louisbourg was both a powerful stronghold and a bustling French city in America. It had some 2,000 citizens (doubling in number over the next decade), a trading centre for ships up from the West Indies and New England, as well as from France or Quebec. But the British authorities in the neighbouring mainland province of Nova Scotia, still largely peopled with French Acadians, worried increasingly about a great hostile fortress so near; while New Englanders grew equally concerned over its constant threat to their own rich Atlantic and West Indies commerce.

This seaboard question rose to crisis in the mid-1740s. And in the meantime, other strains between the empires had developed deep in the western interior, no less important in the long run. Here the French fur trade had had to face the fact that British competition had not merely been confirmed by France's reluctant

Sieur de La Vérendrye. *The cele-brated fur trader who led the French into the western plains during the 1730s is here portrayed on a special Canadian stamp of 1958.*

recognition of Ruperts Land in the Treaty of 1713, but was highly effective, too. British goods laid down in quantity by sea at posts on Hudson Bay were then ready for trade, while French goods shipped out to the St. Lawrence still faced a long, expensive canoe haul westward to the trading areas. Furthermore, inland tribes would willingly travel north to the Bay Company posts for the prices, range and quality of items offered there. Thus, it was virtually essential for the French to reach the natives first, to use their own knowledge of the wilderness and its peoples to tie the Indians into French trading patterns and forestall English contacts. From that need came a sweeping competitive advance of French fur enterprise into the lands of a future Canadian West.

Prominent in leading this advance were the Sieur de La Vérendrye and his four sons. The father, born in Trois-Rivières, but a veteran soldier seriously wounded in 1709 during the war in Europe, had entered the fur trade after his return. In 1728 he was stationed on Lake Nipigon, at one of the French "Postes du Nord" above or beyond Lake Superior, purposely set across Indian canoe routes up to Hudson Bay. Here at Nipigon La Vérendrye took up the idea of thrusting right on to the Western Sea to by-pass the English — to reach the Pacific Ocean itself. He never got there; but from 1731 he and his sons did set up a chain of new posts westward that outflanked the British Hudson Bay trade: from Rainy Lake to the Lake of the Woods, then to Lake Winnipeg and the Red River by 1734, out on open western prairie. In 1738 La Vérendrye further built a fort out at the site of Portage La Prairie, which could intercept parties of Assiniboines heading north for the Bay. His sons went on to the Saskatchewan River that traverses the Great Plains from the Rockies, and erected a post by its entry in 1743, where Plains Cree might be deflected from going up to British York Factory. Though the Western Sea still lay much further, the work of the La Vérendryes and their comrades had carried the French fur trade deep into the Canadian prairies.

Meanwhile, the British Hudson's Bay Company had done almost nothing to move into the western interior. True, in 1691 young Henry Kelsey had travelled inland to the Saskatchewan plains from York Factory, and is often portrayed as the first white man to see a western buffalo. The first buffalo to see a white man has never been portrayed. But Kelsey's trip led to very little. The fact was, that the Bay Company did well enough sitting on the shore. Bulk transport by sea, in wind-driven ships, was more efficient and economical than any number of brigades of the biggest French canoes, that had to be paddled or portaged overland by sheer human effort. So why leave the coasts, when the Indians would travel there themselves — and incidentally, bear the costs of bringing furs down to the shore posts? By and large, the apparent lethargy of the Bay Company was

Voyageurs in Camp. *A rendition of the tough and tireless French-Canadian canoemen who took trading venturers like La Vérendrye and his four sons — plus many others, over time — into the vast Canadian wilderness beyond the Great Lakes.*

actually good business — at least for the time being. Consequently, even later, when in 1754-55, Anthony Henday in Company service made a striking journey from York Factory up the Saskatchewan with a party of Cree, to winter with the Blackfoot in the Alberta foothills, his effort still did not really alter established Hudson's Bay policy. Indeed, the Company's motto might almost have been, "Have furs, need not travel." Things in the West would change; yet not greatly during the remaining days of New France and its own farspread fur enterprise.

Those days were running towards a close, however, even by the mid-1740s. In 1744, Britain and France again met as foes in the War of Austrian Succession in Europe, and from 1745 to 1748 this struggle was also waged in North America. Its results still were inconclusive; but it foreshadowed the downfall of New France. That would not actually take place until the last round in the long imperial contest, the Seven Years War of 1756 to 1763; although the relative positions of both empires — and the useful advantages of historic hindsight — enable us to forecast the decisive outcome well before. We will turn from this negative theme of ultimate French defeat, nonetheless, to examine first something far more positive: the vibrant life and society already created in New France, and the enduring, distinctive heritage it left to Canada thereafter, for centuries more to come.

1

1. Kelsey Reaches the Plains for the Hudson's Bay Company, 1691. *An imaginative reconstruction of young Henry Kelsey first encountering the plains buffalo.*

2. St. John's, Newfoundland, by Mid-Eighteenth Century. *Here is a reminder that this British ocean base was still there and thriving, as suggested by this scene of its harbour looking to the entrance, with fortified Signal Hill on the left-hand side.*

2

The Life and Heritage of New France

By 1745, the settled population of New France along the St. Lawrence had risen to about 45,000, of whom 4,600 were living in the capital and port town of Quebec, and 3,500 in Montreal, the fur-trade headquarters and gateway to the interior. There were several settled Indian groups also present: descendants of the Christian Hurons at Lorette outside Quebec, Mohawks who had turned to the French side, dwelling at Kahnawake and elsewhere near Montreal, and some others drawn from Algonquin tribes, located on a few scattered reserves. Yet the overwhelming majority of the inhabitants were of French stock. This was not really the result of the continuing trickle of immigrants from France. It still mainly stemmed from natural increase within the colony itself, where the birth rate was definitely higher than in the old land, and probably the survival rate as well, thanks to more and better food, and healthier living conditions in a wide new country.

Certainly, the rural residents, the largest element in the French-Canadian population, dwelt fairly comfortably in their square-hewed log farmhouses — though seigneurs and more affluent *habitants* were now building in stone — and their homes were well heated by large fireplaces supplied with plentiful wood, feeding into massive central chimneys. The farm-dwellers had the room they needed, with a loft above and cellars below to keep meat frozen through the winter. They had ample fur and deerskin for clothing; not to mention woven garments of homespun, from the wool of their own sheep. And they had ready access to fish and game in the open countryside. Consequently, the *habitants* faced winter shortages less, and generally lived better, than did their counterparts in northwestern France from where they had largely come; in particular, having more protein in their diet, and wheaten bread to eat, not coarser rye. None of this, of course, should suggest some kind of frontier rural paradise. Wilderness dangers, want and cold, were still never too far away. Work was unending; and women not only tended home and family, but toiled in the fields beside the men. Nevertheless, the rewards were evident, as were the space and opportunities for new farming families. Together, they shaped a robust, self-reliant agrarian society in colonial New France.

This community was built and based along the central reaches of the broad St. Lawrence River, that provided it with vital transportation and valuable fishing at the same time. Hence river-frontage was all-important; and farm-lots extended back in long narrow strips from the great waterway. Dotted along the river-front as they were, the sturdy farmhouses, often boarded or plastered and whitewashed, thus gave the impression of "one continued village" from below Quebec to Montreal — so described by the visiting Swedish botanist, Peter Kalm, in 1749. In time, another range (and more) of farm allotments rose behind the original waterfront properties. But the pattern of ribbon-farms, within long, narrow seigneuries oriented to the St. Lawrence, would last long after New France: as maps or an air flight above the region can still reveal today.

In the 1730s, the *chemin du roi*, the king's road, was run along the north shore of the St. Lawrence from Quebec to Montreal, up to seven metres wide in ploughed dirt, with small wooden bridges over streams, or else fords and ferries. This route, however, was more important at certain periods of the year. In open summer, the river carried far more traffic; in mid-winter the road was good for

Canadian *Habitants*. *We see the typical garb of these country-dwellers — the homespun coat, with a traditional woven sash or* ceinture fléchée, *the knitted* toque *and sturdy boots — along with a pipe for* tabac canadien, *and the riding whips for the* habitants' prized horses.

1

2

sleighs, but the river ice could also be. Nevertheless, the importance of the horse for rural land transport as well as ploughing steadily mounted; so that this imported animal, first called "the French moose" by Indians, became indispensable to the *habitant* farms. It was besides, a favourite source of countryside interest and some expense, not least because of popular winter horse-racing on frozen waterways.

All in all, it followed that the tenant-farmers of New France were far from a downtrodden, exploited European peasantry, but formed a self-respecting and substantial New-World group. They held hereditary possession of their own farms, as long as their seigneurial rents and dues were paid; and these traditional dues were not that burdensome. They freely engaged in litigation before the courts, enjoying many a good land dispute. They were also aware of their own valuable, experienced role in the militia, on raids deep into Indian country. And their life-style was not greatly different from that of most of their *seigneurs*, themselves busy working their home-farm *domaines*: in fact, marriages between sons of the seigneurial order and the daughters of well-to-do *habitants* were assuredly not barred. Hence this was not a closed or oppressive feudal system, whatever its origins in France — any more than it was a merely economic relationship of landlord and tenant, wherein the former could evict the latter from his land for a variety of reasons.

Here was, instead, a system of mutual obligations bound up with land-holding, not land-owning. The *seigneur* himself did not "own" his land, but held it from the crown; and if he failed in his own obligations of service and settlement, might find his land grant revoked. In general, too, the solid *habitant* could not be rashly pushed around by some would-be lordly aristocrat. Yet agrarian New France was still far from a social democracy. There was an engrained sense of deference, as well as of mutual obligation. *Habitants* accepted the *seigneur*'s social leadership, his recognized privileges, although these were largely ceremonial. In short, this was a distinct collective community in at least two ways: distinct from the harsher seigneurialism of Old France; but distinct as well from the individualist farm-ownership of English America.

New France also had an active, influential urban life. Around one-fifth of its population in the 1740s now resided in towns, the centres of commerce and

1. Quebec by the 1740s. *This is a significant view of the main stronghold and city of New France, if still rendered more for art than reality. The major public buildings are too big and tall, done for effect; the smaller dwellings and shops are too small and not numerous enough. Nevertheless, prominent edifices like the Cathedral, Seminary and Hotel-Dieu are plainly shown.*

2. House Scene, *Habitants at Cards*. *While this is a later view, by the famed Cornelius Krieghoff, it still conveys a close family scene in a snug* Canadien *farmhouse.*

3. Winter Transport by *Habitant Sleigh*.

crafts, and of political, religious or military life. Quebec, Montreal and Trois-Rivières also headed local governmental districts; though Quebec, of course, was the seat of government for the whole colony, as well as its prime fortress. In the capital, the structure of royal government continued under its three top figures, governor general, intendant and bishop. Bishops now played a less forceful political part than in the days of Laval; but the power of the Catholic Church was still widespread within a tightly orthodox society, where Roman Catholicism was well maintained by law and supported by tithes — state-enforced taxes for the church. The governors of the period, Philippe de Vaudreuil (1703-25) and Charles de Beauharnois (1726-47), made authoritative leaders throughout, while diligent intendants such as Gilles Hocquart (1729-48), a trained civil servant since boyhood, left their own strong mark on colonial development. Meanwhile, the law courts, the lesser bureaucracy and the officers' class all expanded in a broader but no less hierarchical society; and all were regularly reflected in the ruling official and garrison world of Quebec.

The economic life of the towns was expressed in both their major wholesale merchants and minor shopkeepers; in artisans from carpenters, masons and blacksmiths to shoemakers and bakers; or in seamen, river boatmen and day-labourers. Quebec, as main port, had its considerable export businesses sending wheat and lumber to Louisbourg and the French West Indies, its importers bringing in French goods, and its shipyard and shipwrights building increased numbers of river and seagoing vessels. Near Trois-Rivières, iron-workers at the St. Maurice forges, opened in 1738, were successfully producing stoves, together with other ironware for the colony. At Montreal, there were the warehouses, offices and personnel of the far-extended fur trade: but especially the *voyageurs*, those hard-driving canoemen who left or returned with the seasons, as trade goods and supplies went upriver or western pelts came down to the landing-grounds at Lachine, just above the city. The chief merchants of Montreal, moreover, held a special eminence, since the life of the colony still heavily depended on the fur trade; and it was the Montreal fur merchant, the *bourgeois*, along with his inland agents or partners engaged in dealing with the Indians, who really kept the whole fur empire operating — and therefore, the vast French claims to dominance across the wilderness interior.

In forest sweeps wholly removed from the busy streets of stone-built towns, or the tilled fields of a farming countryside, there lay a very different aspect of New France: the life of the fur trade. By the mid-1740s this largely focused at the farspread inland posts which the French had built; partly for trade with the Indians of a particular area, but partly also to maintain their political and diplomatic presence, and so confirm alliances with native tribes. These posts now ranged far beyond Niagara: from Detroit (established 1701) to Fort Miami (1715) in what now is Indiana, then to Fort Chartres (1717) on the Mississippi in Illinois country, and down the Mississippi to New Orleans (founded 1718). Such places as there were not the same as the northwestern line of trading posts intended to draw off furs from the British Hudson's Bay Company; for the more southerly French forts, lying inland of Britain's Atlantic seaboard colonies, were manned by small but significant French military garrisons, aimed at ensuring Indian loyalties against the wiles and wares of English-American traders penetrating from the Thirteen Colonies along the coast. In other words, the garrisoned posts were meant to keep the Indians tied to French interests in a defensive bulwark

Market Place at Quebec. *Another later picture, but clearly showing the two levels of Upper and Lower Town, and the decidely "city" nature of the setting.*

against any British thrusts westward. And so a "military frontier" under professional officers' command would join the older trading frontier world of free-ranging *coureurs-de-bois*; or now their successors, the hired *voyageurs* and the fur *bourgeois* out of Montreal. It was no less true, however, that this thinly-held inland New France of soldier, trader and *voyageur* continued to shape the very destiny of the town-dwellers and seigneurial farmers along the St. Lawrence.

There is one more element still to be added to the total community of New France: limited in numbers but large in influence, the Roman Catholic clergy. Most of the clergy were town residents, whether in religious orders or serving in parishes; yet their calling not only extended to the farming countryside, but far into the fur-trade world. To take the last first, Catholic priests and friars had repeatedly proved devoted and daring adventurers in the wilderness, from the beginnings of Acadia or the initial French travels to Huronia. They had widely founded Indian missions, in which endeavour the Jesuit efforts among the Hurons had been just one prominent example. They had also accompanied fur trade-explorers on many a classic journey of discovery; such as that of Father Joseph Marquette and the trader Louis Jolliet, the first Frenchmen to trace the Mississippi southward in 1673, although they did not reach its mouth. And Catholic priests were present as well on journeys into the northwest beyond the Great Lakes. As for the agrarian world of New France, from Bishop Laval's day a trained clergy had been sent to serve the growing seigneuries: where, indeed, local parishes would become rural social units in themselves, each under its own priest, or *curé*, and a vestry of leading parishioners. Yet still, the main core of the Church lay in urban society.

Thus at Quebec, there was the ruling Bishop, the Cathedral, the Seminary founded by Laval to train priests for town or country; and the headquarters of the still-weighty Jesuits. In Montreal, which had originally begun in 1642 as Ville-Marie, a religious mission on a dangerously exposed Indian frontier, its affluent merchant community also supported rising urban church activities; but in particular, the Sulpician Order, which had been granted the highly valuable Island of Montreal as a seigneury. It was central in the life of the enlarging eighteenth-century town. There were other male orders also of importance in French Canada's Catholic Church, then and in later days; but the female religious

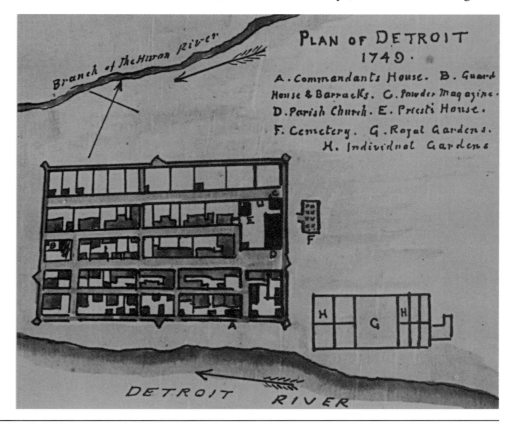

Detroit, 1749. *An early sketch of the French fort at Detroit, on the narrows of the riverway which links Lake Erie and the Upper Great Lakes.*

1

2

3

1. Marquette and Jolliet on the Mississippi. *Here Father Marquette points the way, as the exploring team descends the Mississippi — on a route later completed by La Salle.*

2. Mother Marie de l'Incarnation. *The founder and first superior of the Ursuline Convent at Quebec, from 1639 to her death in 1672. Left widowed in France in 1619 with an infant son, she raised him, then joined the Ursulines; and voyaged to New France at age forty to set up a convent, where successive generations of French Canadian children would be educated. She also wrote catechisms in Huron and Algonquian along with a French-Algonquian dictionary, while her letters to her son would form a mine of information on early New France.*

3. Jeanne Mance. *Stained-glass window depicting the creator of the Hotel-Dieu at Montreal. Another outstanding woman-builder of New France, she had come to Canada with the zealous religious group who established Ville-Marie (Montreal) on dangerous Indian frontiers in 1642. There she supervised her hospital, except for some voyages back to France, until her death in 1673.*

orders which crucially served education, hospitals and welfare work demand special attention.

At Quebec in 1639, Mother Marie de l'Incarnation had founded the Ursuline Convent, one of the earliest teaching institutions in North America. Its first pupils were Indians, taught by nuns who had learned both Iroquoian and Algonquian tongues; but the children of well-to-do French colonists came there increasingly to study both arts and science. The Ursuline nuns were mainly drawn from the colonial bourgeoisie, the commercial middle class. On the other hand, the nursing sisters of Canada's first hospital, the Hôtel-Dieu of Quebec, also begun in 1639, were often the daughters of artisan families; while those of Quebec's Hôpital-Générale, opened in 1693, would largely come from more aristocratic circles. And in Montreal, the Grey Nuns established by Madame d'Youville in 1737 cared for the poor, disabled and infirm, the orphans and the elderly. Here in New France lay the beginnings of modern Canadian social and educational services — and essentially through women's undertakings.

This is heritage, flowing from French Canada well before the British Conquest, but by no means to be forgotten today. Moreover, French colonial women not only worked vigorously in these basic social concerns, but equally showed their own capacity to manage them. And outside the religious orders (which no doubt did give women a scope for their abilities that they would

1

1. Entrance to the Grey Nuns Convent, Montreal. *A nineteenth century picture of a far older edifice, one that exists to the present.*
2. Chateau de Ramezay, Montreal. *This handsome residence of an early governor's family in Montreal still stands as a museum in the present metropolis.*

2

otherwise have lacked), the female residents of New France were not at all the clinging vines of male chauvinist myth. Aside from hard work on the land, country wives might also run their farms while husbands were absent on militia service or engaged in the fur trade. In towns, too, women often had charge of local stores, while the widows of merchants carried on their husbands' businesses — or, like Marie-Anne Barbel, developed as well a thriving pottery works at Quebec from 1745. French law, based on Roman law, gave women more property rights than did English common law then. And Louise de Ramezay, daughter of a governor of Montreal who died in 1724, joined her mother in profitably managing a sawmill and brick-and-tile factory; then herself went on to build a flour mill and a school, and to deal sizeably in lumber up to her own death in 1776. No one could suggest from such particular examples that this unquestionably patriarchal society was somehow gender-equal. Yet it is true that women had wider freedom of life and action in New France than in Old: a state at times deplored by old-country visitors, or even condemned by church authorities: while Peter Kalm himself found it worth commenting that in Canadian society men did not undertake "matters of importance without their women's advice and approval."

In any case, though the heritage that sprang from this life of New France was not just that of Old France, and had been much modified by North American experience, it still certainly did not express modern North American notions of a free society; or even the degrees of liberty already known in the English-speaking colonies of America. In those provinces there were rich and powerful merchants in New England, New York or Pennsylvania, or great estate-owners in southern

1

2

1. Seigneurial Manor House Beside the St. Lawrence.
2. The St. Maurice Iron Forges. *The most technically advanced ironworks in America for virtually a century after their establishment by 1738.*

1. Lady in Town Winter Dress Greeting a Priest.
2. The Jesuit Church and College at Quebec, 1761. *This graphic view, taken after the British capture of Quebec in 1759, still shows the effects of bombardment on the roofs and walls.*

1

2

plantation colonies. Yet there was no seigneurial order of nobility set in a legally superior position on the land. And the average Anglo-American farmer was not by law a tenant but the full proprietor of his own fields and home.

Similarly, in political terms: however well-intentioned was the government of New France — and however far from meek and docile were its subjects — the mass of the people still had very little say in their own public affairs. Power came down from above: the King was the ultimate master of this hierarchical society. True, assemblies of inhabitants might occasionally be summoned to present opinions on special issues; while the home-grown captains of militia, chosen to command their local militia units, held a good deal of community respect, and some authority, as effective rural agents of the intendant. Yet any such expressions of the people of New France were very far from the regularly elected provincial assemblies that were a fundamental part of political life in the English colonies, marking the transfer of the British parliamentary system to those new societies overseas. In sum, whatever the merits (and they were real) of a largely competent, fair and conscientious French system of government, it still gave small place to the ordinary citizen and his views on taxes, policies or individual rights — as would certainly be put forward in words both loud and clear by the elected representative Houses of Britain's Thirteen Colonies in America.

Accordingly, the life of New France was still one where social status, elite privilege and paternal authority in church or state were continually evident. Yet always one must qualify — regarding this unquestionably "new" France in America. There was always open space and opportunity around it, the wilds beyond it, to make this something other than a closely layered, top-run society. There was, besides, the inherent vigour and self-confidence of the French Canadian people (who were no blind followers); and there was, above all, the enterprise and individualism of the fur trade, the sturdy will to survival against all hardships, Indian wars or the increasing weight of the English. These things were rooted in the heritage of New France. They might become somewhat altered over time, or have other aspects added. But French Canada, and all Canada, still owe greatly to the tough inheritance derived from the world of New France — from the eighteenth century right down to the present day.

The Ursulines Convent at Quebec in 1761. *A broad sweep of Upper Town, from fields out to the river, which shows the Convent inside the old town wall.*

The British Conquest of French Canada

In 1745, mounting strains between the British and French in America burst into open conflict, as the War of Austrian Succession spread overseas from Europe. On the Atlantic coast, the long-felt menace of the great French base at Louisbourg — felt both in British-ruled Nova Scotia and in the New England colonies — led to a joint assault by New England troops and the British Navy on that fortress town. It fell late in June, 1745, after a forty-seven-day siege, heavily battered by cannon fire from ship and shore, and after naval reinforcements sent by France had failed to break past the British fleet.

Meanwhile, the continental inland country at first stayed fairly quiet; helped by the fact that the Six-Nations Iroquois Confederacy (the Tuscaroras having joined in the 1720s to make it Six) remained neutral and aloof from either British or French sides. By 1747, however, the dwindling flow of trade goods from France, due largely to British strength on the distant Atlantic, spurred on an Indian conspiracy against the French in the Detroit-Lake Erie region. Once peace was signed in Europe at Aix-la-Chapelle in 1748, a new flood of French goods soon drowned this Indian hostility. Yet it did indicate how vulnerable the French empire really was, even deep in the interior, to superior British naval power on the high seas. Still, aside from some devastating French raids on the New York and Massachusetts frontiers, the war passed off in inland North American without major fighting. Then Louisbourg itself was handed back to France in a stalemate peace of 1748. New Englanders were outraged; and not at all impressed by the return of Madras to Britain in exchange, a key fortified base in southern India. In truth, the contest of worldwide empires simply continued, and the peace was no more than a breathing-space between rounds of combat.

That was clearly perceived by the Comte de La Galissionière, who had replaced an aging Beauharnois as Governor-General of New France in 1747. After the war had ended, the new governor reported to his masters in Paris that, while peace had "lulled the jealousy of the English in Europe, this bursts forth in all its violence in America, and if barriers ... are not opposed at this very moment, that nation will place itself in a condition to invade the French Colonies." Hence La Galissionière particularly sought to secure the link of empire between New France and the French colony of Louisiana down the Mississippi. To this end, he worked to hold the Ohio country — which lay south of Lake Erie and spread west along the Ohio River to its junction with the Mississippi — and his effort was also taken up by his successors. For the Ohio Valley represented a buffer zone between the British seaboard colonies and the French in the interior. If Anglo-American advances westward could be halted here, the French empire might still hope to dominate and develop in the enormous mid-continental heartland. But if the much more populous and economically developed Thirteen Colonies should break through into France's open inland territories, then the

1. Landings of Louisbourg, 1745. *A British fleet, bringing New England troops, comes in to beseige and capture the great French fortress.*
2. British Resentment after the Return of Louisbourg. *This political cartoon, among other things, speaks of "the complaints of the injured Americans" (received here by Britannia) and the need to remove the French "coopt up" in the renewed fortress.*
3. The Defeat of Braddock, 1755. *Attacked from the woods, this British general caught with clumsy transport and inexperienced troops met complete disaster.*

1

2

3

future would almost surely belong to an English America. A great deal hinged on the Ohio Valley, where in the opening 1750s the French began to build a new chain of forts.

At the same time, the British colonies assuredly were looking westward. Most of them had long claimed the lands behind them. In Virginia, which claimed right out to the Western Sea, the Ohio Company had been formed by 1749 to plant settlers in the Ohio Valley. And in 1753 Virginia's governor sent a mission overland to the French forces in the Valley, protesting their military occupation of British territory. The French rejected the protest, inevitably. The next step would be open conflict. It came the following year at the strategic forks of the Ohio where Pittsburgh now stands. Here a small Virginian working party, attempting to build a fort, were driven off by a French detachment who erected a larger structure of their own, Fort Duquesne. In reply, Virginia sent troops and Indian allies under a young major of militia, George Washington. Late in May, 1754, at Great Meadows near Fort Duquesne, the conclusive war for America really began: when Washington suddenly attacked and overran an armed French force, but afterwards was himself attacked and defeated by a greater French concentration. He and his men were allowed to retreat to Virginia, while the inland tribes, impressed by this telling victory of the French, now swung strongly to their side. In any event, although outright war would not officially begin in Europe until two years later, it soon spread widely within North America.

Both France and Britain, moreover, took this undeclared American conflict very seriously, strengthening fortified places, sending out regular troops and naval units, and preparing campaigns; although a supposed peace still lingered on in Europe. Consequently, sizeable British reinforcements were dispatched to take Fort Duquesne and win the Ohio country. Major General Edward Braddock marched a regular army inland from Virginia in the summer of 1755. But as it neared Duquesne, floundering along a crude frontier road little better than a trail, the British column encumbered with siege-cannon and supply wagons was struck from surrounding woods by a withering fire from hidden French and Indians. The column broke; its retreat became a flight, with heavy losses, including that of Braddock himself. New France had gained a major success. Nevertheless, the war was only starting.

And elsewhere, the British did somewhat better during 1755. Colonel William Johnson, British agent to the Six Nations, led New York and New England militia, along with some Mohawk Iroquois, to a limited victory near Lake George on the classic Hudson River-Lake Champlain invasion route into Canada. More significantly, in the Atlantic region combined British and New

1. William Johnson, Superintendant of the Iroquois. *One of Britain's most effective agents in America, he did much to take the still powerful Six Nations into action on the British side, especially the Mohawks from 1755 onward.*
2. Acadian Lands at the Head of the Bay of Fundy. *This old map of 1755 shows farm fields on the Chignecto Isthmus, near French Fort Beauséjour, later to become British Fort Cumberland.*

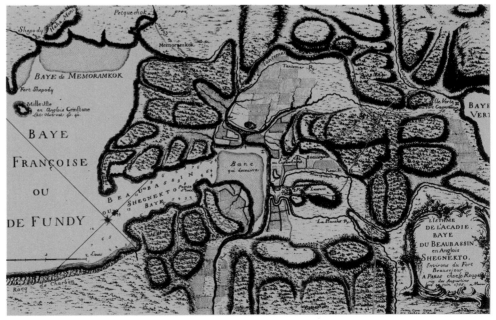

1

2

England forces captured crucial Fort Beauséjour after two weeks of crashing bombardment. With the fall of this main French strongpoint on the Isthmus of Chignecto (where present-day New Brunswick and Nova Scotia meet), France largely lost hold of what had remained to it of former mainland Acadia. But to explain what this implied, and the tragedy that followed for the French-speaking Acadian people, it is necessary to go back in time, to pick up the outstanding story of Acadians and their heritage. In fact, we must go back at least to the Treaty of 1713, when Britain received its lasting title to French Acadia, henceforth the province of Nova Scotia.

In 1713 there had been some 2,000 Acadians present — who had strikingly increased by the mid-1750s to over 13,000, thanks mostly to their own high birth rate. Few immigrants had been sent from France to join them. Even in the seventeenth century, except for brief phases, Acadia had stayed a neglected colony in French hands; or when periodically in English hands as well. Yet at the same time, in very neglect, the original scant French settlers had quietly grown into a distinct society of their own, raising large, healthy families on fertile tidal flats left unoccupied by the native Micmacs — who maintained friendly relations as a result. Acadian village-settlements spread on the low shores of both sides of the Bay of Fundy, and along open reaches like the Annapolis Valley; but not into the Indian-held forest interior. These villages fished profitably, traded grain crops down to New England for West Indies sugar and rum or European goods, and thrived in a simple rural society where the Catholic church and the family unit stood out, but seigneurialism mattered far less: a quiet, withdrawn people wanting just to be left peacefully to themselves. Yet they were not to be; since living where they did, on the margins between two great hostile empires, meant that the Acadians dwelt virtually on an earthquake shockline.

As for the British element who ruled in mainland Nova Scotia from 1713, they consisted of little more than a small garrison centred at the old French

Drafting the Order for Allegiance, requiring Acadians to swear Loyalty to Britain. *Done at Annapolis Royal, formerly French Port Royal, the first seat of government for British Nova Scotia.*

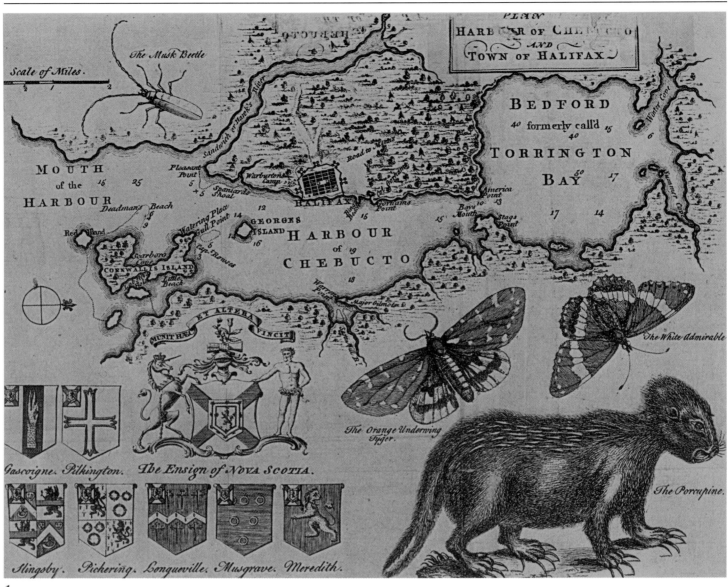

The Musk Beetle

Scale of Miles.

PLAN
HARBOUR OF CHEBUCTO
AND
TOWN OF HALIFAX

BEDFORD
40 formerly call'd 15
40
TORRINGTON
BAY
50 17

MOUTH
of the 16 25
HARBOUR
Deadmans Beach

GEORGES
ISLAND

HARBOUR
of 19
CHEBUCTO

The White Admirable

The Orange Underwing
Tyger.

MUNIT HÆC ET ALTERA VINCIT

Gascoigne. Pilkington. The Ensign of NOVA SCOTIA.

The Porcupine.

Slingsby. Pickering. Longueville. Musgrave. Meredith.

1

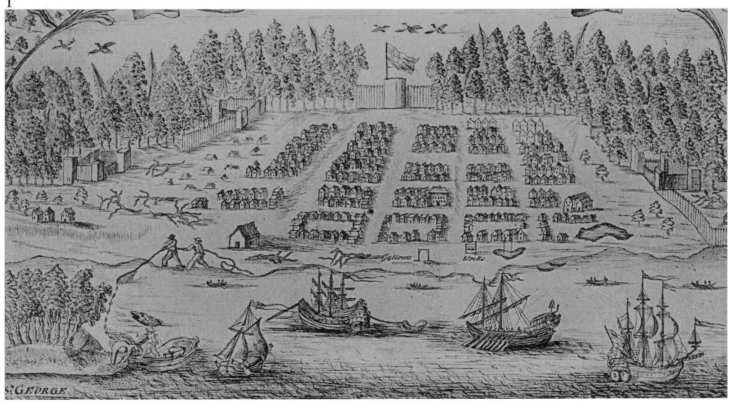

S. GEORGE

Gallows

Stocks

2

capital of Port Royal — renamed Annapolis Royal — plus visiting New England traders and fishermen around the shores. Attempts to draw farm settlers from Britain or New England to this French-peopled territory largely failed. Hence the government of Nova Scotia sought instead to extract oaths of allegiance from the Acadian inhabitants, to make them into safe British subjects. But the mass of Acadians wanted just to remain neutral between contending empires, despite French emissaries who also sought to tie them to the cause of France. To some extent, the British, of necessity, accepted the Acadian stance, while the French spent their efforts on holding the Micmacs, with more success. As the mid-century approached, however, the imperial contest became far more dangerous and critical; even though the would-be neutral Acadians failed to appreciate that fact until too late.

The return of Louisbourg to French control by the peace of 1748 had restored the naval and military power of France in the Atlantic region. And this renewed threat led Britain to reply by founding Halifax in 1749, on the Atlantic coast of Nova Scotia. Under Governor Edward Cornwallis, some 2,000 English settlers were brought from London to establish this new stronghold. Some others of the King's subjects also came from the Crown's holdings, of that age, in Germany; but most of these German-speaking Protestants were placed at Lunenburg, a little further down the coast. In any case, Halifax took shape as a garrisoned port-town, palisaded against Micmac raids, but in time strengthened by a hill-top citadel and batteries to defend the entry to its superb harbour, which could contain whole war fleets. The town was made Nova Scotia's capital as well. And it would build a proud inheritance as a major British and later Canadian base through great wars yet to come.

The French were active also. They strove to keep a grip on inland Acadia beyond the Nova Scotian peninsula, claiming that only the peninsula itself had really been yielded by the Treaty of 1713; so that the areas past the Isthmus of Chignecto still belonged to New France. The Treaty had indeed but vaguely ceded "all Nova Scotia or Acadia with its ancient boundaries" — whatever that meant. Britain, backed by some weight of history, argued that Nova Scotia-Acadia had always extended clear up to the Appalachians. France, which wanted particularly to have winter access overland from Canada down to Louisbourg, contended otherwise. In any case, the French now proceeded to confirm their view that the border should run at Chignecto by exacting their own oaths of French allegiance from Acadians of that area in 1749, and by planting forts upon the isthmus, the chief one being Fort Beauséjour, built in 1751. The British in reply erected Fort Lawrence on their side of the alleged boundary. Skirmishes and raids went on across the line; though all-out war did not come till 1755, when a sizeable British and New England expedition arrived to beseige and capture Beauséjour — as has already been described. But further, Acadians were found in its garrison, even though most had been forced by the French to serve "on pain of death."

The British authorities in Nova Scotia now came to a grim resolve. Faced in

1. Site of Halifax, New Nova Scotia Capital, 1750. *The map (considerably embellished) shows the spacious harbour with a defended townsite beside it, and Bedford Basin, where ships could lie securely beyond. "Chebucto" was the original harbour name.*
2. Initial Settlement at Halifax. *Another early scene, a bit more romantic than real (such as the Mediterranean oared-ship offshore); but showing the military layout of the original town behind defences then threatened by French-allied Micmacs.*
3. Annapolis Royal, 1755. *The former Nova Scotian capital was still there, though now sinking into a local countryside existence.*
4. Edward Cornwallis, Founder of Halifax. *A veteran soldier, later governor of Gibraltar, Cornwallis in his three years at Halifax shaped a flourishing small town and shipping base.*

3

4

1755 with the armed might of Louisbourg, with French agents working among the Acadians or inciting Micmac raids, and surrounded and vastly outweighed by an unsecured, potentially dangerous French-speaking population, the rulers of the Nova Scotian province decided that Acadians must take a full, unqualified oath of allegiance to Great Britain — or be deported. The new governor of Nova Scotia, Colonel Charles Lawrence, was central to this drastic decision. He himself had built Fort Lawrence and met French attacks there. He saw the move proposed as urgent military necessity. And at that moment when English America was reeling from the shock of Braddock's major defeat and the French triumph in the Ohio country, those in authority would very much agree with him, right back to the imperial government in London.

The Acadians, however, did not recognize the demand for an unqualified oath for what it was — a downright ultimatum. From years of previous British failure to enforce such an oath, they had come to believe (wishfully) that it still could be refused. Theirs was the understandable but tragic stand of a small people caught between great forces they did not and would not comprehend. That still is no excuse for what happened to them.

British troops — or rather, keenly Protestant New Englanders quite ready to drive Catholic Frenchmen off valuable lands — were sent to herd the Acadians from their homes, and into waiting ships that would carry them to exile in the British colonies down the Atlantic coast. From Beaubassin and Grand Pré around the head of the Bay of Fundy, from the Annapolis Valley and little Atlantic shore villages, bewildered, unprepared Acadians were driven by Yankee bluecoat troops away from their farms to confused embarkations, where families often were split up. This, after all, was a major transport movement of over 6,000 people, really beyond the hurried plans and limited facilities of those who had supposedly arranged it. Numbers of Acadians never survived their pent-up passage by sea to ports down the seaboard. The wonder is, that so many did, and then managed to eke out a life in the American colonies. Some would go on to France — though they seldom fitted in there successfully — while many others escaped transportation altogether: hiding in the woods, crossing into the forestlands beyond Chignecto, or finding their way to French-held Cape Breton Island and the Island of Saint John (Prince Edward Island to be). Nevertheless, a society of some 13,000 Acadians was effectively broken and removed, reduced to only shattered remnants. Or was it left shattered? Here his lies the "miracle" of Acadian survival: the achievement, above all, of a profoundly enduring heritage.

1. Expulsion of the Acadians. *Here at Grand Pré, near Windsor on Bay of Fundy waters, hundreds of Acadians were harshly driven from their houses and into waiting transport ships that carried them south away from their own cherished homelands.*

2. A Letter About the Acadian Exiles. *From Lieutenant-Governor Belcher of Massachusetts in 1762, regarding these displaced people shipped down the coasts.*

EXILE OF THE ACADIANS FROM GRAND PRE.

1

Boston Septemr 29th 1762.

Honble Sir

The Removing of the Accadians from Halifax, was thought a very necessary Measure, at the time when it was done, & approv'd of by all I have ever heard Speake of it, but as this Province rec'd a great Number of them, some Years ago, who have been an Expence of above Ten Thousand Pounds Sterl: to the Province, & for which they have never been Reimbursted, one Farthing, this has very much Prejudiced the People, against Receiving any more, and the General Assembly have accordingly Refused that the Accadians Sent here, under Convoy of Capt: Brooks, should be Landed in this Province, and He is Obliged, having rec'd no Instructions, from your Honour, nor General Amherst, for his further Proceeding, to Return with them to Halifax. I have done all in my Power, to Serve the Cause, & Immediately Sent a Special Express, to General Amherst, as soon as the Court had Come to their Resolution of Rejecting them, to acquaint him of it, with a Letter, from Govr. Bernard, & Desired his further Directions what to do, Copy of which, with the General's Answer, to me, I here Inclose, who Recommended, that the General Court should Reconsider their Resolution, but before it Come, the Court was prorogued, & will not sett again, 'till after Christmass, in this Case I could not but Advise Capt: Brooks to Return to Halifax, I here Inclose you the Proceedings of the Genl. Court, & Copy, of a Letter Govr. Bernard wrote me on Sunday, as he was going to visit Penobscott, & the Eastward Settlements, & Desired I'd Excuse his not writing to your Honour.

I have agreeable to Your Orders, Supplied Capt: Brooks with Provisions &c. during his stay here, Accounts & Receipts for which I here Inclose, with what I had before Advanc'd for the Province, and as I paid only Cash, for every thing, & Advanc any

The Honble Lieut. Govr. Belcher &c &c &c

1

2

3

4

Acadians might journey on to France or to French Louisiana, where they later became the "Cajuns" of American history. Yet remarkably, many in time came back to their ancestral Acadia, when the Franco-British imperial struggle was over. And in Nova Scotia or Prince Edward Island — but particularly in future New Brunswick — they would renew their own society, language and culture, still in largely rural settings. Their will and courage to make such a return, the devotion of a humble, exiled people to their home territory, not only forms an impressive historic testament in itself, but no less provides a message to all Canada. Today, Acadian communities are vigorously evident in the three Maritime provinces; and in bilingual New Brunswick, they comprise close to half the population. Here is a resolute people's living answer to their terrible time of expulsion, during a deadly contest of empires. But to that contest we ourselves must now return.

In 1756 the Seven Years War began in Europe; although in America the conflict simply continued — witnessing another French success that year, the capture of British Oswego, which was located on the Lake Ontario shore opposite Fort Frontenac, and thus had threatened New France's main water highway to Niagara and on to the Ohio. The French victory at Oswego was won by a new commanding general, the Marquis de Montcalm, a capable soldier of deserved renown; but who had shortcomings of his own. He scarcely seemed aware that he, a trained regular, might make military misjudgments. He was all too disdainful of the colonial authorities in New France, and the whole *Canadien* skill in guerilla warfare developed during years of swift assaults on Indian villages or English frontiers. Montcalm would gain more successes in 1757-8. Yet he disparaged and resisted the strategies of his supposed superior, the Governor-General Pierre de Vaudreuil (Quebec-born son of a notable earlier governor, Philippe de Vaudreuil), who had taken office in 1755 and had pursued a largely successful policy of keeping the British away from New-France by French-Indian attacks amid the forests. Montcalm instead believed that the enemy had to be met and decisively defeated European-style, in pitched battles at strongpoints of defence. Each could be partly right: but their command dissensions scarcely helped to defend New France.

The fact remains that, for all the value of guerilla thrusts in keeping the enemy off balance or disrupting their communications, the crucial battles for America would ultimately be won by regular forces and their well-drilled heavy fire; on open battlefields or in the sieges of key fortresses, not by scattered musket shots from behind trees in the wilds. The French at the start held some advantage in their wilderness knowledge and their ties with the western Indians, not to mention the fact that they were not thirteen unconcerted colonies, moving in varied directions or not moving at all. Yet over time New France's much smaller population and resources were bound to become apparent, as the British colonies began to apply their own real strengths. Furthermore, there was the

1. Governor Pierre de Rigaud de Vaudreuil. *Last governor of New France (1755-60), he was the son (born in the colony) of a distinguished earlier Governor Vaudreuil (1705-25). But the younger Vaudreuil, although able, entered into the corrupt dealing of the French intendant of the time, François Bigot — which lessened his own governing role in the eyes of a disdainful French military commander, the very professional Montcalm.*

2. The Marquis de Montcalm. *Sent to New France in 1756, Montcalm quickly took British Oswego on Lake Ontario, and in 1757, Fort William Henry on the Lake George-Lake Champlain approaches up to New France. The next year he defeated an invading army at Ticonderoga on Lake Champlain: a notable record, till mounting British reinforcements and improved British generalship turned the balance the other way.*

3. William Pitt, Designer of British Victories. *This far-sighted and energetic political leader swung a feeble and corrupt British government into an all-out offensive, using Britain's sea power, sending strong forces overseas, and picking capable men to lead the new armies in America.*

4. Young General James Wolfe. *Already known from service in Germany and the Netherlands against France, Wolfe was a brigadier general during the successful onslaught on Louisbourg in 1758. The resourceful daring he then displayed had much to do with Pitt's appointing him to top command of an even bigger assault — on Quebec itself in 1759.*

5. Louisbourg under its Final Siege: *In 1758, when the town was hopelessly entrapped.*

growing stranglehold of British sea-power on the Atlantic, which in due course let only trickles of French reinforcements and munitions get through, while British regular forces and armaments swelled freely overseas. Finally, there was the guiding genius of William Pitt in the British government from 1757. He shaped a co-ordinated war effort in Britain and America, and chose generals and admirals who could carry it out. Accordingly, though the patterns were not fully apparent till 1758, the greater available weight of British power, once effectively used, spelled doom for France's empire in America. All French aptitudes in forest warfare could do little more than delay the final outcome.

1

1. **Surrender at Louisbourg, July, 1758.** *It came after seven weeks of bombardment, which forced a starving and crumbling fortress to yield — but yet delayed a British attack up the St. Lawrence for another year.*

2. **Fort Frontenac, Taken by the British in August, 1758.** *A rough French sketch, at what is now Kingston, showing the Cataraqui River at its meeting with Lake Ontario, where the fort was set.*

3. **Wolfe's Landing Above Quebec, September, 1759.** *This composite view shows boats going in from the British fleet and a battle under way on the Plains of Abraham — thus blending together a time-span from night into day. Still, it does point to the fact that Britain's sea power not only brought British forces to Quebec, but also carried them past the guns of that fortress, so they could land upstream, on a weaker-defended shore.*

4. **Wolfe's Orders for the Night-Time Landing.** *Only an extract, but it indicates the instructions given to the troops.*

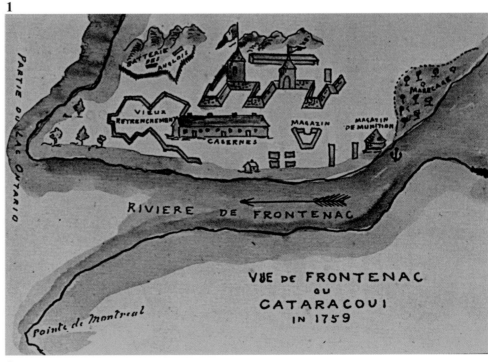

2

3

be irregular, cowardly, and corrupt: a little vigilance however is necessary to prevent surprises, the corps must keep together, must not disperse nor wan- der about the country.

The enemy will soon find, that the artillery and musquetry of this chosen body of infantry is formidable. The troops to hold themselves in readi- ness to land, and attack the enemy.

Captain Shadd has received the General's instructions, in respect to the order in which the troops are to move and land; no officer must attempt to make the least alteration, or interfere with Captain Shadd's particular province, least as the boats move in the night, there be confusion and disorder amongst them: the men are to be quite silent, and when they are about to land, must not on any account fire out of the boats. The officers of the Navy are not to be interrupted in their part of the duty, they will receive their orders from the Officers appointed to superintend the whole; to whom they are an- swerable.

The enemy's forces are now divided, great scarcity of provisions in their camp, and universal discontent among the Canadians; the second Offi- cer in command is gone to Montreal or St. John's, which gives reason to

4

1

2

3

4

The British surge forward showed dramatically in the taking of Louisbourg in July, 1758, after a seven-week siege. That fortress had been much strengthened and better manned since its return to French control. But a powerful British fleet and army that was assembled at Halifax swept up to the great French base; where a successful landing under General James Wolfe led on to massive cannonades that finally forced the shattered town to surrender. This time the British blew up Louisbourg's fortifications. They also occupied Cape Breton Island and the Island of Saint John (Prince Edward), while Wolfe went to seize the fishing coasts of Gaspé. Most important, the way by sea to the St. Lawrence and Quebec now lay open: though it was too late in the season to mount an attack before another year. Meanwhile, there were decisive British successes in the interior, as well. A force under Colonel John Bradstreet repaid the loss of Oswego by capturing Fort Frontenac, which now was weakly held and in poor condition — a strange weakness considering the critical value of this historic post where Lake Ontario met the St.Lawrence. For with its fall, the French chain of forts to westward was broken. The results appeared that November, when Fort Duquesne in the Ohio, itself under British attack and now cut off from supplies, was abandoned and blown up by its own defenders. Fort Pitt appeared in its place: later to become Pittsburgh in the spread of American settlement into the Ohio country.

The war moved toward a climax in 1759. That July, stout, stone-built Fort Niagara fell to the assaults of British troops, New York militia and Mohawk Indians, all under Sir William Johnson (as he now was). With the loss of this major stronghold, the little French fort that had been placed at Toronto harbour was burned by its own garrison. British forces were now converging on the St. Lawrence core of Canada: eastward from Lake Ontario, north from the Lake Champlain region, and up the main St. Lawrence River from the sea, where in June a fleet and army under James Wolfe had arrived at Quebec, the capital and very heart of New France.

For several months Wolfe battered ineffectually at Montcalm's strong French defences along the Beauport shore, on the downstream side of Quebec. But in September he finally struck above the city, his men climbing the steep banks by night; so that the morning of September 13 found a British army of some 5,000 drawn up on the Plains of Abraham outside the city walls. With Wolfe on this less protected flank of Quebec, and across the remaining French supply line to Montreal, Montcalm reacted all too hastily. He hurried the bulk of his forces out of their Beauport lines in a long march around the city, and sent them right into battle. In numbers, they nearly equalled the British, but they were tired, disarrayed, and in their confusion not equal to the ordered discipline of their waiting enemies. Massed British volleys rang out in sequence, blasting down the hastily advancing French, who swayed, then broke and ran. It was all over in half an hour. Montcalm was mortally wounded trying to rally his men. Wolfe died on the battlefield, likely shot by a Canadian or Indian sniper. Yet Quebec was surrendered on September 18, and British forces moved into possession of this main bastion of New France — as indeed it had been, ever since Champlain's time.

The war went on, for there were still many French-held posts, Indian allies, and the French army now centred on Montreal. Moreover, after the Royal Navy had to leave Quebec to avoid being frozen in over the winter, the British forces

1. The General Makes his Way to the Top of the Cliffs.
2. Montcalm Rallies his Men in Response. *Both this and the preceding picture are old-fashioned artists' visions of gallant generals doing noble things — with never a hair awry, and no haste, confusion or sweat. Nevertheless, they do show two brave men who saw the destiny of Canada change between them, before they both fell! on that September 13, 1759.*
3. General James Murray. *He had led a battalion at Louisbourg and fought under Wolfe at Quebec, before succeeding him: to hold the city through the winter until reinforcements could reach his disease-ridden troops. But Murray had also to meet the thrusts of the last French army, down from Montreal under the Duc de Lévis. When in March, 1760, Murray's attempted sally to Ste-Foy was beaten back, he had to wait it out again in Quebec.*
4. French General Lévis at Ste. Foy, 1760. *This itself was a decided French success, which* Canadiens *since have held dear, given the all-too-easy Anglo-assumption that Wolfe and the British had won everything at Quebec in 1759. Yet against any* Canadien *wishful thinking, were the stark facts that more British armies were now converging on New France, and that British sea-power would inevitably bring fresh troops to Quebec in the spring.*

1. The Army of General Amherst en route to Montreal, 1760. *Jeffery Amherst, actual commander at Louisbourg, and Britain's general-in-chief in America, arranged the descent of three strong armies on Montreal. This virtually compelled its fall; to bring the end of French military power in Canada, in September, 1760.*

2. Fireworks in London, England, Celebrating the Peace of Paris, 1763. *Britain had reason thus to hail the end of a long and costly imperial struggle, which in the Treaty of 1763 awarded it widespread control of America north of Spanish Mexico, and complete mastery of a future Canada itself.*

holed up in a badly battered city themselves went through attack. In April of 1760, the French forces led by the Duc de Lévis came down from Montreal. At Ste. Foy, a village just west of Quebec, Lévis fought a battle harder than that waged on the Plains the autumn before, and the British under General James Murray, Wolfe's successor, were lucky to get back within Quebec's defences. But then British warships came up the river when the ice went out. Lévis had to give up his siege, and the very thin hope of a French war fleet arriving instead. The French retired bitterly to Montreal once more. There the British soon closed in from all sides, on a town far less defensible than Quebec had been. And at Montreal on September 8, 1760, Governor Vaudreuil signed the Articles of Capitulation with General Jeffrey Amherst. French authority had ceased in Canada. New France had fallen.

Still, the Seven Years War had not ended in Europe as yet, and so Canada remained under an interim British military rule. Besides, there was always the chance that a peace treaty might again restore some American holdings to France, especially if French fortunes of war happened to improve elsewhere. With such a possibility in mind, France in 1762 indeed contrived to send a naval expedition to seize St. John's, chief centre in British Newfoundland, largely as a counter to use in bargaining back French North Atlantic fishing rights. A surprised St. John's fell easily to this bold attack — but a bigger British expedition sent from New York quickly regained it. In the meantime, peace negotiations were already under way between the principal, mutually exhausted European combatants. They resulted in the Peace of Paris, ratified for Britain by its parliament in February, 1763.

The costliest fighting had gone on in Europe — where scarcely one blood-soaked acre of ground changed hands in the treaty between the main antagonists, France, Spain and Austria, versus Russia, Prussia, and Britain. But in North America, a defeated France gave up her huge empire. She kept only St. Pierre and Miquelon as bases for her Atlantic fishery, two little islands off the southern coast of Newfoundland; and some fishing rights, still, on that big island's empty western shores. Her other domains — Acadia to the Appalachians, French Canada west beyond that, plus the Ohio and Illinois country and all the lands east of the Mississippi — passed into British possession; while Spain was given France's Louisiana territories west of the Mississippi. Now, definitely, New France had disappeared. A century and more of growth and expansion, conflict and courage, had ended in military conquest and total cession.

But it was not all over — not in pride, not in achievement, nor in heritage. The French who had shaped Quebec and many a lasting settlement, who had carried Canada to the Great Lakes and the Great Plains, or ranged from Labrador to the Gulf of Mexico, were by no means going to disappear as a strong and vital factor in Canadian history. New France might have vanished. French Canada and its resolute descendants would not.

1

2

1760s Resident population of
Newfoundland: c. 10,000
New Englanders occupy vacated
Acadian lands in Nova Scotia
(N.S.)

1763 Royal Proclamation prescribes
boundaries, governments and
laws for newly-won territories
of British North America
Population of new Province of
Quebec: 70,000

1763-64 Indians under Pontiac rise against
British in the Great Lakes area

1765 Civil government replaces
military rule in Quebec
Britain passes Stamp Act —
detested by the Thirteen
(American) colonies

1766 Carleton replaces Murray as
Governor of Quebec Province

1767 Some expelled Acadians return to
N.S.
St. Johns Island (future Prince
Edward Island) granted to large
British proprietors

1768 Surge of fur trading around Great
Lakes and Ohio area
James Finlay sets up post on the
Saskatchewan

1769 St. Johns Island provincial
government established

1770s Population of N.S. reaches 17,000
Traders from St. Lawrence
ranging along Saskatchewan
valley

1772 Samuel Hearne reaches Arctic
Ocean via Coppermine River

1773 Scottish immigration flows to
N.S.
First Assembly of St. Johns
Island (Island population now
1,000)

1774 Britain passes Quebec Act
Hudson's Bay Company founds
Cumberland House on
Saskatchewan River

Chapter Four

British Empire and American Revolution
1763 - 1791

1775 American rebel army occupies Montreal

1775-76 American forces under Montgomery and Arnold defeated at Quebec

1776 Declaration of Independence adopted at Philadelphia
British withdraw from Boston; take Loyalists to N.S.

1777 British Fort Howe built at Saint John River, then in N.S.

1778 Captain James Cook lands on Vancouver Island

1779 North West Company formed in Montreal

1781 Surrender of British Army at Yorktown, Virginia

1783 Peace treaty signed between Britain and United States

c.1783 30,000 Loyalists migrate to N.S.

1784 Province of New Brunswick (N.B.) created; Thomas Carleton appointed Governor
Province of Cape Breton created also

1784-868,000 Loyalists and Indian allies settle in western Quebec (future Ontario)

1785 Saint John, N.B. incorporated as a city

1786 Carleton, now Lord Dorchester, returns as Governor of Quebec

1788 Dorchester sets up four administrative districts in western Quebec

1789 Peter Pond establishes first post in Athabasca country
Alexander Mackenzie reaches Mackenzie River
Anglican King's College founded at Windsor, N.S.

1791 Constitutional or Canada Act sets up Upper and Lower Canada, dividing and replacing old Province of Quebec

The Northern Colonies in Britain's America

After the Peace of Paris, a now unrivalled British empire proceeded to organize the great new holdings it had added in America. Accordingly, the imperial authorities in London issued the Royal Proclamation of October 7, 1763, prescribing boundaries, government, law and regulation for gains that stretched from the West Indies to Florida and Canada; although it is only the northern, "Canadian" territories that need concern us. Newfoundland, long in British hands, was thus given charge of Labrador. Cape Breton and the Island of St. John were annexed to Nova Scotia, whose northern boundary would definitely run up to the Gaspé Peninsula and the heights of the Appalachians. And beyond that limit, the Proclamation laid out a new British Province of Quebec, to extend along both sides of the main St. Lawrence River.

On its north, this province was to reach from Labrador's Rivière Saint-Jean in the east to Lake Nipissing in the west, from where its boundary would swing southeastward across the upper St. Lawrence to Lake Champlain, and then run back east again along the Appalachian line. Plainly, such a Quebec province was very much smaller than former New France had been: consisting, basically, of just the farming heartland of French Canada, but leaving out the vast wilderness world of the fur trade that spread west of the Ottawa across the Great Lakes basin, or north and west to Ruperts Land, still held by the British Hudson's Bay Company. The Proclamation of 1763 also announced that this new and far more

Overleaf. Ile Percé, Gaspé Peninsula, 1760.
1. Scene near Berthierville, in Settled Quebec Countryside. *On the Berthier River close to the St. Lawrence, it shows a new bridge, and at the far right a typical* habitant out-door bread-oven.
2. Montmorency Falls near Quebec City. *A dramatically beautiful site that would become a favourite visiting-spot for travellers, or for officers of the British garrison and their lady friends.*
3. The Royal Proclamation of 1763. *This was not an Act of Parliament but was issued by the official Privy Council in Great Britain. Still, if thus more an administrative step, not as solemn as a statute, it was nevertheless binding. The Council of the King's ministers, after all, contained the prime minister and his cabinet colleagues, who sat in and headed parliament itself. And so the Proclamation was very much an expression of imperial government policy for the new British possessions in America.*

1

2

By the Honourable Sir WILLIAM JOHNSON, Bart. His

Majeſty's Surperintendant of Indian Affairs for the Northern Diſtrict of North-America; Colonel of the Six United Nations, their Allies and Dependants, and of His Majeſty's Council for the Province of New-York, &c.

A PROCLAMATION.

WHEREAS I have receiaed His Majeſty's royal Proclamation, given at the Court of St. Jame's the eleventh Day of October laſt, together with a Letter from the Right Honourable Lords Commiſſioners for the Trade and Plantations, of the Tenth of October laſt ſignifying His Majeſty's Commands, that I ſhould cauſe the ſame "to be forthwith made publick inthe ſeveral Parts of my Juriſdiction, and that I ſhould ſtrictly enjoin all Perſons whatever whom it might concern, to pay a due Obedience thereto on their Parts." Which Proclamation is in the Words following.

BY THE KING, A PROCLAMATION.

GEORGE, R.

WHEREAS We have taken into Our Royal Conſideration the extenſive and valuable Acquiſitions in America, ſecured to Our Crown by the late Definitive Treaty of Peace, concluded at Paris the Tenth Day of February laſt; and being deſirous, that all Our loving Subjects, as well of Our Kingdoms as of Our Colonies in America, may avail themſelves, with all convenient Speed, of the great Benefits and Advantages which muſt accrue therefrom to their Commerce, Manufactures, and Navigation; We have thought fit, with the Advice of Our Privy Council, to iſſue this Our Royal Proclamation, hereby to publiſh and declare to all Our loving Subjects, that We have, with the Advice of Our ſaid Privy Council, granted Our Letters Patent under Our Great Seal of Great Britain, to erect within the Countries and Iſlands ceded and confirmed to Us by the ſaid Treaty, Four diſtinct and ſeparate Governments, ſtiled and called by the Names of Quebec, Eaſt Florida, Weſt Florida, and Granada and limitted and bounded as follows; viz.

Firſt. The Government of Quebec, bounded on the Labrador Coaſt by the River St. John, and from thence by a Line drawn from the Head of that River through the Lake St. John to the South End of the Lake Nipiſſin; from whence the ſaid Line croſſing the River St. Lawrence and the Lake Champlain in Forty five Degrees of North Latitude, paſſes along the High Lands which divide the Rivers that empty themſelves into the ſaid River St. Lawrence, from whoſe which fall into the Sea, and alſo along the North Coaſt of the Bay des Chaleurs, and the Coaſt of the Gulph of St. Lawrence to Cape Roſieres, and from thence croſſing the Mouth of the River St. Lawrence by the Weſt End of the Iſland of Anticoſti, terminates at the aforeſaid River St. John.

Secondly. The Government of Eaſt Florida, bounded to the Weſtward by the Gulph of Mexico, and the Apalachicola River; to the Northward by a Line drawn from that Part of the ſaid River where the Chatahou-chee and Flint Rivers meet, to the Source of St. Mary's River, and by the Courſe of the ſaid River to the Atlantick Ocean; and to the Eaſtward and Southward, by the Atlantick Ocean, and the Gulph of Florida, including all Iſlands with Six Leagues of the Sea Coaſt

Thirdly. The Government of Weſt Florida, bounded to the Southward by the Gulph of Mexico, including all Iſlands within Six Leagues of the Coaſt from the River Apalachicola to Lake Ponchartrain; to the Weſtward by the ſaid Lake, the Lake Mauripas and the River Miſſiſippi; to the Northward by a Line drawn due Eaſt from that Part of the River Miſſiſippi which lies in Thirtyone Degrees North Latitude, to the River Apalachicola or Chatahouchee; and to the Eaſtward by the ſaid River.

Fourthly. The Government of Granada, comprehending the Iſland of that Name, together with the Grenadines, and the Iſlands of Dominico, St. Vencents, and Tobago.

And, to the End that the open and free Fiſhery of Our Subjects may be extended to and carried on upon the Coaſt of Labrador, and the adjacent Iſlands, We have thought fit with the Advice of Our ſaid Privy Council, to put all that Coaſt, from the River St. John's to Hudſon's Streights, together with all the Iſlands of Anticoſti and Magdelaine, and other ſmaller Iſlands lying upon the ſaid Coaſt, under the Care and Inſpection of Our Governor of Newfoundland.

We have alſo, with the Advice of Our Privy Council, thought it to annex the Iſlands of St. John's and Cape Breton or Iſle Royale, with the leſſer Iſlands adjacent thereto, to Our Government of Nova Scotia.

We have alſo, with the Advice of Our Privy Council aforeſaid, annexed to Our Province of Georgia, all the Lands lying between the Rivers Altamaha and St. Mary's.

And whereas it will greatly contribute to the ſpeedy ſettling Our ſaid new Governments, that Our loving Subjects ſhould be informed of Our Paternal Care for the Secutity of the Liberties and Properties of thoſe who are and ſhall become Inhabitants thereof; We have thought fit to publiſh and declare, by this Our Proclamation, that We have, in the Letters Patents under Our Great Seal of Great Britain, by which the ſaid Governments are conſtituted, given expreſs Power and Direction to Our Governors of Our ſaid Colonies reſpectively, that ſo ſoon as the State and Circumſtances of the ſaid Colonies Will admit thereof, they ſhall with the Advice and Conſent of the Members of Our Council, ſummon and call General Aſſemblies within the ſaid Governments reſpectively, in ſuch Manner and Form as is uſed and directed in thoſe Colonies and Provinces in America, which are under Our immediate Government; and We have alſo given Power to the ſaid Governors, with the Conſent of Our Councils, and the Repreſentatives of the People, ſo to be ſummoned as aforeſaid, to make, conſtitute, and ordain Laws, Statutes, and Ordinances for the Publick Peace, Welfare and Good Government of Our ſaid Colonies, and of the People and Inhabitants thereof; as near as may be agreeable to the Laws of England, and under ſuch Regulations and Reſtrictions as are uſed in other Colonies; and in the mean Time, and until ſuch Aſſemblies can be called as aforeſaid, all Perſons inhabiting in or reſorting to Our ſaid Colonies may confide in Our Royal Protection for the Ejoyment of the Benefit of the Laws of Our Realm of England; for which Purpoſe We have given Power under Our Great Seal to the Governors of Our ſaid Colonies reſpectively, to erect and conſtitute, with the Advice of Our ſaid Councils reſpectively, Courts of Judicature and Publick Juſtice within Our ſaid Colonies, for the hearing and determining all Cauſes as well Criminal as Civil, according to Law and Equity, and as near as may be agreeable to the Laws of England with Liberty to all Perſons who may think themſelves aggrieved by the Sentences of ſuch Courts in all Civil Caſes or Tryals under the uſual Limitations and Reſtrictions to Us, in Our Privy Council.

We have alſo thought fit, with the Advice of Our Privy Council as aforeſaid, to give unto the Governor and Councils of Our ſaid Three new Colonies upon the Continent, full Power and Authority to ſettle and agree with the Inhabitants of Our ſaid new Colonies, or with any other Perſons who ſhall reſort thereto, for ſuch Lands, Tenements, and Hereditaments, as are now or hereafter ſhall be in Our Power to diſpoſe of, and them to grant to any ſuch Perſon or Perſons, upon ſuch Terms, and under ſuch moderate Quit-Rents, Services and Acknowledgements, as have been appointed and ſettled in Our other Colonies, and under ſuch other Conditions as ſhall appear to Us to be neceſſary and expedient for the Advantage of the Grantees, and the Improvement and Settlement of Our ſaid Colonies.

And whereas We are deſirous, upon all Occaſions, to teſtify Our Royal Senſe and Approbation of the Conduct and Bravery of the Officers and Soldiers of Our Armies, and to reward the ſame; We do hereby command and impower Our Governors of Our Three New Colonies, and all other Our Governors of our ſeveral Provinces on the Continent of North-America, to grant without Fee or Reward, to ſuch reduced Officers as have ſerved in North-America during the late War, and to ſuch private Soldiers as have been or ſhall be diſbanded in America, and are actually reſiding there, and ſhall perſonally apply for the ſame, the following Quantities of Lands, ſubject at the Expiration of Ten Years to the ſame Quit-Rents as other Lands are ſubject to in the Province within which they are granted, as alſo ſubject to the ſame Conditions of Cultivation and Improvements, viz.

To every Perſon having the Rank of a Field Officer, Five Thouſand Acres.—To every Captain, Three Thouſand Acres.—To every Subaltern or Staff Officer, Two Thouſand Acres.—To every Non-Commiſſion Officer, Two Hundred Acres.—To every Private Man, Fifty Acres.

We do likewiſe authorize aud require the Governors and Commanders in Chief of all Our ſaid Colonies upon the Continent of North-America, to grant the like Quantities of Land, and upon the ſame Conditions, to ſuch reduced Officers of Our Navy, of the Rank, as ſerved on board Our Ships of War in North-America at the Times of the Reduction of Louiſbourg and Quebec in the late War, and who ſhall perſonally apply to Our reſepective Governors for ſuch Grants.

And whereas it is juſt and reaſonable, and eſſential to Our Intereſt and the Security of Our Colonies, that the ſeveral Nations or Tribes of Indians, with whom we are connected, and who live under Our Protection, ſhould not be moleſted or diſturbed in the Poſſeſſion of ſuch Parts of Our Dominions and Territories as, not having been ceded to, or purchaſed by Us, are reſerved to them, or any of them as their Hunting Grounds; We do therefore, with the Advice of Our Privy Council, declare it to be Our Royal Will and Pleaſure, that no Governor or Commander in Chief in any of Our Colonies of Quebec, Eaſt Florida, or Weſt Florida, do preſume, upon any Pretence whatever, to grant Warrants or Survey, or paſs any Patents for Lands beyond the Bounds of their reſpective Governments, as deſcribed in their Commiſſions; as alſo, that no Governor or Commander in Chief in any of Our other Colonies or Plantations in America, do preſume, for the preſent and until Our further Pleaſure be known, to grant Warrants of Survey, or paſs Patents for any Lands beyond the Heads or Sources of any of the Rivers which fall into the Atlantick Ocean from the Weſt and North-Weſt, or upon any Lands whatever, which not having been ceded to or purchaſed by Us as aforeſaid, are reſerved to the ſaid Indians, or any of them.

And We do further declare it to be Our Royal Will and Pleaſure, for the preſent as aforeſaid, to reſerve under Our Sovereignty, Protection, and Dominion, for the Uſe of the ſaid Indians, all the Lands and Territories not included within the Limits of our ſaid Three New Governments, or within the Limits of the Territory granted to the Hudſon's Bay Company, as alſo all the Lands and Territories, lying to the Weſtward of the Sources of the Rivers which fall into the Sea from the Weſt and North Weſt, as aforeſaid; and We do hereby ſtrictly forbid, on Pain of Our Diſpleaſure, all Our loving Subjects from making any Purchaſes or Settlements whatever, or taking Poſſeſſion of any of the Lands above reſerved, without Our eſpecial Leave and Licence for that Purpoſe firſt obtained.

And We do further ſtrictly enjoin and require all Perſons whatever, who have either wilfully or inadvertently ſeated themſelves upon any Land within the Countries above deſcribed, or upon any other Lands, which, not having been ceded to, or purchaſed by Us, are ſtill reſerved to the ſaid Indians as aforeſaid, forthwith to remove themſelves from ſuch Settlements.

And whereas great Frauds and Abuſes have been committed in the purchaſing Lands of the Indians, to the great Prejudice of Our intereſts, and to the great Diſſatisfaction of the ſaid Indians; in order therefore to prevent ſuch Irregularities for the future, and to the End that the Indians may be convinced of Our Juſtice, and determined Reſolution to remove all reaſonable Cauſe of Diſcontent, We do with the Advice of Our Privy Council, ſtrictly enjoin and require that no private Perſon do preſume to make any Purchaſe from the ſaid Indians of any Lands reſerved to the ſaid Indians, within thoſe Parts of Our Colonies where We have thought proper to allow Settlements; but that if, at any Time, any of the ſaid Indians ſhould be inclined to diſpoſe of the ſaid Lands, the ſame ſhall be purchaſed only for Us, in Our Name, at ſome Publick Meeting or Aſſembly of the ſaid Indians to be held for that Purpoſe by the Governor or Commander in Chief of Our Colonies reſpectively, within which they ſhall lie; and in Caſe they ſhall lie within the Limits of any Proprietary Government, they ſhall be purchaſed only for the Uſe and in the Name of ſuch Proprietaries, conformable to ſuch Directions and Inſtructions as We or they ſhall think proper to give for that Purpoſe: And We do, by the Advice of Our Privy Council, declare and enjoin, that the Trade with the ſaid Indians ſhall be free and open to all Our Subjects whatever; provided that every Perſon, who may incline to trade with the ſaid Indians, to take out a Licence for carrying on ſuch Trade from the Governor or Commander in Chief of any of Our Colonies reſpectively, where ſuch Perſon ſhall reſide; and alſo give Security to obſerve ſuch Regulations as We ſhall at any Time think fit, by Ourſelves, or by Our Commiſſaries to be appointed for this Purpoſe, to direct and appoint for the Benefit of the ſaid Trade; and We do hereby authorize, enjoin, and require the Governors Commanders in Chief of all Our Colonies reſpectively, as well thoſe under Our immediate Government as Thoſe under the Government and Direction of Proprietaries to grant ſuch Licence, without Fee or Reward, taking eſpecial care to inſert therein a Condition, that ſuch Licence ſhall be void, and the Security forfeited, in caſe the Perſon to whom the ſame is granted, ſhall refuſe or neglect to obſerve ſuch Regulations as We ſhall think proper to preſcribe as aforeſaid.

And we do further expreſsly enjoin and require all Officers whatever, as well Military as thoſe employed in the Management and Direction of Indian Affairs within the Territories reſerved as aforeſaid for the Uſe of the ſaid Indians, to ſeize and apprehend all Perſons whatever, who, ſtanding charged with Treaſons, Miſpriſions of Treaſon, Murders, or other Felonies or Miſdemeanors, ſhall fly from Juſtice, and take Refuge in the ſaid Territory, and to ſend them under proper Guard to the Colony where the Crime was committed of which they ſtand accuſed, in order to take their Tryal for the ſame.

GIVEN at Our Court at St. Jame's the Seventh Day of October, One Thouſand Seven Hundred and Sixty Three. In the Third Year of Our Reign.

GOD Save the KING.

I DO, in Obedience to His Majeſty's Command give this publick Notice to all Perſons reſiding within my Juriſdiction, (being that Country juſtly Claimed by the Six Nations, their Allies and Dependants) that I will, to the Utmoſt of my Power, cauſe the ſame to be obſerved: And I do ſtrictly enjoin all ſuch Perſons to pay due Obedience thereto.

GIVEN under my Hand and Seal at Arms, at Johnſon-Hall, the 24th Day of December 1763, in the Fourth Year of the Reign of our Sovereign Lord GEORGE the Third, by the Grace of GOD, of Great Britain, France and Ireland, KING, Defender of the Faith, and so forth.

WILLIAM JOHNSON.

By Order of Sir William Johnſon.
William Marſo, Secry. for Indian Affairs.

GOD Save the KING.

3

1

2

1. New Northern Lands of British America. *This old map sets out the boundaries of the Province of Quebec prescribed in 1763, by the dotted lines around the St. Lawrence River.*

2. The Pontiac Rising in the Great Lakes West. *Here Chief Pontiac addresses tribesmen gathered in council.*

3. Fort Oswego, on the South Side of Lake Ontario. *Originally built by the British in 1726 to tap the French fur trade at Fort Frontenac on the north shore, it was captured by Montcalm in 1756; but was reoccupied and rebuilt by British forces after New France's final defeat. It would remain a major inland imperial post on through the American Revolution — not to be finally given up, in fact, until the 1790s.*

4. View of St. John's, Newfoundland. *Sketched in the later eighteenth century, it shows the town beside the harbour, and Fort Townsend backing it.*

5. St. John's Harbour Entry. *Another view by the same quick-sketch artist, looking out past fortifications to the sea.*

3

4

5

confined Quebec colony would be given English law and an elected representative assembly in its government, as was standard practice throughout the British Thirteen Colonies in America. Yet a French-peopled British province might not fit so readily into that existing pattern.

As for the western wilds beyond the Province of Quebec, the Proclamation declared them to be Indian Territory reserved to the native peoples: areas under British protection as exercised from military and fur-trade posts, but in which no lands were henceforth to be granted or settled, not until they had been officially purchased by the Crown. The intent was to stop "great Frauds and Abuses," to convince Indians of honest justice at British hands, and to ensure an orderly method of "clearing" native titles to land through official negotiations and binding agreements, before any white occupation took place. From this design came a lasting heritage in itself: in Indian treaties, annual treaty payments and fixed land reserves (*not* "reservations") established for the aboriginal communities. It would be foolish to believe that the design would all work out fairly; or that Indian peoples, who thought in terms of needful land use rather than outright, permanent land ownership, fully recognized what the Europeans had in mind. And the plan was certainly not put forward simply for high-minded reasons of imperial justice; but because at the close of the Seven Years War there was widespread turmoil among the inland tribes, who had largely fought as French allies against the British. In fact, in 1763 a last-ditch effort led by the Ottawa chief, Pontiac, produced a violent Indian rising that laid siege to Fort Detroit and attacked other British-held Great Lakes posts. The British thus sought to restore order, to check white inland contacts and calm native fears. Nonetheless, the imperial Proclamation policy of keeping settlement out of the declared Indian Territory and licensing all fur traders there — of explicitly recognizing Indian land rights and requiring a public, state procedure to deal with them — was to be profoundly significant for a future Canada. No less significant would be the Proclamation Line, thus drawn to bar the Indian Territory against land-seekers pushing west from the older Thirteen Colonies on the seaboard.

But what were the northern colonies like, when the Proclamation programme was set forth in 1763? Looking first at Newfoundland, then moving westward, we find this oldest possession in Britain's enlarged American empire was still dominated by the long-established visiting fishery, in ships that came out from England each summer, although the resident fishery (of island settlers) was steadily growing at the little outports dotted along the coasts. Initially, both the summer fishermen and the fishing settlers had mostly stemmed from

The Town of Halifax in the 1770s.
No longer closed in by log palisades around it, but an expanding commercial town and port, facing seaward to Chebucto Head.

southwestern England, from Bristol around to Plymouth and Poole, with many other points between. Yet though this English West-Country element stayed prominent in Newfoundland, many Irish were added over the eighteenth century, brought by outbound fishing vessels that stopped at Ireland's harbours on the way for more supplies and extra boatmen. These Irish venturers might then remain as fishermen on their own in Newfoundland, or even be abandoned there by ship-captains ready enough to save on return passages home. By the 1760s, at any rate, out of a year-round Newfoundland population nearing 10,000, close to half were Irish. They were chiefly concentrated at outports along the eastern Avalon Peninsula (once the English Shore) and especially around St. John's, the leading port; while the more mobile English had spread out on both the north and south coasts of the island, and were entering the Labrador fishery.

The summer-time population of Newfoundland was of course much larger, rising over 20,000, in total, when the annual fishing fleet arrived from England. One resulting feature of this very distinctive Newfoundland society was its unusually low proportion of women and children. Obviously most of the summer visitors were male, though some female workers did come out with them, at times to stay, marry and begin families. Another feature was the harsh division between the overseas and resident fishermen, still more acute than that between the mainly Protestant English element and largely Catholic Irish. For the two fishing groups were rivals in the basic cod fishery, where the residents had the advantage of earlier starts and longer seasons, and sold their shore-dried cod to trading ships from both Old and New England while avoiding the long Atlantic haul themselves. Still, the visiting fishermen had an enduring advantage in imperial government support. To a British state heavily dependent on seaborne commerce and naval power, the Newfoundland fishery appeared as a vital reservoir of trained, ocean-going seamen available for time of war. The important fishing merchants of West-Country England assuredly pushed that view, and maintained a good deal of influence in the British parliament. Indeed, the "nursery of seamen" argument long led to official measures to restrain settlement in Newfoundland in favour of the overseas fishery — and to the contention that the island was not really a colony at all, but "a great fishing ship anchored off North America."

Hence Newfoundland was left under-governed, even to the edge of anarchy. As a supposed "ship," it had a senior naval officer as governor, the commander of the squadron that escorted the English fishing fleet out and back each summer — and who thus was not there at all in winter, when only a few appointed justices of the peace held sway. The powers of these "winter justices" were feeble, in truth, and there was no general court structure as yet. Newfoundland consequently stayed a pretty wild frontier; even though its fishing yields and its

Halifax from Inland, *showing the Citadel above and behind the townsite — become the main defence work against attacks from the sea.*

resident population both grew, while St. John's became truly a leading town, if so far not organized as such. Finally, the long years of the French wars hit at the visiting fishery, as its sailors were pressed into the Royal Navy while wartime dangers (and insurance costs) mounted on the Atlantic. This overseas fishery did partly recover after 1763, given some helpful government attention; but its position became increasingly uncertain in respect to the economically-advantaged if politically-disfavoured resident fishery. That fact was already indicated by the early 1770s, when Newfoundland's total summer numbers ranged around 26,000, yet over half of them by now were year-round residents.

Nova Scotia held strong fishing elements as well. These were residents, not transients, however; and the colony also developed farming, lumbering and shipping as it traded by sea with New England, Britain or the West Indies. Moreover, while the bulk of its Acadian inhabitants had been expelled (though some were returning even by 1767), New England settlers moved up to occupy vacant Acadian farmlands, from the later years of war on through the 1760s. Wartime perils, and then the Proclamation Line set forth in 1763 to white settlement out of the Indian Territory, had restrained New Englanders from moving westward. Yet they could go north. Some 7,000 of them came to Nova Scotia, until much of the best arable land (not widespread in that province) had been taken up anew.

They settled in the Annapolis Valley and around the head of the Bay of Fundy, planting New England townships that centered on village plots and featured wood-frame Congregational churches. Yankee fishermen gathered in ports like Yarmouth and Liverpool on the southern shores of Nova Scotia. Boston merchants came to Halifax, to serve its garrison and naval base, but also to build up its supply and export trades. Altogether, this influx had made the province virtually a northern extension of New England by 1769. Yet in the early 1770s the arrival of several hundred Ulster Irish Protestants, and then about 1,000 Yorkshiremen in the Chignecto Isthmus — plus the first of Nova Scotia's increasingly numerous Scots Highlanders, who landed at Pictou in 1773 — did work to broaden out the population base. Furthermore, with the emergence of a sizeable British community, not an Acadian one that had rejected oaths of allegiance, it became feasible to introduce representative government as practised in the Thirteen Colonies. Thus in 1758, Nova Scotia's elected Assembly — the first in Canada — met in Halifax. And by the mid 1770s, this flourishing province had more than 17,000 inhabitants, around half of them New Englanders.

By that time, moreover, another new Atlantic province had come into being, the Island of St. John, once Ile Saint-Jean — to be rechristened Prince Edward Island in 1799. Even in 1763, when this island was annexed to Nova Scotia, the imperial government had ordered its generally fertile lands surveyed into large,

Downtown Halifax. *The large mansion between the two churches was Nova Scotia's Government House in the later eighteenth century.*

1

Arrival of
Scottish
settlers,
Pictou, N.S.

Arrivée des
colons
écossais à
Pictou (N-É.)

Canada 8

2

1. **Mill in Annapolis Valley,** *a product of fresh settlement.*
2. **Scots Landings at Pictou, 1773.** *Stamp issued in 1973 to mark the two hundredth anniversary of the arrival of some two hundred Scottish settlers at this location on the Gulf of St. Lawrence shore of Nova Scotia.*
3. **St. John's Island (P.E.I.), 1773.** *Map shows counties, as established for settlement and parliamentary purposes.*

3

20,000 acre estates for settlement; and by 1767 these had all been granted to "proprietors" in Britain, men of rank and good political connections. The aim was to have the proprietors in return establish tenant-settlers on 200-acre lots; but the scheme was a lasting failure. Few of the non-resident owners in Britain made any effort. Few settlers wanted to come and pay rent to absentee landlords, when they could own their own farms elsewhere in British America. Hence, though the island's own provincial government was set up in 1769, actual settlement advanced there very slowly, and the first governor, Walter Patterson, had to have his own log cabin built at Charlottetown. There were some Micmac Indians, but less than 300 white inhabitants when the province began; most of them Acadians who had managed to stay or to return. Still, some Scottish colonists had been

1. The Island Council in Session.
Smaller than the little province's elected assembly in itself — but not a lot.
2. Charlottetown, Island Capital, 1778.

1

2

brought out by 1773 (when the population reached about 1,000), so that the first general assembly was called at Charlottetown that year: just eighteen members meeting in a tavern, and termed "a damned queer parliament." Hampered by the rents required from tenants, and by the payments due from proprietors to meet the costs of government (though left unpaid), the little island province stayed but scantily occupied. Yet its abundant soil and forests, and productive surrounding waters, would in the long run bring its inhabitants a simple but rewarding way of life.

Of these varied northern colonies, the newly-defined province of Quebec had by far the largest population, nearing 70,000 in the year of the Proclamation, 1763; and it went on mounting with a high annual birth rate of 65 per 1,000. Apart from British officials or military garrisons, however, only a small English-speaking, mostly Protestant group collected in the main urban centres of this solidly French Catholic province. In 1764 it was reported that there now were over two hundred "Protestant householders" in Quebec and Montreal. Drawn from both Britain and the Thirteen Colonies, these included artisans, tradesmen and innkeepers; but the key element, rising in wealth and power, were wholesale merchants. In Quebec City they often became importers and exporters. At Montreal, they turned to the long-range fur commerce that still was vital to the colony's economic life. Some who thus moved into Montreal fur enterprise had first arrived as army contractors and suppliers to the British army. Others already had experience on western frontiers, trading there from the older British colonies, particularly out of Albany on the Hudson. But altogether they represented the linking of the great St. Lawrence trade route westward with new access to British manufactures and markets east across the Atlantic. In sum, an Anglo-French fur partnership took shape, one that joined British capital and business expertise with French knowledge of the interior and its peoples — and with the *voyageur* canoe

British Troops in Montreal. *Units which took control of the city in 1760, a city already solidly built in stone.*

brigades that kept the whole system operating.

Success was soon apparent. The inland fur commerce, redeveloping from 1760 after the British victories in the west, did meet a setback in 1763-64 because of the Pontiac uprising and imperial restrictions then imposed on traders going into the Indian country. But the rising was over by 1765, and by 1768 the return of fur-trade control to individual colonies brought on a rapid surge of trading activity all around the Lakes and southwest into the Ohio country, while traders from Montreal reappeared on the Red River in the distant Northwest. In fact, within a few short years, Hudson's Bay employees far to the north in Ruperts Land — long comfortably settled in their posts beside the Bay — were feeling the impact of "pedlars from Canada," as they scornfully dubbed their new rivals. James Finlay from Montreal even reached the Saskatchewan in 1768, where he set up Finlay's House near Nipawin. By the early 1770s the traders out from the St. Lawrence were ranging widely along the Saskatchewan Valley, and looking onward to fresh territory for furs.

The builders of this newly advancing Canadian fur domain would include Scotsmen like Finlay, James McGill and Simon McTavish, Englishmen like John Gregory, Forrest Oakes and the Frobisher brothers, Joseph, Benjamin and Thomas, or American colonists such as Alexander Henry from New Jersey, who had barely escaped massacre at Fort Michilimackinac during the Pontiac rising, or Connecticut-born Peter Pond, a one-time Detroit trader who would push into the Athabaska country north of the Saskatchewan. And this truly was a joint Anglo-French achievement which saw British increasingly present as "wintering partners" at inland posts, or *Canadiens* sharing in headquarter firms of Montreal. Yet there were deep gulfs still to be bridged between two very different societies within Quebec: the one a small though economically powerful minority, the other a large majority, but placed under alien masters from another culture. Hence the question of Quebec, the question of how this province and community could really be integrated into a much enlarged British empire, still stayed crucial — and very far from resolved.

1. Alexander Henry, Montreal Fur Trader. *Significant in the spread of the Canadian fur trade into the North West, American-born Henry moved from the Lake Superior area to the Saskatchewan country, wintering on Beaver Lake by 1776.*

2. Joseph Frobisher, Montreal Fur Trader. *Of English Yorkshire origin, he was in the Athabaska country in the 1770s, and nearly died there of starvation. An original member of the North West Company set up in 1779, Joseph rose within the small directing group which virtually ran this great Montreal-based fur enterprise.*

1

2

beheading — an expressive if perhaps excessive term. It well may be that this colonial community which had stayed under-developed in some respects, and whose top merchants had largely been temporary residents from France, did not have all that much of its own high *bourgeoisie* to lose in any case. On the other hand, it is plain that *Canadien* society after the conquest saw both government and major enterprise left under alien control, without new Champlains, La Salles or d'Ibervilles to supply their once-bold patterns of leadership. In consequence, this society where rural life and the agricultural community remained close-knit, and where continuing *Canadien* seigneurs still drew customary respect, turned inward on itself: to the security of tradition, farm and family, leaving urban turmoil and frantic money-chasing to *les Anglais*. Here too was a Francophone heritage which arose from history; one that would idealize the agrarian world and seek to preserve it, in the classic, cautious social conservatism that hence emerged in the French province of Quebec.

Furthermore, though government and large business had fallen into foreign hands, the religious authority of the Roman Catholic Church had continued in French Canada, and indeed began to grow again following the British conquest. Before then, *Canadiens* had tended to pay somewhat less attention to the moral directives of their clergy. Such an attitude was not quite the worldly scepticism of eighteenth-century France, yet it was far from the original seventeenth-century colony's pious devotion. After the conquest, however, the Church stood out: not only as safeguarding the people's rooted Catholic faith, but also in working to sustain their distinctive language and institutions. Consequently, Catholicism became associated with agrarianism and conservatism, all as vital factors in French Canada's survival within an Anglo-American (and Protestant) empire. More than that, the earnest championing of *Canadien* interests by clerical leaders in their dealings with British government officials within Quebec, gave the Roman Catholic Church a "national" value to the mass of French Canadians, from the very outset of British rule.

After the French surrender at Montreal in 1760, the British military government that took over had made relatively few changes in running the colony: both to avoid trouble with its population while a state of war continued, and because a peace treaty had yet to settle who would finally keep Canada. Thus General James Murray, commander of the British forces at Quebec, ruled as Governor, while lesser commanders served as sub-governors at Montreal or Trois-Rivières much as under the former French regime; functioning locally through *Canadien* captains of militia, just as their French predecessors had done. And this British regime also developed good working relations with the leading Catholic clergy — especially Governor Murray with Jean-Olivier Briand, the vicar-general of Quebec, a principal Church figure after the death of the last French Bishop of Quebec, Pontbriand, in 1760. A tolerant, conciliatory Murray recognized Roman Catholic rights of worship (granted in the Montreal surrender terms) and also respected the Church's religious authority in French Canada. The watchful yet cooperative Briand, later made bishop, not only accepted British state authority, but equally brought it the passive obedience of *Canadiens*. Then came official peace — and soon the Proclamation of 1763 establishing both the new province of Quebec and the structure of civil government which would replace military rule in 1765.

Murray was reappointed Governor for this civil regime. He set up a council

1. Simon McTavish. *He had come from Scotland in 1770 to the fur trade out of Albany, and in 1775 moved his base to Montreal. By 1779 he was one of the main North West Company partners there, and joined with Joseph Frobisher in 1787 in the N.W.C.'s chief supply house, its virtual directorate. He then rose to be the leading company figure, and perhaps the richest man in Montreal (nicknamed "the Marquis") till his death in 1804.*

2. Henri de Pontbriand, Last Catholic Bishop of New France, 1741-1760. *French-born and consecrated, he had headed the Church in the French colony till its surrender, but died in that year, leaving a vital gap to be filled in the* Canadiens' *Catholic inheritance.*

3. Jean Olivier Briand, Catholic Spokesman under Early British Rule. *The effective successor to Bishop Pontbriand, he worked well with British Governor James Murray, but upheld* Canadien *Catholic interests. In 1766, the British authorities thus informally consented to his consecration in Paris as Bishop, with the official title, at first, of "Superintendant of the Church"; although he was received by his Catholic flock as Bishop, and held sway till he retired in 1784.*

4. Sir Guy Carleton, later Lord Dorchester. *Born in Ireland as a member of its ruling Anglo-Irish gentry class, he had a distinguished military career, and first came to Canada to serve in the invading army led by his friend, James Wolfe. On his return to be Governor in 1766, Carleton strove to conciliate the* Canadien *clergy and seigneurial order, with a view to securing a conservative-minded French Canada against the democratic unrest by then developing in the American colonies to southward.*

to assist him, as his new instructions required, and as further instructed, started to introduce English law into French Quebec. English criminal law, with its trial by jury, might win acceptance in time. But civil law, involving the weight of property and business dealings — and also seigneurial tenure, the very basis of the land system under old French law — posed a mass of unfamiliarities and complexities for new British-style law courts. Thus a hesitant Murray did not push legal changes further; any more than he created an elected Assembly, as called for in the Proclamation of 1765. Here the rising English-speaking merchant group in Quebec province made plain their angry displeasure. The Proclamation had promised the English law they relied on, and a representative assembly in which their own views could be heard. Had Old Subjects no rights compared to the New, ex-French, Subjects? Yet Murray, a military man and an autocratic Scot, had small liking for noisy Anglo-shopkeepers and petty demagogues, as he saw them. He really felt more sympathy for the "orderly" French who understood authority — but who might not actually be able to vote, or sit, in a Quebec Assembly under then-existing British laws, which indeed still withheld political rights from Catholics within the Protestant-controlled United Kingdom of Great Britain.

The heated debate grew, and Murray was recalled to London in 1766. In his stead Sir Guy Carleton was sent out; another army officer who had served under Wolfe and had been wounded in the Battle of the Plains of Abraham. Carleton was at first regarded as an ally, if not advocate, of the Quebec English-speaking merchant party. Once settled in the province, however, and facing its critical problems, he soon came around to a very different position. Like Murray, this aristocratic soldier grew to distrust the demands of unruly urban merchants, yet to approve the disciplined-looking seigneurial society of the Quebec countryside. And Carleton also came to appreciate the political value of the Catholic Church led by capable Bishop Briand, which was backed by a dutiful French-Canadian populace — not at all like the increasingly restive citizens of the Thirteen Colonies in British America.

In those provinces, tensions and troubles had been mounting at least since Britain's parliament had passed the Stamp Act of 1765, imposed on legal and other documents in order to raise revenue to meet the common costs of defending

The "Mitred Minuet," 1774. *A British cartoon on the Quebec Act proposed by Carleton. It shows a stately set of bishops wearing their mitres being put through a dance (around the "Quebec Bill") by three top British politicians of the day: Lord Bute, a Scot and former prime minister, playing the bagpipes, Lord North, the current prime minister, and Lord Mansfield, the Chief Justice. Over these three, as well, there hovers a decidedly devilish figure!*

the empire in America. Yet colonists would condemn this step as "taxation without representation," since it had not been levied by their own elected assemblies; and they opposed other imperial revenue measures also. Actually, with the threat of French empire removed, the old colonies no longer felt so dependent on the shield of British power. They became more confidently aware of their own American identity — a new, national identity. Hence over the next decade, issues of imperial taxation, of the Proclamation Line that had officially kept American colonial settlement from expanding west, and other lesser but inflaming clashes that at times developed through sheer official stupidity, all moved the Thirteen Colonies on towards outright revolt. And it was in this ominous setting that Governor Guy Carleton reconsidered the whole question of Quebec within America.

He saw little use in fitting this French-peopled province in with the troubled Anglo-American colonies. It was not, and would not be, a province like the rest. In Carleton's view, "Barring a catastrophe too shocking to think of, this country will remain French till the end of time." And yet, a satisfied French Canada, given the special treatment that it needed, could still become a secure and reliable British imperial base. If Quebec were enabled to maintain the French heritage it held so dear, then it might again be made a bastion of armed strength in North America — but this time on the British side. Out of these considerations came a new policy for the French-Canadian province, which Carleton put forward to the government in Britain when he returned there in 1770 for an extended visit. That policy would be embodied in the vitally important Quebec Act, at length passed by parliament in London in 1774.

This Act effectively dropped the Proclamation plan of assimilation and the promise of an elected assembly for Quebec — even though in 1769 a high judicial decision in London had ruled that British laws denying political rights to Roman Catholics at home need not apply in America. But on the whole, French Canadians had little interest at that time in representative assemblies, which they had scarcely known except for limited, special purposes. And what they otherwise obtained by the Quebec Act would seem much more important to them. To begin with, while the province under that Act was to remain without an elected house and be ruled by a Governor and appointed Council, a new oath would enable French Catholic inhabitants to serve in the Council, or in other

Quebec City in the Era of the American Revolution. *Here a water colour by James Peachey looks from the south bank of the St. Lawrence across to Cape Diamond, topped by the massive stone Citadel, with the Governor's residence, the Chateau St. Louis, to the right of it, and the city itself on the slopes beyond down to the river's edge.*

official posts. Next, although the Act provided for English criminal law, it did maintain French civil law; and with it, the entrenched seigneurial system. Further than that, Roman Catholicism in Quebec now had its own system of tithes constitutionally confirmed. That is, the compulsory dues paid by inhabitants to support the Catholic Church, first authorized by governments in the days of New France, would once again be officially enforced. Such a step in legal taxes did not quite mean a state-established Catholic church, since only the members of that faith would be involved. Nonetheless, it did mean a remarkable commitment by the British state to sustain the Catholic majority's religion. Quebec was plainly not to be a province like the others; but would receive a very distinctive treatment within the British empire.

Finally, the Quebec Act greatly expanded the limits of that province, taking in all Labrador on the east, and in the west extending to the junction of the Ohio and the Mississippi, thence northward to Ruperts Land. Thereby much of future Ontario was added to Quebec, plus all the Ohio country south of the Great Lakes and some further western lands on north to Lake Superior. Such a huge extension had one evident purpose: to bring fur-trading areas already mainly dominated by St. Lawrence commerce within the territorial sway of Quebec Province. At that time, moreover, the southwest fur trade below the Lakes that flowed out to Montreal was much more developed still than the rising trade in the far northwest. Furthermore, this whole great sweep of British imperial territory could be more securely dealt with from a renewed Quebec base: for it covered inland country where old French-Indian ties still mattered; where the fur trade would not endanger existing Indian land rights, but where unyielding American colonial desires to settle on native lands would let loose new frontier bloodshed.

Thus British designers of the Quebec Act might view it. Inevitably, however, that measure brought fierce responses in the already roused Thirteen Colonies. In fact, in American eyes the Act of 1774 became one in a series of "Intolerable Acts" that led to open, armed rebellion against Britain. The American colonials saw the West they had fought over, then been kept from occupying, now brazenly transferred to the keeping of Quebec — to a re-established French and Catholic province sitting north of them, and still under "despotic" rule. This was no doubt a partial and self-interested view; but it was widely shared by Americans, who in their own tradition looked on the continent as naturally destined for them. In any case, events now surged to open war in 1775, between "tory" supporters of imperial authority and rebel "patriots": one year before the would-be United States of America issued a resounding Declaration of Independence. Canadian and American history have frequently been intertwined in a joint heritage — but seldom with more telling effect than in the days of the Quebec Act and the onset of the American Revolution.

British Squadron on Lake Champlain. *The lake lay on a major invasion route from the south into Canada, used in French-Indian wars, in British or American Colonial attacks from Frontenac's time forward, and in 1775-6 by American Revolutionary forces then thrusting against British-ruled Quebec.*

1. General Richard Montgomery. *Born in Ireland, he had become an officer in the British regular army, and had served at Louisbourg and at the French surrender of Montreal. But in 1771 he emigrated to New York, married into a prominent pro-Revolution family, and soon joined the American side. Appointed a brigadier general by commander-in-chief George Washington, Montgomery successfully led the American expedition against Montreal in 1775, but died in the subsequent attack on Quebec City.*

1

2

2. General Benedict Arnold. *Connecticut-born Arnold had also served during the Seven Years War, in the American colonial militia while still a boy. In 1775, he was one of the first militia officers to enlist in the rebel forces, and was joint commander at the seizure of Fort Ticonderoga from the British. Leading troops overland to join with Montgomery in attacking Quebec, Arnold was in full command after the former's death; but failed to take the city. In 1779 he switched to the British side, and for a time lived in Fredericton, New Brunswick. It is ironic that while Montgomery was a traitor to the British, Arnold to the Americans — in United States tradition Montgomery remains a patriot-hero, and "Benedict Arnold" is a veritable term for treachery. That, too, can be heritage.*

The Dividing of Empire

In the autumn of 1775 two American patriot armies marched north to wrest Canada from British "tyranny." One under General Richard Montgomery took the well-travelled Lake Champlain and Richelieu route towards Montreal. The other, led by General Benedict Arnold, struggled overland through dense wilderness to strike directly at Quebec City. Montreal fell quickly; in fact, Governor Carleton evacuated it to move to the stouter defences of Quebec. It was also true, however, that Montreal, centre of influential English-speaking merchants, held numbers of them who were bitterly resentful of the Quebec Act — the French laws and Catholic tithes it had authorized, the assembly it did not grant — while American patriot agents there had been working for months among the disaffected elements in the revolutionary cause of Liberty. At Quebec, Guy Carleton might hope to make a firmer stand until a relieving fleet and army could arrive from Britain in the spring. Yet as winter approached, and both the armies of Arnold and Montgomery gathered around the capital city, the British governor could only face the failed expectations of the Quebec Act he had so confidently pursued.

Far from serving as a restraint on the American colonists, the Act had stirred them to attack. Far from enlisting an army of grateful French Canadians to help keep rebellious colonies in check, it had not drawn the active support of the *habitants*, even if it had won their seigneurs and leading clergy. Carleton, a European aristocrat, had overestimated the deference and obedience of the *Canadiens*, a North American people. The seigneurs might unsheathe their swords and cry "forward"; the priests proclaim the moral calls of loyalty and honour. But the ordinary farmers did not want to go. After long cycles of war, they preferred to sit this one out, to watch as neutrals the engaging spectacle of old foes, British and American, shooting at each other. Furthermore, though still firmly Catholic, the *Canadiens* were by no means overjoyed by tithes being made legal once more; and while they might respect their seigneurs in rural society, did not look to them as military leaders, but rather to their own captains of militia. And so the Quebec Act did not bring the willing popular response that Carleton and London officials had blithely anticipated. Indeed, some French Canadians listened instead to the radical and democratic ideas then being freely spread by American agents.

Over all, Carleton's limited forces in Quebec would include only a small number of *Canadien* militia, about as numerous (or few) as those who actually joined the American side. But his trained British regulars, the stone ramparts of Quebec City, and the besiegers' own serious shortcomings, counted for considerably more. The ill-equipped Americans had scant cannon and inadequate supplies. They suffered badly from disease, as well, during the prolonged siege; and their major attack, in a blizzard on New Year's Eve, brought a blast of fire down on the assailants and the death of General Montgomery. The siege dragged on futilely till spring, when British naval power sent a strong fleet up the St. Lawrence, so that the dwindling, enfeebled Americans had to give up and retreat. The heart of Canada was saved from any further assaults from the United States, because of this enduring fact of British power by sea. Yet it also became evident that, in the wartime alliance reached in 1778 between France and the young American republic, neither partner really wanted to see the other established at

Proclamation by Carleton at Quebec, 1775. *Issued by the Governor as his capital came under American siege, it deals with the problem of disaffection among militia enroled there to help defend Quebec City, and the enemy agents trying to encourage such disaffection. The "useless, disloyal and treacherous" are thus given four days to leave with their families. Not a harshly unreasonable order, in the circumstances, and it probably helped keep Quebec secure.*

22 Nov. 1775

By His Excellency Guy Carleton —

Captain General and Governor in Chief in and over the Province of Quebec, and the Territories depending thereon in America, Vice Admiral of the same and Major General of His Majesty's Forces, commanding the Northern District &c.ª &c.ª &c.ª

A Proclamation

WHEREAS it has been found expedient to raise and — embody a Militia within this City, to co-operate with, and to assist His Majesty's Troops in this Garrison in the Preservation of the City and of the Persons and Property of His Majesty's good — and faithful Subjects resident therein, against certain rebellious — Persons who have invaded this Province, a number of whom have lately appeared in Arms before the Walls of this Town And whereas Information has been given me that some persons resident here have contumaciously refused to enroll their Names in the Militia Lists, and to take up Arms in Conjunction with their Fellow Citizens for the Purpose aforesaid; And that others who had enrolled their Names and had for some Time carried Arms in the Defence and Preservation of the City, have lately laid them down; And also that some Persons are busy in endeavouring to draw away and alienate the Affections of His Majesty's good and faithful Subjects of this City from His — Majesty's Person and Government For these Reasons, and in Order to — rid the Town of all useless, disloyal, and treacherous Persons I have thought fit to issue this Proclamation And I do hereby strictly — order and enjoin all and every person and persons whatsoever liable to serve in the Militia and residing at Quebec who have refused or — declined to enroll their Names in the Militia Lists, and to take up Arms in Conjunction with his Majesty's good Subjects of this City, and — who still refuse or decline so to do; as well as those, who having once taken up Arms, have afterwards laid them down, and will not take them up again, to quit the Town in four Days from the — Date hereof, together with their Wives and Children; And to withdraw themselves out of the Limits of the District of Quebec before the first

Day

Quebec, preferring to have it left to Britain rather than that either of the two new "friends" should hold it.

All the same, as the American Revolutionary War proceeded, British troops (and money) poured in to mount offensives southward from Quebec — now assuredly a powerful military base. Fighting also spread southwest below the Great Lakes, to meet American thrusts into the inland country. In the process, some attitudes in the province of Quebec significantly changed. The leading Montreal merchants thrived on the furs they sent to British markets (from which their American rivals at Albany were now excluded); and their trade was guarded by the British Navy on the Atlantic, by British military power in the interior. These Montreal businessmen accordingly came to see that their own economic stake in the imperial system far outweighed any political discontent over the Quebec Act — and that the Act, after all, had re-attached the valuable southwest fur domains to Canada. And so the merchants' sense of commitment increased with the flow of their trade on into the 1780s; as they recognized that the St. Lawrence commercial realm was tied both to Britain and to Canada's own growth westward. Factors of geography and business interest, in effect, were shaping the prime leaders of Montreal into British imperialists and Canadian economic nationalists combined.

As for the mass of French Canadians in the province, they began to follow the Quebec seigneurial and clerical elites into their own commitment to the British side. Naturally the *Canadiens* still put their distinct community concerns and heritage first; yet they also concluded that the Americans should not be welcomed, but be kept outside. The self-proclaimed republican "liberators" had really turned out to be the same old enemies, *les Bastonnais*, the Puritans of New England; stabling horses in Catholic churches during their invasion, paying in worthless paper money for crops and supplies seized from *habitant* farms. The

1. Death of Montgomery in Attack on Quebec, December 31, 1775. *This surprise assault on the city's Lower Town, cloaked by night and a heavy snowstorm, failed to surprise — and Montgomery himself was killed. Carleton ordered a "genteel coffin," for a former friend and comrade.*
2. After the War: Quebec and its Ramparts. *A few burned-out houses stand in the foreground, but the city generally appears well recovered.*
3. Lunenburg, Nova Scotia, from the Harbour. *A successful farm and fishing centre on the Atlantic coast south of Halifax, it was initially settled by German Protestants brought out by the British government in 1753, it thrived both by supplying food to Halifax and sending fish exports overseas. It also flourished on trading with Britain's West Indies colonies. Yet Lunenburg citizens still feared that they might be "scorched to death" by the fires of the neighbouring American Revolution, and complained accordingly to Halifax.*

1

2

3

Canadiens did not learn to love their British conquerors as a result — why should they? — but did grow to believe that they were better off with them. For the provisions of the Quebec Act had guaranteed French Canada's own special rights and character under British rule, guarantees which the Americans certainly would not have given. Instead angry American outcries had greeted the Act because of the very grants it had made to the "French Papists." Thus for different, but historically sound, reasons neither the Francophone and Anglophone communities of Quebec province took to the American path of the Revolution. They stayed within the remaining British empire — above all, to avoid being swallowed up in another great emerging empire, that of the United States.

A similar set of developments (from disaffection or neutrality to commitment) took place in the adjoining province of Nova Scotia. At the outset of the Revolution, this province had seemed so much a northern extension of New England that many of its inhabitants as well as their Yankee neighbours down the seaboard had assumed that Nova Scotia, too, would come to join the new republic. It looked almost inevitable. Apart from the British naval and garrison base at Halifax, the German-speaking colonists of the nearby Lunenburg area, or some other scattered pockets of Highlanders, Ulstermen and Yorkshiremen, more than half the population were still New England settlers; and they particularly dominated the Bay of Fundy and south-shore stretches, with easy access by sea from the Maine or Massachusetts coasts. Furthermore, these New England Yankees of Nova Scotia were not at all ready to defend their new homeland against American attack. While they had few real quarrels with the British provincial regime, they had no wish, either, to fight their New England kin — as indeed they said in representations to Halifax urging their own neutrality; ironically, much like the Acadians whose lands they had taken over. But then matters rose to a head, with an actual American attempt to seize the province.

In August, 1776, a fairly small and poorly organized offensive was launched from the Maine coast, led by Jonathan Eddy, a fugitive Yankee member of the Nova Scotian assembly. His "army" readily took little Maugerville, a hamlet up the Saint John River, then in November came down to Fort Cumberland on the Chignecto Isthmus to force its surrender. But Yorkshire settlers in the district stood out against the attempt, and messages sent to Halifax brought British reinforcements that quickly ended the venture, with two Indians and one American killed. It was no great invasion. Still it indicated that power based on Halifax could maintain this province: a point that was endorsed by General

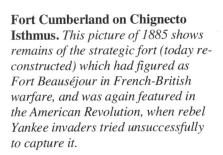

Fort Cumberland on Chignecto Isthmus. *This picture of 1885 shows remains of the strategic fort (today reconstructed) which had figured as Fort Beauséjour in French-British warfare, and was again featured in the American Revolution, when rebel Yankee invaders tried unsuccessfully to capture it.*

1

2

3

1. Yarmouth, at the Entry to the Bay of Fundy. *A busy shipping community on the southwest coast of Nova Scotia, it frankly sought neutrality at first, declaring "we were almost all born in New England." Later American threats of raids did much to change its mind, however.*
2. Farming near Fort Needham outside Halifax.
3. Surrender of Lord Cornwallis at Yorktown, 1781. *This yielding of Britain's main army in Virginia — cut off and surrounded — really spelled the end of the Revolutionary War; although minor combats continued briefly, and the conclusive peace treaty still had to be negotiated. But in real ways, another age of empire in America ended when Cornwallis gave up an increasingly hopeless struggle.*

George Washington, once a major of Virginia militia, now commander-in-chief of the American army, who declared that in the face of British naval strength, no expedition to take Nova Scotia could be effective.

Force or facts of power may obviously shape history; not just desires, plans or firm-held interests. Nevertheless, engagements to the British side also spread in Nova Scotia, to keep it out of the new United States by more than force alone. After the evident failure of invasion by 1777, when a strong Fort Howe was built by the British at the mouth of the Saint John to help guard the Bay of Fundy, the Yankee elements in Nova Scotia grew less inclined to look for a New England takeover, or to contemplate neutrality along the way. Moreover, their own shores and outposts came under attack from New England privateers seeking plunder; and that did bring Nova Scotian Yankees to accept militia service in defence of their homes. Further also, the New Light religious movement arose among them, inspired by Henry Alline, a powerfully evangelical preacher of Rhode Island origin. The "Great Awakening" he brought swept New England-settled districts of the province from 1776 into the eighties. And it drew popular attention away from the earthly American republic towards a new heavenly City of God (not Boston) to be erected in Nova Scotia. In sum, religious fervour replaced political concern for much of the local population, leaving the one-time Yankee province both more aware of its own separate identity and more committed to its British connection — which would not be seriously challenged again throughout the Revolution.

There was still more to commitment: pre-eminently, economic aspects. The town of Halifax, commercial core of Nova Scotia, had been built up by New England enterprise as well as by British military and government activity. Yet its chief merchants, though often originally linked to Boston, depended on their imperial ties in contracting to the armed forces, in shipping to Britain or trading to the sugar islands of the British West Indies. There is no call to suggest hypocrisy here. These town merchants out of New England had arrived when Boston, too, was profiting from the British imperial trading system, and well before revolutionary nationalist views had gained control there. The Halifax commercial elite was virtually a surviving part of the pre-revolutionary empire; and while its members might sympathize with the grievances of former New England compatriots and relatives, they felt small cause to join them in open rebellion. At any rate, an influential Halifax business community cast its lot with the remaining (and still far-reaching) British world-empire. Much the same was

Cumberland House on the Saskatchewan. *Established in 1774, in the Hudson's Bay Company's effort to move inland and meet the mounting competition of Canadian traders from the St. Lawrence.*

true for lesser ports around Nova Scotia engaged in sending dried fish and lumber to the tariff-protected markets of British West Indies — from which far larger New England competitors had removed themselves by act of war. And so Nova Scotia stayed, quite prosperously, on the British side of the dividing empire in America.

The little neighbouring Atlantic province, the Island of St. John, was hardly likely to affect the course of empires. It certainly continued in British keeping — although an American privateer raid on Charlottetown in 1775 carried the acting governor and two officials off to General Washington, who did not want them, and sent them home. The big island of Newfoundland also suffered, more harshly, from American privateering ravages. But here British garrisons and naval squadrons still blocked any real threat to imperial control. And over all, the war years brought the island flourishing times in the essential cod fishery; particularly for its resident boatmen, since many of the visiting overseas fishermen had again been drafted into the Royal Navy. At any rate, Newfoundland, too, stayed surely within Britain's American empire.

At the other, western end of empire, war spread through the inland forests below the Great Lakes, from the Iroquois country to the Ohio and Michigan wilderness. In the upper reaches of New York province, patriot rebel forces contended fiercely against units raised from loyal-minded settlers in the area. But further, the Six Nations Iroquois and their traditional homelands were heavily involved. The Tuscaroras and Oneidas largely sided with the Americans. The rest of the Six Nations, and especially the Mohawks, supported the British; for here old bonds of alliance held strong. They had been well forged under Sir William Johnson as Indian Superintendent till his death in 1774, to be maintained thereafter by his son and heir, Sir John Johnson, later to become Superintendent himself.

Sir John also raised the Royal Regiment of New York from loyal settlers, and fought in many a frontier attack. No less important were Molly Brant, Sir William's consort, an intelligent, forceful and highly regarded Iroquois matron, and her brother, Isaac Brant, powerful war chief of the Mohawks — a skilled statesman in his own right. Bloody raids and battles raged back and forth along the northern New York frontier, between Niagara, the main British western anchor, and Carleton Island, the imperial base on the upper St. Lawrence not far from old Fort Frontenac. The end of fighting in 1782, at all events, found the British and their Indian allies left in possession of a whole belt of land south of Lake Ontario, and on down into the Ohio country. Westward around to Fort Detroit, or on further to Lake Michigan, the same was largely true. Despite temporary reverses, the loyal forces, their Indian allies and fur traders who included *Canadiens*, had kept most of this broad southwestern territory below the Lakes under British rule and Quebec-controlled commerce.

The northwestern lands, above and well beyond the Great Lakes, had still stayed remote from war. Yet in this quarter, the new St. Lawrence-based fur empire that was in the making would far outrange older southwestern fur domains. In fact, its steady expansion to north and west at last brought the Hudson's Bay Company to react against the ever-aggressive pedlars from Canada, who were penetrating deeply beyond the Company's forts along the Bay shores. In 1774 the H.B.C. thus founded Cumberland House on the Saskatchewan, its first inland post, and put it under the capable Samuel Hearne,

Samuel Hearne, Northern Venturer for the H.B.C. *As part of that Company's new push beyond the Bay, Hearne had reached the Arctic coast overland, and he was given charge of Cumberland House thereafter.*

who had already made his name exploring north across the Barren Lands in 1769-72, to reach the Arctic Ocean via the Coppermine River. Still, Hearne's northward journey for the Bay Company had not unlocked fresh fur supplies. It was instead the Montreal trader, Peter Pond, who in 1778-89 opened up a wide new region rich in beaver, by crossing north from the Saskatchewan over the Methy Portage to Arctic-flowing waters, and planting the first post in the wooded Athabasca country. The gains in prospect, and the inevitably high costs of transport, led top Montreal merchants to pool their resources in a joint venture to exploit the Athabascan fur wealth. Set up temporarily in 1779-80, this marked an effective beginning of the great North West Company, and brought Simon McTavish, Peter Pond and the Frobishers together as prominent partners. That company took more lasting form in 1783-84, with McTavish and Frobisher as leaders of an enterprise which in the next ten years would take Nor-Westers to the Arctic and Pacific. Here was another huge emerging empire of the West, essentially Canadian, which well might make the continental divisions wrought by the American Revolution look less ruinous and shattering.

And yet the divisions in America were critical. Out of them came both the United States and modern Canada. Leaving a still unformed West aside for the present, it was to prove tremendously important in history that the northern British holdings, from Newfoundland to mid-continent, did not join the American Revolution but remained apart. This was not just chance, though chance was there. Power, pressures, interests and designs all had their varied parts in laying commitments that built a separate country outside the American republic. But other commitments, of emotion and belief, were largely still to come. They were assuredly developing by the time that peace returned to North America in 1783: thanks to the Loyalist movement, which brought many deeply confirmed supports of the British cause out of the young United States to add their own strong convictions to Canada's future heritage.

Crossing the Methy Portage to Athabaska Country. *This crucial fur route, which was initially opened by the traders from Canada, is here seen being used by H.B.C. rivals, with their characteristic "York boats" (not canoes) initially developed for use on rivers around Hudson Bay. "York" here comes from York Factory, major H.B.C. base on the Bay.*

The Loyalists and their Heritage

Major fighting in America ended with the surrender of the principal British army at Yorktown, Virginia, in the fall of 1781; although it still took two years more to settle the peace treaty. But Britain was badly worn by a war it could not win, against a resourceful and resolute new nation in America, one backed as well by France, Spain and other European powers eager to see a dominant world-empire cut down to size. The final treaty itself, which was signed in Paris in September, 1783, above all recognized the independence of the United States, and drew the boundary that would separate this republic from the British territories remaining on its north. That line began in the east where the St. Croix River flowed into the Bay of Fundy, ran inland between what would be New Brunswick and Maine to the heights of the Appalachians, then stretched westward along the existing border of Quebec to reach the upper St. Lawrence. From here, a wholly new boundary proceeded up this river to the Great Lakes, and on through the middle of these lakes and their connecting streams to the far end of Lake Superior. Finally, the line continued via Rainy Lake and Lake of the Woods due west to meet the upper Mississippi, which was then the accepted inland limit of the United States. This division of the continent would later be extended across the prairies and through the mountains to the Pacific. Yet the Treaty of 1783 first laid down one of the world's longest international borders.

Questions would rise from this boundary settlement, especially since, at war's end, the former western areas of Quebec south of the Great Lakes were still mainly held by British garrisons, St. Lawrence fur traders and resident Indian peoples. More immediately pressing, however, was the question of the American Loyalists, that sizeable pro-British element, perhaps a majority in the Thirteen Colonies when open war began, who had stood by established law and imperial unity against revolutionary upheaval — many of them to fight and die in that cause. Other Loyalist adherents had suffered persecution: had been attacked by mobs, tarred, feathered and ridden out of town on rails; been flung into jail, seen their homes burned, their property confiscated. Consequently, when the peace treaty was being negotiated, Britain recognized its own clear obligation to the Loyalists, and sought at least to provide some protection and restitution for them in the peace terms. To victorious Americans, however, these people were simply traitors who might be best advised to die. Still, the treaty did agree that the American Congress would "earnestly recommend" to the state legislatures of the republic that the rights and estates of Loyalists should be restored, or that they could seek legal compensation for their losses. The federal Congress, however, then had very limited powers, while state politicians felt even less concern.

Mary, or Molly, Brant. *Her own Mohawk name meant "someone lends her a flower." She was really of greater standing among the Six Nations Iroquois, allied with the British, than was her younger brother, Joseph, the war chief: because of her influential place at the head of the Mohawk matrons, her own keen abilities, and her bonds with Sir William Johnson, venerated friend of the Iroquois. Molly Brant was invaluably loyal to the British cause in the Revolutionary War across the interior, and afterwards moved to Cataraqui (Kingston) in her final years.*

1. A Final Boatload of British Troops Leaves New York, 1783. *An artist's reconstruction, it suggests the feelings of the soldiers, British regulars or Loyalist colonials, as they withdrew.*
2. British Ships Ready to Sail from New York Harbour. *One in a series of organized passages (by warships and convoys) which took Loyalists from this last British-held port in the new United States and up the Atlantic to Nova Scotia.*

1

2

Hence Loyalist claims went unhonoured in the United States, while mob abuse and property seizures did not end at all. In such circumstances, more and more Loyalists decided that their only course was to leave a land that had once been theirs no less than the revolutionaries, to find security and justice northward under the British Crown.

Actually, this Loyalist outflow was under way well before the peace negotiations arrived at final terms. In fact, one could trace its beginnings far back into the war years. Even in 1776, when the British forces withdrew from Boston, Loyalist families had sailed with them to Nova Scotia, where they went into camps at Halifax; though later most moved elsewhere, especially to Britain. More significantly, among some fifty Loyalist military units in the Revolutionary War, a number of them fought in the country below Quebec's border, and so ended up based in that colony, to which these soldiers' families were gathered as well. Lesser Loyalist forces operated out of Niagara; their frontier families also made arduous journeys to the protection of that fort. Thus migration paths were already there, as the war wound down.

Those Loyalists who now took a seaboard path to safety up to Nova Scotia, moved in organized fleets of ships out of New York city, which was held to the end by British forces under Sir Guy Carleton as a collecting-point for loyal refugees. In April, 1783, the "spring fleet" carried some 7,000 Loyalists north: men, women and children largely from New York (a notably Loyalist colony), but also from New Jersey, Pennsylvania and New England. About half of them

The Coming of the Loyalists. *A rather idealized old picture of Loyalists landing on a rocky Nova Scotian coast, in all aristocratic finery and courtly manner. Without doubt, they did include some of the former colonies' upper-class society; but the one-time myth that they chiefly consisted of the blueblood element of colonial America has long since been discarded.*

went to Shelburne, close to the southeastern tip of Nova Scotia, where a whole new Loyalist town took form. The rest were landed near Fort Howe at the mouth of the Saint John River on the Bay of Fundy. Here the tent encampments of Parr Town and Carleton arose; and within two years they became Canada's first incorporated city, Saint John. Summer and autumn fleets brought many more arrivals, including Marylanders, Carolinians or other Southerners. In all, some 30,000 Loyalists migrated to Nova Scotia, well outweighing its existing population of about 20,000; and Loyalists also settled on Cape Breton Island and St. John's Island.

Their hopeful town at Shelburne soon began to fade, however, when the land around it turned out to be poor. But they made more successful settlements elsewhere around Nova Scotia. Most successful, indeed, was the Loyalist settlement on the Saint John River. As their pioneer farmsteads spread up that river's broadly fertile valley, and new port centres appeared on adjoining Fundy shores, the colonists of the area sought a province of their own, with its own capital instead of distant Halifax. Accordingly, in 1784, the Province of New Brunswick was set off from Nova Scotia, and its seat of government and legislature was placed at Fredericton, well up the developing Saint John Valley. Thomas Carleton, younger brother of Sir Guy Carleton, was appointed first Governor, a task he would handle till 1803. Cape Breton Island was similarly made a separate province in 1784 because of Loyalist settlement — Sydney being named its capital — although it would be re-attached to Nova Scotia in 1820.

1. Loyalists on the move near Halifax.
2. Saint John, New Brunswick. *It grew with Loyalist settlement around the entry to the Saint John River from 1784, though this picture dates from several decades later. Still it shows the enlarging port and city — the first city to be incorporated in Canada (1785). And Saint John's rise thanks to the Loyalist influx, plus that of farms up-river or along the Fundy shores, had a lot to do with a separate Province of New Brunswick being set up as early as 1784.*

1

2

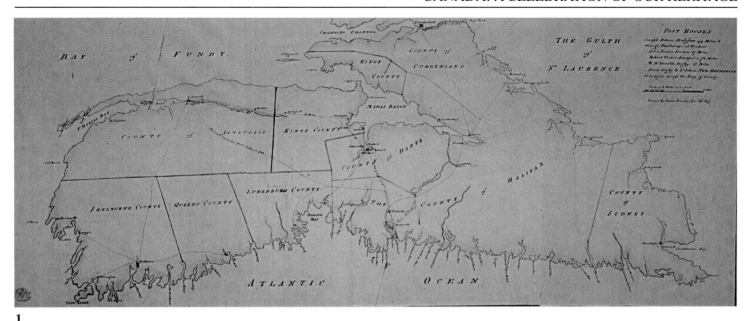

1

2

3

1. Mainland Nova Scotia, 1780s. *In Shelburne County, at the southeast of the province, can be seen the new settlement of Shelburne.*
2. The Loyalist Town of Shelburne, Nova Scotia. *Depicted in a watercolour of 1789, while its settlement was still considerable.*
3. Black Woodcutter at Shelburne, 1788. *Among some 16,000 Loyalists who built this community were about 2,000 Blacks from the old Thirteen Colonies: a group who would form a basic part of Nova Scotia's mounting population.*

1. Thomas Carleton, First Governor of New Brunswick. *Brother of Guy Carleton, he also served in the Seven Years War — and later with the Russians against the Turks. Thomas became quartermaster-general under Sir Guy at Quebec in 1776; then in 1784 was appointed by London to govern New Brunswick. He returned to England in 1803, nearing seventy, after maintaining a regime sympathetic to the Loyalists, but scarcely inspired.*

2. General Sir Frederick Haldimand. *A Swiss-born professional soldier, he had risen in the British army during the Seven Years War; and following peacetime commands in America, was appointed to take over from Sir Guy Carleton as Governor of Quebec in 1778. His work in settling American Loyalists on Canadian lands after the Revolution was widely effective; until he went back to Britain, and was replaced in 1786 by Guy Carleton, now become Lord Dorchester.*

The other main Loyalist migration, overland to Quebec Province, took very different paths, often mere wilderness trails. It moved more by small groups of families and individuals, and came more from inland, backwoods districts of the old colonies, not long-occupied seaboard areas. Large-scale organized movement was not wholly lacking here; however, as was seen in the settling of Loyalist regiments and their families along the upper St. Lawrence, by order of General Frederick Haldimand, Sir Guy Carleton's successor as governor of Quebec. In the spring of 1784, these Loyalists were drawn from their base camps at Sorel below Montreal and set up-river in flotillas of boats under the command of Sir John Johnson, a leading Loyalist himself. Around 4,000 people were thus effectively placed on land grants past Longueil, the westernmost French-occupied seigneury on the St. Lawrence, up to the Bay of Quinte on eastern Lake Ontario. The grants here began with Catholic Scots Highlanders, put nearest to established Catholic French farms, with Scots Presbyterians located next, followed by German Calvinists and Lutherans, then British Anglicans westward in that order. They all were settled by regimental units — as was done with other Loyalist troops on the Saint John in New Brunswick — and undoubtedly, the tested comradeships of war strengthened the new communities. Yet undoubtedly as well, the location patterns made plain the varied religious and ethnic backgrounds of these same Loyalists.

Where the upper St. Lawrence met Lake Ontario, the town of Kingston rose at the site of old Fort Frontenac; both because of the inflow of Loyalists to the area and because the British military base was moved here from Carleton Island, now right on the American boundary. Moreover, groups of settlers organized in militia companies came to Kingston with their families, by sea direct from New York, notably headed by Captain Michael Grass, a Loyalist of German origin who knew the area from having been held a prisoner at Fort Frontenac back in French-war days. Kingston went on growing with the spread of Loyalist farms about it, and the resulting rise of trade. In fact, it came to be the first commercial

1

2

1. Loyalists come to Inland Canada, 1784. *A stamp of 1934, commemorating the 150th anniversary of their arrival in future Ontario: as taken from a sculptured group that stands today in downtown Hamilton — in a province which first took form as Upper Canada, set up in 1791 thanks to the Loyalist inflow.*
2. Loyalist Encampment on the Upper St. Lawrence, 1784. *These ex-soldiers and their families would lay the real basis of settlement in Eastern Ontario-to-be.*
3. The New Town of Kingston, a Loyalist Creation. *The sketch by Elizabeth Simcoe, wife of the first governor of Upper Canada, was done a few years later, in 1793, but shows the town which thus developed at the foot of Lake Ontario.*

1

2

3

1. Joseph Brant, Leader of Six Nations Settlement on the Grand. *When war ended, this major Mohawk chieftain and British ally came with fellow Mohawks and other Iroquois to occupy the large Grand River Reserve, granted to them by the imperial authorities. An able diplomat as well as a cultivated leader, Brant played an important role in early Upper Canada before his death in 1807; and Brant's Ford on the Grand grew into the thriving town of Brantford.*

2. Sir John Johnson.

3. A Newly Cleared Farm by Riverside, 1791. *A typical scene of Loyalist labours in the forests of an opening Upper Canada, it shows stumps left to rot for later removal, and rough rail fences enclosing fields. The buildings do look too far advanced beyond the first log cabin stage; but this contemporary, awkward picture also seems typical in trying to show both what was, and what would come to be.*

4. Essential Domestic Work on an Emerging Loyalist Farm. *Here in an early Ontario settlement, the women of a Loyalist family are carding wool (from their farm's sheep), spinning thread and weaving cloth for garments, while one of the family's men brings in wood, to keep the square-log cabin warm. Tea is also being served, one of the staples even on this distant frontier.*

5. A Winter Road in Upper Canada.

town in future Ontario. Further west, Loyalists also journeyed to Fort Niagara at the far end of Lake Ontario, and were granted farmlands across the Niagara River on what would be the "Canadian" shore; even while still other migrants arrived at British-held Detroit and settled in that fort's vicinity. In addition, over 2,000 Six Nation Iroquois left their ancestral lands in New York Province, now lost to hostile Americans, and took up large reserves granted by their British allies on the Grand River that flowed to Lake Erie — where Joseph Brant led their way to future homes around Brant's Ford. Altogether, some 8,000 or so Loyalist exiles and allied Indians had settled in the western areas of Quebec by 1786, when Guy Carleton, now with the title of Lord Dorchester, returned as the province's Governor.

By this time, the Loyalists' movement to the Maritime Provinces was really over — and only a few had entered Newfoundland — although flows into Quebec went on at a lower rate. Some Loyalists had stayed and settled near Sorel in that province. Others had gone to its eastern fishing shores in the Gaspé Peninsula. But any continued influx went mostly to the western woodlands of Quebec, to the free grants of fertile wild land awarded there to Loyalists by the British authorities. Here, a pioneer farming society rapidly took form on extensive tracts transferred by treaty from the Indian peoples of the region. And over all — whether in Quebec or the Maritimes — the Loyalist communities expressed an earnest will to survive outside the United States, away from republican oppressions and the democratic tyranny of mobs, which they had had good cause to remember.

By and large, these Loyalists were not just hidebound reactionaries, entrenched officials or privileged plutocrats. They were, indeed, mainly conservatives by temperament, people who had rejected the violence of revolutionary change. Moreover, the great majority of them were ordinary farmers or town workers in background; and if some Loyalists had been prominent and well-to-do, or were Harvard College graduates, all in all, they represented a fairly typical cross-section of American colonial society, upper classes through lower. As such, they also comprised varied numbers of Blacks, ex-slaves and slaves, native Indians, and many recent immigrants who had come from Europe to find homes and opportunity in America. In this regard, Loyalism included Gaelic-speaking Catholic Highlanders, and Catholic or Protestant Irish, along with Swiss, French or German Protestants of different churches and sects, who themselves had had to acquire English and had sometimes faced discrimination from the Anglo-American majority in the Thirteen Colonies. Consequently, many immigrant minorities had looked to established British law and institutions which meant security, and they feared revolutionary upheaval with all the mob attacks that could bring. And at the same time, Loyalism also

A Condensed Version of Settlement Growth in Early Upper Canada, I.
Here is a bush farm near where Chatham would appear amid south-western Ontario woodlands around 1795.

drew widely on old Americans, settled since early Virginia or New England, who did not want to overturn the ordered liberties of the British Constitution under Crown and parliament just to suit the demands of radical fanatics and self-seeking demagogues — or so they saw it.

At root, it was political opinions and feelings of this sort which bound the diversity of the Loyalists in a common cause. Many of them had indeed shared colonial grievances and looked earnestly for practical reforms and remedies: but not at the price of tearing down a time-tested governing system for some sudden experiment. Such Loyalists essentially sought to conserve law and order against destruction by illegal force. Right or wrong, they fought and suffered for these views in the Revolution; not through blind devotion to King George III, but in the cause of constitutional change by peaceful evolution, under law. These things would matter in Canadian experience. For the Loyalists brought with them the heartfelt denial of republican excesses and sharp suspicions of mass rule — of an unbridled American "democracy," which to them had mainly meant illegal abuse, rabble-rousing and lynch law. Whether right or wrong, again, they gave new content and purpose to a separate Canadian existence. In effect, Loyalists put decided strength in the idea that there could be another way in North America beside that of the United States.

Furthermore, their settlements in the Quebec interior led to the Province of Upper Canada, the forerunner of the modern Province of Ontario. Immigration into Quebec's western areas had continued with steady trickles of so-called "Late Loyalists," who in course of time came more for free grants of good land than from political convictions. As the western population mounted, however, so did its demands for government services nearer than far-off Montreal or Quebec City, and for local law courts and land-holding based on British, not French law. The Crown itself was officially the seigneur of these newly-opened western Quebec lands; but the Loyalists there wanted to own their farms outright, as in the old colonies, and not be tenants even of a remote and undemanding King George III. Already in 1785 Sir John Johnson had joined with a group of Loyalist officers to petition for British laws and land ownership in western Quebec. And in 1788 Governor Dorchester, once Carleton, set up four local administrative districts and courts for that region, broadly covering present-day Southern Ontario. But the land-tenure issue remained; while Dorchester warned London that the Quebec Act designed to suit French Canadians would no longer do for the English-speaking Loyalist society that had now developed in the populating western districts of Quebec.

Over the next few years the problem was thrashed out, as these districts went

Settlement Growth in Early Upper Canada, II. *And this is Chatham emerging as a village in years that followed.*

on growing. It was involved as well with the problem of taxation, for which representative assemblies would be required to raise local revenues; since during the American Revolution the British parliament itself had adopted the principle that henceforth there should not be colonial taxation without representation. For western, Loyalist Quebec, this meant that elected representatives would accordingly vote taxes, as was already well established in the Maritime colonies. And in eastern, French Quebec, the Anglophone merchants still wanted an assembly, while the *Canadiens* were coming around to recognize its value to their own selves. But how to deal with two very different societies, linked to different law, religion and culture, within one parliamentary body? To the imperial government in London, the plain answer seemed to divide Quebec into two, still very sizeable, provinces named Upper and Lower Canada. Anglophone, Loyalist Upper Canada could thus gain the English law and land ownership it sought, under its own government and assembly. And an overwhelmingly Francophone Lower Canada would not only have its own government and elected house also, but could keep the special provisions of the Quebec Act guaranteeing French law, seigneurialism and the state-recognized rights of the Catholic Church. A draft bill for this new provincial scheme went back and forth between Quebec and London in 1789-90. In 1791 it was passed into effect by the British parliament, as the Constitutional or Canada Act.

The details and implications of this Act of 1791 can best be left for the present. More important, now, is to recognize it as another of the major results of the Loyalist movement that rose out of the American Revolution. Loyalists in particular had produced two new and enduring Canadian provinces, New Brunswick and Upper Canada. But they had done still more — apart from settling countrysides and founding towns from Saint John, Fredericton and Sydney to Kingston and Niagara. Relying on their own American experience, they had cleared thick forest to build bush farms and homes, despite repeated danger, hardship and misery: all too familiar to Loyalist women and wives. The men had turned to fishing and shipbuilding on the coasts, to lumbering and trading as well as farming in the interior. In sum, Loyalist economic and social contributions were widely influential; as were the professional skills and learning which a cultured element among them added, mostly on the seaboard. Beyond all this, however, there was the distinctive heritage of Loyalism. Unlike the much more homogenous, collective French community, Loyalist society embodied ethnic and individual variation, and even the beginnings of multi-culturalism in Canada. For the real diversity of British America was basic in the contributions of the Loyalists — who were not just British in allegiance, but British Americans in outlook and evolution, instead of being "United Statesers." And what they represented finally, in Canada, was almost a Declaration of Independence against the American republic, that had stemmed from revolutionary force.

Sydney, Small Capital of Cape Breton Island. *Here, too, settlement had spread with incoming Loyalists, so that — like New Brunswick — Cape Breton was also set off from Nova Scotia in 1784 as a province of its own. Later, more settlers came; including some Acadians, but particularly Highland Scots, who farmed as well as fished along this ruggedly beautiful island. Yet neither population nor resources developed sufficiently to support Cape Breton's separate provincial existence; so that in 1820 it would be re-attached to Nova Scotia once more.*

-1791	Constitutional Act organizes Upper Canada (Ontario)
	Population of Upper Canada (U.C.): c. 14,000
-1792	Colonel John Graves Simcoe, Governor of U.C., offers free lots to settlers
	Sir John Wentworth becomes Governor of Nova Scotia, till 1808
-1793	U.C. decrees end of Black slavery
	Alexander Mackenzie reaches Pacific
-1794	Jay's Treaty signed between Britain and United States
-1795	North West Company controls two-thirds of Canadian fur trade
-1796	Governor-in-Chief Lord Dorchester (Carleton) returns to England
-1798	Population of St. Johns Island: c. 4,000
-1799	St. Johns Island renamed Prince Edward Island
-1800	Philemon Wright settles on the Ottawa at future Hull, Lower Canada (L.C.)
-1801	Fort William replaces Grand Portage as Nor'Westers' inland fur base
-1802	Annual school grants begun in N.B.
-1803	Population of Newfoundland: c. 20,000
-1805	L.C. conflict in Assembly over funding for jails
-1807	Sir James Craig, Governor of L.C.
	British and American warships clash on Atlantic
-1808	Simon Fraser traces Fraser River to Pacific
-1809	First steamboat put on St. Lawrence by John Molson of Montreal
	British lumber tariffs favour British North America

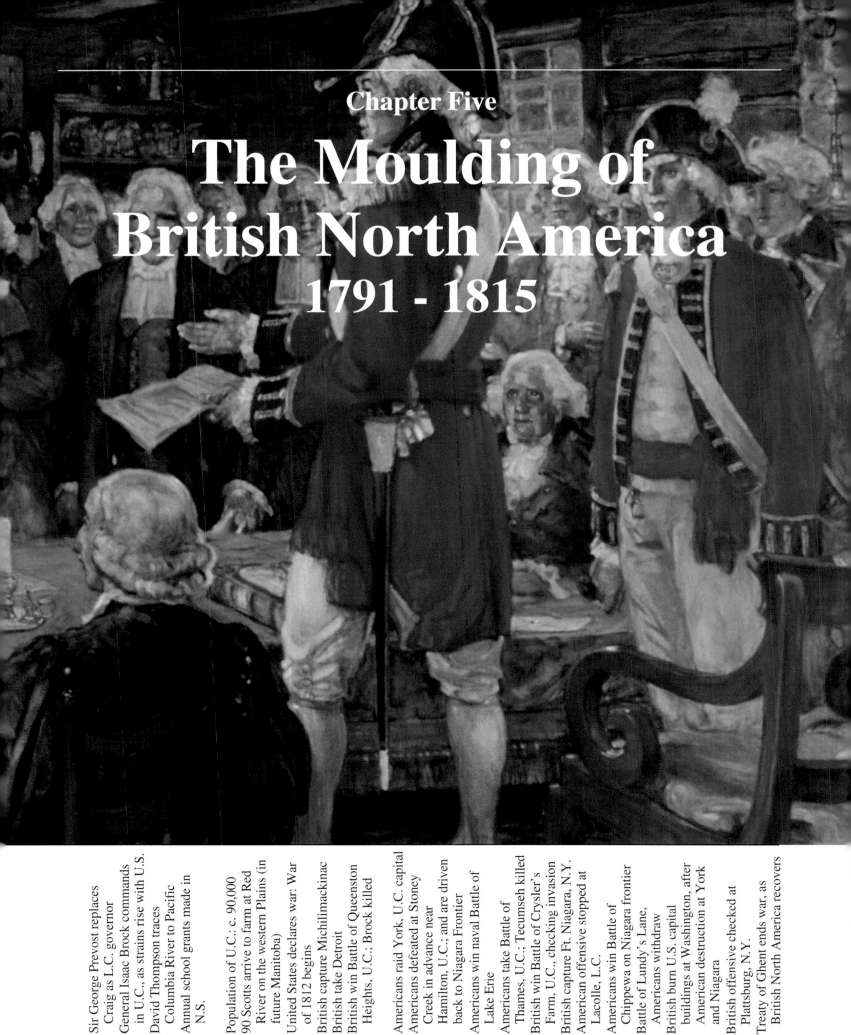

Chapter Five

The Moulding of British North America
1791 - 1815

1811 — Sir George Prevost replaces Craig as L.C. governor
General Isaac Brock commands in U.C., as strains rise with U.S.
David Thompson traces Columbia River to Pacific
Annual school grants made in N.S.

1812 — Population of U.C.: c. 90,000
90 Scotts arrive to farm at Red River on the western Plains (in future Manitoba)
United States declares war: War of 1812 begins
British capture Michilimackinac
British take Detroit
British win Battle of Queenston Heights, U.C.; Brock killed

1813 — Americans raid York, U.C. capital
Americans defeated at Stoney Creek in advance near Hamilton, U.C.; and are driven back to Niagara Frontier
Americans win naval Battle of Lake Erie
Americans take Battle of Thames, U.C.; Tecumseh killed
British win Battle of Crysler's Farm, U.C., checking invasion
British capture Ft. Niagara, N.Y.

1814 — American offensive stopped at Lacolle, L.C.
Americans win Battle of Chippewa on Niagara frontier
Battle of Lundy's Lane, Americans withdraw
British burn U.S. capital buildings at Washington, after American destruction at York and Niagara
British offensive checked at Plattsburg, N.Y.
Treaty of Ghent ends war, as British North America recovers

The Constitutional Act and the Two Canadas

Between 1791 and 1815, British North America took on outlines that it would largely carry into the Canadian federal union of 1867. In the West, its fur-trade territories expanded across the continent to the Pacific. In the East, its Atlantic provinces became more integrated communities, moving beyond basic settlement and meeting new tests of war. And in the Centre, Upper and Lower Canada — the first overwhelmingly English-speaking, the second predominantly French — grew as distinctly different though interrelated provinces, which both faced American invasions during the War of 1812-14. Still further, the two Canadas acquired a common political system, set out for each of them in the Constitutional Act of 1791.

That founding Act provided an imperially-appointed Lieutenant-Governor for each Canada, under a joint Governor-in-Chief, still Lord Dorchester when the measure went into effect. Since Governor Dorchester (Carleton) and his successors normally resided at the fortress in Quebec City, now Lower Canada's capital, the Lieutenant-Governor of that province was sometimes overshadowed. Yet in more distant Upper Canada, the Lieutenant-Governor was in practice all-but "Governor," unless his overlord back at Quebec decided to draw in the reins. An Executive Council, consisting of chief officials and advisors, would work closely with the Governor in either Canada, to carry on his administration and execute his policies, a small, informal but powerful group, somewhat like a little cabinet of ministers.

As well, the Act set up a provincial legislature or parliament for each Canada, composed of two houses, the Legislative Council and the Legislative Assembly. The members of the Legislative Council were named for life by the imperial authorities, and were meant to play an influential role in approving, amending or rejecting laws sent up from the Assembly — much like the House of Lords in Britain. This élite upper house, in fact, was to be a conservative, restraining body in each Canada between governing officials in the Executive Council and the elected representatives of the people in the Assembly. The Maritime Provinces did not acquire this particular new chamber, and each of them still kept an older-style, single Council, which carried out both executive and legislative duties. For the Canadas, however, the anti-democratic doubts left

Overleaf. Upper Canada's First Parliament, Niagara, 1792.
A Pioneer Clearing in Upper Canada. *This presents a somewhat more realistic picture of a cleared farm in the new inland province than the stylized layout previously shown.*

from the American Revolution, or raised afresh by the mass-violence of the French Revolution now exploding in Europe, impelled the planners of the Act of 1791 to place the Legislative Council in their new Canadian design, as a watchful, built-in barrier against popular political excesses.

The Legislative Assembly, the lower house in either Canada, expressed the age-old, vital English inheritance of the people's right to a representative law-making and tax-granting body — vital, as well, to free government under a British Crown controlled by law and parliament. In both Canadas the assembly members would be elected on a fairly wide franchise for that time, open to the solid, seigneurial tenants of Lower Canada and to the ordinary farm-proprietors of Upper Canada; that is, to those holding lands worth forty shillings yearly (no great sum in land-rich colonies), or, besides, to town-dwellers who owned real estate worth five pounds annually or rented property worth ten pounds a year. Money values would change greatly over time; but these qualifications plainly allowed a substantial popular electorate, including female property-holders as well as male. The common people really could share and declare their views in these young Canadian assemblies.

Nevertheless, although elected members in the two Canadas could now voice public sentiments and give consent to taxes (kept fairly low), the Constitutional Act still left the main weight of decision with the Governor and the Executive or Legislative Councils. Moreover, governors had revenues of their own from lands or customs duties outside parliamentary control; while the appointed councils, entrenched and powerful, were pretty effective restraints on the popular will in either province. But one must not overdo the impact of such restrictions, then, on the conservative-minded peoples of both Canadas. In a new Upper Canada, the colonists were generally too busy with the hard demands of pioneering to pay close heed to politics; and most were happy enough with their gains of English law and land tenure, along with having their own provincial government and assembly. In much older Lower Canada, the English-speaking minority also felt content with the new structure which at last had given them British parliamentary institutions. The French-Canadian majority largely took to it as well, seeing that their numbers could dominate the Lower Canadian assembly, while their own special guarantees from the Quebec Act had been maintained in the Act of 1791. Still further, the mass of *Canadiens*, deeply linked in their past to the Catholic Church and the French monarchy, beheld a despoiling French Revolution in Europe which had overthrown both — and thus looked the more favourably on

A Frontier Farm in Lower Canadian Winter. *Painted later by Cornelius Krieghoff, it nevertheless expresses frontier life conditions, as* habitants *pushed new homes into the interior away from their long-occupied St. Lawrence shores.*
Overleaf. Proclamation of the Constitutional Act, November, 1791.

Alured Clarke .:   George the Thir[d]

Faith and so forth To all OUR loving Subjects whom these Presents may concern Gree[ting]
Order in Council dated in the month of August last to order that OUR Province of Quebec sh[...]
Province of Lower Canada by separating the said two Provinces according to the following Line o[f]
lore West of Pointe au Bodet in the limit between the Township of Lancaster and the Seigneurie of
Westermost Angle of the said Seigneurie of New Longueuil thence along the North western B[...]
Ottawas River to ascend the said River into the Lake Temiscanning and from the Head of the[...]
including all the Territory to the Westward and Southward of the said line to the utmost exte[nt]
passed in the last Session of Parliament intituled An Act to repeal certain parts of an Act [...]
Provision for the Government of the Province of Quebec in North America and to make fu[rther]
distance of the said Provinces from Great Britain and the change to be made by the said [...]
between the notification of the said Act to the said Provinces respectively and the day of its com[...]
advice of OUR Privy Council to fix and declare or to authorize the Governor or Lieutenant Governor of[...]
of the commencement of the said Act within the said Provinces respectively provided that such
Ninetyone And Whereas in pursuance of the said Act We have thought fit by another
his Absence OUR Lieutenant Governor or the Person administering the Government of OUR
the Commencement of the said Act within the Province of Upper Canada and the Provin[ce]
wellbeloved Guy Lord Dorchester Captain General and Governor in Chief in and over OUR said[...]
said Province for the time being under OUR Signet and Royal Sign manual bearing date a[...]
necessary measures accordingly Know ye therefore that OUR trusty and wellbeloved Al[ured]
OUR said Governor thereof hath Judged it most adviseable to fix upon Monday the Seven[...]
aforesaid respectively and it is accordingly hereby declared that the said Act of Parliame[nt]
Majesty's Reign intituled An Act for making more effectual Provision for the Governme[nt]
of the said Province shall commence within the said Province of Upper Canada and L[ower]
Year One thousand seven hundred and Ninetyone of which all OUR loving Subjects an[d]
Whereof We have caused these OUR Letters to be made Patent and the Great Seal of OUR sa[id]
[A]lured the Esquire OUR Lieutenant Governor and Commander in Chief of OUR said Provin[ce]
Castle of Saint Lewis in the City of Quebec this Eighteenth Day of November in the Year o[f]
Reign.

Hugh Finlay,
Acting Secretary

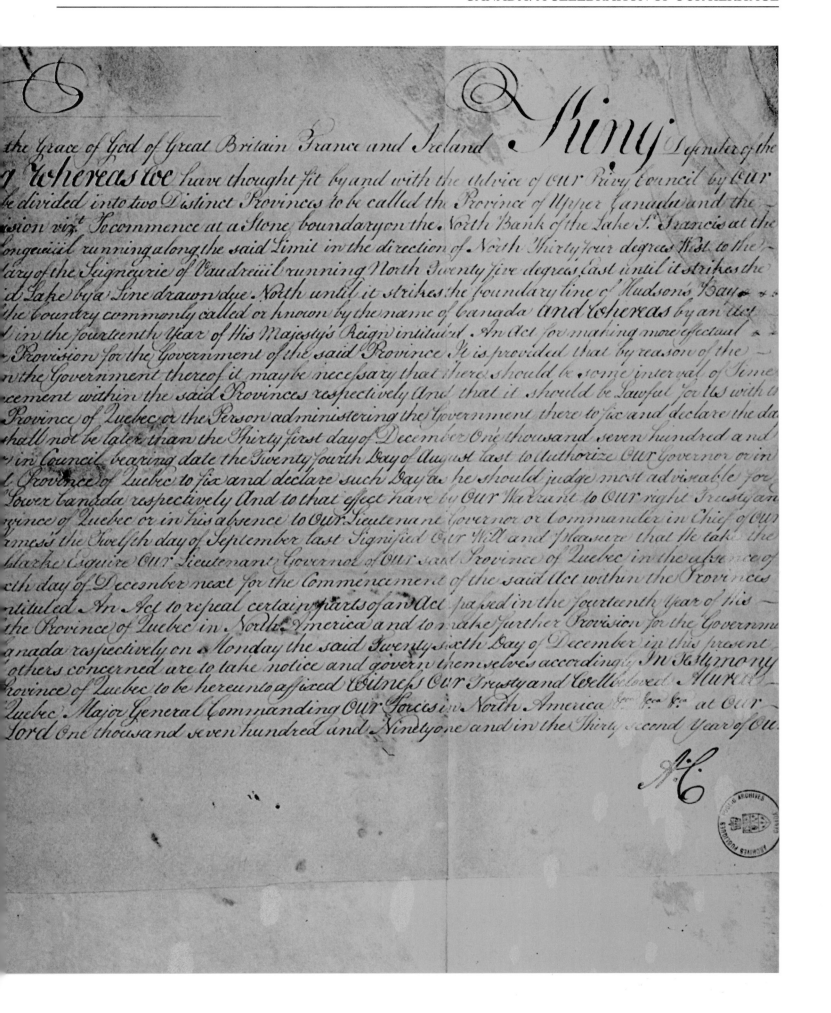

the Grace of God of Great Britain France and Ireland *King* Defender of the

Whereas We have thought fit by and with the Advice of OUR Privy Council by OUR

be divided into two Distinct Provinces to be called the Province of Upper Canada and the

sion viz.t To commence at a Stone boundary on the North Bank of the Lake S.t Francis at the

longitudinal running along the said Limit in the direction of North Thirty four degrees West to the

ary of the Seigneurie of Vaudreuil running North Twenty five degrees East until it strikes the

d Lake by a Line drawn due North until it strikes the boundary line of Hudson's Bay

the Country commonly called or known by the name of Canada *and Whereas* by an Act

d in the fourteenth Year of His Majesty's Reign intituled An Act for making more effectual

Provision for the Government of the said Province It is provided that by reason of the

n the Government thereof it may be necessary that there should be some interval of Time

cement within the said Provinces respectively And that it should be Lawful for Us with th

Province of Quebec or the Person administering the Government there to fix and declare the da

shall not be later than the Thirty first day of December One thousand seven hundred and

in Council bearing date the Twenty fourth Day of August last to Authorize OUR Governor or in

l Province of Quebec to fix and declare such Day as he should judge most advisable for

Lower Canada respectively And to that effect have by OUR Warrant to OUR right Trusty an

vince of Quebec or in his absence to OUR Lieutenant Governor or Commander in Chief of OUR

mes's the Twelfth day of September last Signified OUR Will and Pleasure that he take the

blarke Esquire OUR Lieutenant Governor of OUR said Province of Quebec in the absence of

xth day of December next for the Commencement of the said Act within the Provinces

intituled An Act to repeal certain parts of an Act passed in the fourteenth Year of His

the Province of Quebec in North America and to make further Provision for the Governme

anada respectively on a Monday the said Twenty sixth Day of December in this present

others concerned are to take notice and govern themselves accordingly *In Testimony*

rovince of Quebec to be hereunto affixed Witness OUR Trusty and Wellbeloved Alured

Quebec Major General Commanding OUR Forces in North America &c &c &c at OUR

Lord One thousand seven hundred and Ninetyone and in the Thirty second Year of Ou

1

2

3

their own safely-ordered British constitution. Hence the Constitutional Act, despite its limitations, suited both Canadas reasonably well at the start; so that some time would follow before its restrictive features led on to mounting demands for reform.

Other future issues also would develop from the Act's setting aside lands to maintain a "Protestant Clergy" in Upper Canada. The conservative London designers of this imperial statute had regarded state-backed religion as a bulwark of social order. And, of course, state-enforced tithes to support the Catholic Church had been continued in the Act of 1791 for long-settled Lower Canada. But as for new, underpopulated Upper Canada, so largely Protestant, the Act reserved an amount equal to one-seventh of all the wild lands to be granted to settlers, in order to build up a land endowment that would fund clergy of the Protestant faith — which, in the thinking of the designers, really meant the Anglican Church, the established Church in England. In Upper Canada, however, while Anglicans would remain a leading denomination, there were also German Lutheran and evangelical Protestants present, along with Scots or Irish Presbyterians, and a rising number of Methodists among the Loyalists themselves. Protestantism by its very nature presented variety, not Catholic uniformity. As a result, the Anglican claim on Clergy Reserves — which held back various farm lots and blocks of land from free-grant settlement for later lease or sale — would all but certainly produce lasting grievances in Upper Canada, both for economic and religious reasons. Nevertheless, the fact that initially there were plenty of wild lands available as grants to settlers, also meant that it would take some time before the Upper Canadian Clergy Reserves themselves became a pressing issue.

In any event, an Upper Canada mainly concerned with pioneer settlement might well be pleased with its first Lieutenant-Governor, named when the Act of 1791 went through: Colonel John Graves Simcoe, from Devon in England. He had fought through the American Revolutionary War at the head of the Loyalist Queen's Rangers, and brought that reconstituted regiment with him to Upper Canada to be a construction corps. Devoted to the Loyalist migrants — as most of them were to him — Simcoe aimed at making his new province a very model of British law, liberty and progress, set beside a misguided American republic. Hence, even before he reached Kingston from Quebec and Montreal in 1792, he was full of eager plans for highways, towns and economic enterprises, or for defences against a still unfriendly United States; capably aided in all this by Elizabeth Simcoe, his observant and keen-minded wife, who drew out some of the plans, and wrote or sketched vividly on life in this opening Upper Canada.

An energetic, determined Governor Simcoe (but no less set in his views) issued a crucial proclamation as early as February, 1792, to attract more settlers to his province from the American states, which he earnestly believed still held many people of hidden Loyalist sentiments. Accordingly, his proclamation, widely circulated below the border, offered 200-acre grants to all who would settle them and swear an oath of British allegiance. This open invitation to free land (already known to be fertile from the Loyalists' experience) brought many American frontier families moving westward to make just a minor swing to the northern side of the Lower Great Lakes, and thus locate in Upper Canada. Feelings for allegiance had less to do with this new inflow than Simcoe had optimistically hoped. Some of the newcomers, at first, might still have been

1. First Church Built at York (Toronto). *Notably, this was Anglican St. James, of the denomination officially endowed in Upper Canada by the Clergy Reserves land system, provided under the Constitutional Act. Religious services were widely held across the pioneer province well before many new churches had been put up: at garrison posts or in public buildings, at country inns or in private homes. But non-Anglicans had to rely on their own church-members' contributions to build, while Anglicanism, state-recognized and backed, could draw on the Clergy Reserves funds — at least, once spreading settlement had opened up Clergy lands to lease or sale.*

2. John Graves Simcoe, First Lieutenant-Governor of Upper Canada. *Distinguished commander of the Loyalist Queen's Rangers in the American Revolution, Simcoe would prove a dedicated, energetic and far-sighted governor; though he could also be both dogmatic and over-optimistic in his views. Yet in his years of office to 1796, he accomplished a good deal: bringing in more settlers, building major roads, establishing a new Upper Canadian capital (York, to be Toronto), and generally, in putting the Constitutional Act structure into effective operation.*

3. Elizabeth Posthuma Simcoe. *Scarcely less energetic and eager than her husband — but perhaps more sensibly perceptive — Mrs. Simcoe not only carried on a demanding role as governor's consort, aide, and mother of a young family, but as well produced valuable watercolours of early Upper Canada and a vibrant diary on its life.*

A PROCLAMATION,

To such as are defirous to fettle on the lands of the crown in the Province of

UPPER CANADA;

BY HIS EXCELLENCY

John Graves Simcoe, Efquire;

Lieutenant Governor and Commander in Chief of the faid Province, and Colonel
Commanding His Majefty's Forces, &c. &c. &c.

BE IT KNOWN to all concerned, that his majefty hath, by his royal com-
miffion and inftructions to the governor, and in his abfence the lieutenant
governor or perfon adminiftering the government for the time being, of the
faid Province of Upper Canada, given authority and command to grant the lands
of the crown in the fame by patent under the great feal thereof ; and it being expedient to publifh and declare the royal intention refpecting fuch grants and patents, I do accordingly hereby make known the terms of grant and fettlement to be:

FIRST.—That the crown lands to be granted be parcel of townfhip : if an inland townfhip, of ten
miles fquare, and if a townfhip on navigable waters, of nine miles in front and twelve miles in depth, be
run out and marked by his majefty's furveyor or deputy furveyor general, or under his fanction and
authority.

SECOND.—That only fuch part of the townfhip be granted as fhall remain, after a refervation of one
feventh part thereof, for the fupport of a proteftant clergy, and one other feventh part thereof, for the
future difpofition of the crown.

THIRD.—That no farm lot fhall be granted to any one perfon which fhall contain more than two
hundred acres ; yet the governor, lieutenant governor or perfon adminiftering the government, is allowed and permitted to grant to any perfon or perfons fuch further quantity of land as they may defire,
not exceeding one thoufand acres, over and above what may have been before granted to them.

FOURTH.—That every petitioner for lands make it appear, that he or fhe is in a condition to cultivate
and improve the fame, and fhall, befides taking the ufual oaths, fubfcribe a declaration (before proper
perfons to be for that purpofe appointed) of the tenor of the words following, viz. " I A. B. do pro-
mife and declare that I will maintain and defend to the utmoft of my power the authority of the king
" in his parliament as the fupreme legiflature of this Province.'

FIFTH.—That applications for grants be made by petition to the governor, lieutenant governor, or perfon adminiftering the government for the time being, & where it is advifeable to grant the prayer thereof a warrant fhall iffue to the proper officer for a furvey thereof, returnable within fix months with a plot
annexed, and be followed with a patent granting the fame, if defired, in free and common foccage, upon
the terms and conditions in the royal inftructions expreffed, and herein after fuggefted.

SIXTH.—That all grants referve to the crown, all coals, commonly called fea coals, and mines of gold,
filver, copper, tin, iron, and lead ; and each patent contain a claufe for the refervation of timber for the
royal navy of the tenor following : ' And provided alfo, that no part of the tract or parcel of land here-
" by granted to the faid   and his heirs, be within any refervation heretofore made and
" marked for us, our heirs and fucceffors, by our furveyor general of woods, or his lawful deputy ; in
" which cafe, this our grant for fuch part of the land hereby given and granted to the faid
" and his heirs forever as aforefaid, and which fhall upon furvey thereof being made, be found within
" any fuch refervation, fhall be null and void, any thing herein contained to the contrary notwithftanding.'

SEVENTH.—That the two fevenths referved for the crown's future difpofition, and the fupport of a
proteftant clergy, be not fevered tracts, each of one feventh part of the townfhip, but fuch lots or farms
therein, as the furveyor-general's return of the furvey of the townfhip, fhall be defcribed as fet apart for
thefe purpofes, between the other farms of which the faid townfhip fhall confift, to the intent that the
lands to be referved may be nearly of the like value with an equal quantity of the other parts to be granted out as afore-mentioned.

EIGHTH.—That the refpective patentees are to take the eftates granted to them feverally free of quit
rent and of any other expences, than fuch fees as are or may be allowed to be demanded and received by
the different officers concerned in paffing the patent and recording the fame, to be ftated in a table authorized and eftablifhed by the government, and publickly fixed up in the feveral offices of the clerk of
the council, of the furveyor general, and of the fecretary of the Province.

NINTH.—That every patent be entered upon record within fix months from the date thereof, in the
fecretary's or regifter's offices, and a docket thereof in the auditor's office.

TENTH.—Whenever it fhall be thought advifeable to grant any given quantity to one perfon of one
thoufand acres or under, and the fame cannot be found by reafon of the faid refervations and prior grants
within the townfhip in the petition expreffed, the fame, or what fhall be requifite to make up to fuch
perfon the quantity advifed, fhall be located to him, in fome other townfhip, upon a new petition for
that purpofe to be preferred.

And of the faid feveral regulations, all perfons concerned are to take notice, and govern themfelves
accordingly.

Given under my hand and feal, in the city of Quebec, the feventh day of February, in the thirty-
second year of his majefty's reign, and in the year of our Lord, one thoufand, feven hundred
and ninety-two.

John Graves Simcoe.

BY HIS EXCELLENCY's COMMAND,

THOMAS TALBOT, Acting Secretary.

[Re-printed at Newark, by G. TIFFANY, 1795.]

1. Simcoe's Proclamation of Land Grants for Settlers. *Actually drawn up at Quebec in February, 1792, before he had reached Upper Canada, the new Lieutenant-Governor here both provided for clergy and crown reserve blocks to be set out, and for 200-acre lots to be granted free to farm settlers declaring British loyalty. This measure clearly invited a new frontier inrush from over the American border.*
2. The Garrison at York. *The military base for Upper Canada founded by Simcoe on Toronto harbour in 1793, is seen here a few years later, when it had grown in size; but when it was still the main reason for the town of York, as capital of the province.*
3. Part of the Town of York. *This government village (as it was at first) straggled along the lakeshore at Toronto — portrayed here looking towards the closed-in eastern end of the harbour, where a blockhouse, with flag, then stood.*

1

2

3

1. Peter Russell, Successor to Simcoe. *A former British soldier and official during the Revolutionary War, he had come to Upper Canada in Simcoe's administration, and took over when Simcoe himself returned to Britain in 1796.*

2. The "Highway" from York towards Kingston. *This, the Danforth Road, began through a contract drawn up by Russell with road-builder, Asa Danforth, after Simcoe had laid out Yonge Street and Dundas Street — both of which were not much different, originally, from this mere trail hacked through ancient forests.*

1

2

"Late" Loyalists in sympathy; but more and more they were really land-hungry American frontiersmen, who came with little political concern themselves, and so did not find it too difficult to return to the domains of King George III, under whom they had been born. In any case, this Post-Loyalist American influx would assuredly develop Upper Canada well beyond its original Loyalist foundations. The movement started small under Simcoe — though he had opened the way. But largely because of it, a province of some 14,000 in 1791 rose to around 90,000 before the War of 1812 effectively closed off more entries from the neighbouring republic.

Other than in settlement (most basic) Simcoe worked to get Upper Canada well under way. After a brief stay in Kingston, where he met with his initial Executive Council, the Governor moved deeper into the heart of the province, to Niagara as capital; and here he called Upper Canada's first parliament in September, 1792. But the next year Simcoe decided to shift the government seat away from Niagara on the exposed American border to the northern shore of Lake Ontario: to the harbour of Toronto, where the long-used Toronto Passage gave access overland to Georgian Bay and the Upper Lakes, while the naturally protected harbour could be made a safe naval and military base against American border attacks. And so in mid-1793 the new capital village and garrison centre of York was laid out by Simcoe's Queen's Rangers: later to become the city of Toronto.

Beyond this capital, the Governor had main roads cut by the Rangers: Yonge Street inland, up the Toronto Passage north, Dundas Street west into the heart of southwestern peninsula, where the projected town of London would arise. And to Fort Detroit at the southwest tip of the province, or northward to Lake Huron, the ever-active Simcoe toured and planned a province that should command the Great Lakes. He did still more: under his lead, the province's legislature in 1793 decreed that Black slavery would end in Upper Canada; seventy years before the presumably democratic United States abolished it. Then in 1796 the Governor went home from York, his now-established capital, and was shortly sent instead to command British forces in the West Indies. Peter Russell, his diligent inspector-general (finance minister) followed him as chief administrator of the province. until a new Lieutenant-Governor, Peter Hunter, was appointed in 1799. But Simcoe and Russell together strongly stamped the initial years of Upper Canada.

In those years, too, there were menacing strains along the border between that province and the United States. Since the Treaty of 1783 native Indian peoples below the Great Lakes, who had once been allies of the French and then the British against American thrusts westward, had been left uneasily within territories ceded by Britain to the new United States. Their outlook was bleak, to say the least. The British, however, had not yet given up their forts on what was now, by the peace treaty, the American side of the border. The reason they put forward (and it had weight) was that the Americans had not fulfilled their own treaty commitments to Loyalists. But other reasons were that the Indians still relied on the British fur trade for supplies, obtained at the border posts in

Parliament Buildings at York, 1797.
Ordered built by Simcoe, they were not in use till after his departure.

question; that these posts represented some protection to Upper Canada against American expansion, right from Forts Oswego and Niagara to Detroit and Michilimackinac; and finally, that if the inland tribes were indeed abandoned, they might turn in desperate revenge against the weaker, thinly-held Upper Canada frontiers.

Consequently, Simcoe, instructed by Governor-in-Chief Dorchester, played a tense diplomatic game in the American border areas — not much aided by the Six Nations leader, Isaac Brant, who realistically thought it impossible to create a neutral Indian state there, as Simcoe hoped. American military power soon settled the question in any case, shattering Indian resistance and forcing the western tribes below the border to a virtual surrender in 1794. British-American armed clashes were just barely avoided; but the Indians' defeat was decisive. And at the same time, an American delegation led by John Jay went to London and negotiated Jay's Treaty in 1794, whereby the Americans (belatedly) agreed to deal with neglected Loyalist claims, while the British (belatedly) agreed to evacuate their border forts on the American side, completing the move by 1796.

And so by the late 1790s Upper Canada had settled down to quieter phases of continued immigration and development. Meanwhile, Lower Canada had seen important developments of its own, notably in its political life under the Act of 1791. In that respect, that province's appointed Legislative and Executive Councils were controlled from the start by an English-speaking elite of officials and top merchants; but its elected Legislative Assembly was dominated by the French-Canadian majority — since, after all, they numbered over 145,000 to only some 10,000 in the Anglophone minority. The result was ethnically-based politics, with the British minority elite stressing the demands of commerce, finance and public works, the French popular majority championing *Canadien* rural society, its traditional institutions and cultural heritage. Of course, there were a limited number of English-speaking representatives also in the House of Assembly, largely sitting for the business towns; but the elected house essentially became an instrument of the Francophone community; a process aided by the fact that, from the start, the Assembly established French along with English as an official language in Lower Canada's parliament.

At the same time in economic life, Lower Canadian farmers were prospering on wheat exports sent overseas to feed the cities of an increasingly industrial

Old Fort Niagara Turned Over to Americans. *When Simcoe had first come to Upper Canada and Niagara, this key fort dating from French times had still been in British hands. But it actually lay on the American shore of the Niagara River; which was one good reason for the governor's decision in 1793 to move Upper Canada's headquarters from this border area to York on Toronto harbour. Events proved him right, when under Jay's Treaty, Britain had finally to evacuate the old fort at Niagara by 1796, along with other posts on the American edge of the inland boundary.*

Britain. More than that, while Montreal's chief merchants still thrived on the long-range fur trade, the lumbering, shipping and fishing interests in Lower Canada soon all benefitted from the sweeping rise of wartime prices in Europe. In 1793 Great Britain joined European allies in a general war on France; seeking to quell the furious Revolution there which, quite literally, had just cut off the French monarchy at the neck, by guillotine. The French Wars that followed would last over two decades with little break, widely engaging both Britain and its North American colonies. And if inland Upper Canada mostly experienced distant echoes of the conflict, Lower Canada on the St. Lawrence-ocean highway felt it more considerably, though mainly through busy wartime commerce. Here, however, we now are moving into another era, the opening nineteenth century, which itself demands attention in both Canadas.

1

1. *Canadiens* in Winter Dress at Quebec, 1805. *Perhaps a bit exaggerated!*
2. The Road to Fort Erie Beyond Niagara, around 1800. *This, too, was on the exposed border. Fort Erie, two miles above the Falls, would soon be fought over in the War of 1812.*

2

The Canadas in the New Nineteenth Century

Major economic advances certainly continued in Lower Canada, so much longer settled and more fully grown. As but one example, John Molson, an English immigrant to Montreal of the 1780s, imported a new-fangled steam engine to serve his flourishing brewery; and the technical knowledge he gained led Molson in 1809 to put steam power into a pioneering vessel on the St. Lawrence, the *Accomodation*, running between Montreal and Quebec. Steamboat navigation, thus successfully begun, thereafter spread up-river and on beyond the rapids into the Great Lakes: to prove one of the most significant developments of the young century.

More immediately important, and no less extensive, was the rise of an ever-growing lumber trade out of Lower Canada to Britain. Lumbering, which had been practiced from French colonial times along the St. Lawrence, took on a whole new scale during the wars against Revolutionary France; and then against its supreme dictator, Napoleon, who was proclaimed French Emperor in 1804 and whose conquests soon spread across Europe right to Russia. Only an island Britain, protected by its great naval fleet and carrying on worldwide ocean commerce, managed virtually alone in Europe to withstand Napoleon's tremendous land-based power. But sea-power in that age of wooden sailing-ships still depended on plentiful timber from abundant forests — such as were found in British North America. And even by 1804 Britain was facing a crisis in her domestic wood supply, in that her own home-grown prime timber had become almost exhausted by the heavy construction needs of both warships and merchant vessels, on which her very freedom and economic security depended. She still could look to nearby Baltic European lands for timber; these had indeed become an increasing reliance. But in 1806, the master of Europe, Napoleon issued the Berlin Decrees, intended to choke the economy of an island realm he could not subdue by military force. Among many other things, his decrees prohibited the sending of timber to Britain out of Baltic ports. Some cargoes would still get through. Yet for wood-dependent British shipping, colonial timber was now transformed from a helpful shipbuilding supplement, to a crucial necessity in itself.

Consequently, in 1809, the British government placed high duties on foreign timber, but left colonial timber virtually duty-free; thus giving a strong tariff preference to wood shipped from British North America over closer, cheaper, but unsure Baltic supplies. This imperial preference was also calculated to bring British firms into tackling transatlantic colonial forests, and it did so. Yet above all, it meant that the protective rate set for colonial wood sent to British markets would now cover the cost of ocean shipping — and thus would hugely stimulate

John Molson, Brewer, Entrepreneur and Banker. *One of the most important business figures in Montreal to follow on from the fur barons, Molson not only established a long-lasting brewing firm and applied new steam technology to industry and river transport — he also became a leading banker, and would preside over Montreal's first railway in the 1830s.*

CANADA 34

John Molson 1763-1836

the lumbering already under way from the Maritimes to Lower Canada, and into Upper Canada, for many years to come. In effect, the imperial timber preference (ultimately paid for by the British taxpayer) widely encouraged economic growth across British North America; but nowhere more than on the St. Lawrence, and up its great tributaries, the Saguenay, the St. Maurice, the Richelieu, the Ottawa and more, all offering ample forest resources for imperial trade.

Production for this overseas commerce emerged early on the Richelieu and fast spread to other streams: the square-hewing by broad-axe of giant "sticks" of timber, which then were shipped out from the port of Quebec in roomy if unwieldy sailing vessels. And square-timbering particularly reached up the Ottawa to its own vast forests of red and white pine. At Hull, opposite the present city of Ottawa, Philemon Wright had settled in 1800 with a party of post-Loyalist Americans from Massachusetts. From Hull by 1806 he was already sending large

1. Barrel-Making in Molson's Brewery.
2. Timber Rafts on the St. Lawrence. *The sails obviously help the current move the heavy timbers downriver - and give a bit of aid to "sweeps," oars used to manoeuvre the clumsy giants.*

1

2

rafts of square-hewn timber down to the St. Lawrence and Quebec. And as big lumber firms like Pollock and Gilmour sent agents and partners out from Britain to Quebec — and as William Price from England became "King of the Saguenay" through opening up its timber resources — so the port of Quebec boomed as capital of a lumber empire, while clattering shipyards rose near tight-packed timber coves. French Canadians moved as lumbermen into new forest frontiers, under bosses mainly British or American in background. In any case, not only did Quebec City receive a major economic input, offsetting Montreal's hold on the fur trade and up-river traffic, but also, a Canadian staple export had appeared in timber, to share with wheat in general importance that rose beyond the old trade staples of fish and fur.

More locally important was the settlement of the Lower Canadian region to be termed the Eastern Townships, lying southeast of Montreal and stretching to the Appalachians and the American border. Not occupied by the French Canadians, this wide tract once home to native Abenaki had remained outside the limits of seigneurial holdings; yet the Constitutional Act of 1791 did allow grants of land in Lower Canada to be made by "free and common soccage" (farm proprietorship) beyond the range of established seigneuries. Accordingly, with the thought of attracting more Loyalist migrants, this near-border area was surveyed into townships from 1791, to be granted in such units to "leaders" (with capital) and their "associates" (would-be settlers). But not till late in the nineties did much more than airy speculation take place; and when actual settlers did come in, they were less Late Loyalists than land-seeking post-Loyalist Americans, often drawn from neighbouring northern New England. They made capable pioneers, however, in opening up good farmlands. Hence by 1810 they had added another segment to the English-speaking minority in Lower Canada, one which was largely composed of country-dwellers, not city merchants, and one which would be further enlarged by the British immigrants who came into this Anglophone Townships community after 1815.

All the same, the French speaking populace remained the great majority in Lower Canada: confounding unreal hopes among the Anglophone elite in power (the "British party") that the *Canadiens* could somehow be absorbed into a very much smaller English-speaking population. Instead, an increasingly self-aware "French party" took to political action on their own in the Assembly, to uphold and promote the distinctive interests of French Canada. This political element was mainly centred among an emerging professional class of *Canadien* lawyers, doctors, notaries and the like; though French-Canadian seigneurs, Catholic clergy and government job-holders generally stayed outside as moderates, between the

1. Philemon Wright, Father of Ottawa Lumbering. *An American settler who first came to farm, he took to the timber trade from lack of income; and in this he and his family flourished at Hull on the Lower Canadian side of the Ottawa River.*

2. Timber Base at Montmorency, just below Quebec. *The picture (in the 1810s) gives a distant view of Quebec, both Lower and Upper Town.*

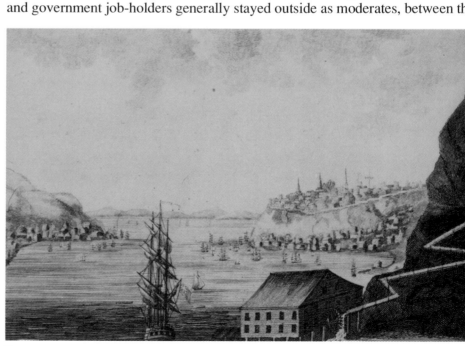

1

2

1. An Ottawa Timber Raft. *A later glimpse (indeed, within the early age of photography), it shows the kind of raft and crew which did develop on the river, and lasted there virtually into the twentieth century.*
2. Square-Hewing the Big Timbers in the Woods. *This picture also falls within the day of photography. But the technique of using the broad-axe to hew "on the square" had not changed.*

1

2

French and British parties. The French-party members largely admired the British parliamentary constitution yet sought to realize it more fully, and thus to enlarge the rights already held by the French-Canadian community, as they beheld them. On such broad questions, however, there were inevitable differences of outlook between French and British sides; and differences on specific issues, as well, brought the Legislative Assembly and the Legislative Council of Lower Canada into mounting conflict.

A particularly sharp clash came in 1805 over an Assembly bill to erect much-needed jails across the province, to be paid for by new import duties on trade. But the Council, petitioned by merchants linked with the British party, sought to meet the costs through a tax on land instead. Angry arguments followed, as the question eventually went right up through the councils and governor to the imperial powers in London. In the outcome, the tax was imposed on land; for this was a local measure for local, not external purposes — and if local residents could afford to build churches, why not jails? Nevertheless, the debate it roused really expressed the basic division between French agrarian interests and British commercial concerns. And it brought on the founding of a self-declared *Parti canadien* in the Assembly to work for change, along with a first Francophone journal, *Le Canadien* of Quebec City, directed by *Parti canadien* members and dedicated to French Canada's institutions, law and customs. Newspaper and party threw themselves vigorously into the cause. Then in 1807 they came up against a formidable new governor, Sir James Craig, a military officer deeply suspicious about the possible spread of French Revolutionary ideas into Lower Canada. His suspicions were much exaggerated; but they did not ease Lower Canadian politics.

Under men like Pierre Bédard and Jean-Thomas Taschereau, strong-minded lawyers, *Le Canadien* not only attacked government favouritism and corrupt land deals, but suggested a potent idea for the future; that members of the government might be held responsible to the elected assembly. The Assembly itself acted to expel two government supporters from its own membership, on what were acceptable legal grounds of that day — though the expulsion of one of them,

1. Governor James Craig in Lower Canada, 1807-1811. *A veteran soldier of the Revolutionary War, and an authoritative general since, Craig was still the wrong man to govern a divided Lower Canada; and besides was ill and dying during his period in office. In any case, his attention to unwise counsellors and his arbitrary acts inflamed French Canadians against him.*

2. Pierre Bédard. *Chiefly instrumental in founding* Le Canadien, *he was illegally imprisoned by Craig in 1810, but later released without trial. He sat in the Lower Canada Assembly from 1792 to 1812.*

1

2

Ezekiel Hart, a Jewish merchant of Trois Rivières, also smacked of religious prejudice. The expulsions, in fact, helped make the general election of 1808 violent, while Craig saw disruptive French democratic nationalism behind it all. When a scarcely-changed new Assembly flatly confirmed the expulsions, both in 1809 and 1810, the governor dissolved the house outright; seized the press of *Le Canadien*, put military patrols in Quebec, and imprisoned Bédard and two others also involved with the paper. But when Craig, backed by the British elite, went on to urge the imperial government to revoke the whole Constitutional Act, the London authorities in 1811 wisely recalled him instead. Thereafter, a different and conciliatory governor, Sir George Prevost (a British soldier but of French Swiss origin), effectively calmed and restored the situation. He changed some members of his Executive Council, appointed *Canadiens* to judgeships, including Bédard, and largely won over French-Canadian support — a matter of grave importance, as renewed strains grew with the United States that would soon burst into the War of 1812. For the time being, at least, Lower Canadian politics and Assembly-Council relations were set on a more even course; although the work accomplished by the *Parti canadien* would not be forgotten by the Francophone community in the years ahead.

Upper Canada saw far less political excitement in the opening nineteenth century. Neither so developed nor divided, the upper province did not yet

Le Canadien, 1806. The influential new mouthpiece of the Parti canadien *in politics, it not only eloquently defended French rights, but also early expressed the idea of responsible government — a government responsible to the colony's own elected assembly.*

produce lasting organized parties in politics, but rather just temporary groups associated with persons more than programmes. And though there might be Assembly-Council disagreements, these hardly roused wide popular responses in Upper Canada, where the governing elite, an oligarchy of firm-set officials, landowning gentry and some merchants, kept much wider support in town or country than in the ethnically split lower province. Moreover, Upper Canada's governors, like its politics, were generally not of strong historic note after Simcoe and on down to the War of 1812. And so other aspects held more significance; particularly the ongoing settlement process in this still very young society.

A continued inflow of Post-Loyalist Americans occupied the shores of Lake Ontario between the Bay of Quinte and the capital of York, spread from the head of the lake through the western peninsula to the Detroit border, and advanced inland up Yonge Street from York itself. Moreover, along with ordinary pioneers, "Plain Folk" also came from the United States: evangelical Protestant group like the Quakers, who located near Yonge, or the German-speaking Mennonites who went into the Niagara peninsula and especially up the Grand River to Waterloo county. Thanks to this whole influx — a spill-over from the westward movement of the great American frontier — the majority of Upper Canada's population was of American origin by the War of 1812; and only a minority of that element were actually Loyalists in background. As for British immigration in this same period, it was restricted both because of the costs and dangers of wartime passage across the Atlantic, and because manpower demands in Britain were high, whether for armed forces, factories or farms. Some Scots Highland soldiers and families were brought to Glengarry in eastern Upper Canada in 1803, to add to the Loyalist Highlanders already there. Some English, Scottish or Irish merchants and artisans also came to Upper Canada's few urban centres, where their qualitative impact mattered more than their limited numbers. But over all, the pre-war province was still largely a land of simple cabins and rough farms occupied by Loyalist or American families, with the latter being decidedly Methodist, not Anglican, and strongly individualist in their views. The British element clustered at the power centres stayed influential. But there was trouble for the future in Upper Canada's

1. Jean-Thomas Taschereau, *like Bédard a lawyer and Assembly member (till 1827), he also helped found* Le Canadien, *and was imprisoned, but ended up a judge.*
2. Sir George Prevost, Governor-in-Chief, 1811-1815. *Both a top general and an adept conciliator, Prevost came from a successful governorship in Nova Scotia to put right Craig's damage in Lower Canada. The amends he made won back much French Canadian good will — though he would prove less successful as military commander-in-chief in Canada during the War of 1812.*

1   2

own division in heritage — whether loyally British or American democratic in origin.

Economic growth accompanied this enlarging Upper Canadian settlement, from the flourishing timber world along the Ottawa to new farms beside Lake Erie, or in the valley of the Thames. Certainly the southern stretches of Upper Canada were now well beyond the fur trade; although it still dominated great northern forest reaches all the way to Fort William at the head of Lake Superior — which was built up from 1803 as a base for the western commerce in furs, now that an earlier base, Grand Portage, was recognized as lying on the American side of the line. But in the southern areas of Upper Canada, livestock and grain as well as timber were emerging as prime exports for the province's settlers, to be sent out the St. Lawrence or down across the Lakes. One can overdo the progress within this frontier community, still with under 100,000 settled inhabitants by the War of 1812. Nonetheless, the evidences of growth in young Upper Canada were plain by then: from the first brick buildings erected at York to the cutting of more main roads, the rise of lake shipping, or even the first provincially-aided schools. And similar growth was no less apparent down to 1812-15 in the Atlantic provinces of a future Canadian union.

1. A Settled Farm in Upper Canada. *Compare this picture of improving farmland in older settled areas of the province with that of an initial forest clearing when the Loyalists had arrived (as shown above on page 158). Now the house is not a log cabin, but a square-timber home with an attic. There is a barn (not a shanty) with a new one apparently under way. There is a bridge, not a ford; the fenced fields have a hay crop. The forest has been pushed back — and the farmer can use a wheeled wagon, now the stumps have been removed.*

2. Fort William on the Kaministiquia. *The new inland headquarters of the North West Company, it did not actually receive its well-known name till 1807, when it was thus named after William McGillivray, by then the top figure in the great Montreal-based fur company.*

1

2

1

2

The Atlantic Colonies and the Wars

From the 1790s on, the three Maritime provinces and Newfoundland were more directly affected than the Canadas by the French Wars because of their Atlantic coastal position; although the American War of 1812 found them less exposed to United States attack — thanks to the British Navy — than were the inland Canadian provinces. And in addition, this whole period down to 1815 brought political and economic developments to the eastern colonies, which further shaped their lasting roles in British North America.

In New Brunswick, the timber trade to Britain became dominant in value, beginning first with tall, straight pines for shipmasts, here in plentiful supply. But the resources of wood up the Saint John and other rivers that could be rafted out to Atlantic harbours came increasingly into trade even, before the imperial timber preference was set up in 1809. From then on the hewing of long squared beams to be sent by merchant firms to Britain spread still more extensively, from Bay of Fundy streams around to the River Miramichi on the province's eastern coast. In fact, thanks to its thick forests extending to the Appalachians, New Brunswick became a timber colony first and foremost. Agriculture of course continued around its shores, along the low Chignecto Isthmus and in the fertile intervales of the Saint John. Fishing and shipbuilding equally grew active on the coasts, while Saint John the city became a focus of rising shipyards, as well as the chief provincial port. And so New Brunswick thrived with wartime markets. Yet also, the quiet return of Acadians brought it new French-speaking farms or fishing settlements from Memracook in the Chignecto area up to the Quebec border. On this eastern side (or "north shore") villages like Buctouche, Richibucto and Shippegan marked the steady building of a restored Acadian community, one which over time would come to form nearly half the population of the province.

But New Brunswick's political life stayed mostly in the hands of a ruling Loyalist oligarchy, a small and powerful ruling group. It featured enduring councillors like Ward Chipman formerly from Massachusetts, to be Solicitor-General from 1784 to 1808, and Chief Justice afterwards; or Edward Winslow, also from Massachusetts (and Harvard), who had worked with Chipman as a top Loyalist officer during the American Revolution, and from 1784 to 1806 sat in New Brunswick's executive until named a Supreme Court judge himself. These are but two leading examples of the Loyalist elite that ran the province — and fairly well at that — under a long-lived Governor Thomas Carleton, who held his own post officially right from 1784 to 1817; though he actually returned to England in 1803, already aged sixty-eight. Thus New Brunswick, in its first age down to 1815, seemed to be what its Loyalist landed-gentry liked to deem a province fit for gentlemen, run in well-mannered style from the placid country capital of Fredericton. Yet plain farmers and fishermen, rough timber-cutters and wood bosses, or striving merchants and port-workers down in busy Saint John, no less represented another growing

1. Winter Lumbering in New Brunswick. *Hauling logs through the woods to riverbank, by oxen.*
2. Saint John from Fort Howe, c. 1815. *A native Indian family is in the foreground, with the bustling port-city beyond.*
3. Fredericton, New Brunswick's Capital, before 1820. *A quiet, "genteel" town well up the long Saint John River.*

3

1

2

1. Winter Scene in Fredericton.

2. Sir John Wentworth, Nova Scotian Governor. *Seen here in younger life, while he was previously Governor of New Hampshire, this notable New England Loyalist held office in Nova Scotia for over sixteen years.*

3. Government House in Halifax, 1819. *The handsome new home for Nova Scotia's governor, it says something about the affluence and power of this seacoast province's top leaders.*

4. Halifax from Georges Island. *Here in the long years of the French Revolutionary and Napoleonic Wars, Atlantic convoys were marshalled behind the protection of guns like these, to cross to Britain under Royal Navy escort.*

5. The Way Inland from Halifax. *An inn stands here beside Bedford Basin, on the path (between the stone walls) that finally leads across the neck of Nova Scotia.*

3

4

5

society of a considerably different outlook. That indeed was shown by the career of James Glenie in the province's Assembly from 1789 to 1803: a Scottish officer-settler (and lumberman) who led a popular coalition in the elected house that attacked the policies of the ruling oligarchy, and even withheld money votes from them through 1795-99. Still, the Glenie opposition largely turned on personalities, not party; and not till long afterward would the conservative political world of New Brunswick effectively be altered.

As for Nova Scotia politics, this older Maritime province at first reflected the problems of absorbing a large Loyalist element that threatened to swamp its existing pre-Loyalist population. To pre-Loyalist "native Nova Scotians" (so they would term themselves), the newcomers were "New York office-grabbers" who demanded only the best — as they scrambled to safety. To the Loyalists instead, the self-styled "native" inhabitants were little more than Yankees who had never faced or fought the American Revolution, yet still pretended to all the hard-earned benefits of British allegiance. Undoubtedly there was rivalry for jobs and positions, as well as mutual prejudice. But in many respects pre-Loyalists and Loyalists in Nova Scotia were much the same people, in their American seaboard origins, their life-styles and largely Protestant faiths, and in their common concerns with farming, fishing and shipping. In short, the two groups settled down quite readily together in society, and thus ultimately in politics besides. In the process, however, there were clashes between Loyalist opposition forces in the Nova Scotian Assembly and the pre-Loyalist old-guard in the Council — which indeed led to the Assembly securing the right to bring in money bills, and even to impeach Supreme Court judges for corruption and incompetence. Being a Loyalist did not mean you could not attack abusers of the King's law!

Nonetheless, reformism among Loyalists rather faded after one of their own became Governor of Nova Scotia in 1792: Sir John Wentworth, once a Governor of New Hampshire, who held his new place in Halifax on to 1808, when Sir George Prevost briefly succeeded him before the War of 1812. Wentworth was well practised in the art of patronage, and free-handedly put relatives and Loyalist friends into his Council or in other official posts. Yet this urbane and capable governor both kept control and his own popularity, despite renewed troubles with the Assembly from about 1802. William Cottnam Tonge, an English naval officer in charge of shipping regulations, had entered the elected house and there organized countryside support against Wentworth and the ruling Halifax group, the "Council of Twelve" (so-called), which sharply challenged their oligarchic power. In many respects the rural opposition front that Tonge built up was a classic case of "country" versus "town" interests. But it broke down when in 1807 Wentworth had its leader dismissed from his naval office and removed the country magistrates who had authorized local, pro-Tonge meetings. Moreover, Wentworth's own public hold, and the loyal conservatism of Nova

Pictou, Nova Scotia. *Around this centre, Scots Highlanders continued to settle in numbers, as they did elsewhere through other eastern areas of the province — thus at last giving an enduring Scottish content to Nova Scotia, the "New Scotland" which had once been granted to a Scots colonizer, Sir William Stirling, by James I in 1621.*

Scotia in the French Wars, allowed him to get away with such legal but overbearing acts. Oligarchy continued to run Nova Scotia, where political parties beyond mere town-versus-country factions would still take years to develop. In truth, a chastened but co-operative Assembly now built Wentworth a fine stone Government House, and voted a stately new Province House for the legislature as well.

Such sizeable expenditures as these at the capital marked the fact that wartimes were good times for Nova Scotia generally: in farming and fishing, in supplying the military, and in sending provisions, saltfish and lumber to British West Indies markets. Convoys massed at Halifax harbour for escort from its naval base to Europe; while Nova Scotian ships under British naval protection reached into Mediterranean trade. Without doubt there were still dangers of enemy attack; but in 1805 Britain's decisive sea-victory at Trafalgar off Spain shattered the main French fleet and its Spanish allies, rendering the high seas safe from all but scattered raiders. Meanwhile, too, Halifax defences had been much strengthened under Prince Edward, Duke of Kent, a younger soldier son of George III, and later the father of Queen Victoria. Formerly in charge of the Quebec garrison, Edward from 1794 was commander-in-chief for Nova Scotia and its Atlantic approaches. And there he worked vigorously (and lavishly) to build up Halifax, the imperial stronghold; in public edifices as well as in the armaments and the stone ramparts of a newly massive Halifax Citadel. He even introduced a semaphore telegraph system. In effect, Prince Edward ministered to the Halifax war boom, that continued long after his own departure in 1800. Assuredly, too, not just Halifax but all the province, enjoyed extensive ocean commerce behind the British naval shield.

At the same time, there was increasing settlement in Nova Scotia, largely composed of Scottish clansmen come from Argyll or Perth, Ross or Sutherland. They still found their way across the wartime Atlantic because of their desperate need to escape starvation-farming in the Highlands, where the thin land was inadequate for an expanding population, and big landlords were "clearing" their estates, replacing tenant crofters with more profitable sheep. The Highlanders, Gaelic-speaking Catholics and Protestants, came to Pictou and Antigonish, or opened farms on rugged Cape Breton Island, not unlike the Highlands in its own stark beauty. Even by 1803 there were probably up to 10,000 Scots in Nova Scotia and Cape Breton, while the island alone held some 6,000 by 1815. A high birthrate helped: Cape Breton might be a rigorous land of pioneer hardships, but for poor croft-tillers accustomed to still worse in their homeland it offered health, room and their own acres — a good recipe for natural increase. Moreover, returning Acadians also settled stretches on the western shores of Cape Breton, as well as establishing new fishing villages at empty harbours around the southern end of mainland Nova Scotia.

Scots and Acadians also went to St. John's Island, renamed Prince Edward Island in 1799, to honour royal Prince Edward, Duke of Kent. Yet despite good lands, fishing grounds and timber reserves, development there took place only slowly, since landholders on the island were not actual landowners, but still tenants of big absentee proprietors back in Britain. Thus in 1797, thirty years after this landlord system had begun, twenty-three township grants held not one occupant, and twelve others only thirty-six families in all. A few of the absentee owners did make more efforts to plant settlers; still, in 1798 there were just over

Prince Edward, and Prince Edward Island. *There was an obvious confusion of too many St. John's — the island, the river, and the cities — and so St. John's Island itself was renamed in honour of Prince Edward, Duke of Kent, in 1799, while he commanded British forces in America. He had, in truth, had considerable connections with British America apart from his busy years in strengthening Halifax: in going to Niagara to see Governor Simcoe in 1792, in establishing close relations with French Canadians during his own time at Quebec, or in serving on campaigns in the West Indies.*

4,000 people in a naturally well-endowed island. One proprietor who did work to establish settlement, however, was the Earl of Selkirk, a wealthy Scottish philanthropist deeply concerned with the fate of evicted crofters in his home country. In 1803 he thus brought 800 Highlanders out to his estate in Prince Edward Island — though at its little capital, Charlottetown, he found an idle governor and a "bad" Council, and everyone "asleep." Nevertheless, Selkirk's colony thrived, and Scottish numbers generally increased on the island — where the much less numerous Acadians also grew well established, notably around Rustico on its north shore.

The big Atlantic island, Newfoundland, grew still more strongly through the war years down to 1815. The quick capture in 1793 of France's fishing bases of St. Pierre and Miquelon, which then were held till peace returned, removed French competition from Newfoundland's basic industry. Moreover, continued decline in the seasonal English fishery (since war had again made it costly for the English fishing ships to cross to Newfoundland, and once more took their men into the Royal Navy) led to the final disappearance of that centuries-old visiting enterprise, quite soon after 1800. This further freed the resident fishermen of the island from competition, leaving them a virtual monopoly of high prices for their catch, even as they sent Newfoundland-built schooners loaded with salt cod to invade Mediterranean markets. As a consequence, more migrants came to settle in a booming Newfoundland, still chiefly drawn from Ireland despite the difficulties of wartime passage. By 1803 there were some 20,000 permanent residents on the island, 8,000 listed as Roman Catholics, 12,000 as Protestants. But in St. John's, where 3,500 of the population lived in a lively, rowdy, jumbled town, Catholics outnumbered Protestants two to one; for this was a chief place of landing, and so of gathering, for recent Irish immigrants. Since 1784, when Reverend James O'Donnell had arrived as Prefect Apostolic, under new arrangements for Catholic toleration in the island, Catholic congregations had grown steadily. But so had Protestant churches, especially Methodist, the first regular Methodist missionaries having arrived in 1785. Over all, with fishing exports soaring and sealing activities rising, with St. John's and outport merchants prosperous, while "men for the boats" were constantly in demand, a better-off society was losing its frontier roughness, spreading its churches or charitable agencies, and setting up new schools.

Yet Newfoundland, the fishing base, still was not a regular colony: having no full-time, civil governor, certainly no provincial legislature, or even full legal rights to private property in land. The last, at least, Dr. William Carson took up, a reform-seeking Scottish arrival of 1808. In 1811-13 he urged that "war gardens" around St. John's, patriotic attempts to raise island food, be legitimized as private property; and he won the concession of plots to individuals. There was a long distance to go. But Newfoundland by 1815 was on its way to recognized property law and provincehood at last.

1. Shipping in the Strait of Belle Isle off Newfoundland, 1810. *This strategic water-passage between the northwestern tip of the great island and the Labrador mainland has been important since early colonial days, for it funnelled seaborne traffic from the Gulf of St. Lawrence out to the North West Atlantic and Europe. Belle Isle was no less important here during the French Wars — where one can see British warships or cargo vessels and American fishing craft all congregating.*

2. The Island of Newfoundland, Map of 1790. *At the top of the map may been seen the just-noted "Straights of Bell Isle"; while at the lower opposite corner lies the most populated area — of course, the shores of the eastern Avalon Peninsula, where between Cape St. Francis and Cape Spear St. John's Harbour is located.*

1

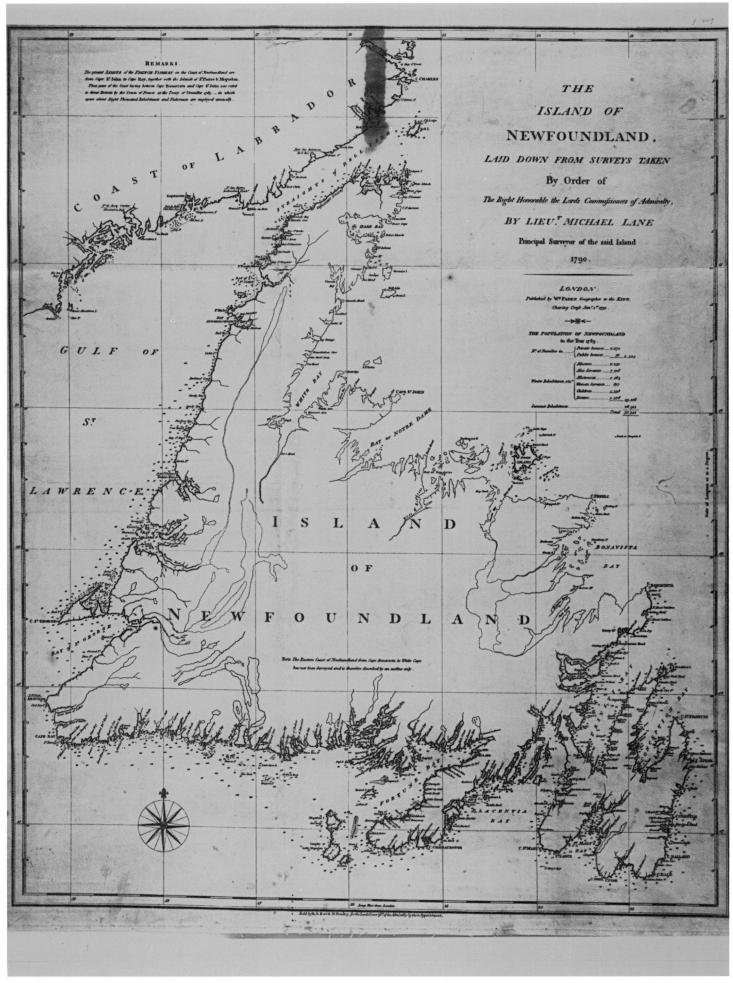

The War of 1812 with the United States

Stemming out of the French wars, new American-British troubles developed on the Atlantic, which actually brought further benefits to the trade of Newfoundland and its colonial neighbours. Napoleon's Berlin Decrees of 1806, blocking off British commerce with Europe, had been matched by Britain's Orders in Council that forbade trading with France and the French-dominated continent. Yet while Napoleon's blockade, for want of sea-power, was only effective in European ports, the Royal Navy enforced the British blockade on the high seas, searching and often seizing neutral ships judged to be blockade-runners — a right recognized in international law. Still, this forceful interference particularly affected the merchant fleet of the United States, which was by now becoming a major maritime nation.

The Americans, in response, passed embargo and non-intercourse acts in 1808-10, officially shutting down their own overseas commerce with the warring powers; though this largely amounted to punishing themselves, especially seafaring New England. But as New England craft lay idle in harbour, or sailed only in local traffic along American shores, so colonial vessels to northward moved in gladly to fill the gap; above all, by taking over more of the carrying trade to the West Indies from New England shipping. Newfoundland dry cod thus reached larger and further Caribbean markets. And a whole new trade emerged, whereby New England ships, illicitly but profitably, ferried goods up to Halifax, Shelburne and Saint John (declared "free ports" in 1808), goods which then were sent to the West Indies in colonial vessels that also took down fish and lumber. In return, they brought back sugar, molasses and rum, much of it to be forwarded them to New England, in a helpful trade that pleased nearly everybody concerned.

What was far less pleasing, however, was the British use of the right of

1. The Right of Search: *Leopard* vs *Chesapeake*, **1807.** *A portion of a letter printed in the* Upper Canada Gazette, *which reports on the clash that had occurred between a British warship, the* Leopard, *and the American* Chesapeake *on the Atlantic. The British vessel sought to exercise the right of search to look for deserters; the American refused. The* Leopard *then fired, killing six and wounding more aboard the United States frigate. This incident came close to bringing an angry American republic to declare war.*

2. Indian Resistance Against the United States. *In the interior, meanwhile, native tribes were suffering from constant inroads by Americans upon their lands. A tribal confederacy was formed to block this frontier grab, under a charismatic leader, the Prophet, and his brother, the Shawnee war-chief, Tecumseh.*

Extract of a letter from a gentleman on board his Majesty's ship Leopard, dated Chesapeak Bay, June 25, 1807.

"We arrived here on the 21ft inft. and, agreeably to the orders of the Hon. Vice Admiral Berkeley, (in the event of meeting the United States frigate Chesapeake, to search her for deserters, of whom we had information) the next morning, the fignal was made from the Bellona to proceed to fea, which we did at 9 o'clock this morning: the Chesapeake was then paffing the Bellona, about 3 miles within us—We ftood to the S. E. with a wind at S. W. until eleven, when it fhifted to E. which retarded the progrefs of the frigate, being obliged to beat—we kept on a wind under eafy fail, until fhe got within two miles of us, when fhe fhortened fail, and we bore down to her, we were about 13 or 14 miles from the land; when fufficiently clofe, the captain hailed, and faid he had difpatches from the Britifh commander in chief—the anfwer was, "fend them on board, I fhall heave too," which he did accordingly—I was fent on board with the Admiral's order, and a letter from captain Humphreys, faying, he hoped to be able to execute the Admiral's order in the moft amicable manner; and,

1   2

Main Events of the War of 1812

1812

June 18	United States declares war
July 16	British capture Michilimackinac
July 19	Americans defend Sackets Harbour, N.Y.
August 16	British capture Detroit
September 29	Americans raid Gananoque, U.C.
October 13	British win Battle of Queenston Heights, U.C.; Brock killed
November 9-10	Indecisive naval engagement off Kingston, U.C.

1813

January 22	British win Battle of Frenchtown, Michigan
February 7	Americans raid Brockville, U.C.
February 22	British attack Ogdensburg, N.Y.
April 27	Americans capture York, U.C., and withdraw
May 15	Yeo takes command of British naval forces on the Lakes
May 27	Americans capture Fort George, U.C.
May 29	British attack Sackets Harbor, and withdraw
June 1	H.M.S. *Shannon* captures U.S.S. *Chesapeake*
June 5-6	British win Battle of Stoney Creek, U.C.
June 24	British win Battle of Beaver Dams, U.C.
July 5	British raid Fort Schlosser, N.Y.
July 11	British raid Black Rock village, N.Y.
September 10	Americans win Battle of Lake Erie
September 27	Americans capture Amherstburg, U.C.
October 6	Americans win Battle of Moraviantown, U.C.; Tecumsah killed
October 26	British win Battle of Chateauguay, L.C.
November 11	British win Battle of Crysler's Farm, U.C.
December 10	Americans burn Newark and Queenston, U.C. while evacuating Fort George and leaving Canada
December 19	British capture Fort Niagara, N.Y.

1814

February 6	British raid Madrid, N.Y.
February 19-24	British raids on Salmon River, Malone, Four Corners, N.Y.
March 30	Americans occupy Odelltown, L.C.
May 6	British capture supplies at Oswego, N.Y.
May 15	Americans raid Long Point, U.C.
May 20-June 6	British blockade Sackets Harbor, N.Y.
May 30	British ambushed at Sandy Creek, N.Y.
July 3	Americans seize Fort Erie
July 5	Americans win Battle of Chippewa, U.C.
July 25	Battle of Lundy's Lane, U.C., Americans withdraw to Fort Erie
August 14	Americans capture British schooner *Nancy*, Lake Huron
August 15	British begin siege of American-held Fort Erie
August 24-25	British burn Washington, D.C.
September 3	British capture American schooner *Tigress*, Lake Huron British capture Castine, Maine
September 5	British capture American schooner *Scorpion*, Lake Huron
September 10	H.M.S. *St. Lawrence* launched at Kingston, U.C.
September 11	British defeated on Lake Champlain off Plattsburgh
September 12-15	British attack Baltimore, Maryland
October 1	Americans lift blockade of Kingston, U.C.
October 20	H.M.S. *St. Lawrence* lies off Niagara, U.C.
November 5	Americans blow up Fort Erie, and retire
December 24	Treaty of Ghent officially ends the war

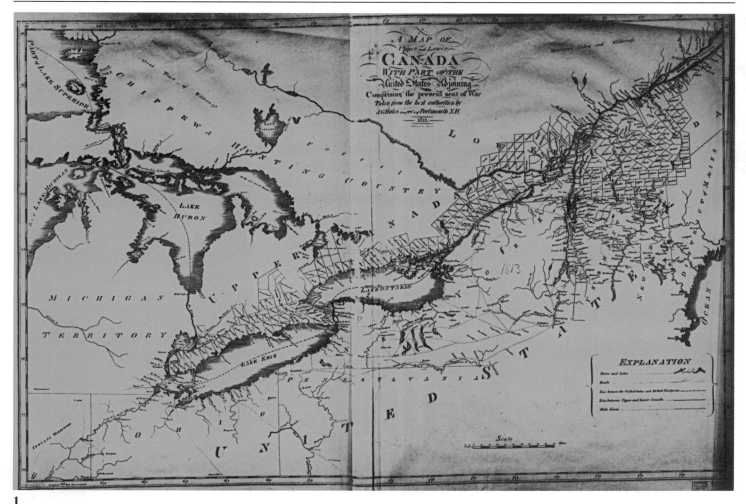

1

2

search to wrest deserters from the British Navy out of United States ships: men who had fled its old-style brutality, or had left for the better pay and opportunity of American merchant service, and by now might even claim United States citizenship. This high-handed British assault on young American national pride mattered in some ways more than the seizures of ships and cargoes. It put patriotic outrage behind American cries for "free trade and sailors' rights" — particularly after individual British and American warships had clashed in thundering combat over the right of search in 1807 and 1811.

In any event, along with these Atlantic troubles that pointed toward the War of 1812, still other strains had arisen in the western interior of the United States. Here there were Indian problems that seemingly involved British influence, and certainly involved the expansionist dreams of western American politicians. An advancing American frontier looked south to Spanish Florida or north to British Upper Canada, where so many Americans had recently been settling; realms that now seemed ripe for taking. And in the centre, land-hungry frontiersmen from Kentucky through Indiana and Michigan were pressing on the remaining native tribes — which brought on desperate armed resistance by an Indian confederacy organized under the pre-eminent Shawnee warrior, Tecumseh, and his visionary brother, the Prophet.

Late in 1811, near the native village of Tippecanoe south of Lake Michigan, the Indian confederates, however, were defeated by American military power. And this fight not only heightened the westerners' resolve to be rid of the Indian barrier, but also their desire to take Upper Canada from the British, viewed in American popular tradition and suspicion as the real force behind the natives' struggle for their own lands. Consequently, western politicians at Washington clamoured for war with Britain, convinced that an Upper Canada full of American settlers could be won easily, especially while British forces were so thoroughly engaged against Napoleon in Europe. In Congress, western expansionists who wanted support for seizing Florida in the south backed those who sought Canada in the north, and *vice versa*. Moreover, although New Englanders stayed largely opposed, sufficient votes were added from other eastern areas irate over the right of search, and ready to see Britain taught a lesson. And so, in June, 1812, Congress voted for war with Britain: well called by one American historian, "a western war for sailors' rights."

It mostly was a western war as far as British North America was concerned, fought largely in outstretched, exposed Upper Canada. Though Lower Canada also underwent attacks, its main St. Lawrence lifeline stayed firmly in British hands; and the eastern, Atlantic provinces were well within the grasp of Britain's sea-power, besides bordering on a New England eager for trade, yet far less eager for war. Upper Canada, however, lay across the open upper St. Lawrence and Great Lakes from much more populous American states. It held little more than one regiment of professional British soldiers when war began. Its own militia forces were small, untrained, and faced the question of whether the Post-Loyalist American settlers would serve at all, since so many of them simply expected an easy takeover from the United States — where one high government official thought it would be "a mere matter of marching." Nevertheless, to offset such ready assumptions, Upper Canada did have several not-so-secret weapons, beginning with the British regulars themselves.

Although only limited British reinforcements could be spared to Upper

1. The Main Battleground Area of Inland Canada, 1812-14. *It is worth noting how thin the belt of organized and settled districts still was by the wartime period, except in the Eastern Townships.*

2. Fort George, from American Fort Niagara. *Fort George had been established by Simcoe on the Canadian side of the Niagara River, when it became evident that the older Fort Niagara across the water would be given up to American control. Fort George was never that strongly placed; but it was a critical post at the entry from Lake Ontario to the river. And so it remained, throughout the War of 1812 on this major fighting frontier.*

1

1. General Isaac Brock. *An idealized picture: Brock did not take time to sit for his portrait. Yet, authentic or not, it suits descriptions of the imposing and inspiring young British General, only forty-two when he died at the Battle of Queenston Heights. Brock, a bold strategist, had risen fast in the French wars, came to Canada in 1802, and was made a major-general in 1811.*

2. The Capture of Michilimackinac, July, 1812. *A sudden attack by British soldiers and fur traders seized this formidable base on Lake Michigan, and thus brought the Indians of the Lakes region gladly to join the British against common American enemies.*

3. General Hull Considers Surrender at Detroit, August, 1812. *Brock's next move took him in person against Fort Detroit, with British regulars, provincial militia and Tecumseh's Indians, to stop an invading American army under General William Hull. Hemmed in by Indians, British cannonades and Brock's strong presence, Hull surrendered an army of some 2,500 to forces less than half the size.*

4. American Invasion over the Niagara at Queenston, October, 1812. *A rough contemporary sketch of American troops landing against British resistance — behind unreal stone walls.*

5. American Retreat from Queenston Heights. *Another composite, imagined view, showing American forces in full withdrawal from the combat still going on the Heights, as they seek safety back across the river. Brock was killed; but the battle was won.*

2

3

4

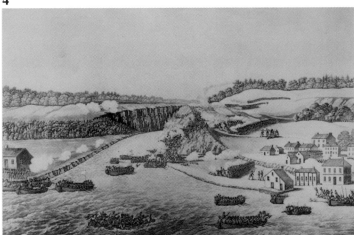

5

Canada till late in the War of 1812, well-trained regulars, skilled and confidently disciplined, could match much larger bodies of American militia, who were raw, loosely organized, and darkly anxious about Indians lurking in ambush. As for the Indians, they had good reason to ally with the British, once they saw that the King George men would fight. They proved invaluable within the forest wilds of Upper Canada, in maintaining or attacking lines of communication, in supplying intelligence on enemy movements, and generally, in spreading alarm and dismay among invaders who had long memories of Indian raids. And then there were the Loyalist, still strongly established in crucial border areas like the Upper St. Lawrence or Niagara peninsula — and grimly determined not to lose their new homes as they had lost their old. Yet beyond all these, there was General Isaac Brock himself: seasoned by the French wars, by service at Quebec from 1802, and in 1811 given command in Upper Canada. A daring but clear-sighted leader, inspiring in his tall, forceful presence, Brock organized Upper Canadian defences, then began the war with bold successes; and so put a very doubtful province on its path to survival and security.

Isaac Brock hit first when war was declared, by capturing Fort Michilimackinac at the top of Lake Michigan: once a French post, then a British, and now American. This sudden surprise blow brought Indians of the whole area to the British side, where Brock and Tecumseh, the Indian leader, worked in close trust. Next the British commander struck at the American troops who had invaded the southwestern tip of Upper Canada from Fort Detroit. He moved swiftly by lake with regulars and York militia to beseige that fort, even though his forces were much outnumbered. The Indians cut off the United States regulars and Michigan militia holed up at Detroit; Brock cannonaded from the river, then boldly demanded the Americans' surrender — whereupon an outbluffed and fearful General William Hull yielded his whole army. This Detroit victory greatly encouraged loyal Upper Canadians, and led uncertain American settlers to do their militia service lest they lose their land grants, since the British were plainly not going to collapse as expected.

Then Brock swung to meet another invading army, which crossed the Niagara River from the New York side near Queenston. Here in October, 1812, he was killed at the Battle of Queenston Heights, leading a typically bold charge up to high ground already held by some American troops. Yet British regulars and militia under General Roger Sheaffe (of Boston Loyalist background) soon hit the Americans from above, driving their whole force back to the river and disaster. And so if Isaac Brock's role was short, it was still decisive in preventing all-too-likely defeat at the outset, and in heartening Upper Canadians to fight. In fact, it helped instill a new Anglo-Canadian patriotism in defence of homeland, such as French Canadians already had long known. Furthermore, Post-Loyalist American settlers, too, could come to share that spirit. They had felt small quarrel with the British authority that had granted them farms, and many came to see the invading troops of the United States not as liberators (from what tyranny?) but as would-be occupiers, crop-looters and barn-burners, whom they must fight in order to protect their own homes built from wilderness.

The next year, 1813, saw further hardening of spirit, as conflict surged back and forth. After breaking through at Niagara, the Americans pushed up to Stoney Creek near present-day Hamilton. There, however, they were compellingly defeated in June, and sent back to the Niagara border once more. Meanwhile,

United States forces raided the capital at York by lake, briefly seizing that town, then leaving it with parliament and government buildings destroyed, along with lasting anti-American memories among its citizens. More widely significant, a United States naval victory on Lake Erie in September, 1813, opened the way for a drive by land into southwestern Upper Canada, bringing British defeat at the Battle of the Thames, where Tecumseh was killed. Nevertheless, this western defeat was offset in November at the eastern end of the province, where a more dangerous American attack across the upper St. Lawrence, which could have snapped the vital supply route from Lower Canada, was beaten at Crysler's Farm near Cornwall. The British units present, regulars and militia, also included *voltiguers*, well-drilled volunteer *Canadien* light infantry, who fought notably in both Canadas, and signified French Canada's own willing response to this war of defence against American aggression.

Voltiguers, moreover, had just played a valuable part at the Battle of Chateauguay in Lower Canada. Here another American army directed at Montreal was driven back at the Chateauguay River as it approached the St. Lawrence, by Canadian forces which comprised ordinary militia, French and English, as well as *voltiguers*. And this success was chiefly due to Colonel Charles de Salaberry, who had raised the *voltiguers*, a distinguished soldier of a leading French-Canadian family, who had already seen long service in Europe

Plan of the Fort at York, Seized in American Raid, April, 1813. *An American fleet laden with troops attacked this provincial capital across Lake Ontario, chiefly to destroy warships being built there. The fort fell to massive American assault, but looting and burning followed — to be recalled in British reprisals later on.*

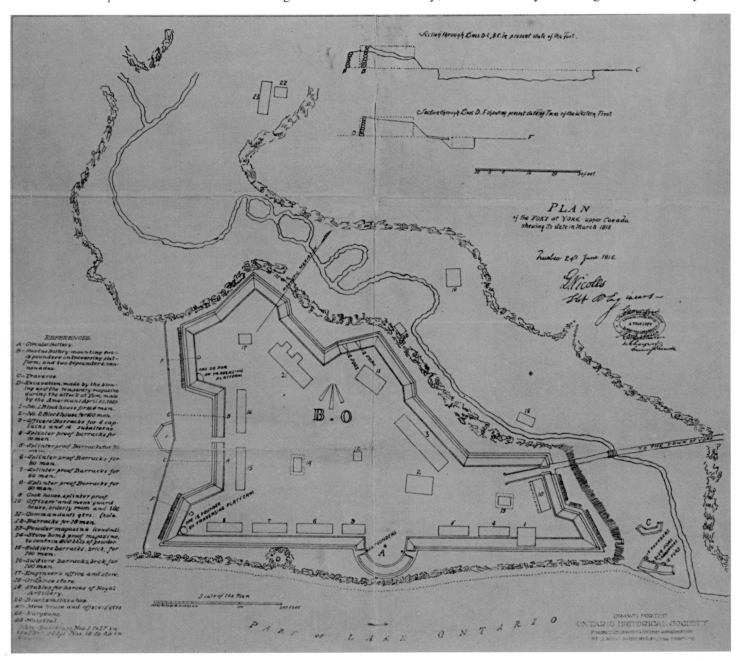

192

against Napoleon. In any event, the year ended with the American war still neither won nor lost. And thus it went on through 1814: with more raids by lake and river, another United States offensive into Lower Canada, checked firmly at Lacolle in March, and a British counter-offensive down to Lake Champlain, checked in turn at Plattsburgh in the fall. The struggle continued, too, in the Niagara border area, where the Battle of Lundy's Lane in June, 1814, was the heaviest and bloodiest of all the war, but ended without a clear decision.

The truth was that both sides were now pretty evenly matched — reinforced British regulars against disciplined American regulars, supported by well-experienced militia on either side. Yet both combatants were wearing down. The United States had wholly failed to take any part of Canada, had seen British naval and military forces occupy Castine in Maine in 1814, and then raid Washington. Britain itself, watching dangerous rifts appear in the European alliance that had finally overthrown Napoleon (while France looked hopefully for its Emperor's return), very much wanted to be freed from a draining, futile war in North America. Accordingly, on Christmas Eve, 1814, British and American envoys signed a treaty of peace at Ghent in Belgium; though the peace would not be known to icebound, warring Upper Canada till well into 1815. Incidentally in June of 1815, Napoleon, back from exile, met his final defeat at Waterloo. And so the long cycle of French wars came to an end at last, along with the American conflict.

The Treaty of Ghent did little more than restore the *status quo ante bellum*, to things as they were before the war. Neither Britain nor the United States made gains or concessions. Still, the treaty did lead to the Rush-Bagot Convention in 1817, limiting warships (and hence armed bases) on the Great Lakes; and also to the Convention of 1818 that ran the American-Canadian boundary out to the Rockies along the forty-ninth parallel. British North America had survived. But more, its existence had further won United States recognition, in a process that at long last — and certainly not in 1815 — eventually brought about a peaceful, undefended border between two great North American nation-states. This was heritage, too, in which the War of 1812 had played its own bloodstained part.

Tecumseh's Death at the Battle of the Thames, October, 1813. *Again the scene is imaginary, from an old American source. But in any case the loss of this outstanding native leader was a serious blow to resistance against United States assaults.*

1. The Battle of Chateauguay, Lower Canada, October, 1813. *Aside from the Battle of Stoney Creek, which stopped the deepest American penetration into Upper Canada near Hamilton that summer, Chateauguay was a valuable defence success in Lower Canada. For here, south of Montreal, a powerful United States advance was defeated by Canadian militia in a joint French-English stand against American invasion.*

2. Charles de Salaberry, Commander and Victor at Chateauguay. *Of seigneurial family at Beauport, he had joined the British Army in 1794 and risen in campaigns in Europe and Europe before the War of 1812.*

3. Lundy's Lane, Niagara Frontier, June, 1814. *The costliest, hardest-fought engagement in the war, between veteran forces on either side, it still saw the American attackers give up the field of battle near Niagara Falls.*

1

2

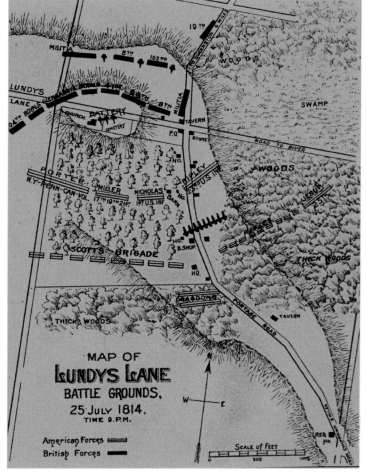

3

1

2

1. Plattsburgh, New York State, September, 1814. *This major contest grew from British counter-invasion, as the reinforced British turned to attack the United States, including a raid by sea on Washington itself. But the main British drives, as here at Plattsburgh, got nowhere: perhaps a good sign that neither side could really win on the other's territory — leading to a lasting peace at the end of 1814, signed at Ghent in Belgium.*

2. Proclamation of the Peace Treaty. *The Treaty of Ghent was simply not known in America when first concluded, given the slowness of transatlantic communications then. Hence this official announcement by Governor Sir George Prevost at Quebec is dated March 9, 1815.*

The World of the Western Fur Trade

Far beyond the developing colonies of eastern and central British North America, far from the impacts of European or American wars, the western half-continent might seem to be little changing into the early nineteenth century. And yet it was changing, as North West Company traders aggressively pushed onward, and as Hudson's Bay Company men offered increasing competition — which finally brought war, fur-trade war, to the West itself. The outcome saw the amalgamation of the two rival companies in 1821 under the Hudson's Bay Company name, and a single fur empire ruled by the new combined organization. All this greatly affected and moulded the emerging West. To tell that heritage story in these pages does require going a few years past 1815. Still the West has often had its own time-frame, which here best takes us to the fur companies' union in 1821.

To begin with the 1790s, an enlarged North West Company centred in Montreal had grown so successfully that by 1795 it controlled two-thirds of the Canadian fur trade, bringing out some 20,000 beaver pelts a year. It spread posts from the Assiniboine to the foothills of the Rockies, to Fort Augustus where Edmonton now stands and to Fort Chipewyan on Lake Athabaska, a new base for the valuable Athabaska trade. It maintained a widely organized system of canoe brigades (fed on pemmican, dried buffalo meat from the plains) which took goods and supplies out to the western posts and brought back their furs. And the Nor'Westers were both more adaptable and enterprising than their Hudson's Bay rivals, for unlike the more rigid older Company, their traders in the interior were not wage-paid "servants," but "wintering partners," who shared in the profits distributed annually. They had good reason to go on expanding trade into rich new country, as long as there was good beaver country left to tap.

Continual expansion, however, meant ever-lengthening canoe routes, and ever-mounting costs of transportation. Increasingly it took first-grade furs skimmed from new territory to meet the heavy transport burden; so that need as well as greed drove Nor'Westers on to fresh resources. But one who sought to do something about transport burdens was Alexander Mackenzie, a wintering partner at Fort Chippewyan. He had heard stories of a great river flowing out to the Pacific, and determined to find it: for then the inland North West posts might be supplied much more cheaply from the western ocean than by costly overland hauls from the east. Accordingly, in 1789, this young Scot set out from Lake Athabaska and reached the great Mackenzie River that ran northward, and which ultimately took him and his party of Indians and *voyageurs* to the Arctic Ocean. Mackenzie actually called this giant stream the River Disappointment, when he realized it ran to chill Arctic saltwater. Yet he had opened a far more practicable route to the northern ocean than Samuel Hearne had earlier done across the Barren Lands: a broad waterway in the long run suitable for bulk traffic to Arctic ports, through a vast wooded valley of high future importance. Mackenzie, in any case, just went on trying. In 1793 he turned westward from Lake Athabaska to

1. Alexander Mackenzie, Who Reached the Arctic and Pacific. *Scottish born, this North West wintering partner in charge of Fort Chipewyan was still in his twenties when he made his way by the Mackenzie River to Arctic shores in 1789, and then crossed the mountains westward to the Pacific coast in 1793. Knighted in 1802 for his discoveries, he remained a major figure in the fur trade till he retired to Scotland in 1808.*

2. Fort Chipewyan, Lake Athabaska. *The important post in the Athabaska country, from which Nor'Westers would thrust to the Arctic and Pacific Oceans.*

3. A West Coast Indian House at Nootka Sound. *Engraved for a 1784 collection of* Voyages Round the World ... of Captain Cook.

1

2

3

the mountain-piercing Peace River, crossed from it to an unknown upper Fraser, and beyond that struck overland by Indian trails through lofty ranges — to come out on the Pacific at Bella Coola inlet: the first European to cross to the West Coast. He and his party here left a concise message painted on a rock in vermilion and melted grease: "Alex. MacKenzie from Canada by land, 22nd July 1793."

Thus, with Mackenzie the drive of the Canadian fur trade spanned the continent; twelve years before the Lewis and Clark expedition from the United States reached the Pacific further south, at the mouth of the Columbia. Yet maritime explorers were already sounding the North Pacific coasts when Mackenzie reached there. In fact, at Bella Coola he just missed a naval expedition headed by Captain George Vancouver of the British Navy. Vancouver was then charting the coastal waters; following on from his old commander, Captain James Cook: the grand explorer of the Pacific from New Zealand and Australia to Hawaii and Alaska, who had landed at Nootka Sound on Vancouver Island in 1778. Moreover, Spanish navigators, working north from Spain's Mexican empire, were also examining what was to be the British Columbia shoreline; until Nootka Sound became the focus of a diplomatic clash between Britain and Spain from 1789 to 1795. Still, in the end British ships won

Map of "Mackenzie's Track." *This map published in London in 1801 has been slightly trimmed for space here, to concentrate it more on northern and western British America as then known.*
Overleaf. Mackenzie Running Rapids in the Western Mountains. *A striking painting by A.H. Heming of Mackenzie's epic journey to the Pacific.*

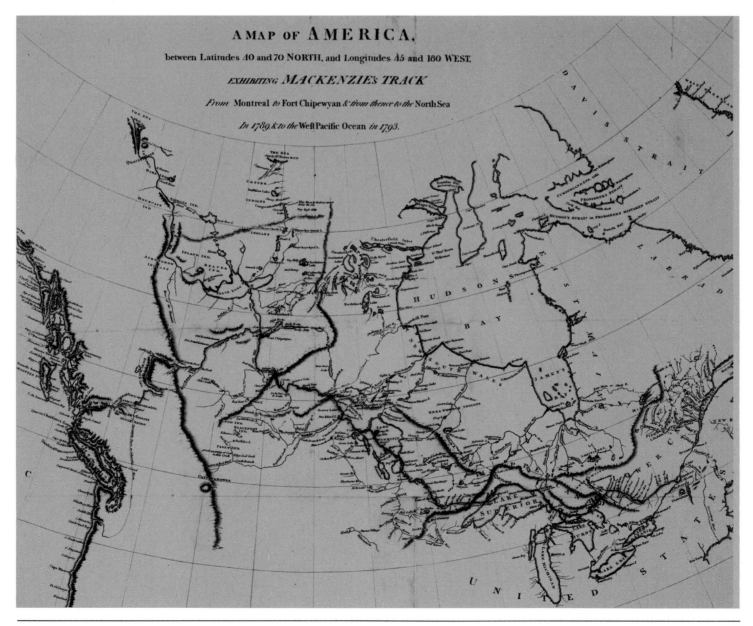

ascendancy in these waters, coming there to trade at Indian shore villages for luxuriant sea-otter pelts that could be sold in China at high prices — a trade, however, in which American vessels soon gave more serious competition.

In any event, North West Company venturers advanced their own fur trade on into the Pacific West, opening better routes across the mountains than Mackenzie's original passage. Outstanding among these pathfinders, who came not just for commerce but to find what lay behind each beckoning range, were Simon Fraser of Loyalist stock, a Company partner in charge of operations beyond the Rockies from 1805, and London-born David Thompson, initially a poor Hudson's Bay apprentice who had transferred to the North West Company as a winterer in 1797, and then spent till 1812 on the plains and Pacific slopes. Simon Fraser in 1808 travelled the river that bears his name to its Pacific outlet, down towering canyons and past the swirling rapids of its own "Hellsgate." And in so doing, Fraser uncovered the great valley carved through mountains which would one day carry transcontinental rails and highways to the metropolis of Vancouver set on magnificent Burrard Inlet — already probed by George Vancouver during his own coastal explorations. As for David Thompson, that eminent map-maker as well as explorer set out in 1806 from Rocky Mountain House, near the head of the North Saskatchewan, to open trade with Indians beyond the Rockies by pack team and canoe. The next few years he spent exploring the Upper Columbia River region, building the first post on that river, Kootenay House, in 1807, and rounding the Great Bend of the Columbia thereafter. In 1811 Thompson followed this waterway to the sea, only to find an American trading base, Astoria, already established at its mouth. And so the

1. Hellsgate, Where Fraser's Party Had to Scramble Along Canyon Walls. *This is a very early photograph, well after Simon Fraser's own day; but it does show the rock-masses and grimly narrow cleft before a road was carved through. It also reveals Indian fishing activities where the salmon crowded into the river gap — including gutted fish set on poles to dry.*

2. The Sea-Otter. *A 1778 painting of the glossy-coated animal that did much to open a Pacific Coast fur trade — for trans-Pacific markets, in fact.*

3. David Thompson, Fur Trader, Geographer, Cartographer. *He is seen surveying, amid vast territories he explored and mapped. The first white man to traverse the whole length of the Columbia River to the ocean, Thompson was also the first to produce a comprehensive map of the western lands that were to become part of Canada.*

1

2

3

Columbia was not to become a Canadian through-route to the Pacific. Yet for many years it carried North West and (later) Bay Company traffic — while the very name "British Columbia" recalls the vast Columbia River inlands that David Thompson first opened.

Meanwhile, through plains and forests stretching back to Upper Canada, the Nor'Westers held dominance: even though lands eastward from the Rockies that were drained by the Saskatchewan into Hudson Bay officially and legally formed part of Ruperts Land, owned by the Bay Company under its Charter of 1670. The Athabaska country and other areas that drained north into the Arctic were not actually within the "English Company's" title; but in any case, title meant little in the wilds, where the Nor'Westers set posts and garnered trade with scant concern about any charges of trespass — quite unenforceable. Their fur cargos flowed back each summer to the Company's interior headquarters at Fort William. Here the wintering partners came down with their canoe brigades in swift *canots du nord*, to meet the Montreal partners and their bigger *canots du maitre* which carried up supplies and could brave Great Lakes storms. Here indeed, Fort William became one of the largest urban places in early Upper Canada when the summer meetings were held; when the *hommes du nord* and the *mangeurs du lard* (the eastern voyageurs who ate salt pork, not pemmican) joined in happy festivities and fights. At the same time, chief Montreal leaders like William McGillivray — who took over from his uncle, "Marquis" Simon McTavish, when the latter died in 1804 — went over the costs and profits with the winterers, and briskly discussed plans for the year ahead. It was anything but a dull session of directors droning over statements!

But as the North West regime continued, so did challenges from its Hudson's Bay opponents. They set up close, competing posts, Brandon House near Fort Assiniboine, Fort Edmonton by Fort Augustus, and many others. They used the efficient York boat to meet their own lack of canoe transport: a roomy, rowed craft that could carry sails, which did well on western rivers. They also made good use of their sea access to the Plains via Hudson Bay — still a much cheaper way west than the Nor'Westers' overland route. And the Bay Company employed its own solid capital reserves, as an old incorporated body, to outlast and outdo the shifting North West partnerships, even buying over the expert services of disgruntled Nor'Westers like Colin Robertson, a capable veteran of the interior.

The critical contest of the fur companies, however, only came to a head after Lord Selkirk (philanthropic, wealthy founder of settlements both in Prince Edward Island and at Baldoon in Upper Canada) bought financial control of the Hudson's Bay Company in 1810, in order to found a new colony within its territory of Rupert's Land. There he obtained a forty-five-million acre grant from the Company in the Red River valley, on fertile prairie accessible by lake and river from Hudson Bay. In 1812, the first group of some ninety poor, dispossessed Scots arrived to open farms on what would be Manitoba prairie, just north of present Winnipeg; and in following years more colonists, including some Irish, were sent out; in all numbering a few hundred by 1816. Yet troubles with Nor'Westers in the area soon developed, even though at first they charitably helped the unprepared settlers. For if the Selkirk colony, in the Bay Company's opinion, represented a living enforcement of its ownership rights on the plains, from the North West Company's viewpoint, this new settlement lay across the

Colin Robertson, Fur-War Figure.
This Scottish Nor'Wester changed over to the Hudson's Bay Company in 1814, to become its chief officer in the Athabaska country. He was an effective agent in the Bay Company's counter-drive against their North West foes, and ultimately became an H.B.C. chief factor, retiring on pension in 1840.

1. Early Settlers Arrive at Red River, 1812. *Seen here in a brief ceremony before the first governor of the colony, Miles Macdonell.*

2. Fort Edmonton on the Plains. *Set at the top of the steep bank of the North Saskatchewan River, where a city would rise in later ages, this is the post as rebuilt and occupied by the Hudson's Bay Company, after Indians had destroyed both its H.B.C. predecessor and the rival N.W. Fort Augustus in 1807-10, during the violence too often promoted by bitter fur-company competition. The fort shown here, with windmill beyond, was demolished in 1915 when Alberta's Provincial Parliament Buildings were erected on its grounds. But it was subsequently reconstructed down in the valley (where the Fort had also once been); and there it remains a popular heritage site today.*

3. The Earl of Selkirk, Philanthropist and Western Colonizer. *More influential, still, in the H.B.C. counter-offensive, was the wealthy Scottish Lord Selkirk, who had already established settlements of evicted poor Highlanders both in Prince Edward Island and at Baldoon in southwestern Upper Canada. Turning to a still larger project, however, to settle impoverished Scots on fertile Western plains, the Earl bought control of the Bay Company in 1810; and thus obtained a large grant within its realm of Ruperts Land, in the Red River Valley. Here in 1812 the first party of Selkirk Colonists arrived via Hudson Bay, to farm in what would be Manitoba. And more settlers followed later to the Red River near its prairie junction with the Assiniboine, where the city of Winnipeg would ultimately emerge.*

vital route from Canada northward into the rich Athabaska fur realm that lay beyond Bay Company territory. It thus implied a dangerous threat to cut off Nor'Westers' trade: a threat which very soon looked real, when because of food shortages in the struggling Red River colony, its governor, Miles Macdonnell from Glengarry, Upper Canada, put an embargo on the export of pemmican from the area. That seemed a flagrant blow at North West Company provisioning, and led to Nor'Westers seizing Macdonnell, driving the colonists away, then burning their settlement.

But this was not all. Though some colonists came back and more arrived, a fiercer attack took place in 1816. This armed assault by Nor'Westers and Métis, the offspring of French traders and local Indian peoples, resulted in the so-called Massacre of Seven Oaks, wherein twenty settlers and their new governor, Robert Semple, were killed in a prairie skirmish. And that in turn brought no less violent response. Selkirk came out to Canada to restore his own colony, equipping himself with magistrate's power in Upper Canada, and with the De Meuron regiment of disbanded soldiers who had fought in the War of 1812. With the De Meurons, he swept powerfully up to Fort William in the summer of 1817, took over the fort, arrested leading North West officers for trial back east, and went on

1

2

3

to the Red River — where Colin Robertson and his own Bay Company men were already securing control. At any rate, Selkirk did ensure that the Red River Colony was enduringly re-established as a pioneer settlement on the plains: quietly living from its crop fields, receiving both Catholic and Anglican missionaries, and generally providing a permanent little core for farming growth within the huge, untilled British North American West.

Nevertheless, the still powerful North West Company hit back at Selkirk for grossly exceeding his limited magistrate's authority at Fort William and in the West. A lengthy series of lawsuits followed which exhausted much of the Earl's fortune and — more — the strength of a sick man ridden with tuberculosis, Selkirk died in 1820, utterly exhausted. But the fur-trade war of North West and Hudson's Bay Companies had come down to near-exhaustion also. There had been fierce ambushes, rival seizures of cargoes. Colin Robertson, the designer of Bay counter-moves, had been arrested by the North West Company. And over all, both sides had lost considerably. Still, the Nor'Westers could not overcome the Bay's advantage of a short sea route to the West, while their own morale had been eroded through years of rising costs and falling profits. Thus by 1821, even William McGillivray, prime Nor'West leader, was ready at last to meet terms — for all his own desires to keep going.

That year, a settlement was reached through the British government, which had faced powerful lobbying from either side. A renewed, combined Hudson's Bay Company took over, holding a fur-trade monopoly, though with McGillivray, his chief associates and Nor'West wintering partners sharing in the amalgamated enterprise. This new monopoly would not only keep charter rights to Ruperts Land, but would also hold control, by licence, to the Arctic West beyond, and to the transmontane West out to the Pacific. And so, by 1821, the West of British North America had been reshaped under this broader Hudson's Bay Company, in a form mainly to last until Confederation. Here was yet another heritage: sprung from the age of western fur-trade giants and bequeathing the first western farm settlement, on the plains of Manitoba.

1. Robert Semple, Governor of the Red River Colony. *Killed at Seven Oaks in the attack of Nor'Westers and Métis on Selkirk colonists, 1816.*

2. Settlers at Red River by Early 1820s. *This sketch by Peter Rindisbacher expresses the multicultural variety of residents in this first Plains western colony, even at the start of settled life. From right to left they are: a Swiss immigrant wife, husband and two children; a German, from the disbanded De Meuron mercenary regiment brought in by Selkirk; a Scots Highlander, seated, and a "French Canadian" — or a Métis? — standing by his side.*

3. William McGillivray, Top Nor'Wester. *The Scots-born nephew of Simon McTavish, who had led the North West Company, McGillivray rose in company service to become chief director after his uncle McTavish died in 1804. In the War of 1812 he commanded voyageurs under Brock at Detroit, and was appointed to the Legislative Council of Lower Canada. But his efforts against Lord Selkirk's Red River Colony led to the Earl arresting him by force at Fort William in 1816. Thereafter, McGillivray worked to negotiate a union between the North West and Hudson's Bay Companies, both hard hit by their strife. When amalgamation was finally achieved in 1821 and enacted by the British parliament, he sat on the new joint Company board; but died in 1825 in London.*

4. The Governor at Red River with his Family, c. 1823. *This scene by Rindisbacher, of driving by sleigh along the Red, probably shows the original log-built Upper Fort Garry in the background. Established in 1822, this key post was so damaged by river floods in 1826 that it was thereafter replaced with a stone structure (constructed by 1835), around which the town of Winnipeg would later arise.*

1

2

3

4

Joseph of Gaspee

1816	Provisions for "common" schools in U.C.
1817	Rush-Bagot Convention between Britain and United States
1818	American-Canadian boundary convention
	15,000 British immigrate to British North America (B.N.A.)
	Dalhousie University founded at Halifax, N.S.
1820s	Scottish, Irish and English immigration to N.S.
1820	Cape Breton Island re-attached to N.S.
1821	Amalgamation of North West and Hudson's Bay Companies into a new Hudson's Bay Company
1823	Irish settle at Peterborough, U.C.
	Capt. Edward Parry, searches for North West Passage
1824	Canada Company chartered in U.C.
	William Lyon Mackenzie founds *Colonial Advocate at Queenston*
1825	Sir Thomas Cochrane is Nfld.'s first resident civil governor
1827	University of King's College, U.C. chartered
	Capt. John Franklin explores along north Alaskan coasts
1828	King's College founded at Fredericton, New Brunswick
1829	Mackenzie first elected to U.C. Assembly
	McGill University opens at Montreal, L.C.
1831	John Ross locates North Magnetic Pole
1832	66,000 immigrate to B.N.A. from Britain
	Representative government established in Nfld.
	Rideau Canal opens
1834	York, U.C. renamed Toronto
	L.C. Assembly passes "Ninety-Two" Resolutions

Chapter Six
Immigration, Colonial Growth and Strife
1815 - 1841

British Settlement and Economic Advance

While the West was still caught up in fur-trade rivalries, eastern British North America had entered a new era in 1815, with the ending of the Napoleonic and American wars. It was an era to be marked by surging British immigration, commercial and agricultural expansion and political strife, as rising reform movements came up against entrenched colonial elites. Moreover, all three factors, British settlement, economic advance and the clash of Reform and Tory elements, were decidedly interlinked. That remains to be shown; but we can start with the mounting tide of migrants from England, Ireland, Scotland and Wales.

In 1815, the barriers to large-scale movement overseas were lifted from a fast-multiplying British population, pent up during long years of war. Transatlantic passages became much more accessible. Their costs fell sharply, for there was now a surplus of ocean shipping, and high wartime insurance rates had disappeared. Furthermore, pushes to emigrate rose powerfully at the same time. There was wide post-war depression as the British economy went through drastic readjustments, while thousands of discharged soldiers were flung into the labour market. And depression was made yet worse by the effects of Britain's ongoing Industrial Revolution. The industrialism of steam and iron machinery had helped defeat Napoleon; but it had also struck hard at traditional cottage handcrafts in Britain, disrupted whole districts and communities, and produced ill-built, crowded factory towns that were hives of misery and disease. Furthermore, unbridled industrial capitalism fostered hectic boom-and-bust cycles, of flush times followed by bleak years, which brought down merchant and farmer alike, and spread unemployment, poverty and hardship among both old-style rural workers and new-style factory hands. Here, then, were compelling drives that sent migrants out to Britain's transatlantic holdings. They were drawn there, as well, by the colonies' demands for workers and their broad lands available; by prospects of new jobs, farms and security, or by dreams of opportunity and a bright future, especially for the children. Such drives and draws are classic in the history of emigrations. And in this movement from Great Britain, they brought around a million people across to British North America between 1815 and the mid-1850s, when the outflow finally subsided from a more securely adjusted and prospering British homeland.

The numbers who thus entered Canada-to-be are not to be measured in terms of our own day, but in those of the much smaller colonial societies of an earlier age. There were only some half a million settled residents in all British North America when this "Great Migration" began. It started in trickles; less than 700 in 1815, though that was not fully a peace-year. It swelled to 15,000 by 1818; then on to 66,000 in 1832 and 109,000 in 1849; sweeping floods for the

Overleaf. Quebec Port, Where Lumber Ships and Immigrants Arrived. *The scene, painted in 1830, lasted on for years as British settlers disembarked from ocean vessels to take river transport onward.*

2. The Emigrants' Welcome to Canada. *This cartoon of 1820 by famed British caricaturist, George Cruikshank, illustrates several things: the awareness in Britain of growing migration out to the Canadian colonies after the Napoleonic Wars; a widespread view, no less, that Canada still was cold and hard; and a sharp parody of the popular "Emigrants Guides" of the day, which not only offered practical advice, but dealt brightly with land tracts, homes and prosperity for the newcomers. Here Jack Frost (who has his snowshoes on backwards) greets a hopeful British settler, duly supplied with silk stockings, dancing pumps and other essentials.*

provinces of the time. As a result, the much older French-Canadian community was placed decisively in a minority. Existing Anglophone inhabitants, moreover, who were largely of North American backgrounds — whether pre-Loyalist, Loyalist or post-Loyalist — were increasingly outweighed by new immigrants from Britain. Hence Canadian society in general became more fully and directly "British" than it had ever been before. Furthermore, that change went on during the very period when the colonies moved towards self-government and then union, on British lines indeed. It may be easy to overdo the British heritage that came with the immigrant waves of the earlier nineteenth century. But it would be thoroughly wrong to underrate it.

"Assisted" immigrants played a considerable part in the earlier years of this transatlantic outflow; for example, those groups brought in by charitable projects such as Lord Selkirk's at Red River, the disbanded soldiers and poor Scots who were sent with government backing to the Perth Settlement in eastern Upper Canada in 1816-17, the needy Irish set down near Peterborough in that province after 1823, or the English rural paupers located in western Upper Canada beyond London in 1832, to get them off parish relief-rolls at home. But increasingly, non-assisted, private efforts took over, as individuals (and their families) scrimped and saved to raise the money for passage and settlers' supplies. Often men would come first, and work as labourers, farm hands or lumbermen in order to earn enough to bring out their wives and children. Women came tending the family young and the old; though some came singly as house or farm servants. The cheapest passages were in timber ships returning empty to Quebec or Saint John for more wood cargoes. Crowded in their dark and soggy holds, on rough tiers of bunks put up for the long, slow voyage, many would-be immigrants went through ordeals for sheer survival; and some of them, among the elderly and the children in particular, did not survive at all.

Not everyone who made the crossing under sail did so in this hardest way — even if the faster, easier voyages of those who could afford them would still have looked grim enough to later travellers, journeying by steamship or even ultimately by air. But along with impoverished crofters, handloom weavers or hard-pressed factory workers in this Great Migration of the earlier nineteenth

1. Clearing a Town Plot, 1834. *For a settlement at Stanley, New Brunswick, north of Fredericton in the woods.*
2. Steamboats at Pointe de Lévy Opposite Quebec, 1828. *Here river steamers waited to carry migrants further inland, toward settlement districts in both Lower and Upper Canadas.*
3. Lachine in 1826. *This village, once at the very edge of settlement in New France, was now a passing sight for immigrants proceeding above Montreal — perhaps in a steamer such as appears here in front of Lachine itself. Across from it, to the right, lies the historic Iroquois reserve of the Caughnawaga or Kahnawake Mohawks.*

1

2

3

1

2

3

4

1. Peterborough Settlement in Upper Canada, c. 1827. *This Irish immigrant community northeastward from York was named for its founder Peter Robinson, who subsequently became Crown Lands Commissioner for the province.*

2. Anglican St. Thomas, St. John's, Newfoundland. *This, the old Garrison Church — the oldest existing church on the island — originated in 1699, but was later destroyed by the French. The building shown here did not go up till the 1830s, to be finally completed in the early forties.*

3. Charlottetown by the 1840s. *Beyond the market place, the new Province House appears — where in 1864 the Charlottetown Conference of delegates from the varied British American colonies would decide to proceed with planning Confederation, a federal union of the provinces.*

4. Downtown King Street, Saint John, 1837. *The St. John Hotel stands at the left, in the city centre.*

5. The Mill Erected at Stanley, 1835.

6. Notre Dame Street, Montreal. *Another main downtown thoroughfare, it displays the tower of new Notre Dame Church (to the left down the way) and the monument to Britain's Lord Nelson and his naval victories against France, put up by a loyal Anglo-merchant population in the city.*

5

6

century there also came solid farmers after fresh, and fertile acres of their own, skilled artisans wanting to better their earnings, and aspiring merchants looking to new business ventures. As well, there were middle-class professionals, lawyers, doctors, teachers and journalists; plus a scattering of upper-class gentry hoping to build more rewarding estates, or half-pay officers, retired after years of war service, who sought to make their limited incomes go further in a new land. In sum, here was a cross-section of contemporary British society.

Of all these varied immigrants, the fewest came from Wales, the smallest national community in the United Kingdom, though with a language and proud culture of its own. The largest and most thickly populated realm, England, sent substantial numbers throughout, on every level, but still ranked second to Ireland. For while Ireland, too, was populous, it was also far worse off: a country bound up in big landed estates and meagre tenant-plots, from which the Irish poor had long sought escape by emigration, even during the French wars. Consequently, after 1815, the largest continuing transatlantic streams of settlers usually flowed from Ireland, both from its heavily Catholic, farming south and from its strongly Protestant northern province of Ulster, where the weavers, artisans and citizens of business towns like Belfast had suffered through stern industrial depressions. Northern Irish Ulstermen, moreover, were staunch defenders of Protestant faith and the British Crown, as seen in the popular Orange Societies they brought with them. The Southern Irish were equally devoted Roman Catholics, and as well kept feelings for an Irish nationalism that had long fought against the British tie. And so the ethnic contests of Orange and Green would be transferred into Canada. As for the Scots, whose rugged northern country contained considerably fewer inhabitants than either England or Ireland, they perhaps made up for quantity by quality. At any rate, whether Catholic Highlanders or Presbyterian Lowlanders, Scots set their own strong mark on English-speaking Canada; assuredly in business or political circles, and often helped by their kin loyalties and excellent Scottish schooling. The Scottish heritage stays powerful in Anglo-Canada still: although a popular notion that this indeed was "a Scotch country" can also be overdone and unhistorical, especially in view of major Irish and English contributions.

The largest number of British migrants went to Upper Canada, which in the provinces of the day had the broadest frontiers of fertile land still to be occupied. Yet other colonies gained many also. In Newfoundland, some incoming Scots settled on its southwestern coast off Nova Scotia, while many more Irish and English entered to the east. The Irish particularly arrived in major waves from 1825 to 1833, after which their influx to this rugged isle rapidly declined. The English came there in lesser flows, but continued on much longer. As a result, Newfoundland kept a small if lasting Protestant majority (such things mattered

St. James Street, Montreal, 1830.
The scale of this chief financial street in the then-largest Canadian city seems evident, even in its winter quiet (probably on Sunday).

deeply in society and politics then), although the Irish Catholics held an emphatic local majority along the eastern Avalon peninsula and in the capital, St. John's. The big island, however, scarcely had frontiers to settle in a harsh interior of rocky uplands and swampy woods. Newfoundland's real frontiers lay in the open surrounding seas; so that population growth and expanding trade activities essentially stayed along its rim of fishing outports and shore towns. Similarly, Nova Scotia's own inland country was often difficult and rugged, without great river highways or rich new Annapolis valleys. More Highland Scots, largely Catholic, came to Cape Breton in the 1820s; more Presbyterian Scots to the flourishing Pictou area; and some Irish and English to Halifax and other older districts. But generally, the stage of pioneering settlement reached its end in Nova Scotia of the 1830s, with few new frontiers then left to occupy.

Prince Edward Island was different — small and mostly fertile. Here more than 10,000 West Country English, from Devon and Cornwall, settled after 1817, taking to the timber trade and sizeable shipbuilding. Effectively, they cleared the island for more farms, although its burden of absentee landlords still slowed farming occupation. There was yet another story in mainland New Brunswick, where the timber trade and British settlement were also closely related, but in a much larger territory. Indeed, that colony's great inland forests, reaching into the Appalachians, were of prime importance in its economic advances after 1815, since most of those areas more suited to agriculture had already been occupied: by the farms of Loyalist descendants beside the Fundy coast or in the Valley of the Saint John; by Acadian village settlements north from the Chignecto along the Gulf of St. Lawrence shore. But timber ships landed regular cargoes of British immigrants (largely Irish, both Catholic and Protestant) at Saint John or at Gulf-shore harbours, from where they widely moved on inward to the lumber

1. Sherbrooke, Lower Canada. *A centre for the settlement operations of the British American Land Company, the village seen here in the opening forties would grow largely as a textile town, soon boasting Canada's first cotton factory.*

2. Timber Coves at Quebec. *Where the lumber ships came and loaded; and where arriving Irish would often stay to work.*

3. Outside London, Upper Canada. *The village is in the far background — a town by 1847 — while nearer at hand, two Indians return from a hunt and a big old tree is being felled.*

1

2

3

camps. They also cleared bush farms or became farmer-lumberers — working at the camps in winter, on their fields in summer — while still others remained in the ports as labourers and shipyard hands. Less Scots and English arrived in New Brunswick; yet more often they were to rise as skilled shipwrights, timber bosses or merchants. At the top of provincial society, however, thriving on a forest trade that was protected by the continuing British timber preference (and was largely based on British immigrant labour), were the timber merchants and chief shippers or shipbuilders: less Loyalist gentlemen, now, than hard-headed business enterprisers.

Lower Canada presented a picture both similar and different. Even more timber shipping (and immigrants) travelled up the St. Lawrence water route to Quebec: which was British North America's leading timber port and by far its prime landing-place for overseas arrivals, right from 1815 into the 1850s. Most of the arrivals there continued on by river to Upper Canada. Yet some migrants instead stayed in the lower province, much increasing the dock and shipyard hands at Quebec or the unskilled labourers and building workers in a fast-expanding Montreal: Catholic Irish especially, for English and Scots more notably took up new farms in the Eastern Townships. Here the British American Land Company, chartered in 1834, bought some 850,000 acres to sell to the settlers; though most of its sales occurred from the forties into the fifties, in the process, building up a major Townships centre, the town of Sherbrooke. And English-speaking traders, manufacturers, professionals and monied men were also added to the dominant Anglophone elite of Montreal and Quebec; while in particular, the largely Scottish business magnates of Montreal maintained and enlarged their power.

Nevertheless, Upper Canada was unquestionably the most affected by the British settlers who poured in yearly. Thanks to this immigration, plus natural

1. Main Thoroughfare in Kingston, 1829, *looking down to the Barracks.*
2. Timbermen's Shanty beside the Ottawa River.
3. Running a Timber Slide on the Ottawa. *These slides, built to carry the heavy timbers past obstacles in rushing water-courses, were risky enough routes in themselves, demanding a good deal of skill and nerve.*

1

2   3

increase, its population climbed from less than 100,000 in 1815 to well over 200,000 in 1831, then on to 450,000 by 1841. Older districts filled in; farm frontiers spread out. And towns grew up, from Cornwall and Kingston to Hamilton, St. Catharines and London; while York became Toronto in 1834, Upper Canada's first city, with some 9,000 residents — its own numbers having nearly doubled in the two proceeding years, largely because it was a focus for arriving migrants. In the east of this province, Ulster and Catholic Irish who had landed at Quebec came on to timber camps up the Ottawa, on both the Upper and Lower Canadian sides of the river. They also chopped out bush farms that provided the northward-advancing camps with hay and oats for their horses, root crops for their axemen. The Ottawa became almost a workers' world itself — of Irish and *Canadien* shanty-dwellers, under Scots and English masters, hewing and rafting the massive square timbers down to Quebec.

In the centre of the Upper Canadian province, newcomers after 1815 cleared farms further inland above Lake Ontario or north of Toronto up Yonge Street: still a rough and muddy route, but by now a busy highway for settlements to Lake Simcoe, bringing farm produce to the city, taking mail, supplies and wholesale goods by return. In the province's western Peninsula, however, the widest growth took place. Along Lake Erie stretched the Talbot Settlement, where Colonel Thomas Talbot, an aristocratic Irishman once secretary to Governor Simcoe, opened main roads and commandingly located British colonists on his half-million-acre grant. There were, as well, lesser "Scotch blocks" or English and Welsh settlements in southwestern Upper Canada. But the biggest project of all was that of the Canada Company, chartered in England in 1826 under the Scottish novelist John Galt. That enterprise obtained two million acres in Crown land reserves scattered across the provinces, and another 1,100,000 in the Huron Tract, a great triangle of fertile wilderness bordered on Lake Huron, with its tip inland at the new town of Guelph, headquarters for the Tract. The Company also built roads, and generally gave good service in filling the Huron area with British settlers during the 1830s and 40s.

Throughout this variegated growth, English arrivals did not just reinforce the established strength of Anglicanism, since their middle and lower ranks considerably supported Methodism or other dissenting Protestant sects in politics. The Scots, similarly, might not only be Tories, both Presbyterians and Catholics, firmly behind the ruling order, but equally firm exponents of new Liberal political views fast making headway in Great Britain. And antagonisms between Ulster Orangemen and Catholic Irish repeatedly erupted in public fights or riots,

1. Colonel Thomas Talbot. *A soldier of old Anglo-Irish family, he first came to Upper Canada with Simcoe in 1792, and in 1803 returned there, after some years of active service in Europe. The rest of his life (till 1853) he spent in settling, directing and developing his huge land grant in southwestern Upper Canada.*

2. John Galt. *This well-known Scottish author actively promoted the Canada Company in Britain and became its superintendent in Canada in 1826; remaining there till 1829, and opening up the Huron Tract. He later backed the British American Land Company (1834), and became its superintendent also, but died before he could return to Canada.*

3. Pamphlet Advertising the Huron Tract. *Dating from after the Union of Upper and Lower Canada in 1841 — since it shows that Upper Canada has now become "Canada West."*

1   2

LANDS IN CANADA WEST (LATE UPPER CANADA).

THE ATTENTION OF

EMIGRANTS, OLD SETTLERS, AND OTHERS,

IS INVITED BY THE CANADA COMPANY TO THEIR

HURON LANDS,

CONSISTING OF A BLOCK OF

ONE MILLION ACRES OF LAND,

Extending Westward from the Gore and Wellington Districts to the Shores of Lake Huron, which bounds it for sixty miles.

The Land in the Canada Company's Huron Settlement is of the finest character, and of the description best adapted to the cultivation of Wheat. This Settlement possesses advantages which render it peculiarly eligible to every class of Settler: scarcely a bad Farm is to be found in it: it is well watered by living Streams, and the climate is most healthy. The principal Port is Goderich, the District Town, which has a population of about 1200—good Stores or Shops, Mechanics, a large Grist Mill, a Fulling and Carding Mill, an Iron Foundry, places of Religious Worship, resident Clergymen, and good Schools, where the higher branches of the Classics are taught, &c. &c. &c.

3

especially at election times. Consequently, British immigrants brought more with them than population increase — their own social and political inheritances as well. But one other thing they brought, no less, was powerful economic stimulus. They greatly enlarged the labour supply of British America. They added fresh capital, skills and enterprise; and much expanded production and demand in every colony — to shape a prosperous, lively era of advance.

The timber trade grew with its largely immigrant workforce; yet also because it was no longer serving wartime ship construction in Britain, but instead the larger and more lasting needs of British industrialism: in beams and deals (heavy boards) for factory or urban building, in shaft-timbers for the vital coal mines, and soon, in ties for new steam railways which had first developed in Britain from the 1820s. Furthermore, the colonial wheat trade rose strongly to feed Britain's industrial population, and was effectively given imperial tariff protection, after 1822. Grain exports continued out of Lower Canada. Still, new high-yielding fields in Upper Canada increasingly entered into the trade, as immigrants' farms, from Peel County near Toronto west to the London District, sent out their grain and flour. And in the process, the pioneer "four corners," where once mill, general store, blacksmith shop and tavern had marked bare frontier beginnings, now widely increased to settled inland hamlets; while down on the "fronts," solid business communities gathered within the rising towns.

The advance of business interests was plain across the provinces — in harbour development companies from the Atlantic ports to the St. Lawrence and Great Lakes, in major wholesale firms from Halifax and Saint John to Quebec or Toronto, and most notably, in the rise of banking. The Bank of Montreal, long to

1. Farmers' Market at Quebec, 1829.
2. Corduroy Road near Guelph, 1832. *Guelph was founded by John Galt as a planned town for the Canada Company's Huron Tract, and roadways like this one were extended from it to serve settlement. Called "corduroy roads" from the resemblance of their surface to the ribbed cloth, their logs laid sideways were emphatically far rougher than any cloth; yet still much better than clogged mud tracks, and able to carry jolting ox-carts, at least.*
3. The Bank of Montreal in the 1830s.

1

2

3

be Canada's premier bank, began in 1817; the Bank of Upper Canada at York (Toronto) in 1820, the Bank of Nova Scotia at Halifax in 1832. At the same time, Montreal merchants quickly recovered from the transfer of the fur trade from the St. Lawrence to Hudson Bay in 1821. For they had turned to the vigorous Upper Canada trade, forwarding goods in from Europe, bringing down grain for export, in a far heavier and more valuable traffic than former canoe-loads of western furs. Thus not just timber yields, wheat crops, or fishing harvests expanded in these years, but major towns and business power, right from Newfoundland through Upper Canada.

Still further, transport by water was vastly improved, thanks to the steamship and canal. The *Frontenac*, first steamer on Lake Ontario, was financed by Kingston merchants and launched in 1817; after which steamboats steadily added to schooner traffic on the Lakes. In 1834, the *Royal William*, built by Quebec interests, was the first vessel to cross the Atlantic wholly under steam — the beginning of a new age of Atlantic steamships, in which Samuel Cunard, Halifax ship-owner, would play a prominent part. Meanwhile, canal construction had come to British America; but especially to the inland Canadas. The Lachine Canal, opened in 1825 to by-pass the rapids in the St. Lawrence just above Montreal, was an initial step in the long development of an Upper St. Lawrence canal system. Then in 1829 the Welland Canal, promoted by William Merritt of St. Catharines, linked Lakes Erie and Ontario for ship traffic, avoiding the huge barrier of Niagara Falls. In 1832, the Rideau Canal was put in service from the Ottawa down to Lake Ontario at Kingston; while Bytown, founded as that canal's headquarters on the Ottawa by its builder, Colonel John By, would one day become Canada's capital city of Ottawa. More canals were also started on the Upper St. Lawrence; although their expensive completion would take till 1848.

In any event, canal routes largely widely constructed by immigrants, Irish in the main, became a notable, large-scale feature of this age of sweeping growth. But no less evident than the costly, government-backed canals were the ever-growing political strains; to which we now should turn.

1. Launching of the *Royal William* at Quebec, 1834. *Here was the next big step, to the open Atlantic. British and American ships had already crossed the ocean with the partial use of steam; but the* Royal William *did so fully.*

2. William Hamilton Merritt: *St. Catharines merchant leader who built the first Welland Canal — the first in a series of ever-larger Welland Canals between Lakes Ontario and Erie.*

3. Locks up to the Rideau Canal at Bytown on the Ottawa. *This canal was constructed in 1826-1832 as a military project to link Montreal and the St. Lawrence with Lake Ontario, by means of a back route via the Ottawa and streams down to Kingston — thus avoiding the Upper St. Lawrence border that had been cut at times by American attackers in the War of 1812. Militarily, the canal did not prove necessary; though its being there did matter. Moreover, the Rideau waterway also promoted the rise of Bytown, its headquarters, brought more advances to the Ottawa Valley lumber empire, and fostered busy traffic in and out through Kingston.*

4. The *Frontenac* in 1821. *This fast steamboat on Lake Ontario was rapidly followed by many others, all along the Lakes.*

1

2

3

4

The Rise of Reform Movements

After 1815, the pace of change accelerated in the politics of the British American colonies, just as in their economic and social lives; all part of a turbulent era of immigration and development. In some ways Newfoundland went through the biggest change, when in 1825 its long reign of visiting naval admirals was ended, and the first resident civil governor, Sir Thomas Cochrane, took office. In 1832 representative government was also established, so that Newfoundland at last became a full-fledged province like the others. Still, quarrels arising between its Legislative Assembly and Council over the control of finances led to factional splits and election violence. Governor Cochrane, once popular, had his coach pelted with mud as he left the province in 1834. Chiefly, he was blamed for showing favouritism to the Council, a small elite group of substantially conservative and Protestant appointees, while the Assembly, looking for wider popular power, had come under the sway of reform-minded members such as Dr. William Carson and John Kent, a young Liberal and brother-in-law of the weighty Catholic Bishop Fleming of St. John's. Backed by formidable Catholic Irish support in and around the capital, the reform elements pushed protests right to the Colonial Office of the British government in 1837; though with little immediate result.

Of course, each province still followed its own political pattern. In Prince Edward Island, for example, politics continued to revolve closely about the enduring question of land-ownership. Governors and appointed Councils largely sustained the legal rights of British absentee proprietors; elected Assemblymen sought their removal, or at least that the distant landowners be compelled to pay the taxes due from their grants to support the province's administrative costs. Even before 1815 there had been groups urging tenant rights in the Assembly, and reform fronts among its members grew increasingly insistent afterwards. Of course, it could be said that these elected populists were not necessarily noble champions of small tenants, but also meant to free the way for local land speculators — in which cause they might even find Council allies. Nonetheless, the land reform question both dominated and bedeviled Island politics for many years to follow.

Nova Scotia did not have such over-mastering problems of land or religion; but that did not prevent a lengthy, if fairly orderly, contest between its ruling Council oligarchy and the representative Assembly. The Halifax oligarchy of officials, big merchants and landowners or shipping and banking magnates — all centred in the "Council of Twelve" around the Governor — was none too inclined to yield its own dignified authority to a rabble-rousing Assembly largely composed of country lawyers, rustic farmers and outport merchants who had rashly proclaimed their own right to speak for the people. (This was the view of the Council gentlemen, of course.) But these superior gentry made a bad mistake when they charged an obstreperous Halifax journalist, Joseph Howe, with libel. Howe, outspoken editor of the popular *Novascotian* since 1828, had been

1. "For Immigration" — a Bitter View. *Let no one think that concern over the flow of migrants is only some present racist reaction. It runs far back, as this cartoon of 1832 suggests, where a disreputable pair stand at "parting hour" in Britain, and look likely to bring more trouble for the decent citizens of their new country. The point is, that not only the immigrant intake in itself, but the doubts and disorders felt as well by established provincial populations (especially among French Canadians fearful of being swamped) would work to heighten popular strains and political feelings in the transatlantic British colonies.*

2. Halifax from Dartmouth, 1834.

1

2

attacking a government beyond control of the representatives of the people. Of Loyalist parentage, he was, besides, a whole-hearted believer in the British tie and British parliamentary institutions. And so, when the oligarchy took him to court in 1835 to set an example to their foes, Howe, defending himself, made a stirring speech on British freedom of the press against tyranny, a speech that resounded across Nova Scotia. He not only won the lawsuit, he won an Assembly seat in 1836, and fast rose to prominence in that house. In fact, he organized and led Reformers as a parliamentary party, and thereby gained concessions from the Colonial Office in 1837 which separated the old oligarchic Council into two bodies, a Legislative and an Executive Council — with four Assembly members henceforth sitting in the latter. It was still a long way to a government constitutionally responsible to the people's house. Yet Howe had taken a sound first step in Nova Scotia.

New Brunswick, too, followed its own political course, one very much concerned with timber, its great staple. The chief political issue here involved crown-land revenues, whether they should be dealt with by governing Council or elected Assembly; yet what was really at stake was who should control the crucial timber leases to these forest preserves — the friends and associates of Council officials, or the big timber dealers who had come to dominate the Assembly. In short, political ideas or constitutional stands really had little to do with it. Not much but timber rivalry divided oligarchy and opposition viewpoints in this province. A good deal of reform-sounding Assembly rhetoric, however, was directed against Thomas Baillie as Crown Lands Commissioner from 1824.

The Novascotian. Joseph Howe, a young journalist of twenty-three, bought this Halifax newspaper by 1828. (They were much cheaper then.) As editor, he made it the most influential paper in the province, pursuing an eloquent campaign of Reform.

THE NOVASCOTIAN,
OR
COLONIAL HERALD.

HALIFAX, THURSDAY MORNING, JANUARY 17, 1828.

1. Howe in Later Years.
By this time (1869) he had led in gaining Nova Scotia effective self-government, became premier himself, and then turned to new federal politics after Confederation — which initially he had opposed — while remaining always devoted to his own home province.
2. "Royal Road" in New Brunswick, 1835.
3. *La Minerve*, Organ of the *Parti patriote*.
Founded at Montreal in 1826, it was linked closely with the Montreal-based leadership of the radical French-Canadian patriotes, whereas the older (and by now somewhat moderated) Le Canadien was felt to be more tied to Quebec-area interests.

1

2

LA MINERVE.

VOLUME I.   MONTREAL, JEUDI 9 NOVEMBRE, 1826.   NUMERO 1.

CONDITIONS.

La Minerve se publie deux fois par semaine, le *Lundi* et le *Jeudi soir*. L'abonnement est de quatre piastres par année, et de cinq lorsqu'on l'envoie par la poste, payables en deux termes. Ceux qui désirent discontinuer leur souscription doivent en avertir un mois avant l'expiration du dernier semestre. Les abonnés qui ne résident pas dans les villes sont priés d'indiquer par quelle voie ils désirent que le papier leur soit transmis.

Les avertissemens seront chargés au taux ordinaire. Ceux qui ne seront pas accompagnés de directions seront insérés jusqu'à ordre contraire, et débités en conséquence.

IMPRIMÉ PAR JOHN JONES,
No. 5, Rue St. Jean Baptiste.

On s'abonne au bureau du Journal, et à la Librairie Françoise de MM. E. R. Fabre & Cie., et chez MM. les Agens dans les Campagnes.

PROSPECTUS.

Un des plus célèbres écrivains du dernier siècle a prétendu que les sciences et les arts n'étoient pas favorables à la cause des mœurs, et que l'éducation étoit inutile et même dangéreuse aux peuples. Si ce paradoxe étoit vrai, si une société humaine privée du flambeau des sciences pouvoit être plus parfaite que celles qui marcheroient à leur lumière, ce ne seroit que chez un peuple encore demi-barbare, qu'un sage législateur auroit prémuni contre une vaine curiosité en lui créant des habitudes simples, en lui inspirant de l'aversion pour le luxe, et du goût pour les paisibles travaux de l'agriculture. Mais lorsque le luxe et la corruption se sont perpétués à travers les siècles, lorsque la plûpart des gouvernemens, accoutumés à se faire obéir sans contrôle, mettent à profit les vices et les préjugés pour conserver une prépondérance que le génie des temps veut leur arracher, ce n'est qu'au moyen des sciences et des arts que l'individu peut reconquérir ses droits sur les masses qu'arme encore contre lui la force des habitudes.

cause commune. Aussi a-t-on vû depuis quelques années s'élever un grand nombre d'établissemens destinés à l'instruction de la jeunesse ; mais comme on ne connoît bien la nécessité des connoissances qu'à mesure qu'elles se répandent, il reste à ce sujet beaucoup à désirer. Puisse notre journal contribuer à remplir les vœux de nos compatriotes !

Nous aurons pour la Religion le respect que lui assure son caractère divin et les sublimes vérités qu'elle enseigne aux hommes.

Nous suivrons avec attention la politique du pays. Ardents à soutenir les intérêts des Canadiens, nous leur enseignerons à résister à toute usurpation de leurs droits, en même temps que nous tâcherons de leur faire apprécier et chérir les bienfaits et le gouvernement de la mère-patrie. Nous donnerons les débats de la Chambre d'Assemblée avec un précis des lois qui y seront proposées. Le peuple a un intérêt majeur à connoître la conduite de ses représentans pour motiver son choix et faire respecter l'opinion publique à ceux qu'il charge de la défendre.

L'histoire de notre pays sera aussi un des objets principaux de nos recherches. Nous prions ceux qui connoissent d'anciennes traditions canadiennes, de vouloir bien nous les communiquer, afin de les soumettre à la critique avant que les monumens qui peuvent servir à leur examen disparoissent entièrement. Tout écrit qui aura rapport à l'histoire naturelle du pays, ou à l'état de l'industrie et des arts parmi nous, sera reçu avec une vive reconnoissance. Nous insérerons aussi toutes les communications qui entreront dans le plan de ce journal, lorsqu'elles seront de nature à y être admises, et qu'elles seront signées de l'auteur lorsque les circonstances l'exigeront.

Enfin *La Minerve* s'occupera de l'Agriculture, de la Littérature, de la Politique étrangère ; elle contiendra aussi les nouvelles récentes, les ventes par décret, et en général on n'y oubliera rien de ce qui peut intéresser ou plaire.

Nous recommandons notre entreprise aux amis de leur pays ; c'est de leur zèle que nous attendons notre succès.

prêts à lui faire ! . . . C'est pour la patrie que Régulus retourne mourir à Carthage au milieu des supplices ; c'est pour la patrie que le Roi Jean, après la honteuse paix de Bretigny, retourne mourir dans la prison à Londres. C'est pour la patrie que les Lacédémoniens Spertis et Buris quittent volontairement leur pays, se rendent en Perse et se présentent devant Xercès, en lui disant : " Nos compatriotes ont fait mourir tes envoyés ; c'est un grand crime, nous venons en subir le juste châtiment ; quel que soit le supplice auquel tu nous condamnes, nous voilà prêts à le subir." Et lorsque Xercès saisi d'admiration pour une si haute vertu, pardonne l'outrage qu'il a reçu, et veut engager Buris et Spertis à rester près de lui, c'est encore la patrie qui dicte leur réponse. " Eh ! comment !" disent-ils, " pourrons nous abandonner notre pays, nos lois, et des hommes tels, que nous venons mourir ici pour eux !"

Une fois allumé, l'amour de la patrie ne sauroit s'éteindre ; ce feu céleste vit et se conserve sous la cendre féconde des souvenirs. J'interroge le Cophte, qui traîne sa misérable existence au milieu des décombres de la ville du Soleil ; il me répond avec un sentiment d'orgueil : " L'Egypte, ma patrie, fut la source des lumières et le berceau des sciences." Le Juif exilé des ruines du Jourdain, errant de contrée en contrée depuis vingt siècles, nourri d'opprobre et de persécutions, se console dans les religieux souvenirs, et n'entend pas sans foi et sans bonheur vibrer dans l'air le doux nom d'Israël.

Née sous le ciel brillant de la Grèce et de l'Italie, la liberté est une plante indigène de ces heureux climats ; le fer des barbares l'a moissonnée ; elle a cessé d'ombrager le sol natal ; mais sous cette terre où pèsent ses oppresseurs, elle a jetté des racines vivaces, indestructibles, toujours prêtes à reproduire des tiges nouvelles.

LA VILLE BATIE EN TERRE.

La ville de Saint Paul, l'une des plus belles et des plus agréables du Brésil, et dont le climat est un des plus sains de l'Amérique, offre plusieurs places, des églises, des couvens, et toutes ses maisons bâties en

3

Baillie, an able but arrogant official, took very seriously the collecting of revenues from timber leases; yet by giving free run to his favoured subordinates he further outraged timbermen forced to pay "tyrannical" taxes. Through the Assembly, their protests went to the Colonial Office, which in 1837 much reduced Baillie's powers. Assembly leaders, in fact, now gained such a hold on timber lands and revenues that New Brunswick seemed a remarkably contented and peaceful province in that very year when armed rebellion broke out in both the Canadas.

The path through reform to rebellion was a complex one in both these much larger provinces. And it was still more complicated in Lower Canada, thanks to the basic ethnic and social division there between French and English-speaking communities. Political issues in this colony would not just express a clash of conservative and reform viewpoints over the governing system, or on matters of financial powers, business projects, land rights and religious rights. All these aspects were present in Lower Canada. But beyond them was the underlying conflict of two distinctive language and cultural communities; the one upholding economic advance, commerce and British allegiance, the other, striving to preserve French Canada's farm interests and heritage in its own national homeland. That conflict ran through almost every Lower Canadian dispute between the governing oligarchy and "British party" on the one side, the French-dominated Assembly on the other. It expressed British commercial Toryism no less than French agrarian Reformism: though fervent *Canadien* Reformers might further express both liberal nationalist hopes and conservative Catholic leanings of their own.

Still further, since political conflict was more deeply seated in Lower Canada, it had arisen there well before 1815, as the pre-war contest of the *Parti Canadien* with Governor Craig had shown. Hence when wartime dangers had passed, the earlier strife between the Assembly and the oligarchy (the "Chateau Clique" in Lower Canada) quickly reappeared; but now in times of rising economic change, and while masses of British immigrants were landing yearly at Quebec and Montreal. French Canadians began to feel more and more embattled. They looked especially to the eloquent, imposing Louis-Joseph Papineau, a lawyer who was chosen Speaker of the Assembly in 1815, after service as a militia captain in the War of 1812 — which saw him at the capture of Detroit. He sat for Montreal West till 1837, almost constantly as Speaker; and he gained wide knowledge of British parliamentary practice, as well as high respect from Lower-Canadian Reformers, who made him their chief leader. Yet Papineau, who gradually became a democratic liberal in his political pronouncements, remained an aristocratic conservative in his own social outlook: a believer in old-regime seigneurialism who became an eminent seigneur himself. Thus he effectively embodied *Canadien* Reformism, which sought to use the new ways in

1. Notre Dame Church, Montreal, 1823-29. *This handsome Gothic structure replaced an older Notre Dame parish Church of French Montreal, on Place d'Armes in the heart of the original town.*
2. Louis-Joseph Papineau. *Seen here in old age, he still displays the impressive stance, the swirl of hair, the dramatic look, which had helped make this lordly "tribune of the people" a commanding popular figure in the Lower Canadian legislature of the 1820s and 30s. After the Rebellion of 1837, Papineau would return to political life in 1848-54; but had less impact in a rather different era, and so retired to his seigneurial mansion at Montebello on the Ottawa, where he died in 1871.*

1

2

politics to preserve the old in society. And so, although some English-speaking liberals or radicals allied with him — largely drawn from American-origin settlers of the Eastern Townships — the chief support he roused came from those French-Canadian liberals who, like Papineau, were beginning to think in terms of national freedom. It was not for nothing that the old *Parti canadien* was reconstituted as the more urgent *Parti patriote* in 1826, with its own journal, *La Minerve.*

Meanwhile, Papineau had directed his political comrades in efforts to wrest financial powers from the ruling Chateau Clique. In 1819 the House of Assembly thus revised a government budget to cut the salaries of disliked officials. That caused the British-appointed upper house, the Legislative Council, to throw out the revised budget in total. And in an ensuing long struggle over finances, the Assembly refused any budget at all in 1827, whereupon Governor Lord Dalhousie dissolved it. Subsequent moves by the British parliament in London, to offer conditional concessions on budget matters, were rejected by renewed Assembly forces; until finally in 1831, the British authorities transferred control of most of Lower Canada's revenues to its own legislature without any conditions. But this victory did not remove the bitter feelings that had mounted. Papineau and his followers went on to still more uncompromising radicalism.

That was evident in 1834, when the Assembly set out its thunderous Ninety-Two Resolutions, proposing an American-style elected, democratic government (though keeping the antique seigneurial system), and hinting at American-style revolution if these demands were not met. In effect, Papineau and the radical liberals with him were toying with prospects of revolt. Yet their aggressive mood was backed by wide popular discontents in the countryside. Here *habitant* farmers faced declining wheat yields from over-used soils, while British migrants streamed in, strengthening the grip of *les Anglais*. These settlers, above all, were filling up the Eastern Townships: thereby depriving French Canadians — who by now were overcrowding the established seigneurial districts — of new lands which they had considered theirs by very birthright.

Accordingly, by 1834, the Reform movement in Lower Canada was reaching a critical threshold. Much the same was true for Upper Canada, although in circumstances decidedly its own. Here there obviously was no such all-important ethnic division. Yet emotional issues of loyalty, of British allegiance *versus* American influence, could sometimes make the struggle between Reform forces in Upper Canada's Assembly and those behind its governing elite look just about as heated. In this upper province, the ruling oligarchy, to be dubbed the Family Compact, was certainly the focus of the chief officials around the Governor,

1. Governor Dalhousie in Canada, 1819-28. *Dalhousie, a British general who fought at Waterloo, had been Governor of Nova Scotia in 1816-19, when he was reappointed to the Canadas as Governor-in-Chief. In Canada, an authoritarian Dalhousie resisted the demands of the* patriote party in the Lower Canadian assembly. His cut silhouette is pictured here, against a painted backdrop of the Quebec Citadel.

2. A Caricature Published in Anglo-Montreal c. 1834. *This shows "Things as They Are" — a devilish-looking Papineau weighing down scales with loads marked "Hatred of British Institutions," "Democracy," "92 Resolutions," and so on; then "Things As They Will Be" — where Justice (whose sword has ended Papineau) levels the balance between "The Happiness and Prosperity of the People" and "Our Glorious Constitution."*

1

2

along with large landowners and top merchants, and was generally supported by pro-British Tory-Conservative opinions which were anti-American rather than anti-French in character. In any event, this Family Compact kept considerable popular backing in an Upper Canada founded on Loyalism and moulded by war against invaders from the democratic United States. After 1815, moreover, the Compact was busily concerned with economic development, a popular cause in itself. Beyond that, it had some capable if keenly partisan leaders: chief among them Dr. John Strachan, Scottish-born Anglican minister and later bishop, and John Beverley Robinson, Canadian son of Virginia Loyalists.

Strachan, York schoolmaster and leading cleric, was as forceful as he was stubborn. He was appointed to Upper Canada's Executive Council in 1818, the Legislative Council in 1820, and made head of the new General Board of Education in 1822. For this first-rate, devoted teacher believed strongly in enlarging education; a belief which also led him to seek, and obtain, a royal charter for a provincial university in 1827 — ultimately to become the University of Toronto. As for Beverley Robinson, the best mind in the Tory Compact and an outstanding lawyer and judge by any measure, he had fought under Brock at Detroit and Queenston Heights while still a law student. Then he had been made acting Attorney-General in 1813 at 21, since his predecessor and legal mentor had been killed at Queenston. Robinson, once John Strachan's prize-pupil, became regular Attorney-General in 1818, and won election to the Assembly, besides, in 1821. Clearly, connection and favour had much to do with his early advancement. Yet he also came to merit it by no less clear intelligence and integrity. Furthermore, Robinson was an effective spokesman in the Upper Canada Assembly, which held a sizeable group of Tory-Conservative members. Indeed, the Tories in the 1820s and 30s elected popular majorities to that House about as often as their Reform opponents did.

All the same, in the age of change after 1815, more Upper Canadians came to question oligarchic rule, and voice grievances over patterns and privileges that no longer seemed acceptable. Hence demands for reform steadily mounted, especially in regard to land policies. The yearly influx of British settlers seeking farms inevitably raised land values. While good, wild land was still available by free grant within the province, it now lay deep in tangled backwoods; and the nearer, semi-opened land — with rough roads to markets, neighbours and some services — had to be bought at ever-rising prices. It had to be bought from big private holders, good friends of the Compact, from the Canada Company close to the government, or else leased (later purchased) from the Anglican Church, which had been granted its extensive land reserves under the Constitutional Act of 1791, in order to support the "Protestant clergy" of this privileged,

1. Entrance to the Grange, York. *Completed around 1820 by Attorney-General and Judge D'Arcy Boulton, this mansion was the kind of elegant home that some members of the provincial establishment would build: people, fairly or not, to be termed "The Family Compact." Certainly the Boultons, originally from England, lived here for generations, becoming mayors, provincial politicians and government members.*

2. John Strachan, First Anglican Bishop of Toronto. *Raised and educated in Scotland, he came to Canada in 1799, and taught school at Kingston and Cornwall. In 1812 he became Anglican rector at York, where he boldly stood up to the American commanders in the raid on York the next year. Strachan pursued provincial education after the war, was named to Upper Canada's governing councils, and obtained a royal charter for a provincial university, King's College, in 1827. Above all, he stayed a major Tory power in government circles on into the 1830s.*

3. John Beverley Robinson, Leading Family Compact Tory. *Robinson as Attorney-General sat in the Assembly (for York), virtually heading the government side there, until in 1830 he was made Chief Justice and Speaker of the Legislative Council. Thereafter his career was largely legal — as an outstanding judge till his death in 1863.*

1

2

3

1. Upper Canada's Legislative Buildings. *Erected at York in 1829-32, they were in use not just until Confederation in 1867, but afterwards for the new Province of Ontario — until replaced by Ontario's present parliament buildings in 1893.*

2. Leaders in Upper Canada Reform: Egerton Ryerson. *Seen here in older years, when he was a well-emplaced and powerful director of Ontario public education, rather than a young, fighting Methodist editor and idealist; although he never lost his religious idealism, nor his loyalism.*

3. Reform Leaders: William Warren Baldwin. *Of top York society and Anglo-Irish family, this well-to-do lawyer-doctor both believed in the tie with Britain and sought to make it operate in freedom, by applying a pattern of British responsible government to the colonies.*

4. Reform Leaders: John Rolph. *A clever English lawyer-physician (not an unusual combination then), Rolph represented southwestern areas of the province, and worked consistently for a radical democratic takeover.*

5. Reform Leaders: William Lyon Mackenzie. *A belligerent and penetrating journalist, he arrived in Upper Canada from Scotland at twenty-four in 1820; but did not settle permanently in York till 1824, when he moved his newspaper there from Queenston. At York, Mackenzie's scorching, anti-establishment paper aroused angry hostility among the powers that be — the Family Compact — and brought on harsh attacks that in the long run mainly helped him win more popular support.*

1

2

3

4

5

semi-official church. There might be resentment in any case against speculative owners holding back empty properties for higher prices. Yet religious differences still more sharply underlined complaints over the tracts withheld as Anglican clergy reserves. As early as 1817 a resolution in the Assembly attacked these reserves as being "beyond all precedent lavish." And criticisms multiplied, leading to calls to divide the clergy land endowment among all the Protestant Churches. The more "advanced" Reformers by the 1830s were even urging secularization, to turn the valuable lands over to the support of public education instead.

Though Anglicanism was still a major element in the colony, and was reinforced by many English immigrants, plus some Protestant Irish, its official privileges regarding the reserves, and more, drew criticisms from other growing church bodies such as the Scottish Presbyterians — but above all, from the Methodists. Rooted among both Loyalists and post-Loyalist Americans, and decidedly strong in the countryside, Methodism now was being further enlarged by arriving English Wesleyan Methodists; to shape a serious challenge to the Anglican church dominance upheld by Compact Tories. In 1829 Egerton Ryerson, a young minister of Loyalist family, became the combative first editor of the Methodists' new *Christian Guardian*. He campaigned tellingly against religious privilege in church, law or public education; and he and Methodist forces became powerful allies of the Reform movement. Still, Ryerson and his co-religionists were really more of a middle group in provincial affairs: in truth, almost conservative-loyal as regards any drastic political change, though determinedly reforming on matters of Anglican dominance, land policy, schools, and some other Upper Canadian problems that typically engaged Reform elements against the Compact side.

Loose-knit reforming forces, moreover, first organized themselves into a definite Reform party in the Upper Canada Assembly of 1824, although it still had no one recognized leader or much party discipline. In response, Tories soon also shaped a distinct Assembly party — beyond former vague factions with little more programme than "support the Governor and his friends." This basic process of party growth, so vital to the rise of parliamentary self-government, took place in all the provinces; but in Upper Canada it went on most clearly under Reform leaders who emerged over the 1820s into the 30s. Among these were Marshall Spring Bidwell, a careful, moderate liberal of American origin, who led a successful struggle to prevent post-Loyalist American settlers being treated as unworthy second-class citizens; and thus tied a sizeable "American" vote closely to Reform. As well, there was the Anglo-Irish Dr. William Warren Baldwin, a wealthy Toronto landowner who wanted to see British responsible government established in Canada, whereby the governing Executive Council would become a true parliamentary cabinet, dependent on the vote of the elected house.

Still further, there was an English radical lawyer and physician, astute John Rolph, and in particular, a fearlessly aggressive Scottish journalist, William Lyon Mackenzie — whose power as an agitator and passion for justice could scarcely be doubted; though his judgement might. By no means the one, prime leader, Mackenzie, who entered parliament in 1829, still led in pressing the pace of Reform in the province, carrying it finally to armed rebellion. That violent outcome took eight more years. Yet since his role in bringing on an Upper Canada Rebellion of 1837 was so influential, we must look at that theme next.

From Reform to Rebellion in the Canadas

Mackenzie had set up his newspaper, the *Colonial Advocate*, at York in 1824, and it rapidly won both friends and enemies for slashing editorials on the Family Compact, a term its editor would do much to popularize. In response, young offshoots of the Compact brainlessly attacked and vandalized his printing-office in 1826, dumping its type into the harbour, and making Mackenzie a hero-martyr of Reform. Two years later he was running for parliament, for a seat in York County above the town, where farm settlers were largely Reform in outlook. And in the Assembly from 1829, this popular champion increasingly led in denouncing the Compact's sins, whether in regard to finance, banking, and canals, lands or education. In fact, Mackenzie's fiery onslaughts brought charges of libel in 1831, in an Assembly that now held a Tory majority, and which carried a vote to expel him. Yet his faithful constituents returned him in a by-election of 1832 — after which more expulsions and re-elections followed until the Tories at last gave up, and Mackenzie was triumphantly confirmed in 1833. The next year, 1834, he was chosen first mayor of the new city of Toronto, though his warmest interest stayed with the provincial struggle. Moreover, he took up radical ideas of American written constitutions and elective democracy to cure the ills of oligarchic rule, especially emphasizing an elected Legislative Council. More moderate Reformers still sought measures within the existing parliamentary structure in order to remove Compact excesses

1. North-West Corner of Front and Frederick in York. *On this corner Mackenzie had his newspaper office, which was assaulted by unruly young Tories in 1826. That gained him public sympathy, and helped elect him as a Reformer to the Upper Canada Assembly.*

2. Sir Francis Bond Head, Governor, 1835-38. *Supposedly aware of Upper Canada's mounting need for reform, he was hopelessly vain and rashly sure of his own ideas. Head proved a disaster, both for the province and for the British authorities who sent him. In fact, along with Mackenzie on the other side, Head really did a good deal to bring on the Upper Canada Rebellion of 1837.*

3. Marshall Spring Bidwell, Speaker of the Assembly. *A prominent, judicious Reform veteran, his political career was effectively ended by the foolish excesses of Head and Mackenzie, between them. Threatened with Head's unjust accusations, Bidwell fled to the United States and did not return.*

1

2

3

or remedy clergy reserves. In particular, Robert Baldwin, the lawyer son of Dr. W.W. Baldwin, had also entered the Assembly in 1829, to seek his father's principle of responsible government, and thus to urge a British constitutional pattern of reform.

But a tirelessly accusing Mackenzie now chaired (and largely compiled) the Assembly's massive *Seventh Report on Grievances* in 1835. This was a shot-gun blast of protests which helped bring a new Lieutenant-Governor to Upper Canada: Sir Francis Bond Head, sent by the Colonial Office presumably as a reform-minded arbiter; yet one who mostly proved opinionated and overbearing — a good match for Mackenzie. Head in 1836 appointed Reformers to his Executive Council, including Robert Baldwin and John Rolph. But when Baldwin sought an all-Reform council, to suit an Assembly once again filled with a Reform majority, Head dismissed his councillors and dissolved an angry house. That brought on a violent election in 1836, wherein the Governor blatantly appealed to the loyalty of the people (especially British immigrants), while Orange gangs attacked or threatened Reform voters. The result was a landslide Tory victory in an anti-republican province; but it also left deep bitterness among more radical Reformers, who felt they had been condemned as disloyal — and might just as well be so.

Indeed, the radicals were becoming more desperate as their support fell off. The Methodists had moved away when Egerton Ryerson broke with Mackenzie in 1833 over the latter's extremism. Moderate Liberals like Robert Baldwin and his followers, seeking responsible government on the British model, were already far from Mackenzie and the American constitutional plans he was proposing. Even Marshall Spring Bidwell and other long-enduring Reformers were dubious of Mackenzie's drift toward revolutionary change. Beyond that, 1837 brought the onset of a major world depression after years of boom; and Upper Canada farmers — their own incomes falling but their debts to banks still high — grew restive and ready to take on city fat-cats or their Compact friends. William Lyon Mackenzie (who had lost his own Assembly seat) hence found eager audiences when he travelled north of Toronto in the summer of 1837, preaching the people's wrongs and the need for emphatic action. That summer, in fact, he was organizing "committees of vigilance" in the countryside, and by mid-October there were secret radical meetings in Toronto, discussing schemes to seize control of the government.

Late in November came the outbreak of actual rebellion in Lower Canada, under Reform leaders with whom Mackenzie had had some, if insufficient, contact. Yet it seemed the moment for an Upper Canadian uprising also: especially when Governor Head, brashly inviting trouble, sent off his own regular troops to help in Lower Canada. Thus in early December, Mackenzie and radical comrades like Rolph called for revolt, without any very clear plan or decision; although Mackenzie issued a glowing Declaration of Independence and a "draft constitution" for Upper Canada, while suggesting its absorption into the

1. The Fight at Montgomery's, December 7, 1837. *This skirmish outside Montgomery's Tavern on Yonge Street, north of the young city of Toronto, was fast over; thus quelling a rebellion that had scarcely been organized as more than a vague armed demonstration. Mackenzie made his way over the border, to new efforts there at raising men and money for his self-proclaimed cause of liberty for Upper Canada.*

2. A Satire on Recruiting New Rebel Forces, 1838. *This "beating for recruits" (with a very unlikely recruiting sergeant) was evidently not expected to be a great success in Canada.*

1   2

American union — some independence! At any rate, some seven hundred uncertain farmers gathered on Yonge Street north of Toronto, many thinking it just a demonstration, but all deluded by Mackenzie's rosy-bright yet utterly vague promises. If this sounds harsh, he did throw away farm families, their lives and hopes, for his own airy schemes — which he later rejected, when he said that he was sorry.

This inept little Yonge Street Rising ended on December 7, 1837, as loyal militia from Toronto, backed by men from the Hamilton area, scattered the disorganized rebels in woods and fields near Montgomery's Tavern above Eglinton, which was then well outside the city. One rebel was killed; Mackenzie and Rolph escaped to the United States; and Marshall Bidwell went there also (when pressed by Governor Head) although he had not been involved himself. It was the sorry outcome of a futile effort; which does not lessen the true facts of grievances — or of the determined men like Mackenzie, who faced up to them courageously, if not well. An even more limited rising of a few hundred in the western London District quickly collapsed without fighting. For Upper Canada might assuredly want reform, but not on Mackenzie's radical pro-American terms.

1. Lord Aylmer, Unsuccessful Governor in Lower Canada, 1831-35. *Aylmer and his successor, Gosford, both failed in spreading oil on troubled Lower Canadian waters: placed as they were between an imperial government that would have liked to compromise, but did not know how, and a French patriote party led by a militant Papineau who did not believe in compromise in any case.*

2. Lord Gosford, (1835-7). *Under him, the oil he was seeking to spread caught fire — in a much more serious rebellion than that in Upper Canada. Issues ran deeper in this lower province, divided between the heritages of its French and English-speaking communities. Hence the military actions taken to suppress rebellion in Lower Canada would assuredly be larger — though it still stayed limited and localized, even here.*

3. Wolfred Nelson, Leader of Rebels in Arms. *A Montreal-born Anglophone surgeon, he entered the Assembly in 1827 and for ten years was one of Papineau's principal lieutenants. Then, while Papineau stayed out of the fight, Wolfred led in battle. He soon was captured, to be exiled to Bermuda in 1838. But later that year he was amnestied, and returned to his profession in Montreal.*

4. Robert Nelson, Leader of American Invasions. *A surgeon like his brother, and a member of parliament for Montreal, Robert avoided the fighting of 1837; but the next year raised American sympathizers in Vermont and invaded the Eastern Townships — declaring himself president of a new republic. After his defeat by loyal forces he again fled to the United States, to live for some time in California.*

1

2

3

4

More could be said, and will be. At this point, however, the much larger and more serious rebellion in Lower Canada demands our attention: to trace its rise from 1834, where we left reformism in this lower province. After Papineau's resounding manifesto, the Ninety-Two Resolutions, British authority had got nowhere in looking for solutions. The Resolutions, in truth, demanded the impeachment of Lord Aylmer, the Governor since 1831; and he was recalled in 1835; not in blame, but because he simply could not make contacts with an unyielding Papineau and his Assembly majority. Governor Lord Gosford followed him till late 1837, instructed to conciliate but not concede — an absurdly futile policy which certainly confirmed that the faults lay not only on the Assembly side. All that Gosford's most charming efforts did was to alienate a suspicious British Party without winning over their French-Canadian opponents. Then came the inflaming Ten Resolutions of the British parliament in March of 1837, refusing self-government and elective institutions, while authorizing the Lower Canadian oligarchy to take revenues without Assembly consent. The Ten Resolutions were an outright challenge to revolt; and within months they brought that very result.

Papineau and his party had by no means been doing well. The extremist doctrines of the Ninety-Two Resolutions had taken John Neilson and many moderates away — Neilson, a bilingual Scot devoted to French Canada, but who wanted it reformed, not made into a revolutionary American state. On the other

1

2

1. St. Denis, November 23, 1837. *East of Montreal and south of Sorel,* habitants *under Wolfred Nelson here defeated a mismanaged British attack on the village.*
2. Colonel Wetherall's Force en route to St. Charles. *This picture, however, shows the scale of British response, with massed professional soldiery that could not long be withstood by untrained opponents.*

hand, the brothers Wolfred and Robert Nelson, English-speaking radicals though of Loyalist descent, stayed with Papineau, as did most of his French *patriote* supporters; notably Augustin Morin, part-author of the Ninety-Two Resolutions, and Elzéar Bédard, son of Pierre Bédard, the pre-war leader of the *Parti canadien*. And Papineau's support, at least in the Montreal district, continued strong among *Canadiens* of town and country — although it grew evident, as the time of test approached in 1837, that he had little left to offer except noble messages. Like Mackenzie in Upper Canada, in fact, this Lower Canadian champion of the people was long on words but short on decisions. Events, not Papineau, carried the march through to open rebellion.

In Montreal, ethnic fears among the English-speaking populace spawned the Doric Club, whose rowdy members paraded in semi-military style or fought with their French counterparts, the Sons of Liberty. As street violence spread, the authorities ordered *patriote* leaders arrested, and Papineau fled the city. Still a talker, not a doer, he went to orate at grand countryside rallies. Yet attempts to arrest him and his friends brought on armed resistance against troops sent out from Montreal. At St. Denis in the Richelieu Valley, a blundering military column was repulsed on November 23 by *Canadien* rebels under Wolfred

1

1. St. Charles, November 25, 1837. *Here on the Richelieu, accordingly,* patriote *resistance failed to keep out the regulars.*

2. St. Eustache, December 14, 1837. *At the other, western side of Montreal on the mainland shore, the decisive battle fought here saw British troops capture the church and presbytery fortified and held by the* patriotes: *a battle in which Dr. Jean Olivier Chénier, the rebel leader, was killed.*

2

Nelson. In nearby St. Charles two days later, *patriotes* with only old muskets and pitchforks were effectively defeated. And at St. Eustache north of Montreal, on December 14, the heaviest fight saw rebel leader Dr. Jean-Olivier Chénier killed in a crushing attack by regulars under Sir John Colborne, the veteran British commander-in-chief for both Canadas. This broke the back of a revolt which its political inspirer, Papineau, had never really commanded. He fled safely to exile in the United States instead.

Another attempt came in February, 1838, at Lacolle, when Robert Nelson led rebels and American supporters back over the American border into the Eastern Townships, but was driven out by loyal militia. The same thing happened to him in November at Odelltown, in a second abortive invasion from Vermont. All in all, it was a hopeless rebellion: limited to the Montreal district alone, opposed by many French Canadians as well as British, and strongly condemned by the Roman Catholic Church, whose influence was still great. Yet compared with the little Upper Canadian affair, this Lower Canadian revolt was far more serious; involving many more people, if still a restricted minority of the *Canadiens*. It also produced many more casualties and prisoners, and it revealed considerable passive sympathy for the *patriotes*, if not as much active willingness to back them. In any case, the rebellion in Lower Canada was rightly taken far more seriously by the imperial government in Britain; though even an undoubtedly loyal Upper Canada raised other compelling problems, as American border raids followed its own small internal uprising.

1. Odelltown, November 9, 1838. *This was less a further round in an internal rebellion, already checked, than it was an external attack in the border warfare that had spread along the American boundaries of both Canadas. At Odelltown, around two hundred of "Her Majesty's Loyal Volunteers," drawn from the largely Anglophone Eastern Townships defeated some 1,200 so-called patriotes led by Robert Nelson, but largely composed of American adventurers.*

2. British Reinforcements from New Brunswick. *It might seem that Britain had the military power on hand to keep control. Yet with regulars shifted from Upper Canada to the Lower Canadian outbreaks, and with dangers rising far along inland American borders, the trained forces available needed strengthening as much as possible. And so these men of the 43rd Regiment were sent up overland, here crossing the St. John River in the winter of 1837-8.*

3. Footnote to Invasion, 1838. *A notice at Burlington, Vermont, to those Americans who had provided guns for "Canadian Patriots."*

1

2

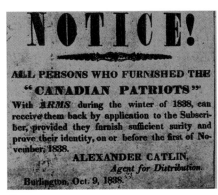

3

Border Warfare, Durham Report, and Union of the Canadas

While the last outburst of revolt in Lower Canada came briefly in November, 1838, in its neighbour-province an undeclared frontier war went on recurrently throughout that year, thanks to armed attacks from a most un-neighbourly United States. These were unofficial, private efforts to wrest Upper Canada by force from British rule, although for months American state authorities did little effective to check them. At first, with the flight of Upper Canadian rebels to the republic after their own rising had failed, there was a significant Canadian share in new attempts to carry on the fight, while the refugee radicals appealed to American sympathizers for help. Thus William Lyon Mackenzie and others reaching Buffalo in early December, 1837, sought to thrust back across the Niagara frontier. Indeed, Canadian "patriots," and increasing American supporters, occupied Canada's Navy Island in the Niagara River in mid-December, as their base camp for invasion. But the Canadian patriot role was very soon outweighed, when more and more Americans took up warlike forays into Upper Canada.

Among these raiders, at the one extreme, were those termed "border ruffians," out for plunder. At the other were visionary, democratic idealists, seeking revolutionary freedom for a people groaning (of course) under imperial British tyranny. In between were seekers after excitement, fortune, power — and fertile lands, which Mackenzie for one, promised lavishly. And over all, there was general American expansionism, which then was pushing south to Texas and Mexico as well as north into British territory: full of a belief in Manifest Destiny, the God-given right of the United States to extend its own empire over a whole continent.

Navy Island, held by largely American invaders, was soon sealed off, then bombarded by Upper Canada's militia forces. While Mackenzie was busy there drafting further governing schemes for the State of Upper Canada, his supporting forces drifted away; until by mid-January, 1838, Navy Island was evacuated. Yet this was only the start of border troubles. Raids took place that winter along the Detroit frontier. In March, a sizeable American invasion across Lake Erie to Pelee Island was defeated by combined British regulars and militia. In May, the Canadian steamer *Sir Robert Peel* was seized and burned off Brockville by "river pirates," and in June the Short Hills raid was repelled in the Niagara area. These were only some of the alarms and incidents of 1838, which ended at last at the Battle of Windsor in December, throwing back one final American foray. But the "war" had really climaxed at the Battle of the Windmill in November near Prescott, where a mass of American invaders who had crossed the Upper St.

1. Brockville, Upper Canada, 1838. *This quiet waterside town on the Upper St. Lawrence would soon be faced by the tensions and violence of undeclared war, as were a host of other places along the exposed inland boundary.*

2. Seizure of the *Caroline* at Navy Island. *Mackenzie's intended invasion army collecting on Navy Island was supplied from the American mainland side of the Niagara River by the steamer* Caroline. Late in December, 1837, seven boatloads of Canadian militia crossed the river at night to seize the vessel at her moorings. They cut her adrift, empty, and sent her burning down-river towards the Falls. But despite this highly imaginative American picture, the Caroline did not go over Niagara Falls, but grounded above them — where her burnt-out hulk stayed visible for years.

1

2

Lawrence caused as many British deaths as had the Battle of Queenston Heights, during four days before they surrendered.

In fact, if Americans liked to think that this was a second American Revolution, it was really much more a second War of 1812 to Upper Canada's defenders, constantly resisting attacks from the United States. Consequently, an angry Tory reaction swept this province that had been subjected to lootings, burnings and bloodshed, following its own far-from-popular local revolt. Revolt, in truth, to most Upper Canadians seemed only treason that meant misery, not freedom. And so, "traitor" rebels were flung into prison — though only two of them were hanged. Moderate Liberals like Robert Baldwin, while no friends of rebellion, had to lie low; and Reformers gave way to vehement Orange Tories, especially in Toronto. Yet things began to change in both the Canadas from mid-1838, when a new Governor-General, Lord Durham, reached Quebec: commissioned by the imperial government to inquire into the Canadian rebellions, and to recommend full-scale remedies for them.

John Lambton, Earl of Durham — known as "Radical Jack" — was a keenly reforming Liberal himself. In fact, he had been a thorn in the side of Britain's established Whig-Liberal government, now under Lord Melbourne, which finally recognized that a lot would have to be dealt with in British North America, and did not mind giving the task to a major political critic — who would either get rid of the problem or himself in the attempt. Durham, as imperious in conduct as he was democratic in beliefs, acted all too imperiously when, in dropping charges

1

2

1. The Battle of the Windmill, Prescott, November 1838. *The scene displays the massive stone windmill occupied by attacking Americans, under siege and bombardment. British steamers, pressed into service as gunboats, fire from the St. Lawrence: two of them from Kingston with naval seamen and artillery aboard; the smallest from Brockville, with just two small cannon.*

2. A Cynical Comment on British Government Reactions, 1838. *In this British cartoon, Prime Minister Lord Melbourne is explaining to a young Queen Victoria that rebellion in Canada was all due to reform in parliament: thereby portraying him as anything but liberal-minded. Still, realizing the involved (and expensive) nature of the colonial troubles, the Melbourne ministry did appoint Lord Durham to investigate.*

1. The Earl of Durham. *A demanding political reformer, if a commanding social aristocrat, Durham could be difficult to deal with — expecting his own way, and upset when he did get it. His lifelong illness, tuberculosis, which killed him at forty-eight, probably contributed to his feverishly eager or dejected moods. Nonetheless, bold in ideas, brilliant in grasp, Durham contributed hugely to Canada's heritage, even if he was only in the country for short months. His Report, completed after he had left, opened the way to self-government within the British provinces in America; and ultimately to a wholly free Canadian nation.*

2. Robert Baldwin, Upper Canadian Father of Responsible Government. *Durham, on the imperial stage, had vitally backed the idea of responsible cabinet rule. William Lyon Mackenzie and Louis Joseph Papineau in the Canadas had voiced keen colonial grievances, but hardly offered acceptable remedies. Yet the moderate Reformer, Robert Baldwin of Upper Canada, (building cautiously on the views of his father, Dr. Baldwin) saw prospects of using the parliamentary system which Mackenzie or Papineau did not; and which Durham himself had only partly recognized. In fact, Baldwin — a "man of one idea" ever since his entry to the Upper Canada Assembly in 1829 — foresaw that making the government ministers, or cabinet, collectively responsible as a party group to the elected Assembly, would effectively transfer control to the colonial people through their own representative party majority in parliament.*

3. Proclamation by Durham as Governor-General, 1838. *This extract expresses his policies on arriving in Canada: to open up all questions and hear from "honest" advocates of reform without distinctions of party or race; but not "disturbers of the public peace" or "enemies of the Crown and British Empire."*

against all those still held for rebellion, he sent eight others already convicted in Lower Canada to a mild exile in Bermuda: a move attacked as beyond his powers by his enemies at home, who gleefully pushed him into resigning. But in the five months before Durham returned to England in November, 1838, this governor-commissioner did monumental work; mostly in Lower Canada, yet including a fruitful trip to Upper Canada besides. For Lord Durham both saw for himself and took solid advice; including on the Atlantic provinces, which were within his mandate as well. And in Upper Canada he heard particularly from Robert Baldwin on the principle of responsible cabinet government, as applied to meet colonial problems.

Durham's findings and answers all came out in the great Report he produced on his return to England, published in February, 1839. Its creator never saw its results, since in 1840 he died from the tuberculosis he had battled for years. Yet the Durham Report would prove a milestone in Canadian history and heritage, by helping to bring on a different era of political advance well beyond the ineffectual colonial strife of the 1820s and 30s. To begin with, the Report of 1839 dealt trenchantly with old grievances: with abuses of oligarchy, high-level favouritism and speculation in land grants; with Anglican privilege and clergy reserves, or problems of finance, canal-building, local administration and more. But far more important, it put forward two main recommendations: responsible government and the union of the Canadas, each of which demands a closer look.

Durham asserted that a maturing British colony should run its own affairs as Britain did at home, under a government duly responsible to its parliament. Given the British constitutional inheritance, he argued, the inhabitants of such a colony would scarcely stay content with less. True, he felt that the external aspects of colonial affairs — for instance, foreign relations, defence or overseas trade — could still remain under imperial control. But in all internal matters, a colony's government should stand or fall by the votes of its own elected, representative assembly, just as the British cabinet stood by the will of the House of Commons in London. This parliamentary approach cut out all talk about elected upper houses, the Legislative Councils. For while select, small upper chambers might usefully amend and improve laws, they should not interfere with the popular Assembly's right, alone, to give or withhold confidence in the government — in the ministers who composed the ruling Executive Council. With this assertion Durham clearly echoed Robert Baldwin's own submissions on responsible self-rule for British North America; although it should be noted that he did not go as far as Baldwin did in recognizing the need for complete party government, and thus still tended to see the Governor, not a party premier,

1

2

By His Excellency
The Right Honorable John George
Earl of Durham, Viscount Lambton
&c &c Knight Grand Cross of the
most Honorable Military Order
of the Bath, one of Her Majesty's
most Honorable Privy Council, and
Governor General Vice Admiral,
and Captain General of all Her
Majesty's Provinces within, and
adjacent to, the Continent of North
America &c &c &c &c

Durham

A Proclamation.

The Queen; having been graciously
pleased to entrust to me the Government of British North
America, I have this day assumed the Administration of
affairs.

In the execution of this important
duty, I rely with confidence on the cordial Support of all
Her Majesty's Subjects, as the best means of enabling me
to bring every question affecting their welfare to a Successful
issue, especially such as may come under my cognizance
as Her Majesty's High Commissioner.

The honest and conscientious advocates
of Reform, and of the amelioration of defective Institutions,
will receive from me, without distinction of Party, Races,
or Politics, that assistance and encouragement which
their patriotism has a right to command, from all who
desire to strengthen and consolidate the connexion between
the Parent State and these important Colonies; but the
disturbers of the public Peace, the violators of the Law,
the enemies of the Crown, and of the British Empire,
will

3

as directing government policy; even though that Governor was only to act through ministers who held majority-party support in the Assembly.

Accordingly, responsible government was still not fully envisaged by Durham, and would have to evolve further. Nonetheless, his powerful advocacy was vital in getting the whole process moving. The words of the Earl of Durham plainly carried more weight, in the power centres of London, than those of a mere loyal colonial like Robert Baldwin. But in any case, it still took time before even the Durham Report's call for responsible rule was conclusively accepted by the imperial authorities.

As for a union of the Canadas, however, this was quickly taken up by the British government. At first, Durham had looked for a complete or legislative union of all the colonies. Yet he soon had found that even a federal union, which would still leave provincial governments in being, was unacceptable to the Atlantic provinces. From the information he received, they were not interested, or were even opposed, to joining with the big, distant and unruly Canadas. New Brunswick appeared quite happy and "harmonious," with full Assembly control of its revenue already. Newfoundland and Prince Edward Island were caught up in their own particular internal contests; and in Nova Scotia, the issues were those of ordinary party manoeuvring, not of deep and dangerous conflict. In consequence, Durham came to a union of the Canadas alone as a fundamental part of his Report.

For one thing, that union could make responsible government safely possible in these two colonies. His months spent in a still bitterly divided Lower Canada, had convinced this imperial investigator that the only final answer to what he indelibly described as, "two nations warring in the bosom of a single state," was French Canada's own absorption into a larger, loyally British unit. In such a unit, Francophones would not only enjoy the benefits of British economic progress, but would share in responsible rule — yet could be outvoted by the combined weight of the Upper and Lower Canada British. From Durham's own national faith in Britain's constitution and industrial progress, it seemed self-evident that the *Canadiens*, a small, backward people without any real history or future, could in time become peaceably and happily assimilated in a far greater society. Here was a typically biassed (and wrong) assumption of many a complacent Anglophone before and since, which only led *Canadiens* to keep up a lively defence of their own distinct society and culture. In effect, Durham himself re-stimulated French heritage in Canada.

All the same, his analysis seemed convincing in other respects. What both Canadas surely needed, economically, was a broad union which would remove the barriers on their common St. Lawrence trunkline to mid-continent, and which would have the capabilities and credit to complete the expensive St. Lawrence canal system. In economic terms, such a union promised richly to both the leading merchants of Montreal and the business interests of Upper Canada; and there is little doubt that it also promised growth in lumbering, farming and settlement for ordinary residents along the way. Yet further, even a union without responsible government — which the Melbourne ministry in Britain still did not mean to concede — should bring new development and prosperity, spread peaceful progress and help contain the French element within one securely British united province.

In the calculations of the imperial government, such a union could win

Title Page of Durham's Report, 1839. *A rather plain presentation of powerful findings and history-making recommendations.*

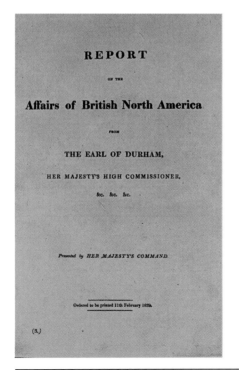

REPORT

on the

Affairs of British North America

from

THE EARL OF DURHAM,

HER MAJESTY'S HIGH COMMISSIONER,

&c. &c. &c.

Presented by HER MAJESTY'S COMMAND.

Ordered to be printed 11th February 1839.

(3.)

Assembly consent in an Upper Canada close to bankruptcy because of its canal expenditures, if union was backed substantially by an imperial loan. And as Lower Canada was being ruled by a small, emergency Special Council, there would be no French-dominated Assembly to refuse its own approval. Hence the Melbourne ministry went after a Canadian union without responsible government, although with considerable political improvements as well as new financial aid. Furthermore, the ministry sent smooth Charles Poulett Thomson, later Lord Sydenham, to Canada as Governor General, charged with promoting some of the particular reforms proposed by Lord Durham; but above all, with carrying through the Canadian Union project.

Thompson was no radical aristocrat like Durham, but a Manchester business representative and a skilled political manager. In the fall of 1839 he arrived in the Lower Canadian province, where he set adroitly to work to ensure union. That was relatively easy in Lower Canada, since its Special Council approved his business-like arguments; even though a voiceless French-Canadian majority was left with gloomy doubts. In Upper Canada it took more effort; but here Thomson's commercial knowledge and promised British funding for development drew the Tories, while his vague talk of responsible rule attracted many Reformers. He even brought Robert Baldwin into the government in 1840; and that year, too, steered a significant change in the Upper Canada clergy reserves system through the Assembly: whereby some share of the money from the sale of clergy lands would go to other Protestant churches besides the Anglican. Also, he made plain that the proposed union scheme would give less populous Upper Canada as many seats in a united legislature as Lower Canada. Accordingly, by mid-1840 the convincing Governor had achieved his basis of consent; and that summer the Act of Union passed the British parliament, while in recognition Thomson was named Baron Sydenham of Kent and Toronto.

The Union Act went into effect in February, 1841, as Lord Sydenham stayed on as first Governor-General of the United Province of Canada. This Act, and what it did, can best be discussed in the next chapter. But it does bear saying, now, that it led on to responsible self-government and ultimately to the federal union of all British North America; although neither of these historic consequences looked like near possibilities when the Union of the Canadas actually began in early 1841. At the present point, however, it seems better to look back. Out of a quarter-century of immigration and economic advance — both of which had by no means ended in 1841 — out of the accompanying discords which had exploded into the Canadian rebellions, two much more politically aware colonial societies had developed. Their heritage of revolt might rest for Upper Canada in what were largely myths about William Lyon Mackenzie's gifts to Canadian self-government — mostly non-existent. But in Lower Canada, they had enshrined a romantic but real Francophone nationalism, to last right on into separatism in modern Quebec.

1. Burnt-Out St. Eustache: Heritage of Rebellion. *In Upper Canada in 1837-8, the losses of life had stemmed mainly from external attack. Only a few persons were killed or executed because of the internal rising. But the Lower Canadian internal revolt itself cost some 350 lives. The death toll still was not that large, in a province by then of more than half a million. Nevertheless, the impact was hard felt by a close-knit Canadien community, including the exiling of some rebel prisoners to Australian penal settlements, till they at last were freed to return home in the later 1840s. Over all, the Lower Canadian revolt understandably left much greater marks and harsher memories.*

2. Charles Poulett Thomson, later Lord Sydenham. *He came to Canada in 1839 as governor, essentially to carry out the British cabinets's own views on Durham's Report; that is, to provide for a union of the Canadas and economic aid, but not responsible government. After carrying union forward, to be put into effect by the Union Act of 1840; Sydenham continued as governor of the United Province of Canada thereafter, until his accidental death in 1841. He achieved a lot, politically and materially. But his own superficial smoothness left major questions unanswered, to rise once more in the future.*

1

2

TERRITORIAL EVOL

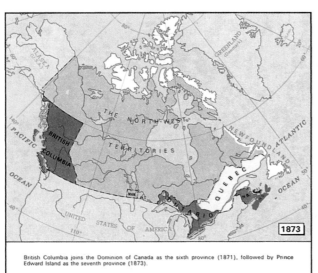

British Columbia joins the Dominion of Canada as the sixth province (1871), followed by Prince Edward Island as the seventh province (1873).

1873

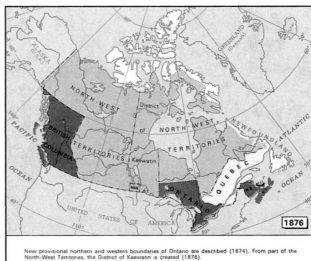

New provisional northern and western boundaries of Ontario are described (1874). From part of the North-West Territories, the District of Keewatin is created (1876).

1876

British rights to the arctic islands pass to Ca (1881), but the extension to the east is con Saskatchewan, Athabaska, and Alberta are c

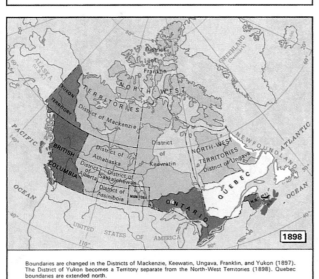

Boundaries are changed in the Districts of Mackenzie, Keewatin, Ungava, Franklin, and Yukon (1897). The District of Yukon becomes a Territory separate from the North-West Territories (1898). Quebec boundaries are extended north.

1898

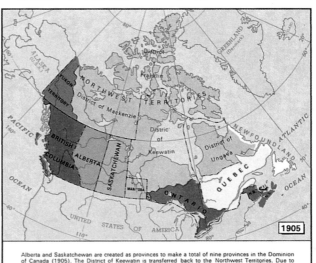

Alberta and Saskatchewan are created as provinces to make a total of nine provinces in the Dominion of Canada (1905). The District of Keewatin is transferred back to the Northwest Territories. Due to changes in adjoining areas the boundaries of the Northwest Territories are redefined (1906).

1905

Ontario and Manitoba attain their present bou Quebec is extended northward to Hudson B Hudson Strait, thereby absorbing mainland Quebec-Labrador boundary remains unsettled.

TION OF CANADA

1882

The boundaries of Manitoba are extended ...ario. The provisional Districts of Assiniboia.

1889

The Ontario-Manitoba boundary dispute is settled by the Ontario Boundary Act. Ontario is enlarged west to Lake of the Woods and north to the Albany River.

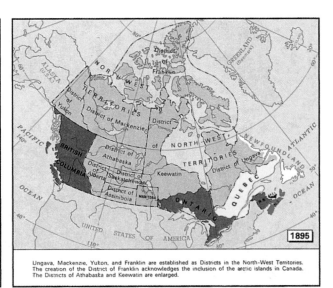

1895

Ungava, Mackenzie, Yukon, and Franklin are established as Districts in the North-West Territories. The creation of the District of Franklin acknowledges the inclusion of the arctic islands in Canada. The Districts of Athabaska and Keewatin are enlarged.

1912

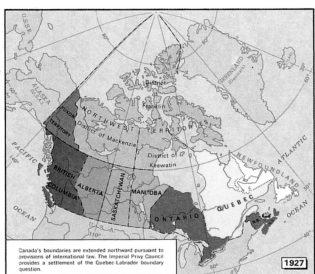

1927

Canada's boundaries are extended northward pursuant to provisions of international law. The Imperial Privy Council provides a settlement of the Quebec-Labrador boundary question.

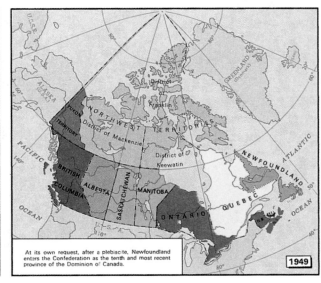

1949

At its own request, after a plebiscite, Newfoundland enters the Confederation as the tenth and most recent province of the Dominion of Canada.

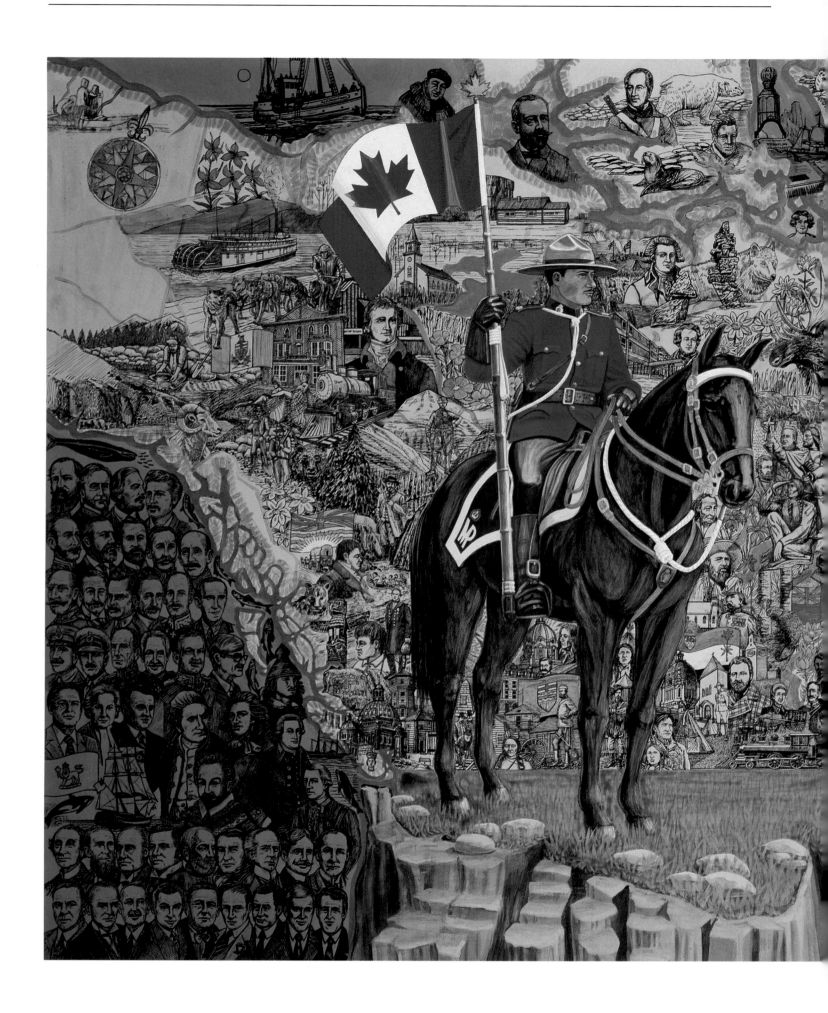

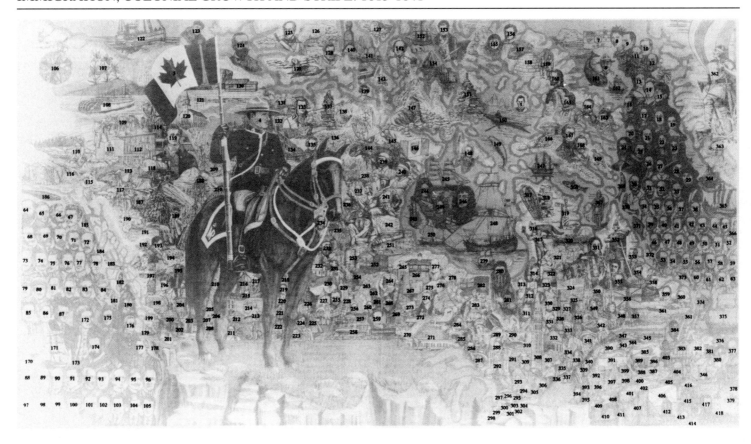

Key to *From Sea Unto Sea* by Brian Romagnoli

NATIONAL

1. Royal Arms of Canada
2. Provincial Coat of Arms
3. Flag of Canada
4. Royal Canadian Mounted Police
5. HRH Prince Charles - Heir to Throne
6. Lord Baden Powell - Boy Scouts

ROYAL HEADS OF STATE

7. Queen's Personal Canadian Flag
8. Queen Elizabeth II
9. King George VI
10. King Edward VIII
11. King George V
12. King Edward VII
13. Queen Victoria
14. King William IV
15. King George IV
16. King George III
17. King George II
18. King George I
19. Queen Anne
20. Queen Mary II
21. King William III
22. King James II
23. King Charles II
24. King Charles I
25. King James I
26. Queen Elizabeth I
27. Queen Mary I
28. King Henry VIII
29. King Henry VII

FATHERS OF CONFEDERATION

30. Adams George Archibald
31. George Brown
32. Alexander Campbell

33. Frederic B.T. Carter
34. George Etienne Cartier
35. Edward Barron Chandler
36. Jean-Charles Chapais
37. James Cockburn
38. George Coles
39. Robert Barry Dickey
40. Charles Fisher
41. Alexander Tilloch Galt
42. Col. J.H. Gray
43. John Hamilton Gray
44. Thomas Heath Haviland
45. William Alexander Henry
46. John Mercer Johnson
47. Hector Louis Langevin
48. Johnathan McCully
49. A.A. Macdonald
50. John A. Macdonald
51. William McDougall
52. Thomas D'Arcy McGee
53. Peter Mitchell
54. Oliver Mowat
55. Edward Palmer
56. William Henry Pope
57. Ambrose Shea
58. William H. Steeves
59. Sir Etienne-Pascal Tache
60. Samuel L. Tilley
61. Charles Tupper
62. Edward Whelan
63. Hewitt Bernard, Sect.

GOVERNOR GENERALS

64. Viscount Monck
65. Lord Lisgar
66. Earl of Dufferin
67. Marquis of Lorne
68. Marquis of Lansdowne
69. Lord Stanley
70. Lord Aberdeen
71. Earl of Minto
72. Earl Grey

73. H.R.H. Duke of Connaught
74. Duke of Devonshire
75. Lord Byng
76. Lord Willingdon
77. Lord Bessborough
78. Lord Tweedsmuir
79. Earl of Athlone
80. Lord Alexander
81. Rt. Hon. Vincent Massey
82. General George P. Vanier
83. Rt. Hon. Roland Michener
84. Rt. Hon. Jules Leger
85. Rt. Hon. Edward Schreyer
86. Rt. Hon. Jeanne Sauve
87. Rt. Hon. Ramon Hnatyshyn

PRIME MINISTERS

88. Rt. Hon. Sir John A Macdonald
89. Hon. Alexander Mackenzie
90. Hon. Sir John J.C. Abbott
91. Rt. Hon. Sir John S.D. Thompson
92. Hon. Sir Mackenzie Bowell
93. Rt. Hon. Sir Charles Tupper
94. Rt. Hon. Sir Wilfred Laurier
95. Rt. Hon. Sir Robert L Borden
96. Rt. Hon. Arthur Meighen
97. Rt. Hon. W.L. Mackenzie King
98. Rt. Hon. Richard B. Bennett
99. Rt. Hon. Louis St. Laurent
100. Rt. Hon. John G. Diefenbaker
101. Rt. Hon. Lester B. Pearson
102. Rt. Hon. Pierre E. Trudeau
103. Rt. Hon. C. Joseph Clark
104. Rt. Hon. John N. Turner
105. Rt. Hon. M. Brian Mulrony

YUKON TERRITORY

106. North Point Compass Card (Alaska U.S.A.)
107. Floral Symbol - Fireweed

108. Sternwheeler
109. Dog Sled
110. Prospector Panning For Gold
111. Provincial Flag
112. Palace Grand Opera House, Dawson City
113. Gaslight Follies
114. Legislative Assembly
115. Bighorn Sheep
116. Elias-Coastal Mountains
117. Prospectors Mining - Klondike Gold Rush
118. Engine No. 51 White Pass - Yukon Railway

NORTHWEST TERRITORIES AND ARCTIC

119. Alexander Mackenzie
120. Mission Church, Fort Providence
121. Arctic Tundra
122. R.C.M.P. Patrol Boat St. Roch
123. Sergeant Henry Larsen
124. Ronald Amundsen
125. Comdr. Robert McClure
126. Polar Bear
127. Baby Seal
128. Vilhjamur Stefansson
129. Sea Lion
130. R.C.M.P. Post, Pierce Point, Darnley Bay
131. Franklin Camp, Coppermine River
132. Rocky Defile Cliff
133. Samuel Hearne
134. Legislative Assembly, Yellowknife
135. Thomas Simpson
136. Floral Symbol - Mountain Avens
137. Inukshuks, Pelly Bay
138. Arctic Wolf

139. Lady Franklin
140. Franklin Cenotaph
141. Franklin Ship, Erebus
142. Sir John Franklin
143. Franklin Expedition Cairn,
     King William Is.
144. Moose
145. Mace of Territorial Council
146. Provincial Flag
147. Walrus
148. Arthur Dobbs
149. Beluga Whale
150. Inuit Kayak
151. Inukshuit, Igloolik in Foxe
     Basin
152. Parry's Ship
153. Sir William Edward Parry
154. Icebergs
155. Inuit Kridlak
156. Capt. Leopold McCintock
157. Muskoxen
158. Igloo snow hut
159. Inuit Ipilkvik and Tukkolerktuk
160. Dr. John Rae
161. North Atlantic Right Whale
162. W. Baffin/R. Bylot Ship,
     Discovery
163. Knud Rasmussen
164. Carl Peterson
165. Capt. John Davis
166. Snowy Owl
167. Sir John Ross
168. Sir Martin Frobisher
169. Rock Ptarmigan

BRITISH COLUMBIA

170. Orca Whale
171. Cook's Ship, Resolution
172. Capt. James Cook
173. Drakes's Ship. Golden Hinde
174. Sir Francis Drake
175. Capt. John Meares
176. Capt. George Vancouver
177. Don Juan Bodega y Quadra
178. White-Beaked Dolphin
179. Hudson Bay Company
     Steamer, Beaver
180. Maquinna
181. Tuna Fish
182. Pink Salmon
183. Sablefish
184. Pacific Sardine
185. White Seabass
186. Pacific Gray Whale
187. Grizzly Bear
188. Conrad Kain
189. Judge Mathew Begbie
190. Floral Symbol - Pacific
     Dogwood
191. Provincial Flag
192. Covered Wagon, Cariboo
     Gold Rush
193. Simon Fraser
194. Fraser Descending Fraser
     River
195. Sir James Douglas
196. David Thompson
197. Indian Totem Pole
198. Mackenzie's Rock
199. Giant Douglas Firs, Cathedral
     Grove
200. Provincial Parliament Building
201. Queen Victoria, City s
     Namesake
202. Point Atkinson Lighthouse,
     Vancouver
203. Fort Langley, Vancouver
204. Hudson Bay Co. Bastion at
     Fort Nanaimo
205. Last Spike Cairn at
     Craigellachie

206. Sanford Fleming
207. William Van Horne
208. Lord Strathcona, Donald Smith

ALBERTA

209. Floral Symbol - Wild Rose
210. Rocky Mountains
211. Sioux Chief Sitting Bull
212. Fort Macleod, Calgary
213. Commissioner James Macleod
214. Provincial Flag
215. Commissioner George French
216. Legislative Building,
     Edmonton
217. Blackfoot Chief Crowfoot

SASKATCHEWAN

218. Poundmaker's Grave
219. Cree Chief Poundmaker
220. Fort Battleford
221. Superintendent James Walsh
222. Fort Walsh
223. Sioux War Chief Spotted Eagle
224. Blood Chief Red Crow
225. Plains Indian Teepee
226. Legislative Building, Regina
227. R.C.M.P. Chapel
228. Wheat Fields
229. Grain Elevator
230. Provincial Flag
231. Maj. General Frederick
     Middleton
232. St. Antoine de Padoue,
     Batoche
233. Gabriel Dumont
234. Cree Chief Big Bear
235. Floral Symbol - Red Lily
236. Rev. George McDougall
237. Father Albert Lacombe

MANITOBA

238. Buffalo
239. Anthony Henday
240. Henry Kelsey
241. Pierre de la Verendrye
242. Hearne's Rock
243. Jens Munk's Ship at Churchill
244. John, Lord Churchill
245. HBC Barque, Prince Rupert
246. Prince Rupert
247. Red River Colony Ship,
     Wellington
248. HBC Ketch, Nonsuch
249. Pierre Le Moyne d'Iberville
250. York Boat
251. Cannon, Fort Prince of Wales
252. Provincial Flag
253. White Birch
254. Canadian Beaver
255. Louis Riel
256. Marie Anne Gaboury
257. Red River Cart
258. C.P.R. Countess of Dufferin
259. Earl of Selkirk, Thomas
     Douglas
260. Superintendent Samuel Steele
261. Saulteaux Chief Peguis
262. Col. Garnet Wolseley
263. Floral Symbol - Prairie Crocus
264. Viking Heritage, Gimli
265. Ring-necked Pheasant
266. HBC Post, York Factory
267. Fort Garry Gate, Winnipeg
268. St. Michael's, Gardenton
269. Legislative Building, Winnipeg

ONTARIO

270. Canada Goose
271. Great Hall, Fort William
272. Voyageur Canoe
273. North West Company Flag
274. William McGillivray

275. Hudson Bay Company Flag
276. Sir George Simpson
277. Simon McTavish
278. Floral Symbol - White Trillium
279. Hudson's Barque, Discovery
280. Henry Hudson
281. Captain Thomas James
282. Provincial Flag
283. Samuel de Champlain
284. Pierre Radisson
285. Medard des Groseilliers
286. Robert de La Salle
287. Etienne Brule
288. Father Jacques Marquette
289. Louis Jolliet
290. Jolliet & Marquette in canoe
291. Sainte-Marie Among the
     Hurons
292. Martyr's Shrine, Midland
293. Queen's Park, Toronto
294. William Lyon Mackenzie
295. Sir John Graves Simcoe
296. Sir Isaac Brock
297. Six Nations Chief John Norton
298. Shawnie Chief Tecumseh
299. Mohawk Chief Joseph Brant
300. Sir Allan MacNab
301. William Hamilton Merrit
302. Laura Secord
303. Niagara Falls
304. Navy Hall, Niagara (Newark)
305. Kingston City Hall
306. Sir John A. Macdonald,
     Kingston
307. Changing of the Guard, Ottawa
308. Peace Tower of Parliament
     Buildings
309. National War Memorial,
     Ottawa
310. Holland Tulips

QUEBEC

311. Louis-Joseph Papineau
312. Lord Durham
313. Lord Elgin
314. Lord Grey
315. Louis Hebert
316. Gray Fox
317. Snow Shoes
318. Ungava Cairn
319. Payne Bay Cairn
320. Mistassini Cree in Canoe
321. Floral Symbol - White Garden
     Lily
322. Maple Sugar Tapping
323. Sir Guy Carleton
324. Provincial Flag
325. The Citadel, Quebec City
326. National Assembly, Quebec
     City
327. Marquis L.J. de Montcalm
328. Wolfe-Montcalm Monument
329. Plains of Abraham
330. General James Wolfe
331. Brig. Gen. James Murray
332. Bonsecours Market, Montreal
333. Jacques Cartier
334. Col. C.M. de Salaberry
335. Ste. Sulpice Clock, Montreal
336. 1st Railway: Laprairie - St. Jean
337. Jeanne Mance
338. Madeleine de Vercheres
339. Marguerite Bourgeoys
340. Paul de Maisonneuve
341. Count Frontenac
342. Marquis de Vaudreil
343. Cartier's Cross at Gaspe
344. Perce Rock
345. Micmac Hut and Canoe
346. Cartier's Grand Hermine Ship
347. Duck

348. Marie de La Peltrie
349. Louis XIV
350. Ste. Anne de Beaupre Church

NEWFOUNDLAND

351. Mikak of Labrador with son
352. Gasper Corte-Real
353. Dr. Wilfred Grenfell
354. John Guy
355. William Carson
356. Provincial Flag
357. Floral Symbol - Pitcher Plant
358. Lord Rodney
359. Joey Smallwood
360. Sir Winston Churchill
361. L'Anse aux Meadows
362. Leif Ericsson (Greenland)
363. Reindeer (Greenland)
364. Saint Brendan
365. Leif's Viking Ship
366. Ocean Perch fish
367. Thorfinn Karlsfni
368. Arctic Char
369. Northern Pike
370. Atlantic Salmon
371. Halibut
372. Herring
373. Mackerel
374. Giovanni Cabotto (John Cabot)
375. Cabotto's Barque, Mathew
376. Guglielmo Marconi
377. Sir Humphrey Gibert
378. Grand Banks
379. Cod Fish
380. Cape Spear
381. Cabot Tower
382. House of Assembly, St. John's
383. Colonial Building
384. Last Beothuk, Shanawdithit

PRINCE EDWARD ISLAND

385. Provincial Flag
386. Joseph Des Barres
387. Potato Crop
388. Floral Symbol - Lady's Slipper
389. Province House,
     Charlottetown

NEW BRUNSWICK

390. Acadian Flag
391. Provincial Flag
392. Abenaquis Family
393. Edward Winslow
394. Ward Chipman
395. Marie de la Tour
396. Floral Symbol - Purple Violet
397. Carleton Martello Tower
398. Loyalist Landing Rock, St. John
399. Legislative Building,
     Fredericton

NOVA SCOTIA

400. Floral Symbol - Mayflower
401. Joseph Howe
402. Province House, Halifax
403. King's Bastion, Fort
     Louisbourg
404. Alexander Graham Bell
405. Silver Dart, 1st Flight
406. Provincial Flag
407. Schooner Bluenose
408. Pierre de Monts
409. Jean de Poutrincourt
410. Port Royal
411. Acadian Evangeline
412. Old Town Clock, Halifax
413. Samuel Cunard
414. Royal William, 1st Steamer
415. United Empire Loyalists
416. St. Paul's Anglican Church
417. Giovanni da Verrazano
418. Peggy's Cove

Events Relating to the Rebellions in the Canadas

Upper Canada

1834

When York becomes the City of Toronto in March, William Lyon Mackenzie is chosen its first mayor.
Reformers in October win the provincial elections, in a general leftward swing.

1835

That winter, Reform radicals in the Assembly, with Mackenzie in the lead, manage to carry the inflammatory Seventh Report on Grievances.

1836

Governor Bond Head arrives in January to make changes. He appoints Reformers Robert Baldwin and John Rolph to the Executive Council; but they resign in March.

Head dismisses the Reform-dominated Assembly in April, after which new elections (marked by violence and Head's interference) return a Tory majority.

Radicals grow more embittered and extreme as their support falls off.

1837

Trade depression, bad harvests and farmers' debts to banks promote rural unrest, through winter into spring.

June-September, Mackenzie tours countryside around Toronto, speaking to large audiences on the people's wrongs, and organizing "committees of vigilance."

In October, Head sends all the regulars in the province to Lower Canada, because of the surge of unrest there.

Into November, Mackenzie holds secret meetings with Reform leaders from around Toronto, to plan taking over the government. Publishes Draft Constitution for Upper Canada in his paper, November 15.

December 1, Mackenzie writes a Declaration of Independence.

December 4, would-be rebels gather from rural areas to Montgomery's Tavern up Yonge Street north of Toronto.

December 5, Rebel forces march down Yonge to Gallows Hill below St. Clair, where they clash with a sheriff's picket, and flee back.

December 7, Rebels are scattered in a brief skirmish with loyal militia at Montgomery's.

December 13, Mackenzie and a force mainly of American "patriots" occupy Navy Island in Niagara River, where he declares himself head of the Provisional Government of the State of Upper Canada.

December 14, Rebels from the Brantford-London area, collecting at the village of Scotland, disperse on hearing of Mackenzie's defeat at Montgomery's, and the close approach of loyal militia toward themselves.

December 29-30, "Patriot" supply-ship *Caroline* seized off Navy Island by loyal Canadian forces.

1838

January 14, Mackenzie and followers depart for Buffalo and beyond.

February 25, American attackers driven back from Fighting Island, on the Detroit River in west of Upper Canada.

March 3, British regulars and Canadian militia defeat a more serious invasion of U.S. "patriots" at Pelee Island, Lake Erie.

May 29-30, Canadian steamboat, *Sir Robert Peel*, seized near Brockville and destroyed by Americans.

June 5, at Quebec, a newly arrived Governor-General Durham protests strongly to the United States about the river "outrage," the destruction of the *Sir Robert Peel*.

At the Short Hills in June, an American attack into the Niagara Peninsula lasts some days before being dislodged by British-Canadian troops — one in a number of further border raids too numerous for all to be named here.

July, Durham goes from Quebec to Montreal and on to Upper Canada — then to Buffalo where, as a good democrat and able diplomat, he wins considerable favour. But in Toronto he meets with Reformer Robert Baldwin particularly; and hears Baldwin's views on responsible rule for Canada.

November 1, Durham, having resigned, returns to Britain, although new violence erupts on the Canadian-American border.

November 11-16, Battle of the Windmill, at Prescott on the Upper St. Lawrence.

November 21, U.S. Proclamation states that armed Americans crossing into Canada will not be protected.

December 4, Battle of Windsor: the last major border attack is here defeated.

1839

February, the publication of Durham's Report points to a new era for all Canada.

Events Relating to the Rebellions in the Canadas

Lower Canada

1834

The *Parti patriote*, combining liberal-radical doctrine with conservative *nationaliste* defence of *Canadien* institutions, continues its majority hold on the Lower Canadian Assembly.

The Ninety-Two Resolutions pass the Assembly in February, pushed by the *Parti patriote* leader, Louis-Joseph Papineau. Aside from rooted anti-British charges, these resolutions call for an American system of elective government (implying another American Revolution if not accepted), the impeachment of current Governor Aylmer and his "wicked" advisers, and the protection of seigneurial tenure, French law and Catholic religious bodies.

1835

Lord Gosford succeeds the recalled Aylmer as Governor-in-Chief; but in trying to deal with a "non-negotiable" Papineau and his party, loses his own support and fosters resentments among the Anglo-minority in Lower Canadian politics.

1836

By now, thanks to British efforts at reform under Aylmer and Gosford, there are more French legislative councillors and judges now than English, and proposals already set forth to turn over government revenue to full Assembly control. Yet all this comes too late. Increasing communal friction, plus agricultural hardships and growing economic depression, set the stage for outright revolt in French Canada.

1837

In March, the Ten Resolutions pass the House of Commons in England: bluntly denying the Ninety-Two Resolutions' claims; but more than that, allowing the taking of revenue in Lower Canada without Assembly consent — a harsh reply to Papineau's own hard stand.

Over the summer, strains mount in Lower Canada, as the Assembly under Papineau's lead again refuses funding to the government. Demonstrations spread in the Montreal area, and radical *Fils de la Liberté* are organized in the city (imitating the Sons of Liberty in the American Revolution) as shock troops for local conflict.

October, a large public meeting at St. Charles in the Richelieu Valley moves to organize a provincial government for Lower Canada — though a vehement Papineau now begins to lower his oratory and urge caution — too late.

November 6, Fighting breaks out in Montreal between the *Fils de la Liberté* and the Doric Club — a counter Anglophone gang-organization. Civic and provincial authorities take alarm at the disorders.

November 16, government officials seek to arrest *patriote* leaders who flee from Montreal, including Papineau — thereby inciting more violence.

November 23, The sending out of troops to seize *patriote* leaders and ensure order simply moves rural opposition on to open warfare. At St. Denis, a military column is repulsed while trying to occupy that village.

November 25, Government forces take St. Charles.

November 30, Troops now capture, and burn, St. Denis.

December 14, At St. Eustache a decisive battle crushes rebel resistance, and brings the burning of the village, while *patriote* leaders escape to the United States.

1838

In late May, Lord Durham arrives at Quebec as High Commissioner and Governor-General, and soon offers amnesties.

In September, Durham exiles a few top rebel prisoners to Bermuda; but his political rivals in England attack this move as exceeding his authority — and a proud Durham resigns.

November. Durham returns to England, to complete his "Report on the Affairs of British North America."

November 9, At Odelltown in the Eastern Townships, a last armed outbreak in Lower Canada is defeated — mostly an invasion by American sympathizers and landseekers.

1839

February, the issuing of the Durham forecasts another day: with Upper and Lower Canada soon to be united, and to achieve effective self-government during the 1840s that follow.

- 1840s Renewed British immigration, especially to Canada West
  - Rev. Peter Jones, native missionary, upholds Indian
  - State-supported school systems emerging, notably in the Canadian Union
- 1841 Governor Sydenham says Union government will rule according to elected House
- 1842 Webster-Ashburton Treaty settles border dispute between Maine and New Brunswick (N.B.)
  - Reformers Baldwin and LaFontaine brought into Canadian Union's government
- 1844 Elections bring Conservative victory in C.W., but Reform victory in C.E.
  - Brown founds Toronto *Globe*
- late 1840s Increased emigration from Ireland to B.N.A.
- 1845-47 Franklin's search for North West Passage results in his and his crews' deaths
- 1846 Britain begins policy of free trade, removing its imperial Corn Laws. Its Colonial Secretary Grey announces B.N.A. colonies will have responsible rule
  - Lord Elgin named Can. Governor-General, to put responsible government into full effect there
- 1847 Reformers win elections both in Can. and N.S.
- 1848 Tory ministry defeated in Can. House; responsible Reform cabinet under Lafontaine and Baldwin takes over
  - St. Lawrence canal system completed
- 1849 Rebellion Losses Bill introduced in Can. Assembly
  - Imperial timber preference removed
  - Vancouver Island established as a colony under H.B.C. control
- 1850s World trade and colonial commerce revives
  - Railway boom develops in B.N.A.

Chapter Seven
Self-Government and Federal Union
1841 - 1867

1850	Reformers win elections in P.E.I., to begin responsible rule there
1851	Capt. Robert McClure finds North West Passage
1854	Reciprocity Treaty established between U.S. and B.N.A. "Liberal-Conservative" coalition replaces Can. Reform government Seigneurial tenure abolished in C.E., and clergy reserves system in C.W.
1855	Nfld. begins responsible rule
1856	Representative assembly given to Vancouver Island
1858	Province of British Columbia (B.C.) set up on mainland "Double Shuffle" in Can. keeps Macdonald and Cartier Conservatives in power in the Union
1859	Nor'Wester founded as first newspaper at Red River Led by George Brown, Toronto Reform Convention adopts plan to federate the two Canadas
1860	Grand Trunk Railway completed across then-Can. union
1861	U.S. Civil War begins — and strains relations with B.N.A.
1864	Political deadlock in Can. parliament; but Great Coalition of Conservative and Reform leaders, Macdonald, Brown and Cartier, agrees to pursue general federation Charlottetown Conference accepts B.N.A. federation in principle (September) Quebec Conference works out detailed plan for Confederation (October)
1865	Quebec Resolutions approved by Can. parliament
1866	Fenian Raids from U.S. into Canada Pro-Confederation government wins in N.B., while a hesitant N.S. comes round
1866-67	London Conference adopts the revised "Quebec scheme"
1867	Resulting British North America Act takes effect, July 1

Gaining Responsible Rule

By 1841, good times had largely returned to the British North American colonies after the harsh depression of the late thirties. St. Lawrence commerce had begun flourishing again in 1840, while British immigration, which had all but stopped during the rebellions and their troubled aftermath, rose in another ascending curve to run on through the forties. And if economic conditions had much improved, so had relations with the United States. Border warfare ended, as American adventurers gave up beating themselves against stubborn Canadians who did not want to be liberated, and as federal authorities in the great republic properly enforced its official neutrality. Moreover, the question of New Brunswick's uncertain inland border with Maine (which had seen both American and British forces move into disputed lumber territories in 1839) was peacefully put to diplomatic settlement. The results came in the Webster-Ashburton Treaty of 1842. This defined New Brunswick's boundary north above the headwaters of the St. Croix River, while disposing of some other outstanding Anglo-American issues. Consequently, even as the decade opened, and the Act of Union took effect in the new Province of Canada, the way was clearing for more colonial growth — but especially, for the advance of responsible self-government.

To start with, the Act of 1840 that had combined the two Canadas in one province had given it a single government and parliament without much changing the existing constitutional patterns. Under a Governor-General for the Union, there again would be an Executive Council, an appointed Legislative Council and an elected Legislative Assembly; so that, apparently, the old separate Canadas had simply been merged in one. And yet they had not. English-speaking, largely Protestant Upper Canada with its English-based law, and mainly Francophone Lower Canada, French in civil law and strongly Roman Catholic in religion, would remain as notably different halves of a United Province of Canada. And while these two sections henceforth would officially be labelled Canada West and Canada East, even their former names, Upper and Lower Canada, would stay in wide public use. Furthermore, the very Act that set up the new province embedded sectional division right within it, in its structure of parliamentary representation.

At union, much older Lower Canada had a population of some 650,000 to Upper Canada's 450,000. Lord Durham himself, in proposing a union, would have left its representation to a common basis of population, confident that the younger Upper Canadian community would continue its rapid growth through

Overleaf. Canadian Government Leaders Arrive by Steamer for the Charlottetown Conference, 1864. *At the gangway stands John A. Macdonald; to his left is George Brown; to his right are George Étienne Cartier at the front and D'Arcy McGee a little back, between them.*

1. Francis Hincks, Shrewd Reform Go-Between. *A close associate of Baldwin in Upper Canada, and a persuasive correspondent of LaFontaine in Lower, Hincks did a great deal to promote the Reform alliance for responsible government. Entering the Union parliament in 1841, he became a chief member of Baldwin-LaFontaine governments, in the 40s, and later, a Reform premier himself (1851-54).*

2. Louis-Hippolyte LaFontaine. *He sat in the old Lower Canadian Assembly from 1830 as a Papineau supporter, but rejected rebellion. French-Canadian Reformers rallied afterwards to his steady common sense; and he effectively became their leader in 1841, premier in 1848-51; then chief justice of Lower Canada from 1853 till his death in 1864. Above all, he was Robert Baldwin's constant partner in responsible government, and invaluable Francophone colleague.*

1

2

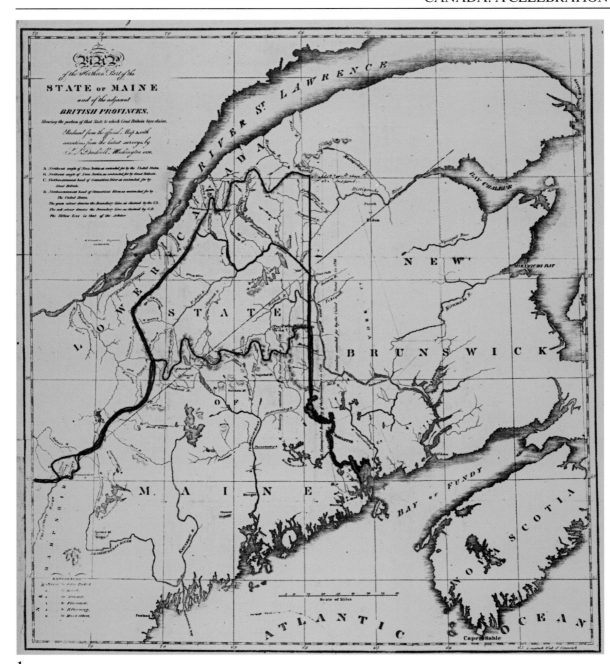

1

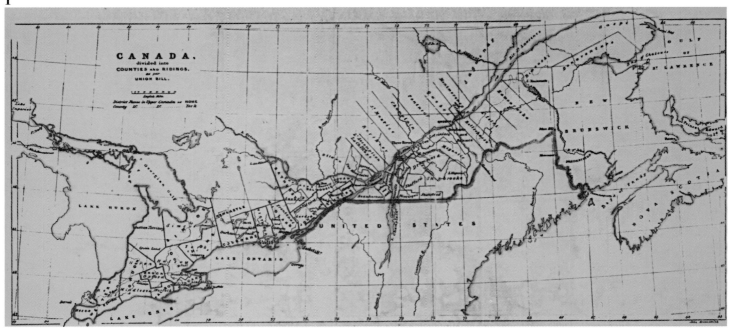

2

1. Maine-New Brunswick Areas in Dispute. *Essentially, the question here was settled by the Treaty of 1842 awarding the upper, marked portion of the disputed territory to Britain, the larger, lower portion to the United States.* **2. Counties and Electoral Ridings of the New Canadian Union.** *As laid out under the Union Act, and showing many a name still in use today; though others have gone, as growing populations required new units.*

1. Royal Proclamation of the Union Act, February 10, 1841. *As the document shows, this Act "to reunite the Provinces of Upper and Lower Canada," passed the British parliament in 1840, then was put into effect early in the following year, under Lord Sydenham, as still Governor-General.*

2. Sir Charles Bagot, Governor-General, 1842-43. *Bagot's short period in office was crucial; for under him responsible rule was actually applied in the Union of Canada, when he accepted Baldwin and LaFontaine as his ministers because they controlled a majority in parliament. It then was a pragmatic and uncertain step, but still a basic move forward. Incidentally, Bagot was painted for this well-known picture in sixteenth-century costume — not his usual dress as an esteemed diplomat previously in the United States or Russia, or even as Canadian governor at the Union's new capital of Kingston.*

3. Sir Charles Metcalfe, Governor-General, 1843-46. *A top figure in India's civil service, who thereafter was made governor of Jamaica, Metcalfe had real abilities, though no experience in handling the popular parliaments and politics of a North American province. Seeking "balance" with the best of intentions, he brought on political turmoil, Reform defeat and Tory manipulation; but did not long check the effective growth of responsible government in Canada.*

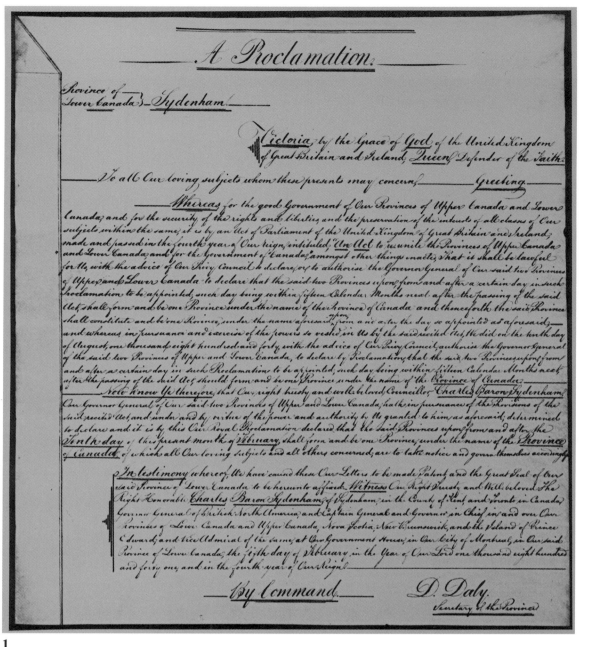

1

2

3

British immigration, and so before long obtain a majority of seats in the intended joint legislature. But the imperial government, seeking both to appease Upper Canada's worries over being swamped in a new union, and to limit French Canadian influence in it from the start, had opted instead for equal representation. Each section, the much more populous Canada East and the far less numerous Canada West, was thus to be allotted forty-two members in the new united Assembly. The result was to divide the Province of Canada politically, as well as culturally and socially, into two equal parliamentary segments. That led on to sectional power-blocks, to sectional parties and policies, and even double-headed ministries. The Union Act of 1840 by no means abolished two distinct Canadas: anything but.

Nevertheless, the Union would do well in forwarding their joint economic development — and also their march to responsible rule itself. That march really began while Canadian union was still in the planning stage, when some perceptive Reformers saw how it might be used to benefit their cause in both Canadas. Francis Hincks, acute Protestant-Irish editor of the new Toronto *Examiner*, which championed Robert Baldwin's principle of responsible government, began a close correspondence in 1839 with Louis-Hippolyte LaFontaine of Montreal, who was a prominent former supporter of Papineau yet one who had opposed rebellion, and who now was rising to the fore as the most capable figure in French Canadian Liberalism. Hincks pressed the view on LaFontaine that a party alliance of Upper and Lower Canadian Liberals could use the Union to build a solid majority in its joint Assembly: a majority which would stand firm upon responsible government, and could win it constitutionally, in parliament, from British imperial authorities who anxiously wanted peaceful progress, not embarrassing new conflict in the colonies. LaFontaine seized upon the thought that responsible government would amount to Canadian home rule, the best means of defending the *Canadiens'* own rights. He told voters in his Canada East constituency of Terrebonne County, during the first Union parliamentary elections in the spring of 1841, "I am in favour of the English principle of responsible government." And though he was defeated in Terrebonne (largely by Anglo-Tory mob violence), through Robert Baldwin's willing aid this *Canadien* leader was elected in Canada West's York County, thus personally confirming the growing Anglo-French Reform alliance.

Nevertheless, in the first Union parliament of 1841, Governor-General Sydenham used his amply persuasive powers to satisfy Assembly members that his coalition government containing both Conservatives and Reformers would rule in "harmony" with the interests of the elected House, if not actually be

1. William Henry Draper, Conservative Leader. *Seen here in his old age (as a chief justice) Draper was a skilful manager wholly relied on by a dying Metcalfe to keep control of parliament. He ran the Union government almost like a prime minister himself, in handing out patronage; thereby probably teaching a young Conservative colleague, John A. Macdonald, something of the art.*

2. Lord John Russell, Head of Britain's Free-Trade Liberal Regime in 1846. *An outstanding figure in British Reform politics for many years, Russell led his new Liberal ministry to complete the shift to free trade begun under Conservative Sir Robert Peel; and so to a changed imperial policy which enabled major British colonies to introduce responsible government under their own majority party rule.*

1   2

responsible to it. He also guided through some useful measures on local government, banking, schools, canal loans and more. Yet Baldwin left the ministry, in order to protest Sydenham's refusal to bring it under clear Assembly control And the Governor-General would have faced other signs of mounting opposition, had he not met with a fatal accident while out riding that autumn near Kingston, the Union's first capital. The hard issues thus were left to his successor as Governor-General, Sir Charles Bagot, a distinguished British diplomat more insightful than the overly self-confident Sydenham.

Bagot tried especially to gain better acceptance from the French Canadians, many of whom still wanted to repeal the Union. And he did so through being fully at home in French, and by appointing Francophones to a fairer share of official posts. Yet he could not break down the increasingly powerful opposition alliance of Upper and Lower Canadian Reformers in the Assembly, based on the mutual understanding and trust established between the two leader-partners, Baldwin and LaFontaine. Thus in September, 1842, as Bagot strove to prevent a crucial Reform majority vote in the Assembly against his government, he had to

1

2

1. The Earl of Elgin, Governor-General, 1847-54. *This moderate Liberal-Conservative, another ex-governor of Jamaica, was appointed to Canada by Lord Grey, Colonial Secretary in the Russell cabinet, to carry out the new imperial policy of recognizing responsible rule. When the elections of 1847-8 brought a Reform sweep in both halves of the Canadian Union, Elgin duly called on Liberal leaders LaFontaine and Baldwin to head a new government as co-premiers. And afterwards he steadily backed his Reform ministers, despite Tory outcries, because they held majority support from the people. Here the Governor is seen giving formal, legal assent to bills passed by parliament — such as the Rebellion Losses Bill, which would rouse so much Tory anger.*

2. The Burning of the Parliament Building in Montreal, April, 1849. *This was a result of the Rebellion Losses Bill passed that spring: a measure which seemed only fair to French Canadians seeking compensation for serious damages done during the Lower Canada revolts of 1837-38, but which to many Anglophones in Canada East looked like indemnifying rebels. When Lord Elgin, however, assented to the Bill, as constitutionally backed by his responsible ministers and the Assembly's vote, Tories (who would not see how a "British governor" could so desert the loyal) attacked and fired the parliament houses in Montreal — which in 1844 had replaced Kingston as Union capital.*

bring both Baldwin and LaFontaine into office; for neither would come without the other. Bagot saved his ministry, but at the price of making it Reform-dominated, a significant step towards responsible party government. Still, Tories found the sky did not fall, while the Governor got on very successfully with his changed ministers; although his own health began rapidly to fail, leading to his death in May of 1843.

The next Governor-General, Sir Charles Metcalfe, a veteran imperial administrator, was able and well-intentioned, yet firmly resolved to yield no further to creeping responsible government. The quarrels that soon rose between him and the Reform ministers he had inherited from Bagot brought their resignations in the fall of 1843. Metcalfe accordingly dissolved the Reform-controlled Assembly, and tried new elections in 1844; acting as a forthright partisan himself in strenuously appealing to public loyalty. In Canada West his "loyal" appeal worked; here Tory Conservatives carried the elections. In Canada East, LaFontaine's French Liberals still kept control. Hence Metcalfe (at damaging cost) achieved just a bare overall majority for his own allies in the Assembly. But thanks to the skills of his chief Conservative minister, William Henry Draper, an urbane Toronto English lawyer known as "Sweet William," the Governor's side kept a narrow hold. Nevertheless, Metcalfe, too, was ill — now dying of cancer — and he increasingly relied on Draper: letting that talented advisor become almost a prime minister himself, directing policies and dispensing government patronage to Conservative party interests in order to keep afloat. In fact, Draper was virtually performing as a party premier, even before responsible government had been officially established.

Metcalfe went home to die late in 1845: Canada had been sadly hard on its recent governors. For a year or more, the Canadian union went through an uncertain interim, while the Draper ministry still managed to stay in office. During this same period, however, far more influential developments took place in Britain. There the Conservative regime of Sir Robert Peel, which had sent out both Bagot and Metcalfe, was replaced in mid-1846 by a new Liberal ministry under Lord John Russell. But Peel had already committed Britain decisively to free trade, by abolishing the protective British Corn Laws; and the Russell Liberals would go still further in freely opening British markets to international commerce. One major effect, soon evident, was a changed attitude towards colonial policy. If the economic life of colonies was no longer to be imperially controlled, why should their political life be? There was, besides, a decline in Britain's concern for overseas possessions; now that its industrial supremacy, free trade and unequalled Royal Navy meant that the whole world could be Britain's oyster, while colonies largely produced more costs than benefits. Few British free traders then thought of actually abandoning colonies, but rather of guiding them on to self-government, to run their own affairs at their own expense. But whatever the moral obligations, there was a whole new desire in London government to move away from colonial "burdens."

Consequently, in November, 1846, the Colonial Secretary, Lord Grey, declared a crucial change in imperial policy, first set forth to the Governor of Nova Scotia, though it was later transmitted to Canada and elsewhere. Grey announced that the British North American colonies were henceforth to be governed only according to the will of their own inhabitants. Governors from now on would take their ministers from whatever group or party held the

Burning of Parliament, from the Toronto _Globe_. _Very plainly, this report in a leading Reform journal did not favour the Tory side._

BURNING OF THE PARLIAMENT HOUSE BUILDINGS IN MONTREAL.

The Tories of Canada have at length unmasked themselves before the world. The garment of loyalty under which they have concealed their deformity, has been cast off by their own hands, and they stand revealed as the enemies of social order, the enemies of British connexion—the enemies of constitutional liberty—the abettors of mobs, and the destroyers of property. We know there are many exceptions to this description, but we challenge any man to show that this is not now their legitimate character as a party. We could not have conceived it possible that men moving in a respectable rank in life would do such things, if we had not heard assassination defended by magistrates in Toronto, and did not know that burning and rioting had become the favourite pastime of the Tories of Montreal.

The intelligence of the signing the Rebellion Losses Bill by Lord Elgin reached Toronto on Wednesday evening, by telegraph. On Thursday morning came the astounding news that the Parliament Houses had been burnt down by a mob. Circumstances have been added, such as that Lord Elgin was personally insulted, which formed no part of our telegraphic despatch, and are only backed by the apocryphal authority of Tory journals. This intelligence has been received by these journals in a manner most discreditable to them. The _Patriot_ took the lead on Thursday morning, in using the language of menace. He calls on all "Conservatives to do nothing rashly—to think well before they act : and above all things to act unitedly." What did he mean by _acting_ after the Bill had finally passed the Legislature? Resistance unquestionably to the law. He makes a mock talk of appealing to the Queen, and the Imperial Parliament, although he admits it is too late. He gloats over the alleged pelting of Lord Elgin, giving it in Italics. He pities him,—styles him an enemy of his countrymen,—recommends the Tory members of Parliament, to resign their seats, and winds up with asking the ludicrous question, "Is our loyalty to be contemned or not?"

The _Colonist_ is more rabid—although the intelligence of the Montreal disturbances was known in Toronto when he wrote. He speaks of the burning of the Parliament Houses—their valuable libraries and public records, like one who is quite pleased with what he styles _the result_—talks of the Bill as outraging _morality and decency_, and holds the Governor General and his Councillors as answerable for all the consequences. A slight qualifier of _regret_ follows over these " occurrences," but he is immediately consoled by the reflection that they are but a "consequence" of the measures of the government. Then follows a plain hint that enough had not been done.

" Nor do we conceive, from present appearances, that the evil consequences have as yet fully developed themselves. The nature and full extent of them, will be exhibited from day to day, while the people are labouring under the effects of the gross insult that has been offered to their better feelings and judgments,"

He see-saws along, hoping and expecting— talking of no good resulting from wild exhi-

majority in a colony's Assembly, give them full support, and change them only when the Assembly produced a new majority. In sum, truly responsible government was thus authorized for a colony's domestic affairs, under a party cabinet and premier, with the Governor simply responding to confidence votes in the elected House, though he would still have his own role to play in external relations. This, then, was the climactic move in the advance to self-government; soon to be acted upon in the big Province of Canada.

There early in 1847 a new Governor-General arrived, the Earl of Elgin, balanced, clear-headed and tough-minded, though with a ready grace of humour. A Liberal-Conservative statesman, he also firmly believed in responsible government, perhaps helped by the fact that Lord Durham was his wife's father. And in Canada, Elgin worked convincingly and capably to carry out the new colonial policy: at first giving cordial support to Draper and his Tory associates in the Canadian ministry since they still held a small Assembly majority. But at the end of 1847, general elections in the Province of Canada brought a decisive Reform victory in both East and West. Thus when the new parliament met in 1848, the existing Tory administration was crushingly defeated in the House, and resigned in early March. Elgin promptly called on the Reformers to take office in a ministry jointly headed by LaFontaine and Baldwin — in that order, since LaFontaine had the larger parliamentary following. Thereby, responsible rule was plainly acknowledged and put in full effect, under a one-party cabinet led by the two Reform leaders as co-premiers. Self-government was granted. But it already had been earned; earned by the will and common-sense of Canadians of two languages, and as a constitutional heritage of far more value than that of empty revolt.

This LaFontaine-Baldwin cabinet soon got to work on major reforms. A critical test of the responsible system, however, came a year later, when early in 1849 the Ministry brought in a Rebellion Losses Bill to compensate for damages done during the Lower Canada revolt of 1837. Damages in Upper Canada had already been dealt with. Still, many Tories, especially Lower Canadian British, denounced this Losses Bill as "payment for treason," and eagerly looked to the British Governor-General to veto it. But Elgin would not reject a measure advised by his responsible cabinet and resting on an Assembly majority. In April, outraged Tories reacted with sheer mob-violence, burning down the parliament

From the Halifax Hotel, 1840s. *To Nova Scotia's capital, elections in 1847 had already brought Reform victory and a responsible cabinet for that province at the start of 1848, two months ahead of the Province of Canada.*

building in Montreal, the capital of the Union since 1844. Still, Governor Elgin calmly held firm in face of mob attacks against him, refusing to call out military forces that could well provoke more violence. And so the Tory extremists played themselves out, and sullenly gave up — while responsible rule in Canada came through its crucial test by fire.

In other British North American colonies, self-government arrived far more quietly than in an ethnically divided Province of Canada. Nova Scotia, as Joseph Howe himself declared, "achieved a Revolution without bloodshed." There Howe out-talked and out-manoeuvred both Tory opponents and governors alike, as he shaped the solidly popular Reform party; even bringing over John Boyle Uniacke, a formidable Tory leader who became a powerful friend and party colleague instead. Reformers swept the Nova Scotian elections of late 1847. Consequently, in January, 1848, a Liberal party cabinet was called into office: actually, the first responsible colonial government in the British Empire (or any other, for that matter). Uniacke officially became premier, Howe Provincial Secretary, though the key inspiration and achievement remained Howe's throughout. As for neighbouring New Brunswick, that timber province had stayed quite happy in its Assembly's control of forest revenues, under mixed Tory and Liberal ministries during the 1840s. In 1848, however, the Colonial Office here applied its new principle of responsible rule to endorse a government led by Reformer Lemuel Allan Wilmot as attorney-general — though he proved more interested in power than principle. Not till Charles Fisher took over as premier in 1854, with a clearly Liberal party, did responsible self-government gain real meaning in New Brunswick.

Similarly, Prince Edward Island and Newfoundland were given the new imperial policy already put in practice elsewhere. In the former colony, the Reformers who took the island election of 1850 received responsible cabinet government the next year, under George Coles as first premier; although the old absentee-land ownership question continued to plague this province's politics. In Newfoundland — which of course was later in its political evolution — responsible rule was only instituted in 1855; again by imperial authority, and after it had been granted to other British possessions from Australia to South Africa. Nevertheless, it may generally be said that by the early 1850s, internal self-government was an accomplished or nearly accomplished fact in all of settled British America; if still excluding the wilderness domains of a vast North West ruled by the fur-trading monopoly of the Hudson's Bay Company.

1. Wilmot and Responsible Rule in New Brunswick. *An active Reformer in the provincial House from 1836, Lemuel Allan Wilmot resigned from the Executive Council in 1845 to protest the governor of the province making appointments without consulting his Council. Wilmot seemed more concerned about matters of office, however, than responsible ideas. Still, in 1848 he was appointed to lead an intended responsible ministry in New Brunswick; although he left that position in 1851 to become a provincial Supreme Court judge.*

2. George Coles and Responsible Rule in Prince Edward Island. *First elected there in 1842, he rose in the Assembly as an advocate of responsible government; and the victory of his Reform forces in elections held in 1850 led to his being chosen as head of the Island's first responsible regime in 1851. Coles was also to be a notable Father of Confederation in later years.*

1   2

Social Changes and the Coming of Railways

In the West of British America, wild lands and native peoples still were but little altered. Yet across the East, the frontier age was plainly passing in the 1840s, as renewed British immigration and economic development brought ever-mounting social changes in their wake. To generalize, intensive growth was taking over from extensive spread. Frontier settlement was no longer continually advancing into fresh territories. The Atlantic provinces, of course, had largely occupied their own arable lands by now, including Newfoundland, leaving aside its empty and inhospitable interior. Canada East was certainly still pushing out bush farms into rugged country north of the fertile St. Lawrence valley, but this was only a limited sort of frontier extension, considerably inspired by efforts of the French Catholic clergy to spread true faith and simple life away from the corrupting influences of *les Anglais*. Moreover, in Canada West, long the most expansive frontier region, good new lands were fast running out, as farm clearings came up against the thin soil and rock masses of the enormous Precambrian Shield.

Accordingly, already-opened areas of the Upper Canadian inlands now became far more intensively settled — there still was lots of room for that. Fully tilled and fenced acres replaced roughly cultivated fields; frame farmhouses and planked barns supplanted log buildings and squared timber homes. And as local roads improved, with more farmers living along them to do the required road labour, so earlier backwoods hamlets became well supplied and organized country villages. Here the rural elites erected handsome houses. Here churches, stores, mills and workshops clustered, along with the doctor's office, lawyer's office — and often a little newspaper office, too. Much the same could be said of other maturing countrysides across the British American provinces; but the Upper Canadian farm world most markedly revealed by 1850 the social change away from raw frontier existence.

The passing of the frontier also appeared in another, very different way: in the declining role and status of native peoples within much of eastern British North America. This decline indeed was not new or even recent; but it was lamentably evident by the 1840s. Once the Indian tribes of the East had been vital to entering Europeans, as agents or suppliers in the all-important fur trade. And the Indians' abilities in forest warfare long had made them both feared as enemies and sought as allies. But since the War of 1812, their military role had largely vanished, as settled countrysides steadily cut into forest wilds. The fur trade had no less disappeared across much of the East; although it remained significant in more northerly reaches, where traditional Algonquian hunting bands particularly endured. Nevertheless, the main weight of the fur trade now lay westward in the huge realms of the Hudson's Bay Company. As for Indian peoples in changing eastern worlds of settlement, they lived largely neglected, nearly ignored, on reserves which often were inferior tracts in back townships. Lands which turned out to be good in quality sometimes had a way of being

1. First Canadian Postage Stamp.
Thanks to the transfer, the "three penny beaver" was issued by the Post Office of the Province of Canada in 1851.

2. Country Scene in a Maturing Canada West. *This picture might be compared with earlier ones in Upper Canada, on page 158 and page 177. Now the farm is machine-reaping grain; a large verandahed farmhouse stands by trim outbuildings, and a buggy carries its passengers on a much improved road across open countryside.*

1

2

reassigned; though it could be noted that ancestral native claims and binding treaty provisions were duly recognized in many other instances. The trouble was, there were all too many cases where they were not. In fact, even the big Six Nations Reserve along Upper Canada's Grand River suffered from developers' greedy incursions, and the legal disputes which followed.

The Iroquois of the Grand had been settled farmers when their European neighbours arrived about them. They had established themselves on working farms; their tribal leaders from Joseph Brant's time lived in ample homes like "Chiefswood"; and they had adapted effectively to dwelling amid a European society. Other smaller Indian groups, once roaming hunters, did less well. Confined to unproductive acres with no more open horizons, they were afflicted by poverty, disease and drunkenness, or by white policies which varied from keeping them segregated to seeking their absorption — always for their own good, of course. Nevertheless, native conversions to Christianity, earnestly pursued by white missionaries, did some social good as well as harm. While uprooting age-old cultural and religious supports, they still helped native communities to cope with the white world all around them; especially when native Christians themselves took up that cause of adjustment. This was strikingly exampled when Kahkewaquonaby, or Peter Jones, the son of a white surveyor and a Mississauga (Ojibwa) mother, became the first Methodist native missionary in Upper Canada: translating the Christian gospels into Ojibwa, arguing vigorously for Indian land rights, and winning enthusiastic support for native interests from lecture audiences in England during the 1840s. Yet the dominant white societies of eastern British North America mainly regarded Indian peoples as inevitably dwindling fragments. Whether they saw them as vanishing, romantic creatures of the wild, or as incapable and outmoded savages, the whites showed little concern for Indian heritage or future. Only the natives would prove such views were wrong; by surviving still in close-knit communities of their own.

1

2

1. Rural Mail Service in a Wintry Canada East. *Both sections of United Canada were increasingly served by regular mail routes into their rural areas. These particularly improved when in 1851, under responsible rule, the postal system was transferred from imperial to Canadian control.*
2. Six Nations Reserve on the Grand River. *These are Onondaga lands near Brantford, though the town itself lies beyond the hills.*

But nothing altered the fact that colonial society itself became far more interconnected, as transport and communications improved over the 1840s, even before railways arrived in the next decade. In 1848, the massive upper St. Lawrence canal system was finally completed, providing through navigation from ocean to Great Lakes, and much lowering freight costs in the process. On land, earth and mud highways were being macadamized, surfaced with interlocking, water-draining crushed gravel, while plank roads for "fast" transit by coach or buggy linked up major towns. Cheaper postal service would also help improve communications, and the spread of newspaper readership in the countryside. But more than that, the electric telegraph appeared between Niagara, Hamilton and Toronto in 1846, to which lines east to Montreal next were added. Today we may easily underrate this primitive start of immediate, electric news — but soon items were being flashed within minutes from New York via Buffalo to Toronto, or to Montreal from Boston and Portland. Modern immediacy did not just begin with television or fax. In consequence, the provincial societies off British America moved all the faster out of frontier isolation.

At least as important was the rise of publicly supported education. New Brunswick made bare beginnings with small annual school grants in 1802, Nova Scotia in 1811. Upper Canada provided for local "common" schools in 1816, while Lower Canada maintained various church-directed institutions. Yet it was only in the 1840s that a state-backed school system really developed; notably in the Union of Canada, where an Act of 1841 established non-denominational public schools for Canada West, and Protestant or Catholic-connected schools with public funding for the English or French residents of Canada East. This provincial system was enlarged on into the fifties, particularly to ensure state-aided but Catholic-taught "separate schools" for the Roman Catholic minority of Canada West. At all events, even by 1850 public education was a sizeable reality in the Canadian union; though less so in the Atlantic provinces.

On higher educational levels, however, the Maritimes had early led in developing colleges and universities. In Nova Scotia, Anglican King's College had been founded at Windsor as far back as 1789; and only 134 years later would it move to Halifax, to join in association with Dalhousie University, which itself had been founded at Nova Scotia's capital in 1818. In New Brunswick, another King's College began operating in Fredericton in 1828, to become the University of New Brunswick by 1859. And within the Province of Canada, its own Anglican King's College at last opened at Toronto in 1843; but then was secularized in 1849 as the non-denominational public University of Toronto, in an act put through by Robert Baldwin. Meanwhile, by 1841 Methodist Victoria University had taken shape at Cobourg under Egerton Ryerson as first president, and Presbyterian Queen's emerged the next year at Kingston. McGill in Montreal, had begun teaching in 1829, although its own first building only went

1. Kahkewaquonaby or Peter Jones, Native Methodist Missionary, 1802-56. *Both talented and trained, "Sacred Feathers" not only ministered to the Upper Canada Ojibwa for over twenty years, but wrote and published their history. He also was elected chief of two Ojibwa bands, and eloquently set forth the Indian case to white society.*

2. Mail Steamers Reaching Halifax Through Ice. *They are the English and Newfoundland mail ships, the former likely a "Cunarder." For Samuel Cunard of Halifax had won the transatlantic steam-mail contract from the British government, to form a basis for the great ocean shipping company, the Cunard Line.*

1

2

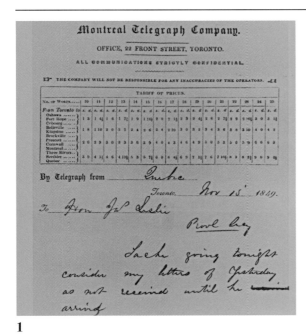

1

2

3

4

5

1. The Electric Telegraph. *This telegram sent in November, 1849, from Quebec to Toronto evidently concerned business between Étienne Taché and James Leslie, both members of the LaFontaine-Baldwin Reform government of the time.*

2. Dalhousie University in Halifax. *Originally endowed with customs duties collected in Maine while British forces from Halifax occupied the coast during the War of 1812, this institution began as a college founded in 1818 by then-Governor Dalhousie, and did not get university status till 1841. Henceforward, despite difficult periods, it grew to be a major Atlantic centre of higher education. Here the University, set in snows, is backdrop for the gathering of the Tandem Club, in a social kind of winter-sleighing.*

3. McGill University, Montreal. *While McGill had been chartered in 1821, it only started teaching (medicine) in 1829. Not till 1843 did it commence in arts, and come to occupy its lasting site on the slopes of Mont Royal — where this and other buildings began going up.*

4. Victoria University at Cobourg, Canada West. *It stemmed out of the Methodists' Upper Canada Academy, operating since 1836 at Cobourg, which in 1841 obtained a university charter. The imposing structure consequently erected in Cobourg would then be Victoria's home until the 1890s, when the university moved to Toronto to become a federated partner in the broader University of Toronto — and there a new home for it would be built beside Queen's Park in 1892.*

5. King's College in Toronto. *Chartered in 1827 as a provincial university for Upper Canada, it was only in 1843 that it finally opened, while this new building was erected for it, located in Queen's Park-to-be. In 1849, however, Anglican-controlled King's College was replaced by the non-denominational public University of Toronto. The building shown here became a provincial mental asylum, then was later demolished; while the new University of Toronto in a few years began a much grander structure, University College, completed beside the Park in 1859.*

up in 1843. As for Laval at Quebec, dating back to 1663, this Catholic seminary would not be chartered as a public university until 1853.

Not only teaching and learning, but original literature as well was growing in the British American provinces. To mention just a few classics among many works, there was François-Xavier Garneau's *Histoire du Canada* in three volumes (1845-48), a powerfully *nationaliste* interpretation of French Canada's heritage; Susanna Moodie's best-known book, *Roughing It in the Bush* (1852), a sternly graphic account of Upper Canadian frontier life; her sister, Catharine Parr Traill's more cheerful *Backwoods of Canada* (1835 and 1846); and Thomas Chandler Haliburton's humorous work of fiction, *The Clockmaker* (1836 and 1840) offering the "sayings and doings of Sam Slick," a sharp-eyed Yankee trader peddling his timepieces in the Nova Scotian society of that day. There were many other new cultural voices: including the *Literary Garland* of Montreal, a periodical which during the 1840s published the writings of Moody and other rising Anglophone authors; while in the same city in 1847, *L'Avenir*, a Francophone weekly, took up the zesty cause of radical *Canadien* nationalism, both in letters and politics. All in all, this era expressed a whole new stage in cultural activity — as it equally did in economic development as well.

In fact, good times and healthy immigration rates through most of the 1840s assuredly fostered the social and cultural growth just surveyed. Lumber and wheat markets flourished, merchants prospered, while British immigrants on the whole came well prepared and found employment. That is, until late in the decade, when another world depression struck hard. And at the same time, famine rose in Ireland, where a disastrous potato blight ruined that country's most vital food crop. Refugees now poured out of Ireland, desperate, near-starving, and soon riddled with deadly infections such as typhus and cholera. They came to American ports, to Saint John in New Brunswick or up the St. Lawrence into Canada, crammed in "coffin ships," in which large numbers died. The surviving Irish migrants brought a flood of helpless misery and disease to hard-pressed colonial communities. The great mass of the 109,000 British who reached the North American provinces in 1847 indeed were Irish-born; and their

1. Good Conduct Certificate, "Upper Canada Public Schools." *This not only marks the growth of public schooling by the 1850s, but also testifies that the terms "Upper" and "Lower" Canada did not simply disappear after the Union of 1841. They not only continued in popular use, but for some official or state concerns as well — such as public education.*

2. An Anti-Annexation Cartoon from "Punch in Canada," 1849. *This was directed against French Canadian radicals (dubbed* Rouges*) in the National Democratic Club of Montreal, who endorsed calls to join the American republic; although the mass of* Canadiens *held aloof. Here* Rouge *monkeys, under their master, Papineau (back in politics for a while), prepare "to trample on the British lion."*

GOOD CONDUCT.

A good name is better than precious ointment. Eccl. VII. 1

Goodness and mercy shall follow me. Ps. XXIII. 6.

Do that which is good. Deut. VI. 18.

Hold fast that which is good. 1 Thess. V. 15.

PUBLIC SCHOOLS, UPPER CANADA.

W. C. Chewett & Co. Lith. Toronto.

THE "CLUB NATIONALE DEMOCRATIQUE."

1   2

influx continued, although diminishing, on into the early fifties. In the new land these tragic Irish died in thousands at quarantine camps on Partridge Island off Saint John, at Grosse Isle outside Quebec, or in the "emigrant sheds" of Montreal, Kingston, and Toronto. Still, the majority survived and struggled through, to work largely in towns or lumber camps; and to add another heritage of fortitude — women even more than men — which descendants of the Famine Irish rightfully remember to this day.

Meanwhile, as problems of disease and welfare soared, bleak depression idled ships and trade in Canada of the late forties, closing down businesses and jobs and leaving the new canals almost empty: blows which particularly hit the major port of Montreal, and so partly explained the fierce mob-violence there over the Rebellion Losses Bill in April, 1849. Moreover, Britain's switch to free trade in 1846 had removed the imperial Corn Laws that had protected colonial exports of wheat and flour; and in 1849 the imperial timber preference was also sliced away. Consequently, even after the anger over the Rebellion Bill had subsided, bitter feelings remained among powerful Montreal business elements. Their sense indeed of being abandoned by imperial interests led a number of their leaders to sign the gloomy Annexation Manifesto of October 1849, proclaiming that a failed and neglected Canada should give up and join the United States. This was colonial heritage too — a tendency to sell Canadians' own abilities short, and look to a new dependence to help out. (If Mother would no longer help, try Uncle.) Significantly also, the Manifesto was not only backed by Montreal Anglo-Tories, but by *nationaliste* French radicals, who now included a returned but scarcely altered Louis-Joseph Papineau. Yet the decisive mass response across both Canada East and West, French and English, was to condemn outright any idea of joining the Americans. And the business Tories of Montreal felt their own Canadian loyalty come surging back, as world trade and colonial commerce revived in 1850.

All the same, Montreal politically had proved too feverish as a governing centre, so that from 1850 the Union's government would be shifted periodically between the two old provincial capitals, Toronto and Quebec — for sectional divisions in Canada prevented either being permanently selected. In 1858, however, the young city of Ottawa, once a canal and lumber village, was chosen as permanent seat of government by Queen Victoria (advised, of course, by her ministers and instructed by Sir Edmund Head, then Canadian Governor-General). But grand new Parliament Buildings, in stately Victorian Gothic style, would not be finished for use in Ottawa till 1866. And well before, in the earlier fifties, a much better economic phase had opened for the Canadian Union.

At that time, returning prosperity had effectively advanced to boom, as the St. Lawrence canals filled with traffic, grain and lumber again poured out to

1. Monument at Montreal to Irish Immigrant Dead of 1847-48. *Put up by the men who built the first great bridge across the St. Lawrence, it remembered the many Irish victims of "ship fever" in the disastrous famine migrations of the latter forties.*

2. The Champlain and St. Lawrence R.R., 1849. *The newspaper announcement here illustrates this line's short "portage" nature: between Laprairie on the south side of the St. Lawrence and St. Johns on the Richelieu River that led to Lake Champlain.*

3. The Montreal Annexation Manifesto, October, 1849. *This article on the Manifesto, from the Toronto* Mirror, *needs some explanation. The* Mirror, *an Irish Catholic paper (when such things mattered strongly), was considerably more pro-American than the bulk of the Anglo-press — whether the Liberal but British-oriented Toronto* Globe, *or still more emotionally "loyal" Conservative journals in Canada West. The* Mirror, *not too surprisingly, thought annexationism a reasonable idea for consideration. But it did not take hold to any serious extent, despite the opinions of this paper.*

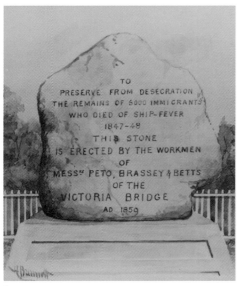

ANNEXATION AND REPUDIATION.
(From the Toronto Mirror.)

The *Mirror* was the first journal in Canada, honest, or clearsighted enough, to announce the Annexation fact. Of course, but little attention was bestowed upon a subject of such trivial importance, and the more especially as it had been introduced to public notice by so humble an organ as the *looking glass:* but truth is very strong, however weak may be its promulgators. The Annexation question is no longer a thing to be laughed at: neither do we think it will be found a farthing candle, to be puffed out by a Government *bellows-man*, whether in the shape of a newspaper *hack*, or a Law Officer of the Crown.

The Merchants, and Proprietors, of the first Commercial City in British America, have issued a Manifesto, which will be read by every inhabitant of Canada, with the most serious consideration. The question of, *British Connexion or American Annexation*, is put before them, in plain and honest language. No mystery,—no oracular ambiguity,—no half and half talk,—is allowed to obscure the purposes and views of the signers of the document. They have faced their work, like men who fear not truth, and will not shrink from upholding it. They cannot but have been aware, that in taking this bold step, they were about to subject themselves to a most unsparing public ordeal, and that they would very soon, have arrayed against them, a vast host of prejudice; political, national, and religious intolerance; loyal hypocrisy, rotten liberalism, and sycophantic selfishness. But we very much mistake the characters of many of the men, whose names we observe appended to the Montreal Manifesto, if they are to be frighted from their consistency by the ordinary scare-crow exhibitions, to which recourse is had, in these days, for the purpose of intimidating the agitators of measures of sweeping reform.

The Montreal Annexationists must be reasoned with,—not denounced. They have shewn pretty clearly, by the cool and logical manner in which they have submitted their proposition to public opinion, that they are capable of arguing their case both coolly and calmly; and they have not taken their ground without reckoning on consequences.

1
       2
       3

British markets or into the United States, and a whole new era of railway building took form. Railways had first reached the colonies in the 1830s. The sixteen-mile Champlain and St. Lawrence had opened successfully in 1836, linking Laprairie opposite Montreal with the Richelieu water route down to New England; while the Albion Mines Railway in Nova Scotia had begun in 1839 to carry coal out to the port of Pictou. Yet little more track was built; although the 1840s saw new lines chartered in provincial parliaments. By 1850, there still were only sixty-six miles of operating track in all British North America. Then, however, the return of general prosperity — plus the fact that railways now were well established in Europe and the United States, thus freeing capital for their construction in Canada — brought on a railroad era that virtually transformed land transport in the British American provinces, and raised wide new prospects for their future.

By 1853, the new St. Lawrence and Atlantic reached south from Montreal to Portland, Maine, thus giving Montreal commerce a winter outlet to salt water when the St. Lawrence was frozen solid. And the Northern Railway, started in 1851, by 1855 connected Toronto with Collingwood on Georgian Bay, an iron road pointing to the Upper Lakes and the vast North West beyond. The Great

1

1. An Early Great Western Railway Locomotive. *This engine, with its broad, spark-arresting smokestack for wood fuel, worked out of Hamilton to Niagara, Toronto or Windsor.*
2. The Suspension Bridge across the Niagara River, 1859, *linking the Great Western with American lines to New York.*

2

Western was open in 1854 from Hamilton to Windsor on the Detroit River, via London, and from Hamilton to Niagara Falls, there linking with American tracks to New York. By 1856 the G.W.R. was also extended to Toronto. Other, smaller lines were constructed in both sections of Canada. But the biggest project of them all was the Grand Trunk Railway, chartered in 1853 to span the entire Canadian Union. By 1860 it was completed: from Rivière du Loup on the south shore of the Lower St. Lawrence to Sherbrooke in the heart of the Eastern Townships; from there to Montreal, crossing the St. Lawrence over the magnificent new Victoria Bridge; then on through Kingston, Toronto and Guelph, finally to Sarnia on Lake Huron — one of the world's longest rail routes at that time. The Grand Trunk's construction by an influential British-based company had still deeply depended on grants and backing from the Canadian government. That brought unhappy private-public entanglements in railway politics, leading to extravagance and heavy public debt, political-insider deals and outright corruption. Nonetheless, the Grand Trunk forged a vital transport bond across the central province of Canada, one that would last on to the present.

Railroads were not begun in Newfoundland until the 1880s. Yet even by 1848 large designs were under way in the Atlantic mainland provinces for a

1

2

1. The Victoria Bridge over the St. Lawrence at Montreal. *A marvel of engineering in its day, it ran in a long wrought-iron "box" above the river, and was completed for the Grand Trunk Railway in 1860.*
2. A Locomotive for Newfoundland. *Again a broad-stack design, this is a "tank engine" without a tender, carrying its own fuel and water — convenient for smaller-traffic lines.*

1

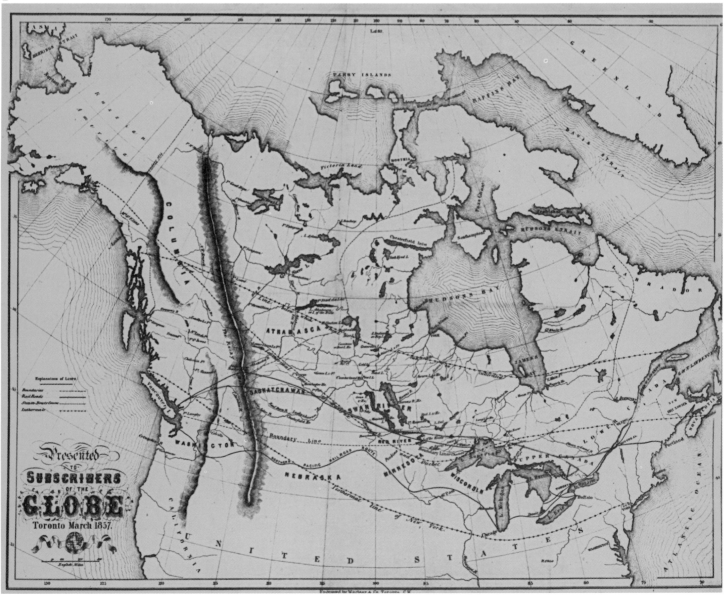

2

Halifax-to-Quebec line through safely British territory, to join the Maritimes with Canada and the St. Lawrence. Difficulties over route and division of costs, however, halted this first Intercolonial Railway project; though it would come up repeatedly in years to follow. In the meantime, Nova Scotia built a line from Halifax up to Truro, ready to go on into New Brunswick. This latter colony took up the European and North American Railway, which connected Saint John with Portland by 1857, and by 1860 extended to Shediac on the province's eastern shore. But a forecast of what railways could do — Intercolonials or even more — came in a glowing speech by Joseph Howe at a railway banquet in Halifax in 1851, where Howe prophesied that many in his audience well might live to hear "the whistle of the steam locomotive in the passes of the Rocky Mountains."

They might, indeed — for railways met the challenge of continental distance. Passengers and bulky freight now could move by rail in North America throughout the year, at regular speeds far beyond the fastest horse. This conquering of distance also brought the need for accurate railway scheduling, resulting, indeed, in Standard Time to replace local "sun time": an international achievement successfully pushed by its Scots-Canadian originator, Sandford Fleming, initially the chief engineer on Toronto's Northern Railway. As well, rail technology really introduced the machine age into British North America; in metal foundries and engineering shops, locomotive works and rail-rolling mills; thus developing skills in steam and iron to serve wide new factory industries. Such industrial plants would mainly emerge later. More immediately important here is the fact that the Railway Revolution gave practical meaning to dreams of wider colonial union: to visions of bringing all British North America into one much stronger unit, able to withstand the pulls and pressures of the United States and even reach to the Pacific — as a united country joined by and flourishing through its rail lines. Furthermore, if rails alone could bind a great new interprovincial union, only such a union would have the credit and tax resources needed to get the costly lines constructed. Railways and ideas of British North American Union hence came together in the 1850s, to thrust on to Confederation in 1867 — and to still greater rail routes afterward.

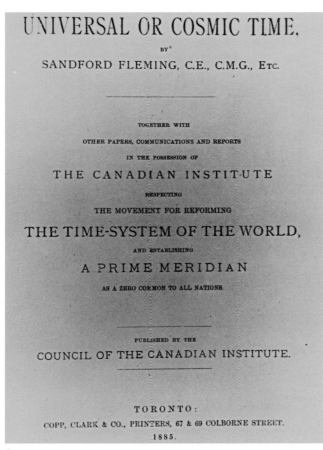

UNIVERSAL OR COSMIC TIME,

BY

SANDFORD FLEMING, C.E., C.M.G., ETC.

TOGETHER WITH

OTHER PAPERS, COMMUNICATIONS AND REPORTS

IN THE POSSESSION OF

THE CANADIAN INSTITUTE

RESPECTING

THE MOVEMENT FOR REFORMING

THE TIME-SYSTEM OF THE WORLD,

AND ESTABLISHING

A PRIME MERIDIAN

AS A ZERO COMMON TO ALL NATIONS

PUBLISHED BY THE

COUNCIL OF THE CANADIAN INSTITUTE.

TORONTO:

COPP, CLARK & CO., PRINTERS, 67 & 69 COLBORNE STREET.

1885.

3

1. A Grand Trunk Engine. *Following the initial broad-stack era, after coal-firing grew more general.*
2. Railway Hopes in the Toronto Globe, 1857. *The map from the newspaper shows isothermic (temperature) lines across the continent as then understood; but more than that, a hoped-for railway to the Pacific, through western mountain ranges obviously not very specifically shown.*
3. Standard Time: a Result of Railways. *Title page of papers given by Sandford Fleming to Toronto's Canadian Institute (later Royal), which set out his proposals for world-wide standard time: eventually adopted by an international conference held in Washington in 1884. Moreover, Fleming, Scottish-born. was not only an eminent distinguished railway construction engineer and manager, but as well designed Canada's first postage stamp, and surveyed a route for a future transcontinental railway, the Canadian Pacific to be.*

Growing Forces for Union, and Disunion

Developments in trade no less than transport opened new vistas for the provinces, as they moved away from former reliance on exports to Britain or the West Indies and into growing American markets. The loss of the imperial protective tariff system, when Britain turned to free trade between 1846 and 1849, had proved to be more a shock than a disaster. Colonial wheat and timber again found ready British sales during the booming fifties. But no longer was there the rooted colonial belief that things would always stay that way. Instead, grain, wood — and a lot of Atlantic fish — now were also going to the United States, where northeastern factory centres needed more foodstuffs, and midwestern towns and farms more building lumber. This mounting commerce brought on the Reciprocity Treaty of 1854 between the republic and British provinces: a major agreement which established reciprocal free trade in natural products to run for ten years from 1855, then be renewed or abrogated (cancelled). And while the colonists thus gained free entry to the United States for their raw produce, the Americans, too, got what they particularly wanted, free access to the rich fisheries in colonial waters up the Atlantic coast.

Over all, the Treaty of 1854 did very well; although the good times it gained credit for were also due to railway building and internal colonial growth. As time went on, however, the colonies became concerned about the future, when the Treaty necessarily faced renewal. If the Americans then should abrogate the agreement, the best economic choice well might be to unite all the provinces in order to combine and develop their own home markets. Consequently, by the early 1860s, the forces both of railways and commerce were pointing towards union. And so, eventually, would issues in the great North West between the Lakehead and Pacific, the wilderness British territory ruled since 1821 by the re-made Hudson's Bay Company that had absorbed its old Nor'Wester rivals.

This powerful London-based fur enterprise had set its North American headquarters at Fort Garry in the Red River Colony, the small but persevering farm community first established by Lord Selkirk on the prairie sweeps of Ruperts Land. Ruperts Land itself — the vast forest, plains and tundra country that drained into Hudson Bay — was still the Company's domain by chartered right. But beyond it, both the North to the Arctic Ocean and the Far West over the Rockies were also held by the Company, under British parliamentary acts which

Hamilton, C.W., 1854. *A growing lakeside place, but about to grow much farther through two factors: the railway-building age just under way — which would give the city's Great Western access southward over Niagara or westward past Detroit, while its own rail industries developed — and the Reciprocity Treaty of 1854, which opened American markets to a flow of natural products shipped out via Hamilton.*

from 1821 had licensed it to maintain government and fur-trade monopoly in these huge regions also. Since 1821, moreover, the Bay Company had generally managed this whole wild empire profitably, peaceably, and in ordered style; though its quiet condition largely rested on good relations with the native inhabitants, Plains Cree, Assiniboines, Peigans (Blackfoot) and many others to the north or west. Good relations, too, depended especially on Indian women who had married fur traders according to "the custom of the country." They provided a bridge connecting two very different societies; and some of them besides served as respected diplomats or mediators between one side and the other. In later days, the increasing entry of white women into the fur-trade West largely ended these older "tender ties" across racial lines. But during generations which produced the Métis as a vigorous new people, sprung from mixed Indian and French or British origins, the recognized fact of white-native family bonds did a great deal both for tranquil Company control and the mutual adjustment of European and Indian elements throughout the North West.

Throughout this realm, as well, the Bay Company's York boats carried on transport by the Saskatchewan or other Plains waterways. And they were increasingly supplemented by Red River carts, sturdy two-wheeled vehicles drawn by oxen that plodded south down rutted prairie paths to American posts in the Minnesota Territory, or north and west along the Carlton Trail, which in time stretched out to Fort Edmonton. All this traffic linked the Great Plains region by the mid-century (if crudely thus far), while pack-trains crossed on over the mountains to the Pacific West. Yet still more routes by land and water led far northward, past the Arctic Circle into the icebound homelands of the Inuit.

Here British explorations, particularly by sea in Royal Navy ships, had steadily opened up the Arctic expanses; although only a few examples can be offered here. In 1823, Edward Parry of the Navy had pushed the search for the North West Passage through Fury and Hecla Strait west above Hudson Bay, while in 1827 John Franklin, R.N., had probed from the Mackenzie River delta

1. Fort Garry at Red River. *This is the Lower Fort, called the "Stone Fort," which was built on the Red in 1831, and became the seat of the Hudson's Bay governors of Ruperts Land in 1843. Some miles away, Upper Fort Garry, already established at the forks of the Red and the Assiniboine (where Winnipeg would arise), was less elaborate and massive; yet became far more the real focus of the Red River Colony.*

2. The Red River Cart. *These ox-drawn carts, originally made without metals — and built to be knocked down and floated with wheels removed across prairie rivers — also initially went ungreased, so that the shriek of their axles could be heard for miles.*

3. Rewards for Finding Sir John Franklin in the Arctic, 1850. *This poster from the British Admiralty offered very large sums in the money of the time.*

1

2

3

out along the north Alaskan coasts. John Ross located the North Magnetic Pole west of the Bay in 1831 — still a long way from the geographic Pole itself. And Sir John Franklin's expedition of 1845-47, at last to determine the North West Passage, starkly resulted in his own death and those of the crews of his two vessels; yet brought on a stream of searches to "find Franklin." These certainly were futile; nevertheless, they widely increased Arctic knowledge and contacts with the Inuit. Thus parties under John Rae or Richard Collinson mapped icy Arctic islands closest to the continental shores, and in 1851 Captain Robert McClure finally uncovered the elusive North West Passage Franklin had died in seeking; though it was not be navigated successfully for some sixty years to follow.

Arctic explorations would matter greatly to Canada in the long run. During the mid-nineteenth century, however, events within the heartland of the Hudson's Bay Territory, at the Red River Colony, mattered considerably more. Here the Company's rule in America remained for decades in the capable hands of Sir George Simpson, as Governor-in-Chief of Ruperts Land from 1826 to 1860: a brisk forceful Scot, the "Little Emperor," who strongly upheld Company interests and pushed exploration besides. He himself crossed the continent westward — and on around the globe — in a monumental journey of 1841-2. But by the 1850s, times were changing; and at Red River the old, sequestered world of fur-trade monopoly was beginning to pass away. In 1849 the Company had been compelled to let free traders operate out of the Red River (population by then about 5,000) to posts down across the United States border. In 1855 American railroads reached St. Paul in Minnesota. In 1859 the first American steamboat came up the Red to Fort Garry, where a little commercial hamlet to be called Winnipeg was already rising just outside the stone walls. And eager American venturers came up also; some looking forward to the annexation of the British territories to northward — a project even endorsed by resolution in the Minnesota legislature.

Not only Americans, but Canadians too, began showing a decided interest in the Red River and the Hudson's Bay Territory. Late in the fifties, settlers started to reach there from Canada West — and the first newspaper at Red River, the *Nor'Wester*, was founded by two young Toronto journalists in 1859. Meanwhile in 1857, the future of the Hudson's Bay Company empire had come before a Select Committee of the House of Commons in Britain, to consider whether the Company's licence to its leased western territories should be renewed. The Committee's report recommended, among other things, that fertile areas in the plains, such as the Red River and Saskatchewan Valleys, might be acquired by Canada for settlement. That recommendation proved inconclusive; yet it was handwriting on the wall. A thinly-held fur empire of the Hudson's Bay Company

1. Sir George Simpson, Bay Company Governor. *Of Scots origin, Simpson came with the Hudson's Bay Company to North America in 1820; began by competing with Nor'Westers at Lake Athabasca, then was made governor of the Northern Department when the fur companies amalgamated. By 1826 he was governor for all the H.B.C. trading domains in British America, remaining so to his death in 1860. His knowledge of the trade and its territory was unsurpassed, and he travelled it to its limits.*

2. H.M.S. *Investigator* **Caught in Arctic Waters, 1851.** *One dangerous result of renewed search activities in the Far North (Published in 1854 — the ship got away).*

3. The *Nor'Wester* **Founded at Fort Garry, 1859.** *This paper was begun by William Buckingham and William Coldwell, two journalists associated with the Toronto* Globe *under George Brown, who was himself much interested in Canada acquiring the Red River and the North West beyond the Lakes — and so valued the channel of communication provided through the Nor'Wester.*

1

2

THE FIRST NEWSPAPER AT RED RIVER.

PROSPECTUS

OF

"THE NOR'-WESTER,"

A JOURNAL TO BE PUBLISHED AT

FORT GARRY, RED RIVER TERRITORY.

THE undersigned, will, without delay, commence the publication of a Newspaper at Fort Garry, Red River, to be entitled THE NOR'-WESTER and to be devoted to the varied and rapidly growing interests of that region.

Exploring parties organized under the direction, respectively, of the Canadian and British Governments, have established the immediate availability for the purposes of Colonization of the vast country watered by the Red River, the Assiniboine, and the Saskatchewan ; and private parties of American citizens, following Captain Palisser, are engaged in determining the practicability of rendering this the great overland route to the gold deposits of British Columbia. The Red River Settlement is the home of a considerable population, hardy, industrious, and thrifty ; occupying a fine farming country, with all the advantages of prairie and timber combined. It has churches many ; and educational advantages which will endure comparison with those of more pretentious communities. And for hundreds of miles beyond, stretches one of the most magnificent agricultural regions in the world, watered abundantly with Lakes and navigable Rivers, with a sufficiency of timber, with vast prairies of unsurpassed fertility, with mineral resources, in some parts, of no common value, and with a climate as salubrious as it is delightful. Such a country cannot now remain unpeopled. It offers temptations to the emigrant nowhere excelled. It invites alike the mechanic and the farmer. Its rivers and rolling prairies and accessible mountain passes, secure to it the advantages which must belong to a highway to the Pacific. It has mail communication with Canada, *via* Fort William ; and regular communication with the Mississippi, *via* steamboat and stage to St. Paul. What can impede its development ? What can prevent the settlement around Fort Garry from becoming the political and commercial centre of a great and prosperous people ?

The printing press will hasten the change, not only by stimulating the industrial life of the Red River Settlement, but by assisting the work of governmental organization, the necessity for which is admitted on all sides ; not only by cultivating a healthy public sentiment upon the spot, but by conveying to more distant observers an accurate knowledge of the position, progress, and prospect of affairs.

THE NOR'-WESTER starts on an independent commercial basis. Indebted to no special interests for its origin, and looking to none for its maintenance, it will rely wholly upon the honest and efficient exercise of its functions as the reflex of the wants and opinions, the rights and interests, of the Red River Settlement. Its projectors go thither tied to no set of men, influenced by no narrow preferences, shackled by no mean antipathies. Their journal will be a vehicle of news, and for the pertinent discussion of local questions ; governed only by a desire to promote local interests, and a determination to keep aloof from every entangling alliance which might mar its usefulness at home or abroad. It will be a faithful chronicler of events—a reporter, assiduous and impartial. Especially will it aim to be the medium for communicating facts, calculated to enlighten the non-resident reader with regard to the resources and the geography, the life and the sentiment, of the district in which it will be published. Nor will efforts be wanting to render it equal to the tastes of the Red River settlers ; arrangements having been made that will secure reliable correspondence from Canada and elsewhere.

During the early winter months of its existence, THE NOR'-WESTER will be published fortnightly, to meet the mail arrangements with Canada ; next Spring it will be published weekly, and will be continued regularly thereafter.

The connection which the subscribers have maintained with the Toronto press, is referred to as an evidence of their practical ability to carry out the task they have undertaken.

Price Two DOLLARS per annum, payable invariably in advance. Letters may be addressed to Box 699, Post Office, Toronto, until the 20th September, proximo ; after that date, communications to be addressed to Fort Garry—in all cases pre-paid

WILLIAM BUCKINGHAM
WILLIAM COLDWELL

AUGUST 22, 1859.

3

would surely be supplanted — whether by takeover from the powerfully expansionist United States or by union with a hopefully enlarged Canada. That was really the question emerging for the North West: one that had already revealed itself upon the Pacific shores.

The question there took shape, in fact, in the Oregon Country, a great reach of territory which bordered the Pacific between Russian-ruled Alaska on the north and Mexican-held California on the south, a territory which had been jointly occupied by Britain and the United States since 1819. By the 1840s, however, American westward expansion was rapidly filling in the southern half of this Oregon Country; and, as ever, fur posts could not stand long against the tide of settlement. Furthermore, as disputes arose, an aggressive United States threatened war, during the presidential election of 1844 demanding "Fifty-Four Forty or Fight" — all the country right up to Alaska. That would have cut off a future Canada completely from the Pacific; though it was largely election noise. Instead diplomacy brought the Oregon Treaty of 1846, which broadly divided the disputed territory in half, by extending the Canadian-American boundary along the 49th parallel onward from the plains over the mountains to the Pacific, then dipping southward around Vancouver Island. In many respects, this Treaty was a reasonable solution. Yet the British colonists had faced renewed American dangers along their borders, not to mention extravagant American claims and talk of war.

In any event, the valuable Columbia waterway to the ocean now decisively fell to the Americans, since the lower Columbia lay south of the newly extended boundary line, thus compelling British traders and colonists to rely on the more difficult Fraser route to the sea further northward. Nonetheless, there was ample

1

1. "The Dalles" on the Columbia River, 1846. *These flagstone-like formations marked a vital water route through the Oregon Territory to the Pacific. But Britain was not fated to control it; and under the Oregon Treaty of 1846 would have to give up the original Fort Vancouver set by the Bay Company at the mouth of the Columbia.*

2. Fort Victoria on Vancouver Island. *This was begun in 1843 by the H.B.C. as a West Coast port and base, in anticipation of the loss of Fort Vancouver in the Oregon Country. It was to become the capital of a whole new British colony on the Pacific.*

2

space left for a great province of British Columbia to arise in time. And more immediately significant, the Hudson's Bay Company established a new west-coast headquarters, Fort Victoria, at the southern end of Vancouver Island. This, in fact, became the focus and capital of a colony of Vancouver Island, set up in 1849 under Company control in order to provide a firm basis of British settlement on this fertile and well favoured isle: to pin down the western end of the American border, and make sure another Oregon did not happen.

The Hudson's Bay Company sent shiploads of English settlers to Victoria, right around Cape Horn at the bottom of South America. Dorset farmers, Stafford miners and varied town workers arrived — 140 migrants, for example, by the nicely-named *Tory* in 1851. Company servants and retired officials also settled in; and though the colony stayed small, farming thrived in the mild island climate, where spring flowers opened before March. Moreover, lumbering and fishing resources soon were tapped, as well as productive coal mines up the island near Nanaimo. Relations with the native peoples, besides, generally stayed amicable: with the local Salish, the formidable Cowichans up the coast, and the majestic Haida who travelled in sea-going dugout canoes down from the Queen Charlottes far northward. And thanks considerably to the decisive leadership of James Douglas as Company chief factor and governor, the young province advanced steadily; indeed was given its own representative assembly in 1856.

Douglas, a Nor'Wester in background (though born in British Guiana), had

1

2

3

1. Nanaimo on Vancouver Island, 1859. *Valuable coal deposits that were opened near here added to the rising trade of Vancouver Island — not now in furs, but increasingly in fish and lumber, and in coal that went down to San Francisco. The Island thus was growing in its settlement and economy, while its capital, Victoria, became a small city in the early '60s, if mostly because of new gold finds made on the B.C. mainland.*

2. Sir James Douglas, Builder of British Columbia. *Douglas, born in British Guiana, educated in Scotland, had joined the H.B.C. in 1821, and by 1823 was sent to Fort Vancouver on the West Coast. After dealing for the company from California to Alaska, he was put in charge of building Fort Victoria in 1843. Then, after the Bay Company had received title from Britain to Vancouver Island in 1849, in order to plant a colony there, Douglas was also named its Governor in 1851, and supervised that colony's slow yet real growth. But gold discoveries on the mainland in 1857-58 brought a turbulent inrush of miners from California. Hence in 1858 Douglas was also made Governor of a new mainland province of British Columbia. He ruled it almost absolutely, but effectively: so that up to his retirement in 1863-64, the continuance of British Columbia in British, not American, hands owed a great deal to him.*

3. John Robson, Journalist and Politician. *Settling in 1861 at New Westminster, infant capital of the mainland province of British Columbia, Robson used his* British Columbian *there to seek responsible rule and then union with Canada, just as de Comos did on Vancouver Island. Both men would subsequently be premiers of British Columbia, but of a larger province which from 1866 combined both island and mainland in one united British Columbia.*

THE BRITISH COLONIST.

VOL. 1.　　　　VICTORIA, V. I., SATURDAY, DEC. 11, 1858　　　　NO. 1.

THE BRITISH COLONIST

Will be published every Saturday, at Victoria, V. I.
By A. DE COSMOS.

Subscription, for One Year,　　　　6 dols.
"　　　　Six Months,　　　　3 "
"　　　　Three Months,　　　　2 "
Single Copies—Twenty-five Cents.

ADVERTISEMENTS will be inserted at the rate of
Five Dollars per square of 12 lines per month.
TERMS—CASH.

THE FRASER MINES VINDICATED; OR, THE HISTORY OF FOUR MONTHS. By ALFRED WADDINGTON.

The above is the title of a work just issued from the press, written by a gentleman not unknown in literary circles. The work treats, as its title indicates, of matters concerning the interests of Vancouver Island and British Columbia; gives a short history of the times, and the blunders which have been committed by various parties, and to which, in a great measure, may be attributed the slight depression in our affairs; and suggests a number of remedies which, if applied at once, will assist materially in bringing back the thousands who have left our ?es.

We give below one or two rather inter ... g extracts from the work spoken of, which is neatly printed, and well worth a perusal:

"Every candid reader will now be convinced, (and I am speaking to those abroad, for those here know it well), that the disappointments attending this unfortunate gold crusade have had nothing to do with the existence of the gold itself, and that in presence of the numerous obstacles which have had to be contended with, the quantity so far extracted may compare most favorably with the beginnings of any other gold field, and is of itself a sufficient proof of its abundance. Indeed the state of the country has alone hindered a much greater quantity from being taken out; and the steady increase in the amount coming down, and which will probably amount to near 500,000 dollars for November; though with a relatively small number of miners, and all the impediments of the winter season to compete with, adds a new proof to the fact. If the above calculations could have been carried down to the present date (Nov. 15) this would have been still more apparent; but it is becoming every day more difficult to obtain the real amount exported, for every other store deals now in gold dust, besides which many get their friends to take it down at a small premium, to avoid the expense of the Express.

"Moreover, and with respect to the future yield, hardly a spot beyond the bed of the river had been prospected in the whole country, and now within a fortnight bank diggings have been discovered extending on both sides of the Fraser to the foot of the mountains, including thousands of acres. These are in fact a species of dry diggings, but it is beyond doubt that the other kind of dry diggings exist plentifully in the north; and indeed they have been found wherever the miner has been able to search for them with any persistency. Again, leads of gold quartz are well known to exist on Pitt river, and quite latterly coarse gold has been discovered 60 miles up the Squamish river, on Howe's Sound; leaving little doubt that gold will be worked before long on this side of the coast range north of Fraser river.

"So much for the gold mines. And now taking a farewell look at Victoria, and though comparisons are said to be invidious, let us recapitulate and confront what has been done there.

"We will say nothing of its climate, its unrivalled position and other natural advantages. But where, in spite of the stifling influences of monopoly, shall we find so much progress in four short months as in Victoria? Where now are her rivals, Port Townsend, Watcom, Sehome, and the two Semiahmoos, for which so much has been done or attempted? Where in so short a time have there been so many streets laid out, built up and some of them graded, macadamized, planked, and even lighted up, as in Victoria? Eight substantial wharves carried out into the harbour, two brick hotels and other brick buildings, numerous frame houses and stores, besides those going up, twenty or thirty restaurants and coffee houses, steamboats built and launched, in short all the beginnings of a large city. Where a more orderly population, or more law-abiding? Where in the United States a city without taxes, lawyers, or public debt? Where in the United States the town or city, where there is more money to be made, even now, by the industrious trader or craftsman who is at all decently started in his business, than in Victoria? And as a proof, rents are higher at this moment than in San Francisco, and in spite of the sudden revulsion in business and the departure of so many jobbers and traders, there are scarcely six business stores empty. A proof, bye the bye, that the prosperity of the country could do without them. Could San Francisco boast of as much at the end of four months? And yet she had at her disposal a whole territory possessing the greatest possible facilities for internal communications and commerce, without restrictions or monopoly to cope with, or a neighbouring hostile press to calumniate her and drive every body away from her shores."

In the following paragraph the author makes a thrust at the army of scribblers who infested the country a few weeks since, and who seemed to delight in misrepresenting every thing connected with our advancement:

"It is to the newspapers of San Francisco that, with one or two exceptions, we owe our bad name abroad, and the consequent check on foreign emigration. If I recollect right there exists in San Francisco an association, which has not been over successful, for the promotion of immigration. The newspapers have done better than the association, for they have succeeded not only in stopping all our immigration, but in keeping it to themselves. Much could be said on their way of treating every thing in this country, but their strictures have been so evidently tinctured with jealousy that it would be hardly worth while; and as to their correspondents, some of their letters have been so ridiculous, not to say worse, that I rather suspect they must have been tinctured with rum.

"Assuredly there has been enough to find fault with, without having recourse to all these exaggerations. Most of them have been totally unfounded, and I may truly say that, under a different regime, the almost superhuman difficulties we have had to contend with would have been overcome, and our short history instead of being chequered with reverses would have presented a brighter page.

"Providence, for wise reasons, had ordained that it should be otherwise, and that our exaggerated dreams of prosperity, our castles in the air should be roughly interrupted and destroyed. We have been brought to our senses, and some of us have been taught the lessons of adversity. Over speculation is at an end, and land agents in despair. A flock of men, the scouts of civilization, and who would have converted this country into a second California, have left our shores. Many immigrants too, of a much better class, but who were not suited to the country, have left us. Men who wanted impossibilities—Miners who have their wives and children, their homes, their claims with which to gain an independence, and all the comforts of a congenial climate in California, were not the men to stop here. Besides they had been spoiled, and no ordinary gains could satisfy them. Nor did we want so many jobbers and importers. Where goods can be thrown into the market from San Francisco in a fortnight, speculation is out of the question, and instead of 59 jobbing houses (about as many as in San Francisco,) all that is wanted for the present trade with the mines and back country is a small number of wholesale merchants.

"We have then reason to be thankful, and if our short sighted disappointments have been a severe trial to all, we have still a good aftergrowth of hope before us. The truth is already spreading abroad; all the assertions of those who have left us will not diminish one ounce of the gold in our mountains, and those who are gone will soon be replaced by another population as active, more hardy and less ambitious. Let that population once reach our shores, and measures be taken to encourage them, foreigners or not. Let miners be allowed to make their own bye-laws and regulations for each bar or district, subject to the approbation of a council of miners; instead of starving them out, let the country be entirely thrown open, so that provisions may be as cheap as possible in the interior, and let the tax on goods be modified, so as to be levied on the superfluities and not on the necessaries of life. Let every one be allowed to buy land at American prices and not at five dollars an acre; and instead of throwing obstacles in the way of the colonist, give the poor bona fide settler a right of preemption, and a premium of land, taken from the wild waste, to the deserving father of a numerous family. Above all, let us have no tardy measures to drive emigrants away once more and make us lose the advantages of another year. Let all this and more, if possible, be done, and the progress of this favored country will be as sure as it will be rapid."

NOVA SCOTIA.—The Tories and Liberals are working lustily for the "loaves and fishes." The late election for two members of the Lower House, resulted in favor of the Liberals. W. Forman Chief Engineer of the Railroad, has been removed, and Mr. Laurie appointed in his place. The Government charge him with incompetency. The Opposition say he was removed for interfering in the Hants election, which ended unfavorably to the government.

Religious feeling is enlisted in support of each party. A Protestant alliance is ranked on the side of the Liberals. The Catholic influence, one-fifth of the population, supports the Johnston administration.

The Hon. Dr. Tupper, Hon. R. B. Dickey and W. A. Henry, Esq., have been appointed delegates to England on the subject of an Inter-Colonial Railway.

It appears that just now there is great excitement in Canada. The Bowmanville Statesman says:

"Never since the troublous times of 1856,—'57 was the province in such a state of political excitement; and most assuredly there never was greater cause for alarm than at present exists."

HALIFAX AND QUEBEC RAILWAY.—We have sufficient authority for stating that the British Government will guarantee the interest on money enough to build the above Railway—to be constructed by the Company which was recently represented at the Colonial Office by Lord Bury, Mr. Cunard, etc.—St. John News.

1

continued in the reorganized Hudson's Bay Company, and had moved the Company's Pacific headquarters to Victoria. Made Governor of Vancouver Island in 1851, he not only shaped that colony, but also a still newer colony, British Columbia, which emerged on the mainland when gold was discovered on gravel bars along the Fraser River in 1857-8. Miners flocked to the canyons of the lower Fraser: via Victoria from California, whose own gold fields were beginning to play out, across the continent from the eastern British provinces, and around the globe by sea from Britain and Europe. To deal with this frantic, disorderly rush, Douglas swiftly took it on himself to establish law and security on the mainland, where Britain in 1858 set up the province of British Columbia, placing it also under his governorship.

Thereafter, Victoria boomed as the supply base for the Fraser gold fields. And when the original fields were dwindling around 1860, big new finds made further up the Fraser, in the Cariboo district, brought a whole fresh surge of growth both to Vancouver Island's capital and to mainland British Columbia; now with its own capital of New Westminster near the Fraser's mouth. Yet though these young British colonies seemed fast flourishing, they faced serious future problems: of costly inland communications through rough mountain country, problems of finding a wider economic basis if the gold ran out, and worries about the constant, powerful presence of so many American miners from across the border. Would the Oregon case be repeated, after all, if the small Pacific settlements could not withstand American annexationism? Could fur-company rule endure — or was union with distant Canada the one, ultimate, effective answer? These questions rose with the 1860s, and as new colonial leaders came forth. One was grandly called Amor de Cosmos, once plain Bill Smith from Nova Scotia, until he changed his name in California. He moved up to Victoria in 1858, founded a paper there, the *British Colonist*, and soon went into politics to seek responsible government for the colony. Another was John Robson, born at Perth in Upper Canada, who in 1861 began his own *British Columbian* at New Westminster, and also took up the quest for responsible rule. Both men would be crucial in the cause of union with Canada. Indeed, from the earlier 1860s, that issue took on mounting force: for the Pacific West no less than the Plains country.

On the prairies, the world of Selkirk settlers tilling their near-subsistence holdings beside the Red, or of Métis buffalo hunts out on open plains, would increasingly be challenged by commercial farming, brought by new arrivals who

1. The *British Colonist* of Victoria, 1858. *In a sense, this paper founded by an eccentric Amor de Cosmos continues today within the present Victoria* Times-Colonist. *But in its opening days the record of the Fraser gold mines took top news place — followed by reports from Nova Scotia, and more briefly, Canada.*
2. A Street in New Westminster, 1860s.

2

ploughed up ancient grasslands. And in the Far West, the world of Company posts and transient mining camps would increasingly be replaced by enduring villages and shaft-mines, by cattle-ranching and lumbering. Furthermore, back East, where earlier frontiers had so largely been occupied in the British provinces, eyes there were turning westward more and more. Nowhere was that more evident than in Canada West, former Upper Canada, the most populous and rapidly growing community in all British North America. Expansionism indeed was not just an American trait. By the 1860s Canada West, future Ontario, was strongly displaying it — especially in the Upper Canada Reform or Liberal party as headed by George Brown.

Brown, a hard-driving Edinburgh Scot, whose Toronto *Globe* became the most widely circulated newspaper in British North America, had rebuilt failing Upper Canadian Liberal forces into a sweeping popular movement. To go back and explain, Robert Baldwin's Reform party, that had seen responsible government triumph in the United Province of Canada in 1848, had split wide open in 1850-1, under attacks from new or revived radical elements. These included both Reform veterans like William Lyon Mackenzie and John Rolph, safely returned from exile, and young democratic idealists like William McDougall, who looked for men who were "clear grit" to move on beyond fancy-dancy British parliamentary self-government to "cheap" American-style elective rule and "simple" written constitutions. Such radicals were inevitably dubbed Clear Grits, notably by George Brown's *Globe* (which added "bunkum-talking cormorants"). Brown himself was an ardent supporter of Baldwin and British responsible government, having founded his *Globe* in 1844 to back them. But Clear Grit onslaughts led Baldwin to resign in disgust in 1851. And his vital Lower Canadians partner, Louis LaFontaine, soon followed, worn down by similar attacks from the French-Canadian radicals termed *Rouges*.

The chief lieutenants of Baldwin and LaFontaine, Francis Hincks and Augustin-Norbert Morin, then replaced them in office. Soon, however, this Reform or Liberal Hincks-Morin ministry ran into even more party divisions; until in 1854 it fell apart in utter sectional confusion. In its stead a new Liberal-Conservative Coalition took power, headed by Sir Allan MacNab, an old-guard Tory politician from Hamilton, with Morin still as his Lower Canadian co-premier. In fact, their middle-ground coalition effectively combined Upper Canada Tory-Conservatives (plus some moderate Liberals formerly led by Hincks) with Lower Canada mainstream Liberals, who had grown pretty moderate themselves. Yet it won and lasted; and not just because of its broad political basis. It also embraced powerful railway-building interests: even crusty old Sir Allan said genially, "my politics now are railways." Besides, this MacNab-Morin Coalition moved successfully in 1854-55 to remove two outstanding grievances: by secularizing Upper Canadian clergy reserves, and turning their income over to municipalities; by abolishing Lower Canadian seigneurial tenure and paying the seigneurs compensation for their rights. But finally, this new political formation gained immeasurably when in 1856 John A. Macdonald, Kingston Scot — and undoubtedly the ablest politician in Canada — replaced MacNab as cabinet head; while in 1857, George Étienne Cartier of Montreal became Canada East co-premier, a powerful fighting colleague for the strategic-minded Macdonald. Their partnership, in truth, would shape a national Canadian Conservative party, which successfully joined Anglophones and

The Gold Regions of British Columbia. *From a map of 1862.*

Francophones within one lasting political formation.

But meanwhile, as the Liberal-Conservative Coalition of 1854 was first taking hold, the Liberal fragments left in opposition were coming together themselves, thanks largely to George Brown, who had entered parliament in 1852. By 1855 he had made peace with his former Clear Grit foes. They already shared some major causes; among them, resisting enlarged Catholic separate school rights in Canada West as ruinous inroads into its non-denominational common school system; or urging "representation by population," in order to give the western half of the Canadian Union the larger number of seats in parliament which its greater population warranted. But along with "rep by pop" and other sectional causes, both Brown and the Grits ardently wanted westward expansion — to bring the British North West into union with Canada. To that end, Brown's influential *Globe* waged a vigorous public campaign from mid-1856 for the acquisition of the Hudson's Bay Company Territory. Here its owner was decidedly helped by William McDougall, now on the *Globe* staff, whose own paper, the *North American*, had earlier pushed for gaining the West; but had since been absorbed into the *Globe*. At any rate, in January, 1857, a Toronto Reform Convention celebrated the reunion of Canada West Liberalism and called for the annexation of the North West: joining Brown's Toronto business-leadership group, who eagerly looked for new western markets to develop, with the Clear Grits' rural following of land-hungry farmers, who sought fertile western tracts to settle.

Consequently, this Brownite-Grit-Liberal combination swept Canada West in provincial elections held late in 1857, while old Grit radical aims were submerged in a respectably British Victorian Liberal party hereafter moulded by George Brown. Furthermore, the ruling Conservative Coalition was tossed into trouble, since John A. Macdonald's forces were now a minority in the western half of the Union, although Cartier's support held in the eastern section. Hence 1858 proved a hectic political year; even marked that summer by a sudden, four-day Liberal government headed by an all-too unprepared Brown. But swiftly, deftly, his Conservative opponents who had left office as the Macdonald-Cartier ministry slipped back in as the Cartier-Macdonald cabinet, after a shady, so-called "Double Shuffle" of their ministerial posts. All the same, the shuffled Conservative administration did return with one significant fresh policy: to inquire into forming a federal union of all the British American colonies. It was only an initial promise to take up the question of union with the other provinces: but it signalled the opening of a path that led to Confederation. Adopted partly by the Conservatives to outplay the Brownite Liberal thrust for western expansion, this federation venture made no immediate headway with the Atlantic colonies, still bound up in their own internal concerns. Thus it was soon dropped by the Canadian Conservative government itself. Nonetheless, it heralded a rising era of plans and policies aimed at union, of strains and dangers of disunion, as the momentous Confederation years got under way.

1. William McDougall, Prominent Early "Clear Grit," 1822-1905. *An idealistic, optimistic Toronto lawyer, he founded the* North American *in 1850 to back the cause of radical Reformers old and young. For a few years McDougall and his Grit associates fought strenuously with Brown, the* Globe *and mainstream Liberals; but after 1854 they buried the hatchet to work jointly against revived Conservative forces instead.*

2. Ottawa, Future Capital of Canada, 1861. *Its choice in 1857 to be the permanent seat of government (and thereby end the periodic shifting of Canada's capital since 1849 between Toronto and Quebec) was put forward to provide a mid-point between the two former capitals in a sectionally-divided Union. But this Ottawa choice roused sectional discords anew, which further plagued Union politics in 1858-59. Still, by 1860 the decision had been confirmed: though new parliament buildings would not be ready in Ottawa for several more years.*

1

2

1. George Brown, *Globe Editor and Leading U.C. Reformer, 1818-1880. Scottish-born Brown, who came to Toronto at twenty-four in 1843, after six years in New York, made his* Globe *(begun in 1844) a powerful Reform organ. Entering the Canadian Union's parliament in 1852, Brown rose to head the Upper Canada Reform party by 1858, urging annexation of the great North West to Canada, representation by population within the Canadian Union, and, from 1859, a new federal form of union for the Province of Canada. All this led him in the 1860s to seek Confederation for British America — and to be a vital factor in the process which achieved it by 1867.*

2. Leader of the Conservative Coalition Government of 1854: Sir Allan MacNab, 1798-1862. *Combative, wily, and staunchly Tory, MacNab had made his name (and won his knighthood) commanding loyal militia forces in the Upper Canada Rebellion against insurgents and American invaders. He sat in parliament for his Hamilton home-area right from 1830, and led the Tory opposition against the Baldwin Reform ministry from 1848. But in 1854, now mellowed — and happy mostly to build railways — Sir Allan joined with former, moderate Liberal foes from Lower Canada to head a strong new majority Liberal-Conservative government.*

3. Co-Leader of the Coalition of 1854: Augustin-Norbert Morin, 1803-1865. *He also entered politics in 1830 — in the Lower Canadian Assembly as a* patriote *follower of Papineau who actually drafted the resounding Ninety-Two Resolutions of 1834. In hiding, though not in arms during the Lower Canada Rebellion, Morin afterwards re-entered parliament as a supporter of LaFontaine: and being earnest and cultivated, in due course became LaFontaine's chief lieutenant, then his successor. Hence when the Coalition of 1854 was formed, Morin was the obvious leader for its eastern contingent, by now mainly composed of rather conservative French Liberals. But neither MacNab nor Morin would long stay as co-premiers, since more resourceful leaders soon took over — Macdonald and Cartier.*

4. Lasting Leader of the Coalition: John Alexander Macdonald, 1815-1891. *A talented statesman and a tireless politician, Macdonald came from Scotland to Kingston with his parents as a boy of five. Admitted as a lawyer in 1836, he was elected to the Union parliament for Kingston in 1844, and first entered government under the Conservative Draper. Macdonald believed firmly in Canada, the British link, and a French-English partnership; while his own shrewd realism played an influential role in constructing the Liberal-Conservative Coalition of 1854. In this he became Attorney-General West; and in 1856 replaced MacNab as Upper Canadian leader and co-premier. His long career that followed, however, must be left for future (and frequent) references.*

5. Lasting Leader of the Coalition: George Étienne Cartier, 1814-1873. *As a young lawyer and* patriote*, he fought at St. Denis and St. Charles in 1837; had to flee to the United States, but returned to Canada in 1838. Ten years later Cartier was elected to the Assembly, at first as a LaFontaine Liberal for Verchères; later for Montreal until his death. Appointed to the Conservative Coalition cabinet in 1856, he became its eastern leader and co-premier the next year; thus beginning his lasting comradeship with John A. Macdonald. Indeed, his tough courage and warm trust were as necessary to Macdonald as were the solid body of votes Cartier supplied from Canada East — where he ruled all but unchallenged from 1858 to his death.*

3

4

1

2

5

The Path to Confederation

1. Alexander Tilloch Galt, 1817-93. *Son of John Galt of the Canada Company, he himself had been Commissioner of the British American Land Company in the Eastern Townships during the 1840s, and in the 1850s became a leading railway builder, who looked as well to Canadian expansion. Hence in 1858 Galt laid his resolutions for a broad B.N.A. federation before parliament; and joined the Cartier-Macdonald Conservative cabinet on condition that it would pursue them. Afterwards he remained a major figure in the Confederation movement.*

2. Antoine-Aimé Dorion, 1818-91. *A noted parliamentary debater and Montreal lawyer, Dorion as a young man in the 1840s had been a noted radical liberal, or French-Canadian* Rouge *democrat. In parliament from 1854, he came to head the small but able* Rouge *contingent there, largely through sheer intellectual force. Thus he became chief leader of the Lower Canadian Liberals in opposition to the now-Conservative French majority group, to be known as* Bleus.

3. Thomas D'Arcy McGee, 1825-68. *Superb speaker, powerful editor, and ardent believer in a "new nationality" for Canada, Irish-born McGee gave his eloquence and fervour to the cause of Canadian Confederation. As spokesman of the numerous Catholic Irish community in Canada East, he entered parliament for Montreal West in 1858; and held cabinet posts first as a Liberal, later as a Macdonald Conservative — but always with a ruling concern for Canada, to which he brought his own poetic Irish heritage.*

Politicians' talk of a British North American union had been going on for years — with the American federal example so close at hand, how could it be otherwise? Back in 1849, Canadian Tories had vaguely proposed federation as some sort of answer to British free trade and colonial responsible government. Yet not till the hot political summer of 1858 were meaningful resolutions on the subject laid before the Canadian legislature, placed there by Alexander Galt, a top Montreal businessman and a leading representative of the English-speaking minority in Canada East as independent Liberal member for Sherbrooke. But Galt was also a powerful Grand Trunk promoter and contractor who had been moving much closer to the rail-minded Conservatives, although he still kept his own horizons. At all events, he put resolutions before the Canadian Assembly in 1858, calling both for the transfer of the great North West to Canada and for a general confederation of all British North America, in which the western territories (and rail links) would take their place. Galt's resolutions remained undecided. Yet when the Cartier-Macdonald cabinet took power that August after the notorious Double Shuffle, Galt was brought in as finance minister, along with his own Confederation proposal. And while that scheme got nowhere then, it was too hopefully appealing just to be forgotten. Henceforth in the Province of Canada the Conservative side kept touch with the idea of a broad federal union, an idea which re-emerged from time to time. Liberal ties with the federation concept soon followed as well.

In 1859, an Upper Canada Reform Convention of over 600 delegates meeting in Toronto adopted a plan to federate the two very distinct Canadas, powerfully urged and steered by George Brown. This scheme proposed provincial governments for Canada West and Canada East, to handle such sectionally different matters as education, culture and local affairs, and one general, "joint authority" for matters of their common concern, like finance, transport and economic development. Here, too, were the germs of future Canadian federalism. Moreover, Lower Canadian Liberals joined their Upper Canadian counterparts in endorsing the dual federation idea; among them, Antoine-Aimé Dorion, keen-minded French-Canadian leader of the *Rouges*, and Thomas D'Arcy McGee, an eloquent voice of the Catholic Irish community particularly strong in Montreal.

These Liberal forces, however, made little progress when in 1860 they put the dual federation scheme before the Canadian legislature. Their Conservative opponents, especially in Francophone Canada East, feared to change the existing Canadian union because of the new sectional difficulties which could arise. In fact, Conservatives, over all, preferred to keep the present union going, until

1

2

3

Major Events Leading to Confederation

1858

August	Conservative cabinet in Province of Canada raises question of B.N.A. federal union with the Maritime Provinces: no interest yet

1859

November	George Brown and Canadian Grit Liberals advocate a federation of the two Canadas

1861

April	U.S. Civil War begins, raising pro-Southern sentiments in Britain and serious questions of defence for B.N.A.
November	U.S. warship stops the neutral British *Trent* and seizes two official Southern emissaries to Europe; Britain and U.S. move near war

1863

	Hudson's Bay Company empire taken over by London financial group willing to sell its lands to Canada for settlement

1864

March-April	Nova Scotia, New Brunswick and Prince Edward Island pass resolutions to discuss a Maritime Union among themselves
June	In Canada, G. Brown offers to back a government willing to remake the existing Canandian union
June 14	"Great Coalition" of Brown Reformers and Conservatives formed in Canada to pursue B.N.A. federal union, ie. Confederation
September 1-9	Charlottetown Conference: Canadian delegates bring Maritime provinces to drop Maritime union for a general Confederation
October 10-27	Quebec Conference: Canadian and Maritime delegates formulate detailed plan for Confederation in 72 Resolutions
	Prince Edward Island and Newfoundland reject Confederation

1865

February	A.J. Smith's anti-Confederate government elected in New Brunswick, while Nova Scotia stays uncertain
March	Quebec Resolutions gain legislative approval in Canada
June	Britain gives its support to Confederation

1866

April	Irish-American Fenians attack across New Brunswick's border to little effect, but stimulate pro-Confederate sentiments there
June 1	Fenians strike over Niagara frontier, repelling Canadian militia at Ridgeway
June	S.L. Tilley's pro-Confederate government elected in New Brunswick
	Constitutions for future Ontario and Quebec adopted existing Canadian parliament
December 4	London Conference begins deliberations, and ends by delivering the completed draft scheme for Confederation

1867

March 29	British Parliament enacts B.N.A. Act establishing an original Confederation of four provinces (Nova Scotia, New Brunswick, Quebec, Ontario), and setting up a federal system of government
July 1	B.N.A. Act takes effect in the new federal Dominion of Canada

1

2

some distant day when a general Confederation might actually be established. As for the Liberals, they divided: since numbers of them, especially in eastern Upper Canada, also felt uncertain about a change to federalism, and still hoped to make the existing union of the Canadas work better through the "double majority" principle, whereby critical votes in parliament would have to carry majority support from both halves of the province, east and west. Indeed, when in 1861 George Brown left parliament temporarily, both ill and defeated, an older Reformer, Sandfield Macdonald from Cornwall in eastern Upper Canada, moved the Grit Liberal forces towards the double-majority idea — though this was really an improbable notion, since it would require joint majority votes from Protestant Brownite Grits and Catholic Cartier Conservatives alike: two fiercely determined opposites.

But also in 1861, new external threats began to grow. That spring, the Civil War erupted in the United States, between the Union forces of an industrial North and the rebel Confederacy proclaimed by a slave-owning South. Out of their bloody conflict incidents soon arose involving Great Britain and the Union North — which would steadily develop into the world's strongest military power. These incidents inevitably affected the British provinces in America, set right beside the embattled Union. There was a good deal of sympathy within the provinces for the anti-slavery cause of the American North, and Canada West particularly had become a haven for Black slaves fleeing from the South. Nevertheless, high-handed Northern talk of using force against Southern sympathizers in adjoining British territories increasingly put the colonies on the defensive once more, to guard their borders against renewed American dangers. Then came the "Trent Affair" late in 1861, when an American Union warship stopped the British mail steamer *Trent* on the open Atlantic and took off Confederate diplomatic envoys bound for Europe. It was an outright violation of British neutrality — though not unlike what British naval vessels had done to American ships before the War of 1812. As a result, war fever rose between Britain and the United States, until cooler counsels on both sides prevailed.

British regulars still were rushed overseas, and militia companies were raised in Canada in 1862 to meet possible American attacks. From then on, the question of colonial defence loomed large, reinforcing the idea of an interprovincial union to bring greater military efficiency and strength. Other dangerous episodes followed from Lake Erie to the Atlantic coasts. In Nova Scotian waters, Northern warships hung off Halifax to catch Southern "blockade-runners," and there late in 1863 they seized the coastal vessel *Chesapeake* back from its Confederate captors, setting off a furore in the Maritime provinces. But most serious of all was the Confederate raid on St. Albans, Vermont, in October, 1864, when a band of Southern conspirators crossed from Lower Canada to rob banks in this small town, then escaped back into Canada with their loot. The St. Albans Raid outraged Americans. Union troops were ordered to pursue any further raiders right into Canada — a sharply menacing threat. In fact, the real peril of border war gave fresh urgency to the question of defence, while D'Arcy McGee warned Canadians that they might sleep no more, except under arms.

And meanwhile, internal troubles within the existing Canadian union had continued, as its two widely different halves — with equal blocks of seats within one parliament — clashed stubbornly in politics. Canada West still demanded representation by population to recognize its decided lead in numbers, now over

1. Volunteer Regiment Receiving Colours at Toronto, 1863. *This was part of the response to the* Trent Affair, *to the threats and dangers it raised, which produced a sizeable militia movement to add volunteer forces to the defence of inland Canada. Here the "Tenth Royal Regiment, Toronto Volunteers" is having its regimental flags, or colours, presented at a parade ceremony.*

2. Montreal from Mont Royal, 1863. *A view across Canada's then-largest city to the new Victoria Bridge, showing the city reservoir in the foreground and McGill University just beyond it.*

ten years old, and by the census of 1861 standing approximately at 1.4 million for the western section to 1.1 for the eastern. Beyond that, the western section sought an end to "French-Catholic domination," which had imposed Catholic separate school measures on Upper Canada, thanks to Lower Canadian French votes added to those of the Upper Canadian Catholic minority; and had also placed larger tax burdens on Canada West in support of Montreal's business interests. That, of course, was the one-sided but heartfelt opinion of the Anglo-Liberal West; while in the French Conservative East no less emotional views upheld Catholic faith and cherished *Canadien* heritage against wild English Protestants of the western section, who would surely destroy true faith and culture, if they ever gained the larger share of seats in the United Province. Yet these opposed, uncompromising sectional stands threatened sheer deadlock for the Canadian Union.

For a time, that threat seemed to have been put off, when in May, 1862, a middle-ground Liberal ministry headed by Sandfield Macdonald replaced the Cartier-John A. Macdonald cabinet, which had fallen over a too costly Militia Bill. The new government, bringing together wishful moderates of both sections, tried to keep the Canadian union going on the basis of the double-majority principle. But that principle failed flatly when a new separate school bill for Upper Canada still went through by virtue of Lower Canadian votes. Thus in mid-1863, Sandfield Macdonald's ministry was reorganized in order to save it — in which effort George Brown, now back in parliament, played a major role. New elections did not help the remade Liberal regime, however; for while Brownite Grits carried Canada West in a revived campaign for rep by pop, Cartier Conservatives swept Canada East as strongly against it. Nothing had worked. Though the Reform government struggled on amid the sectional impasse, it finally collapsed in March, 1864. In its place a no-less shaky Conservative administration took over, led by John A. Macdonald, as cheerfully genial as ever, and by Sir Etienne Taché, a French Canadian elder statesman dating from LaFontaine's time (though under Taché's nominal control, Cartier still managed the French-Canadian contingent). In any case, this Macdonald-Taché government itself gave up after three months of futility: equally unable to cope with the sectional deadlock, wherein Liberals controlled the western votes of the Union and Conservatives the eastern. Essentially, the constitution itself would have to change. And here George Brown took a deliberate, dramatic step — which went on to Confederation.

1. John Sandfield Macdonald, Moderate Liberal, 1812-72. *From Cornwall, Canada West, he was a veteran Reformer in parliament, which he had first entered in 1841. Yet though able and astute, Sandfield was also cantankerous and overconfident: in fact, not likely to make a success of trying to steer a middle course between the demanding Upper Canada Grits and the unyielding Lower Canada Bleus. And so he failed — yet would reappear after Confederation (which he had previously opposed) as the first premier of the new Province of Ontario.*

2. Sir Étienne Taché, 1795-1865. *After serving through the War of 1812, he became a country doctor in Lower Canada; but entered parliament in 1841, rose in Reform ranks, and in 1848 was made a member of the La-Fontaine-Baldwin cabinet. Continuing in office, Taché joined the Coalition ministry of 1854. Through 1856-57 he was its Lower Canada chief, whereupon he retired and received a knighthood. In March, 1864, however, he returned to politics, to head the short-lived Taché-John A. Macdonald regime, and the Great Coalition which followed. Thereafter, he served as an excellent chairman of the crucial Quebec Conference held in October, 1864.*

1   2

When the Macdonald-Taché government resigned on June 14, Brown made known that he stood ready to support a new ministry solidly committed to settling the sectional problems of Canada. Keenly aware of the deadlock themselves, John A. Macdonald, Cartier and Galt met privately with Brown in the then-capital city of Quebec. Out of their discussions came a transforming agreement: to seek first a general federation of all British North America, or if that failed, the dual federation of the Canadas. Brown and two Liberal colleagues would join a new coalition government under the official premiership of Taché, as a figure respected by both sides. Thus arose the Great Coalition — the strongest government of all the Union era — with substantial eastern and western, Conservative and Liberal, majorities behind it in the common cause of federation. And once it was formally announced to a loudly cheering Assembly on June 24, 1864, the Coalition launched a telling approach to the other British American colonies.

It came at ideally the right time. By mid-1864, the forces for union were reaching critical heights across the wide expanses of British North America. In the Hudson's Bay Company empire of the North West, a group of top London financiers (who also had connections with Grand Trunk Railway interests) had bought control of the Company in 1863; and were ready to see its old fur-trade monopoly replaced, at a price, by farm settlement and telegraph or railroad lines all the way to the Pacific. No less influential in the East, the Intercolonial Railway project had powerfully re-emerged, stimulated by American border dangers, which made a wholly British rail route between the Maritimes and inland Canada seem even more vital. An Intercolonial Railway conference in London between Canadian, New Brunswick and Nova Scotian representatives had broken down in the fall of 1862, over final financial terms. But though a sense of Canadian bad faith was left with the Maritimes, the prospect of a binding railway was not at all forgotten — something which an intercolonial union might far better accomplish. By mid-1864, that prospect appeared even more attractive to the two main Atlantic provinces, not only worrying about their future on the edge of a great American military power, but also seeking new means for their own development. Confined as they were to the northeast corner of the continent, the flourishing seaboard colonies of New Brunswick and Nova Scotia looked for new expansion inward, along their own rail links into the vastness of British

The Charlottetown Conference, September, 1864. *The delegates are photographed at the entrance to the Government House of Prince Edward Island. Too numerous to name in full here, the following at least may be singled out. John A. Macdonald is seated at the centre on the steps, Cartier standing to his right, beside him. Galt sits at the front left of the picture; Brown (with one foot raised on the steps) is at its far right; Dr. Charles Tupper, premier of Nova Scotia, is behind Galt. Samuel Leonard Tilley, premier of New Brunswick, stands forward from, and to the right of, the gentleman with his hat raised to shade the sun.*

Report of Resolutions
adopted at
A Conference of Delegates
from the

Provinces of Canada Nova Scotia and New Brunswick and the Colonies of Newfoundland and Prince Edward Island held at the City of Quebec tenth day of October one thousand eight hundred and sixty four as the Basis of a proposed Confederation of those Provinces and Colonies.

One The best interests and present and future prosperity of British North America will be promoted by a Federal Union under the Crown of Great Britain provided such Union can be effected on principles just to the several Provinces.

Two In the Federation of the British North American Provinces the system of Government best adapted under existing circumstances to protect the diversified interests of the several Provinces and secure efficiency, harmony and permanency in the working of the Union — would be a general government charged with matters of common interest to the whole country and local Governments for each of the Canadas and for the Provinces of Nova Scotia New Brunswick and Prince Edward Island, charged with the control of local matters in their respective sections — provision being made for the admission into the Union on equitable terms of Newfoundland the North West Territory British Columbia and Vancouver.

Three In framing a Constitution for the General Government, the Conference, with a view to the perpetuation of our connection with the Mother Country, and to the promotion of the best interests of the people of these Provinces, desire to follow the model of the British Constitution so far as our circumstances will permit.

Four The Executive Authority or Government shall be vested in the Sovereign of the United Kingdom of Great Britain and Ireland and be administered according to the well understood principles of the British Constitution by the Sovereign personally or by the Representative of the Sovereign duly authorised.

Five The Sovereign or Representative of the Sovereign shall be Commander in Chief of the Land and Naval Militia Forces.

Six There shall be a General Legislature or Parliament for the Federated Provinces composed of a Legislative Council and a House of Commons.

Seven For the purpose of forming the Legislative Council, the Federated Provinces shall be considered as consisting of three Divisions — First Upper Canada — Second Lower Canada Third — Nova Scotia, New Brunswick and Prince Edward Island, each division with an equal representation in the Legislative Council.

Eight Upper Canada shall be represented in the Legislative Council by twenty four Members, Lower Canada by twenty four Members, and the three Maritime Provinces by twenty four Members of which Nova Scotia shall have ten, New Brunswick ten, and Prince Edward Island four Members.

America, whose exports could then flow down to their Atlantic harbours. And growing evidence that the United States now aimed to end reciprocal free trade and raise its own high tariff walls, further turned the Maritimes towards economic and political union with Canada and the North West beyond.

Indeed, the three Maritime Provinces were already seeking to strengthen their own position by discussing "maritime union" among themselves at a conference to be held at Charlottetown in early September, 1864. But to this meeting representatives from Canada also asked admission, in order to present far wider proposals for union. The Charlottetown Conference planners agreed. On September 1 a group of Canadian visitors from the new Canadian Coalition ministry arrived by government steamer at the little island capital, glowing amid late summer sunshine and the excitement of a visiting circus. Chief among the Canadian party were John A. Macdonald, Brown, Cartier, Galt, McDougall, and McGee. They enthusiastically outlined a grand scheme for general federation which had been drafted at long, gruelling cabinet sessions in Quebec. The Maritime delegates responded as enthusiastically. Within days the project of Confederation was endorsed in principle; and it was agreed to hold a further, larger interprovincial conference at Quebec to work out and decide the plan in detail. Seldom could a new nation have had a more amiable and enjoyable start than in that warmly golden Charlottetown September.

In October, 1864, during cooler, working autumn weather, the monumental Quebec Conference met in the Legislative Buildings high above the sweep of the St. Lawrence. Taché presided as its august Chairman. Along with the main Canadian delegates — Macdonald, Brown, Cartier and Galt, Langevin, McGee and McDougall — there were outstanding Maritimers like Samuel Leonard Tilley, the astute Liberal premier of New Brunswick, Dr. Charles Tupper, tough Conservative master of Nova Scotia, or capable George Coles and J.H. Gray of Prince Edward Island. And there were also representatives from Newfoundland this time, such as F.B. Carter and Ambrose Shea. This list still leaves out other noteworthy members including Charles Fisher and E.B. Chandler from New Brunswick, Adams Archibald and Jonathan McCully of Nova Scotia; but out of 33 delegates in total it should serve.

The Quebec Conference did work hard from October 10 to 27; although with splendid evening social occasions in a hospitable Quebec City. Out of the Conference came the future constitutional structure of Canada, in seventy-two resolutions all debated and accepted. For instance, they provided an appointed federal upper chamber, the Senate, based on equal representation for the main settled regions of British America (then the Atlantic, Quebec and Ontario sectors), and set up an elected federal lower chamber, the House of Commons, based on the democratic majority principle of representation by population. Furthermore, federal governments would stand or fall by the votes of this popularly elected House of Commons. Thus federalism and responsible parliamentary government were to be combined in the central sphere of a new constitution.

1. The Quebec Resolutions. *The first eight of the Seventy-Two passed at the momentous Conference in Quebec, as originally transcribed by hand.*
2. Saint John, New Brunswick, 1864.

2

That was also true for the provincial sphere, where provinces would operate similarly, although within their own prescribed list of powers. The division of powers, so basic to a federal system, led on to plentiful later discussions. But let it briefly be said here, that matters assigned to provincial control were broadly to cover property, civil rights and civil law (so different for French Canada), education and municipal affairs, land resources and welfare institutions. And the "general parliament" would look after criminal law and justice, defence and external relations, native rights and aliens, plus trade, transport, shipping and fisheries. Further, any unspecified, residuary powers would also fall to the central regime, along with a considerable wider taxing authority. Over all, this was an effective division, which certainly did not mean that it would not face future challenges. Yet beyond all such concerns, the Quebec Conference resolutions no less called for the completion of the Intercolonial Railway "without delay," between Canada East and Truro in Nova Scotia — and for provisions to admit "Newfoundland, the North West Territory, British Columbia and Vancouver Island" into the new Confederation. The intended scope was clearly continental.

The Quebec Conference plan won wide public acclaim when it was made known: but gradually reactions set in. No doubt inevitable, considering the breathtaking scope of change proposed, these reactions variously arose from old regional or local feelings and resentments, doubts about the complexities (or generalities) of the Quebec plan, its inability to satisfy every special concern — and fears about its costs, certainly in new taxes. But more specifically, some particular elements and areas turned against the scheme. In Lower Canada, for example, the *Rouges* rejected it as "a Grand Trunk job" to bail out railway interests; but also because these heirs of Papineau's radical *nationaliste* tradition

The Battle of Ridgeway. *The defending Volunteers had the numbers but the invading Fenians had the experience, dating from the American Civil War. In fact, the enthusiastic Canadian militia advancing too fast, fell into confusion, and were driven off. Still, the Fenians themselves soon retired back over the border — finding once more that Canadians just did not want to be saved from outside.*

Leader Extra.

4th EDITION

The U. S. Government Stirring.

Regts. to be sent to the Front.

REPORTED CAPTURE OF BRITISH SOLDIERS.

False rumors from various quarters.

20 minutes to 11.

Large numbers of Fenians have left Oswego for Port Hope and Toronto in steamers. Another steamer has left Lewiston. The United States steamers too late to catch them.

2,000 Fenians left Buffalo this morning for Fort Erie. They have torn up portions of the track, and are causing much excitement.

Rouses Point report all quiet there, and no strangers except ordinary travellers arriving by train. 100 laborers at Rome, supposed to be Fenians, are on the way to Potsdam Junction.

BY TELEGRAPH TO THE LEADER.

ST. ALBANS, Vt., June 1.—Three hundred Fenians arrived here this morning.

The second edition of the morning *Express* contains the following:—

"BUFFALO, 3:30 a. m.—Two reporters, who left at midnight to reconnoitre the river shore between here and Tonawanda, have just returned, and report that they found that the straggling parties whose movements were so skilfully confused at first, kand proceeded to Black Rock and down the river toward some point of crossing below. The number in the several columns observed was not less than 600 men moving in perfect order with silence and celerity under capable officers. At Lower Black Rock a train of nine waggons heavily loaded with arms and ammunition was found waiting in consequence of some delay. The train consisted of five large double waggons. Between one and two o'clock the train which had halted for some time started forward.

BUFFALO, June, 1, 4:30, A. M.—Intelligence is received that 1,500 Fenians effected a crossing of the river and landed in Canada about half-past three o'clock this morning. The crossing took place at Pratt's Iron Furnace and the landing was made at a point about a mile below Fort Erie. The ferriage was accomplished by means of two tugs, with two canal boats, conveying about 1,500 men about 200 of whom the boats could not accommodate were left on this side. They expect to follow shortly. The invaders met with no interference or opposition. When they landed on the opposite shore loud cheers were given, which could be plainly heard on this side, together with the sound of the fife and drum. Sweeny was vigorously cheered at Fenian head quarters, and all sorts of statements are made as to his present position and further movements. It was announced at Fenian headquarters, Townsend Hall, this morning, that a mass meeting would be held in the evening and a call is to be issued for a general gathering of all the friends of Ireland. The entire Irish population are wild with excitement. It was confidently stated among those gathered at the hall that Sweeny is now in Canada at the head of a large number of men.

The telegraph cable has been cut at Fort Erie and the Grand Trunk rails said to be torn up. Several English soldiers are said to be prisoners.

BUFFALO, June 1, 11 a. m.—It has just been reported that Port Sarnia and Windsor have been captured by the Fenians.

It is also reported that they have taken possession of the Welland Canal.

[A late report says there is no truth in the statement regarding Windsor, Port Sarnia, and the Welland Canal.—ED. LEADER.

[SPECIAL FROM OUR OWN CORRESPONDENT.]

BUFFALO, June 1, 11:20 A. M.—The Fenians have possession of Taylor's heights, one mile and a half below Far Erie, near the place called Waterloo and the highest lands in the vicinity. They have commenced throwing up earthworks there, and some have struck off towards the Brantford road. The town here is in a great state of excitement at present and the newspaper offices are besieged.

The last report from Erie ferry is to the effect that the steamers are crossing and that everything is quiet. It is reported that the Fenians turned the people out of their homes at Fort Erie.

5th EDITION

The Fenians Burn a Bridge.

PORT COLBORNE, June 19—noon. Refugees from Fort Erie report the burning of the Sowerwines bridge, five miles west of Fort Erie.

6th EDITION

Doings of the Fenians at Fort Erie.

Fenian Reinforcements.

VOLUNTEERS AT DUNNVILLE.

The Queen's Own at their Destination.

2 o'clock, noon.

The Fenians at Fort Erie have opened a recruiting office, and are now enrolling volunteers. They have seized the Newbigging House, and made it their headquarters. When opposition is offered by people of the town, the Fenians at once set fire to their houses.

PRESCOTT, June 1, 12:30.

We hear that a party of 116 men supposed to be Fenians were ticketed at Rome for Ogdensburgh this a. m. They expect to be reinforced before night at Ogdensburg. Fenians are sauntering about town.

DUNNVILLE, June 1—12 o'clock, noon. Captain Booker, with the Hamilton force of volunteers, is here.

PORT COLBORNE, June 1—12 o'clock, noon. The Queen's Own, under the command of Major Dennis, has arrived here—all right.

7th EDITION

THE LATEST FROM BUFFALO.

The Fenians Opposite Black Rock.

The Encampment said to number 2,000 or 3,000.

The work of plunder commenced.

Horse stealing their favorite practice.

(BY SPECIAL TELEGRAPH FROM OUR OWN CORRESPONDENT.)

BUFFALO, June 1, 1:30 P. M.

I have just returned from Lower Black Rock 4 or 5 miles from the city and had a view of the Fenians encamped on the opposite bank; some say to the number of 2000 or 3000. A tug boat carried over a large number, and cheers for the new arrivals were distinctly heard on this side. The ferry-boat is now stopped, but the Fenians appear to have full liberty to ply in tug boats as often as they please. A man on a white horse appeared to be very active, he being distinctly seen on the bank of the river riding amongst his men. About half-past six the host of the Fenian army proper went over in canal boats and took with them twenty wagon loads of munitions of war. They have sentinels posted for miles around their encampment, and are enjoying their favorite occupation of stealing all the horses in the locality. The stars and stripes float from a flag-pole at Erie, opposite Black Rock, but the general impression here is that if the Canadians have the least spark of that spirit they are supposed to possess the Fenians will soon have to skedaddle. It is said that they intend going on to Chippewa forthwith. The steamer Michigan has steam up to prevent the Fenians coming back.

All kinds of rumors are afloat here—one that Windsor has been burnt down, and another that Fenians have crossed in thousands from Ogdensburg—all of which are, I think, incorrect.

Special messengers have been sent to the Fenian encampment and are expected back in an hour.

The greatest anxiety exists here as to the result of to-day's movements. If the Fenians get well thrashed at the first engagement, it will give great satisfaction to a large number of the Buffalonians who detest them as much as Canadians do.

Public Meeting.

A public meeting will be held by request of the citizens, this day at four o'clock in the St. Lawrence Hall, to organize a Home Guard.

The Lord Chamberlain has received The Queen's Commands to notify to The Honⁱᵉ Robert Wilmot that Her Majesty will be graciously pleased to receive _____ Lin _____ at a Court to be held at Buckingham Palace on Thursday the 7ᵗʰ of March 1867 at ¼ to 3 o'clock.

Full Dress.

1. The Fenians Invade across the Niagara River, 1866. *This Toronto* Leader *extra, reporting on developments early that June, represented the accepted way to get the latest news out to people on the streets, in the dark ages before radio and television.*
2. The London Conference, 1866-7: Reception at the Palace. *The final meetings to settle the Confederation plan were indeed royally entertained. Here is an official invitation to attend the Queen at Buckingham Palace, extended to a New Brunswick delegate, Robert Wilmot (later to be a lieutenant-governor) who was a cousin of L.A. Wilmot of previous days, and who had switched from the anti-confederate to confederate side during New Brunswick's crucial political changeover in 1866.*
3. Halifax from the Citadel, with Sentries on Guard.

deemed it an Anglo-power drive that would swamp the French-Canadian people.

Yet more still in the Maritimes, little Prince Edward Island itself felt swamped by the rep-by-pop principle, which would allow it only a scant five seats in the federal House of Commons. The island colony withdrew, not to enter Confederation until 1873. Moreover, Newfoundland, which was still remote from the mainland ("Her face turns to Britain, her back to the Gulf," sang anti-Confederate Newfoundlanders) also rejected union with Canada, and was not to join it till 1949. Nevertheless, these rejections were not disastrous. A viable federal union could still be formed between the big Province of Canada and the two main Maritime provinces, New Brunswick and Nova Scotia. Then in New Brunswick, Tilley's pro-Confederation government was defeated in the provincial election of March, 1865, though to a large extent over local issues. Furthermore, in Nova Scotia Tupper did not even dare to put Confederation to a test in the Assembly: for his formidable Liberal opponent, Joseph Howe — who had not been at either Charlottetown or Quebec — was heading a powerful movement to save his beloved home province from what he called "the Botheration Scheme."

All the same, there was reason to hope that Maritime opinion could be won back. And in the Province of Canada itself, the Quebec Resolutions gained commanding legislative approval in March, 1865, following historic parliamentary discussions duly published as the *Confederation Debates*. The opposing *Rouge* group was simply flooded under. The main body of Cartier's Conservatives held firm, usefully aided by public pronouncements from the Catholic bishops of French Canada in favour of Confederation. Moreover, Brown's Upper Canadian Liberal majority stayed heartily with the Quebec plan. But more also, John A. Macdonald now rose to the fore as virtual leader of the Coalition ministry, thanks to his patient generalship and amiable wit — not to forget his sharp skill as an in-fighter or his always dexterous and tolerant diplomacy.

Later in 1865, besides, new influences strengthened the cause of the Quebec federal plan. Much stemmed from Britain, still a powerful factor in colonial decisions across the Atlantic. The imperial government was anxious to reduce its commitments and burdens in North America, and was aware, too, of closer problems rising in Europe with the emergence there of a strong German nation-state and other new potent nationalisms. Thus in the early summer of 1865, an official Canadian mission to England by Macdonald, Brown Cartier and Galt, won the British government's agreement to use its legitimate influence to help create a new Confederation; to guarantee defence aid to it, and arrange for the transfer of the whole North West to such a federal state. And when the Canadian mission returned home, assured of British backing for the Quebec plan, American influences were also working in its favour — if quite unwittingly.

The American Civil War had ended in April, 1865. With a sigh of relief, British Americans watched the mighty Union armies being rapidly demobilized. But there was still a huge pool of trained United States military man-power available, and American expansionists again were looking northward, particularly across the western plains. Furthermore, American high-tariff interests exploited anti-British sentiments that rose after the St. Albans Raid of 1864 to ensure the abrogation of the Reciprocity Treaty. It indeed would disappear in 1866. These looming problems hence led anti-Confederation elements in the

The Proclamation of Confederation, 1867. *Note that it was issued on May 27, to take effect on July 1 — the first Dominion Day, now Canada Day.*

BY THE QUEEN.
A PROCLAMATION
For Uniting the Provinces of Canada, Nova Scotia, and New Brunswick into One Dominion under the Name of CANADA.

VICTORIA R.

WHEREAS by an Act of Parliament passed on the Twenty-ninth Day of March One thousand eight hundred and sixty-seven, in the Thirtieth Year of Our Reign, intituled " An Act for the Union of Canada, Nova Scotia, and New Brunswick, and the " Government thereof, and for Purposes connected therewith," after divers Recitals, it is enacted, that " it shall be lawful for the Queen, by and with the Advice of Her Majesty's most Honorable " Privy Council, to declare by Proclamation that on and after a Day therein appointed, not being " more than Six Months after the passing of this Act, the Provinces of Canada, Nova Scotia, and " New Brunswick shall form and be One Dominion under the Name of Canada, and on and after " that Day those Three Provinces shall form and be One Dominion under that Name accordingly:" And it is thereby further enacted, that " such Persons shall be first summoned to the Senate as " the Queen, by Warrant under Her Majesty's Royal Sign Manual, thinks fit to approve, and " their Names shall be inserted in the Queen's Proclamation of Union:" We therefore, by and with the Advice of Our Privy Council, have thought fit to issue this Our Royal Proclamation, and We do Ordain, Declare, and Command, that on and after the First Day of July One thousand eight hundred and sixty-seven the Provinces of Canada, Nova Scotia, and New Brunswick shall form and be One Dominion under the Name of Canada. And We do further Ordain and Declare, that the Persons whose Names are herein inserted and set forth are the Persons of whom We have, by Warrant under Our Royal Sign Manual, thought fit to approve as the Persons who shall be first summoned to the Senate of Canada.

FOR THE PROVINCE OF ONTARIO.	FOR THE PROVINCE OF QUEBEC.	FOR THE PROVINCE OF NOVA SCOTIA.	FOR THE PROVINCE OF NEW BRUNSWICK.
JOHN HAMILTON,	JAMES LESLIE,	EDWARD KENNY,	AMOS EDWIN BOTSFORD,
RODERICK MATHESON,	ASA BELKNAP FOSTER,	JONATHAN M'CULLY,	EDWARD BARRON CHANDLER,
JOHN ROSS,	JOSEPH NOËL BOSSÉ,	THOMAS D. ARCHIBALD,	JOHN ROBERTSON,
SAMUEL MILLS,	LOUIS A. OLIVIER,	ROBERT B. DICKEY,	ROBERT LEONARD HAZEN,
BENJAMIN SEYMOUR,	JACQUE OLIVIER BUREAU,	JOHN H. ANDERSON,	WILLIAM HUNTER ODELL,
WALTER HAMILTON DICKSON,	CHARLES MALHIOT,	JOHN HOLMES,	DAVID WARK,
JAMES SHAW,	LOUIS RENAUD,	JOHN W. RITCHIE,	WILLIAM HENRY STEEVES,
ADAM JOHNSTON FERGUSON BLAIR,	LUC LETELLIER DE ST. JUST,	BENJAMIN WIER,	WILLIAM TODD,
ALEXANDER CAMPBELL,	ULRIC JOSEPH TESSIER,	JOHN LOCKE,	JOHN FERGUSON,
DAVID CHRISTIE,	JOHN HAMILTON,	CALEB R. BILL,	ROBERT DUNCAN WILMOT,
JAMES COX AIKINS,	CHARLES CORMIER,	JOHN BOURINOT,	ABNER REID M'CLELAN,
DAVID REESOR,	ANTOINE JUCHEREAU DUCHESNAY,	WILLIAM MILLER.	PETER MITCHELL.
ELIJAH LEONARD,	DAVID EDWARD PRICE,		
WILLIAM MACMASTER,	ELZEAR H. J. DUCHESNAY,		
ASA ALLWORTH BURNHAM,	LEANDRE DUMOUCHEL,		
JOHN SIMPSON,	LOUIS LACOSTE,		
JAMES SKEAD,	JOSEPH F. ARMAND,		
DAVID LEWIS MACPHERSON,	CHARLES WILSON,		
GEORGE CRAWFORD,	WILLIAM HENRY CHAFFERS,		
DONALD MACDONALD,	JEAN BAPTISTE GUÉVREMONT,		
OLIVER BLAKE,	JAMES FERRIER,		
BILLA FLINT,	Sir NARCISSE FORTUNAT BELLEAU, Knight,		
WALTER M'CREA,	THOMAS RYAN,		
GEORGE WILLIAM ALLAN.	JOHN SEWELL SANBORN.		

Given at Our Court at Windsor Castle, this Twenty-second Day of May, in the Year of our Lord One thousand eight hundred and sixty-seven, and in the Thirtieth Year of Our Reign.

God save the Queen.

LONDON : Printed by GEORGE EDWARD EYRE and WILLIAM SPOTTISWOODE, Printers to the Queen's most Excellent Majesty. 1867.

Maritimes to have new thoughts — over the economic future, and the need as well to shape a united front against American threats, to show that the colonies could not be absorbed piecemeal. The reality was that Maritime anti-Confederates had little positive to offer, only criticisms. In both New Brunswick and Nova Scotia they now began to come around; not saying they liked the Quebec plan they had so thoroughly condemned, but suggesting (vaguely) that some other union scheme might suit. Then came the Fenian Raids, to complete the popular defeat of Maritime anti-Confederation forces.

The Fenians were Irish-Americans, many of them Union ex-soldiers, who sought confusedly to free Ireland from British rule by invading Canada instead. Yet more important, an unfriendly United States let them do so, and thus let loose another round of border warfare. That unofficial conflict spread violence into British American territory from April, 1866, thereby spurring a colonial resistance that looked still more towards the strength of union. The Fenians raided into Lower Canada, and ultimately struck at Red River. Most serious, however, were their push across the Niagara River at Fort Erie (leading to bloody combat in the little Battle of Ridgeway) and their invasion over the New Brunswick frontier from Maine, which proved even more significant in the response it roused. The Upper Canadian raid struck a community already fully in support of Confederation. But the rapidly collapsing New Brunswick assault rallied much less convinced Maritimers to the cause of union — especially when grand Fenian pronouncements condemned Confederation as a design for British anti-republican tyranny. If so, angry Maritime citizens might only think Confederation a good idea! New elections were held in New Brunswick. Its weak anti-Confederate government (with no fresh answers) was swept away in June,

The New Parliament Buildings in Ottawa. *They would now be put in use for a whole new federal Dominion, soon to extend from ocean to ocean.*

1866, replaced by Tilley and his Quebec-plan supporters. Moreover, in Nova Scotia, Premier Tupper now felt it safe to reopen the federal union question; and soon delegates were being readied for a final constitutional conference to be held in Britain, the centre of empire.

This London Conference met at the Westminster Palace Hotel in December, 1866, with many of the former Quebec Conference delegates present, but not George Brown. While his determined drive had essentially launched the successful Confederation movement, he had left the cabinet in 1865, less suited for the long haul which his great rival, Macdonald, had effectively taken over. Brown, however, remained a strong supporter of Confederation; and he shared in shaping a new provincial constitution for Ontario in 1866, when at the first legislative session held in the newly completed Parliament Buildings in Ottawa, constitutions for both the future provinces of Quebec and Ontario were debated and accepted. As for the London Conference that ran on into 1867, it made some revisions in the original Quebec scheme; but basically it approved a federal system built upon the Quebec Resolutions which then was put through the imperial Houses of Parliament in the spring of 1867 as the British North America Act. That founding Act went into effect on July 1, 1867. John A. Macdonald stood out on that great day, rightly, as the first prime minister of a confederated Dominion of Canada. But Brown, Cartier and Galt, Tilley, Tupper, and McGee, nonetheless shared signal honours for its creation.

The new federal Dominion thus born in 1867 began with only the provinces of Nova Scotia and New Brunswick, Quebec and Ontario, once Upper and Lower Canada. Yet steps to bring in the whole western half of British America were already well under way. Within three more years, the great North West of plains, sub-Arctic and Arctic expanses would be added to the union. Within four years, British Columbia and Vancouver Island (combined as a single, larger British Columbia in 1866) would join Confederation as well. Still, these western changes, from centuries of fur-trade dominance, must be left for now; since while in process, they only were to be realized after the original achievement of Confederation.

Nevertheless, it can and should be said that on July 1, 1867, the established British-American communities heralded the birth of a "new nationality" — the favoured term of that day. It had varied elements: Native peoples, French Canadians, English, Irish, Scots, and Welsh, along with Germans, Blacks and still more; all in a growing blend of ethnic heritages, regional outlooks and economic interests. Together these elements formed one broad Canadian state, soon to reach transcontinental size. The members of the new nationality thus joined on July 1, 1867, to celebrate the birthday of their federal union; with pomp and proclamation at Ottawa, the capital of Confederation, with parades, military reviews and public ceremonies in other major centres. But above all, the day was a summer holiday for ordinary citizens: marked by regattas on lakes or rivers, games and picnics in parks or fair grounds; fireworks and bonfires gleaming from the heights, as the warm July night came on. The people happily enjoyed federal Canada's birthday — as they have ever since.

1867   Sir John A. Macdonald heads first federal government at Ottawa

1868   Britain passes Ruperts Land Act, to transfer North West to Canada

1869   Red River Rebellion led by Louis Riel

1870   Manitoba Act passed in Ottawa

1871   B.C. joins Confederation

1872   Dominion Lands Act, providing settlement arrangements for a new, vast West

1873   P.E.I. joins Confederation in the East

1875   North West Territories Act passed

1879   National Policy of tariff protection introduced

1880-81 Canadian Pacific Railway (C.P.R.), rechartered

1885   North West Rebellion under Riel Execution of Louis Riel at Regina C.P.R. completed at Craigellachie, B.C.

1887   Interprovincial Conference at Quebec

1896   Liberals under Laurier replace Conservatives in power at Ottawa

1899-1902   South African War; Canadians participate

1905   Grand Trunk Pacific and National Transcontinental railways launched Alberta and Saskatchewan erected as provinces

1911   Conservatives under Borden take office

1914   First World War begins in August; Canada raises troops for overseas

1917   Imperial War Conference in London

1918   First World War ends in November Canadian Northern Railway nationalized

1919-23 Grand Trunk & Grand Trunk Pacific Railways nationalized

1919   Versailles Peace Conference National Progressive Party set up

1921   Liberals under Mackenzie King take over in Ottawa

1929   Wall Street stock crash heralds Great Depression of 1930s

1930   Conservatives under Bennett form federal government

Chapter Eight

Canada Since Confederation

Building a Transcontinental Nation

It will take a second volume to trace Canadian heritage onward from Confederation to our own day. Yet this first volume still can close with a broad survey of the century and a quarter that was to follow the federal union of 1867. And while such a survey may undoubtedly leave out aspects of the full and complex story, its key features should be there: beginning with the first major period after 1867, which ran to the mid-1890s, and saw a transcontinental Canada gain lasting shape.

In 1868, the British parliament passed the Ruperts Land Act, providing for the new Canadian dominion to take over the North West, once terms of compensation had been reached with the Hudson's Bay Company. In 1869, that company accepted a Canadian offer of £300,000 plus large western land grants. But the actual transfer of the territory did not go smoothly. It was held up by armed Métis resistance at the Red River — and the impact of this Red River Rising must be looked at in a moment. More immediately important, however, is

1

Overleaf. Competing Rail Lines. *Canada's new era of railway building assuredly grew from the transport needs of its expanding national economy; but the results might look overdone — as here, where two rival mainlines run side by side through level country.*

1. Cariboo Road in the Far West. *This major route up the Fraser shows what "good" land transport was like in British Columbia before railways — which only a union with Canada would bring.*

2. Execution of Thomas Scott in the Red River Rising, 1870. *Shot at Fort Garry in March, after a court martial by Riel's provisional government, Scott's death brought on fierce responses in English Canada.*

2

the fact that the uprising ended peaceably with the Manitoba Act of 1870, whereby Canada erected its first new western province. The Act recognized French-language and Catholic-education rights for the Métis in particular, in setting up a small and thinly populated Manitoba not much changed in size from the old Red River Colony. In 1875, Canada's North West Territories Act next organized the huge expanses beyond, under the control of a lieutenant-governor and appointed council. But in the meantime, across the Rockies, the province of British Columbia entered Confederation in 1871. Negotiations between British Columbian delegates and the federal regime in Ottawa had brought an agreement which ensured responsible government and financial aid to the struggling Far West province (large in area but still scant in numbers), and also promised it a transcontinental railway within ten years. Thus Canada would truly reach from sea to sea — though with still more problems on the way.

One of these was certainly the Red River Rising of 1869-70, which left bitter consequences. With some cause, the Métis people of the area had felt sharply anxious about their own land and cultural rights once a distant, unknown Canada took charge. In Louis Riel, of Métis and French Canadian descent, they found a resourceful leader, though one inclined to erratic judgements also. Riel skilfully used the threat of Métis armed power to win them negotiated terms in Ottawa's Manitoba Act. Yet his rash misuse of that power to "execute" a Canadian Orange foe, Thomas Scott, did much to turn a successful, almost bloodless western protest into a hot dispute between French and English Canadians back East. The former hailed Riel, not all that accurately, as a noble defender of the claims of French Catholics in the West. The latter, no more accurately, damned him as a traitor, murderer, and the arch-enemy of the Anglo-Protestantism destined to take over in the western regions. And though temporarily stilled, this angry split over Riel was to re-emerge in years to come.

All the same, the sea-to-sea Dominion went on developing. In the East, the Intercolonial Railway forged ahead, while Prince Edward Island joined Confederation on July 1, 1873; largely to obtain finances for an Island railway, and to buy out its absentee landlords at last. Newfoundland, however, still failed to support union with Canada. Otherwise, Canadians mostly turned their eyes westward; particularly when the federal government controlled by Sir John A. Macdonald and his Conservatives chartered a private Canadian Pacific Railway Company to build the transcontinental line to British Columbia. But in the summer of 1873, the sensational Pacific Scandal became known, revealing that top Conservatives like Macdonald, Cartier and Langevin had received sizeable election funds from the chosen C.P.R. interests. The Macdonald ministry collapsed, as did its huge Pacific Railway scheme. A Liberal cabinet took office

1. Prince Edward Island Railway Pass. *The need to finance this railway, which was said to wind across the Island from one crossroads to the next, was a significant factor in P.E.I. coming to accept union terms in 1873.*
2. Alexander Mackenzie, 1822-92. *He came from Scotland in 1842, settling permanently in Sarnia, C.W., as a builder and soon a Reform editor. He also became George Brown's chief political comrade in parliament from 1861, supported Confederation, and after it was achieved, rose as a leading Liberal in the new federal House — and replaced John A. Macdonald as Prime Minister in 1873, thanks to the Pacific Scandal. But resolute and diligent as Mackenzie was, he could not overcome the depression problems of the 1870s or build the Pacific Railway as fast as was demanded, particularly by B.C. Thus he lost office to John A. in 1878, and gave up the Liberal leadership two years later.*

1

2

THE LIBERAL PROGRAMME;

OR, THE ERA OF PURIFICATION.

1

"ANTI-SECESH."

"Let me go, you old deceiver."
"By no means, my dear. What? leave, when our honeymoon is hardly over. Come, I'll let you have a little more pin money"

2

3

under Alexander Mackenzie, George Brown's former chief lieutenant, and tried instead to build the railway in stages, by government contract. Progress was painfully slow, however, since world depression had struck again; drying up trade, capital and tax revenues. By 1876, dissatisfied British Columbians were voicing ideas of secession, though were largely talked out of them. Then in 1878, a conscientious but uninspiring Mackenzie was replaced by the old master, John A. Macdonald, whose Conservative party swept back into power with a powerful new programme — the National Policy.

This called for a high protective tariff to defend Canadian home markets against foreign competitors, especially American. Yet it was tied in as well with settling the West and constructing the transcontinental railway. In such a three-part project, the protective tariff would foster the eastern industry and capital, that would serve or supply western farm settlement, which in turn would feed its products eastward. And the railway would link both sides, taking settlers and supplies out to the West, carrying grain or other produce back to the East and the world abroad. All three factors thus were basic in Macdonald's grand design for nation-building. He set out to achieve all three, beginning with the National Policy of tariffs, as laid down in Finance Minister Leonard Tilley's budget of 1879. It levied duties of up to 25 per cent on imported manufactures, which stimulated new industrial enterprises from Nova Scotia to southwestern Ontario. Next, the Canadian Pacific Railway was rechartered in 1880, and awarded to a strong new syndicate centred in Montreal. As for filling in the West, important steps for western settlement had already been taken, such as the Dominion Lands Act of 1872, that offered free homesteads of 160 acres to farm entrants; or the North West Mounted Police, established in 1873 to maintain order across the plains; or the series of federal Indian Treaties, which after 1870 "cleared" lands for incoming settlers, by moving native tribes off their ancestral ranges to fixed reserves, where they received federal support. Not a great deal more farm settlement would actually occur, however, until the C.P.R. went through.

Its construction began anew at Yale, B.C., late in 1880, and in 1881 back east. From near North Bay, where rails came up from Montreal, the new line reached out across the forests, rock and muskeg of Northern Ontario. It raced over the prairies west of Winnipeg, and climbed into the giant western mountains; until at Craigellachie in Eagle Pass, on November 7, 1885 the last spike was driven home, binding Canada from east to west. Nonetheless, grave troubles accompanied this whole immense achievement.

In the spring of 1885, another and more serious western rising broke out on the North Saskatchewan, centred around Batoche near Prince Albert. This was

1. The Liberals Clean House, 1874, after Evicting the Macdonald Conservatives. *In this cartoon from the popular journal,* Grip, *Mackenzie scrubs the Pacific Scandal from the floor; George Brown (still the dominating* Globe *owner, if out of parliament) fumigates the air; Richard Cartwright, Liberal finance minister, tends the tub of Honesty; and Oliver Mowat, new but lasting Liberal premier of Ontario, raises purging vapours from Constitutional Law.*
2. John A. Meets B.C. *Talk of Secession from Union, 1879. Another cartoon, conveying that Macdonald, now re-elected, was taking his customary approach: spending funds to handle issues; not least, to realize the long-promised Canadian Pacific Railway.*
3. C.P.R. Construction on the Fraser, 1881. *Here between Yale and Boston Bar the new rail line curves below the old road along the rugged mountain valley.*
4. C.P.R. near Jackfish, Ontario, 1885. *At this trestle in the Precambrian rock above Lake Superior, the rail link "between the Rockies and Montreal" was finally closed.*

4

1. Troops Moving by C.P.R. to the Northwest Rebellion, 1885. *The new railway shows its value, as soldiers sent to quell the second Riel-led revolt travel over its track from eastern Canada.*
2. The Taking of Batoche, 1885. *The capture of this Métis village and headquarters by the troops sent west spelled the end of rebel resistance, despite the courage of the defenders.*

AN OCCASIONAL SPILL.

COLD COMFORT IN A FLAT CAR.
INCIDENTS IN THE MARCH OF THE ROYAL GRENADIERS

1

2

the North West Rebellion, made by Métis settlers in that area who again feared for their lands and culture, and were joined as well by Cree Indians who had been left ill-fed on inadequately supplied federal reserves. More notably, too, Louis Riel had returned to head the revolt, urged back from years of exile in the United States. But Riel now was far more erratic, a religious visionary preaching a new faith of heavenly schemes and dreams, while his own Métis people died hopelessly at their barricades. For the C.P.R., though yet unfinished, moved militia forces from eastern Canada in days, not months, to bring the decisive crushing of revolt at the gun-pits of Batoche. Riel was seized, to be tried by judge and jury at Regina that autumn. His mental state suggested mercy to French Canadians. But the trial verdict, and English Canada, demanded that he hang for treason. Prime Minister Macdonald grimly but resolutely concurred. Riel, died on the Regina gallows in November. His ill-fated rebellion had reopened the inflamed rift between French and English Canada, and had lastingly damaged Conservatism within Quebec — although as well, it had proved the value of the C.P.R., and secured the prairies for enlarging settlement.

Nonetheless, only trickles of new settlers arrived even after the Canadian Pacific was open — its first through train reaching the Pacific in 1886, near where Vancouver was soon to rise as the western rail terminus. Depression had hung on, all the same, despite a temporary lifting in the earlier eighties when the building of the C.P.R., and industrial developments stirred by the National Policy, had brought on hopeful upsurges. But while world food prices still stayed low, there seemed little need for vast new grain fields in Canada's West. In fact, as times grew dull once more, many in the Canadian Dominion lost faith in John A. Macdonald's bold plan of nation-building. A disappointed Nova Scotia for

1. Execution of Louis Riel, November, 1885. *His death left a heritage of bitter memories between French and English Canada, far from gone today.*
2. The Old Man in His Last Election, 1891. *In this poster, Macdonald, now seventy-six, is supported by figures representing agriculture and industry — as he holds the flag, which then was meant to signify no free-trade takeover by the United States, a basic Conservative stand.*

1

THE OLD FLAG.
THE OLD POLICY.
THE OLD LEADER.

2

1. Sir Charles Tupper, 1821-1915.
This leading Nova Scotian Father of Confederation had become a close political associate of John A. in federal politics. Minister of railways when the C.P.R. was under construction, he later was Canada's High Commissioner in Britain; but in 1896 he returned to Ottawa to head the Conservative government, till it fell in elections later that year.

2. Wilfrid Laurier, 1841-1919. *Fluently bilingual, courtly and acute, Laurier took law at McGill, and practised it at Arthabaska, south of Quebec, till he entered active Liberal politics in 1871. He sat for Quebec East in parliament from 1877 to his death. Briefly a member of the Mackenzie cabinet in 1877-78, he became Opposition leader in 1887; and after his election sweep of 1896 formed a powerful government that did well amid a new era of prosperous development in Canada. Knighted in 1897, Laurier did much to keep Francophones and Anglophones together in politics; but all his earnest efforts would not succeed during their deep split over wartime conscription in 1917-18.*

some time even talked of secession. Quebec, sharply wounded over Riel, decried Anglo-Conservative federal dominance, and elected *nationaliste*-minded provincial Liberals to fight Ottawa power. Then a very substantial Ontario complained that it was paying excessively for the Dominion in its taxes, and wanted to see federal powers reduced. All these discontents with the federal nation-state — and more — were displayed at an Interprovincial Conference gathered at Quebec in 1887; though, aside from letting off provincial and regional resentments, its results proved limited. Besides, John A. Macdonald meanwhile held firm in Ottawa, re-elected there by a Canada that had found no other statesman-leader. Somehow he kept things going. But in 1891 John A. fought his last big political battle.

His Liberal opponents, led by a talented and eloquent *Québecois*, Wilfrid Laurier, were pressing for free trade with the United States, or more specifically, Unrestricted Reciprocity. That term, harkening back to the prosperous mid-century years of the Reciprocity Treaty, appealed widely to Canadians disappointed by depression and the National Policy, and ready to open Canada to the American republic (by now a far greater economic giant) for the sake of more immediate trade returns. Yet Macdonald stood unyieldingly for Canadian economic nationalism — for "The Old Man, the Old Flag, and the Old Policy" — and won a popular victory at the polls. The strain was too great: he was dead within months. Yet, for good or ill, the Old Chieftain had saved his nation-building programme. A series of brief-ruling Conservative prime ministers followed him, including Charles Tupper, John A.'s old Nova Scotian comrade of Confederation days. Then in 1896, Laurier and the Liberals at last took power; although by then the central election issue was "Manitoba Schools," concerning the educational rights of Catholics in that province. Otherwise, very significantly, the Laurier Liberals dropped their former talk of American free trade and now maintained Macdonald's National Policy. Beyond that, a fresh cycle of world prosperity opened in 1896: which meant for Canada that the West rapidly became settled, the C.P.R. thrived, and major protected industries bloomed. Macdonald's transcontinental nationalism thus eventually paid off: even if, finally, in a new, Liberal, era.

1

2

"Canada's Century" — and the First World War

From 1896 to the eve of the First World War in 1914 Canada enjoyed an all-but unbroken boom, which led Liberal Prime Minister Sir Wilfrid Laurier to proclaim that the twentieth century would belong to Canada as the nineteenth had to the United States: a glowing national forecast that did not sound too far unlikely at the time. In truth, the young Dominion grew amazingly fast in these pre-war years, particularly in the West — which within a single generation changed from raw frontier expanses to prosperous wheat lands dotted with towns; from sod cabins and plank shanties to frame or brick homes with telephones, electric light, and even some automobiles; all within a well-organized Western regional society. For, as grain demands rose steadily in thriving industrial Europe and eastern North America, so farm settlers flocked to develop Canada's "last, best West."

Migrants came from the eastern provinces and the British Isles, the old, traditional sources; yet they also moved up from the American West, by now largely occupied. And they arrived as well from continental Europe. These last newcomers formed the smallest part of the population inflow, but were highly significant for the future. Indeed, sizeable non-English or French-speaking communities now appeared across the Canadian plains — whether Scandinavians, Germans, Slavs or Hungarians, and Jews or Christian religious sects like Mennonites and Russian Doukhobors. Moreover, others in this latest influx of European heritages went on to Far West mines, logging camps and fisheries, settled down in Northern Ontario mining and lumbering, or else became workers and shopkeepers in major Eastern cities and factory towns. In total, these added multi-ethnic elements spread widely within a booming Canada after the

1

2

1. Sod House in Saskatchewan. *Often the first home of settlers on tree-less, grassy prairies.*
2. The New Prairie Homestead. *At Moose Jaw in 1905, this brick house shows an earlier wooden home behind it — made of sawn lumber, no doubt brought in by rail.*

1. The Last Best West. *This 1909 federal government poster for "Canada West" certainly did not mean the old "Canada West" that disappeared at Confederation, but the new West beyond Ontario, fast developing from 1896 onward.*

2. European Immigrants aboard Ship. *They came in mounting numbers to Canada from about 1896, out of both Central and Eastern Europe, and adding to older but continuing inflows from Britain or the United States.*

3. Inside an Immigrants' Home on the Plains, c. 1900-10. *This scene is actually a re-creation, exhibited in a western provincial museum.*

4. A Prairie Town about 1900. *The "Town" is not identified here, yet is quite typical of those springing up across the Plains West, as transport and supply centres for spreading grain farms.*

2

3

4

mid-1890s; but above all, across its rapidly-filling West.

From the new granaries of the Canadian plains huge crops began to pour east to world markets via the C.P.R.; to the rising Lakehead ports of Port Arthur and Fort William, then on by lake freighter to grain elevators at Montreal and other export points — including Saint John and Halifax when winter froze in the St. Lawrence route. Prairie grain, in time, also made its way out via Vancouver, burgeoning as Canada's chief rail and port-centre on the Pacific; though this flow rose chiefly after the opening of the Panama Canal in 1915, and later grew still larger when trans-Pacific sales to Asian countries became important. In any case, by 1914, an east-west national Canadian economy was working well from coast to coast, shaped mainly by tariff walls, railways, and fast-increasing population. Prime Minister Laurier reaped returns from this grand economic success. But he faced political problems, nonetheless, within a soaring Canada.

The rooted French-English division appeared once more over a British imperial war in the South Africa colonies against the tough-minded Boers, a farming people largely of Dutch origin who had long subjected the native black inhabitants there, but who fought strenuously for their own national freedom in the South African War of 1899-1902. This struggle overseas found English Canada ready to heed Britain's call for aid (as were Australia and New Zealand); but saw French Canada unwilling to join in distant imperialist battles, and somewhat sympathetic to the Boers as another non-British people caught within

1

1. C.P.R. Railyards at Fort William. *They repeatedly were enlarged, as the growth in wheat traffic from the West to the Lakehead ports urged on still more rail construction.*

2. Grand Trunk Grain Elevator at Montreal, c. 1910. *Whereas the National Transcontinental Railway fed to the harbour of Quebec, a still bigger Montreal remained the chief entry-exit port on the St. Lawrence, served by the Canadian Pacific, the Grand Trunk and Canadian Northern together, and by a whole set of massive elevators along its foreshore.*

2

the Empire. The Anglo-Canadians, however, were not just knee-jerk imperialists, as the Francophones assumed, but felt that Canada now was no mere colony, and should show it by taking on responsibilities in the world at large, instead of staying safe, colonial isolationists in North America. Laurier coped with these very different approaches through putting enlistments for the Boer War on a voluntary basis, while providing government support for those troops who went there. Thus Anglo-Canadians could fight and die in crucial battles like Paardeburg, and French-Canadians keep out of an "imperialist assault." In consequence, the Liberal majority still held together to give Laurier more election victories in both 1900 and 1904. By the latter date, however, another major issue had emerged: concerning railways.

The very success of western wheat farming had overloaded the C.P.R., transcontinental route. More rail links seemed essential. A confident new-century Canada went after them. The Canadian Northern, a conglomerate of prairie railways, built its own line to the Lakehead and planned to go on east. The Grand Trunk, the biggest eastern rail company, sought to extend westward to the Pacific. These two projects might well have reasonably been combined into one new transcontinental — but public optimism and private ambition produced two more instead. The Canadian Northern set out to complete a route of its own between Vancouver and Halifax. The Laurier regime chartered the Grand Trunk Pacific in 1905, as a Grand Trunk subsidiary to reach from Winnipeg to Prince Rupert on the British Columbian coast; and it also enacted a measure to build the National Transcontinental from Moncton, New Brunswick, to Winnipeg, as a government line to link with the Grand Trunk Pacific rails. These giant schemes would later run into grave financial difficulties, although their construction certainly fed the boomtime growth. Moreover, in 1905 as well, the two new provinces of Alberta and Saskatchewan were erected out of the then-existing North West Territories; while in 1912 Manitoba's northern limits were enlarged to match, and Ontario and Quebec were similarly extended northward to their present boundaries.

Other issues had come to the fore by then, however, to affect a Laurier Liberal government basking in high prosperity. By 1909, another pressing imperial problem had arisen out of the close naval-building race between Britain and a German empire expanding its own world power. Naval security on the oceans seemed crucial to Canada. Hence the Laurier ministry brought in a bill

Reciprocity Election Campaign in 1911. *Here the Toronto* Star, *a popular Liberal paper, has set up a display to help the Laurier Liberals in elections that turned considerably on their proposed reciprocal free trade agreement with the United States.*

that established a small Canadian navy; meant to support the giant British fleet in time of war, thus satisfying Anglo-Canadian feelings, but otherwise to be under Canadian control, thus easing French-Canadian concerns. Yet the Naval Service Bill passed in 1910 pleased neither side that greatly. Many Francophones still thought it a dangerous external commitment. Many Anglos considered it a feeble gesture, creating only a "tin-pot navy." The naval question would continue on.

In a very different area, the Laurier Liberals found that the western farm community (a rising power itself) largely saw the National Policy as enriching eastern manufacturers alone, and instead wanted low tariffs, even free trade, as did some Maritime interests as well. Consequently, when Laurier went to the polls again in 1911, he offered a new Reciprocity agreement with the United States, while also upholding his compromise naval scheme. Both policies failed him. Anglo-Canadians, except on the prairies, rejected any need for new trade deals with Washington — where Congressional leaders unwisely hailed Reciprocity as advancing the Stars and Stripes northward to the Pole! At the same time, French Canadians still saw Laurier's naval programme as enlisting their sons to die in foreign wars. The Liberal regime and its expressive leader were soundly defeated. The Conservatives took office in their place, headed by the cautious but determined Robert Borden of Nova Scotia.

Borden now advocated an emergency money contribution to help build big battleships for the Royal Navy, long Canada's chief world defence. Yet the Naval Aid Bill he put forward late in 1912 was blocked the next year by a Senate still dominated by the Liberals. Borden, however, had not just proposed paying Britain cash to cover Canada's external responsibilities, but in return to claim a national voice in shaping imperial decisions. For him, the other side to Canadian naval aid was to share in making a common British Empire foreign policy — by no means a meekly colonial stand. In the end, the First World War broke out before the issue was settled. But this tremendous conflict led to a settlement itself, since its grim years of warfare earned Canada the right to be treated as a nation in world affairs, a right won in bloodshed.

Britain's declaration of war against Germany in August, 1914, bound Canada also, as still officially a British colony although internally self-governing. Yet what that fast-maturing young Dominion did in response, was very much its own decision. And Canada under Borden reacted strongly to the threat of German world aggression. Canadians joined both the Royal Navy and the new Royal Canadian Navy, or soon the increasingly important naval and military air services. Mainly, however, they flocked into the army divisions of the Canadian Expeditionary Force, in which some 425,000 served overseas, at a cost of nearly 60,000 young lives. At Ypres in 1915, Canadian troops stubbornly withstood a first German gas attack — without gas masks. In 1916 they plodded and died in the costly Anglo-French Somme offensive. In 1917, they made a brilliantly

1. Robert Borden, 1854-1937. *Pre-eminently a lawyer, and a leading one in Halifax, this somewhat aloof, gruff Nova Scotian saw politics more as a duty than a way of life. Yet had tenacity, insight and forcefulness; and after ten years as leader of the Conservative Opposition in Ottawa (he succeeded Tupper) finally defeated Laurier in 1911. Then Borden ruled as prime minister himself till 1920, through the strains of the First World War. He was knighted in 1914; this picture dates from a London visit of 1912.*
2. Well-Dressed European Arrivals at Quebec, c. 1910.

1

2

successful strategic attack at Vimy Ridge. And in 1918 they shared in the final victorious Allied sweep forward, in which, as the war was ending that November, a Canadian commanding general, Sir Arthur Currie, led his forces into Mons in Belgium, where four years earlier British units had met the original German onslaught. Thanks to Canada's effective commitment, Prime Minister Borden could thus play a prominent role at the Imperial War Conference held in London in 1917, which resolved that the British Empire should in future become a Commonwealth of free and equal nations. And thanks to the powerful Canadian war effort, Borden was also made an influential member of the British imperial delegation at the Versailles Peace Conference of 1919; where Canada signed and ratified the peace treaty on its own behalf, and also became an initial member of the worldwide new League of Nations. Unquestionably, the First World War had put this country plainly on the international scene.

Yet at home, the war also deeply divided Francophone and Anglophone

1

2

1. Recruits Off to the Canadian Army in 1914. *In that summer and fall, crowds of volunteers joined up across the whole country. This scene was in Toronto; but it was much the same elsewhere.*
2. Canadians at Vimy Ridge, 1917. *Here three Canadian soldiers look out on the scene of one of their greatest successes in the First World War.*

Canadians, over the key question of military conscription. Both groups at first had readily volunteered for military service abroad; but the former viewed it as an heroic crusade for those who wished to go, the latter as a grim necessity to preserve security and freedom for everyone. In time, the supply of eager volunteers dwindled; yet the heavy losses of trench warfare kept up the demand for more recruits. The Borden government tried hard to maintain enlistments — although in Quebec their efforts were too often ill-conceived. Nonetheless, understrength army units not only lose morale, but suffer higher casualties. Borden consequently decided that conscription was inevitable. In August, 1917, it was passed into law. That fall the government faced an angry wartime election — which returned the Borden regime, yet split Canada between opposed French and English votes. When conscription was actually applied from January, 1918, the responses proved less violent than might have been feared. Still, the bitter memories left remained through years to come; since French Canadians again felt they had been steam-rollered by a permanent Anglo-majority — as in the Riel case, or on other occasions thereafter. And their resentments against the Conservative party would particularly last.

In the economic sphere, however, the War of 1914-18 brought strong advances to Canada: in western farming, northern lumbering and mining, or in industrial and labour growth, especially at major eastern centres. Here war needs for munitions, ships, aircraft, trucks, and a great deal more, fed busy factory developments in Ontario and Quebec, though the Maritimes or the West Coast shared some of them as well. Generally speaking, industrialism stimulated by the National Policy in the 1880s, then fostered by the good times after 1896, now climbed much further, amid high wartime demands. Not all the growth would last once peace returned. Yet the bigger industrialized Canada that had thus emerged by the 1920s would continue; in the automobile factories of Windsor or Oshawa, in heavy steel and engineering works at Montreal or Hamilton, or, in specialized electrical plants based on hydro-power — more widely scattered, but considerably centring around Toronto.

Meanwhile, big transcontinental railways also took new form. Soaring

1. Automobile Plant in Oshawa after the War. *Its lines of new cars express the mass automotive age largely brought to Canadian industry by the demands of war transport, and the new manufacturing techniques they fostered.*

2. Power Machinery on Western Farms. *Similarly, this use was stimulated in prairie agriculture by the needs and markets of war.*

1

2

wartime prices and inflated costs had brought financial failure to the overoptimistic Canadian Northern and Grand Trunk Pacific projects. The former line was nationalized by the federal government in 1918; the latter between 1919 and 1923, along with the original Grand Trunk itself. Moreover, the National Transcontinental and the much older Intercolonial (both already government-owned) were further added, in order to form the huge public Canadian National Railways System. This "C.N." has sometimes been condemned as a money-wasting public enterprise. But it is largely a monument to failed, extravagant private enterprise — while the successfully "private" C.P.R. was in truth funded heavily by the taxpayer through huge, rich public land grants, government subsidies and repeated guarantees.

In any case, by 1920, Canada was deep in its own peace-time readjustments, as the soldiers came home, war industries closed down, and post-war depression struck the land. Prime Minister Borden, worn down by wartime issues, retired that July. He was replaced by Arthur Meighen from Manitoba, who had commandingly combined the railways; yet proved an all-too-forceful minister of justice in putting down the disruptive Winnipeg General Strike of 1919. Indeed, Meighen only held office until December, 1921, when federal elections returned the Liberals to Ottawa under William Lyon Mackenzie King. They marked the opening of a new era in many ways — but far from least, in that those elections saw women now able to vote federally in Canada on an equal basis with men.

1. The Canadian National Railways Appear. *As seen in Port Arthur station at the Lakehead in the early 1920s.*

2. The Winnipeg Strike, 1919. *Brought on by post-war inflation, labour anxiety and hopes of overall collective bargaining, this broad-based strike virtually shut down the city. Hence it led to government responses by force, such as this advance by the Mounted Police against strikers on June 21 that brought 30 casualties. When it all subsided, Arthur Meighen, uncompromising federal minister of justice, was hero to some in Canada fearing another Russian revolution; villain to others, especially in union labour ranks.*

3. Arthur Meighen (1874-1960). *Undoubtedly talented, he successfully handled the complex business of railway restructuring; but his rigid attitudes also brought him hostility, and helped defeat him as Conservative prime minister just a year after succeeding Borden in 1920.*

1

2

3

Progressive Twenties, Depressed Thirties, and Return to World Conflict

1. Mackenzie King, 1874-1950. *Liberal prime minister for over twenty-one years, he entered politics not through law, but the civil service. After studies at Toronto and Harvard, this Ontario-born labour economist became Ottawa's first deputy minister of labour in 1900, then first labour minister in Laurier's cabinet in 1909. In parliament for North York, King was defeated in the 1911 election, however; and again in 1917, when he held to Laurier's anti-conscription stand. That still helped bring him the leadership of the Liberal opposition in 1919, following Laurier's death. And he won the election of 1921: to begin his prime ministerial years that ran with a short break to 1930, and continuously from 1935 to 1948. Lacking Macdonald's wit and friendly charm, King was quite arguably his equal in adroit political management, and in calculated tactics of delay.*

2. Canadian Legation in Washington, c. 1926. *This first Canadian official post in a foreign country marked King's development of Canada's external relations. The Canadian "legation" here was raised to an "embassy" in 1944, a higher level of diplomatic mission. The flag being flown in the picture is Canada's old one — the Red Ensign bearing the Canadian coat of arms.*

The new prime minister had none of the grace and elegance of his Liberal predecessor, Sir Wilfrid Laurier, who had died in 1919. But Mackenzie King, staid or even dull in manner, proved a born master of political management. He was besides, the grandson of the Upper Canadian radical Reformer, William Lyon Mackenzie. Cherishing that heritage, King sought to end remaining imperial constraints on Canada's national freedom; though that largely meant taking as isolationist position in North America and looking more towards the United States than Britain — rather as his grandfather had done. Accordingly, in office, Mackenzie King dropped Borden's quest for a joint Empire foreign policy, urging instead Canada's claim to shape its own. In 1923 he won imperial acknowledgement of this self-governing Dominion's right to make treaties abroad, and in 1926 he initiated the first Canadian diplomatic mission to a foreign country: in Washington. Finally, in 1931, the British parliament passed the Statute of Westminster to cover the basic changes in the empire. It confirmed that Canada and the other Dominions were full-fledged and freely associated nations, although revisions in their own constitutions such as they might want henceforth would yet go thorough the British parliament. Still further, the Governor-General in Ottawa was now only to represent the Crown as the linking symbol of the free Commonwealth of Nations, not any central British authority. By 1931, in fact, Canada's long passage to nationhood had mostly been achieved — and very much in a Canadian constitutional way: by evolution, not violent revolution.

King's bland managing skills no doubt eased this orderly advance to nationhood. Nevertheless, it can be said that he was virtually seeking Canada's right to avoid more external obligations, in a post-war era where most Francophones opposed continuing imperial entanglements, while many Anglophones tired of costly ventures overseas no less looked to a North America set at presumably safe distance from European bonfires. At any rate, an isolationist King by and large managed to outplay the older-style imperialism of his Conservative rival, Meighen. Yet internal, not external, issues really did more to affect the Liberals' hold on federal power.

They had won the lead, but less than a majority in 1921, when regional

1

2

grievances were dividing a troubled Canada. Quebec was still embittered over wartime conscription — blaming both the Tories and Anglo-Canada in general — although the fact that King had stood with his old chief, Laurier, in opposing conscription helped keep a solid French-Canadian block behind the Liberal regime at Ottawa. Elsewhere, however, the Maritime Rights movement was seething in the Atlantic provinces, which repeatedly had felt outweighed and undervalued in Confederation. And, above all, Progressivism had arisen on the western plains: a farmers' revolt against the two old parties, Liberals and Conservatives, which had seemingly traded power back and forth between them with scant regard for ordinary citizens. This peaceful but potent farm revolt had been spurred on by the collapse of wartime wheat prices and the ending of the federal board that had marketed grain during the war. Yet, western Progressivism really expressed the far deeper resentments of prairie producers against big-purse eastern interests — banks and loan companies, railways or tariff-sheltered manufacturers — all of whom apparently dominated the old-party elites at Ottawa, despite anything that western voters might do. Still, it is worth adding that this strong protest, which put new Progressive parties into provincial power across the Plains West, also appeared in Ontario, where a United Farmers government (with labour support) had won office at Toronto in 1919. And notably, it was an Ontario Progressive, Agnes Macphail, who was the first woman elected to the federal parliament in 1921.

In Ottawa, however, Mackenzie King bided his time with a shaky uncertain House of Commons, while wooing the unseasoned Progressive members there as "Liberals in a hurry." He deftly gained enough fringe support (or wordily evaded dangerous decisions) to survive through the next federal election, held in 1925. True, in 1926 Meighen briefly returned to power in a confused House of Commons; yet he was decisively defeated by King in a fresh election that October. By this date, Progressivism too, had lost its drive federally, even while Meighen Conservatism had been foiled. King had at last secured himself in power; more through cool calculation and resolve than any mere chance.

In the meantime, economic prosperity was returning across Canada: by 1924 at least. Wheat prices and sales went up; resource industries and manufacturing did even better; while automobile highways spread, skyscrapers climbed, and radio arrived in the twenties' boom. As well, there was a renewed inflow of immigrants. Many still came from Britain, but also increasingly from southern

1. Reviving Immigration: Arrivals at Winnipeg in the 1920s. *Here is a party of Central Europeans, many of whom would continue to flow into the West through the good years of the later twenties.*
2. Agnes Macphail, 1890-1954. *The first female member of the House of Commons, an Ontario rural school teacher, she was elected as a Progressive in 1921, and sat in parliament till 1940; then in the Ontario house, 1943-45, and 1948-51. She became a founding member of the C.C.F., and as well a noted prison reformer, anti-militarist and feminist.*

1

2

and eastern Europe: Italians and Greeks, Ukrainians, Poles, Finns and others, who went variously to the West and North or into eastern cities. But this influx would soon end, after the good times peaked in 1928-9. The Wall Street stock crash of October, 1929, signalled the onset of a vast world depression, in which Canadians, and Mackenzie King's government, faced bleak new challenges for survival.

The decade of the thirties hence began in darkening gloom, with business cutbacks and swelling unemployment. The federal Liberals, facing repeated provincial demands for help (essentially for poor relief) responded cautiously, inadequately. In 1930 they fell — amid a tide of public distress and anger beyond even the management arts of Mr. King. The Conservatives took over, now led by Richard Bedford Bennett, a wealthy lawyer of New Brunswick origin and Alberta career. Dynamically confident, if overbearing too, "R.B." promised to end the Depression. It ended him instead. He tried futile high tariffs and oppressive relief work-camps. He negotiated a system of Empire preferences in 1932, to expand Canada's still sizeable trade with Britain and some of the other dominions; though the results proved not that great. In 1934 he also reintroduced a wheat marketing board; but world grain prices stayed low, while much of the Canadian West was hit by devastating drought. Finally, in 1935, Bennett put forward a surprising new programme (for a big-business Conservative) of widespread government intervention and controls, minimum wages and unemployment insurance. All the same, his socio-economic reform programme came too late, when he was nearing a new election after five disastrous years. The Bennett New Deal thus was readily condemned as a "deathbed conversion."

Downtown Montreal, 1930. *The Royal Bank skyscraper is centrally located opposite some of the city's many docks. This aerial view was taken from the British airship R 100, which crossed the Atlantic on a tour that summer.*

1

2

3

4

1. Depression — and Drought, 1931. *The Great Depression, that spread from 1930 through finance, factory and farm, hit western farming especially hard in dryer prairie regions, where rainfall failed, crops withered and soils blew away; as here near Kincaid in southern Saskatchewan.*

2. Relief Project, 1933. *A hospital under construction at Dundurn, Saskatchewan, in a province heavily affected by farm failures and relief costs, while welfare needs soared steadily.*

3. The March on Ottawa, 1935: Unemployed Boarding Train in Alberta. *This mass "box car" protest achieved little directly; but did impress on public opinion the desperate state of sufferers in the West.*

4. Richard Bennett, Who Did Not Beat the Depression, 1870-1947. *Wealthy Calgary lawyer and Conservative businessman, Bennett aspired to replace the "do-nothing" Liberal King and beat the Depression by bold, aggressive moves. In parliament at Ottawa from 1911, and a member of Meighen's short governments, Bennett won the election of 1930; but though a telling orator, shaped few effective programmes, despite lots of effort. And so he fell in 1935.*

Its key reforms, moreover, were declared by the Judicial Committee of the imperial Privy Council — still the top constitutional authority — to be beyond the scope of federal powers in the Canadian constitution, as set forth by the basic British North America Act of 1867. In fact, about all that came out of Bennett's hopeful tries were some significant ideas for the future and the public Canadian Broadcasting Corporation, set up in that form in 1936.

Mackenzie King himself returned to power in October, 1935. Careful as ever, he put the matter of federal government powers before a Royal Commission in 1937, which usefully postponed the problem. He also did what he could to improve the flow of trade by reaching new, if limited, reciprocity agreements with the Untied States in 1935 and 1938; and these did help at least to enlarge Northern resource exports and activities. Inevitably, however, King like Bennett before him came up against the regional discontents and new political forces rising from the relentless impacts of depression. In overburdened cities, unemployment, poverty and hardships brought extreme responses: from small but

1

1. C.B.C. in Operation: "Opportunity Knocks." *A popular radio talent show on the young C.B.C., which first began as the public Canadian Radio-Broadcasting Commission, erected by Bennett in 1932.*

2. King Returns: Reciprocity Agreement with U.S., 1935. *A limited deal, not a comprehensive pact, is signed here at Washington in November, with U.S. Secretary of State Cordell Hull and President Franklin D. Roosevelt at hand.*

2

militant communist or fascist groups ready for riot and violence, since they dealt in class and racist hatred. Yet far more widely supported political movements, that stayed within the constitutional, democratic system, emerged in both city and countryside. Such was the new *Union Nationale* party in Quebec, led by Maurice Duplessis, which in 1936 defeated the provincial Liberals and began another reign of Quebec *nationalisme*, feuding constantly with Ottawa. In Ontario, the aggressive Mitchell Hepburn replaced a tired Tory provincial regime in 1934; but though officially a Liberal, this lively, rabble-rousing "Mitch" despised the withdrawn and canny Mackenzie King (the feeling was mutual). More lastingly significant, however, were whole new parties that developed in the West — Social Credit and the C.C.F., the Co-operative Commonwealth Federation.

Social Credit, except for its initial "funny-money" attempts to create paper credits for hard-hit western producers, really expressed a right-wing prairie conservatism. It first emerged in Alberta, where in 1935 the gospel-preaching

1. **William Aberhart, Social Credit Premier of Alberta, 1937.** *"Bible Bill" is heading a party rally in Calgary, while his successor-to-be, Ernest Manning, sits beside him by the post.*

2. **Re-armament: Aircraft at Vickers Plant in Montreal, c. 1938.** *These "Deltas" for the R.C.A.F. would soon be overshadowed by more advanced aircraft building in Canadian factories. But they do indicate two things: preparations for the looming conflict with the Fascist powers overseas, and the mounting significance of air power — which would produce the giant Commonwealth Air Training Plan in Canada by 1939-40.*

3. **James Shaver Woodsworth, 1874-1942.** *Seen here when first elected as a labour representative to parliament for North Winnipeg in 1921, Woodsworth was chosen leader of the C.C.F. at Regina in 1933; and by clear integrity and ability, built a role at Ottawa markedly larger than his own party following.*

1

2

3

1

2

3

4

1. Canadians Crossing a Military Bridge in the Second World War in Europe. *Presumably, this London Bridge, erected by Royal Canadian Engineers, did not fall down.*

2. Troops Enter a Regained Dieppe in Normandy. *Marching down the street, in the distance, come Canadian forces: a welcoming moment after their earlier losses in the gallant but costly Dieppe raid of 1942.*

3. Woman Worker in Vancouver Shipyard, 1943. *The home front in the Second World War saw historic developments of its own, especially in the employment of women for war industry, in many ways exceeding that of the First World War.*

4. Canadian Delegation at First Session of U.N. Assembly, 1946. *The group illustrated includes: Louis St. Laurent, then external affairs minister, beside the "Canada" sign; Paul Martin, minister of health and welfare, next to him; John Bracken, then Conservative Opposition leader, next but one beyond Martin; and beside Bracken, M.J. Coldwell, by then leader of the C.C.F.*

William Aberhart defeated an old, disreputable Progressive government and built an enduring party that in time would spread to British Columbia also. The C.C.F. was very different, as a left-wing party of democratic socialism. Founded in Calgary in 1932 by a coalition of farmer-progressives with labour and socialist idealists, it really took off in 1933, when the Regina Manifesto set forth its goals, while James Shaver Woodsworth, an independent labour member at Ottawa, and once a leader of the Winnipeg General Strike, became the party's revered chief. In 1935, Woodsworth headed the seven C.C.F. members who entered the federal parliament; thus opening a political development that would reach widely across Canada, and ultimately continue into the N.D.P., the New Democratic Party of later eras.

Yet as the dirty thirties trudged toward their close, internal strains were gradually overtaken by external tensions. The Depression at last began to lift, when the world from 1937-38 moved into a new armament boom. Ironically, times improved as the western democracies hastened to rebuild their own defences, let lapse through wishful post-war dreams of easy isolation and disarmament. The truth was that totalitarian aggression would not let anyone withdraw in isolation from the world; not even "secure" Americans — as they learned from Japan's attack on Pearl Harbour in late 1941. And Canadians had already recognized as much, when in September, 1939, they joined with French and British allies to fight German onslaughts across Europe. This time Canada, as a full nation, made its own declaration of war; soberly and responsibly, not at all forgetting the terrible costs of the First World War. But Nazi Germany's expansion by force across the heart of Europe, Italy's thrust into Africa, Japan's into China, plainly marked the spread of ruthless conquests that could not go on; even while the communist Soviet Union, no less totalitarian and oppressive, brooded darkly — yet allied with Nazi Germany in its lawless march against free nations.

And so Canada was swept into the urgent dangers of World War II. Again Canadian troops went overseas, mainly to Britain and France, but this time to fight as well in Italy or the Pacific. It truly was a global war, where Canadian airmen served off India or Malta, in fighters above England, or especially in heavy bombing raids over Germany: a war where Canadian sailors saw action from the Caribbean and Mediterranean to the Russian Arctic, yet particularly in the cruel Battle of the Atlantic against the German U-boat, to keep the convoys of supplies flowing to Britain, the free world's bulwark. As for Canadian army divisions, they at first did dull if necessary garrison duty, sharing the defence of

The Hundred-Millionth Projectile — and C.D. Howe, 1944. *The hard-driving "C.D.," wartime production boss for Canada. here receives this munition of war from the Cherrier plant in Montreal.*

Britain against the Nazi power which in 1940 had conquered western Europe, until Italy was at length invaded by Anglo-American and Canadian forces in 1943. But Canadian troops mostly went into action with the Allied re-entry to France, begun in June, 1944. From their landings on the Normandy beaches they fought onward to Belgium and the Netherlands; and units of the First Canadian Army pushed through the German Rhinelands until the final Nazi surrender came in May, 1945. Japan's collapse followed in August, before major Canadian forces could be redeployed to the Pacific. In any event, it all constituted an outstanding military record for a nation of some twelve million people. The Second World War, in fact, decidedly affirmed and enlarged Canada's international presence.

This involved still more than military operations: including an ample Canadian programme of Mutual Aid for wartime allies, the opening of Canadian diplomatic offices right around the globe, and, above all, a prominent Canadian role in the new United Nations that after the war sought to maintain peace and collective security, which a former, weaker League of Nations had failed to do. Canada under King had joined in designing the U.N.; and then worked actively in the many-sided tasks of that world body. Canada also led in establishing N.A.T.O., the North Atlantic Treaty Organization, in 1949, and took a determined share in the Korean War of 1950-53, fought under U.N. command to check North Korean communist aggression. Not a leading great power, but still a large and influential one, Canada since 1953 would thus continue to play a highly responsible role in world affairs — especially through its many later commitments to international peace-keeping from Cyprus to Viet Nam, Somalia to Yugoslavia.

But to return to the Second World War, on the home front it again had brought French-English discords over conscription. Prime Minister King had tackled that problem in careful stages. In 1940 he won a new election, and had then enacted compulsory service for home defence, after the Germans overran Europe. In 1942 he held a national vote, which supported overseas conscription "if necessary," but by a large Anglo-majority ranged against a determined French opposition. Still, French Canada at least had had prior notice, when draining losses in Normandy brought a very reluctant King to impose full conscription late in 1944. Hence, although there were Quebec outcries, the government edict took orderly effect. For most French Canadians grudgingly considered that King had tried; while Louis St. Laurent, his chief Quebec cabinet minister, cordial but

1. Louis St. Laurent, 1882-1973. *King's heir as prime minister in 1948 (seen here being ratified by a Liberal Convention in Ottawa) was an accomplished bilingual corporation lawyer. St. Laurent started poor in the Eastern Townships but rose high; not only by ability, but by force of character. He shared in building NATO and Canada's role in it. His government's good record (in good times) helped him win sweepingly in elections of 1949 and 1953; though thereafter he seemed to tire and withdraw — leading to his defeat in 1957.*

2. War in Korea, 1950-53. *The soldiers under fire are from the highly distinguished "Van Doos," the Royal 22nd Regiment of* Canadien *fighting renown.*

1

2

calmly judicious, stood staunchly by him. Accordingly, the Liberal party not only held together, but King went on to win the election of 1945 at war's end; and to retire in 1948, after thirteen unbroken years in office. He was succeeded by a fluently bilingual — and much more affable — St. Laurent: who in 1949 had the satisfying task of announcing the entry of Newfoundland into Canadian Confederation at last; a change led forward by the Canada-Newfoundland interconnections made necessary during the wartime Battle of the Atlantic.

The war had also added greatly to Canada's economic development. Huge new resource enterprises were established to provide the materials of modern warfare; as were giant steel and shipbuilding works, tank, artillery and automotive factories, or aircraft, electronic and petro-chemical plants. In sum, very valuable "high-tech" components grew out of Canada's industrial war effort of the 1940s; and they would last on into the future. As a matter of fact, this large and complex industrial war economy was refitted to peacetime needs with considerable success: in part, a tribute to government planning, to many business and labour leaders, and also to C.D. Howe, King's powerful wartime Minister of Munitions and Supply. Compared to troubled post-war readjustments after 1918, this time at least there was no such painful phase of downturns and disruptions. Perhaps hard Depression years had made both Canadian citizens and governments more careful; while the King federal regime was certainly better prepared to deal with the social and economic problems of transition to peace than the Borden-Meighen cabinet had been. No doubt, as well, pressing demands for rebuilding a devastated Europe, heavy American investments there, and extensive housing and supply demands within post-war North America itself, all aided in Canada's rapid resurgence in the later 1940s. That resurgence, moreover, climbed into another boom phase as the 1950s opened — to shape a whole new era for the country.

Newfoundland Enters Confederation, 1949. *The Ottawa* Journal *reports a great occasion: when the easternmost portion of North America, long frequented by Europeans, became Canada's newest province after years of negotiation.*

The Latest Decades

We now have reached a period that lies within the experience of many Canadians alive today: the last four decades down to the present. As such, these years form a continuing sequel to the past centuries of history and heritage already traced out in this book. And though but briefly summarized here, this latest period provides a fitting conclusion to our long story — a conclusion that starts with the tremendously prosperous decade that doubled Canada's gross national output between 1950 and 1960.

The thriving Canadian community of the fifties now may tend to be seen as smugly concerned with material growth and comfort, with raising neat families in neat suburban ranch houses while ignoring greater issues. One might note, instead, that those who had gone through the terrible shocks of the Depression and the Second World War, to face the threats of Cold War and atomic annihilation were not quite so thoughtlessly complacent as later contemporaries might deem them. But there is no question that material growth swept impressively across Canada of the fifties in north or south, from rich new iron mines near the Quebec-Labrador border to huge projects for aluminum and power development at Kitimat in British Columbia's coastal ranges. In between, Alberta became a major world oil-producer from the opening of its Pembina field around 1954; pipe lines for oil and natural gas were built from the prairies west to Vancouver or east to Toronto and Montreal; and by 1959 the magnificent St. Lawrence Seaway had been completed jointly with the United States: not just to carry ocean shipping into the heartlands of the Great Lakes, but to add vast new hydro-electric power supplies from the Upper St. Lawrence.

As well, there were uranium fields for nuclear power; first tapped in the North West Territories, then in northern Saskatchewan by 1953 and northern Ontario by 1955. There were expanding lumber, pulp, or mining operations also, from B.C. to Quebec and New Brunswick. But above all, Canada's cities swelled steadily, from Halifax to Victoria. In fact, by 1956, about half of the Canadian population were city-dwellers — a long way from historic forest or farm frontiers. Urban growth indeed was illustrated by the opening of the first city

The Polymer Plant: Petrochemicals at Sarnia, 1946. *This in a real way was another economic result of the Second World War for Canada: the creation of a major new industry, at first to supply synthetic rubber when war with Japan cut off natural rubber supplies across the Pacific; and then to produce a wide range of products chemically derived from oil shipped from the Canadian West.*

1. Setting out a New Townsite, Yellowknife, N.W.T. *An early start on post-war expansion at this northern capital centre, August, 1945.*
2. Logging by Truck in British Columbia, 1951.
3. Drilling for Oil in Northern Forests, 1953.
4. Constructing the St. Lawrence Seaway, 1955. *In this work-in-progress scene, a spillway tunnel for the new canal goes right under the old canal, which carries a small lake freighter — about as large as the old route could manage.*

1

2

3

4

subway system in 1954 at Toronto, which also began metropolitan government that same year. Yet these are just a few dates among many possible that could be noted, such as the start of Canadian television programming by the C.B.C. in 1952. And with them go the building of the first expressways; the development of great airports for jet travel; not to forget massive downtown-office skyscrapers, high-rise apartment blocks, or the suburban shopping malls, increasingly under way by the 1960s. Still further, there were strong new streams of immigration, which accompanied and enlarged this whole process of economic and social change. Nearly a million and a half new migrants arrived in the 1950s, continuing on from the post-war flows of European refugees. British newcomers still were prominent (many now came by air); but Dutch, Germans and Slavs, Italians and other southern Europeans, entered in growing numbers — along with West Indians — to alter the major cities above all. In the mid-fifties Canada's birth-rate for its own post-war "baby boom" generation was one of the highest in the world. Yet a great ethnic change no less was under way.

That did not show in national politics, however. Here the old traditional

1

1. Mobile Television Unit for C.B.C. Toronto, 1956.
2. Post-War Refugee Immigrants, 1950. *They are receiving passports for Canada at the office of the Canadian Christian Council for the Resettlement of Refugees, in Breman, Germany.*

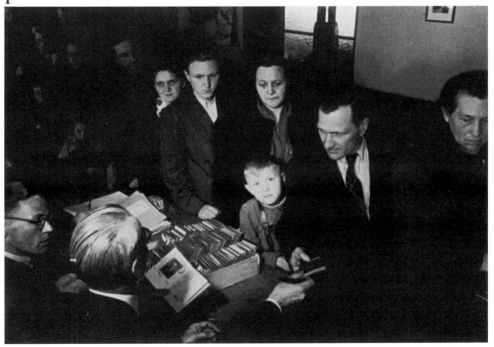

2

1

2

3

1. Lester "Mike" Pearson, 1897-1972. *Born in Ontario, he entered the civil service in the 1920s, and in the 30s and 40s held major posts as a capable diplomat in both London and Washington. Made deputy-minister of External Affairs in 1946, Pearson was active both at the U.N. and in developing NATO. In 1948 he was appointed minister (i.e., political head) for External Affairs in the St. Laurent government. This role brought perhaps his greatest moment, when he defused the world-threatening Suez Crisis of 1956, by successfully proposing a U.N. peacekeeping force to stabilize the area — the first of such forces — and for this he received the Nobel Prize. When St. Laurent retired from politics, following his government's defeat in 1957, Pearson became Liberal Opposition leader. He finally won power in 1963; to continue as prime minister until his own retirement in 1968. During his regime, the present Canadian flag was adopted.*

2. John George Diefenbaker, 1895-1979. *Pearson's very different Conservative rival was a populist prairie lawyer and parliamentary veteran from Prince Albert in the Plains West, not from the international and Ottawa elite. And he gave a fighting account of himself: from entering the federal House in 1940 to becoming Conservative leader in 1956, then taking over the government from 1957 to 1963. A glowing orator, an ardent party politician, he did less well with problems of government; and after his fall from office, reluctantly gave up his party leadership in 1967.*

3. Thomas Clement Douglas. *An early picture of "Tommy" about the time the Baptist minister from Weyburn, Sask., was elected to parliament in 1935 as a C.C.F. member. In 1944 this witty, masterful debater had shifted to Saskatchewan politics: so successfully that the socialist government he led to power there lasted on after his own departure in 1961 — when he moved back to the federal parliament as first leader of the N.D.P. Though he had no such success in Ottawa henceforth, he remained a much regarded political figure until he left politics in 1979.*

1

1. Founding Convention of the New Democratic Party, 1961. *At this Ottawa gathering, the N.D.P. became heir to the C.C.F., and joined forces also with the Canadian Labour Congress (C.L.C.).*

2. Ernest Charles Manning. *Once a student then a cabinet minister of William Aberhart's in Alberta, he took over as Social Credit premier of that province in 1943; and was elected seven times till he retired in 1968, leaving a strong government and a prosperous Alberta. No religious spell-binder like Aberhart, Manning was careful but constantly efficient; especially in the financial direction of an expanding provincial economy.*

3. William Andrew Cecil Bennett. *Born in New Brunswick, he moved to Kelowna, B.C. in 1930; did well in the hardware business, then entered the B.C. house as Conservative member for Okanagan in 1941. Becoming an independent in 1951, Bennett was elected for a swelling Social Credit party the next year, and successfully formed the new provincial government. He led British Columbia through two prosperous decades of development, to retire following his defeat by N.D.P. forces in 1972. But his son, William Richard Bennett, succeeded him, and became Social Credit premier from 1975 to 1986.*

2

3

patterns still held. St. Laurent, by now an affable "Uncle Louis," easily took the federal elections of 1953. But in 1957, the Liberal party so long in office — and not helped by an arrogant C.D. Howe pushing his trans-Canada pipe-line scheme too hard — was beaten (barely) by revived Conservatives under John George Diefenbaker. This Saskatchewan lawyer, good on emotional speeches if not on critical decisions, won a new and convincing election triumph over Liberalism the next year. It was unfortunate that he could not use it better, given his own conspiracy-minded fears. At all events, Diefenbaker threw his sweeping gains away during the early 1960s. And so the Liberals returned to power in 1963, under Lester Bowles Pearson: a likeable and very able diplomat who had won the Nobel Peace Prize; but who himself proved no strong prime minister, after he was induced from government service into active politics. Consequently, through most of the 1960s, Canada did not have the commanding national direction earlier exercised by a King or Borden.

The 1960s, too, saw strong provincial regimes not greatly contained by federal authority. One of the earliest of these (and very successful in its own domain) was Canada's first socialist regime, the C.C.F. government set up in Saskatchewan under capable Tommy Douglas in 1944. It lasted on till 1964, and established the first medicare system in Canada; though Douglas left in 1961 to become federal leader of the New Democratic Party, formed that year to join the C.C.F. with the powerful unions of the Canadian Labour Congress. In British Columbia, a Social Credit government was elected in 1952 under W.A.C. ("Wackie") Bennett, who ruled his majestic West Coast empire until 1972 when N.D.P. forces defeated him. In Alberta, Ernest Manning, heir to William Aberhart, ran a long-enduring, formidable Social Credit principality of his own till his retirement in 1968; and it continued three years more. Ontario's provincial Conservative dynasty (headed by suave Premier John Robarts, from 1961 to 1971) was perhaps a bit more amenable, if not much. But Quebec above all, experienced its Quiet Revolution to modernize that province, carried out by Liberal Jean Lesage, as its vigorous premier in 1960-66. Beyond that, it soon saw a vehement René Lévesque break with Lesage's nationalizing moves as still inadequate — to urge the separation of a sovereign Quebec from Canada, through the *Parti Québecois* which Lévesque came to lead in 1968.

Such an issue of separation, a vital question in relations between Canada's two chief cultures, really mattered a good deal more than the popularly noted radical movements in the universities of the sixties, where students protested "elitism" and the (American) Viet Nam War or held teach-ins, love-ins, and smoke-ins — American copies again. And yet, whatever the hopeful student idealism of the 1960s, the world went on its way, while Canada thus far survived Quebec's neo-separatist stirrings. In fact, it celebrated Expo, the brilliant World Fair held in Montreal in the summer of 1967 to mark one hundred years of

Social Credit Convention in British Columbia, 1953. *This right-wing movement, with strong evangelical underpinnings, also grew in British Columbia; but took on its own dimensions, as if influenced by the grandeur of Pacific mountains. The Vancouver assemblage of 1953 here also shows two Social Credit premiers inset, Bennett of B.C. and Manning of Alberta.*

1. Expo at Montreal, 1967. *This dazzling Canadian exposition, marking a century of Confederation, gave the country (and its visitors) a real sense of Canada's accomplishments, despite gnawing evidences of Quebec separatism rising at the time.*

2. Pierre Elliott Trudeau, Power and Enigma. *Born at Montreal in 1919 to an affluent French Canadian father and a mother of Scottish descent, Trudeau studied in Montreal, Harvard and London before becoming an influential radical writer and a law professor in his home province — critical both of social wrongs there, and the simplistic answers of Quebec* separatiste *nationalism. He sought a united Canada, with equal bilingual rights and opportunities for Francophones or Anglophones. Entering parliament as a Liberal in 1965, two years later this talented yet difficult man was made minister of justice under Pearson. In 1968 he was chosen prime minister, and energetically held that office right to 1979: when he was briefly beaten, but returned to govern quite as powerfully from 1980 to 1984. Then Trudeau retired undefeated — and as admired or deplored as ever.*

3. René Lévesque. *Journalist born in New Brunswick, a war correspondent, then a Quebec TV commentator, he joined the Quebec legislature as a Liberal in 1960. He became a prominent member of the Lesage provincial government, till he left it in 1967 and founded the Parti Québecois to seek constitutional separation between Quebec and Canada. He and his party won provincial power in 1976; and although their Quebec referendum for "sovereignty-association" was beaten in 1980, they stayed in office until 1985, when an ailing Lévesque resigned and the P.Q. was defeated. He died two years after.*

4. Queen Elizabeth Signs Proclamation of the New Constitution Act, 1982. *Done at Ottawa in April, with Trudeau seated beside the Queen.*

Confederation. Extreme separatists might plant deadly bombs in a few Quebec mail boxes; but most Canadians, Anglophone or Francophone, native or immigrant, took pride and pleasure in their country's centenary.

Prime Minister Pearson, however, who had sought to follow a course of "co-operative federalism" to meet the demands of the major provinces for more powers and funds, by now had had enough. His own friendly diplomacy and good will had eased the daily workings of the federal system; which indeed had looked in need of changes at least from King's time on. But not much more than transitory adjustments had been achieved between rival, entrenched, federal and provincial positions. The call to remake the constitution had almost become part of Canadian heritage in its own right. Pearson would not be coping with it much further. After the glow of Expo, he announce his own retirement. And in April, 1968, a Liberal party convention chose a very different successor, Pierre Elliott Trudeau.

Wholly bilingual, of both French and British heritage (plus solid Montreal wealth) Trudeau was at once the intellectual and the activist. A highly-regarded lawyer, teacher and writer, he could coolly plan or give hot, stirring speeches; contrive no less than King had done behind the scenes, or stand boldly forth like Bennett. His abilities were outstanding. So were his faults: of arrogance, impatience and chip-on-the-shoulder rudeness. Thus he would become one of Canada's most successful and longest-serving prime ministers; yet in some quarters would be reviled as well, most plainly in the Canadian West. In any event, this brilliant French-Canadian who had been Pearson's Minister of Justice now began years of fighting for a bilingual and bicultural Canada against Anglo-reluctance, while no less striving to block Franco-separatism. In brief, Trudeau wanted both main language groups to share fully in a federal nation open to each through bilingual national services and facilities.

There is no time here to go into his devoted, and at times risky, campaigning

1

2

3

4

1

2

3

4

during the 1970s. Suffice it to say that this sharp but seemingly off-hand prime minister really outplayed a keenly quick Lévesque himself: who won control of Quebec for his potent *Parti Québecois* in 1976, but then could not bring it to a deal that would carry the French-Canadian community out of Canada. Superbly influential as ever, Pierre beat a floundering René in Quebec on the provincial referendum vote of 1980. No doubt, pro-Canada Quebec Liberal leaders like Claude Ryan played a valuable part; as perhaps did Anglo-Canadian feelings expressed to keep the founding Francophone community within a continent-wide Canada. Yet Trudeau's personal triumph was as large as Lévesque's defeat: though it scarcely settled the future of Canadian Confederation.

In truth, although Québecois separatism had for now been vanquished, nothing yet was clear for years to come. Trudeau, logical as ever, sought to define and enact a revised constitutional structure suitable to either French or English-speaking Canadians, and put in Canada's own hands. Hence he worked to "patriate" the constitution from its existing place in the keeping of the British parliament. In 1982 all this was accomplished, after a great deal of negotiation with the provincial premiers that still left Quebec under René Lévesque's government in flat disagreement over both the contents and the methods involved. Thus — too typical of a superior, impatient Trudeau — this deep problem was overridden rather than solved. Nonetheless, Canada's constitution was now brought home to Canada, where further federal changes could yet be settled; a Trudeau achievement marked by Queen Elizabeth's visit in April, 1982, that signed and sealed Canada's full control over future constitutional changes.

And so, by the early 1980s, top Canadian political issues had at least been met by Trudeau Liberalism; and there seemed to be time to address other questions.

In that regard, Pierre Trudeau's accomplishments had not only included bringing the constitution under Canadian control, but adding a basic Charter of Rights to it, as well as developing federal bilingualism for Canadians of either main language group. Still further, in his years of office he had pushed the strong central governmental authority he believed in, enlarging the basic federal provisions for health and hospital care launched under Pearson, and in general promoting ample Canada-wide social programmes. Yet Trudeau's regime was less concerned to deal financially with the constantly increasing costs of this Canadian social welfare state. Nor did he cope effectively with growing inflation and public deficits from the early seventies on, hence amassing fiscal problems for the future. In any event, he was beaten, if marginally, in an election of 1979, and yielded power to the Conservatives now led by an Albertan, Joe Clark. But Clark's government proved uncertain and short. In 1980, "old pro Trudeau" came back; to hold office until early in 1984, when he decided to retire — after a solitary walk in a snowstorm.

The office he left would soon be filled by a new Conservative leader, convivial Brian Mulroney from Baie-Comeau in eastern Quebec. Of

1. Brian Mulroney, Prime Minister, 1984-93. *A bilingual, affable Quebec lawyer, and a prominent corporate executive, this new Conservative leader won the elections of 1984, and set out to soothe and strengthen a sorely troubled Canada. But though both determined and perceptive, his attempts were often lessened by his frothy talk, his backstage deals, and his constant insider croneyism — so that he often did not seem believable, even when he meant it. When he retired in 1993, the resentments he had gathered surely had something to do with the fact that his successor, Kim Campbell, lasted mere months, while the elections that beat her in 1994 only returned two Conservative members to parliament from a once-great party.*

2. Jean Chrétien, Liberal Prime Minister, 1994. *Another bilingual lawyer from Quebec (Chicoutimi), he was different from Mulroney in more than politics — accented in his English, folksy instead of smooth, and with down-to-earth humour, not chief-executive style. Yet Chrétien had a distinguished record in government, first as a revenue minister under Pearson, then in posts from Indian affairs to finance under Trudeau; and he directed the anti-separatist side in the Quebec referendum of 1980, as well as becoming a key figure in the constitutional negotations that followed. Thus he came to the prime ministership well prepared for the job.*

3. Recent Immigrants: Women from the Philippines.
4. A Vietnamese Family.
5. From Honduras: a Mother and Son.

5

Irish-Canadian worker origins, this former Iron Ore Company president was lively in his colloquial French, if pretentious-sounding in his public English. He kept close ties with old cronies, and nursed a deep ambition for political power. But moderate and conciliatory, as well as an acute party manager, Mulroney won a huge election majority in 1984, built essentially on a Quebec base and strong Western support. He now sought to govern Canada in a bright new Conservative business image: one which embodied free trade with the United States, the privatizing of various large government enterprises, cutting away the heavy public deficit, and decentralizing the Canadian federal system through new constitutional negotiations with the provinces. With such grand designs — and the eager business optimism of the roaring later eighties — Mulroney again carried the federal elections of late 1988. He also reached a free trade agreement with the United States, carried some privatizations forward, such as "de-nationalizing" Air Canada, and established the new Goods and Services Tax (a productive cash-cow) to help finance the expensive work of deficit reduction.

Yet as the 1990s opened, recession settled in on Canada: without the worst shocks of the Great Depression, but dragging on relentlessly. Mulroney's designs lost all their dazzle. While it was still too soon really to weigh the effects of free trade and privatization (though claims *pro* and *con* rose loudly), it was very plain that the G.S.T. had won little love. In fact, consumers held back in times when jobs were being slashed, so that sales and tax yields went down together. Furthermore, a great new wave of constitution-revising turned out a total flop. It was, assuredly, not all the fault of Mulroney's ready blarney, or of backroom party "experts" and costly public relations campaigns that backfired. But by 1992 the Canadian public, both French and English, was anxious economically and fed up politically with party posturing, with special interests and insider deals, not to mention the blather of self-important "statesmen." And so, in another referendum, the citizens — the democracy — flatly rejected a final structure of complex constitutional proposals. It was back to square one, at least for the near-future. Meanwhile, Mulroney's dwindling support sank even lower, until in the spring of 1993 he decided to retire. That June, he handed over his office to his former Minister of Justice, Kim Campbell of British Columbia, who was chosen to be Conservative leader by a party convention in Ottawa, and became Canada's first female prime minister. She was disastrously beaten, however, in the elections of late 1993 by Jean Chrétien, once a leading Trudeau minister, who thus restored the Liberals to power in Ottawa.

That in itself might signify the start of still another era in Canada, just over a century and a quarter after its Confederation in 1867. If John A. Macdonald had now returned, he would have found many things he might not have expected, such as N.D.P. socialist regimes in British Columbia, Saskatchewan and Ontario; or free trade in place instead of his National Policy, or a greatly enlarged governing system within a vastly more complicated country. And yet, always shrewd and pragmatic, John A. might not be that surprised: not to see the federal union he and his compatriots had put together still operating, still including French Canada, still functioning responsibly, and still balancing out the diverse demands of regions, interests, peoples and heritages within an immense transcontinental nation-state.

That nation-state, by the 1990s, contained an even greater blend of multi-cultural inheritances. Italians and Portuguese, Greeks, Macedonians and other Balkan elements, came in migrations on through the seventies, while Middle Eastern, Caribbean and Latin American arrivals brought still more variety to Canada's main cities. The 1980s, however, particularly saw an immigration shift to Asia. Although previous inflows did not cease, now there were rising numbers from India, Pakistan and Sri Lanka, from China, Viet Nam or the Philippines. Much bigger urban Black communities also arose, drawn not only from the West Indies but Africa as well. Montreal notably gathered French-speaking Haitians, while Toronto gained more Jamaicans and Trinidadians. And while Chinese communities expanded generally, Vancouver especially received a major influx from Hong Kong, often with valuable skills and capital, as Hong Kong citizens left their home city which was soon due to be turned over to Communist China's rule.

The years of Trudeau and Mulroney not only witnessed these big new ethnic inflows, but cultural and social changes that were larger still. For example, within greatly expanded university and research facilities Canadian talent made pathfinding gains in the physical or social sciences and in biological or medical fields, while the arts, humanities and architecture also produced top Canadians of world stature. Computerization, xeroxing, "faxing" and electronic data exchanges spread throughout the workplace, as well as in the research centre. Hence old-style material manufacturing yielded somewhat to rising service-and-information enterprises — which meant at least two things: that the impacts of free trade which struck at old industry would be somewhat offset by the growth of new; and that women would play an ever-wider part in the workforce, as minds increasingly took over from muscle power. Canadian society in the eighties and nineties (French or English) thus showed the steady rise of two-income families. Yet this had further cause, since the climbing inflation and over-loaded mortgages of the money-grabbing eighties meant that fewer Canadians could reach their traditional goal of the single-family, one-income home. In fact, close-packed dormitory suburbs, along with quadruplexes, apartment blocks and condominiums, took over more and more. As one instance,

Welding by Robot, General Motors, Oshawa.

Mississauga rose from open farmlands between Hamilton and Toronto as a small town by 1968, a full city by 1974 — and by 1985 was the ninth largest place in Canada, with some 350,000 residents.

Other urban centres had their own ballooning growth and influence. Not just Montreal, Vancouver or Toronto (the largest Canadian metropolis from the 1970s), but Calgary, Edmonton and Ottawa as well, or Winnipeg, Quebec and Halifax in lesser degree. And Hamilton, Victoria, Regina and Saint John — or St. John's in Newfoundland — must not be discounted in any way. These chief Canadian centres of productive hinterlands and regional social life can never be dismissed. Yet always, beyond the continual changes of today's urbanized world, there is the age-old inheritance the Canadian peoples built upon their giant land, right from prehistoric eons down to the present.

They have survived there, struggled and grown: from earliest Inuit settlements in the Arctic to recent hard-fought Iroquois land claims at Oka in Quebec; from long-contested native rights in northern British Columbia to those in question on the shores of Labrador. Other than facing such problems, non-native groups, too, have sought to defend endangered environments; from the magnificent, wild Tatshenshini River on the Alaskan border to the immense James Bay watershed, where hydro-schemes have threatened to destroy the natural world in Northern Quebec. Beyond these, there have been a host of other confrontation points between ancient legacies and later developments, which would become repeated issues for Canadian inhabitants and political leaders alike. Yet all this is Canada, whether during recent eras since Confederation, or back through the far longer past since its historical records first began. We still must leave those records here, well aware of how much more has to be explained and substantiated in our second volume to follow. Nonetheless, it may be said of past ages to Confederation, and thereafter, that a native Micmac or Assiniboine chief, a Samuel de Champlain or an Alexander Mackenzie, might yet have judged that whatever had been gained by humankind in this northern America still rested on the wealth and heritage of the huge natural environment — which no one in Canada might ever dare to ignore.

West Edmonton Mall. *Beyond this giant mall the skyline of modern Edmonton appears.*

Chapter Nine

Partners in Progress

Piet J. Koene

Abitibi-Price Inc.

Ranked among Canada's largest forest products enterprises, Abitibi-Price manufactures newsprint and uncoated groundwood papers at eleven mills located across North America and markets its products to customers around the world.

The development of Abitibi-Price can be traced through the individual and combined histories of its two founding companies — Abitibi Power & Paper Company Limited and The Price Company Limited. William Price arrived in Quebec in 1810 as an agent of the British Admiralty, seeking a new supply of wood to keep its frigates on the seas. Seeing opportunity in the vast tracts of virgin timber, he remained in his adopted land after fulfilling his commission and established a thriving lumber industry for the Saguenay and Lower St. Lawrence regions of Quebec.

In 1909, the enterprising Frank Anson grubstaked two McGill University students on a prospecting trip in Northern Ontario. The students returned having found no gold, but enthusiastic about the rich forests and fast flowing rivers. Realizing the potential that lay ahead, Anson obtained forest limits rights near Iroquois Falls from the Ontario government and proceeded to construct a whole town, power plant and dam and, of course, a pulp and paper mill. By the summer of 1915, the first roll of newsprint was produced at the Iroquois Falls mill.

The two companies underwent a period of rapid growth and expansion, acquiring subsidiaries in Quebec and Ontario before the onslaught of the Great Depression. Undergoing extreme financial difficulty, Abitibi was placed in receivership in 1932, while the Price company was forced into bankruptcy in 1933. As the economy gradually picked up both companies recovered and began to expand once again. In 1961, Price merged with the Anglo-Newfoundland Development Company, another major natural resources company with holdings throughout Quebec and Newfoundland.

Abitibi obtained a controlling interest in Price in 1974, and later, in a dramatic takeover, acquired the remaining shares. In 1979, recognizing the significant contribution of Price, and to bring all operations under one name, Abitibi changed its name to Abitibi-Price Inc.

Abitibi-Price underwent another significant change in 1981 when Olympia & York, a major Canadian real-estate developer, acquired a controlling interest in the Company. Over a decade later, in the face of its own financial diffi-culties, Olympia & York relinquished its control block to a consortium of lenders. In early 1994, the lenders offered and sold their shares to the public making Abitibi-Price, once again, a widely-held company.

Abitibi-Price's facilities produce more than two million tonnes of paper annually which are used for telephone directories, business forms, advertising inserts, flyers, magazines, catalogues, and, of course, newspapers. About half the company's production — one million tonnes — is made with old newspapers that have been de-inked and repulped to produce paper with recycled contents ranging from five to sixty per cent.

In charting its course for the future, Abitibi-Price has implemented sweeping changes in its vision, goals and strategies to focus on becoming the world's finest in the groundwood industry — the finest in shareholder returns, the finest supplier, the finest employer, and the finest in corporate citizenship and environmental leadership.

1., 2. The history of Abitibi-Price Inc., a world leader in the groundwood paper industry, is closely intertwined with the development and utilization of Canada's forest resources.

1

2

ALBATours International Incorporated

Founded in 1977, ALBATours International is one of Canada's leading tour operators.

Italy has always been ALBA-Tours' flagship destination. Over the past 18 years, ALBATours has expanded to include seven Cuban destination resorts; Acapulco, Puerto Vallarta, Ixtapa, Manzanillo and Cancun in Mexico; popular Caribbean destinations such as the Dominican Republic, St. Lucia, St. Maarten, Jamaica, Bahamas, Aruba and Barbados; and Venezuela in South America. Florida charters are also offered, as well as domestic and international flights, to complete a vital diversification of products.

ALBATours represents an industry that has largely developed since the mid-1960s, where tour operators put together packages that are sold to the public through travel agencies. These tour operators take care of everything from chartering airplanes to making hotel reservations for the traveller. The travel agent essentially buys the package from the tour operator and sells it to the public.

Unlike other tour operators, however, ALBATours is owned by a group of travel retailers. In 1977 ten travel agents with a high percentage of Italian-Canadian clientele realized a market niche that was not being met, and came together to see what they could do to fill it. They noted that the Toronto area has a remarkably high number of Italian immigrants, many of whom were interested in returning to Italy to visit family. Realizing that their needs were simple these travel agents decided to charter aircraft to Italy. This plan worked so well that the next summer ALBATours was officially set up to handle the new charter operation as a tour wholesaler.

The travel to Italy took place mainly in the summer, and so ALBATours, under the leadership of General Manager and Vice-President Gianni Bragagnolo, immediately set out to organize packages to Mexico and Florida for winter vacationers. Although the founding travel agents provided a solid customer base that helped get ALBA-Tours off the ground, the company deals on an equal basis with more than 3,000 retail agents across Canada that sell its products. Says Bragagnolo, "There is no way we could survive by playing favourites with ten retailers over 3,000 others."

Since those early start-up years, ALBATours has expanded steadily, to the point where 75 per cent of its business is now actually outside Italy. However, Bragagnolo knows the dangers of over-rapid growth in a very competitive and volatile industry, and is therefore careful to see that expansion is controlled: "It does not pay to take on more than the company, now with over 70 employees, can efficiently handle."

Besides this close management scrutiny, the company's success is also due to the close contact it maintains with the retail aspects of the industry, offering professional service from a dedicated staff that operates with the use of the most sophisticated and advanced technological systems available. At monthly board meetings the owners make suggestions and give advice from a travel agent's perspective; however, the day-to-day administration of the company is left strictly to the company management, who have obviously proven themselves capable in handling the over 100,000 people who flew from Pearson International Airport last year with ALBA-Tours packages.

The current shareholders of ALBA-Tours International, eight of whom who were also co-founders: (seated, from l. to r.) Nick Ciarelli, Nino Sinicropi, Gianni Bragagnolo, Leonardo Cianfarani, and Enzo Comar; (standing, from l. to r.) Danny Boni, Roger Battista, and Joe Ancona; (not appearing) Bruno Crugnale, Mike Giambattista, and Anthony Sarracini.

ADT Canada Inc.

Over one hundred years ago, speedy ADT (formerly American District Telegraph) messenger boys could report a fire in three minutes flat. Today, ADT's fastest detection system works in less than three one-thousandths of a second. From humble beginnings to world-wide operations, ADT has become a leader in providing new technology for the protection of people and their property, moving from the early telegraph signal to today's sophisticated state-of-the-art electronic equipment.

ADT Canada Inc. is the Canadian division of ADT Security Systems Inc., (itself a division of ADT Limited), the world's leader in electronic security protection serving the United States, Canada, Britain and Europe. In North America, ADT is the largest provider of electronic security services, serving 493 of the "Fortune 500" companies. Delivering peace of mind to customers in the home and the workplace, ADT designs, installs, monitors and services security systems that match the client's specific needs. But it is not technology alone that has made ADT the premier supplier of security systems for business, industry and private homes, it is commitment — a constant commitment to product innovation and customer service — to deliver the best.

ADT's earliest roots can be

1

traced to several Canadian companies. B.C. District Telegraph and Delivery Company Limited was incorporated in 1891, obtaining a 50 year franchise for the operation of district telegraph systems in Vancouver and Victoria. Initially, the company provided the transmission and delivery of telegrams to its customers. This service soon evolved into the provision of signal boxes for watchmen and guards, by which the individual could signal his well-being at specific intervals to the central office. Call boxes were also provided to customers. By operating these simple electro-mechanical telegraphic call boxes on their premises, subscribers could have a messenger at their door within minutes — usually to take a message for telegraphic transmission but also at times to perform other errands or summon assistance.

As the company grew, B.C. District Telegraph expanded into new areas, and in 1908 the first complete premises were installed with the company's fire alarm system. Thus, the company's first comprehensive burglar alarm system was inaugurated.

After World War I, B.C. District Telegraph and Delivery extended its services to many areas throughout the province. By the 1950s, with the popularity of the telephone, expansion in the area of telephone line facilities occurred and the name was shortened to B.C. District Telegraph Company Limited.

The eastern roots of ADT began

1. Incorporated in 1891, B.C. District Telegraph and Delivery Company Limited became part of ADT in 1956.
2. Dominion Electric Protection Company was founded in 1905, providing the eastern roots of ADT Canada.
3. ADT Security Systems began in 1874 as American District Telegraph in Baltimore, Maryland, with 22 messenger boys.

in 1905 when S.B. McMichael founded Dominion Messenger & Signal Company Limited in Toronto. Engaged in similar activities as B.C. District Telegraph, Dominion Messenger soon began to expand. In 1906 it opened an office in Hamilton, in Winnipeg in 1909, and an Ottawa location in 1914. In 1918 Dominion Messenger purchased Holmes Protection of Canada. Founded in 1897 in Toronto to provide messenger services, Holmes Protection had been the first company to offer burglar alarm services in Canada.

Becoming Dominion Electric

2

3

Protection Company in 1924, the all-Canadian enterprise grew to become Canada's largest full-service alarm company, with a manufacturing plant in Montreal and central stations across the country. In cities and towns where a central station was not located, local or self-contained systems were connected to the fire or police department. The company manufactured, installed and operated electric signalling systems for the protection of property from fire and theft, and included watchman patrol and manual fire alarms, automatic fire alarm systems, automatic sprinkler supervisory systems, and burglar alarm systems.

During World War II, part of Dominion Electric's factory located in Montreal was converted to the manufacture of gyro-compasses for "Mosquito" low level bombers. So well manufactured, enquiries continued to be received at ADT Canada's corporate headquarters in Toronto as late as 1994, regarding repairs and parts. In recognition of its important contribution to the war effort, the company received a "Meritorious War Service" award in 1943.

In 1956 controlling interests were obtained in Dominion Electric Protection Company, British Columbia District Telegraph Company, and Alberta Alarm Company by ADT Security Systems. ADT itself had been incorporated in 1901 when Western Union consolidated 57 district telegraph companies in the United States under the umbrella of its oldest member, American District Telegraph, founded in 1874. Through its emphasis on tech-

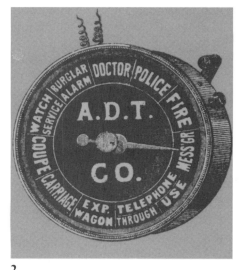

1

2

nical research efforts, ADT grew rapidly in the areas of burglar, hold-up and fire alarm systems.

With its entrance into the Canadian market, ADT became the primary provider of security systems in Canada. Its Canadian branches, sharing in ADT's technology, were able to offer business and industry in Canada the same high quality systems and services as ADT did in the United States. Becoming an independent corporate entity in 1961, ADT Canada has continued to expand through dynamic sales and marketing efforts as well as several strategic acquisitions. Embarking aggressively on a program to pursue the residential market in the 1970s, ADT Canada is now the largest commercial and residential security firm in Canada.

ADT also actively participates in programs designed to reduce crime and drug abuse. It is a strong supporter of the National Crime Prevention Council and was instrumental in the development and implementation of a program to respond to increasing conjugal violence. Initiated at ADT's Winnipeg office in cooperation with the local police, telephone company and social service agencies, the AWARE programme (Abused Women's Active Response Emergency) provides a short-term protective signalling security system for women who are in high-risk situations of spousal violence. Its success has encouraged other cities across North America to

implement the program — some 48 at year-end 1994.

Today, ADT maintains its leadership position in the security industry by ensuring customer satisfaction through its commitment to quality service and technical innovation. All its product lines are constantly updated with state-of-the-art components that provide better, more efficient service to its customers.

Dedicated to protecting customers and their property through sophisticated yet easy-to-use electronic security systems, it is this vital commitment to service that ensures ADT Canada's leading role in the security industry, now, and in the future.

1., 2. The early ADT call box evolved from a single purpose messenger service unit (1) into a multi-service call box (2). 3. A typical early Central Station, where fire alarms and watchman signals were constantly supervised. 4. Today's ADT modern monitoring centres involve fibre optics communications lines and advanced computer technology.

3

4

Alfield Industries Limited

Alfield Industries Limited, a wholly Canadian owned corporation, is primarily engaged in the design and fabrication of precision tooling and the manufacture of stamped metal products. Since it was established in 1969, Alfield has experienced such steady and continuous growth and stability that it has drawn attention from researchers from the University of Western Ontario, and from customers as far afield as Japan, Germany, Mexico, the United States and Canada. Much of this success can be directly credited to Manfred Muntwyler, the company's president and chief executive officer.

Manfred Muntwyler was also one of the original founders of the business. After immigrating from Switzerland in 1953, Muntwyler received his training in tool and die making and design engineering, and subsequently began working in the industry. In 1969 he co-founded Alfield Industries with one other partner, in Weston, Ontario. The company operated for the first two years with just two employees in 400 square feet, mainly designing and building custom tools and dies, as well as some special machinery.

Company growth followed a consistent pattern from the start; by the mid 1970s Alfield, no longer being able to expand within its present building, was ready to move to a larger site, also in Weston. Here operations were started in one unit of the building, moving into extra units as it became necessary. By 1986 Alfield occupied the entire building, totalling 15,000 square feet, with 35 employees. By this time the company had also added stamping to its tool and die works, and its five metal presses increased the demand for space. As a result, the company moved across the road to a 22,000 square foot building, one of the four buildings it now occupies.

1

After Muntwyler acquired sole ownership of Alfield in 1987 the company saw very rapid growth and technological upgrading, especially through the incorporation of computers in the design, manufacture, and communication processes. At this time Manfred Muntwyler's son, Derrick Muntwyler, also joined the company, having completed post-secondary studies. Although he now holds the position of Vice President in charge of Finance and Administration, Derrick Muntwyler, as all others in management positions, first learned what it is like to "get his hands dirty" in the plant.

Manfred Muntwyler maintains a conservative approach to managing the company, and hence the administrative end is kept to a minimum; he has never employed sales or marketing people, relying instead on personal contact with long-term customers. This also includes a "hands-on" management style, with

1. Manfred Muntwyler, co-Founder, President and Chief Executive Officer, and his son, Derrick Muntwyler, Vice President of Finance and Administration, examining an Alfield engineered product.
2. Alfield's Mexican facility, constructed in 1992, is located in the city of Puebla and its output is destined for the automotive market.

Muntwyler often seen on the shop floor solving problems, in direct contact with the employees. Each of Alfield's five engineers also makes a point of spending time with the customers on a weekly basis, as well as on the floor with the toolmakers.

The "lean-production" principle exercised by Muntwyler means maintaining the labour force at proficiently low levels and using robotic technology as needed, to meet customer requirements efficiently. Just-in-time production is practiced to reduce the need for warehousing, thereby further increasing productivity. Due to working with long-term customers, through its research and improvement programs, Alfield has been able to perfect its technology and

2

expertise, enabling production of the highest-possible quality of products. Presently Alfield is undergoing ISO 9001 and Q.S. 9000 implementation, for certification by end-summer, 1995.

In addition to an apprenticeship program at Alfield, the other employees also receive on-going training. Each employee is usually able to perform several jobs, and the work is done in small groups. A group works on a particular part from design to completion, avoiding an assembly-line effect and mentality. The large number of long-term employees attests to the level of satisfaction experienced within the organization as well.

Part of the company's stability is due to the fact that, as the name implies, Muntwyler is careful to maintain customers in diverse fields. As throughout its history, Alfield's largest customers continue to be the automotive and electrical industries. However, it also produces various components for other industries, from office furniture to "go chairs" (a newly-conceived type of wheelchair) and items for the medical field. It is also due to this wide customer base that the company has seen continued business growth, and has never had to lay off an employee due to lack of work.

In the last few years Alfield has seen rapid expansion in its exports to include North American, Asian, and European markets. It has achieved significant recognition

from automotive manufacturers and their suppliers, and now produces components for Toyota, Volkswagen, General Motors, Chrysler, and Ford.

Alfield is also participating in a 50 per cent joint-venture in Mexico. The plant in Mexico, built in 1992, covers 60,000 square feet and employs 135 people, focusing primarily on the automotive industry. Much of the design and testing of the items produced in Mexico is carried out at Alfield's Toronto facilities where the necessary equipment is often more readily available.

Today, about 60 per cent of the work done at the Toronto operations is for the automotive industry, and this plant has grown to where it requires four separate buildings, totalling 66,000 square feet and 130 employees, producing about 250 different components each week. About three-quarters of the work is metal stamping, requiring presses that range from 20 to 600 tons; the rest is in the design and fabrication of tools and dies. Approximately half of the work done in this plant is for export.

One of the strengths of this company has been its flexibility in meeting the needs of the client. Alfield provides full assembly of the products for some customers, participating in initial design and testing stages of what it produces; for others it simply manufactures accord-

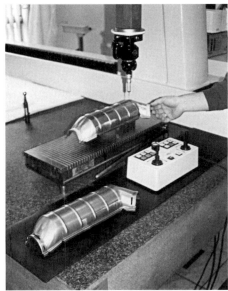

2

ing to the customer's specifications. Whether the requirement is for exhaust systems for cars, or for specially-made medical bone implants tailored to each particular patient, the competent engineers at Alfield are available to design the right part, and workers experienced in the trade are there to manufacture it.

As Alfield looks to its promising future, it plans to maintain its employment of new technology for efficiency, and its diverse customer base for stability. As the venture in Mexico attests, its long-range goal is to participate in the globalization of the automotive industry, responding to the opportunities presented in that process. If its history can be taken as any indication, it seems that the careful, visionary management of the company can be counted on to lead it to further prosperity.

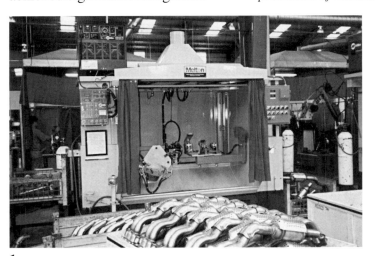

1. *A robotic welding installation for the production of exhaust system components.*

2. *The company's high-technology quality control is stringent and exacting.*
3. *Computers are a vital aspect of the design and manufacturing processes at Alfield Industries, including CADD (Computer Aided Drawing and Design) based workstations.*

1

3

AlliedSignal Canada Inc.

A pioneer in Canadian aviation and a recognized leader in technological innovation and engineering design, AlliedSignal Aerospace Canada is a premier market supplier of aviation, defence and aerospace products. The company supports a corporate-wide mandate to constantly seek out and develop new solutions that will enhance the performance and reduce the operating costs of commercial and military aircraft.

AlliedSignal Aerospace is a unit of AlliedSignal Canada Inc., an advanced technology company with businesses in aerospace, automotive products, chemicals, fibres, plastic, and advanced engineered materials worldwide. Originally established to support AlliedSignal's corporate products in Canada, AlliedSignal Aerospace has developed its resources and capabilities, and now also internationally markets its own products, systems and services. It has developed into an acknowledged leader in the specialized fields of electronic controls systems, window heat control systems, de-icing/anti-icing systems, communications systems, electro-optics, aircraft engine controls and accessories, power management and generation systems, and support systems.

AlliedSignal Canada began as two separate Canadian companies: Garrett Canada and Bendix Avelex, that now form today's world-leading entity. In 1952, The Garrett Corporation, based in the United States, established a sales office in Montreal, offering the products and services of AiResearch Manufacturing Company of California. Three years later, it opened a repair and overhaul facility in Toronto because of both the increasing level of business and Garrett's commitment to provide responsive and meaningful support of its products marketed in Canada.

The limited manufacture of avionics was initiated in 1956, and in 1960, Garrett Canada, as it was then known, obtained the contract to build the central air data computer for the CF-104 airplane. Creating the technology base and capability to manufacture and test highly sophisticated electronic systems, the following year the complete electronic temperature control systems product line contract was obtained. Since this transfer, these and many other products have been designed, developed and manufactured exclusively in Canada and sold worldwide as major aircraft subsystems.

In 1989 Garrett Canada combined with Bendix Avelex, to establish AlliedSignal Aerospace Canada. Bendix Aviation was first begun in Montreal in 1931 as Aviation Electric Limited. Growing into a world-class supplier of high-technology defense electronics, aerospace products and services, in 1985 it became Bendix Avelex Inc.

With customers around the world, AlliedSignal aerospace has become a major participant in the complex international arena of today's aerospace industry. Through international collaborations in North America, Europe, the Middle East and the Far East, AlliedSignal Aerospace Canada is an experienced partner in multinational programs. The company's activities span a wide range of intricate products and technologies in both commercial aerospace and defence programs, worldwide as well as in its traditional markets in Canada and the United States.

Today the majority of the western world's military and civil transport aircraft carry electronic environmental control systems designed, developed, manufactured and supported by AlliedSignal Aerospace Canada. Environmental control systems maintain flight deck and cabin temperature and humidity, as well as control air conditioning and related temperature, pressure and flow sensors.

Another of the company's core

1. *Garret Canada was established in 1952 and came to specialize in the design and manufacture of major aircraft electronic control systems.*
2. *Bendix Aviation began in 1931 and grew into a world class supplier of high-technology defense electronics and aerospace products.*

1

2

products is engine control systems. AlliedSignal Aerospace supports a range of sophisticated engine control systems and related accessories for aircraft engines. The company has manufactured more than 100,000 fuel control systems which have amassed more than 125 million flying hours, including highly demanding use aboard tactical aircraft such as the F-16 and F-18 fighters. This area of expertise was one of the cornerstones of the company's business in the early years and continues as an important component today.

Regulations prohibit the departure of an aircraft if its wings or other aerodynamic surfaces are contaminated by ice, frost or snow. To help protect aircraft from the dangers of icing, AlliedSignal Aerospace has developed its Electro-Thermal Ice Protection Systems. The company is also developing a Contaminant Fluid Integrity Measuring System, which will be the first automated system to provide the pilot with this critical flight-safety information.

In addition to its broad experience in electronic control systems for aerospace and aviation applications, AlliedSignal Aerospace has achieved an international reputation for its expertise in the design, development and manufacture of sophisticated electro-optical systems, notably thermal imaging products. Thermal imagers are ideally suited for use in fog or smoke, at night or in daylight, for applications such as surveillance, drug interdiction,

1

weapon sights and targeting systems. The company is now a leading supplier of night vision devices to the Canadian Armed Forces.

AlliedSignal Aerospace's emergency locator transmitters work in conjunction with the international search and rescue satellite system, and are carried aboard more than 90% of the western world's commercial aircraft on transoceanic flights.

Employing more than 1,200 Canadians, AlliedSignal Aerospace has full-service operations in Toronto and Montreal; a regional airliner service centre at Summerside, Prince Edward Island; an Electronic System Centre at Cornwall, Ontario; and an Aeromarine Facility based in Richmond, British Colombia. Furthermore, the company has developed extensive repair and overhaul facilities at three locations across Canada.

Reflecting its high standards of excellence, AlliedSignal Aerospace has been honoured with various trib-

1. AlliedSignal Aerospace has produced more than 100,000 fuel control systems for aircraft manufacturers around the world.
2. The company's automated test stations enhance its global reputation for leading edge manufacturing and state-of-the-art products.
3. The majority of the western world's transport aircraft carry sophisticated electronic environmental control systems designed and manufactured by AlliedSignal Aerospace Canada.

utes, including the Merit Certificate from the Canada Award for Business Excellence and the Good Corporate Citizen Award from the Etobicoke (Ontario) Chamber of Commerce. Knowing that the company makes a difference in the quality of life within the community it resides is also a source of pride for Allied-Signal; many local and national charities benefit from the company's assistance.

AlliedSignal Aerospace Canada became an industry leader through its ongoing mission to exceed beyond the technical, quality and reliability requirements of its customers. Its dedication to customer focus, quality, people, commitments, and growth through innovative new product developments will propel it into the future.

2

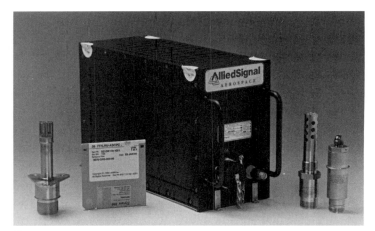

3

Artistic Glass Inc.

With the strength of a tradition of beauty and artistry in a centuries-old craft, Artistic Glass Inc. proffers its wares of stained glass. Understanding individual designs for both traditional and contemporary settings, the craftsmen of Artistic Glass work with pride, always conscious that what they create will bring joy and inspiration to those who see the results.

The history of Artistic Glass is essentially the story of Josef Aigner and his dedication to his trade. Acquiring the skills in early childhood in his native Germany, he learned the art of stained glass from his father, a master craftsman, who in turn had learned it from his father. After studying at the Luiesen School of Art and the Maische Academy of Art, both in Munich, he began designing, constructing and restoring stained glass windows throughout Europe for several years.

Coming to Canada in 1968, he founded Artistic Glass the following year, where he specialized in individual custom commissions.

Met with success, the company moved to its present location on Dundas Street West, an 18,000

1

1. *Josef Aigner, Founder and President of Artistic Glass Inc., with then Minister of Indian Affairs and Northern Development, Jean Chrétien.*
2. *Artistic Glass offers a wide range of stained glass possibilities for many settings, both traditional and modern.*
3. *In addition to stained glass, the company also custom creates sculptured glass from individually designed moulds.*

square foot facility. Large enough to handle even the biggest requests but with the intimacy and warmth of a smaller work force, each project receives the utmost of attention, carried out carefully and professionally.

Josef Aigner points out that in the mid 1980s Artistic Glass looked into mass production centred around standard designs, but soon returned to the basic method of selecting each job based on its own merits, and working the craft as a labour of love. As a result, Artistic Glass is now asked to engage in work destined for clients around the

world, from Hong Kong and Japan to the Middle East, Europe, and the United States.

In Canada, Artistic Glass' creations can be found from Vancouver to St. John's, including such projects as La Societe de Banque Suisse in Montreal, the Seagram Tower in Niagara Falls, Brock University in St. Catharines, and the Hilton in Quebec City. Toronto area installations include several fashionable restaurants, such as Winston's, The Old Mill, Fisher-

2

3

man's Wharf, Spaghetti Factory, Bo-Fingers and the Four Seasons Sheraton Hotel.

Along with secular commissions, works have been created for numerous religious buildings of many different denominations: Catholic, Lutheran, Anglican, United, Baptist, Jewish, Buddhist and Sikh, among others. All have had the uplift that comes from some very beautiful work, making a lasting impression of beauty and faith which is also a worthwhile investment.

Restoration is a very important aspect of Aigner's work. He has often been commissioned to restore very beautiful and historically important pieces, which, through time, neglect and the elements, have fallen into serious disrepair. With great respect for the craft, these valuable early works are disassembled, then painstakingly reconstructed with the original pieces, where possible. Replacement pieces are made using the same techniques and materials as were originally used. The piece is replaced looking exactly as it did when first installed generations ago.

The range of work available is amazing — and not limited to glass art. A small selection includes: massive bronze doors for a Ukrainian church in Toronto; a sculptured, carved glass dividing wall for a doctor's residence in Boston; Gothic shaped frameless glass doors for an Anglican church in Toronto; and doors with fused facetted glass jewels, which are the entrance to the head office of the Toronto Sun newspaper.

Josef Aigner also created carved glass doors with a wheel-cut design as the entrance to the Financial Post's head office in Toronto. An innovative security system was employed here, with invisible magnetic locks. There are facetted Dalles de Verre, one inch thick glass, carved with a chisel and constructed into breathtaking walls of colour, used as exterior walls for buildings.

1

There have been mosaics and murals, stained glass domes and ceilings, and frescoes. Many oil paintings have been commissioned, ranging from original works to faithful reproductions of art treasures (one has just been completed for the Mother Superior of the Carmelite Nuns in Italy).

There have even been furniture and interior designs, such as elegant and beautiful carved glass dining tables — one is currently being made for a residence in Barbados.

The possibilities are limited only by imagination! By supplying quality work, and taking care of each customer as an individual — understanding their needs and desires, the success of such a business cannot be far behind.

1. *A portion of the "Donor's Wall" — created by Artistic Glass and a clear example of the role that decorative glass can play — at Brock University in St. Catharines, Ontario.*
2. *The company's craftsmanship can also be seen displayed in many churches located throughout Toronto and across Canada.*

2

Bayer Inc.

A research-based, highly diversified company with businesses in chemicals, health care, life sciences and imaging technologies, Bayer Inc. is one of Canada's leading corporations. As a vital part of the worldwide Bayer AG family, one of the world's largest chemical companies, the Canadian arm, together with its sister company, Bayer Rubber Inc., is intrinsically linked to international resources and research and is positioned among the top 25 research and development spenders in Canada. Headquartered in Toronto, Bayer Inc. operated previously as Miles Canada Inc., but in 1995 the Canadian entity changed its name to more accurately reflect the wider global appellation.

Bayer AG is one of the most highly diversified companies in the chemical industry: over 400 operations involving approximately 146,000 employees in 140 countries, more than 100 manufacturing plants on five continents, and a portfolio of some 10,000 products all testify to the scale and dynamism of Bayer AG's development. Reflecting its status as one of the world's most research-intensive companies, nearly 60 per cent of sales come from products Bayer itself has developed during the last 15 years. Indeed, Bayer research is directly tied to the history and progress of chemistry itself.

Bayer AG was founded in Germany in 1863 by Friedrich Bayer and his partner Johann Friedrich Weskott. Producing aniline dyestuffs, also called coal tar dyes, Bayer's North American presence began already in 1865, when it acquired an interest in a coal tar dye plant in New York.

With decisive foresight, in 1883 the company hired three chemists, launching the firm on a path to scientific achievements and marking the beginning of Bayer's impres-

sive development. The first pharmaceutical to be produced was the pain reliever phenacetin in 1888. By 1897 a Bayer chemist had discovered the method to produce high quality acetylsalicylic acid, and Aspirin* was registered as a worldwide Bayer trademark in 1899. The now well-recognized Bayer cross was first used in 1904 to market Bayer pharmaceuticals.

As the company expanded and its list of innovative products grew, it also experienced difficulties with its global subsidiaries. After the first World War, Bayer AG temporarily lost its assets including name and trademark rights in several countries around the world, including Canada and the United States, where they were acquired by a predecessor of Sterling Winthrop Inc.

In order to re-establish its North American presence, Bayer AG acquired a number of companies, among them Chemagro in 1967 and Cutter Laboratories in 1974. In 1978, Bayer AG acquired the pharmaceuticals company Miles Laboratories Inc. of Elkhart, Indiana, and its subsidiary Miles Canada Inc. Miles Laboratories itself began in 1884 when a country medic, Dr.

1

Franklin L. Miles, began bottling his "restorative nervine" to treat a number of chronic illnesses. Opening its first offices in Elkhart, Indiana in 1888, all the early remedies were initially formulated by Dr. Miles.

Among the many medicinal products eventually produced by Miles Laboratories was Alka-Seltzer*. First formulated in 1929, it quickly became the major sole product of the company, accounting for the majority of sales and selling two billion tablets annually worldwide. To meet the Canadian and British demand for Alka-Seltzer*, in 1936 Miles Laboratories, Ltd.

2

1. *David M. Hillenbrand, Ph.D., President and Chief Executive Officer of Bayer Inc.*
2. *To commemorate the occasion of its historic name change from Miles Canada Inc. to Bayer Inc., over 500 employees at the Etobicoke head office formed a living logo as part of their celebrations in April 1995.*

was formed in Canada, and an Alka-Seltzer* production facility was established in Toronto two years later. Other pioneering Miles' products included One-A-Day* vitamins in 1940, Flintstones* vitamins in 1969, and the skin wound cleanser Bactine* in 1950.

A pivotal turning point for the Bayer companies in Canada and the United States occurred in 1994, when Bayer AG purchased Sterling Winthrop's North American OTC (over the counter) drug business, including all trademark rights in Canada and the United States related to the Bayer name and Bayer Cross. With this acquisition, Bayer was once again able to use its name and the Bayer trademark without restrictions, to strengthen its presence in Canada. As a result, in April 1995 Miles Canada Inc. was renamed Bayer Inc.

"By operating under a single company name worldwide, we can take full advantage of the synergies that spring from Bayer's pre-eminent profile. Now, we can use the Bayer name to strengthen the Bayer presence in North America," explains David Hillenbrand, Ph.D., President and Chief Executive Officer of Bayer Inc.

Today, Bayer Inc. is involved in six distinct activity areas in Canada.

Bayer's Healthcare Division has developed many leading prescription drugs for the prevention, diagnosis and treatment of a wide range of ailments, including cardiovascular diseases, microbial infections, diabetes and haemophilia. Its

diagnostics group has provided the means to diagnose many diseases and health problems, including thyroid problems and cancers, analyzers for blood examinations, and laboratory information systems involving state-of-the-art computer solutions.

In Canada, the Consumer Care Division is responsible for Bayer's numerous over-the-counter health care products, including such well-known names as Alka-Seltzer*, Midol*, and Aspirin*.

The Chemicals Division produces a wide range of chemical products, including resins for paints and coatings; synthetic iron oxide pigments for paints and concrete products; process chemicals for water treatment, chemical processing and other industries; dyes for textile dyeing and printing; processing chemicals for the textile and leather industries; and aroma, flavour and food ingredient enhancers offered by the Haarmann & Reimer group.

Bayer's Polymers Division is a leading Canadian supplier of plastics and polyurethane resins to automotive, appliance, construction and furniture manufacturers as well as the packaging and construction industries. The company offers 210 different products to its customers and, like the Chemicals Division, is ISO 9002 certified.

Bayer Inc.'s Agriculture Division is involved in crop protection, with products for controlling weeds, insects and diseases; and animal health, with pharmaceuticals, insecticides, vaccines, biologicals, flea

products, dewormers and anti microbials supplied to veterinarians and producers for pets and livestock.

The Agfa Division offers equipment, software and film for the graphic arts, printing and publishing industries; film, paper, chemistry and equipment for the photographic market; and film and equipment for medical and industrial imaging, micrographics, and cinematography.

Bayer Rubber Inc., a sister company also belonging to the Bayer AG group, is located in Sarnia, Ontario and is one of the world's leading producers of synthetic rubber. It manufactures 175,000 to 200,000 tonnes of synthetic rubber a year and is a leading worldwide researcher in the area of rubber applications.

Standing at the leading edge of technological development, Bayer's expertise is complemented by a thorough sense of responsibility to society. It is this continuing commitment to applying its expertise responsibly that will ensure Bayer's success well into the next century.

* Names appearing with an asterisk are trademarks of Bayer AG, Bayer Inc., or Bayer Corp. Bayer Inc. is a licensed user of the Bayer AG and Bayer Corp. trademarks.

1. *In addition to the head office located in Etobicoke, Ontario (a suburb of Toronto), Bayer in Canada also has sites and offices in Vancouver, Winnipeg, Sarnia, Ottawa and Montreal.*
2. *Bayer Rubber Inc. is a major manufacturing, research and development site for Bayer in Canada. Based in Sarnia, Ontario, it is one of the world's leading suppliers of quality synthetic rubber for a multitude of purposes.*

1

2

Birthright International

1

Believing in the right of every woman to give birth to her child with dignity, and the right of every child to be born, Birthright International is an interdenominational organization comprised of a loving, caring group of people dedicated to helping any girl or woman who is pregnant and has problems.

The history of Birthright International began in 1967 when the federal government passed legislation partially legalizing abortions in Canada. Louise Summerhill, a busy housewife and mother of seven children, felt that something should be done to assist those women who wanted to carry their pregnancies to term.

Summerhill convened a meeting, hoping that others would see and share her vision. As a result, Birthright was founded in 1968 in Toronto with a handful of volunteers and $300 in the bank. The need was great, and through Summerhill's foresight, steady leadership and faith, along with an overwhelming response from the grassroots level, branches sprouted rapidly throughout Canada, the United States and South Africa.

Summerhill's enduring principles, clearly formulated in the or-

ganization's charter, continue to direct Birthright's work today. From the outset it was decided never to charge for services, that it would not become involved in adoptions, and that it would not use pressure tactics or be involved in the political debate. Volunteers, always the mainstay of Birthright and approaching 5,000 in Canada alone, must be non-judgemental, listening and supportive in a personal, caring way to anyone who calls for help.

The services and assistance that Birthright offers depends on the individual situation: from crisis telephone support to help in telling parents, aid in finding shelter, legal or medical assistance, referrals to social service agencies for financial assistance or professional counselling, referrals to reputable adoption agencies, maternity and baby clothes, transportation, and friendship throughout the pregnancy.

Without the benefits of any large endowments, Birthright relies exclusively on the generosity and goodwill of churches, other organizations and individuals. The support has been great and has forged Birthright into a well-planned and well-managed organization.

In recognition of the important work that she accomplished, Louise Summerhill was granted numerous

awards including The Christian Culture Award from the University of Windsor, and the Canada Volunteer Award Certificate of Merit. Summerhill was also awarded honourary degrees, from Molloy College, Long Island, New York; St. Joseph College, Rensellaer, Indiana; and St. Michael's College, University of Toronto.

Before her death in 1991, Summerhill prepared for the future of Birthright International. Her oldest daughter, Mary Berney, has worked since 1984 at the international headquarters on Coxwell Avenue in Toronto and oversees the administrative aspects, serving as co-President along with two other daughters — Louise R. Summerhill, a lawyer, and Stephenie Summerhill Fox, a chartered accountant.

In 1993 Birthright International celebrated its 25th anniversary with more than 550 chapters worldwide, including 70 in Canada, 450 in the United States, and others in South Africa, Ghana, Cameroon, Nigeria and Hong Kong. With an average of 28,000 women per month making their initial visit to a Birthright centre, unknown numbers of grateful women will come to rely on its services in the future, as it continues to provide a loving alternative to women in a time of special need.

1. *Louise Summerhill, who founded Birthright in 1968 in Toronto, Ontario, and served as its President until 1991.*
2. *The worldwide headquarters of Birthright International, on Coxwell Avenue in Toronto.*

2

B'nai Brith Canada

1

Canada's largest and most senior Jewish organization, B'nai Brith is widely recognized as a preeminent Jewish advocacy organization in Canada, particularly in the area of human rights. Throughout its 120 years of service to the Canadian community, B'nai Brith has been active in fostering the development of a positive Jewish identity and a devotion to community service among its members.

The greatness of B'nai Brith Canada lies in its sustaining a strong program of community volunteer service, education, athletics, and social and cultural programming alongside an active involvement in the monthly publication of *The Jewish Tribune* featuring organizational news and current affairs writing, and, most significantly, an advocacy operation which has drawn on the strengths of existing members while bringing in new supporters. Specific involvements include the spawning of the Canadian Jewish Law Students' Association, organizing North America's largest soft-ball league, the development of seniors' housing projects in Canada, the development of health clinics and other community services in Israel, and the mounting of its Community Volunteer Service program.

The history of B'nai Brith Canada is one of pride in accomplish-

ments on many levels. The first Canadian B'nai Brith lodge was founded in Toronto in 1875. Canada Lodge, as it was known, was the 246th Lodge in the international fraternal order. Active until 1894, it served a significant purpose, providing members with opportunities for socializing and undertaking benevolent activities on behalf of the wider Jewish community. Montreal Lodge opened in 1881, providing fraternal functions and working with early social service organizations until its closing in 1903.

B'nai Brith activities began again in Canada in 1913 when Mount Royal Lodge was established in Montreal. From this point onward, the organization began to have a greater and more meaningful impact on the life and vitality of Canadian Jewry. By the mid 1920s, a number of lodges were operating with concerns in community development, education and advocacy. After a well-organized and wide spread war effort during World War II, by the late 1940s efforts were also turning to assisting the newly established State of Israel.

As more and more community activities were begun, goodwill toward the organization grew and the number of lodges increased. In 1970 the League for Human Rights of B'nai Brith Canada was organized. Since then, it has initiated a se-

ries of educational programs in regard to anti-Semitism, and has played a leadership role in advancing Christian-Jewish dialogue. The League was also a significant player in Canada's recent constitutional debates, and it has been formally recognized by the federal government for its contributions to the advancement of human rights.

Through its Institute for International Affairs, B'nai Brith Canada has become a leading public educator in international human rights, with one area of intense involvement being the quest to bring World War II war crime suspects residing in Canada to justice.

B'nai Brith programs have made the organization a credit to its people and to the community at large throughout the country. Having demonstrated the virtue of community service for over a century, and having shown leadership in the Jewish community and more generally in the quest for the full enjoyment of human rights by all citizens, B'nai Brith now looks forward to even greater accomplishments in the next century.

1. *Frank Dimant, Executive Vice President, has been instrumental in leading B'nai Brith Canada to become the primary Jewish Advocacy Organization in Canada.*
2. *B'nai Brith Canada's National Headquarters located in North York, Ontario.*

2

BT Canada Ltd.

One of Canada's foremost suppliers of internal materials handling equipment, BT Canada Ltd. has established itself as a market leader in service and support. Offering much more than simple lifts, BT Canada is able to analyze its clients' needs, recommend a solution, individually customize a wide range of materials handling equipment, and follow-up with an ongoing commitment to after-sales support.

Canada was first introduced to BT materials handling equipment in 1953 when Strathmos Scales Ltd., a Toronto based subsidiary of BT Industries' parent company in Sweden, began distributing BT hand pallet trucks. When BT Industries acquired Strathmos Company in 1975, the company's name was changed to BT Lift Canada Ltd., and relocated to 16,000 square foot premises on Steelcase Road West in Markham, Ontario.

As demand for its products increased, a custom designed, 48,000 square foot facility was constructed on Royal Crest Court in Markham, as a base for continued expansion. Concurrently, the company became BT Canada Ltd. — dropping the world "lift", and more accurately reflecting the ever widening product range.

With a strategically located and highly trained network of dealers operating throughout Canada, BT Canada Ltd. is now the largest supplier in its industry niche — electric powered lift trucks and hand operated pallet movers. Its comprehensive list of internal materials handling equipment includes manually operated trucks, walkie trucks, stackers, order pickers, reach trucks, and, BT Canada's specialty products, narrow trucks for constricted aisleways and high stacking demands. BT Canada is also acknowledged as a leading supplier of automated handling systems, designing and installing some of the most sophisticated systems in the world.

As part of the larger BT Industries group of companies, founded in Sweden in 1946 for the manufacturing of hand pallet trucks, BT Canada is one of 14 subsidiaries operating around the world. BT Canada's equipment is shipped from its parent company, while final assembly is undertaken in Canada. Furthermore, the customization of the equipment for individual client requirements is done at the Markham facility, including specialty lifting devices, forks for specialty uses, and extra wide or long forks. Certain components, such as forks, batteries and chargers, are sourced locally.

But BT Canada supplies much more than just equipment. Paul Bennett, President of BT Canada, emphasizes, "by utilizing proprietary software, we are able to analyze a

1

customers' needs and design a solution. From recommending the right machines to designing complete warehouse operations, and providing turn-key solutions with the racking installed, BT Canada is able to fill a client's materials handling requirements."

From its early beginnings in simple hand pallet trucks to a well-established successful company, BT Canada Ltd. has built its reputation on service, a foundation that strongly supports its further pacesetting role in the industry.

1. *Paul Bennett, President of BT Canada Ltd.*
2. *The company's head office, located in Markham, Ontario.*
3. *BT Canada is a leading supplier of electric powered lift trucks and hand operated pallet movers.*

2

3

The Canada Life Assurance Company

1

Hugh Cossart Baker, a bank manager in Hamilton, Canada West, established The Canada Life Assurance Company on August 21, 1847. The first Canadian life company by some twenty years and now one of the eight oldest in North America, it received a charter in both English and French from the Province of Canada.

Canada Life, in step with the forward march of a young nation, became a national institution with steadily growing international status. The first policy on a resident of the British Isles was placed in 1848, followed a year later with the first policy on a resident of the United States. The United States Division was established in 1889, and the Division now serving the United Kingdom and the Republic of Ireland in 1903.

A leader in the Canadian insurance field, Canada Life published the first Canadian mortality studies after recording experiences from 1847 to 1893. Furthermore, the company provided policies to women at normal rates from its beginning while some other companies refused to insure them or asked for higher premiums. Canada Life became one of the pioneers in the group insurance field in 1919 and in introducing non-medical life insurance three years later.

Originally, in 1847 the founders wished to establish a mutual company with all assets owned by policyholders, but in those early days in the Province of Canada this was not allowed. However, when legislation in the mid-twentieth century permitted the change, policyholders and shareholders of Canada Life voted overwhelmingly for mutualization.

In 1848, Hugh C. Baker stated: "That life assurance societies will succeed in this land, I cannot for a moment doubt. Originating as they do in the purest motives of humanity, based upon the surest calculations and conducted upon the most impartial principles of equity, they must run a triumphant course, lessening the sum of human misery and exerting a healthy moral influence."

Down through almost a century and a half, Canada Life has been motivated by the first president's guiding principle: "The interest of the policyholder is paramount!"

The company has pioneered in the use of advanced electronic data processing, including as early as 1970 the first fully-leased telephone channel for the transmission of voice, data and correspondence between any nations in the Commonwealth and the United Kingdom.

The directors and senior officers of the Canada Life have included many distinguished business and professional people including the first Canadian Ambassador to the United States, the first Governor of the Bank of Canada and Alternate Governor of the International Monetary Fund. All are dedicated to providing the most security for the clients of Canada Life and its companies.

2

1. *Hugh Cossart Baker, who founded The Canada Life Assurance Company in 1847, the first Canadian life company.*
2. *The company's head offices, located on University Avenue in Toronto.*

Canada Post Corporation

The first organized postal service in what was to become Canada began in 1693 when the government of New France paid Pedro daSilva for carrying a packet of letters from Montreal to Quebec City.

Although the first government post office opened in Halifax in 1755, and the first Canadian postage stamp — the red "Three-Penny Beaver" — was issued in 1851, Canada did not get an "official" postal service until after Confederation.

On April 1, 1868, the Post Office Act came into effect, uniting the postal systems of Prince Edward Island, Nova Scotia, New Brunswick, Quebec and Ontario. During the Post Office's first year of service, annual mail volumes included nearly 22 million letters, 19 million newspapers, and 39,000 parcels — a total of about 41 million pieces of mail.

Canada's postal service was managed as a government department until the 16th of October, 1981, when the former Post Office Department became Canada Post Corporation through an Act of Parliament.

Today's Canada Post Corporation collects and processes on average 40 million pieces of mail every business day, to be delivered to nearly twelve million business and household addresses.

Canada Post's workforce includes over 54,000 full- and part-time employees. The Corporation operates a network of 22 major mail processing plants, a fleet of 5,500 vehicles, and contracts for the services of over 7,000 air, surface and marine transportation contractors to move the mail. Canada Post's business generates annual revenues of close to four billion dollars.

Canada Post has become recognized as a world leader in postal technology. One example of the

1

Corporation's use of technology is the National Control Centre, located at Canada Post's head office in Ottawa. Electronic systems at the Centre provide real-time information on various aspects of mail operations and alert operators of potential system failures. Control Centre staff keep an eye on everything from surface and air shipments to machine down-time and adverse weather conditions, and they monitor the movement of mail 24 hours a day, seven days a week.

Canada Post also works in cooperation with foreign postal administrations, benefiting Canadians by paving the way toward more efficient global mail services. The Corporation markets its technology and expertise to other countries through its wholly-owned subsidiary, Canada Post Systems Management Limited.

Canada Post Corporation has been in the message transfer business for 300 years. For most of those years, messages moved in hard-copy format by ship, by rail, by road, and, in this century, by air. Today, Canada Post also moves messages electronically, thus continuing its unique role as the nation's universal and cost-effective information transfer and distribution system.

1. Canada's national postal service has been providing a vital communications link for Canadians since it was founded, one year after Confederation, in 1868.
2. Today's modern and efficient Canada Post Corporation collects and processes approximately 40 million pieces of mail daily.

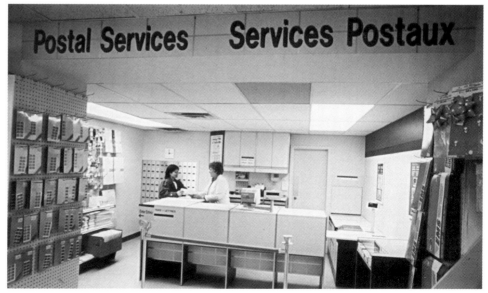

2

Canadian National Exhibition

Toronto's Canadian National Exhibition (the CNE — also affectionately known as the "Ex") remains one of the greatest links to the early years of Canadian agriculture, commerce, industry and the arts. The annual Exhibition was established in 1879 by the Ontario Provincial Legislature through "An Act to Incorporate the Industrial Exhibition of Toronto." Since then, it has acted as an annual celebration of community spirit, a gathering place for Canadian manufacturers and farmers, and a showcase for the latest technological developments from around the world.

The CNE's litany of firsts began in 1882 when the Exhibition grounds became the first fairgrounds in the world to be lit by electricity. Two years later, the first electric railway was introduced to Canada at the CNE. The early years of the Canadian automotive industry were also linked to the early years of the Exhibition as automobile shows became a favourite attraction (reflected by the construction of the Automotive Building in 1929).

Communication technologies, many of which are taken for granted today, were introduced to Canadians at the CNE. Early experiments with the telephone were conducted in full view of the public on the CNE grounds. Similarly, some of the earliest phonograph recordings in existence today were recorded at the CNE.

The CNE has played an on-going vital role in presenting music and the arts to Canadians. From Metropolitan Opera soprano, Lilly Pons, on the Bandshell just prior to World War II, to the more recent "Scottish World Festival Tattoo" in Exhibition Stadium, the CNE has featured every variety of performance artist on its many stages.

Over the course of more than a century, the CNE has moved with

1

the times and adapted to new economic realities and public tastes. New technologies like virtual reality continue to be introduced to many Canadians at the CNE and artists like the Rolling Stones and Bette Midler have taken over the stages. Today, the CNE draws more than 1.5 million visitors annually — making it one of the top three largest annual exhibitions in the world.

By the summer of 1997, Exhibition Place will be home to a new exhibit facility called the National Trade Centre. Encompassing the existing Coliseum Complex and a new exhibit hall, the National Trade Centre will become Canada's largest

and most modern trade and consumer show building.

Like previous structures built on the site of the CNE in their time, the National Trade Centre will help bring the CNE into the future. And though the CNE will change with time, it will continue to serve as a catalyst for commerce and community spirit for millions of Canadians in the future.

1. The CNE at 50 years of age, along the Princes' Boulevard looking east toward the Princes' Gate, with the Electrical and Engineering Building on the left and the Automotive Building on the right.
2. The CNE today has more than 1.5 million visitors annually.

2

Canadian Holidays Ltd.

Ranking among the largest tour operators in Canada, Canadian Holidays Ltd. offers the travelling public a wide range of destinations encompassing the most popular resort locations across North America and around the globe. Catering to a broad spectrum of market segments, its comprehensive litany of tour products range from the traditional fully escorted and inclusive tour program, to the more flexible holiday packages. Reflecting its well-known standards of performance, Canadian Holidays, in a recent national study of Canadian travel agents, was the preferred tour operator named by travel agents and ranked first when rated for performance.

Canadian Holidays — also the oldest tour operator in Canada — began in 1926 when Joseph Nordman formed the company's predecessor, Treasure Tours Registered. A wholesale tour operation promoting escorted European tours, it had offices in New York and Montreal, the headquarters of the company.

From the beginning, Treasure Tours organized, in cooperation with several shipping companies, its own tours as well as Foreign Independent Travel (FIT's) to Europe. Blocks of cabins were booked on transatlantic ships and guided tours sailed to Europe, where they were welcomed by Treasure Tours' receiving staff and escorted through the program.

In 1939 the tours were suspended until 1946 when, after the war, the European service was resumed. Expanding its activities, it soon became one of the major Canadian tour operators. The largest area of business was the company's Outgoing Department, which was selling Treasure Tours' programs through retail agencies and to professional and scientific organizations.

Tours were prepared in coopera-

tion with steamship lines, and printed programs were offered to the public through travel agents, the steamship lines themselves, and special interest groups on a national basis. During the early postwar years Treasure Tours held appointments with most of the major ship lines, including Cunard, Star Lines, Holland-American, French Paquet Lines and GAL Polish Lines, among others.

As transatlantic air traffic became established and popular, travel business gradually shifted from ships to airplanes. In response, Treasure Tours received IATA (International Air Transportation Association) and ATC (Air Transport Committee) appointments and subsequently also was appointed by all the major airlines.

By 1970, Treasure Tours had 28 programs with airlines and 11 special programs; furthermore, the Outgoing Department was also handling Group Tours, FIT's, hotel and car reservation, and individual and group insurance. The Incoming Department was active in organizing congresses and conventions in Canada, as well as tours for special interest groups from many countries. Always in the forefront of the industry, in 1970 the first Inclusive Tour

Charter (ITC) aircraft flew from Montreal via Toronto to Freeport, launching the company on a new road to success as an ITC operator.

In the early 1970s, in addition to its Incoming Tours, Treasure Tours had programs to Europe, the Orient, the Middle East, and South America. A sampling of prices of the 1973-74 winter season for a tour — including round trip air transportation, hotel and breakfast — reveals a cost of $279.00 for two weeks to destinations in Florida, and starting from $269 per week to the Bahamas. By 1974, Treasure Tours was the second largest ITC tour operator offering all-inclusive tour packages in eastern Canada.

In 1975 Treasure Tours was purchased by Nordair Ltd., giving Treasure Tours better access to flights and allowing it to expand as an ITC operator. New destinations were added and departures increased, with Treasure Tours pioneering new destinations such as Cancun in Mexico and Cuba.

During the 1980s, as the travel industry consolidated, Treasure Tours strengthened itself through a series of mergers. In 1985 Canadian Pacific Airlines purchased Nordair Ltd., including Treasure Tours. The following year Canadian Pacific

Treasure Tours, Canadian Holidays' predecessor company, was founded in 1926.

Airlines' tour operator, CP Air Holidays — established in 1980 in Western Canada and by 1985 itself having become Canada's largest tour operator — was merged with Treasure Tours. Subsequently, Pacific Western Holidays, established in 1981, was also merged with Treasure Tours, creating Canada's largest national tour operator servicing over 450,000 travellers annually.

In 1989 the company became even larger with the integration of Wardair Holidays, which had been offering vacation packages to the Canadian traveller for over 25 years. That same year, reflecting the increased utilization of Canadian Airlines charters and the recent mergers, Treasure Tours became officially known as Canadian Holidays.

Today, the company offers the leisure traveller nationally and internationally a broad and comprehensive range of high quality and competitively priced tour products on charters as well as on the Canadian Airlines international scheduled route network. Current destinations include numerous locales in the United States, Mexico, Costa Rica, Nicaragua, Bahamas, Cuba, Dominican Republic, Grand Cayman, Jamaica, Barbados, St. Kitts and Puerto Rico.

Each destination, selected by experienced product managers, represents a range of hotels to choose from and a holiday selection to accommodate all travellers. Each year new hotels and destinations are added, all meeting the high standards of quality, value and service that have become Canadian Holidays' keys to success.

Canadian Holidays attends to the traveller's needs with attention to the smallest detail, ensuring a pleasant, memorable and relaxing stay. Reflecting the perception of the consumer and their concern for value, the company is experiencing rapid growth to all its international destinations.

The company's 600 employees are each committed to offering consumer efficiency, value and service.

1

To ensure continuing excellence, seminars and familiarization trips are undertaken to keep employees up-to-date and aware of both new and existing destinations. The management team itself has had years of experience in the travel field providing innovative leadership, and is engaged in all aspects of producing quality package holidays. Furthermore, promotion from within provides a supervisory and management team fully aware of the operating structure of the company and its objectives and long term goals.

Currently servicing over 600,000 customers annually, Canadian Holidays is a leader in its field, having built its reputation on a long heritage of quality service and customer satisfaction. From Disneyland to Aukland, Las Vegas to Los Cabos, Canadian Holidays Ltd. has developed hassle-free holiday packages and tours suited to every class of the travelling public.

1. *Canadian Holidays offers a wide range of holiday packages and tours to meet the needs of the travelling public.*
2. *Errol Francis, President, has been with the company since 1978.*

2

The Canadian National Institute for the Blind

The world's largest private reha-bilitation agency for blind and visually impaired people, The Canadian National Institute for the Blind is Canada's national voluntary agency providing services to individuals across Canada for whom loss of vision is a central problem in personal and social adjustment. The aim of the CNIB, as the organization is commonly known, is to help blind and visually impaired people find ways to lead more satisfying lives.

Underlying all CNIB services and actions is the belief that blind and visually impaired individuals can be integrated into the mainstream of community life, each according to his or her ability. It is this continued, single-minded focus on a defined goal, along with a willingness to adapt to the changing needs of a growing clientele, that has propelled CNIB to the forefront of creating new and unimagined opportunities for blind and visually impaired Canadians.

Having celebrated its 75th anniversary in 1993, CNIB has a long and vital history. It was founded in 1918 in the post World War I period of Canadian history, established in response to the need for a national service and rehabilitation organization to help blind veterans and others achieve an independent lifestyle.

During the night of October 9, 1915, Lieutenant Edwin Baker, making his way through the trenches, was blinded by a sniper's stray bullet. The first Canadian officer to lose his sight during World War I, he returned to Canada after a period of convalescence in England, only to find that rehabilitation services for blind and visually impaired people were few and very fragmented.

Looking to remedy the situation, Edwin Baker and six others worked to convince the public of

the need for a national organization. In 1918 their efforts were rewarded when they obtained a charter from the federal government to form The Canadian National Institute for the Blind, with the mission "to ameliorate the condition of the blind of Canada and to prevent blindness." That same year, the Canadian Free Library for the Blind amalgamated with the CNIB and became its library and publishing department.

Determined to place blind men and women in productive and gainful employment, in 1918 the CNIB also opened its first industrial department. The men made brooms while the women made reed baskets, engaged in machine sewing and knitting, and loom weaving. By 1920 these departments had created almost 200 jobs for blind Canadians, while providing much needed income for the organization from the sale of the products.

In 1920 Edwin Baker became the Managing Director of the CNIB, a position he held until 1962, dedicating his life to preventing blindness and improving the quality of life for blind and visually impaired people. The values that he instilled in the organization are part

Lieutenant-Colonel Edwin A. Baker, C.C., O.B.E., M.C., Croix de Guerre, B.Sc., LL.D., was a leading force in the establishment of The Canadian National Institute for the Blind.

of his enduring legacy today.

Formed at a time when government social services were virtually non-existent and many of its clients needed help obtaining food, clothing and shelter, the CNIB soon realized that, in addition to offering direct assistance, training and rehabilitation services, it also needed to educate and lobby government concerning its role in aiding blind Canadians. Under Edwin Baker's direction, the CNIB spearheaded activity in the areas of blindness legislation which was unprecedented, and its advocacy and lobbying resulted in many new public services, important federal entitlements including disability pensions and income tax exemptions, and much more, including blind voters' legislation.

During Lieutenant-Colonel Baker's tenure, the CNIB also branched out into new areas such as blindness prevention measures showing the importance of silver nitrate drops in the eyes of new-born babies, as well as the beginning of rehabilitation in the home that involved the teaching of braille and other independent living skills.

After World War II, the CNIB expanded its services to meet the needs of its clients by building 21 residences and service centres in major cities across Canada. These centres allowed the CNIB to reach more blind people, and helped blind and visually impaired persons gain more recognition in their communities.

In the 1950s and 1960s, rapid advances in technology and automation increased the need for training and retraining of people for work. New blindness prevention initiatives were begun, such as the

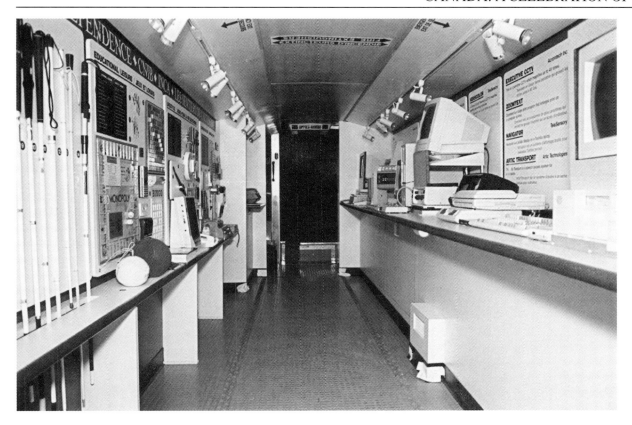

Inside the CNIB Technibus, a travelling technology exhibit and an example of the future direction of the CNIB — bringing technology to people and people to technology. A wheelchair accessible 40-foot intercity bus, it was specially designed and outfitted with over 100 high and low tech aids for blind and visually impaired persons. During 1993, the CNIB's 75th anniversary, the Technibus visited 156 communities in its nation-wide tour.

Ontario Eye Bank in 1955, followed by other Eye Banks across the country. More than 33,000 donated eyes in Ontario alone have helped many regain their vision through transplants.

By the mid 1970s, as more community-based service facilities and centres were developed, the need for CNIB residences diminished. The 1980s saw the CNIB, ever evolving, undergo several important changes, including the decision to extend services offered by the CNIB to all Canadians experiencing serious functional visual difficulties; the prioritization of CNIB services into seven core rehabilitation and library services; the development of a national service equity program to respond to regional and local disparities in access to the core services; and the development of CNIB technology services for blind and visually impaired persons, soon giving it leadership in this specialized field.

Today, approximately 25,000 volunteers and 1,500 staff complement the work of the CNIB, providing direct services to over 75,000 Canadians through a network of more than 60 Service Centres

across Canada. These services are grouped in the seven core areas on which the CNIB has decided to concentrate: counselling and referral; rehabilitation teaching; orientation and mobility instruction; sight enhancement; technical aids; career development and employment; and library services. A priority of the CNIB continues to be the provision of special programs and services to seniors, children and their families, and deaf-blind people.

Throughout its history, the CNIB has encouraged blind individuals to take an active part in the development of the Institute. The National Council, CNIB's governing body, is comprised of blind and sighted volunteers from across Canada, and throughout its history the organization's President has always been a blind or visually impaired individual.

Internationally, the CNIB has been instrumental in promoting and aiding the development of services for blind and visually impaired people, and in the prevention of blindness in developing countries. Recognized worldwide as a leader in its field, the CNIB has welcomed personnel from sister organizations in

other countries to participate in CNIB training and study programs in Canada. From the outset, CNIB officials have served on many international bodies and on assignments abroad, beginning with Lieutenant-Colonel Baker who was selected as the first President of the World Council for the Welfare of the Blind (now the World Blind Union) and served for three consecutive terms.

Looking at the many landmark initiatives already achieved, the CNIB sees itself further developing its pioneering role in all areas, but, in particular, its leadership role in the use of technology to help blind and visually impaired people find ways to lead more satisfying lives.

As it moves forward to the future with enthusiasm and pride, the work is undeniably more pressing and needed than ever before. With its strong heritage and its respect both in Canada and throughout the world, The Canadian National Institute for the Blind looks forward to creating yet more pathways to independence for Canada's blind and visually impaired people, as it continues to make the impossible a reality.

Canadian Tire Corporation, Limited

The leading hardgoods retailer in Canada, Canadian Tire Corporation, Limited has 425 stores from coast to coast. Its mission is to be the first choice for all Canadians in automotive, leisure, and home products, by providing total customer value through its "customer-driven service." In its own words, "Canadian Tire's vision is to be the best at what our customers value most."

But the long history of success of Canadian Tire is no accident. It has been the result of concentrated efforts, dedication and a commitment to achieving a goal. The store's founders had a vision and the courage to realize it. They worked long and hard, despite difficult times, and were shrewd and innovative. They understood their business, they commanded company loyalty, and they instilled their values in their employees, endowing the company with the enduring legacy of their driving commitment to a successful enterprise.

In 1922 two brothers, A.J. and J.W. Billes, used their accumulated savings of $1,800 to purchase Hamilton Tire and Rubber, a small garage, with a few automotive parts and some tires. Located on Gerrard and Hamilton streets in Toronto, Ontario, a city with 40,000 cars, the store stocked a small range of repair parts, such as tires, batteries, and a homemade brand of antifreeze, for the two most popular car makes of the time. A portent of the future was the introduction, later that same year, of windshield wipers, an automatic starter, and an improved car heater.

Meeting with early success, the company was incorporated as Canadian Tire Corporation, Limited in 1927. That same year it issued a one-page listing that featured tire values on one side and an Ontario road map on the back. This venture into direct marketing was followed

1

2

by the production of a mail-order list that was sent to car owners in Southern Ontario and New York state. The success of these two promotions gave birth to the first Canadian Tire catalogue in 1928.

In 1931 Canadian Tire introduced its unconditional tire guarantee for its Super-Lastic brand of tires. It was the first time in Canada that a tire was guaranteed for other than manufacturing defects, and it also signalled that Canadian Tire was coming of age as an emerging force in the retail world.

Despite the Great Depression, Canadian Tire's policy of offering quality merchandise at low prices al-

lowed the company to grow and prosper, and in 1934 the first Associate Store opened in Hamilton, Ontario. The annual catalogue that year was 24 pages long, promoting the company as the "largest direct automotive supply house in Canada, a 100 per cent Canadian company."

In 1939 there were 71 associate stores, a number that grew to 116

1., 2. *J.W. Billes* (1) *and A.J. Billes* (2), *co-founders of Canadian Tire Corporation, Limited.*
3. *Canadian Tire's flagship store at Yonge and Davenport in Toronto, as it was in 1936.*

3

by 1946. In 1956 the 150 stores, located throughout Eastern Canada, had outgrown the Toronto warehouse's capacity and construction began on a new, specialized distribution centre, the Sheppard Distribution Centre, especially designed to meet the needs of a growing and prosperous chain of retail stores.

When J.W. Billes passed away in 1956, A.J. Billes assumed the role of President. Under his leadership the business continued its expansion march across the country. Gas Bars were introduced, and Cash Bonus Coupons, the "Canadian Tire Money" now so familiar to Canadians, were subsequently offered, first to Gas Bar customers in 1958, and then extended to store purchases in 1961. Believing that excellent performance deserved recognition and had to be rewarded, A.J. Billes pioneered a profit-sharing plan for employees that remains one of the best in Canada.

Canadian Tire's long-distance hauling operation began in 1967, and, reflecting the quantities of merchandise handled, a second major distribution facility was built, in Brampton, Ontario. In 1981, the Edmonton Distribution Centre was inaugurated to service Western Canada. The company's cross-country odyssey reached the west coast in 1980, with the establishment of a Canadian Tire location in Vancouver, British Columbia, and later expanded throughout the Western provinces.

Today, the approximately 425 stores are stocked from a selection of 55,000 products, including automotive parts and accessories, sports and leisure equipment, hardware and housewares, as well as providing auto repair service. In addition, the Petroleum Division, which has 206 outlets, is the largest independent retailer of gasoline in Canada.

A growing part of Canadian Tire is Canadian Tire Acceptance, established in 1968, which is engaged primarily in financing and managing customer credit accounts that arise from the sale of goods and services at Associate Stores and Petroleum's gasoline outlets. In addition, Acceptance performs third-party transaction processing, operates a national emergency roadside service for Canadian Tire Auto Club and markets a variety of insurance products to Canadian Tire customers.

The stores have always been innovative in customer services. When the chain's flagship store at the corner of Yonge Street and Davenport Road, Toronto, was a counter-service operation, the clerks took orders for goods at the counter and then fetched them from the stock shelves at the back on roller skates, gaining them a reputation for speed! This commitment to customer service continues, as Canadian Tire strives to deliver "customer-driven service."

Always providing the greatest value possible, the Canadian Tire house brands, including Motomaster and Mastercraft, have become a Canadian institution since they were first introduced in 1931. Over the years they have achieved a wide level of recognition and have been integral to the company's growth — for example, Motomaster is Canada's leading line of automotive replacement parts; it is Canada's number one replacement tire, as well as the leading battery, motor oil and antifreeze brand.

An important priority for Canadian Tire is the stewardship of environmental quality. With a strong commitment to recycling, it has shown leadership in its efforts to offer customers environmentally responsible products, services and packaging.

Canadian Tire has long been involved in giving something back to the communities in which it is located, from local event sponsorships and bike rodeos, to special areas of concern, such as child safety and protection through programs such as the Cycle Safe Helmet Program, the Learn Not to Burn Program and the Stay Alert ... Stay Safe Program, offered by the Canadian Tire Child Protection Foundation. The Foundation was formed in 1993 and is funded by the Corporation and Associate Dealers to support community based programs for the protection and well-being of children. The Corporation also offers twenty-four A.J. Billes Canadian Tire Scholarships annually to the children of employees, in recognition of the efforts of those who strive to be their best.

Employing more than 27,000 people, Canadian Tire Corporation, Limited and its Associate Dealers are a well recognized Canadian establishment. With a strong enterprise, a clear vision, excellent employees and management, and an outstanding dealer network, Canadian Tire is poised for future success, firmly rooted in its history of serving Canadians for over 70 years.

Today's Canadian Tire is Canada's largest retailer of automotive parts and accessories, home products — including housewares and hardwares, and sporting and leisure goods, at 425 locations across the country.

Cara Operations Limited

Cara Operations is the parent of respected Canadian restaurant and retail brand names such as Harvey's, Swiss Chalet, and Grand & Toy. Through these companies and others, Cara touches the lives of thousands of Canadians every day. Its story is a history of entrepreneurship and growth, paralleling the development of the Canadian nation. It is the story of a Canadian company that grew from vending its newspapers on the Grand Trunk Railway to today's sizeable concern.

Cara Operations Limited began as the Canada Railway News Company (CRNCo.), incorporated in 1883 with the modest aspiration of selling newspapers and magazines to the Canadian travelling public. The business partners and founders of CRNCo. had seen the need to formalize their working relationship after a number of years of selling news material on railways and at railway and steamboat stations in Southern Ontario. The original partners included Thomas Patrick Phelan, the grandfather of Paul J. Phelan — the company's Honourary Chairman today, his brother Frederick Phelan, and their two cousins Hugh and Colin Chisholm.

By the late 1880s both the Chisholms had left the company, leaving the Phelans as majority shareholders from that time forward. Under the entrepreneurial guidance of T.P. Phelan, CRNCo.'s president until 1932, the company experienced rapid growth until the onset of the Great Depression.

In 1902 CRNCo. moved its head office from Montreal to Toronto and expanded its charter "to carry on the business of catering and keeping restaurants and hotels." Two years later, the company purchased its first hotel, the first in a long series that the company would own or operate, which included such prestigious names as the

T.P. Phelan, the founder of Canada Railway News Company (CRNCo.), the predecessor to Cara Operations Limited. Well-known for his willingness to help the less fortunate, he used to run a virtual gauntlet between Union Station and Bay Street's National Club, armed with a pocketful of bills which he dispensed en route. But, on days when philanthropy palled, his assistant was under instructions to bring a stepladder round to a certain office window so that "T.P." could clamber down unseen, making his escape from indignant cronies "who were trying to put the bite on him." Today, Cara's concern for the community is expressed through more conventional means, including corporate environmentalism and participation in the "Imagine" program, whereby participating Canadian companies donate at least one per cent of their pre-tax earnings to charity.

Queen's Hotel in Palmerston, Ontario; Wawa Hotel, near Huntsville, Ontario; and the Highland Inn, located in Algonquin Provincial Park in Ontario.

To meet the needs of its customers in their new Canadian nation, company operations quickly expanded into railway restaurants and the sale of food products, on the trains and in amusement parks. As steamships became more and more deluxe, the company kept pace, expending considerable sums in order to satisfy all clients. Although certain dealings remained on a low budget basis, such as the newsstands on the docks, other stands of varying sizes appeared aboard ships, followed by company lunch counters and full-scale dining rooms.

By 1919, CRNCo. officially spanned the continent with the opening of its newsstand at the Grand Trunk Pacific station in Prince Rupert, British Columbia. CRNCo.'s employees were riding the trains of

the Algoma Central and Hudson Bay route from Sault Ste. Marie, Ontario to Hearst, Ontario; the National Transcontinental from Moncton, New Brunswick to Winnipeg, Manitoba; and the Grand Trunk Pacific across the West.

CRNCo's success came through a combination of factors. The company's dedication to the spirit of enterprise, its willingness to go anywhere, anytime, and its tight managerial controls enabled it to gain a large share of the marketplace. From early on, the company was dedicated to treating its employees very well and was rewarded with a high degree of staff loyalty. Management of the company remained in the hands of the Phelans who sometimes gave up promising professional careers to serve the company.

The Great Depression hit the company hard, and closures began in 1931. When T.P. Phelan died in 1932, the presidency went to his brother-in-law, J.D. Warde, who had been with the company since 1908. With his eye for detail, he was able to guide the company through troubled times. By 1937 the company was beginning to re-cover, and when Warde fell ill in 1938, Harry Warde Phelan, the son of the founder, became CRNCo.'s new president.

After building a strong network based on water and land transit, the company recognized the vast impor-tance of the next step in public transportation — the commercial airlines. CRNCo., like the modern Cara, was determined to be where the customer is. In 1941 Canada's first airport restaurant opened at Montreal's Dorval Airport and CRNCo. was asked to manage this experimental facility. Flight kitch-ens soon evolved at all the major airports, and restaurants, news-stands and gift shops were estab-lished as air terminals spread across the country. In 1944 CRNCo. formed Aero Caterers Limited to serve the airline industry.

Eugene D. Phelan, a nephew of the founder, became CRNCo.'s president in 1945, overseeing CRNCo. until 1961, when Paul James Phelan, a grandson of the founder, became the president. Upon assuming the presidency, P.J. Phelan began to form the business empire that exists and thrives today. He merged CRNCo. and Aero into a new entity, Cara Operations, and began to reorganize the company; flight kitchens were upgraded, retail outlets were built in the nation's air-ports and shopping centres, and in 1968 Cara became a public com-pany. Of great significance, P.J. committed to professional manage-

1

ment to lead the company.

Boyd Matchett became presi-dent in 1969 and under his leader-ship the company acquired Winco Steak N'Burger, a chain of family-style restaurants, in 1976. The fol-lowing year Cara obtained Food-corp Limited, which brought with it the ownership of Swiss Chalet res-taurants, founded in 1954 with its hallmark strength of spit-roasted chicken and barbecued ribs, and the Harvey's fast-food chain, founded in 1959. In 1984 M. Bernard Syron

2

became Cara's president and C.E.O., assuming the Chairmanship in 1990 with Gunter Otto as presi-dent and C.O.O.

Further expansion occurred in 1990. Cara acquired Grand & Toy Limited, Canada's market leader in both the retail and commercial of-fice products business. In 1991 the Arvak Group of companies was ob-tained, including Beaver Foods Limited, one of Canada's foremost institutional catering companies pro-viding service across Canada, and

1. *An early CRNCo. news-stand in Halifax, Nova Scotia, c. 1910.*
2. *Appreciative passengers receiv-ing a meal pre-pared by Aero Caterers Limited, a subsidiary of CRNCo. started in 1944.*

Summit Food Distributors Inc., a full-line wholesale food distribution company operating primarily in Southern Ontario.

The shift to professional management was accompanied by changes in information technology. In the early days reporting systems, which were sophisticated for the time, enabled CRNCo. to award bonuses, but were no substitute for on the spot family management. Computerization gave professional management the tools to control the business and to allocate capital based on performance. Today, information technology at Cara is evolving to be a key component of satisfying customer needs. Whether the customer is an airline tracking down the cost of a special meal, a business buying office supplies or food products, a family wanting a home delivered Swiss Chalet meal — information technology is the key to prompt, economic service.

The entrepreneurial spirit is alive at Cara today in the form of franchising, with staffing about equal between employees and franchisees (with their staff). The company demonstrates its dedication to staff and franchisees through training at Cara College, the encouragement of long term franchise relationships, competitive compensation, in some cases, partially based on stock performance, employment equity, and team building.

Today the main Cara divisions — Airport Services, Beaver Foods, Grand & Toy, Harvey's, Swiss Chalet, and Summit are leaders in their field. However, Cara, a well-established Canadian company, is but beginning to explore the wider world, with the recent establishment of a Harvey's in Prague, Czech, and a task force analyzing market feasibility in China. The entrepreneurial spirit continues in the decentralized way the company is managed, joint ventures between the divisions, and continued expansion. With ever more professional management, Cara is always ready to go anywhere, anytime to serve its customers.

1

1. *Swiss Chalet, famous for its hallmark spit-roasted chicken and barbecued ribs, is one of Cara's retail divisions.*
2. *Grand & Toy Limited is Canada's market leader in both the retail and commercial office products business, and has been a member of the Cara family of companies since 1990.*
3. *Cara's individual subsidiaries join forces from time to time in displays of interdivisional co-operation, such as at this educational institution cafeteria. Operated by Beaver Foods Limited, it offers choices from the Harvey's fast-food menu and its own brand "Roasters."*

2

3

Credit Suisse Canada

The largest non-North American bank operating in Canada, Credit Suisse Canada is a Canadian chartered bank providing comprehensive financial services in corporate banking, corporate finance, private banking and treasury services. With a Canadian presence for over 40 years, Credit Suisse Canada (CSC) strives to be a customer-oriented organization with a long-term commitment to Canada and a focus on the highest quality service. Through its offices in Toronto, Montreal and Vancouver, CSC services corporate, government and individual clients across Canada.

Credit Suisse, a leading international bank founded in Zurich, Switzerland in 1856, first established a Canadian presence in 1951 in Montreal, Quebec. This agency office, initially staffed with 8 employees, was opened for the purpose of providing Canadian securities safekeeping and custodial services to Credit Suisse branches and clients, as well as a private banking operation.

With the 1980 revision of the Canadian Bank Act, Credit Suisse Canada converted its financial operations into a chartered bank. The head office was moved to Toronto in 1981, and by 1982 CSC had 58 employees. Subsequently, a branch was also opened in Vancouver in 1985. With the expansion in services, the number of employees rose to the current level of 135; loans grew from approximately $325 million in 1982 to over $2.3 billion currently; and total assets rose from $425 million to approximately $3.8 billion.

CSC provides its customers with quality services and sophisticated products tailored to individual needs. Its Corporate Banking section offers credit products such as term loans, revolving credit facilities and standby lines of credit. CSC is active in structured finance transactions including gold loans, oil and commodity monetizations, credit enhancement products and asset securitizations. In cooperation with Credit Suisse in the United States, CSC arranges and participates in project financing for the mining, energy, chemicals, oil and gas, and pulp and paper industries.

Corporate Finance offers a full range of financial advisory services to companies, providing innovative solutions to the strategic and financial needs of corporate customers. It assists clients in maximizing shareholder value through the identification and implementation of domestic and international transaction opportunities. Credit Suisse Canada is recognized as a major player in the syndicated loans market. Its experience in syndicating large transactions includes cross-border and multicurrency term and revolving facilities. The Corporate Finance Group will structure and arrange private placements for the corporate, provincial and municipal customers of Credit Suisse Canada and place the resulting debt with institutional investors including life insurance companies.

Treasury services, with its solid reputation among the leading members in the Canadian marketplace, includes foreign exchange, risk management, money market and precious metals. This area is also responsible for managing the Bank's capital and liquidity position which includes overseeing the hedging of interest rate and currency risks.

Private banking specializes in the management of wealth by extending the highest level of expertise and customer services. It offers sophisticated investment management, financing alternatives, and advisory services to high net worth individuals, private companies and institutions. Portfolio management services are offered on a fully discretionary basis through its wholly-owned subsidiary, Credit Suisse Inc.

In addition, as a vital member of the Credit Suisse worldwide network, which includes over 80 foreign branches, subsidiaries and representative offices, Credit Suisse Canada works closely with its colleagues to provide its Canadian clients with a comprehensive international approach.

Over the years, Credit Suisse Canada has developed a strong position in the Canadian marketplace. Its reputation has been hewn from the same principles of strength, quality, reliability, professionalism and complete confidentiality which have been the hallmarks of Credit Suisse for well over a century — traits that will continue to underpin its success in the future.

1. The head office of Credit Suisse Canada's parent company, Credit Suisse, is located in Zurich, Switzerland.
2. Credit Suisse Canada's head offices are located on University Avenue in Toronto.

1

2

CHIN Radio/Tv International

CHIN Radio/Tv International has been celebrating the differences of the Canadian people for almost three decades. From its roots in radio broadcasting for the people and businesses of Toronto's "Little Italy," CHIN has expanded to radio and television broadcasting in more than 30 languages to over 30 distinct cultural communities in the Southern Ontario area.

After serving in the Second World War, CHIN-founder Johnny Lombardi came home to Toronto and established a grocery business in the area known as Little Italy. Lombardi, who later became known as the "unofficial mayor" of Little Italy, saw the potential of radio programming and went to the air to promote the businesses of his area. However, finding his program passed from station to station by owners who were not as dedicated as he was to the rapidly growing multicultural community, he became determined to establish a radio station which would serve all the minority cultural groups which make up Canada's pluralistic society.

When Lombardi won his radio broadcasting license in 1966, he and several partners formed CHIN radio. But since Lombardi's partners did not share his vision of CHIN radio as a truly multilingual and multicultural radio station, he decided to take the risk of becoming the sole manager of CHIN. Though many thought that a unique, multilingual radio station to serve the ethnic communities was not financially possible, Lombardi knew there was a need that he could fill, so he proceeded to obtain his solo license from the Canadian Radio-television and Telecommunications Commission (CRTC).

Lombardi could now run the station as he thought best, but he still had to convince the CRTC that there was a need for programming

1

in more than Canada's two official languages of French and English. Lombardi persisted in urging the CRTC to accept his multicultural concept and to recognize the need to speak to the immigrant new-comers in their own languages.

CHIN was first heard in 1966 on CHIN-AM 1540, which in 1984 extended its broadcasting time to 24 hours a day. Only a year after CHIN-AM began, Lombardi added CHIN-FM 100.7 to his enterprise. To serve its listeners better, CHIN-FM's broadcasting output was doubled by the replacement of the 4,000-watt transmitter on the CN Tower by an 8,500-watt transmitter in 1992. Culminating 40 years of determined effort by Lombardi, CHIN-FM was granted "special considera-

tion" by the CRTC which cited it as a unique, multicultural broadcasting vehicle in the 1980s. This, however, is by no means the extent of CHIN communications.

When the Global Television Network began broadcasting in 1974, Lombardi recognized another opportunity to expand the extent of CHIN's ability to reach the people beyond Metropolitan Toronto. Global accepted his proposal for CHIN to become an independent producer of language programming on its network. In September of 1994, after airing for two decades on the Global Television Network, CHIN's roster of language programming moved entirely to CITY-TV, and is now beamed to its television viewers from The CHIN Building. Lombardi has provided weekly programs on CITY-TV since 1984. His Italian Variety Show is live-to-air each Sunday from the lobby of The CHIN Building.

More recently, in 1989, CHIN achieved "superstation" status and is now broadcasting satellite pro-

1. *Johnny Lombardi (far left) in a photo taken in Zutphen, The Netherlands, during his service in the Canadian Army in the Second World War.*
2. *A billboard from CHIN's early years in the late 1960s. Its 18-language voice has since increased to more than 30.*

2

gramming nationwide (Anik E1, Channel 2, C Band 7.875 MHz) and to parts of the United States.

In addition to CHIN's broadcasting programs for the ethnic communities throughout Metro Toronto, it also sponsors many ethnic events in this multicultural city, reaching out to the communities it serves to bring people of all ages and backgrounds together. Most famous of these is the annual CHIN International Picnic, the largest free picnic in the world. Originally held on Toronto Island, it has grown so much in popularity and attendance that it now takes place on the grounds of Exhibition Place. CHIN and Lombardi host approximately a quarter of a million people where they "celebrate our differences" over the Canada Day weekend.

CHIN also hosts an annual Italian Day at Ontario Place and an Italian Celebration at Paramount Canada's Wonderland. These festivities provide a place for the community to celebrate "being fiercely Canadian and very proud of heritage." Lombardi and CHIN also bring internationally known artists to perform at such concert halls and stadiums as Massey Hall, Roy Thomson Hall, Maple Leaf Gardens, the O'Keefe Centre, and the SkyDome. CHIN, via its radio and television broadcasting and its staging of events, reaches out and touches, with great impact, the very diverse

1

fabric of the Greater Toronto Area.

A dream come true for Johnny Lombardi was the opening of The CHIN Building in 1992, a self-contained complex which houses CHIN's new home with state of the art radio and television studios, an adjoining shopping mall and housing for seniors. The "Leonardo Court" seniors' housing, named after Johnny's father, is an integral part of The CHIN Building complex, and the product of hard work by Johnny and his family. In 1986, after extensive lobbying, the family was granted the necessary permits to build a senior citizens' home. This home is Johnny's gift to his community for its ongoing loyalty and support throughout the years.

Although Johnny Lombardi is

the president and founder of CHIN Radio/Tv International, he is not the only Lombardi who has devoted his or her life to CHIN. His son, Lenny, is active as CHIN's executive vice-president and his daughters, Theresa and Donina, are busy in their roles as administrator and TV director respectively. However, Theresa points out that her father expected them all to earn the positions they have at CHIN. Beyond family members, CHIN now employs well over 100 producers, announcers and support personnel.

CHIN's multicultural and multilingual programming has preserved the varied cultural heritages of its listeners who have come to Canada from all over the globe. It has introduced the varied cultures of our modern communities to all, so that better understanding and communication can exist between Canadians of all backgrounds. CHIN's goals as a communications organization reflect what Lombardi himself once said, "Let us live in peace together. Let us, the all of us, 'celebrate our differences' together."

The contribution of CHIN to the cause of multiculturalism, understanding and goodwill between people of every national, racial and religious origin has been recognized and acknowledged throughout Canada. With its multiple programs including the recent addition of satellite broadcasting, CHIN Radio/Tv International is very capable of leading multicultural programming in Canada into the future as strongly and surely as it has in the past. Its varied voices echo each other in their desire to create a better understanding of Canada and its multicultural mosaic, whose vibrancy and colour make up Canadian society.

1. *Johnny Lombardi, C.M., O.Ont., OStJ, CavUdR. He is Founder, President and Chief Executive Officer of CHIN Radio/Tv International.*
2. *CHIN's home as it leads multicultural and multilingual programming in Canada into the twenty-first century.*

2

Coffee Time Donuts Inc.

With an insatiable appetite for donuts, the Canadian retail donut industry generates sales approaching one billion dollars annually. Capitalizing on this extraordinary market, Coffee Time Donuts Inc. has become one of the fastest growing franchisors of stores selling coffee and donuts in Canada. A success story which has been developing over the past ten years, Coffee Time now has approximately 200 stores currently located largely in Toronto and around the Golden Horseshoe in Southern Ontario, with plans to expand beyond into new geographic areas throughout Canada and internationally.

The history of the growth of the Coffee Time network in many ways reflects the vision and hard work of its founder and President, Tom Michalopoulos. Aggressively pursuing the development of the chain, and with his personal background and experience in the real estate field, he has been able to successfully direct Coffee Time, capably choosing new sites and communities where to open a new Coffee Time store.

In 1982 Michalopoulos opened his first donut store in Bolton, Ontario. Able to make the venture a success, he opened a second location in Etobicoke and a third in Scarborough in 1983, which became the first to display the Coffee

1

1. *Tom Michalopoulos, Founder and President of Coffee Time Donuts, and his wife Tina Michalopoulos.*
2. *Danny Grammenopoulos, Executive Vice President.*
3. *An innovative and highly successful marketing concept has been the Coffee Time café.*

Time name. Over the next six years several more stores were opened, but it was not until 1989 that the vast groundswell of expansion began to occur.

The Coffee Time chain has experienced a dramatic growth since then, fuelled by a constant flow of quality entrepreneurial franchisees who are attracted by the level of support that the organization provides to all its locations and the comparably low costs of beginning a Coffee Time franchise. Consequently, the demand for franchises continues to grow, allowing the company to be highly selective and

choosing from among only the best.

By the fall of 1990, 25 Coffee Time locations had opened. The following year the number had doubled, and by the fall of 1992, there were over 85 sites. During 1993 and 1994 the growth has been even more sensational, with in excess of 200 stores displaying the Coffee Time name by the end of 1994.

This rapid growth in locations has occurred through the establishment of new Coffee Time branches as well as the conversion of existing donut stores operating under another name. As the industry continues consolidating from an

2

3

independent group of disorganized, scattered and competing producers into an organized group of large franchisors, one may expect more individual and independent locations to continue to convert their facilities into a Coffee Time location.

In 1991 Coffee Time opened its present corporate head offices on Ellesmere Road in Scarborough. Future plans include moving all corporate functions to a new centralized inhouse distribution business, including a 40,000 square feet distribution warehouse, which will offer centralized purchasing along with tighter inventory and operational controls.

The head office operation provides management support, advertising, distribution, and employee training support to its franchises. But one of the most substantial assets that Coffee Time offers is its widely recognized name, signage, logo and store standardization. Michalopoulos, with his personal style of management and as a former real estate agent, spends time reviewing the potential sites as well as attempting to stay in direct contact with the individual operators once the site and franchisee have been selected. Indeed, franchisees often identify him and his support as one of the key elements leading to their success.

Coffee Time stores offer their patrons an ample selection of fresh, quality products — whether for a meal or as a snack. With a focus on a wide variety of donuts and gourmet blended coffee, the menu ex-pands into luncheons such as soups and sandwiches, along with baked goods including muffins, croissants, pastries and other desserts, and a choice of hot and cold beverages. One of the major reasons for the success of a Coffee Time location is precisely the broad spectrum of people it attracts, from the breakfast crowd to the luncheon rush to evening snackers. And for customers who do not wish to take the time to come into a store, many full-producing and satellite Coffee Time stores now also have drive-through capabilities.

In addition to the traditional donut store style, Coffee Time has developed several innovative new concepts in retailing. One highly successful concept has been the development of café style locations, encompassing the idea of two stores in one — something for everyone at one location. On one side is the typical Coffee Time store. However, occupying the other portion, there is a fully licensed café style setting, complete with distinctive colours, a sit-down menu and table service. Three of these café style locations have been opened to date.

Another novel marketing concept being implemented is the Coffee Time "Express" consisting of kiosks, carts and free-standing drive-through locations. With a modular design showcasing the menu, they are fashioned for use in high traffic areas, such as in educational institutions, service stations, hotels, office buildings, and other institutions.

Coffee Time has carefully con-centrated its development focus within a manageable geographic area, but plans are in place to extend into other cities and towns, first in Ontario and then into other parts of Canada, the United States, and beyond. It is careful to develop and pursue its geographic expansion cautiously, where demand is sufficient to allow for rapid growth and a strong market presence.

Reflecting on Coffee Time's remarkable success, Michalopoulos attributes the accomplishments to the ideal combination of advertising support, product assortment, careful site selection, rigorous training, ongoing follow-up support, superior design and construction; and the Coffee Time team, including its franchisees, among the best in the industry, as well as its head office staff, committed to the success of the company, such as Danny Grammenopoulos, Executive Vice President and a key performer in the company's rapid expansion.

The fastest growing company of donut store franchises in Canada, Coffee Time Donuts is poised for the future, anticipating continual sustained growth because, as the company's slogan succinctly emphasizes, "Coffee Time Is Anytime."

1. Coffee Time kiosks — a modular design fashioned for high traffic areas — can be found in educational institutions, service stations, hotels, office buildings, and other institutions.
2. An important milestone — celebrating the opening of Coffee Time's 100th store.

1

2

COSTI

COSTI is Canada's largest education and social service agency with a specific mandate to provide services to new Canadians and their families. Reflecting a holistic view of their needs, COSTI programs encompass immigrant orientation, education, training and employment.

COSTI (incorporated as COSTI-IIAS Immigrant Services) originated with the amalgamation, in 1981, of two major service agencies, COSTI (formerly Centro Organizzativo Scuole Tecniche Italiane) and the IIAS (Italian Immigrant Aid Society), each of which had a lengthy and proud history of service in the immigrant community.

COSTI was established in 1962 to help recent Italian immigrants obtain the professional qualifications required to practise their trades in Canada. Its first operations were based in a church basement in Toronto and were soon moved to an old unused mansion at 136 Beverley Street owned by the Italian government. Whereas COSTI currently operates with a ten million dollar annual budget, its first fund drive raised $3,600 through the diligent work of volunteers campaigning door to door.

COSTI's first Director and Co-Founder, Joe Carraro, believed that the best way for immigrants to become full contributors to their new society was to become a genuine part of it. "Integration through education" became COSTI's motto. Integration, in this context, was seen as the ability to interact productively with Canadian society while maintaining one's own cultural identity and independence, if so desired. To prepare immigrants for the English-language licensing examinations which they were required to pass in order to work, COSTI workers organized English language instruction programs. For those who wanted to enter apprenticeship programs, COSTI also provided upgrading instruction in math and English.

The programs at COSTI soon outgrew its facilities and the organization began working in collaboration with technical education centres in the area. As the number of clients increased, a need was perceived not only for vocational counselling, but for general and family counselling as well. By the end of the 1960s, the agency had opened counselling offices in Hamilton, suburban North York and elsewhere in Metropolitan Toronto.

In 1966, the Worker's Compensation Board contracted COSTI to begin a program to rehabilitate injured workers. People who were unable to continue working at their present job because of injuries were retrained for new occupations. Due to the increasing number of people being helped by COSTI, the retraining shop was moved to a 20,000 square foot facility in 1976. In 1969, COSTI became part of the United Way network and at the same time began serving immigrants from other countries in addition to those from Italy.

During the 1970s, COSTI's services expanded once again to include aid for refugees coming to Canada. Recognizing a pressing need for many of the Vietnamese "boat people" to confirm their true level of education, COSTI developed an examination and certification process in conjunction with George Brown College, the first program of its kind in Canada. Due to increased refugee immigration and COSTI's record of success in meeting the needs of refugees, the number of COSTI clients who are refugees has since increased to 18 per cent.

Like COSTI, IIAS was formed to help recent immigrants in Canada. Also first meeting in a church, IIAS was established in 1952. Originally, its main purpose was to provide newcomers with their basic necessities. Meeting immigrants at Union Station in Toronto, workers would then help them find places to stay, jobs to go to, and would follow up with orientation counselling designed to help the immigrants be more comfortable in their new country. IIAS also expanded its services to include helping immigrants with

1. COSTI's founding in 1962 was in the basement of a church. It subsequently moved to this lovely mansion, which now serves as the Italian Consulate. COSTI now provides services out of 11 different locations in the Greater Toronto Area.
2. In the 1960s COSTI was founded to help thousands of Italian skilled tradesmen to obtain their provincial certificate of qualification. Today COSTI continues that tradition by providing training and counselling to thousands of newcomers from all over the world.

1

2

paperwork to qualify for Unemployment Insurance and other government benefits and assistance they were entitled to. Because the goals and work of IIAS and COSTI were very similar, negotiations were initiated in 1980 to amalgamate the two agencies. On January 24, 1981 this goal was achieved and the organizations were merged under the official name of COSTI-IIAS Immigrant Services.

COSTI, as the amalgamated organization is commonly referred to, has expanded so that it now assists 30,000 people annually. Its largest single program is instruction in English as a Second Language, with some 2,000 students enroled in its classes at any given time. While the main target group identified within the education programs is recently arrived immigrants, service is also provided to disadvantaged adults, youths, and women. The courses offered range from basic literacy to college and university entrance level classes.

There are, however, many additional programs offered by COSTI. They include aid in preparation programs to obtain citizenship papers, services for seniors, vocational and placement services, immigrant settlement services, post-settlement support, programs designed specifically for women, family counselling, and public education. Through these programs, COSTI has expanded to be able to make positive changes in the community as a whole.

COSTI's 160 full-time staff, collectively fluent in more than 30 different languages, are not only multilingual but also multicultural. By hiring workers and counsellors who are familiar with immigrant communities, and largely come from immigrant backgrounds themselves, COSTI is able to reach the community and bring about changes which otherwise would not take place. People are generally more comfortable coming for help to someone who knows their language and culture than going directly to a school or other organization which may not have these advantages. This also enables the staff to better anticipate potential problems with integration into Canadian society and to solve these problems more effectively. In addition, COSTI benefits from many hours donated by willing volunteers who bring new ideas, enthusiasm, and their personal touch to the organization through their involvement.

From its Toronto base, COSTI has expanded throughout Metropolitan Toronto and York Region, opening five different employment and training centres, a Family Counselling Centre that responds to the psychological and social needs of the Italian-Canadian community, and, more recently, a 100-bed Reception Centre for people who have recently come to Canada as refugees.

COSTI strives to be a leader in community service by using a client focused, proactive, and innovative approach in planning, developing

1

and delivering services. Its programs ensure that regardless of language or cultural barriers, people who arrive in Canada are able to use their existing skills, learn new ones, and participate actively in all aspects of Canadian life.

Responding to the immediate and longer-term needs of immigrants is a never-ending process. As one need is met, another emerges. For this reason, COSTI is continually evaluating new programs and making improvements to existing programs to serve the immigrant community which has been able to rely on its service, and to ensure that this community can always continue to do so.

1. *COSTI's work with refugees has led to the establishment of a 50-room Reception Centre. Refugees can be accommodated and provided with orientation, counselling, and assistance in finding permanent accommodations.*
2. *Computers challenge students' hands and minds in one of many COSTI skill training programmes. COSTI provides English language instruction to 16,000 newcomers on an annual basis.*
3. *Injured workers learn to adapt at COSTI's Rehabilitation Centre.*

2

3

The Dominion of Canada General Insurance Company

The biggest natural catastrophe in Canadian history occurred on September 7, 1991 in Calgary, Alberta. In just 30 minutes, a hailstorm ravaged parts of the city and the surrounding area, causing over $300 million in damage to automobiles and property. Miraculously, there were no personal injuries.

The Dominion of Canada General Insurance Company was on the scene, helping hailstorm victims restore their lives to normal by sending 64 employees from across the country to Calgary to assist in the crisis situation. Three weeks after the storm hit, 6,700 automobile and property claims had been made with The Dominion.

The frequency and severity of hailstorms, especially in Alberta, is increasing each year from June through September. The Dominion's stability makes it possible to provide comfort when such disasters occur.

The story of The Dominion of Canada General Insurance Company runs parallel with the history of Canada. It is a story of people working to achieve personal success while providing their fellow Canadians with insurance services vital to their businesses, their homes, and their lives. It is the story of a company that grew over a period of more than one hundred years, with Canada, and for Canada. Formed by George Gooderham and Sir John A. Macdonald, it was the first wholly Canadian casualty insurance company, founded when the new nation of Canada was large, healthy, strong and twenty years old, when a railroad spanned the country and

1. *The Right Honourable Sir John A. Macdonald, Prime Minister of Canada, 1867-1873 and 1878-1891; and President of the company, 1887-1891.*
2. *George Gooderham, co-founder and President, 1891-1905.*

the pioneer was turning townsman.

George Gooderham was the son of William Gooderham, who, together with James Worts, had founded the venerable Gooderham & Worts Distillery in Toronto. When William Gooderham died in 1881, George Gooderham took over as President, while at the same time serving as President of the Bank of Toronto and the Canada Permanent Mortgage Corporation. George Gooderham saw great opportunities ahead for an insurance company designed to serve this growing nation; it would be truly interwoven with the growth of Canada.

Sir John A. Macdonald, as Canada's first Prime Minister, had a particular interest in the building of our new nation, and wanted a transcontinental economy based on an east-west axis. He had confidence in George Gooderham's new business venture, believing that the new company would serve the country's

1

2

best interests, and he agreed to be President of the company.

Originally, the company was to be incorporated under the name "The Manufacturers' Life and Accident Insurance Company," but it was recommended that two companies be formed, one for accident insurance and one for life insurance. Therefore, on June 23, 1887, Bill 125 was passed in Canada's Parliament and The Manufacturers' Life Insurance Company was born.

When the company commenced business in Toronto at 38 King Street East on November 5, 1887, the city had a population of 181,000. The company's first President was Sir John A. Macdonald and its Vice President was George Gooderham. By early 1890 the Head Office was moved to the Traders Bank Building at the corner of Yonge and Colborne Streets, the rent for which was $600 a year, including taxes, heating and cleaning. At the same time, a typist received eighteen dollars a month and a policy-writer five cents per policy.

When Sir John A. Macdonald died in 1891, George Gooderham was appointed President of the company. The company applied to and was granted by Parliament permission to amend the Act of Incorporation, enabling the company to transact guarantee bond insurance and to change the company's name to "The Manufacturers' Guarantee and Accident Insurance Company."

In 1895 there was a feeling of confidence in the Canadian air, and Prime Minister Sir Wilfred Laurier proclaimed: "The twentieth century will be Canada's." In 1896, the company engaged in a new concept and opened a permanent branch office in Montreal. In the same year, the expanding business required larger quarters and the Head Office was moved to the McKinnon Building, at the corner of Jordan and Melinda Streets in Toronto. Two years later, in 1898, the company received permission to change the company name to "The Dominion of Canada Guarantee and Accident

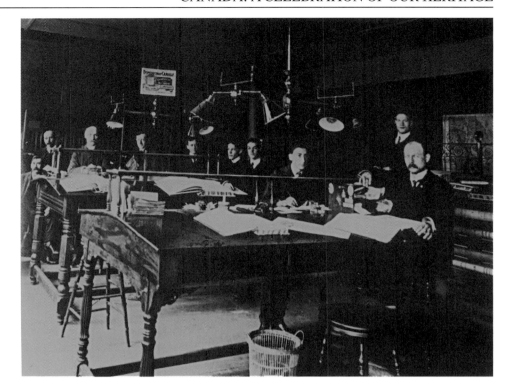

Insurance Company."

In 1905, George Gooderham died and was succeeded as President by his son, Colonel Albert E. Gooderham. The company's first branch office in Western Canada was established in Calgary in 1907. The company prospered in Western Canada and another branch was soon opened in Winnipeg. In 1910, Col. Albert Gooderham was appointed Chairman of the Board and J.E. Roberts became President. It was during this period that new and innovative products, including plate glass and burglary insurance, were added to the company's line of business.

The company celebrated its twenty-fifth anniversary by opening a branch office in Vancouver. In 1914 automobile insurance was included in the company's policies, and, one year later, fire insurance was also included. When J.E. Roberts died in 1916, Col. Albert E. Gooderham was re-appointed President. He continued to strictly adhere to the principle laid down by his father: "We are building for the future, not the immediate present." To this principle of building slowly but surely the company owes much of its growth and success.

During World War I, Col.

The Dominion's Toronto Head Office staff, 1904.

Gooderham, a Colonel of the 10th Royal Grenadiers regiment, co-operated as fully as possible with the government towards the war effort. For example, he provided funds to build a huge complex of laboratories on the outskirts of Toronto to help produce an anti-toxin to combat tetanus poisoning in wounded soldiers.

In 1921, the company opened a new branch in Ottawa. A year later, celebrating its thirty-fifth anniversary, the company moved to the new Dominion Building at 26-28 Adelaide Street East in Toronto. The anniversary brochure proclaimed that "Fairness and promptness in making settlements are a firm policy of the company, as attested by the record that 96 per cent of all claims are settled within one day of receipt of proof." Two years later, the company was authorized to engage in the life insurance business.

The Casualty Company of Canada, which was transacting general insurance business in all the provinces of Canada, was acquired in 1926. In 1927 electrical machinery and inland transportation insurance were added to the company's list of products. During that same year, the company changed its name once again, to The Dominion of Canada General insurance Company.

In 1935, a few months before his death, Col. Albert Gooderham was granted Knighthood in recognition of the extensive public service performed by both himself and his wife, Mary.

He was succeeded as President by his brother, George H. Gooderham. In that year, the company had over 20,000 accident policyholders in every province in Canada, and also in Newfoundland, England and the West Indies; its policies were written in three languages, English, French and Spanish.

The post-war years were years of unbridled optimism and the company prospered. In 1951, Harry W. Falconer was elected President, succeeding Edward D. Gooderham, who had been President from 1943 to 1950. Falconer passed away a few months after being elected, and Henry Stephen Gooderham was appointed President, renewing the continuity of a member of the Gooderham family occupying the Chief Executive position.

In 1961, the company applied for and received a listing on the Toronto Stock Exchange. A new Head Office building was officially opened in 1962, with Henry S. Gooderham stating, "During the past seventy-five years, Canada has developed from a young Dominion to become one of the leading trading nations of the world, and our company, fully owned by Canadians and providing complete insurance coverage for Canadians, has kept pace with that growth." The scene was set for the company to enter the fourth quarter of its first century — a period of twenty-five years in which the annual written premiums for The Dominion would increase more than twenty-fold.

In 1969 the Board of Directors voted to join with The Empire Life Insurance Company as wholly-owned subsidiaries of a new hold-

The company's product range is illustrated by marketing brochures produced between 1941 and 1949.

ing company, E-L Financial Corporation. With a long history of association between the Gooderham's and the Jackman's, who controlled The Empire Life, the move made good financial sense for both companies. While preserving their independent character, the combined organization would result in a stronger entity. Henry R. Jackman, Chairman of the Board of The Empire Life, became President of E-L Financial, and Henry Gooderham became Chairman. Although E-L Financial's interests have expanded, the operating independence of each of the component parts has been a cardinal principle.

In 1969, Henry Gooderham retired as President and was appointed Chairman of the Board, a position he held till his retirement in 1972, when he was succeeded by his son Peter S. Gooderham. A decision was made by The Dominion's Board of Directors to open the position of President to all employees, and H. Norman Hanly was elected President. In 1972, Kenneth G. Hutchison was elected President, overseeing the company till 1978.

One of the more significant corporate decisions of the seventies was to establish a presence in the

Maritime Provinces. A branch office was established in Halifax and a service office in Charlottetown. Both quickly proved successful and The Dominion became a truly national company, from sea to sea. The driving force behind this expansion was Frederick G. Elliott, President from 1978 to 1981.

The company has long been involved in the process of automation, and has been an industry leader in the adoption of new and improved methods. In the 1990s, The Dominion continues to upgrade its information systems. By the 1950s, the old manual computing systems had been mechanized into a new punch-card system. By 1960, the company began the transition to electronic computerization. Today, high speed electronic communication links every office from the Atlantic to the Pacific, paralleling Sir John A. Macdonald's early vision.

In keeping with its commitment to the people of Canada, the company established The Dominion Group Foundation in 1978. Funds are maintained and distributed by the Foundation, which supports a variety of Canadian activities including the arts, athletes with disabilities, education, charitable agencies and institutions, and research projects across Canada.

During the late seventies the company enjoyed productive and profitable times, but soon the world economy weakened and severe recession hit the country. The company's fortunes followed those of the industry with large underwriting losses.

Donald A. Waugh, who began his career with the company as a Claims Supervisor in the Montreal office in 1956, was elected President in 1981. He prepared the company to take its place in the forefront of today's competitive insurance industry. The company retained its strong financial position, and 1983 and 1984 were two of the most successful years in the company's history.

Several new branches were

1

opened in Ontario in the 1980s. By 1985, in addition to the Head Office, The Dominion had a total of twenty-nine offices, including ten full service branch offices, across Canada.

In 1985, The Dominion purchased The Canadian Indemnity Company, a company strong in Western Canada where The Dominion wanted a more prevalent presence. By 1986, the establishment of a single Head Office organization was completed. In that same year, The Dominion sold the American operations of The Canadian Indemnity Company, enabling The Dominion to focus its energies and resources in Canada.

In 1987, The Dominion sold its life insurance operations to Empire Life, another company in the E-L Financial family.

The Dominion continues to seek out new opportunities to develop into the best, the most effective, and the most profitable operation in the Canadian general insurance field. In 1990 the Board of Directors of The Dominion appointed a President and Chief Executive Officer from the financial sector — one of the first insurance companies to do so. Rowland W. Fleming, an experienced senior banker, filled the position of President and Chief Executive Officer on September 1, 1990.

On March 12, 1991, a Letter of Intent was signed whereby The Dominion of Canada General Insurance Company agreed to purchase

the Canadian operations of SAFECO Corporation. This acquisition put The Dominion in the top level of general insurance companies in Canada.

George L. Cooke joined The Dominion as President and Chief Executive Officer on February 17, 1992. Again, the company displayed its progressive edge by seeking a leader who had experience and knowledge of other sectors of the economy in addition to the insurance industry. Mr. Cooke has a distinguished record in both the public and private sectors.

Mr. Cooke joined the company as the property and casualty industry began to face challenge, change and opportunity reflective of the 1990s economy. 1992 saw the introduction of federal and provincial legislation that will significantly affect the industry. A consolidation of the industry is likely, whether through mergers, acquisitions, or withdrawals. The industry must position itself for new competition expected under deregulation from non-traditional players such as banks. It is important to continue to maintain close constructive cooperation with policy makers at federal and provincial levels of government to ensure the interests of the industry are effectively communicated.

To prepare for those imminent changes, during 1991 and 1992, The Dominion underwent a major restructuring of its operations by consolidating branch operations which led to regional centres providing efficient and effective service to brokers and policyholders. Future profitability in the industry is dependent on improved operations management and The Dominion believes its restructuring will accomplish this goal. Both employees and the broker community supported The Dominion through a difficult year of restructuring with a view to the longer term competitiveness.

Reflecting on the hopes for a future equally successful as the company's illustrative history of growth, George Cooke emphasizes, "The insurance industry is faced with many challenges and must change in order to survive. The Dominion is preparing for the future by making those changes."

1. *The Dominion of Canada General Insurance Company's logo, which was once the Canadian Coat of Arms, reflects how the history of the company is closely intertwined with the history of Canada.* 2. *Henry (Hal) N. R. Jackman became Ontario's 25th Lieutenant Governor in 1991. Like his father before him Henry (Harry) R. Jackman, His Honour served on The Board of Directors of The Dominion having first been appointed a Director in 1964 and Honourary Chairman when he accepted his current appointment.*

2

Dovercourt Electro-Plating Co. Ltd.

Automotive parts, appliance parts, and food service products all have one thing in common: each receives its finish through a process known as electro-plating. In an industry whose basic technique is much the same as early in this century, Dovercourt Electro-Plating Co. Ltd. has become an innovator and industry leader, able to rise to the top in a field one could term a "phantom" industry — electro-plating is inherent to many items common to our daily lives, but few people know what is involved in the process or even that the article received such a finish.

Electro-plating is how the vast majority of metal products receive their final finish, through the electro-deposition of one metal over another. The basic process consists of chemically cleaning the parts prior to being placed in a plating tank. The electro-plating itself involves a source of power, a plating solution which acts as an electrolyte, an anode which is usually made from the same metal that is being deposited, and the part that is to be electroplated, which serves as the cathode. As a controlled electrical current is passed from the anode to the cath-

ode, the nickel ions (in a nickel plating tank, for example) are attracted to and adhere to the surface of the cathode, the metal part. Modern, automated facilities may require in excess of sixty individual steps from initial cleaning to finished product.

Electro-plating serves both a cosmetic and protective function. Although a thin layer readily serves to beautify the part, additional corrosion resistance can be obtained through the application of a somewhat thicker finish. Where corrosion resistance is critical, such as with high quality automotive parts, several specialised layers of metal are deposited.

Dovercourt Electro-Plating has been a family business since 1921, and is currently owned by the third generation, Rob and Dave Edwards. Dovercourt began as a modest concern, with a staff of four in a 1,200 square foot facility on Dovercourt Road in Toronto. It was during Bob Edwards' tenure as President, the second generation to be involved with the company, that the company began to expand. Under his management the company grew in equipment, volume and physical

plant size, expanding first to 3,000 square feet, then moving to a 5,000 square-foot factory where it started chrome plating wire work. In 1969 the company moved to a 15,000 square foot location, which was subsequently expanded to 20,500 square feet.

By 1969 the company employed 80 people in a facility which included plating tanks for nickel, zinc, chrome, brass and gold, and was electro-plating washing machine and electrical appliance parts, automotive parts and substantial wire work.

During the 1970s, as the industry began to consolidate, the decision was reached to specialize in high-volume nickel-chrome plating work, and fully-automated equipment for high production was obtained. During the 1980s, as automotive work began to comprise more and more of the work, a second company, known as Autotek Electroplating Inc., was formed in 1987 by the Edwards family. Dave Edwards explains the critical link of the metal finishing industry as an essential service to the manufacturing sector. "If local manufacturers can not obtain quality finishes at competitive prices for their products, then the manufacturing sector will be forced to relocate to an area where they can."

Dovercourt Electro-Plating Co. Ltd. approaches its 75th anniversary as a successful, family-run business, spanning three generations and with the potential of a fourth generation joining the firm — a remarkable accomplishment in today's economy. And with a dedicated workforce of 150 men and women working at two facilities, its high environmental standards, and plans for a third facility based on projected growth, this company will assuredly continue its role as a leader in the electro-plating industry.

Bob Edwards, former President of Dovercourt Electro-Plating, at the company's original premises on Dovercourt Road, c. 1955.

Etobicoke General Hospital

A dynamic and innovative hospital, Etobicoke General employs leading-edge medical technology and progressive management techniques to provide the best and most cost-effective patient care services. Responding to the diverse needs of its growing community, Etobicoke General Hospital provides a comprehensive range of emergency, surgical, obstetrical, paediatric, psychiatric, transitional care, and internal medicine services to residents of the City of Etobicoke, the Malton area of the City of Mississauga, the Town of Vaughan, and some areas of the Peel and York Regions.

Etobicoke General Hospital's story is one of support and concern. Often described as "a testimony to the efforts of the people of Etobicoke," the propelling thrust behind the building of the hospital came from a Founding Committee of concerned citizens. Thanks to that committee, and the efforts of the Auxiliary formed shortly thereafter, the quest for a new hospital to serve the expanding community received much needed volunteer and fundraising support. Officially opened on September 25, 1972, Etobicoke General was heralded as Canada's most modern community hospital.

Built at a cost of $22 million, the 508-bed hospital soon became an innovator in several fields. Etobicoke General Hospital was one of the first health care facilities to combine its obstetrical and surgical suites, complete with 10 major operating rooms, for more effective utilization of equipment and personnel. A pioneer in the use of electronically controlled conveyance of medical and linen supplies, this remote control technology helped to minimize handling of materials for more efficient delivery of fresh goods and return of soiled materials from all points in the hospital.

Throughout its history, the Hospital has continued to monitor and respond to the changing health care needs of its community. Incorporating the latest technological advances and a patient centred care model, in 1992 Etobicoke General opened a newly renovated Emergency Department complete with an After Hours Clinic. Having these side by side services has enabled Emergency Department staff to focus on the care of patients with potentially life-threatening injuries and illnesses, while those requiring less urgent services are also seen in a more timely fashion.

Thanks to the high profile enjoyed by the new hospital, Etobicoke General was able to recruit top-flight surgeons who pioneered unique techniques to use the body's own tissues in breast reconstruction surgery. Used successfully in over 300 patients since 1990, this revolutionary technique enables women who have experienced partial or total breast removal through disease or injury, to have their breasts restored with amazing cosmetic results. This practice helps to enhance self image without further risks associated with implants and their deterioration over time.

One of the first Canadian hospitals to develop an expertise in laparoscopic surgery, the Hospital has always placed a high priority on searching for ways to reduce patient discomfort, scarring and recovery time. Laparoscopic surgery is performed through a special tube inserted in the patient's belly button, virtually eliminating all external scarring. This technique is now used to dramatically reduce the trauma to the body in a wide variety of procedures ranging from hernias to hysterectomies. Surgeons and clinicians from across Canada and around the world have either visited the hospital, or attended international seminars given by Etobicoke General surgeons, to learn these techniques for the benefit of their patients.

Today, Etobicoke General continues to be a testimony to the dedication and compassion of its people, and to the support and involvement of its community. Thanks to advances in medicine and technology, a growing focus for the Hospital is in the areas of day surgery and out-patient services. With more than 90,000 patient visits in 1994, including some 2,600 births and over 55,000 emergency cases, Etobicoke General Hospital remains as vital a resource as when it was first envisioned.

Opened in 1972, Etobicoke General Hospital takes great pride in its role of having served area residents for over 20 years.

The Dufferin Group of Companies

For close to three decades, the Dufferin name has stood for Canadian craftsmanship in the billiard equipment industry. Its tradition of quality and service, that is part of every Dufferin product manufactured, is renowned wherever the game of billiards is played.

The creation of the Dufferin group of companies began with Al and Elizabeth Selinger and Dufferin Cue Ltd. Out of a single wood specialty business four highly successful Canadian companies have been developed: Dufferin Cue Ltd., Selinger Wood Ltd., Dufferin Leisure Ltd. and Dufferin Game Room Store Ltd., as well as Dufferin Inc. in Chicago, Illinois.

It was in 1967 that the Selingers purchased Dufferin Patterns & Wood Specialties. Renamed Dufferin Cue, it was refocussed to produce the highest quality cue at the best possible price. Manufacturing approximately 5,000 cues in the first year, the name soon became associated with the highest cue value on the market. In order to construct the straightest cues, Dufferin Cue hired expert wood craftsmen and built its own custom cue manufacturing equipment to incorporate traditional hand-craftsmanship with high-technology processes.

To ensure a consistent supply of the highest quality maple hardwood needed for cue production, in 1978 the Selingers purchased their principal lumber supplier, a woodworking facility in Goderich, Ontario, and thereby established Selinger Wood Ltd.

With an expanding market for Dufferin products in the United States, in 1981 the Selingers started Dufferin Inc., a sales and distribution facility located near Chicago, Illinois. Six years later, the Selingers continued to expand their presence in the billiards industry with the purchase of a billiard table manufacturing plant that produced

1

2

approximately 300 billiard tables per year, renaming it Dufferin Leisure Ltd. Included in the purchase were the company's existing retail outlets in Edmonton, Calgary, and Winnipeg.

This early foray into retailing lead to the development of the Dufferin Game Room Store, the first of which was opened in 1986 at the Square One Shopping Centre in Mississauga, Ontario. During the next two years, 12 additional stores were opened across the country, including several operated by individual franchise owners.

When Al Selinger passed away in 1992, Elizabeth A. Selinger carried on, with the dual responsibilities of Chief Executive Officer of the Dufferin group and President of Dufferin Cue. A second generation

of Selingers have also joined the management team. Robert Selinger is President of Selinger Wood, Catherine Selinger is President of Dufferin Game Room Store, Roy Selinger is President of Dufferin Leisure, and several other family members are also involved in the family business in other capacities.

Today, Dufferin Cue, Canada's largest manufacturer of billiard cues, is the most technically advanced volume cue manufacturing facility in the world, producing more than one-half million cues annually in 35 different models. Approximately 75 per cent of the production is for export, including large volumes to the United States

1. *Al P. Selinger, who passed away in 1992, was co-Founder of the Dufferin group of companies.*
2. *Elizabeth A. Selinger, co-Founder and Chief Executive Officer of the Dufferin group, and President of Dufferin Cue.*
3. *Dufferin Cue is a premiere supplier of billiard cues worldwide.*

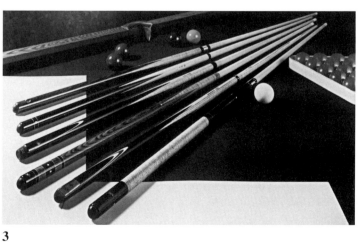

3

and over 50 other countries in six continents. Dufferin's one-piece cue is an industry standard and is considered the "house" cue by most commercial establishments worldwide. In fact, an estimated 75 per cent of North American clubs insist on Dufferin cues. Furthermore, its two-piece cues are also favourites of both leisure and professional pool, snooker and carom players.

Selinger Wood now processes five million board feet of hardwood per year, one-third of which is for sale to the export market. The wood is used as the raw material for Dufferin cues and billiard tables, as well as flooring, toys, furniture, tool handles, bowling lanes, bowling pins, and other leisure items.

Dufferin Leisure is Canada's largest billiard table manufacturer, producing more than 5,000 tables annually in 15 different models. More than 80 per cent of Dufferin tables are sold for residential use, with the remaining 20 per cent sold in the commercial billiard club market. In addition, Dufferin Leisure also produces many billiard room accessories such as cue racks, scoreboards and bars. The vast majority of billiard clubs in Canada use Dufferin billiard equipment.

Dufferin Game Room Store has developed into a highly successful and rapidly growing national retail chain. Offering all the essentials for a good time with family and friends, its retail outlets sell a wide range of items, from Dufferin billiard tables and Dufferin cues to table tennis, dart boards, board games, electronic games, puzzles, and other game room accessories. There are currently more than 50 Dufferin Game Room Stores nationwide, and both in 1993 and 1994 Dufferin Game Room Store Ltd. was named as one of Canada's fastest growing companies. To ensure it offers the very best products and services, Dufferin Game Room Store retains the services of several official technical advisors, including Canadian and Former World Snooker Champion Cliff Thorburn,

1

other professional pool players, table tennis and dart players.

Despite its growth, the Dufferin group of companies has retained a family feeling. "Our customers are families and we are a family business," explains Elizabeth Selinger. "The tightknit family atmosphere among ourselves and our staff is the essential core of the business." It is an approach that has allowed Dufferin to grow significantly, while maintaining unsurpassed quality standards, and the personal touch of a family-run enterprise.

To better realize the combined synergies of the individual companies in the Dufferin group, in early 1995 the three principal companies — Dufferin Leisure, Dufferin Cue and Dufferin Game Room — moved into a unified 163,000 square foot facility in Mississauga, Ontario. The new site houses two

manufacturing plants, a warehouse for the Toronto area retail operations, plus head offices for the three companies.

Since the early attempts to produce the world's straightest billiard cue in 1967, the Dufferin name today is considered to be synonymous with the best in billiards. An established industry leader, the Dufferin group of companies is now well poised for further accomplishments based on the principles — quality, tradition and family fun — that brought Dufferin such success in the past.

1. Dufferin Game Room Store began in 1986 and has more than 50 locations across Canada, including this franchise store in Victoria, British Columbia.
2. Dufferin Leisure is the largest billiard table manufacturer in Canada, producing over 5,000 tables annually in 15 different models.

2

EM Plastic & Electric Products Limited

The roots of this dynamic business organization can be traced back to August of 1967, when James Gutmann, Dr. Otto Röhm and Dr. Gerhart Ziener established their first distribution business venture in Canada. Two years later, they expanded the business significantly with the purchase of an electrical wholesale company, Eugen Meth and Associates, which had locations in Montreal and Toronto. With the financial counsel of Joe Melotek of Akler Melotek, Chartered Accountants, those early years in the company's history were marked by entrepreneurship tempered with a sense of evolving market economics, focused on materials distribution.

In the early 1970s, the company name was changed to EM Plastic & Electric Products Limited reflecting the broader base of product in the company's portfolio. The EM prefix is linked to the original founder, Eugen Meth, whose energy and foresight provided much of the foundation of the business enterprise. Meth retired shortly after selling his business, turning over the stewardship to James Gutmann. In the early years, under Gutmann's leadership, the business prospered and was soon ready to begin a period of expansion that has continued to this day.

In 1972 EM Plastic made an important strategic move to acquire William H. Steer, a Vancouver based company that was primarily engaged in the distribution of electrical and neon materials supplies to support the signage and display markets. With the addition of plastic products, this company later became EM's British Columbia operation. Throughout this time EM Plastic began to shift its operations to include the distribution of a wider range of plastic sheet goods, chemicals, adhesives and paints in addition to products required by the sign industry.

While EM Plastic consequently found extended markets for its ex-

1

panding product lines it also found a need to open new branch facilities in Manitoba and Alberta. Under the management of Russ Thompson, a branch was opened in Winnipeg in 1974 and the following year an Edmonton location, directed by Stuart Barker, was put into place. Both Barker and Thompson have proven to be capable managers, with acute sensitivities to the customer, while continuing to set their sights on even greater opportunities for growth.

Since then the company continued to expand, adding warehouse facilities and offices in Dartmouth, Nova Scotia in 1979 and St. John's, Newfoundland in 1983. During this period of expansion, the EM Company continued to be decentralized in nature while developing critical commercial mass. It was also coming to terms with its longer range goals and experimentation with its business strategy. It was during these latter years that the Board of Directors made the conscious decision to step

1. To provide superior levels of service, EM Plastic delivers over two-thirds of its customers' orders with its own trucks.
2. Advanced paint mixing facilities in all branches, like this one at EM Vancouver, allow EM to provide one more instant, customized, value adding service to its sign and graphics customers.
3. With state-of-the-art conversion equipment in every warehouse, EM Plastic can custom cut any substrate, saving its customers time and waste material, and ultimately making them more profitable.

back from the operational aspects of the business and bring in a dedicated business manager entrusted with leading the company's future prosperity and growth objectives.

The process of soul searching and business planning introspective was further facilitated by the purchase of Neo Valves in 1987. This valve distribution company, served three primary engineering market segments: commercial, industrial and waste water treatment. At this same time, Gutmann was ready to retire from running the consolidated EM Group of businesses and selected his long time acquaintance, Rae Townsend to succeed him as

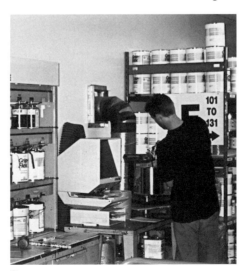

2

3

President and Chief Executive Officer in 1988.

With the adroit financial skills of Sam Landzberg, of Akler Melotek Frimet & Landzberg, Chartered Accountants, and the insightful legal counsel of Chris Dymond, of Dymond & Associates, as well as Townsend's considerable international business skills and his uncompromising passion for operational excellence and market focus, Gutmann's high hopes for management succession could now be realized.

One of the first tasks was to crystallize the EM Groups' Vision, Mission and Operating Objectives in order to renew the company's business energy, enterprise and focus. Simply put, EM Groups' vision is to be an internationally competitive, integrated, market driven organization that through a selective strategy of materials distribution enhances the long term prosperity of its customers, suppliers, employees and EM Group of Companies as a whole.

Its mission: to maximize and capitalize on its business strengths, diversities, synergies of products and materials application technologies to maintain or become the dominant market leader. In 1992, it acquired selected assets of Geiger Plastics & Rubber to further expand its "readiness to serve" capabilities in the Windsor, Ontario market and, subsequently, in 1993 opened a sales office in Detroit, Michigan. To date, this exceptional company

is one of Canada's largest materials distribution companies serving the signage, display, fabrication, screenprint, glazing, industrial valve, and waste water treatment industries.

With warehouses and offices across Canada, including locations in St. John's, Dartmouth, Quebec City, Montreal, Toronto, Windsor, Winnipeg, Edmonton, Calgary and Vancouver, it is clear that the company provides a most significant link between international and North American manufacturers of plastic sheet goods, valves, electrical products and chemicals within the confines of the Canadian market place.

Throughout the United States, Neo Valves enjoys a broad base of sales through sales agents in 24 states, with a view to expanding its commercial representation throughout North, South and Latin America. Waste water and sewage treatment facilities will singularly remain a critical issue to expanding commercial, industrial and residential growth and prosperity.

With EM Plastic and Neo Valves well positioned, The EM Group now has its current sights on further business expansion. There is little doubt in its capabilities to realize its business objectives if the past is any indication of the future.

Whatever the need — from plastic for motorcycle wind shields and industrial glazing, ballasts and lamps for signage, resilient seal gate valves for water treatment facilities,

3

absorbents to pick up and contain environmentally dangerous chemicals, or screenprint inks and emulsions to be used in retail displays — this company has no equal in North America. EM remains singularly focused as having materials distribution expertise with market and customer focus. It simply provides seamless applications solutions based on the most technologically advanced materials.

Today, with in excess of 130 employees, the EM Group of materials distribution businesses provides over 5,000 products for thousands of clients both large and small. Of note, in each of the markets it chooses to serve, its customers remain the who's who of industry and market leadership.

The transformation of a good business into one which is a great business has been based on the strong contingent of human resource talent and management direction at the EM Group. There is little doubt that EM Plastic & Electric Products Limited and Neo Valves takes a great deal of pride in its past, but most importantly can look to the future with even greater promise.

1. *Sign vinyls can be cut to customer specified length — meeting customers' exact requirements.*
2. *Modern, efficient warehouse facilities, conveniently located across Canada, provide customers with local access to the full spectrum of The EM Group's broad product offering.*
3. *EM's head office, located in Downsview, Ontario.*

1

2

Etobicoke Ironworks Limited

Etobicoke Ironworks Limited is the largest manufacturer of scaffolding in Canada. The scaffolding produced at Etobicoke Ironworks is used throughout Canada, the United States, Mexico, Taiwan, Japan and Italy. In addition to this, the company is rapidly expanding to other markets around the world. Not limited to scaffolding, the company also produces structural steel and miscellaneous ironwork for use in the construction industry.

The story of this unique company originated when it was incorporated in 1945 as a division of Dundas Iron. In 1956 Hank Rosati acquired the miscellaneous ironworks division from Dundas, moved to a new location in the City of Etobicoke and appropriately renamed the company Etobicoke Ironworks Limited. It began as a small business, manufacturing and installing steel railings and miscellaneous ironwork. The company succeeded in the early years, and by the late 1960s Hank Rosati invited his brother Al Rosati to join him in the running of the company. Al accepted the challenge, and took over much of the administrative work. Continuing to prosper under the new arrangement, within a few years the company moved from its original premises in Etobicoke to a new building at its present location in Weston, remaining in the Toronto area.

At this same time, Etobicoke Ironworks added the manufacture of structural steel to its ironworks.

The amount of work done in structural steel increased as demand grew, and thus it became the mainstay of the company through the 1970s and 1980s. It continues to be an important element of the business today. Meanwhile, the Rosatis consistently expanded the facilities at the Weston location, constructing and purchasing new buildings as it became necessary.

In the early 1970s the company added the manufacture of quality scaffolding to its operations. Carrying on with the manufacture of structural steel, scaffolding and its miscellaneous ironworks, Etobicoke Ironworks continued to flourish under the steady management of the Rosati brothers until their retirement in 1988.

With the retirement of the Rosatis, John Brasil became president and took over the management of the company. Brasil, in the early 1980s, was involved in setting up the company's robotic welding process for the manufacturing of scaffolding. Under the new ownership and management Etobicoke Ironworks introduced the innovative and new generation Total Scaffold System.

Scaffolding, unlike structural steel, can economically be shipped long distances and is not limited to local markets. In order to take advantage of the opportunities this created, Brasil began the expansion of Etobicoke Ironworks' scaffolding market. As a result of this new strategy, the company now has inde-

1

pendent distributors throughout Canada and the world. Each distributor buys scaffolding, shoring and formwork systems from Etobicoke Ironworks and then sells or rents them independently. In 1988, the manufacture of scaffolding comprised 20 per cent of the company's

1. *Over the years, Etobicoke Ironworks Limited has fabricated many iron stairways and handrails.*
2. *Structural steel for the construction of industrial buildings is another area of specialty for the company.*
3. *Etobicoke Ironworks has provided scaffolding systems for construction projects around the world, including this bridge project in Hong Kong.*

2

3

work. Today it has grown to where it accounts for some 60 per cent.

Part of the reason for this extraordinary success is the versatile design of the scaffolding. The Etobicoke Ironworks' Total Scaffold System is based on a sophisticated completely modular system, with all components engineered to lock onto a unique rosette, minimizing the number of pieces and keeping all parts standard and flexible. In addition, the components are hot dipped galvanized, resulting in a much longer maintenance-free life span, and robotically welded with state-of-the-art equipment. All standard components are kept in stock to allow for fast delivery to the customer with specialized components manufactured on demand. There are no loose fittings such as nuts, bolts or clamps to be lost, and the scaffolding is shipped ready for use. This allows the scaffolding to be set up quickly and easily, (one person with a hammer can erect the system) without compromising safety.

Etobicoke Ironworks' Total Scaffold System can be put to countless uses. In new construction it is set up both inside and outside buildings for purposes including brick-laying, electrical and painting. Because it can easily be adapted to overcome steep angles and irregular shapes, the scaffolding is also ideal for use in restoration and renovation projects. A recent example of this application is the extensive restoration work completed on Ontario government build-

1

ings at Queens Park in Toronto, where Etobicoke Ironworks supplied all the scaffolding.

In addition to new construction and renovation, the Total Scaffold System can also be erected in or around the most complex structures, such as pipes or smokestacks or inside large tanks. For this reason, the scaffolding is used widely in the oil industry, where it is applied both to the repair of above-ground pipelines and for work at refineries (on- and off-shore) where it may be seen stacked hundreds of feet high. In the pulp and paper industry the Total Scaffold System is used inside large boilers for cleaning and maintenance.

The versatility of Etobicoke Ironworks' Total Scaffold System even allows the scaffolding to be easily converted to temporary grandstands or stages for use at special events.

Although the production of scaffolding accounts for most of the work done at Etobicoke Ironworks today, the company continues to

1. *The company's shoring and form-work systems, renown in the industry, are used in the construction of many concrete buildings, such as this edifice in Kochi, Japan.*
2. *The company's scaffolding was employed for the reconstruction work of the Canadian National Exhibition's Princes Gate in 1994.*
3. *The scaffolding is also used in such venues as musical concerts.*

manufacture structural steel and miscellaneous ironwork such as the fabrication of handrails and metal stairways. The structural steel the company produces is used primarily in the construction of industrial buildings.

Etobicoke Ironworks Limited currently employs 70 people at their 65,000 square foot facilities. It occupies five buildings and, due to its growing market, will soon be adding another building to provide them with a much-needed additional 25,000 square feet. Some 50 per cent of its business is for export, to markets that have been largely developed over the past few years.

It seems certain that the company's unique products, combined with the careful management that has characterized this company, will continue to make further inroads into the global market in the future.

2

3

Hakim Optical Laboratory Limited

When a nine year old boy in Tehran, Iran went to work to help support his impoverished family, little did he realize that one day he would be presiding over one of the most successful optical companies in Canadian history. Karim Hakim, combining his tradesman background, an innate marketing savvy, and an unflagging work ethic, has been able to carve a formidable niche in the Canadian optical market. By consistently offering value, selection and customer service over the years, Hakim has carefully nurtured Hakim Optical Laboratory Limited from a one-man operation into Canada's largest optical retailer.

To understand the growth and unequalled success of Hakim Optical, one must understand its history, and its history is very much the story of Karim Hakim and his ability to learn from his experiences and see opportunities where others saw only difficulties, obtaining success where others have been met with failure.

Forced to quit school and go to work at the tender age of eight because his father had died and he was needed to help support his mother, he found work at a blacksmith's shop, blowing the bellows for the fire. A physically demanding job, the slender boy could not handle the punishing hours at the forge and left after six months. Soon after, he began working for a man who ground magnifying glass from old window panes. It was here, under the watchful eye of an unforgiving mentor, where he became well-versed in the many aspects of the optical field, from the intricacies of lens grinding to the maintenance of equipment and upkeep of worn machinery.

Yearning for an education, he decided to run away to the Soviet Union in search of schooling. Caught by a border guard and re-

Forced to seek employment to aid his impoverished family, Karim Hakim, founder and President of Hakim Optical Laboratory Limited, began learning the lens-grinding trade at the young age of nine in his native Tehran, Iran.

turned home, the enterprising teenager enlisted in night school at the age of 14 to learn how to read and write.

Enlisting in the Iranian navy at 19, he tasted the savoury experiences of the outside world, and decided to emigrate. Arriving in Germany, he worked at grinding precision lenses for instruments before leaving for Switzerland and engaging in similar work. It was during this period that he perfected his craft as a lens grinder, learning modern methods for the grinding of optical lenses for precision instruments and eyeglasses.

Immigrating to Canada in search of a successful future, he found work in the ophthalmic lens grinding field, saving his hard-earned money and gaining expertise in his new land, all the while biding his time — waiting for the chance to strike out on his own. In 1967 he was able to set up a laboratory (in a dance hall in the former Elmwood

Hotel) with basic equipment, and soon after opened a laboratory on Elm Street in Toronto. Later on, he bought old equipment from a retiring lab. in Chicago and brought the 30 year old machinery to Canada where he rebuilt it himself and made millions of pairs of lenses with the old equipment.

He began by selling his lenses to opticians and optometrists. The shops supplied him with the frames and he would grind, polish and mount the lenses, and then deliver them to his clients for $3.50 to $4.00 per pair. He soon began receiving patients directly with their orders from ophthalmologists and business rapidly expanded through word-of-mouth advertising.

Grinding lenses day after day, he quickly realized that it did not make sense to sell lenses for four dollars and then watch the final product retail for as much as $80, and vertical integration soon appeared as the next logical step.

Although able to make a good living as a wholesaler, opportunities in the retailing aspect of the business were too intriguing to pass over, so he decided to launch into retailing as well.

A key factor in the growing success of Hakim Optical was that while in the wholesale trade the profit margin was less than a dollar, by selling directly to the public he was able to earn over five dollars as profit, and still be able to retail much cheaper than other shops. During the day he would sell as many as 80 pairs of glasses, and then it was not unusual for him to stay at the business most of the night grinding the lenses, as he always promised the finished product would be done in 24 hours.

By giving honest value, he attracted more and more people, and the retail portion of sales soon dominated the business. Hakim recalls, "The place was rather small, and at times it became so full that customers had to wait outside until someone else left." Needing to expand to make more space for the showroom at the front of the store, he moved his machinery first to the back of the store and later to the basement, when the store took over the entire main floor for eye examinations

1

and the showroom.

The success of Hakim Optical can be in many ways attributable to Hakim's philosophy of giving personal attention to each customer. Pleased eyeglass wearers would leave and many times come back, bringing with them new customers. Not wanting to turn away a single customer, including those with other than regular prescriptions, he ambitiously began to grind specialty lens orders, such as those required for cataract patients.

Furthermore, by maintaining the lens grinding operation, he was able to keep his prices down. Hiring young workers, he personally trained them in his successful techniques, and many of his early workers are still with the company as opticians and technicians. Letting his able staff run more and more of the technical side of the operation under his tutelage, Hakim himself began to concentrate on the business

1., 2. With 70 showrooms and 45 one hour factory locations across Southern Ontario, Nova Scotia and Florida, Hakim Optical sells as many as 1,000 pairs of prescription eyeglasses daily, and is able to supply any type of lens that its customers may require, from contact lenses to specialty lenses.

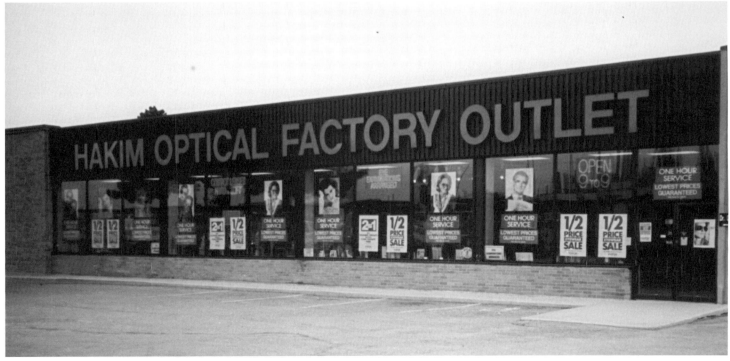

2

1

aspects of the operation in search of further growth in new retail areas.

The company's quest for customer value is one of the key factors to the extremely loyal client base the company now enjoys. Looking to offer more value to his customers, Hakim began buying frames at bankruptcy sales — as many as he was able and at bargain prices — and was able to offer these free to the customer for the price of a pair of lenses.

Realizing the successful nature of this innovative marketing con-

cept, Hakim began buying thousands of fashion frames at value prices directly from manufacturers at middle man prices, thereby widening the selection of free frames for the customer. Quality is always of prime concern, as the company offers a certificate that guarantees against breakage on all Hakim frames for a period of one year.

At one point, Hakim Optical had potential difficulty with the federal Department of Consumer and Corporate Affairs over claims of having

the lowest prices in town. The company was thoroughly investigated but, to the competition's surprise, no prosecution ensued, because it was revealed that Hakim Optical's claim was indeed a valid one.

1., 2. Emphasizing the fact that eyeglasses are a vital fashion accessory, Hakim Optical's customers are able to choose from a wide selection of more than 3,000 free fashion frames imported from around the world, with brand name and signature frames also available for a small additional charge.

2

Many customers appreciate Hakim Optical's emphasis that eyeglasses are a vital fashion accessory and are attracted by the store's philosophy that eyewear should look good on the person. Often, just the right frame can give someone that total fashion look. "A pair of glasses isn't just a device to aid your eyesight, they're fashion," Hakim emphasizes. Hakim Optical supports these sentiments with a selection today of more than 3,000 fashion frames imported from as far away as the Far East, Italy, France and Germany.

Having moved into its current head office in 1987, Hakim Optical now has over 500 employees in total, including many who are trained technicians and qualified opticians, some of whom have over 20 years of experience. On a good day, the company sells as many as 1,000 pairs of prescription eyeglasses at its 70 showrooms and 45 one hour factory outlets located across Southern Ontario and in Nova Scotia and Florida.

Providing complete eyeglass services, Hakim Optical is able to supply any type of lens that its customers may require, from contact lenses to specialty eyeglass lenses, and is now believed to be the largest in Canada in retail sales. In addition to the wide selection of free quality fashion frames, brand name and signature frames are also available for a small additional charge.

With the ongoing success of his stores, Karim Hakim himself now has some time to relax at his home, which includes such amenities as tennis courts, and indoor and outdoor swimming pools — the outdoor model, which he points out, is the largest residential pool in Canada. When on vacation, he can be found many times cruising on his own 39.5 metre long luxury yacht, whose layout and furnishings were chosen personally by himself.

Today, Hakim Optical has proven Hakim's philosophy that a successful enterprise must be built on service. He points out that he

1

was not trained as a businessman, but as a good lens grinder; when he started in business, he was only aware of his skill and giving the customer the best quality at the best price. His golden rule, instilled into all the employees, "serve as you would be served," has paid off well, with close to 80% of the store's clientele being repeat customers.

Having sold over eight million pairs of eyeglasses, Hakim Optical Laboratory Limited stands as a motivating rags-to-riches testimony of one man's drive and determination to overcome obstacles, an inspiring symbol to the Canadian en-

trepreneurial spirit, and an overwhelming success in the retail optical industry.

1. *Hakim Optical is now believed to be Canada's largest optical supplier based on retail sales, employing over 500 trained technicians and qualified opticians, with its success attributable to the company's all-encompassing emphasis on customer service — giving the customer the best quality at the best price.*
2. *By consistently offering value, selection, and customer service over the years, Karim Hakim has carefully nurtured a one-man operation into one of the most successful optical companies in Canadian history.*

2

Harcros Pigments Canada

From initially producing iron oxide for its pigmentary value, Harcros Pigments Canada has moved to the forefront of its field as a quality manufacturer of iron oxide. Today, Harcros iron oxides are used to meet the unique needs of a broad base of worldwide industries. From bricks to paints, from toy finishes to cosmetics, and from the electronics industry to rocket propellant, Harcros iron oxides have become an essential ingredient in a wide array of indispensable products.

Harcros Pigments Canada began in Toronto in 1929, founded as Northern Pigment Ltd. by Norman Zoph, when wages were $18 a week for a 48 hour work week. Northern Pigment's ferric oxide pigments were originally destined for the paint industry, the only manufacturing segment to employ oxide pigments at the time. The company began by producing yellow iron oxides, serving both the Canadian and export markets. Equipment for the production of red oxides was installed as demand grew. With a strong emphasis on developing new markets and products, Northern Pigment's technical group was responsible for pioneering a number of new products and uses, such as in the electronics field.

In 1945, a devastating fire destroyed a major part of the plant fa-

1

cility. The following year, Zoph and his partners sold their interest to Canadian Corporate Management Co. Ltd. A program of reconstruction was undertaken and expansion ensued, as markets increased and demand grew. In 1986, the business was purchased by Canadian-based Federal Industries. Then, in 1992, the business was acquired by Harcros Pigments. As an integral member of this global company, the Toronto facility was renamed Harcros Pigments Canada.

There was much synergy in this acquisition, since Harcros Pigments had been in the iron oxide business since the mid-1800s. Today, Harcros Pigments has iron oxide operations in Great Britain, France, Mexico, Canada, and the United States

and serves customers in over 165 countries.

Since 1992, Harcros Pigments Canada has been transformed into a customer service operation. Instead of manufacturing iron oxide particles, the Toronto operation focuses on providing a quick response to marketplace requirements. This is achieved by sourcing quality iron oxides from Harcros Pigments' worldwide operations and customizing them to meet individual customer needs. Harcros Pigments Canada's extensive blending operation, when combined with its field sales and technical service team, creates a highly responsive centre able to match customer colour and physical property targets within a very short

1. c. 1942. Since its founding in 1929 as Northern Pigment, Harcros Pigments Canada has been dedicated to the manufacture of iron oxides.
2. In 1945 a disastrous fire destroyed a large portion of the plant and manufacturing facilities.
3. Recovering from the fire, the company returned invigorated and ready to meet the expanding demand for its product.

2

3

period of time.

Harcros Pigments has the broadest range of iron oxide colours on the market, many of which have become worldwide standards. The company is one of the largest manufacturers of natural and synthetic iron oxides in the world, with over 200 separate products. Harcros' expertise and resources have enabled it to produce the finest quality iron oxide pigments supported by a strong technical service and field sales organization.

Harcros Pigments, today, is proud to offer a product line that is developed from the broadest range of iron oxide manufacturing process options in the world. For over a century Harcros has evolved these processes with continuous improvement and innovation. Generally, the processes may be categorized into two types: precipitation and calcination. Some products, however, are manufactured by a combination of these two general process routes.

Engineered to be non-toxic, non-hazardous and environmentally friendly, Harcros' iron oxides play an important role in our life. Iron oxides are essential pigments in most coating systems, from primer paints to architectural paints and wood stains. They are also the primary colouring agent for construc-

1

tion products such as concrete block, concrete brick, paving stone, concrete retaining walls, and mortar. They are even found in concrete roof tiles and asphalt shingles, providing the varied shades that we see atop of each house.

Harcros iron oxides also play a major role in the electronics field. Soft ferrite magnets are found in televisions and computers. Other specialty uses include toner for copier machines and laser printers, propellant for automobile airbags, and burn control for the solid rocket boosters used on the space shuttle. Harcros iron oxides are also used as a colourant in pharmaceutical, cos-

metic, and pet food applications.

Committed to being the preferred worldwide source of iron oxide pigments, Harcros Pigments Canada is investing in capabilities and technology to meet the unique and ever-changing needs of its broad customer base.

1. *Known as Northern Pigment throughout most of its history, the company has played an important role for the Canadian construction and manufacturing industries.*
2. *In 1993 Northern Pigment was renamed Harcros Pigments Canada, becoming a vital member of a global company that serves over 165 countries worldwide.*

2

Hearn Pontiac Buick Limited

"A business has to exceed customer expectations to stay at the top," explains Hugh Popham, President and General Manager of Hearn Pontiac Buick Limited. Indeed, quality sales and service people dedicated to treating the customer with respect have been the key to the success of the dealership since its founding. The oldest dealership in Etobicoke, Ontario, Hearn Pontiac Buick Limited is now well-represented with four locations, including the central car dealership, a burgeoning truck centre, a body shop and a remote compound.

The dealership was first opened on October 29, 1948, by Elliott Stedelbauer. Known as Elliott Stedelbauer Pontiac Buick GMC, it was located at 3180 Lakeshore Boulevard in Toronto. After the founder retired in 1959, when an average new car sold for $2,795, the dealership became Hearn Pontiac Buick Ltd. under the able partnership of Frank A. Hearn and Herbert A. Kearney. Hearn was President and Kearney, having distinguished himself previously as a top sales person with several other dealerships, served as Vice President.

When Hearn passed away in 1967, Kearney became President. During his tenure, the dealership grew and expanded. Devoted to the industry, in 1971 Kearney became a panel member of the Commercial Registration Appeal Tribunal, an appointment he held until his death.

Kearney was also a loyal hockey fan, offering jobs to players during the off-season and helping

1

2

former Toronto Maple Leafs' stars Bobby Pulford and the brothers Barry and Brian Cullen get started in their own successful car businesses. Involved in the community as well, Kearney managed College Hockey School and sponsored an annual charity-benefit summer baseball all-star game of hockey players.

As the dealership expanded, it outgrew its original location and in 1978 moved to its present site on The Queensway in Etobicoke. With truck sales blossoming in the early 1980s, more employees were added, bringing the total to over 50.

After Kearney passed away in 1990, Hugh Popham became President. Having an academic background in business, a career in the automotive industry, and with the dealership since 1987, Popham came well-prepared. He oversaw the expansion of truck sales and an enlarging dealership to over 75 employees.

In 1992 the new Hearn GMC Truck Centre opened, across the street from the car dealership. The

Centre more than doubled the dealership's truck sales and brought the total square feet of all locations to over 38,000.

Reflecting the dealership's emphasis on customer treatment, Hearn Pontiac Buick recently twice received the corporate President's Triple Crown trophy, in 1989 and 1992, based on sales and overall customer satisfaction. As Popham emphasizes, "Our focus is on the customer. But customer satisfaction must begin before the sale and continue afterwards. If customers are treated right, they will return, ensuring their happiness and our future success."

1. *Herbert A. Kearney, Vice President, 1959-1967, and President, 1967-1990, with his wife, Joyce Kearney, who served as President of Hearn Leasing Limited.*
2. *Hugh Popham, President and General Manager since 1990.*
3. *Hearn GMC Truck Centre, opened in 1992, brought an increase of over 100 percent in truck sales.*
4. *Hearn Pontiac Buick Limited, located on the Queensway, is the oldest dealership in Etobicoke, Ontario.*

3

4

Hertz Canada Limited

With its familiar yellow and black logo in over 5,000 locations and 130 countries, Hertz, the largest car rental company in the world, can point with pride to a long litany of "firsts" directed towards improving customer service.

Founded in 1918 by Walter Jacobs in Chicago, Hertz commenced business with a fleet of 12 Model T's. Known at the time as the Rent-A-Ford Company, it was acquired in 1923 by John D. Hertz. As president of the Yellow Cab and Yellow Truck companies, Hertz gave the rental car company both his name and its widely recognized colours. During his tenure at the helm he built the foundation of today's global company.

In 1924 Hertz began the world's first international rental network when Brigadier General Gordon Secord obtained the rights to the initial Canadian Hertz location in Toronto. With a fleet of three cars, the Toronto licensee serviced those wealthy travellers who were landing on the grass fields of what was then Toronto's Malton Airport (now operating as Pearson International Airport). Always innovative, Secord offered the airplane crews at the time a commission to refer their passengers to Hertz.

Another early Canadian location was in Montreal, where Hertz introduced the Drive Yourself System in 1926. That same year, Hertz was the first rental company to introduce advance reservations, enabling its customers to plan ahead for their car rental.

In 1933 Hertz introduced its pioneering "Rent-It-Here/Leave-It-There" program, allowing customers to rent in one location but leave their vehicle in another location. The following year Canada's tenth licensee operation was opened in Kitchener, Ontario by Samuel (Skee) Wicks and his wife, Katherine. At the time, the daily cost to rent a Hertz vehicle was $3.50, which included 100 free miles and gas. This Kitchener licensee operation has gone on to become the oldest continuously operated Hertz licensee in the world. Now in its third generation as a family business, the head office of this five-site operation is only two blocks from the original location.

In the 1940s, when commercial air traffic became more popular, Hertz continued to blaze new trails by locating inside airport terminals. In 1947 Hertz was the first car rental company to issue uniforms for its Customer Sales Representatives, adding an air of professionalism to the business. In 1971 Hertz offered the first toll-free reservation number and in 1972 introduced its #1 Club for business travellers — an express service allowing club members to bypass airport counters and go directly to their car.

The five largest Canadian Hertz licensees became part of the Hertz Corporate system in 1973, when Montreal, Ottawa, Toronto, Calgary and Vancouver locations were sold to the Hertz Corporation. Close cooperation between corporate and licensee locations has allowed the Hertz Canada network to strengthen over the years, and it remains one of the key ingredients to the company's continued growth and success. Today, Hertz provides a number of unique value-added benefits for its customers including Computerized Driving Directions — a touch screen computer capable of generating and printing driving routes and instructions in the customer's choice of language. As well Hertz offers an Instant Return Check-In Service, Emergency Road Service, Cellular Phone Service and even an Inflight Reservations Service, all in the name of adding convenience to their customer's rental experience.

Dedicated to innovation and customer service, Hertz Canada Limited — the oldest rental car service in Canada — needs only to look at its history for inspiration for the future.

The new "Drive Yourself System" was first introduced in Montreal, as described in this ad in The Gazette *on May 10, 1926.*

Horn Plastics Ltd.

1

2

1. *Horst A. Hornung, Founder, Chairman and Chief Executive officer of The Horn Group, which includes Horn Plastics Ltd.*
2. *In October 1994 Horn Plastics achieved its ISO 9002 registration, a globally recognized quality certification. From left to right: Michael Lynch, Quality Manager, Ernest Gourley, President, and Allan Firhoj, ISO Coordinator.*
3. *The company's head office and Pickering, Ontario manufacturing facilities.*

Supplying custom molds and high precision components that have earned international recognition, Horn Plastics Ltd. has expanded into a group of companies whose growth has been honed through a strict adherence to precision and quality. With the pursuit of quality being a constant goal of Horn Plastics, the delivery of close tolerance parts has become the standard manufacturing procedure. But providing a superior product is not enough. Service to its partners in industry, from concept to completion, is the cornerstone of the Horn philosophy.

Headquartered in Pickering, Ontario and with additional facilities in Whitby and Markham, Horn Plastics is a world-class manufacturer of custom components and assemblies, integrating injection molding and associated fabrication technologies principally for the office equipment, electronics, automotive and medical industries.

Horst A. Hornung, Chairman and Chief Executive Officer of The Horn Group, first established D&E Precision Tooling in 1969 in Pickering, Ontario. A toolmaker by trade, he immigrated to Canada from Europe with the desire to establish a company specializing in the manufacture of small precision molds. Convincing original equipment manufacturers of the merits of both designing and fabricating the molds and the injection molded plastic parts, Hornung seized the opportunity, and in 1978 Horn Plastics was born.

Horn Plastics and D&E Precision Tooling formed a natural partnership, combining engineering know-how and experience to produce a steady stream of high precision molds and molded parts. Eventually, it began to form partnerships with companies for whom Horn would combine plastic as well as metal parts into subassembled components.

A decade later, Horn Plastics, wanting to expand its capabilities to include the molding of larger parts, established Hornco Plastics in Whitby to house heavier machines. And, in 1994, to extend their capabilities even further, a 4,200 square foot Class 100,000 clean room was created within this facility to produce components for the medical industry.

It was during this time that Hornung gradually stepped back from the day-to-day management and appointed Ernest Gourley as President. Continuing in the same tradition, Gourley has continued to lead Horn Plastics to new heights in industry-recognized quality standards.

Horn Plastics holds the distinct honour of being Canada's first certified plastic supplier to Xerox Corporation as well as maintaining the manufacturing excellence standards

3

of the internationally recognized Motorola Six Sigma quality program. In addition, the company has received, more than once, the Xerox World Wide Award of Excellence, an award based on quality, cost control, early supplier involvement, delivery performance, flexibility, lead time, and progressive management.

Furthermore, after close to one and a half years of preparation, Horn Plastics applied for its ISO accreditation. In late 1994 the company received its award after the first audit, certifying that the Quality Management System of Horn Plastics Ltd. complies with the requirements of ISO 9002, including: part quality, manufacturing processes, customer service, quality of personnel and the technological level of equipment.

Hornung explains, "Quality is a commitment, not just a word. It means having proactive personnel ready to respond to the exciting challenges that lie ahead in an expanding international marketplace. The Horn Group believes that excellence is the foremost standard of quality demanded by our industry partners. To consistently meet that standard, we combine molding experience, statistical process control, advanced technology, and, most importantly, the skills and dedication of our people."

Indeed, Horn Plastics places a high degree of emphasis on employee selection and training. Embracing a corporate philosophy that encourages advancement, Horn

1

Plastics is committed to maintaining an environment that encourages the development of its people. Gourley emphasizes: "The ability to meet the precise tolerances that are required by our customers is only achievable through years of training, experience, and pride in one's work."

Horn Plastics has expanded from its earlier status as a local supplier to its current position as a global competitor, enlarging its international customer base to include an impressive list of companies serving world-wide markets. The company today ships to the United States, China, Singapore, Ireland and the United Kingdom.

As part of its vision for the future, Horn Plastics is currently undertaking preliminary expansion studies in the United States. In addition, the company has also begun the production of proprietary products. One such product, the Cycle Caddy, a patented plastic carrier for bicycles, has enabled Horn Plastics to maintain a level of independence from the up and down market swings of supplying original equipment manufacturers.

As a responsible corporate citizen, Horn Plastics is committed to the well-being of the community and the environment in which it works. Benefiting local charities and events, the company also encourages its employees to become involved.

Today, Horn Plastics' primary commitment continues to be the provision of high quality technical and manufacturing services to fully satisfy its customers' requirements, from initial concept to the finished plastic product. Working together with its customers to meet industry's demands of tomorrow, the people of Horn Plastics are ready to face the exciting challenges of the global market.

1. *Hornco Plastics Inc. was established as an affiliate company in 1988 in Whitby, Ontario.*
2. *The Whitby facilities includes a 4,200 square foot Class 100,000 clean room to produce components for the medical and pharmaceutical industries.*
3. *Horn Plastics Ltd. supplies custom designed and manufactured moulds and high precision components for an international customer base.*

2

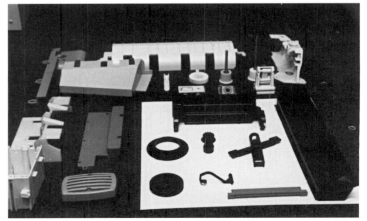

3

The Hospital for Sick Children

On March 13, 1970, a pleasant-looking man with a fringe of white hair edged around the cashier's counter of the Hospital and opened a canvas travel bag, pulling out more than $5,000 in crumpled and musty bills "for the poor kids." In 1937, in the box for donations at the door of the Hospital, a large diamond was found wrapped in cotton batting. Officials speculated that perhaps it was from the engagement ring of a mother whose child had been saved by the Hospital in the polio epidemic and who gave the gem in gratitude.

These unexpected gestures of thanks are indicative of how The Hospital for Sick Children, known affectionately for generations as "Sick Kids," has found a special place in the hearts and minds of all who are associated with it. The Hospital, now one of the largest paediatric hospitals in North America, is essentially a health care community dedicated to excellence in the compassionate care of children and their families. Working in partnership with other institutions to expand the horizons of patient care, education, and research, the Hospital places emphasis on the treatment of children with severe illness and injury, while providing basic medical care

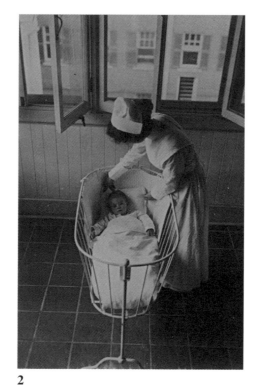

2

to children in the local community.

The Hospital also reaches beyond provincial and national boundaries to serve a global community through the provision of scientific and medical knowledge, teaching, and quality patient care. Of the 17,073 admissions in 1992, 16,645 were from Ontario, 245 from other areas of Canada, 47 from the United States, and 136 from other countries.

A community hospital, a national resource, and an international

1. *The boy is in an oxygen tent: these early contraptions were the forerunners of today's modern ventilation techniques.*
2. *Published in the 1916 annual report, this photo was taken on a balcony at the old hospital on College Street. In those days, children frequently stayed in hospital for weeks and months.*
3. *Assisted by fresh air and sunshine, Sick Kids nurses tend to their young patients on the balcony of the Baby Ward. The photo is one of hundreds carefully preserved in the Hospital's archives.*

leader — the intertwining of these roles has earned the Hospital its present stature, a position that has been built throughout its history, which itself is a heartwarming story of human dedication and medical progress, pioneering new research and new levels of proficiency.

Sick Kids was founded in the spring of 1875 when Elizabeth McMaster and a group of friends opened The Hospital for Sick Children in a small downtown Toronto house that had 11 rooms rented for $320 a year. In the first year 44 patients were admitted and 67 others were treated in outpatient clinics. Under the direction of John Ross Robertson, publisher of the *Evening Telegram* and chairman of the Hospital's Board of Trustees, the Hospital opened its first brand new build-

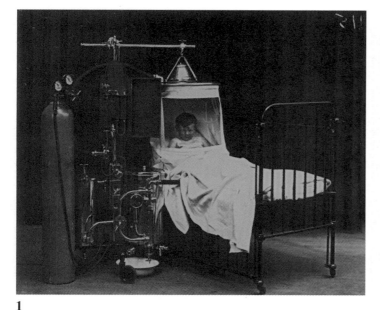

1

3

ing on College Street at Elizabeth in 1892.

A few years later, in 1908, the Hospital installed the first milk pasteurization plant in Canada, with staff leading the fight in Canada for compulsory pasteurization. Pablum, a precooked baby cereal, was developed at Sick Kids in 1930. In 1953 the Research Institute was established. Through the 1980s, advances in genetics that made worldwide headlines led to the identification and cloning of a number of genes including those responsible for causing hereditary diseases such as Duchenne muscular dystrophy and cystic fibrosis. Today, more than 800 staff, including senior scientists, physicians, and students, are engaged in more than 400 research projects in 75 fields.

Hospital physicians also pioneered renowned surgical developments such as the Salter operation to repair dislocation of the hip and the Mustard operation to correct a heart defect that often was fatal. In the 1960s, the Hospital opened one of the first intensive care units in North America devoted exclusively to the care of premature and critically ill newborn babies.

By the early 1980s, it was evident that Hospital staff needed new facilities to support family-centred care and to offer state-of-the-art therapy to critically ill and injured children. After more than 10 years of planning, five years of construction, and a move schedule that spanned three months, the process was complete by early 1993.

The Hospital's new home is an eight-storey tower described as one of the most complex buildings in Toronto. Renovations will create new outpatient clinics, laboratories and offices in the old building. The two structures, old and new, are linked and fully integrated on a number of levels.

The Atrium, at the heart of the new facility, vibrates with natural light, fountains, full-size trees,

whimsical papier-mâché sculptures, and a multi-panel mural of children at play.

The new 817,000-square-foot facility features many improvements and innovations, such as single bed patient rooms with private washrooms and accommodation for one parent to remain overnight; a paediatric Intensive Care Unit with the capacity to care for almost twice as many patients as before; a trauma-orthopaedic-neurosurgical unit — the first of its kind in Canada — designed to meet the needs of children admitted with profound injuries; a suite of state-of-the-art operating rooms; a much-needed Magnetic Resonance Imaging unit; a bone marrow transplant centre; an expanded gastroenterological procedure suite; and a large, multi-windowed playroom on each nursing unit. The new facility has allowed the Hospital to continue its important commitment and encompass-

ing mission: to continue to provide leadership in the paediatric health care field, joining with families as partners in care, while striving to be sensitive to the physical, spiritual, and emotional needs of the multicultural community it serves.

Today, in all of its many roles, as a teaching hospital for the University of Toronto, as a research institute, and as a treatment hospital for children from Toronto and from around the world, The Hospital for Sick Children continues with the same spirit and compassion that first led Elizabeth McMaster to establish a hospital dedicated entirely to the care of children.

Soaring glass wings outline the Atrium of The Hospital for Sick Children. This new facility, designed by the Zeidler Roberts Partnership, opened in January 1993. Designed around a central atrium with trees and a fountain, the Atrium provides all-new accommodation in private rooms for patients and parents.

Houghton Canada Inc.

1921 - 1996
- 75th Anniversary -

Celebrating its 75th anniversary in 1996, Houghton Canada Inc. is an independent manufacturer and supplier of specialty processing chemicals and lubricants. As an integral member of the Houghton International family of companies, Houghton Canada can also draw on the more than 130 years of Houghton's worldwide experience and quality products. Industry, especially today, demands innovation, and Houghton has a long history of quick response and leadership.

Houghton Canada Inc. first began in 1921, as British American Fuels & Metals Ltd. in Toronto. The purpose of the company, as stated in its incorporation papers, was to "produce, procure, sell, manufacture and manage coal, coke, peat, wood, mines, mining, and tramways." Changing its name to Production Materials Ltd. in 1924, the company continued to grow and expand, and in 1947 relocated to its present three acre site on Symes Road in Toronto. Becoming E.F. Houghton & Company of Canada Ltd., the facility has undergone five major expansions and modernization to meet the ever increasing demand for its products and services. In 1993, it adopted its current name, Houghton Canada Inc., in keeping with its parent company's change from E.F. Houghton & Co. to Houghton International Inc., to better reflect its worldwide scope.

In addition to its manufacturing plant, laboratories and offices in Toronto, Houghton Canada also has warehouses in Montreal and Vancouver. Internationally, Houghton has multiple locations in 28 countries, including the United States, Mexico, South America, United Kingdom, Continental Europe, the Middle East, Asia, India, Pakistan, Australia and Africa, supplying manufacturing industries around the globe.

The Houghton product line is continuously expanded and renewed through its worldwide development effort to provide safe, effective fluids for industry. Produced through years of research and testing, each product is designed to increase production, improve safety, reduce cost, be environmentally friendly and improve the quality of their customers' products.

Serving a wide gamut of industries, Houghton's customers are among the key manufacturers in the pulp and paper, automotive, steel making, aluminum processing, die casting, off-shore oil and appliance sectors. The Houghton line of products, especially formulated for these industries, includes all types of fire resistant hydraulic fluids, water soluble and straight cutting oils and coolants, rolling oils, wire drawing and press forming lubricants, cleaners, rust preventatives, polymer and oil based quenchants, and numerous pulp and paper process aids, such as Yankee dryer coatings and release agents, defoamers, de-inking chemicals and dispersants.

But Houghton goes beyond manufacturing and supplying products; its mission is to provide innovative and reliable solutions to industry's challenges. The solutions include advice, testing, information, product research and rapid service.

When reviewing the success of the company, Frank Heath, President of Houghton Canada, emphasizes, "Houghton has always been customer focused and heavily involved in technical service — not willing to end the sale without full support. We go on-site to provide that essential back-up. Furthermore, Houghton is adaptable with its ever-changing technology reflecting a wider range of products to suit industry's changing needs." It is precisely this continual innovative response by a highly trained, professional, long serving and dedicated staff that has ensured Houghton's success in its quest to solve today's problems, while planning tomorrow's solutions.

Houghton's reputation for integrity, quality and performance is a source of pride and motivation.

1. *Houghton Canada moved to its current site on Symes Road in Toronto in 1947. Since then the facility has undergone five major expansions and modernization.*

1

Humber College of Applied Arts & Technology

One of Canada's largest community colleges, Humber College of Applied Arts & Technology serves approximately 12,000 full-time and 65,000 part-time students from Canada and around the world. With several campus locations in Etobicoke and York in Metropolitan Toronto, Humber is recognized as a socially responsive, adaptive institution accountable to its community.

Accessible, responsible and flexible, Humber is a comprehensive college of applied arts and technology offering 135 full-time diploma and certificate programs at the post-secondary and post-diploma levels, as well as over 4,000 part-time courses, seminars, conferences and client training programs. Its programs are current and relevant to the workplace — in part as a result of the high degree of interaction and cooperation between Humber College and the business world — and Humber's graduate placement rate is consistently high. Indeed, many graduates have gone on to become leaders in their field in Canada and abroad.

Humber College can take pride in its aggressive exploration of new fields and opportunities, intrinsically linked to its connections to business, industry and the arts. The College has developed and managed many training projects for clients both nationally and around the world. Recently, Humber College has played a vital role in developing contracts to provide business and health assistance to such far-flung areas as Bahrain, Brunei, China, India, Kenya, St. Vincent, Thailand and Ukraine. Proving its commitment to stay on the cutting edge of technological changes are the College's Digital Imaging Training Centre and the Canadian Plastics Training Centre which meet the training needs of both students and industry.

According to Humber College President, Dr. Robert A. Gordon, "In today's climate of increased global competition and economic restructuring, it's vitally important to keep abreast not only of new technologies but also of the significant training and re-training needs of current and future employees. At Humber College, we keep an eye on emerging trends, and structure our programs and courses so that they are of maximum benefit to the career development plans of our students and to the hiring needs of employers."

Internationally, Humber College attracts students from all parts of the world, offering a number of programs and services to help international students succeed. Furthermore, in addition to a number of productive local and offshore alliances, Humber College has had a strategic partnership with Kiev State University of Economics in Ukraine since 1990.

Founded in 1967 in the former James S. Bell Elementary School on Lakeshore Boulevard West, Humber College's excellent and modern facilities have now grown to include a large North Campus, in Etobicoke, with stores, cafeterias, dining rooms, day care centre, medical clinic, and athletic complex; a smaller Lakeshore Campus, with its small-town feeling, historical buildings and parks extending to the very shores of Lake Ontario; a 300 acre Arboretum located along the Humber River Valley offering a wildlife sanctuary, grasslands, ponds, bike paths and gardens all connected by tranquil walkways; the Keelesdale campus, in the City of York; a Business and Industry Service Training Centre; a new Learning Resources Centre; and residence facilities for 760 students.

Looking at Humber College's success, it is not hard to see that it is linked to Humber's reputation, which itself is based on the quality and diversity of its programs, the expertise of its faculty and staff, its high placement rate, and its strategic Metropolitan Toronto location.

1. *Gordon Wragg, Humber College's founding President.*
2. *Dr. Robert "Squee" Gordon, Humber College President since 1982.*
3. *The North Campus is Humber's largest campus. Construction of the campus began in 1967.*

1

2

3

Hudson's Bay Company

The Hudson's Bay Company, one of the oldest commercial organizations in the world, traces its roots back to 1670 when King Charles II of England granted a group of investors a charter and a trading monopoly covering a vast region of Northern North America. The territory granted to "The Governor and Company of Adventurers of England Trading into Hudson's Bay" covered much of present-day Western Canada and parts of the Northern United States. Later, the Company's trading territory would extend to the Pacific Ocean.

For 200 years the Hudson's Bay Company played a major role in the development of the North American fur trade, first from trading posts located around Hudson Bay and James Bay, and later extending inland into the heart of the continent and beyond.

The history of Canada is, to a remarkable extent, also the history of the Hudson's Bay Company. A Company man, Henry Kelsey, was the first European to see herds of buffalo on the plains of Western Canada, and Company explorers such as Samuel Hearne and Anthony Henday opened large uncharted areas of the North and West to commerce, trade and subsequent settlement. Canadian cities such as Winnipeg, Edmonton and Victoria began as outposts of the Hudson's Bay Company's fur trade and many small communities across the Canadian North grew up around a Company post, many of them dating back to the earliest years of the Company's activity in North America.

For the first 200 years of its history, the Hudson's Bay Company was primarily concerned with the fur trade, but as the years went by other activities were undertaken. The Company, over its history, has been a land company, a transportation company, and a store-keeper.

In 1870 the Hudson's Bay Company's chartered territory in the West was transferred to the government of the newly-created Dominion of Can-

1

ada in return for a modest cash settlement and a portion of agricultural land in the "fertile belt," which was sold to settlers over the next 85 years.

During the nineteenth century as well, the Company became a major factor in Western transportation, moving goods to isolated communities and posts by canoe, York Boat, steamer, and, in the twentieth century, by airplane. In the twentieth century, also, the Company brought radio communication to the North.

As settlement increased in the

West, the Hudson's Bay Company became increasingly involved in the retail trade, and by the early years of the twentieth century sales shops and stores existed in major centres across Western Canada and in the North.

The first Hudson's Bay Com-

1. *The Company store on Cordova St., Vancouver, c. 1890.*
2. *Port Burwell, 1934. The flag is raised upon the arrival of Hudson's Bay Company Governor Patrick Ashley Cooper, while indigenous people listen to an interpreter reading the Royal message.*

2

pany "department store" opened in Winnipeg in 1881, not far from Upper Fort Garry, and for years was a major hub of the fur trade. The store was described as "Ali Baba's Treasure Cave" and sold everything from farm implements to Russian caviar and Brussels lace.

Plans to expand and enhance the department store business in Western Canada were halted by World War I (Company ships were involved in the transfer of war supplies to Europe), but expansion began in the first years of peace, resulting in the creation of a chain of modern department stores in major cities across Western Canada. The fur trade, meanwhile, continued in the North, with the Company still holding a major position as trader and store-keeper in remote Northern communities, where Company men often served as the stand-in doctor, dentist and peacekeeper.

By 1970, its 300th anniversary, the Hudson's Bay Company had transferred its head office from London, England, to Canada, and cross-Canada expansion had begun in earnest. The Company had already made forays into Eastern Canada with the purchase of the Montreal-based department chain Henry Morgan and Co. in the late 1950s. In the late 1970s two large Canadian retailers, Zellers and Simpsons, were added, and the Company expanded its operation in downtown and suburban locations throughout Western and Central Canada.

In the difficult business climate of the 1980s, the Hudson's Bay Company, electing to concentrate on its retail activities, moved away from participation in the resource and property development industries. Simpsons was absorbed into the Hudson's Bay Company identity and the Company's Northern Stores operation was sold, ending a direct association with the Canadian North that went back to 1670. In the mid-1980s the Company also sold off its wholesale and fur divisions.

As the Company moved into the 1990s, profits increased dramatically and expansion resumed with the ac-

1

quisition of the Woodward's and Towers chains. As the 325th anniversary draws near, the future looks bright. The Hudson's Bay Company — the Company of Adventurers — continues to play a major role in the unfolding story of Canada.

1. The unique logo and crest of Hudson's Bay Company, an enduring enterprise whose history is integral to a complete understanding of Canada's history.
2., 3. The Hudson's Bay Company store in Winnipeg, c. 1920 (2) and c. 1939 (3).

2

3

Imperial Oil Limited

Having played a leading role in the Canadian petroleum industry for more than a century, Imperial Oil Limited has grown to become one of the country's largest corporations. Imperial Oil is Canada's largest producer of conventional crude oil and bitumen (a type of very heavy oil), a major producer of natural gas, the largest refiner and marketer of petroleum products, and one of the country's major chemical suppliers.

The company's origins go back to September 8, 1880, when 16 oil refiners in southwestern Ontario pooled their resources to form The Imperial Oil Company, headquartered in London, Ontario. The young company was quick to find ways of upgrading its products — in those days mainly lamp oil, axle grease and other lubricants, wax and candles — and to extend its marketing reach to cities such as Montreal and Winnipeg. To raise badly needed capital to finance further expansion, Imperial sold a majority interest to an American firm, Standard Oil Company (New Jersey), which already had affiliates in Canada. In February 1899, Imperial took over all of Standard's Canadian assets, including a refinery in Sarnia, where the company moved its operations and head office.

The alliance helped underpin a period of rapid expansion in Imperial's distribution network. Imperial opened Canada's first gasoline station in 1907 and, while the Great War of 1914-1918 raged, it built four new refineries. These were also the years when Imperial became an active explorer and producer as well. In 1920, the company discovered oil at Norman Wells, N.W.T., just south of the Arctic Circle. Later in that decade it helped develop the Turner Valley field south of Calgary, Alberta. In February 1947, Imperial made a landmark oil discovery at Leduc, Alberta, that ushered in a period of major expansion in Canadian oil reserves and production.

In the late 1940s and into the 1950s and 1960s, Imperial was busy growing to accommodate its expanding oil-field operations, by enlarging its refining capacity and its pipeline network. On the marketing side, service stations changed their appearance to become more compatible with the neighbourhood, highway service centres became a new landmark, and self-serve stations, the first in Canada, joined the Esso chain in 1970. In 1990 the company introduced several environmentally friendly products including a new reformulated gasoline aimed at reducing summer smog, and lubricating oil that is more than 50 per cent re-refined oil.

By the 1960s it had become apparent that the sedimentary basin of western Canada — although still rich in natural gas — was not likely to yield major new discoveries of crude oil. As a result, Imperial moved its search for petroleum into frontier areas of the Far North and East Coast offshore. In 1985, the company completed a major expansion of its Norman Wells oil field, discovered more than 60 years earlier. Imperial also moved its search for oil into another kind of "frontier" — the huge resources locked in the molasses-like deposits of bitumen at Cold Lake, Alberta, and in the tarry sands of the nearby Athabasca region. At Cold Lake, after more than two decades of experimentation into techniques for producing heavy oil from deeply buried oil sands through steam injection, Imperial started commercial bitumen production in 1985.

One of the most significant developments in the history of Imperial was the purchase of Texaco Canada on February 23, 1989. This purchase was the largest in the company's history and the second largest acquisition in Canada to date.

Throughout its long history Imperial has endeavoured to be a leading member of the Canadian business community by providing quality products and services at competitive prices, by undertaking an active program of research and development, by maintaining an ongoing contribution program and by wholeheartedly accepting its responsibility to protect the environment. As the company proceeds through the second decade of its second century of operation, its mission continues to be the creation of shareholder value through the development and sale of hydrocarbon energy and related products.

The Mackenzie River at Normal Wells, N.W.T., c. 1920. Imperial Oil Limited has made pioneering use of aircraft in opening the Canadian North with a discovery, that through subsequent development, has become the company's largest single source of conventional oil.

Jessan Transportation Limited

A growing trucking company serving manufacturers and other transport companies in the greater Toronto and Southern Ontario markets, Jessan Transportation Limited has built its reputation on a history of personal service and dedication to on-time delivery. The company's current fleet of approximately 60 units is based out of Jessan's four acre terminal in Etobicoke, Ontario.

Jessan Transportation was founded in April 1975 by Peter Burns and Harold Scott, who were joined the following year by Bill Campbell as a third partner. The company began with one truck providing local cartage services in Toronto. Burns, with his previous experience in another transport company, piloted the growth of Jessan which quickly earned a name for quality service. With a growing customer list, by May 1976 Jessan had 10 trucks on the road.

In 1981 Burns and Campbell bought out Scott, and the following year Burns became the sole shareholder, purchasing the remaining shares from Campbell. Annual increases in sales occurred each year, except for a period during the recession in the early 1980s. Expansion quickly resumed until 1986, when poor economic times, combined with a slowdown in the transport industry as a whole, dampened Jessan's rapid growth rate.

After extensive review and study, in 1990 the decision was reached to divide and refocus Jessan's primary business, changing from solely a local cartage carrier to adding an intermodal service to railheads in the United States and Canada for Southern Ontario freight. The intermodal service consists of tractors moving railway trailers between Southern Ontario manufacturers and the rail ramps in Detroit, Michigan; Buffalo, New York; and Welland and Toronto, Ontario.

Jessan's cartage services consists of straight trucks and tractor trailer combinations moving mixed general freight in the greater Toronto area and, to a lesser degree, to other Southern Ontario points. Customers include other transport companies — providing back up by supplying these companies with tractors and drivers on a short term basis — and various Ontario manufacturing concerns based in the Toronto area.

Always on the leading edge of technological advances in the transit industry, Jessan Transportation engages in extensive EDI (Electronic Data Interface) connections between its head office, railways and other companies. EDI allows the easy transfer of customer service requests and invoicing; furthermore, extensive computerization of the dispatch functions provides up to the minute information on each load consigned to Jessan for handling, reduces paperwork, and facilitates and expedites the transfer of cargo.

Current key members of Jessan's management team include Peter W. Burns, President; John A. Mcdonald, Vice President and Controller, who joined Jessan Transportation in 1982 and brought both accounting and North America wide transportation experience; and Bram Everitt, General Manager Intermodal, who joined Jessan in 1990 with over 30 years in previous marketing positions with major North American railways, bringing with him the critical knowledge that allowed Jessan to launch its intermodal service.

Looking at its success, Burns attributes it largely to Jessan's history of service, of knowledgable personnel, dedication, and hard work — strengths that will allow Jessan Transportation Limited to continue to prosper in the future.

Peter Burns, President and Co-founder of Jessan Transportation. Starting with one truck in 1975, the company now operates a fleet of more than 60 units out of its four acre terminal in Etobicoke, Ontario.

Insurance Crime Prevention Bureau

As business and commerce prospered in the early decades of the twentieth century, so too did the incidence of insurance fraud in Canada. In 1923, tired of being cheated by policyholders who set fire to their own properties to collect insurance, the association of Canadian fire underwriters organized the new Fire Underwriters' Investigation and Loss Information Bureau (FUILIB) in Montreal.

Popular opinion of the day said it was virtually impossible to obtain a conviction for arson, but the underwriters believed their new agency could help overburdened public officials with their work and — at the same time — reduce fire insurance claims.

The brand new FUILIB set out to prove that arson was indeed a convictable crime that first winter, when the two original employees — General Manager Harry Rethoret and the Bureau's first Special Agent, former RCMP investigator H.F. McDonald — trudged through blizzard conditions and bitter cold, with a photographer in tow, to scour the site of a local incendiary fire.

Later, the court commended the new Bureau for its excellent work, then sentenced two men to five years each in penitentiary, for arson. The "impossible" had been achieved, and this landmark conviction earned huge headlines in all the Montreal newspapers of the day.

Another early investigation — and the resulting establishment of the first "Loss Information Cards" — again proved the fledgling Bureau's effectiveness. The owner of

three local retail stores had, over a number of years, filed claims for several suspicious fires, each time receiving substantial insurance compensation. As a result of the FUILIB's "Card", circulated to member companies, the retailer had difficulty obtaining new coverage, and the fires — probably not surprisingly — ceased to happen.

In 1926, the FUILIB became an independent organization and expanded its operations beyond Quebec and Ontario to all provinces. About the same time, the first of two similar organizations moved into action to fight automobile fraud, another burgeoning crime of the Roaring Twenties.

The fact that for several years there were two agencies fighting auto fraud caused a most unusual incident in 1930. On January 27 that year, the car owned by the manager of the Automobile Loss Investigation Bureau was stolen — although locked and in gear — then found three days later thanks to information provided by the rival organization, the Canadian Automobile Recovery Bureau. Total cost of repairs for the broken car door, cut wires

1

and a smashed instrument panel was $26.05.

Today, more than 70 years and well over 100,000 investigations later, the Insurance Crime Prevention Bureau is still hunting down fraud on behalf of its 1920s predecessors.

There are currently about 185 employees at the Bureau's head office in Toronto and its regional offices in 32 cities across Canada.

1. *Harry Rethoret, the first Fire Underwriters' Investigation and Loss Information Bureau (FUILIB) employee and Founding Manager, 1923-1948.*
2. *A FUILIB Special Agents training seminar, c. 1940. The value of the Bureau was such that the number of investigators grew rapidly.*

2

More than half of these employees are investigators — Special Agents — who are all former police officers with at least ten years of experience, including investigations and extensive courtroom experience.

Property-casualty insurance experts estimate that approximately 10 to 20 per cent of all insurance claims in the 1990s are fraudulent, resulting in losses of between one and two billion dollars annually. Every insurance buyer — and taxpayer — pays for this fraud, with higher insurance premiums, and through escalating costs for firefighting, police investigations and court proceedings.

Funded by the majority of Canada's property-casualty insurance companies, the Bureau presently fights fraud under the banner of three branches: the Fire Underwriters' Investigation Bureau, the Canadian Automobile Theft Bureau, and the Casualty Claims Index Bureau.

The main difference between insurance frauds in the 1920s and now is their complexity. While there are still many individual cases of fraud reported to the Bureau, much more of the Insurance Crime Prevention Bureau's work now involves tracing and exposing the activities of professional fraud rings. These highly-sophisticated scams often involve several principals and hundreds of crimes, most in the area of faked bodily-injury frauds and vehicle thefts. Many are inter-provincial and, increasingly, international.

While the Insurance Crime Prevention Bureau continues to be best known for its investigations of property and vehicle fraud — still scouring fire sites and other suspicious claims for clues to fraud — a crucially important tool for preventing insurance crime is the sizeable pool of loss information the Bureau manages on behalf of its member companies and other organizations fighting fraud. This entire loss information database — more than one million subjects — is available to members electronically through the Bureau's computer network, the Automated System for the Prevention of Insurance Crime.

Other services provided by the Bureau include working with auto manufacturers and governments to develop systems to discourage motor vehicle thefts, including better locking devices, visible vehicle identification numbers, secondary serial numbers and improved registration procedures. Education and training are also key: the Bureau provides regular seminars and workshop programs for insurance company employees to promote the most effective handling of automobile and property-loss claims, as well as seminars at police and fire teaching facilities.

Although insurance fraud will never be completely eliminated, it can be decreased. In the 1990s, this translates to tens of millions of dollars in savings to the member companies as a result of claims being dropped or reduced following Insurance Crime Prevention Bureau investigations for fraud.

In the late years of the 20th century, as in 1923, the Bureau continues to carry out its mission of helping reduce insurance crime as much as possible, while saving both lives and property in the process.

Harry Rethoret, the FUILIB's first manager, would be proud.

1. *An Insurance Crime Prevention Bureau Special Agent examining a burned-out vehicle. Serial numbers from burnt wreckage can help support a claim or confirm suspicions of insurance fraud.*
2. *With more than 1.3 million references in its growing electronic database, computerized data is key to preventing and detecting insurance fraud.*

1

2

J.J. Muggs Gourmet Grille

An innovative Toronto based restaurant company, J.J. Muggs Gourmet Grille is regarded as an industry leader in casual dining and catering. Starting with its Bloor Street West location, the Mug Restaurant, as it was first known, introduced the public to the "definitive" eatery: an innovative menu combining traditional fare with creative flare, and an extensive selection of large portions of great quality food enjoyed with personable, efficient service.

Ted Nikolaou, the founder of J.J. Muggs, is proud to say that his restaurants are still among the most beautiful and comfortable around today. All four locations in the greater Metropolitan Toronto area reflect the J.J. Muggs philosophy of developing and operating restaurants at the highest possible standards. In addition, J.J. Muggs' catering division has its own production facilities, providing its rapidly growing clientele with some of the most stylish high quality catered food available.

Nikolaou emigrated from Greece to Canada with his family in 1955. Being the eldest child in the family, he needed to help with the family finances and soon was employed as a shoeshine boy in downtown Toronto. Maintaining a strong work ethic, he boasts that since that time he has never had a day when he was unemployed. After working at several other jobs in Toronto, at the young age of nineteen he had saved sufficient money to buy Rex Grille in 1960. Successfully operating the twenty-two seat restaurant located at Lakeshore and Mimico for ten years, he then sold it to allow himself the opportunity to begin the J.J. Muggs tradition.

The success story of J.J. Muggs began in 1971, when the Mug Restaurant and Eatery opened on Bloor Street West. The "Mug," as it was known then, quickly became one of

1

Toronto's most popular gathering places, an eatery style restaurant offering large portions, low prices and plenty of variety. In a city with an ever-growing number of theme or specialized eating spots, the 120 seat Mug was an oasis in a crowded desert, and an instant success. The Mug's concept was enduring — high quality food, excellent service and great value.

The first large scale Mug opened in the Eaton Centre in 1982. The concept included spacious surroundings and a decor featuring leaded stained-glass windows, decorative brass railings, a giant spiral stairway leading to an entire upstairs level of dining, and a beauti-

ful concave stained-glass dome adorning the ceiling. Guests cannot help but feel the warmth and intimacy of the restaurant.

In 1985 the Woodbine Centre location overwhelmed guests with a greenhouse atrium, seven levels of dining, a mezzanine overlooking a spectacular convex stained-glass dome and a completely open kitchen. A new name was also introduced, J.J. Muggs Gourmet Grille.

1. *Starting with the Bloor Street West location in Toronto, the public was first introduced to the "definitive" eatery in 1972.*
2. *The first large scale J.J. Muggs opened in Toronto's Eaton Centre in 1982.*

2

In 1987 the Bloor Street location was expanded and refurbished. When it reopened as J.J. Muggs, it had been refitted with Italian marble columns and floors, neon accents, stylish artwork and more comfortable surroundings. The dark mirrored glass highlighted by a large green awning identifies the restaurant and augments the spectre of the entire Bloor Street annex.

Recently the newest location was unveiled, J.J. Muggs Erin Mills Town Centre. Located in Mississauga, this spectacular showpiece of marble, granite and quarry cast stone has three floors of dining, two backlit illuminated marble bars and a kitchen which is completely open to the dining room.

While J.J. Muggs boasts decorative and spacious surroundings, with both intimate and party-style seating, its true pride lies in culinary imagination. With an emphasis on excitement and a concern for convenience, J.J. Muggs is open daily for breakfast, lunch, dinner and late night snacks. From classical to modern cookery, the menu crosses multi-cultural borders to include Italian, Greek, Mexican, Jewish, Eastern, French and, of course, North American dishes. Nikolaou points out, "Because of the wide range of clientele, the menu must have something for everyone." Children are also welcome, receiving special attention with a colouring book menu.

The J.J. Muggs catering division has been operating since the early 1980s. To ensure a successful event, catering representatives assist in developing the proper menu for each client, whether it be selections from the catering menu or special requests to fill individual requirements. Capable of catering to functions from 10 to over 1,000 people, J.J. Muggs Catering is seen at a wide range of events, from business meetings to banquets, and from wine and cheese parties to weddings. Some of the more specialized arrangements including catering to the private suites, media

1

personnel and private functions at Maple Leaf Gardens in Toronto from its full service kitchen on the premises; and operating a unique, restaurant style cafeteria at the Toronto Star Building.

Realizing that the location of each restaurant is very important to the eventual success of the establishment, Nikolaou personally undertakes a critical approach to site selection, carefully applying criteria to ensure a successful location. In many other areas of management there is this same hands-on approach. For example, Nikolaou works closely with the professional interior designers to create J.J. Muggs' unique atmosphere. In addition, Nikolaou credits the entire J.J. Muggs team, and in particular his Operations Manager, Tony Palermo, with the smooth operation of the restaurants.

Looking back over the twenty years of development of his restaurant enterprises, Nikolaou also acknowledges the support he has received from his family. As he warmly comments, "It takes a special kind of family to give the support needed for the type of hard work required for this business. Without the encouragement of Joan [Mrs. Nikolaou] and my children, Steven and Lisa, all this would not have been possible." Steven has also joined in the business and manages one of the restaurants.

Today, the excitement is just beginning at J.J. Muggs Gourmet Grille. With an ever-changing concept, new ideas are only limited by the people that create them. With the finest food available, this multipurpose dining establishment and catering service looks forward to continued growth and success.

1. *In 1985, the Woodbine Centre location, also in Toronto, overwhelmed guests with a greenhouse atrium, seven levels of dining, a mezzanine overlooking a spectacular convex stained-glass dome and a completely open kitchen.*
2. *Located in Mississauga, Ontario, the newest J.J. Muggs was recently opened in the Erin Mills Town Centre.*

2

The King Edward Hotel

The oldest and one of the most prestigious hotels in Toronto, The King Edward Hotel's impeccable service and world class style are the domain and a favourite resting place of the world's contemporary elite. A historic landmark, it is fully restored to its original turn-of-the-century elegance of grandeur and glamour. In style, service, ambiance and decor, The King Edward embodies the elegant era of the monarch for whom it was named. Famous around the globe, it has been repeatedly classified among the best hotels.

The King "Eddie," as it is fondly called, has always attracted the elite. Its guest books carry such famous names as Rudyard Kipling, Mark Twain, Lady Astor, Elizabeth Taylor, Richard Burton, and the Beatles (who needed barricading in when over 3,000 fans stormed the lobby). Canadian prime ministers and governor-generals, His Royal Highness Prince Philip, and foreign heads of state, including Charles de Gaulle,

1

Aga Khan and Baroness Margaret Thatcher, have all called The King Edward their home away from home while staying in Toronto.

First opened in 1903, The King Edward was built by George Gooderham, then the richest man in Toronto and owner of the venerable Gooder-

1. *The King Edward Hotel first opened in 1903, realizing a wealthy Toronto businessman's dream of building a grand place for the rich and famous from around the world to stay.*
2. *A nine-storey tower was added in 1928, bringing the number of rooms to almost 800 and included a ballroom on the top two floors.*
3. *A favourite retreat of Toronto business and social life, The King Edward has always attracted the elite. Its guest list has included such famous names as Mark Twain, Rudyard Kipling, Theodore Roosevelt, Lloyd George, Anna Pavlova, John Diefenbaker, and His Royal Highness Prince Philip. Designated as a historical site in 1975, it was destined for a $25 million restoration and facelift in 1979.*

ham and Worts Distillery. A visionary who staked his money and political clout on an ambitious plan to build a grand gathering place in which the rich and famous from around the world could stay, he was a latter-day King Canute, pouring money into the project to realize his

2

3

dream.

Gooderham hired the foremost architect in Canada, E.J. Lennox, who was already world famous for his designing of the recently completed Toronto City Hall. Technologically, The King Edward was a structure ahead of its time, constructed as Toronto's first completely fireproof hotel.

The hotel's sumptuous and splendidly proportioned interior included massive marble columns and a natural skylight in the lobby, while the hotel's exterior was completed in French Renaissance style using terracotta trimmings. Construction costs totalled $6 million, in addition to its antique furnishings, which included 17th century tapestries, a Constable painting, Greek statues, and the jewel box of Diane de Poitier.

The lavish, Edwardian oasis of extravagance and elegance established the hotel as Toronto's fashionable centre, and it immediately became the favourite haunt of Toronto business and social life. When it opened, a single room on the European plan cost $1.50 per day, while prices for a bedroom with parlour and private bath attached ensuite started from $7.00.

In 1928 a new wing was built, including a nine-storey tower rising above the original eight-storey structure. The addition brought the number of rooms to close to 800, and included a convention room and a ballroom on the two top floors of the tower.

Designated as a historical site in 1975, in 1979 The King Edward was closed for 18 months for a $25 million restoration and facelift, painstakingly removing the years of accumulated grime and soot, restoring the hotel to its former beauty as an architectural gem that boasts some of the most luxurious hotel suites in Canada. Each of the 315 spacious rooms and suites were meticulously refurbished — elegantly appointed and tastefully furnished, combining Edwardian charm with the latest in modern amenities.

When it reopened in 1981, The

1

King Edward had joined the ranks of Forte Hotels' list of premiere hotels. One of the world's leading hotel and catering companies, Forte Hotels was founded in 1935 in Great Britain and currently has over 1,500 locations worldwide in 37 countries.

Management and staff, dedicated to the comfort of each and every guest, strive to make a visitor's expe-

rience the most pleasant and memorable as possible. The service is immaculate, friendly, and aimed at providing a regal atmosphere, complemented by the hotel itself, with its vaulted ceiling lobby, skylights and marble pillars that evoke images of another unhurried age.

Many guests come to savour the dining experience in The King Edward's two restaurants. Indeed, the Café Victoria is almost as famous as the hotel itself. Its baroque ceilings are preserved by the Ontario Historical Board as a reminder of the art and craftsmanship that is so rare in newer buildings.

Other services provided by The King Edward include 14 ample rooms for meetings, conferences or banquets. Furthermore, guests can also enjoy the hotel's health spa and daily live music.

The King Edward Hotel today continues to realize its builder's dream of establishing a palatial resting and meeting place as a reprieve from life's sojourns for people from Toronto and around the world, an abode to gather and stay in lavish settings inspired with a grand sense of occasion.

1. *The King Edward Hotel today, fully restored to its turn-of-the-century elegance of grandeur and glamour, an architectural gem boasting some of the most luxurious hotel suites in Canada.*
2. *The hotel's lobby, with its vaulted ceiling, skylights and marble pillars, evokes memories of another unhurried age, embodying the elegant era of the monarch for whom the hotel was named.*

2

Kisko Products

The largest manufacturer of private label brand freeze pops in Canada, Kisko Products represents the entrepreneurial spirit, dedication and perseverance that are characteristic of many newcomers to Canada. Founded by an immigrant from Jamaica, Kisko Products is now a successful industry leader, dominating its market segment.

The story of Kisko Products begins with Leslie Josephs in his native Jamaica. After successfully establishing a freeze pop manufacturing operation that grew to service the entire island, he and his family immigrated to Canada in late 1975. After analyzing various business opportunities, Josephs reached the decision to begin a freeze pops operation in Canada.

In the face of well-established competition, Kisko Products was founded in 1977 with one machine in a 5,000 square foot facility in Scarborough, Ontario. The original product manufactured was a drink in a plastic pouch with an attached straw. Assorted freeze pop lines were subsequently added to the product line.

Initially unable to penetrate the wholesale and grocery markets, Kisko Products began selling its product at convenience and corner stores. With innovative marketing, demand quickly grew and Kisko expanded into adjoining industrial units. Needing larger facilities, the company moved to a 32,000 square foot building at its current site in Markham, Ontario. Recently enlarged to 52,000 square feet, the state-of-the-art automated facility now houses the manufacturing and warehousing operations, with additional off-site warehousing facilities.

After gaining success at the convenience store level, Kisko began making inroads at wholesalers and then supermarkets. With superior quality and outstanding service, Kisko Freeze Pops soon became

1. *Leslie Josephs, President, and his wife, Glenor Josephs, co-founders of Kisko Products.*
2. *Kisko Products is now the largest manufacturer of private label brand freeze pops in Canada.*

available nationwide. Demonstrating the company's exceptional success, it has become the number one brand in Ontario and the number two brand nationally. Furthermore, the company is also exporting approximately 50 per cent of its production to the United States, Eastern Europe, Puerto Rico and the Bahamas.

Reflecting on the company's success, Josephs attributes it not only to quality products and excellent service but also to loyal customers and the dedication of the management and all employees at every level of the company. Furthermore, his family has also been heavily involved in the company's accomplishments. His partner and wife, Glenor, has been with the company

since the beginning, and three of their sons, Mark, Peter and Randolph, are now part of the management nucleus, functioning as Sales Manager, Production Manager, and New Product Development Manager, respectively. In addition, the extended family has been involved in many capacities.

From a kitchen production centre in Jamaica to Canada-wide and global marketing, Kisko Products is an archetypal example of hard work, commitment, and immigrant tenacity. With distribution centres in Regina, Vancouver, Moncton and Montreal, demonstrated market leadership, and innovative new products under development, Kisko Products today is well-positioned for further growth.

Kodak Canada Inc.

A leading supplier of products for copying, document management, printing and publishing, health care, photography and the motion-picture industries, Kodak Canada Inc. is a major Canadian manufacturing, marketing and service organization. Employing over 2,000 Canadians, Kodak Canada's Canadian-made consumer and commercial imaging products are sold both domestically and internationally.

The company first began with a small office in downtown Toronto at 41 Colborne Street in 1899, when George Eastman — Eastman Kodak's founder — sent John G. Palmer to evaluate Canada's incipient photographic business. Convinced of the viability of the Canadian market, Palmer became the first President of Canadian Kodak Ltd., as the company was then known. Two years later, the company moved to a large building on King Street West.

By 1912, Canadian Kodak had approximately 400 employees, and its new plant manufactured film, mounts and paper. The following year the company purchased its present site at Weston Road and Eglinton Avenue in northwestern Toronto and began construction of new facilities. When the company celebrated its 25th anniversary in Canada, over 900 employees worked at the seven building plant and office complex.

By 1960 more than 1,700 Canadians were employed by the company. 1963 marked the introduction of the Kodak Instamatic camera, and within two years more than 200,000 units of this popular item were sold. The Kodak Pavilion at Expo '67 allowed the nation to see Kodak's stunning achievements at the time of Canada's Centennial, and how photography impacted daily life.

In 1979 the company adopted its current appellation, Kodak Canada Inc., as it continued to thrive and expand into new areas of imaging beyond photography. During the mid 1980s Kodak Canada began a $50 million consolidation program in manufacturing, marketing, distribution and customer support to upgrade the major manufacturing equipment and improve and expand its distribution centre.

A member of the worldwide Eastman Kodak community of companies, Kodak Canada has the corporation's world mandate to produce micrographic film and Duraflex display material. Kodak Canada also manufactures a large portion of the world's supply of Eastman colour print film, the film projected in movie houses.

Today, Kodak Canada serves the Canadian market through its marketing centres in Montreal, Toronto and Vancouver, and its offices in Calgary, Edmonton, Winnipeg, Ottawa, Quebec and Halifax.

Quality driven and customer focused, Kodak Canada was the first in the Eastman Kodak organization to be accredited Class "A" under MRPII, a difficult manufacturing resource planning discipline. As well, the company has received ISO 9000 certification for its key manufacturing and supply, customer service and customer equipment service divisions. A company-wide commitment to total quality, driven by Kodak Canada's Quality Leadership Process, is the underpinning principle behind its high performance.

With its ongoing dedication to detail and quality, its well-established reputation, and its historic litany of achievements and pace-setting accomplishments, Kodak Canada is assured of a continuing leading role in the imaging industry.

1. *Founded in 1899, Kodak Canada Inc. quickly established for itself a dominant role in the photographic trade.*
2. *With its precise attention to quality and detail, Kodak Canada Inc. is a leader in the Canadian imaging industry.*

1

2

Knud Simonsen Industries Limited

1

2

Firmly established as a world leader in the food packing industry, Knud Simonsen Industries Limited (KSI) has a long history of being engaged in practically every aspect of meat processing. Over the years, the company has gained a remarkable reputation for its innovative solutions to the needs of its clients. Its customers operate modern processing plants around the world, each one designed and constructed from start to finish by KSI.

KSI was founded in Toronto in 1961 by Knud Simonsen. Having become a machinist in his native Denmark, he acquired further experience in South Africa and Sweden before immigrating to Canada. Upon arriving in Toronto with his wife, Bente, their daughter Ingrid, and later, their daughter, Marie, he founded Knud Simonsen Industries Limited.

Working out of their home — with a welding machine in the garage, three designers in the family room, and two installers on the road — the Simonsens directed KSI towards its future success. In the early years the company manufactured and sold mainly single pieces of meat processing equipment.

As sales increased, KSI expanded and moved to a 5,300 square foot facility in Rexdale, Ontario. Renting more and more production space, in 1972 KSI purchased its present 3.5 acre site and began the construction of specially designed facilities dedicated to the manufacture of meat processing equipment. KSI now occupies approximately 55,000 square feet in its own facility, and rents an additional 30,000 square feet.

KSI's meat processing expertise also expanded into the poultry, fish, dairy and other food processing fields. KSI provides clients with a "start-to-finish" package. The prospective plant owner supplies the land and KSI supplies the rest — feasibility studies, layout, buildings, equipment, plant installation and service, and even staff training. The plant can be as sophisticated, or as simple, as the client needs.

The company's worldwide reputation for innovative problem solving, engineering capability, consistency, reliability and product integrity is based on KSI's wide range of experience. Its cosmopolitan approach to business allows the plant equipment to incorporate the latest in technology from around the globe. The company's experts understand the industry's specific needs and adapt each plant to suit the needs and requirements of each customer.

KSI's modern manufacturing facilities are capable of designing and fabricating meat processing facilities for beef, hogs, lambs and horses, total cooler systems, and many forms of alternate processing. In the thermal processing field, KSI is a world leader in continuous

3

1. *Knud Simonsen, Founder and Chairman of Knud Simonsen Industries Limited (KSI).* 2. *The company's 55,000 square foot head office and manufacturing facility is located in Rexdale, Ontario.* 3. *Skilled employees and advanced machinery enhance KSI's international reputation for precision manufacturing.*

cook/chill systems, for mass production of processed meat.

From the smallest meat hook to boning tables, batch and continuous smoke/cook systems, pickle injectors, buggy lifts, vat dumpers, and conveyor systems, KSI manufactures them all. In addition, it also offers a full range of engineering services especially tailored to the food processing industry — activities include specialist plant manufacture, pre-investment feasibility studies for new and existing facilities, appraisals, conceptual design, detailed plant layout and project engineering.

Strong emphasis at KSI on research and development has ensured that the company has led the industry in technological changes. The company's design engineers continually strive to improve on today's standards for tomorrow's needs, ensuring that KSI will continue to be an innovator in years to come.

Approximately 80 per cent of KSI's production is for export, with customers in approximately 25 countries, including Denmark, Sweden, Germany, France, Italy, England, Bulgaria, Venezuela, Argentina, Chile, Japan and United States. Most of the major meat and poultry packers across North America are KSI customers. Indeed, the world's largest hog operation, bacon, ham and wiener plants have been installed by KSI.

Looking at the phenomenal growth and success of KSI, Knud Simonsen, now Chairman, attributes continuity as one of the keys to the prosperity of KSI — continuity of suppliers, customers and staff. "At KSI, we consider every one of our employees to be important," Simonsen explains. "This is probably one of the main reasons why our staff stay with us. This continuity allows staff members to obtain a broad and thorough knowledge of the equipment designed and manufactured by the company, resulting in an advantage for the company as well as the customers."

But above all, Simonsen sees

1

God's blessing on the company from the beginning. "I am a firm believer in 'when man listens, God speaks; when man obeys, God acts.' This has been the key and background to our entire success. We have had our difficulties, ... but we have always survived and have been strengthened through God's guiding hand."

Simonsen also explains the company's operating philosophy: KSI doesn't merely sell machinery; rather, it goes beyond supplying the facilities, to solving associated problems and providing follow-up and service as well. Its objective is to continue to share its accumulated knowledge and expertise with its

customers worldwide.

For more than a quarter of a century, Knud Simonsen Industries Limited has been in the forefront of development in the food processing and meat packing industries. With approximately 150 employees, including representatives around the globe, KSI can now truly be called a pacesetter and a world leader in its field, a company whose future will undoubtedly be as strong as its past.

1. KSI custom designs and produces a wide range of equipment for the meat processing industry.
2. KSI also has been the sole agent in Canada since 1968 for Multivac automatic packaging machines.

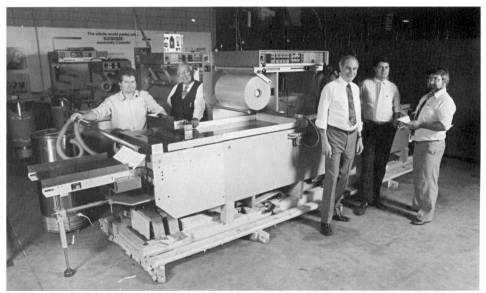

2

Kubota Canada Ltd.

The leading distributor of compact diesel tractors in Canada, Kubota Canada Ltd. has achieved its success by offering the Canadian marketplace innovative products and outstanding service. As one of 17 world affiliates of Kubota Corporation, based in Osaka, Japan, Kubota Canada is able to offer world leading technology rooted in over 100 years of experience.

1

Founded in 1891, Kubota Corporation entered the Canadian market in 1975 with an office in Markham, Ontario. Finding a dearth of suppliers of compact diesel tractors in North America, Kubota Canada was formed to fill the niche. Introducing 12 to 25 horsepower diesel tractors, the company quickly met with success. Although competition grew, Kubota Canada has successfully maintained its status as the industry's leader in its market segment. A major reason for the success and growth of Kubota, is that it is a corporation which remains in a constant state of improvement, making subtle changes based on customer feedback, assembly-line experience, and a large research and development team.

Expanding its product line to include diesel tractors up to 100 horsepower, Kubota Canada, now offers over 50 different models of compact diesel tractors. In addition, other products offered by Kubota Canada include Kubota's large line of diesel engines, gasoline powered generators, a series of pumps, compact excavators and articulated wheel loaders for the construction industry.

With three regional distribution centres, in Richmond, British Columbia, Drummondville, Quebec, and at its head office facility in Markham, and over 190 specially trained dealers located across the country, Kubota Canada is in constant contact with its customers, able to anticipate and fill their needs. Kubota Canada's clients outside of direct agriculture applications include landscapers, city governments, hospitals, golf courses, mines, private individuals, and the light construction industry, all of whom find Kubota's small equipment, customized for specific uses, more practical and durable than other equipment available.

As a member of the worldwide Kubota family, Kubota Canada has access to leading edge technology. Kubota Corporation is one of Japan's leading manufacturers of a comprehensive range of machinery and products, including farm equipment, iron pipes, industrial castings and machinery, environmental-control facilities, residential building materials and prefabricated houses. Another Kubota company, Kubota Metal Corp., is located in Orillia, Ontario and is that city's leading employer. Worldwide, Kubota Corporation employs over 20,000 people in 20 plants, and annually sells in excess of $9.5 billion U.S., including one-half million gas and diesel engines, one of its hallmark lines.

In addition to superior products, Kubota Canada also offers superb after-sales service. With a product line that is constantly evolving to match the needs, dealership training is highly emphasized in order for all dealers to be technically well-trained concerning all of the Kubota products they offer.

As it celebrates 20 years of service to the Canadian market in 1995, Kubota Canada Ltd., which now dominates the Canadian compact diesel market by outselling all its competitors combined, looks forward to many more decades of success in Canada.

1. The company's head office is located in Markham, Ontario.
2. Kubota Canada offers a wide range of compact diesel tractors and other prodcuts.

2

Le Hage Industries Int'l. Inc.

1

3

With over three decades of experience in the plumbing and drainage product field, Le Hage Industries Int'l. Inc. offers, through its subsidiary Ancon Inc., modular drainage products designed for the construction methods of the 1990s. As a licensee for Sloan Valve Company, Le Hage offers a complete line of sensor operated faucets and flush valves for the modern "no hands" washroom.

The history of Le Hage Industries begins with C.L. Hagedorn, the company's President, who first started in the plumbing and drainage product field in 1953. Forming Wade International Ltd., it began as a distribution company to market plumbing products made by Wade Inc. of the United States. In 1960 Hagedorn established Le Hage Industries Int'l. Inc. as a parent company to manage Wade International.

During the 1960s, Le Hage Industries formed and acquired several successful companies to manufacture specialty products for the plumbing trade that were subsequently sold. One of these success stories was Watrous Inc., formed in 1964. Located in the United States, it manufactured flush valves and soap dispensers. Under Le Hage's guidance, its product lines were redesigned and expanded to include washroom accessories for non-residential buildings and hospital specialties, before being recently sold.

After selling its holdings in Wade International Ltd., in 1972 Le Hage Industries began to operate internationally through F.C. Frost Ltd. Located in the United Kingdom, it was jointly formed by Le Hage Industries and F.C. Frost to manufacture the Watrous line for sales in the United Kingdom and the Middle East.

In 1978 Le Hage Industries formed a new corporation, Ancon, which began to manufacture and market a new modular concept system for the plumbing and drainage specialties. With a complete product line that contained fewer parts than other systems on the market, the Ancon system was designed to be an economical modular system, allowing wholesalers to easily maintain a complete inventory.

Focusing on the non-residential construction market in industrial, commercial and institutional buildings, Ancon rapidly gained market dominance. With its modular system impulsing its growth, Ancon has grown to become the largest company in the drainage industry in Canada.

In 1991 Le Hage also became a licensee for Sloan Valve Company of the United States. With over 80 years of experience in the plumbing products industry, Sloan's flagship product line is its "no hands" washroom, which includes a wide range of sensor operated bathroom accessories.

In 1993 Le Hage sold its Ancon division and Sloan license to Watts Industries of the United States, giving it important access to Watts' well developed marketing division, which will fuel further growth in the future.

Analyzing the achievements of Le Hage Industries, Hagedorn emphasizes that one of the key reasons for its success has been the company's foresight to understand the future needs of the marketplace and subsequently develop the products to match those needs. It is this foresight, coupled with the company's wealth of experience that will allow Le Hage Industries Int'l. Inc. to continue as a leader in the plumbing and drainage industries.

2

1. C.L. Hagedorn, the Founder and President of Le Hage Industries Int'l. Inc., located in Toronto, Ontario.
2. Through its subsidiary Ancon, the company offers a complete modular drainage products line.
3. As a licensee for Sloan Valve Company, Le Hage Industries distributes sensor operated faucets and flush valves for the modern "no hands" washroom.

The Learning Enrichment Foundation

Its record has drawn international acclaim; its model for community economic development is unique; and its programs are instruments for local, community, cultural, economic, and social development. A non-profit, charitable agency functioning in the City of York in Metropolitan Toronto, The Learning Enrichment Foundation (LEF) provides education, training and related support in order to encourage and prepare individuals to achieve meaningful integration into society and the world of work.

Through its innovative family of programs working in a synergistic relationship, LEF strives to meet the ever-changing needs of its diverse communities. Programs include the provision of quality child care, the promotion of intercultural sensitivity, the provision of employment training, small business support, job creation, and the fostering of full employment and community economic development.

The Learning Enrichment Foundation was born of necessity. With a higher than average rate of unemployment in the multicultural City of York in the late 1970s, the Foundation was created in 1978 to respond to this critical situation with an education/business partnership. By 1980, LEF had started a range of programs designed to meet the economic needs of the community. As new needs and areas of concern were identified, specific programs were developed to address those inadequacies.

Today, the Learning Enrichment Foundation is in many ways the sum of its component parts, with each program strengthening the others. In addition to several specific entities operating under the auspices of LEF, there are many related areas of activities. LEF's skill training programs for unemployed people offer courses in many areas, such as computer training, indus-

1

trial construction and maintenance, and child care assistant training. In addition, the centre offers extended employment skills including literacy and numeracy programs.

LEF's Child Care Program arose out of the need to offer daycare to give people the freedom to participate in training programs or employment. The ingenious model of community-based, non-profit centres combines professional and dedicated Early Childhood Educators and Certified Assistants in partnership with responsible and concerned parents. The 14 centres administered by LEF provide a warm and nurturing environment to over 600 children who are honoured as unique individuals and where their dignity and rights are respected.

The Food Services Program began as the most efficient method to

provide hot lunches and morning and afternoon snacks for the children in LEF's child care centres. Today, with over 200 employees, Food Services also provides cafeteria facilities for other LEF employees.

Realizing that a major barrier to employment for the many immigrants living in York was their lack of English, LEF began its LINC (Language Instruction for Newcomers to Canada) program. It provides immigrants with the basic communication skills that are essential to function effectively in Canadian society.

In response to youth employ-

1. *The Learning Enrichment Foundation located in the City of York.*
2. *LINC students in the ESL Computer Lab during supervised self-instruction.*

2

ment, the JOY (Job Opportunities for Youth) employment counselling centre was opened, with a multilingual and multicultural staff. JOY clients are composed of over 80 per cent immigrants of visible minority status whose income and educational levels often bar them from other educational and employment opportunities. JOY provides assistance in finding the most suitable job, training program or apprenticeship, and offers direct referrals to employers, in addition to pre-employment training and job maintenance workshops. For employers, JOY provides the right people for the job, along with information on cost-shared training and wage-subsidized programs.

TEAM (Towards Employment Action in Metro) engages in career exploration and pre-employment training programs designed to provide the skills one needs to obtain and maintain employment. Aspects include the evaluation of current skills, individual career counselling and career planning, pre-employment and team building workshops, basic computer training, on-the-job training experience and skill training. TEAM is where individuals develop action plans resulting in training and employment.

YBOC (York Business Opportunities Centre) assists in the establishment of new small businesses and thereby the creation of new jobs. It is designed to help businesses take advantage of shared services, space and management assistance in an interactive entrepreneurial facility. YBOC's self-

employment training program assists qualified candidates in becoming self-employed by developing their entrepreneurial abilities, teaching them knowledge in small business management, and preparing them for their own business start-up.

Over the years, LEF's network of services have developed a unique inter-related and inter-dependant relationship as they work together to serve the community. For example, the skills training programs work co-operatively with employment counselling services. Child care centres attend to the children of clients as well as assist in the education of trainees. Construction trainees and participants in the Cook's Training Program create items for the child care centres. The Construction Training Program helps renovate space for other activities, such as the York Business Opportunities Centre.

Eunice Grayson, Executive Director of The Learning Enrichment Foundation since its inception, points out that the staff reflects the clientele composition. Among the more than 200 employees, approximately 42 languages are spoken, helping immigrants that have come from around the world to benefit from the programs. Furthermore, LEF works in cooperation with other community development organizations and agencies for the mutual benefit of all involved. LEF's focus has always been within the City of York, where all its programs are located, but clients from across Metropolitan Toronto are welcomed. As to funding for the pro-

1

grams, Grayson explains that it is derived from a variety of sources, including from the federal, provincial and municipal governments, from fees for certain services, and a portion from fundraising. To remain effective and relevant, LEF is soliciting members who will help to support and direct its goal of community economic and social development.

Looking to the future, The Learning Enrichment Foundation can draw strength from its sound past: the growth and development of an organization innovative in meeting needs, skilful in developing programs, and resourceful in helping people of various backgrounds, as it continues to enrich vast numbers of individuals and the community as a whole.

1. *Forklift safety training.*
2. *Every day, Food Services prepares over 600 meals for the children in LEF's Child Care Centres.*
3. *A group of youth participating in a pre-employment training workshop at the JOY Centre.*

2

3

Leland Industries Inc.

A Canadian company using Canadian steel successfully competing against offshore competitors on international markets, Leland Industries Inc. is a rapidly expanding manufacturer and distributor of fasteners and ventilation equipment. Serving manufacturers, industry and construction, Leland has established rigorous benchmarks of quality that surpass the test of today's exacting needs.

As a manufacturer of specialty fasteners, Leland Industries is now the single source of grain bin fasteners for almost all North American grain bin manufacturers. In addition, Leland also produces and distributes steel and stainless steel nuts, bolts, and screws for sheet steel fabricators, metal building manufacturers, professional contractors, and manufacturers of culverts and sectional garage doors.

With the support of his wife Dianne, Leland Industries was founded in 1983 by Byron Nelson, the company's President. After acquiring experience as a fastener distributor company which he himself had founded, he came to the realization that to be a successful Canadian fastener manufacturer involved the development of a niche market.

Entrepreneurial, innovative, hardworking and willing to do what was needed to realize his vision — practical skills acquired in his youth while working at the family farm in Saskatchewan — Nelson established Leland Industries with one machine. Incorporating in 1984, Leland moved to a 2,000 square foot unit in Scarborough, Ontario, with five employees. Concentrating on the steel clad building and grain bin industries, Leland was successfully able to expand its production, convincing manufacturers to switch to its product line.

Although the company moved to a 12,000 square foot location on Gibson Road in Markham, Ontario, in 1991 Leland Industries was forced to relocate once again because of growing sales, to its current 40,000 square foot facility on Torbay Road in Markham. In 1992 Leland opened branches in Edmonton and Calgary, with a third western location established in 1994 in Vancouver. In 1995 a new branch was also opened in Quebec.

Always responsive to customers' needs, Leland initiated an inhouse painting operation to provide superior painted fasteners matching the colour of the cladding. Indeed, Leland's innovation led to the creation of a proprietary paint machine utilizing powder paints rather than liquid. Ideal for the environment, the new paint is also tougher and longer lasting. Other in-house services include special engineered fasteners, custom coatings, trimming and assemblies, distinct coloured painting, and individualized packaging and labelling.

Looking at the success of Leland, Nelson attributes it to the quality of service that the company offers in its niche markets. Since the company's founding, service has always been one of Leland's top priorities. From the placement of an order to the delivery of the final product, employees work together to guarantee customer satisfaction.

The next generation of Nelsons is already involved with the company. Duane Nelson oversees the computer

1

operations of the company, while Jason Nelson is in charge of production and scheduling.

With approximately 75 employees currently handling 6,000 tons of raw material annually, Leland is once again poised to expand its facilities and production capacity. But as it continues to grow, Leland Industries remains committed to sustaining the quality of manufacturing and service that has made it so successful.

1. *Byron Nelson, Founder and President of Leland Industries Inc.*
2. *The 40,000 square foot central manufacturing facilities of Leland Industries, located in Markham, Ontario.*

2

Louis Interiors Inc.

With over 30 years of manufacturing experience, Louis Interiors Inc. has become one of the leaders in the Canadian furniture industry, specializing in sales to the design industry and commercial trade. Its understanding of design trends and product philosophy has distinguished the company as one which strongly focuses on product, quality and commitment to clients.

Louis Interiors today is the culmination and vision of its founder, Louis Muller. For more than a third of a century, Muller has piloted the company to its present situation as one of the eminent furniture manufacturers in Canada.

After immigrating to Canada from Hungary in 1956, Muller began saving money, with the dream to start his own furniture company. That dream became a reality in the summer of 1961 when Muller founded Louis Interiors in Toronto, beginning from the garage of his house. Engaged in high quality custom upholstery work, he soon needed to move to a rented facility on Avenue Road. Muller recalls, "Because of the high quality, business picked up quite fast. Quite simply, the value was in the work."

The following year, with expanding sales and three employees, the company moved to larger premises on Yonge Street. Engaging also in design work, the company soon needed to move to 2539 Yonge Street where it expanded to fill all three floors.

1

Bill Muller, the founder's son, joined the company in 1981 in a period when Louis Interiors was beginning to branch into large commercial work such as restaurant chains and hotels. In 1988, having outgrown its facilities once again, the company moved to its current 30,000 square foot building on Orfus Road.

As sales began to slow down with the recession of the late 1980s, Bill Muller successfully navigated the company to increasing its furniture sales in the Unites States market and across Canada. Export sales now account for approximately 25 per cent of production.

The staff of approximately 30 employees include skilled furniture craftsmen, frame designers and assemblers, as well as technical and administrative support staff. Regarded as a premier high-end manufacturer, it is through a special blend of old

world skills and modern technology that the company ensures its clients the best of quality and styling. Each piece reflects the dedication and skills of the employees. Craftsmen hand-tie coil springs, hand-sew the skirts, and complete the upholstery with each piece of fabric matching perfectly, particularly emphasizing the finishing details.

Having evolved into a diverse company offering a wide range of custom and contract design, the company's two most recent complete furniture lines include the Showroom Collection, offering ten graceful seating styles suitable for both contract and residential settings, and the Louis Collection, a contemporary furniture collection consisting of six full seating styles all varied yet distinctive.

Excellent quality, an unwavering commitment to delivery schedules, and competitive prices have made Louis Interiors the choice supplier to over 200 restaurant and hotel installations across North America, including such prestigious locations as the Skydome and the Royal York Hotel in Toronto.

The company's products have emerged from a simple idea: "To build furniture to exceptional standards of quality and workmanship." It is this concept that has been the force behind all of the furniture pieces that leave the shop of Louis Interiors, and it will be the underpinnings of further success.

1. From the beginning, Louis Interiors was dedicated to craftsmanship and quality furniture, c. 1965.
2. Louis Muller, Founder and President, with some of the company's products designed for the commercial restaurant industry.
3. Bill Muller, the Founder's son, has been with the company since 1981.

2

3

Lever Brothers

Keeping clean is what Lever Brothers is all about. Its hallmark brand, Sunlight, is the soap that became the foundation of a dynasty of products that today are as popular as ever. In fact, Sunlight products are now found in two-thirds of all Canadian homes, and Sunlight dishwashing liquid is number one in all of Canada.

The Sunlight legacy, built around a family of quality products that were marketed with care and met by a receptive public, has more than a century of strength and tradition. Its heritage of distinctive value has given Lever Brothers the necessary corporate foundation to launch new soaps and detergents over the years that reflect the scientific and technological advances in cleaning that the company has integrally helped to achieve.

The history of Lever Brothers can be traced to William Hesketh Lever, who joined his father in the Northern England grocery trade at the age of 16. The family business had been selling a variety of soaps, but since 1874 it was dispensing one type exclusively. However, the inherent difficulty in retailing the soaps of that time was that the soap turned rancid when exposed to air. Lever, in an early display of his marketing and business genius, turned to a solution unique for the era. It was commonplace to sell the soap in large unwrapped bars which were subsequently cut up into smaller pieces. But Lever began selling his product in smaller sizes — tablets of soap wrapped in imitation parchment.

Realizing that the grocery trade would not continue to hold his interest, Lever decided to dedicate his energies to the soap industry. With a clear intention of establishing his soap as a product of distinctive quality, he needed a distinguishing trademark, and in 1875 the Sunlight heritage commenced.

1

In 1885, together with his brother James Darcy, Lever opened his first factory in the Lancashire town of Warrington. Through a series of experiments and trial soaps, Lever Brothers, as they became known, obtained the ideal formulation for a pure soap, uniquely prepared for the cleaning of hands and clothing.

With an exceptional product labelled with a good name, wrapped properly and sold at a fair price, the lacking ingredient for success was a loyal market. To this end the com-

2

pany began its now legendary marketing campaign, spending vast amounts on publicity to encourage the wholesaler to buy the products, along with the important corollary of targeting the end-user — the

1., 2. From the outset, Lever Brothers placed unprecedented emphasis on marketing and advertising. Targeting both the wholesaler and the end user, it projected its flagship product, Sunlight Soap, into a dominant position in the retail soap market, first in Britain and later around the world.
3. The Canadian Sunlight Soap Works first began production in 1903, manufacturing its product for the growing Canadian market. Insisting that its soap be 100 per cent pure, it wholesaled Sunlight Soap in boxes that clearly displayed the company's legendary reward.

3

working class family.

In 1888 Lever Brothers built a huge soap factory on the south shore of Mersery River, and nearby constructed a unique model workers' village, christened Port Sunlight, which still exists today. (To ensure the following day's production schedule, the company shut the pubs at 8:00 every night.)

Well established in Britain, the company began looking farther afield. Travelling to Canada in 1888, Lever realized the potential of the Canadian marketplace with its affinity for British goods, and established a sales agency in Montreal. Lever Brothers initially found it somewhat difficult to successfully establish itself because of Sunlight's relatively high price — the consumer was able to buy a much larger bar of conventional soap for the same price as a smaller bar of Sunlight soap — and so once again Lever turned to marketing. One famous ploy was the establishment of the Sunlight guarantee: "A $5,000 reward will be paid by Lever Brothers Limited, Toronto, to any person who can prove that this soap contains any form of adulteration whatsoever, or contains any injurious chemicals." No records exist to indicate that the company ever needed to pay.

Sunlight soap was also advertised as "The purest laundry soap in Canada." The claim was that the product provided many extra hours of leisure on wash days because its efficiency and absolute purity saved the user from many "weary hours of wash tub drudgery."

By 1892 business was improving. The company moved its Montreal agency to Toronto and opened offices in Saint John and Halifax. With confidence in the future, it also purchased 23 acres of land on the east side of Toronto's Don River on which to build its first Canadian factory. Going into production in 1903, it was described as "the finest soap factory on the American continent" and produced approximately 1,250 tonnes of Sun-

light soap in its first year of operation. The goal was to produce Sunlight soap with skill and experience, rather than with cheap labour, and without the common foul smelling air because, unlike much of the common soap of the day, no rancid grease or slaughterhouse offal was used, only pure oils and pure fats. Reflecting its concern for its employees, Sunlight Soap Works also included a kitchen where employees' meals were prepared for serving in the adjacent dining hall.

By the mid 1940s yearly production of Sunlight Soap in Canada had risen to over 7,000 tonnes, and as a result in 1948 the current plant was constructed. Although the arrival of synthetic detergents posed a possible threat to the future of Sunlight soaps, the name itself was so strong that the synthetic cleaning products which Lever Brothers itself began to produce were also highly successful. Sunlight Liquid for Dishes first appeared in 1963, and Sunlight Powder, a synthetic laundry detergent, came in 1966.

Today, Lever Brothers remains a significant force in the Canadian detergents market. It has the leading share in dishwashing liquids and personal wash products, and has the leading brand in bar soaps with Dove, launched in the late 1950s. Lever 2000, launched in 1990, is the leading deodorant soap in Canada. Sun-

light, the original Lever brand, has a strong share of the laundry detergent market.

Reflecting on the company's successes, E. Peter Elwood, President of Lever in Canada, attributes it largely to "a commitment to providing products that more than satisfy consumer needs, based on the latest technology, and positioning them to grow and become a force within the industry."

Lever Brothers can also take pride in the leading role it has played in the industry with its environmental program, recognized by government and environmental groups alike. The company has taken the initiative with suppliers to reduce the size of its containers and hence the amount of packaging, along with an increased use of recycled plastics.

Well-established in the marketplace, Lever Brothers can look to its heritage as a continuing source of inspiration. A family of quality, good value products, renowned for their cleaning capabilities, backed by a dedicated company — in Canada alone Lever employs approximately 500 people — has given the company the basis for yet more successes in the future.

The Canadian head offices and manufacturing facilities of Lever Brothers are located on Sunlight Park Road in Toronto near where the Don River meets Lake Ontario.

Magna International Inc.

One of the largest manufacturers of automotive systems and components in the world, Magna International Inc. is headquartered in Markham, Ontario. The company has annual sales of approximately five billion dollars and employs 21,000 people in more than 80 manufacturing and product development centres throughout North America and Europe.

The story of Magna is in many ways the story of its founder, Frank Stronach. An Austrian immigrant trained as a tool and die maker, Stronach arrived in Canada in 1954. A year later he moved to Toronto, where he found a job working as a tool and die maker. In 1957 he opened his own business — Multimatic Investments Limited — in a rented garage in the Dufferin and Dupont Streets' area of Toronto's old manufacturing district. It was here, working long hours and sleeping on a cot next to his lathe, that Frank Stronach began building his one-man tool and die shop into one of Canada's largest corporations.

Following an initial order to produce metal brackets for General Motors, the company expanded into the production of stamped automotive components and began to increase operations. In 1969, Multimatic merged with the Magna Electronics Corporation Limited, a publicly-traded aerospace and defense company. Soon after, the company was renamed Magna Interna-

1

2

3

tional Inc., with Frank Stronach as Chairman and CEO.

By the 1970s, the auto parts business was booming — and so was Magna. One of the main reasons for the company's strong growth was its strategy of building small factories with no more than 100 people. Undertaken in order to foster a close working relationship between managers and employees, the small factories helped create an environment which encouraged individual initiative and involvement.

Another reason for the company's growth was its decentralized operating structure, with each factory set up as a separate profit centre. This approach, designed to avoid bureaucracy, made the company more responsive to customer needs and changing market conditions.

In order to attract and maintain top-notch, entrepreneurial managers, Stronach introduced a pre-determined profit-sharing arrangement. By sharing ownership and profits with his new managers, he was able to harness their entrepreneurial energy and creativity, further helping to fuel Magna's growth.

Initially, only managers participated in the profit-sharing plan. But when Magna eventually became a

1. Frank Stronach, shown here working at a lathe in the tool and die shop he started in 1957. The small, one-man operation he started has grown into one of the largest and most diversified automotive parts suppliers in the world.
2. Magna International Inc. founder and Chairman, Frank Stronach.
3. Don Walker, President and Chief Executive Officer of Magna International Inc.

public company in the early 1970s, with Stronach as the controlling shareholder, he expanded the principle of profit and equity participation to include every employee. Frank Stronach's business philosophy, which came to be known as "Fair Enterprise," provided the foundation of Magna's unique operating structure and corporate culture.

By the end of the 1970s, Magna had 40 plants — almost all of them in Canada — and revenues of $180 million. In order to focus on the development of its automotive technologies, the company sold its aerospace/defense division.

A decade later, Magna had 17,000 employees in more than 100 factories throughout the world. With annual sales approaching two billion dollars, Magna was opening a new factory every six to eight weeks. The company, which had undertaken a major diversification strategy in the mid-1970s, was making more than 5,000 different automotive components.

Today, Magna is a global company with manufacturing divisions in ten different countries supplying systems and components to all of the world's major carmakers. Magna's unique corporate culture is one of the main reasons for the company's success. At the heart of this culture is an operating philosophy based on profit-sharing between the three driving forces of the business: investors, employees and management. Each of these key groups receives a pre-determined percentage of annual pre-tax profits. This profit-sharing principle — what one business study referred to as Magna's "success formula" — is enshrined in the company's governing Corporate Constitution.

Magna employees receive 10 per cent of the annual pre-tax profits: three per cent is in the form of a cash payment, and the remaining seven per cent in the form of Magna stock, making each employee a shareholder with a real stake in the success of the company. In fact, ever since the introduction of the Employee Profit and Equity Participation program in 1976, Magna has grown at the remarkable average rate of more than 20 per cent per year.

In addition to Magna's unique Corporate Constitution, the company has an Employee's Charter, which guarantees a number of employee rights, including competitive wages, a safe and healthful working environment, and fair treatment. A key feature of the Employee's Charter is the Magna Hotline, a toll-free number which employees can call if they have any concerns or if they feel their rights have been infringed.

The company also recently established employee "Fairness Committees" at many of its operating divisions. These committees give employees the chance to democratically resolve concerns that arise on the shop floor. Together with the Hotline, the Fairness Committees provide another avenue for ensuring fairness and employee democracy in the workplace.

Magna's expansion into Europe in the mid-1980s has taken on more strategic prominence since the mid-1990s. The company made several key acquisitions in 1994 in order to expand its presence in the large European market and add several new technologies, including air bag systems.

The automotive diversification strategy that Magna implemented in the 1970s has today made the company the most diversified automotive parts supplier in the world. Magna's wide range of product and manufacturing expertise allows the company to supply complete interior and exterior automotive body systems at a time when automakers are contracting more and more automotive systems development to suppliers such as Magna.

Magna's highly skilled and highly motivated employees give the company a key competitive advantage. Of Magna's 21,000 employees, 1,000 are engineers involved in developing new automotive products and re-engineering current products and processes, while 1,500 are tool and die makers. The company's shares are listed and traded on The Toronto Stock Exchange and Montreal Exchange in Canada, and on the New York Stock Exchange in the United States.

The vision of founder Frank Stronach and the entrepreneurial spirit which has guided Magna's growth over the past five decades is still strong and vibrant. As a corporation which focuses on innovations in its human resources and automotive technologies, Magna will continue to be a business pioneer for many years to come.

1. *Magna is founded on an entrepreneurial culture that rewards innovation. This dual cavity fender mould doubled parts production and reduced manufacturing costs.*
2. *Magna's unique Corporate Constitution inspires pride and ownership in all its employees. The Constitution gives employees a stake in the success of the company through its profit sharing and equity participation programs.*
3. *State-of-the-art technology and advanced engineering processes allow Magna to produce world-class, quality products at globally competitive prices.*

1

2

3

Mattel Canada Inc.

1

A worldwide leader in the design, manufacturing and marketing of toys, Mattel Inc. can trace its roots back to 1945 and the garage of a Southern California couple, Ruth and Elliot Handler. From this modest beginning, Mattel has grown to become one of the most respected and recognized names in the toy industry. Known as "The University of Toyland" for its many contributions to the toy industry, Mattel has been established in Canada for more than 30 years.

The history of Mattel starts when partners Harold Matson and Elliot Handler began manufacturing doll furniture in the Handler's garage workshop. The fruits of their labour were marketed under the name "Mattel," a name they coined by combining the letters of their last and first names, respectively. In 1946 Matson sold his interest in the young company to Elliot and Ruth Handler and, together, this husband and wife team built their company into a multi-million dollar business. Their vision and ingenuity were aided by the burgeoning children's market of the post-war baby boom.

Already an expanding success story, Mattel made toy industry history when, at the 1959 New York Toy Fair, it introduced its first Barbie® doll. This $11\frac{1}{2}$ inch fashion doll went on to become the best-selling doll of all time and the toy industry's most successful product line. In 1993, worldwide Barbie sales exceeded the U.S. $1 billion mark.

In 1968 Mattel made the successful transition from dolls to toy vehicles with the introduction of Hot Wheels®. These miniature die-cast cars were such a hit with little boys that they generated in excess of U.S. $25 million in the first year of sales.

During this exciting period of growth and expansion, Mattel Canada Inc. was created in 1963 to service the growing toy market in Canada. In the years which followed, Mattel Canada grew from a branch office operation to a full-scale corporate entity, controlling all marketing and distribution for the Canadian market. To meet the challenge of servicing a national market in a country as vast and regionally diverse as Canada, Mattel Canada opened sales offices in Montreal and Vancouver.

Based in Toronto, Mattel Canada today employs more than 120 people and is Canada's largest toy company. The current President, Ian Bradley, joined the company as Director of Finance in 1983. President since 1990, Bradley has seen Mattel Canada through its most intensive growth period ever, including several acquisitions and the 1995 merger with Fisher-Price Canada.

With the addition of Fisher-Price, Mattel now has four principle core brands — Barbie, Fisher-Price, Disney and Hot Wheels — which are recognized the world over and account for 80 per cent of total sales.

In 1994, the original of these global power brands, Barbie, celebrated a landmark 35 year anniversary. In Canada, the occasion was marked by the opening of Mattel Canada's second exclusively Barbie destination shop, *Barbie on Portage* in Winnipeg. Based on the success of this store and the flagship *Barbie on Bay*, opened in Toronto in 1993, Mattel Canada will open two more Barbie boutiques in 1995.

At the heart of the Mattel business philosophy are four fundamental strengths: time-tested core brands, unsurpassed international marketing presence, a worldwide manufacturing network, and financial discipline. Despite changing economies and consumer buying habits this unique and powerful combination of qualities continue to propel Mattel to new heights and record sales.

1. *Mattel Canada President, Ian Bradley, traces his own roots to Kirkland Lake, Ontario.*
2. *The head offices of Mattel Canada in Etobicoke, Ontario.*
3. *Barbie, introduced by Mattel in 1959, is Mattel's most successful product ever.*

2

3

MSA Canada

In 1914, two engineers with the U.S. Bureau of Mines started a small, one-room business to produce safety and rescue equipment to fight all-too-frequent mine tragedies. They called their fledgling business "Mine Safety Appliances Company" and its stated mission was "That Men Might Work in Safety."

One of their early notable achievements was to persuade Thomas Alva Edison to scale down his heavy nickel-iron alkaline battery to a size small enough to be worn on a miner's belt. As a result, open-flame lamps soon disappeared in favour of electric cap lamps, a giant advance towards eliminating fiery mine explosions and saving lives.

In January 1937, Mine Safety Appliances Company of Canada Limited was founded in Montreal, where it remained until 1942, when the head office was relocated to Toronto. It was the first international subsidiary of what was by then the largest company in the world devoted exclusively to the manufacture and distribution of mining and industrial safety products. The name was officially shortened to MSA Canada Inc. in the 1980s.

Its goal was to bring the now established Edison Electric Cap Lamp into widespread use in Canadian underground mines and to introduce Canada's resource and heavy industries to the company's extensive range of respiratory protection devices, gas detection instruments and a myriad of other safety products which had been developed expressly to protect the lives and health of the workers in the primitive and relatively unregulated workplaces typical during those times.

The early years of MSA Canada's existence were dominated by the Second World War and the

1

need to support the Canadian war effort. The extra effort to reach maximum production at this time made worker safety a more important issue than ever. Consequently, MSA Canada began sponsoring a mine safety trophy in 1941. Named the John T. Ryan Trophy in honour of the co-founder of Mine Safety Appliances Company, the trophies have since become the most prestigious safety awards in the Canadian mining industry. They are still sponsored by MSA Canada and are now presented nationally and regionally in three mining categories: metal, coal, and select other mines such as potash, salt, gypsum, etc.

After the War the company diversified to include products for industries in addition to mining, and

2

the focus of MSA Canada broadened to cover all segments of Canadian industry where workers might be exposed to physical danger or health hazards.

Now, more than half a century after its founding, MSA Canada Inc. brings its proven safety technology not just to the mining industry, but to steelmaking, firefighting, defense, oil refining, utility operations, construction, and so on. As part of the world's largest organization dedicated exclusively to the manufacture and distribution of safety products, it remains committed to the values of its co-founders "That Men (and Women) Might Work in Safety."

1., 2. *Throughout its history, MSA has been dedicated to the manufacture and distribution of mining and industrial safety products, from early model gas masks (1), to award winning state-of-the-art personal "multi-gas combination indicators" (2).*
3. *The head office facility of MSA Canada is located in Toronto, Ontario.*

3

Mount Sinai Hospital

Rich in the dual traditions of caring and service, Mount Sinai Hospital is an internationally renown institution and a leader in the health care industry and biomedical research. Located in Toronto, Ontario, Mount Sinai is committed to providing excellence in patient care, education and research.

Having celebrated its 70th anniversary in 1993, Mount Sinai Hospital has a history of growth in relation to the community it serves, evolving through the years in response to the changing and growing needs of its community.

Mount Sinai Hospital was founded in 1923 through the work of an active group of women from Toronto's Jewish population who had a dream. It was a dream of a hospital that would serve the Jewish community, providing a strong teaching centre for young Jewish doctors; and, in many ways the most important impulse, to give something back to the broader community and country which provided for so many in their grave periods of need.

Beginning as a 33 bed hospital located on Yorkville Avenue, by 1933 it had grown to 84 beds. But Mount Sinai wanted to be more than merely an important community hospital, its vision was to become one of the foremost teaching hospitals within Canada that would be perceived as a vital force in the health care community.

By 1953, that vision was one step closer to being realized when the new Mount Sinai Hospital opened its doors on University Avenue with over 330 beds, at the current site of Queen Elizabeth Hospital. Three years later, the hospital received its accreditation status and also became formally affiliated with the University of Toronto.

These two events signalled that, in addition to the advancement into new and challenging areas of medicine, Mount Sinai was much more than a Jewish community hospital. It was evolving into an institution committed to accepting full responsibility for the general patient community along with its new role as a teaching institution.

During the 1950s and 1960s, the health care services Mount Sinai provided grew in leaps and bounds with a rapid expansion of programs to meet the ever increasing needs of its community. It soon became clear that more space was once again required.

In 1973 the hospital moved to its current site on University Avenue, with Her Majesty Queen Elizabeth and Prince Philip present for the official opening of the ultramodern and well-equipped facility.

Mount Sinai Hospital has historically been guided and supported by a vast network of community members. In the early 1980s, the Board recognized there was a large void in the area of basic science research. More importantly, there was an exciting opportunity to integrate basic science research with the hospital's many patient care programs.

As the hospital's commitment to research expanded, new and dedicated quarters were needed, and in 1985 the Research Institute of Mount Sinai Hospital was founded.

Later renamed the Samuel Lunenfeld Research Institute, the fundamental philosophy behind the creation of the Institute was to create an environment where clinicians could work alongside basic science research, bringing the most current treatment from research and experience directly to the bedside.

In 1992 an event occurred which clearly proved that Mount Sinai had achieved senior level status in the healthcare sector. The hospital became the recipient of Canada's first four-year accreditation award, issued by the Canadian Council on Health Facilities Accreditation — the highest honour a Canadian hospital can achieve in the accreditation process.

Today, Mount Sinai Hospital has evolved into a 487 (adult and newborn) bed acute care hospital and a major teaching centre affiliated with the University of Toronto. Wanting to better focus its energies and resources, the hospital has committed itself to becoming a leader in six strategic program areas.

In the area of perinatology, Mount Sinai offers specialized services in low risk and high risk obstetrics, fetal assessment, therapy and neonatal intensive care. Its medical surgical respiratory/thoracic program encompasses a whole spectrum of problems including lung cancer, asthma and breathing disorders during sleep. The oncology specialization area includes the treatment of orthopedic, breast, col-

1. *Mount Sinai Hospital first opened in 1923 on Yorkville Avenue in Toronto.*
2. *In 1953 the hospital moved to a new 330-bed facility on University Avenue.*

1

2

orectal, head and neck, hepato-biliary, thoracic, oculoplastic and oral soft tissue cancers. The gastro-intestinal section focuses on inflammatory bowel diseases such as Crohn's disease and ulcerative colitis. The musculoskeletal specialization features bone and soft tissue surgery, including a major program involving bone and cartilage transplants.

The sixth strategic program area of Mount Sinai Hospital is its research, which encompasses a wide range of collaborative programs between Mount Sinai Hospital and its Samuel Lunenfeld Research Institute, all focusing on a "bench to bedside" approach. The Institute is widely recognized as one of Canada's premier biomedical research facilities, with an annual budget of over $20 million, of which three-quarters is secured from international peer-review funding and contracts with biotechnology and pharmaceutical companies.

The Institute's research programs range from basic studies on the molecular biology of development and cancer to clinical research in a wide spectrum of patient care areas. The Institute's major programs include Development and Fetal Health, Cancer and Molecular Biology, and Clinical Epidemiology. The Institute is also planning a major expansion of its laboratory space to establish a new program in Human Genome Re-

2

search aimed at understanding the molecular determinants of human health and disease.

Mount Sinai Hospital has also formed a major collaborative association with the internationally respected cancer centre Princess Margaret Hospital/Ontario Cancer Institute, which will be relocated beside Mount Sinai Hospital. Furthermore, the hospital has a special relationship with Baycrest Centre for Geriatric Care and has a number of collaborative associations with other area hospitals.

Many of the hospital's programs are internationally recognized. The orthopedic oncology program is the largest of its kind in North America. The hospital's Rachel and David Rubinoff Bone and Tissue Bank is the only facility accredited with the American Association of Tissue Banks and supplies medical centres across North America. The Miles Mount Sinai Cardiovascular Clinical Research Laboratory, which opened in May 1992, is a unique North American human research laboratory dedicated to cardiovascular research.

The hospital is also a national leader in laser and laparoscopic surgery for gallstones, ileostomies and bowel resections. The otolaryngology program features clinicians and scientists who are involved in an ambitious international scientific exchange program. In addition, the Hospital also has a multidisciplinary diabetes clinical research unit that monitors and treats approximately

1,800 outpatients at regular intervals; a widely recognized psychiatry department; important referral programs in perinatology and rehabilitation medicine; and is a recognized University of Toronto Centre of Excellence for oculoplastics in the Department of Ophthalmology. The hospital's internationally respected Department of Nursing, committed to theory-based practice and innovative research, was recently established as a World Health Organization Collaborating Centre — the only nursing service department in the world to hold such a distinction.

Admitting over 23,000 patients and with more than 538,00 outpatient visits in 1993, Mount Sinai Hospital continues with its tradition of caring and with an ongoing commitment to serving its ever growing community. Founded with a vision for the future by a group of pioneering individuals, it is this vision, coupled with ongoing phenomenal community support, that has guided Mount Sinai throughout its history on its road to becoming an internationally renown centre of research and a leader in the Canadian health care field.

1. *One of the hospital's many areas of specialization is bone and cartilage transplants.*
2. *Mount Sinai Hospital today, a world renown institution.*
3. *Dr. Barry Smith, Pediatrician-in-Chief at Mount Sinai, administering care to a premature infant.*

1

3

National Research Council of Canada

As Canada's principal public sector science and technology agency, the National Research Council of Canada performs, supports, and promotes scientific and industrial research for the economic and social benefit of the country. NRC has more than 3,000 dedicated men and women applying science and technology in a wide range of areas, from pharmaceuticals to plant research, from cell biology to clean fuels. Since its founding in 1916, NRC has been devoted to promoting the innovative research necessary to improve the quality of life of all Canadians.

NRC's beginnings were modest. A federal Order-in-Council on June 6, 1916 created an Honorary Advisory Council on scientific and industrial research. The Council members' activities were at first limited to directing research projects, granting scholarships, and serving on committees.

In 1918, the Advisory Council recommended to the government that it build and operate central laboratories in Ottawa. After a long struggle for authorization and financing, a new research organization was formed, soon to be known as the National Research Council. In the mid-1920s, Parliament approved the funds to buy property where the Rideau River joins the Ottawa River. While NRC researchers waited for new laboratories to open in an imposing building next door at 100 Sussex Drive, they carried on their work in converted lumber mill buildings.

In 1928, Dr. Henry Marshall Tory was appointed as NRC's first

1

full-time President. It was under his direction that the organization began to grow and make its presence felt nationally and internationally. A national research journal, the *Canadian Journal of Research*, was launched in 1929, the predecessor of today's 13 NRC research journals.

The agency began to attract and hire top scientists and researchers in their fields, filling appointments in the newly established divisions of chemistry, physics and biology. Studies were undertaken in areas such as plant diseases, animal diseases, and finding commercial use for waste natural gas in Western Canada.

During the Great Depression, funding was tight, but NRC was laying the foundation for a place of pre-

eminence in Canadian research by the time World War II broke out. During the 1930s, researchers were already developing pressure suits for pilots, making advances in medical research, and working on radio detection devices that helped the Allies develop one of their most effective weapons: radar. From 1939 to 1945, the number of NRC employees grew tenfold, from 300 to almost 3,000.

In 1945, NRC expanded its nuclear research role by establishing an atomic energy division at Chalk River, Ontario. The division became Atomic Energy of Canada Limited in 1952.

NRC's reputation continued to grow in the postwar period, attracting

1. *The National Research Council has carried on research in its building on Sussex Drive in Ottawa since 1932.*
2. *At NRC, researchers are innovators and explorers, questioning and probing with patience and persistence while forming a partnership of intellect and imagination, equipping Canada with the scientific and technological tools needed to meet the challenges of the future.*

2

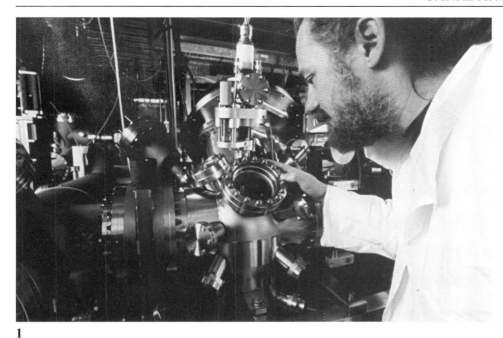

1

researchers from around the world. Its Post-Doctoral Fellowship Program, established in 1948, became a major factor in the expansion of science and technology research in Canada.

The decades of the 1950s and 1960s were an exciting and fruitful time in NRC history. Among the many accomplishments were the development of canola as a major cash crop, the design and building of the cesium atomic clock (which helps set the standard for world time calibration), studies of the northern atmosphere, and the perfecting of the crash position indicator, an automatic distress signal to help rescuers find downed aircraft.

When the energy crisis occurred

in the early 1970s, NRC played a leading role in research into alternative energy forms, including solar energy, wind energy and biomass.

The 1980s saw a flurry of expansion. With the construction of laboratories in different regions of the country, NRC forged stronger ties with research and industrial communities in such centres as Saskatoon, Winnipeg, Montreal, Halifax, and St. John's.

During the 1990s, NRC has been undergoing a comprehensive reorganization, sharpening its focus to help Canadian industry become more competitive internationally. As stated in its long range plan for the years 1990 to 1995, NRC has three main objectives: to preserve and strengthen

the base of research in NRC laboratories; to build partnerships with industry, government and universities to advance national research and development interests; and to set up new research programs in key economic areas in which Canada could become a world leader.

Reflecting this new emphasis, NRC is undertaking research programs and forming partnerships that have resulted in advances in areas such as information technology, environmental clean-up techniques, advanced manufacturing processes, and aeronautics. NRC is also actively engaged in research in the public interest. Recent work includes improving building and fire codes, developing sensitive bomb sniffers, producing anti-counterfeit optical chips incorporated in Canadian bank notes, and doing research to help clean the St. Lawrence River.

As part of its effort to advance science and technology in Canada, NRC provides specialized services to the research and industrial communities. The Canada Institute for Scientific and Technical Information (CISTI) has the largest Canadian collection of international information in science, technology and medicine. The Industrial Research Assistance Program (IRAP) provides technical advice and financial assistance to Canadian industry through a national technology transfer network.

Today, NRC has 19 research institutes across the country, forming a vital research and development network that strengthens Canada at home and around the world. Looking to the future, the National Research Council of Canada will continue as a catalyst for the technological changes needed in Canada to create a more prosperous and competitive nation. NRC's past has given great cause for celebration, and the same will be true in the future.

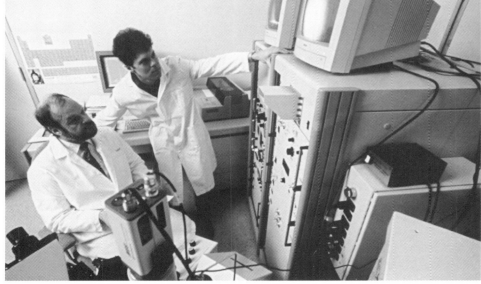

2

1., 2. As Canada's principal national science and technology agency, NRC is dedicated to improving the social well-being and economic prosperity of Canadians.

Noranda Inc.

Noranda Inc. is a diversified natural resource company that operates in three sectors — mining and metals, forest products, and oil and gas — primarily in North America.

Noranda Minerals, part of Noranda's Mining and Metals group, is an integrated base and precious metals mining, smelting and refining group, producing a significant share of the world's zinc, nickel, copper, gold, silver, lead, potash, cobalt, and sulphuric acid. Noranda Aluminum smelts aluminum and produces a wide range of downstream products, and Wire Rope Industries manufactures steel wire rope.

Noranda Forest Inc., one of Canada's largest producers of forest products, has three principal business segments: building materials, pulp, and paper.

Noranda's Oil and Gas group is made up of two companies that explore for, develop, and produce natural gas, natural gas liquids, and crude oil. Noranda's Oil and Gas group is one of Canada's largest in terms of natural gas and oil reserves.

Noranda is one of Canada's largest investors in research and development. The Company operates two technology centres — the Noranda Technology Centre in Pointe Claire, Quebec, and Falconbridge's (46 per cent owned by Noranda) centre in Sudbury, Ontario.

Noranda is committed to employing advanced technology, employee development and training, and open lines of communication with its customers and all of the Company's stakeholders. Taken together, these practices are establishing each of Noranda's individual businesses as industry leaders.

The Company's history all started with a prospector named Ed Horne, whose search for gold led him to the fire-ravaged wilderness of western Quebec in the late 1800s. After several trips into the same general area, Horne was convinced that it was there where the next big gold stakes were to be won.

In 1921, the men who put up the original $225 grubstake sold out to a syndicate of 12 residents from New Liskeard, Ontario, who developed the prospect. It turned out to be a supermine — "the Horne" — and Noranda was born. Incorporated in 1922, the Company's name is a contraction of "Northern Canada".

The cost of placing the Horne property in production was financed through the sale of shares, largely to the Canadian public, together with a $3 million loan with a share bonus from Hollinger, another Canadian company. Currently, 90 per cent of Noranda's shareholders are Canadian, owning approximately 98 per cent of Noranda's shares.

As time went on, Noranda explored many other territories that were just as isolated and inaccessible as western Quebec: Manitouwadge in Ontario, Murdochville and Matagami in Quebec, and Granisle in British Columbia. Each of these territories eventually expanded into a full-fledged region in their own right. Modern facilities were set up on each site, along with infrastructures for the new and evolving communities.

Originally formed as an exploration and development company, Noranda began a program of integration and expansion after establishing its operating base with the discovery of the Horne orebody in 1928, leading to the development of the Noranda Inc. of today. The first stages of the program were construction of the Canadian Copper Refiners plant in Montreal, Quebec, and acquisition of an interest in a neighbouring wire and cable plant.

Today, Noranda employs 31,000 people at its operations and sales offices around the world, and its total assets were approaching ten billion dollars in 1993. A Canadian-owned company, its common shares are listed on Canada's major stock exchanges.

c. 1911. Ed Horne's search for gold led him to the wilderness of western Quebec and the beginnings of Noranda.

Normerica Building Systems Inc.

With its distinctive custom designed homes, club houses and resort lodges located throughout Canada and the United States as well as overseas, Normerica Building Systems Inc. is now one of the most important creators of timber homes and panelized buildings in North America. Offering true country homes with grace, strength and enduring beauty that express the personal taste and ideals of each individual owner, Normerica works closely with every client, from concept to completion, to ensure that their home is the realization of their dream.

Normerica was founded in 1979 by David McFarlane as Upper Canada Post & Beam, focusing on the potential of developing a market niche in Canada for quality built homes using the 4000 year old tradition of post and beam construction. With headquarters in Markham, Ontario, it remains a private company with majority ownership by David McFarlane, Brian Love and Norbord Industries (a subsidiary of Noranda Forest).

Building on the post and beam concept, "Upper Canada" developed a leadership role in applying innovative production methods, while incorporating state-of-the-art energy-efficient panelized building technology.

Today Normerica offers three individual building system choices. The company promotes these beautiful homes under the Normerica Custom Country Homes banner within the United States, and as Upper Canada Custom Country Homes throughout Canada and the rest of the world.

Its Post and Beam portfolio consists of traditional timber frame homes featuring bold, exposed pine posts and beams connected with mortise and tenon joints enclosed with an energy-efficient panelized construction method. Normerica's Panelbeam homes combine panelized wall construction with unique pine beamed ceilings to create elegant energy-efficient homes. Lastly, Panels-Plus delivers a precision, factory-crafted home using Normerica's "openwall" panelized building system, allowing for easy site-assembly and assuring superior quality at an affordable price.

Throughout the production process, thorough attention to design and construction details, in conjunction with careful factory-fabrication of most major components, assure the highest levels of quality. Furthermore, all three categories of homes meet the Canadian government's R-2000 criteria and standards, assuring extremely energy-efficient homes.

With an ever increasing range of home designs coupled with Normerica's unique and innovative design system, individual tastes and needs are readily satisfied. Standard designs can be modified, or Normerica is able to custom-design a home based on a client's or architect's plans. David McFarlane, President, emphasizes, "The essential character and quality of a Normerica home is very personal. We create custom homes."

As Normerica's reputation spread across North America, it also became renowned around the world. Multilingual staff manage the principal overseas markets of Japan, Spain, and Turkey, with other sites of Normerica installations including Estonia, Germany, and Argentina.

Sophisticated technology, unequalled quality control, and outstanding design creativity have all helped bring Normerica to the leadership position it now enjoys. As one of the world's major manufacturers of prefabricated timber and panelized structures, Normerica Building Systems' founding mission continues to be its guide for future growth: To design and manufacture beautiful, energy-efficient custom country homes of abiding grace and value.

1. Normerica Building Systems offers classic designs in a variety of building systems.
2. Inside a post and beam constructed house, with the company's trade mark fiddlehead window.

1
2

Northwestern General Hospital

With more than 40 years of growth and service to its community, Northwestern General Hospital is a 240-bed acute care community general hospital. Located on Keele Street in the City of York, the hospital primarily serves residents of the Cities of York, Toronto and North York in Metropolitan Toronto.

The hospital's full range of medical, surgical and diagnostic services ensure the provision of quality patient care, while maximizing the efficient use of limited resources and ensuring the long term viability of the hospital. Northwestern General specializes in compassionate care to patients that addresses the physical, psycho-social, emotional and spiritual needs of each individual, yet respecting the diverse needs of its multi-cultural community and staff.

The history of Northwestern General begins in the post World War II period of growth of Metropolitan Toronto. The Township of York was growing rapidly with unprecedented immigration, but without the facilities of a local hospital. The first concrete ideas for Northwestern General can be traced back to three men of vision who realized that with strength, co-operation and human caring, the dream of a community hospital could become a reality.

Canon Albert Jackson, an Anglican minister, rallied the community in support of a hospital that they could call their own. He approached Rabbi David Monson and Father Francis Gallagher to help realize the dream. The trio planted the seed and then oversaw the development of its roots. The community, the politicians, everyone, came to recognize the need for a community hospital.

In 1950, 15 acres of land were obtained along Keele Street for $15,000. Exemplifying community support, much of the initial financing for the hospital was obtained through a special property tax levy, approved by a ratio of three to one by the residents of the Township of York.

Construction began in 1951 and on August 10, 1954, with the most modern equipment available at the time and with 104 beds, Northwestern General Hospital first opened its doors. But soon, crowded corridors and a shortage of beds were becoming an everyday occurrence and plans ensued for expansion.

In 1961 the first addition was constructed, adding four floors to the original building and raising capacity to 248 beds. The need for further enlargement again became evident, and in 1976 the East Building was opened, bringing bed capacity to 287 active treatment beds, greatly increasing facilities, and providing new and specialized departments.

The Harold and Grace Baker Centre was built in 1984, a 120-bed nursing home and 120-bed retirement residence. The same building also incorporates the Ernie Boccia Creative Child Day Care Centre which provides care for 45 children.

Northwestern General's vision for the future — a vision held with great enthusiasm — is to expand the vital role it plays in its community to providing care to the "total being." The dream is to encourage healthier lifestyles which will in turn prevent a variety of diseases, illnesses and injuries.

A dream originally helped build Northwestern Hospital General, and its vision now carries it into the future, as the hospital continues to deliver excellence today for a healthier tomorrow.

1. *Northwestern General Hospital provides a broad range of medical, surgical and diagnostic services to the residents of the Cities of York and North York.*
2. *The acute care community general hospital recently celebrated its 40th anniversary. Helping to cut the cake are Moe Emer, former Board Chairman; Brent Chambers, President; Fergy Brown, Mayor of the City of York; Frank Seymour, former Administrator; Rabbi David Monson, one of the Hospital's founders; Douglas Anderson, former Board Chairman; and Tony Canale, current Board Chairman.*

1

2

OPS Business Systems Inc.

Founded in 1979 as Office Photocopier and Suppliers by Daniel S. Haywood, OPS' President, the company began rather modestly with Haywood's brother, Glen Haywood, and four employees in a 2,000 square foot location on Torbay Road in Markham, Ontario. From the beginning OPS marketed Toshiba products, because, as Haywood explains, "Toshiba has a worldwide reputation for quality and reliability, and its expertise in electronic excellence has long been the foundation of this forty billion dollar giant."

Canada's largest distributor of Toshiba office equipment, OPS Business Systems Inc. has grown through its dedication to service and customer support. Realizing that a newly completed sale is but the first step on the road to a potentially long-term business relationship, OPS is committed to providing the best ongoing support in the industry, matching the high quality of the products it sells.

With a growing list of clients, OPS paid close attention to providing the best support possible, and was rewarded with a loyal customer base, many of which are now third and fourth generation user clients. As facsimile machines began to become part of the office environment, OPS seized the opportunity and began offering several Toshiba models to its customer base and became Canada's largest distributor of Toshiba facsimiles. To better reflect its wider product offerings, the company adopted it current name.

As the need for better showroom facilities and larger office space increased, OPS expanded into neighbouring units in the same complex, and in 1991 the company moved to its current highly visible site on Woodbine Avenue, with 15,000 square feet offering one of Canada's largest showroom facili-

ties to showcase its broad range of office equipment.

With a marketing background and an initial exposure in the technical end of the office equipment field, Haywood has stressed after-sales support from the beginning. All OPS technicians and sales people are first trained by the company itself, ensuring that each one is very familiar with all OPS products and its underlying philosophy of building the business on exceptional customer service. Then, factory trained from Toshiba on the equipment and on-going advancements in technology, continual training is emphasized to ensure that OPS personnel are considered to be the top performers in the industry.

One clear example of OPS' attention to customer after sales support is its unique Customer Satisfaction Link program. Through customer surveys, OPS staff have been trained to be proficient in meeting their customer demands and expectations. If a customer has any difficulty or question concerning any office equipment or service provided by OPS, they can fax it on pre-supplied "Customer Satisfaction Link" forms and expect an immediate response. Haywood explains, "This innovative service gives our customers a clear cut means to having problems solved without having to go through the aggravation of contacting the proper department and personnel to help solve their dilemma. This is the OPS 'moment of truth' that demonstrates how quickly we

react and give the customer the comfort that we care by showing that we have the ability to solve problems outside the normal day-to-day support."

Reflecting the company's proactive maintenance program, OPS provides an all encompassing "perfect copy" guarantee with all of its photocopiers: if every copy is not a perfect reproduction, the customer need not pay.

As a result of this dedication, OPS has enjoyed a consistent pattern of growth, doubling in size in the last four years. Its clients are located throughout the greater Metropolitan Toronto area and range in size from small and mid-size organizations to some of Canada's largest corporations such as Eaton's of Canada, Ernst & Young, National Grocers, and Grand & Toy, to name a few.

Today, with approximately 60 personnel, OPS Business Systems, under the direction of Daniel Haywood and a staff of loyal professional managers and employees, is poised for further success, devoted to customer service and support, now and into the future.

1. Daniel S. Haywood, Founder and President, with the support of his family, has guided the success of OPS Business Systems since its inception.
2. Located in Markham, Ontario, OPS is now the largest distributor of Toshiba office equipment in Canada.

1

2

Peerless Enterprises

1

Specialists in all types of roofing systems, Peerless Enterprises is a Canadian company that has earned its credentials as one of Canada's premier sources of roofing expertise. Committed to providing leadership and innovation, Peerless Enterprises manufactures and installs built up roofing, metal roofing, steel roof deck, metal siding, and all related services to provide a weather tight environment.

Founded in 1943 in Toronto by Otto Minialoff, the father of the company's current President, Peerless began with its first roofing shop behind the Minialoff residence. Through hard work and a dedication to quality results, the company expanded into new facilities, and in 1957 a new five acre complex at Queensway and Kipling Streets in Toronto was opened. Ex-

panding from flat asphalt roofing into metal decking, in 1958 Peerless became one of the first companies in Canada to roll-form steel roof deck.

Diversifying further in the 1960s, the company became engaged in metal siding. The decade was also an important period of innovation, with Peerless introducing the Canadian industry to hot asphalt transport tankers, pitch pumps, and new methods of installation.

The 1970s saw expansion through the acquisitions of subsidiaries and the establishment of a new manufacturing site. Northern Roofing, based in London, Ontario, was acquired in 1972; subsequently, Julian Roofing (Ont.) Ltd. of Stoney Creek, Ontario was also procured, providing Ontario-wide roof installation services. In 1977, Peerless opened a new two and one-half acre complex on Carlingview Drive, dedicated to the manufacture of the Peerless metal product line.

Committed to Canada-wide sales, Peerless Enterprises Alberta was established to provide the complete Peerless product line in Western Canada. In Eastern Canada, Peerless Enterprises Maritimes was recently inaugurated to complete the company's nation-wide service.

Today, Peerless provides a total service for new roof construction, roof repair, restoration, maintenance, or roof replacement using

the most current methods and roofing technologies. Fully-trained crews bring a tradition of quality workmanship to every job, from incidental repairs to major installations. Furthermore, Peerless is a leading manufacturer of architectural metal roofing systems, custom metal panel systems, insulated metal siding and steel roof deck. As technology advances, Peerless takes pride in expanding its capabilities to bring new materials and applications to its customers.

Upon the retirement of the founder in the late 1950s, the second generation of Minialoff's assumed the helm. Currently, Joe Minialoff, the eldest son, is President, while his two brothers, Jerry and Nicolas Minialoff, oversee the Metal Products Division, and equipment maintenance, respectively.

With a total commitment to customer satisfaction, from manufacture, sales, supply and installation to ongoing maintenance, Peerless Enterprises has over 50 years of experience, expertise and motivation to meet the future challenges of the Canadian roofing industry.

1. *Otto Minialoff, founder of Peerless Enterprises.*
2. *Peerless uniquely designed, manufactured and installed all the metal cladding for Darlington Nuclear Generating Station in Clarington, Ontario.*
3. *Peerless provides its leading roofing expertise across Canada.*

2

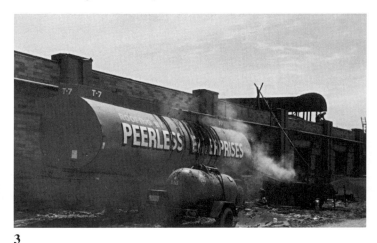

3

Pindoff Record Sales Limited

Celebrating its 35th anniversary in 1995, Pindoff Record Sales Limited — a wholly owned and operated Canadian company — now represents one of the largest audio/video companies in Canada, with over $200 million in annual sales. Music World, a major division of Pindoff Record Sales, currently has over 110 stores from coast to coast and itself is celebrating its 25th anniversary.

The history of Pindoff Record Sales is to a large extent the story of Kroum T. Pindoff and his wife, Eva Pindoff, and their hard work and dedication. Immigrating to Canada from Germany in 1955, the Pindoffs had a dream to begin their own company. After working in a variety of capacities, in 1960 Kroum Pindoff founded Pindoff Record Sales, working out of his house selling albums to independent convenience store owners. Operating out of his station wagon, he covered many miles, working 14 hours a day and seven days a week.

Soon, his efforts began to bear fruit, and in 1962, in response to expanding sales, the first Pindoff Record Sales warehouse opened. The Pindoffs' continuing hard work, diligent efforts and sound business practices led the company to attain major accounts, such as The T. Eaton Company Limited in 1970.

Realizing that to expand Pindoff Record Sales further required broader marketing control in the future, in 1970 the company opened up its first Music World store in Fairview Mall in Toronto, thereby setting the direction for future successes under the able guidance of Eva Pindoff as President. By 1972, four Music World stores were in operation. As Pindoff Record Sales Limited expanded into new accounts, Music World also continued to grow, opening more and more stores and increasing its presence across the country during the 1970s and 1980s

Today, the company's head of-

1. *Eva and Kroum Pindoff, co-founders and executive management of Pindoff Record Sales and Music World.*
2. *The company's head office and central distribution centre, in Toronto, Ontario.*

fice and distribution centre is located in a 55,000 square foot facility in Toronto. The Montreal branch boasts over 20,000 square feet; in addition, there are also two sales offices for Western Canada, in Vancouver and Calgary. Ensuring that the company functions as a unified entity and is efficient and competitive, Pindoff Record Sales has implemented advanced technological and electronic systems that allow for instant communications with its suppliers and customers anywhere.

Wanting to share their prosperity with those less fortunate, in 1993 the Pindoffs established The Pindoff Project after a visit to Bosnia. Working with the Canadian Red Cross, the goal has been to aid those less fortunate in war torn Bosnia. Currently, The Pindoff Project is engaged in the building of an orphanage to house over 200 children and elderly in Bosnia. Treating the project as in a businesslike fashion, the Pindoffs ensure

that all monies are sent directly to the end user without any administration costs. To date, The Pindoff Project — funded primarily by the Pindoffs — has raised over $750,000, with plans to extend funding to other places of need around the world. The Pindoffs were recently publicly recognized by the Canadian Red Cross for their humanitarian efforts.

In recognition of his achievements, on May 3, 1995, Kroum Pindoff was inducted into the Canadian Music Hall of Fame.

The success of Pindoff Record Sales Limited has stemmed from one of Kroum Pindoff's basic philosophies of "health and happiness." It is his belief that the health and happiness of his suppliers, his customers, and his employees is important to each other because only the health and happiness of all will ensure that the company continues to be an industry leader for years to come.

Pizza Pizza Limited

1

One of the most successful pizza companies in Canada, Pizza Pizza Limited's well known orange and white boxes along with the familiar phone number are constantly putting smiles on the faces of pizza consumers everywhere. Now located in hundreds of neighbourhoods across Ontario and looking to expand across Canada and internationally, Pizza Pizza has become an industry leader through its commitment to excellence in product quality and service, and its ongoing emphasis on developing new and innovative marketing ideas and products.

The history of Pizza Pizza is very much the story of Michael Overs, who has guided and steered the company from the outset. The first location was founded in 1968 in little more than 300 square feet at the corner of Wellesley and Parliament Streets in downtown Toronto. A rather small outlet, it was nevertheless a bold experiment, with Overs involved in every aspect, including the carpentry work, which he himself completed to a large extent.

Realizing that to be a successful pizza store it needed to be run like a business, Overs started what eventually became a pizza revolution in Toronto. He began with marketing. Seeing that when the store issued

coupons the business boomed — and without them his customers went elsewhere — he came to the conclusion that promotion and advertising were at the heart of a prosperous business and, therefore, began a persistent coupon and marketing campaign which continues on a much larger scale today.

A second early problem was keeping the pizza hot during delivery. This issue was resolved when Michael Overs designed an insulated bag that acted as a portable heat retention unit which became the prototype of the delivery bags which are now copied and used in proliferation throughout North America.

The business started to grow and by 1979, a turning point for the chain, Pizza Pizza had over 20 stores. It was in 1979 that Pizza Pizza centralized its already extensive operations around one, now very well-known phone number to Torontonians. The popularity of the "967-11-11" jingle is legendary in light of contemporary advertising campaigns. The phone number, and the supporting system that made it the first computerised, one-number, centralized pizza ordering phone

system in the world, gave Pizza Pizza operators the means to easily obtain all the information needed to help them fill each customer's order.

The new system was able to keep track of all aspects of a customer's pizza needs. In addition to the routine information of name, address and phone number, the system also recorded special order requests and most frequently ordered toppings. Calling Pizza Pizza became like walking into a friendly restaurant, where a customer could ask for "the usual" and receive it.

The ensuing success of the centralized phone number spurred the company's growth, and by 1984 there were 65 Pizza Pizza locations across Toronto. With his entrepreneurial foresight, Overs began to analyze future opportunities for further expansion and realized the need for a new marketing tool — the third component of the company's success. Customers wanted their pizza delivered fresh, hot, *and* fast.

In 1985 the 30 minutes-or-free campaign was launched, impulsing new corporate growth. One year later, the chain had soared to 99 stores. And despite time-conscious

1. *Michael Overs, Founder and Chairman of Pizza Pizza Limited.*
2. *First located in downtown Toronto, Pizza Pizza has expanded into Ottawa, Hamilton, London, and over 70 towns across Ontario.*

1

2

customers carefully monitoring their clocks, only one-half of one percent of all pizzas are delivered after the 30 minute deadline.

January 1992 heralded the grand opening of Pizza Pizza's first restaurant outside Canada. Splendidly located in a converted historical landmark in San José, Costa Rica, it became an instant success and soon after, four more Pizza Pizza restaurants opened in the country.

Recently, Pizza Pizza has deployed resources into developing non-traditional slice locations. There are now more than 250 of these sites, established in such diverse locales as convenience stores, sport centres, universities, cinemas, gas stations, golf courses, bingo outlets and high schools.

Always insisting that its employees have the skills of the highest calibre, Pizza Pizza has its own school for training. "Pizza Pizza University" teaches cooking, marketing and management skills to prospective and existing franchisees, cooks, corporate management and market managers, in order that they can operate and manage their stores confidently and successfully. This is an intensive program, lasting six weeks.

With over 250 franchise stores and an additional 250 slice locations, Pizza Pizza has become an unparalleled achievement. But to continue to build further success, the company continues to nourish its

roots, working together to build stronger, healthier communities in which it grew up. The company's extensive community involvements include the sponsoring of over 300 baseball, hockey and soccer teams for youngsters, and actively raising money for dozens of charities. The company is also a good local employer, hiring people from each community in which it is located.

Helping to guide the company to future success is Lorn Austin, the company's Chief Operating Officer. He explains, "Anticipating trends and creatively responding to those trends ahead of the competition, and in ways that meet customer needs, has been the secret of our success since Pizza Pizza began. We are, and always will be, a Canadian based operation doing things the Canadian way, and that means outperforming the competition, being more innovative and creative, and offering people better service and value."

Austin continues, "As we grow, we will be challenged by others who will try to imitate our success. To meet those challenges, we must continue to maintain our well-established commitment to quality, competitive pricing and exceptional service, and we will continue to be the number one choice of consumers everywhere looking for top quality and value in the pizza industry."

Today, Pizza Pizza is still a young company, maintaining an energetic and aggressive marketing

program in a highly competitive marketplace. While the future will see many more international sites and a global presence, it will continue to be a Canadian, community-based organization that relies on the personal attention given to customers by every employee in each store. Ultimately, no matter what else changes, personal service, quality and value will always be the strong foundation that has built Pizza Pizza, and will be the keys to guide the company to further growth in the future.

1. Pizza Pizza's community involvement is widespread, involving the sponsorship of sports teams and the support for thousands of local charities.
2. In recent years Pizza Pizza has been developing non-traditional slice sites in a wide range of locations, including gas stations, cinemas, universities, and convenience stores.
3. Leading Pizza Pizza into the future is Lorn Austin, the company's Chief Operating Officer.

3

Precision Engineering Company

Established in 1945 by John E. Pratt and George Wheaton, Precision Engineering Company was located at 545 Keele Street in Toronto in a modest 1,200 square foot facility. Wheaton was succeeded the following year by William F. Phillips. In these early days, journeyman tool makers earned $1.25 per hour as the company supplied tools, dies, jigs and fixtures for domestic manufacturers. In 1952 the building was expanded to 5,000 square feet and personnel increased to approximately 15 employees.

In 1963 Phillips died, and, subsequently, Al Sunnucks (Shop Superintendent and General Manager) became a partner. In 1964 the company was incorporated as Peco Tool & Die Limited, and continues to trade as Precision Engineering to this day. During the 1950s and '60s the company designed and built progressive dies and specialty machinery for a wide range of industries and products, including steel door and window frames, fridges, stoves, washers and dryers, camping equipment — gas stoves, lanterns, coolers, canoes — aluminum pie plates and roast pans, hospital beds and much more.

After Pratt died in 1972, Adolf Kurz (Shop Foreman) became a

1

partner. Under the direction of Sunnucks and Kurz, by the mid 1970s the company increased its production facilities and focused attention on the automotive industry. Securing a large contract with General Motors to produce hood latches, the company needed to expand further and in 1982 moved to Iron Street in Etobicoke, occupying 14,000 square feet. A few years later, as new opportunities were realized, a second 14,000 square foot facility was added.

When Sunnucks retired in 1988, after 42 years with the company, Kurz became President and R. Lawrence Pratt, son of the co-founder, who joined the company in 1985, became a partner and is currently Vice President.

Continued growth and diversity prompted the most recent move to the present-day location at 22 Iron Street. Currently the company occupies 80,000 square feet and employs approximately 150 people. An array of products are made supporting both domestic and transplant automobile manufacturers. Applications

include restraint systems, such as driver- and passenger-side air bag modules, sub-assemblies for lumbar support systems and numerous parts for engines, drivetrain and brake systems. Support services include research & development, design, prototype, test and validation procedures.

As Precision Engineering Company marks its 50th anniversary, Adolf Kurz notes "Progressive change has been the hallmark of our company. We have successfully integrated traditional expertise with new skills and innovative methods. We look forward to another half-century of growth and continuous improvement focused on respect and mutual satisfaction for those associated with Precision Engineering."

1. *The first home of Precision Engineering Company, located at 545 Keele Street, Toronto, c. 1970.*
2. *Adolf Kurz, President (l.), and R. Lawrence Pratt, Vice President (r.).*
3. *The company's current head office and manufacturing facilities, on Iron Street in Rexdale, Ontario.*

2

3

Providence Centre

The history and heritage of Providence Centre expands over 140 years from Old York to Scarborough, Ontario. Four Sisters of St. Joseph arrived in Toronto in 1851, when the care of orphans was a pressing concern due to frequent recurrences of typhus, especially among refugees from the Irish Potato Famine.

To support the Sisters' ministry, the House of Providence was founded in 1855 on Power Street to provide hope for orphans, the mentally challenged, the abandoned, the chronically ill, the aged and the dying. During the 1890s the House of Providence was home to some 700 residents. Over the years, the building was gradually enlarged to four times its original size.

In 1905 the Sisters of St. Joseph purchased a farm on Warden Avenue, east of Toronto. The carefully managed farm supplied provisions for the House until the late 1950s, but it had other benefits as well: it provided much-needed employment and rehabilitation for many men who came to the House for aid. This was particularly important through the Great Depression of the 1930s.

By the late 1950s the House of Providence building was falling into disrepair. A feeder lane of the new Don Valley Parkway was slated to be built through the House of Providence property. Thus, the Sisters decided to relocate to the Warden Avenue farm site.

In 1962 the House of Providence was replaced by the new Providence Villa and Hospital (renamed Providence Centre in 1990), the most modern geriatric centre in Canada.

Currently, the Centre includes 292 beds in its long term care facility, and the 285 bed chronic care and rehabilitation hospital. The Centre also includes palliative care on an inpatient basis as well as commu-

1

nity outreach for the terminally ill who live in their own homes. The hospital provides rehabilitation and is part of the Regional Geriatric Program.

Continuing in the traditions of the Sisters of St. Joseph, the Centre welcomes people of various faiths and cultural backgrounds. The underlying values of the Centre are declared in a Philosophy of Governance. The main points stress sanctity of life, human dignity, compassionate service, community, social justice and social responsibil-

ity. This heritage and philosophy continues to be demonstrated daily through the care and services offered at Providence Centre.

1. *Women in their dormitory in the House of Providence, Power Street, Toronto around the 1940s. About 35 women per dormitory each had a bed, bedside table, straight-back chair and a rocker.*
2. *A resident, volunteer and patient participate at the annual fundraiser, Spring Festival, on Providence Centre's grounds, where over 15,000 people attend during the last Saturday in May.*

2

Reuters Information Services (Canada) Limited

Paul Julius Reuter, who founded his news agency in 1851, dedicating it to speed, accuracy and independence.

Reuters is information. Around the clock, never sleeping, whether covering wars or movie stars, flashing out vital financial figures or maintaining complex trading systems, Reuters is there. The world's leading information organization, Reuters informs its global clients instantly by the latest electronic means, then helps its customers to analyze the facts. It is the leading provider of information to banks, brokers and other organizations involved in financial markets. But inseparable from this is the company's other main activity — the supply news, pictures and video to the world's media.

Customers in all parts of the world depend on Reuters to provide them with reliable and objective news and financial information. Reuters financial clients watch current and historical news and prices on more than 280,000 screens in over 150 countries. In Canada, Reuters services approximately 900 customers, including virtually all the major names in the financial services, print media and broadcast sectors.

Reuters worldwide coverage of general, political, economic, financial and sports news is supplied by a network of some 1,200 journalists, photographers and television cameramen based in 75 countries, including 13 correspondents and three photographers in five cities in Canada. Its comprehensive coverage of the financial markets worldwide embraces more than 180 exchanges and over-the-counter markets from Toronto, London and Tokyo to Kiev, Nairobi and Shanghai.

But throughout the international organization, the key values instilled by its founder continue to be the key to its success. Paul Julius Reuter endowed his new agency with three basic principles: speed, accuracy, and independence from bias, with a commitment to rapid technological innovation and reliable service. His vision of fast, dependable news coverage, delivered using the latest technology, is the company's heritage.

Reuter first applied these principles in 1850, when he used a pigeon post to bridge the last gap in European telegraph lines between Aachen, Germany, and Brussels, Belgium. Carrying financial information in small, silk bags under their wings, the pigeons delivered the news for Reuter faster than anyone or anything else.

Emigrating to Britain, he founded his telegraphic agency in London in 1851. From a two-room office just outside London's stock exchange, he began his transmission of stock market quotations between London and Paris using the first undersea cable. The service was soon extended to other European countries, with an expanding content to include general and economic news. By 1859, in addition to serving financial institutions, Reuter was also supplying all leading British and many Continental European newspapers.

News breaking information quickly enhanced the reputation of the service, with the first major "scoop" being the rapid transmission to London in 1859 of Napoleon III's Paris speech foreshadowing France's war against Austria. Branch offices quickly sprang up, and by 1861, Reuter agents were located as far away as Asia and South Africa.

The firm continued to be held within the Reuter family until 1915 when it became a private company, Reuters Limited. In 1925 Britain's Press Association acquired the majority shareholding and for the next 59 years, Reuters was owned by a combination of press groups. In 1984, it became a public limited company, registered in the United Kingdom as Reuters Holdings PLC. This company owns Reuters Limited, the operating company. Reuter shares are widely held around the world and are traded on the London Stock Exchange and on NASDAQ.

Reuters has remained committed to innovation. In 1923 the company pioneered the use of radio to transmit news internationally, and in 1962 Reuters transmitted its first story to the United States on the Telstar satellite — the first venture into space communication by private enterprise.

In 1964 Reuters launched the world's first international, computerized information retrieval system — Stockmaster. Following the deregulation of the Bretton Woods fixed foreign exchange rate system in 1971, Reuters devised an information data network to serve the needs of the decentralized money markets and in 1973 the Reuter Monitor was born. The Reuter Monitor Dealing Service was launched in 1981 allowing transactions to be completed on screen. Reuters now offers international computerized matching systems for futures options and foreign exchange.

Continuing to exploit the latest advances in information and computer technologies, Reuters' array of products and services has greatly expanded. Reuters financial information and products, which comprise the vast majority of Reuters services, provide the global business community with real-time financial data, transaction systems, and access to current and historic databases. Clients then can employ Reuters software, such as the Reuter Terminal, to analyze market trends, negotiate deals with chosen partners, or find their counterparts through an automatic deal matching process.

For broadcasters, newspapers and magazines, Reuters supplies television news coverage, as well as 24-hour text services, news pictures and graphics. In addition, it operates the largest international television news agency, whose daily coverage is estimated to reach some 500 million households worldwide via more than 650 broadcasters in over 80 countries. To provide these services, Reuters has developed the world's most extensive international private satellite and cable communications network.

In 1921 Reuters began a 600 word daily service for Canada. By 1964 Reuters began to sell its wire services directly to Canadian clients, operating out of a Toronto office. The Reuter Canadian Financial Report was started in 1974, also based in Toronto, with Reuters hiring its first Canadian journalists at this same time. The first Canadian clients for Reuters financial information services were signed in 1975.

During the mid 1980s Reuters made a number of important acquisitions worldwide, including two in Canada. In 1987 it obtained Securities Clearing International Corp., a small Toronto-based consulting firm that was strong in the area of com-

1

puter financial software development. Reuters then acquired I.P. Sharp Associates Limited. Based in Toronto, and with a significant international presence, I.P. Sharp's data processing, software development and financial database operations strongly complemented Reuters financial services.

Reuters Information Services (Canada) Limited now has approximately 100 employees with sales offices in Toronto, Vancouver, Calgary, Ottawa and Montreal. The Reuters Canada team is committed to delivering innovative, flexible information and technology solutions that provide competitive advantage to its clients.

Reuters provides a more complete newsfile from Canada than any other international news agency. Its Canadian domestic news service provides comprehensive coverage of local financial markets, the economy and politics. Reuters was the first international news agency to report the extent of the sweeping victory of Jean Chretien's Liberal party in the October 1993 national election.

Reuters provides a strong file of political and sports pictures from

Canada. Both of Reuters Toronto-based photographers have won Canadian photography awards. A Reuter photograph of Jean Chretien on election day was published around the world and was nominated for a prestigious Canadian national newspaper award.

Reuters Canadian sales and support structure combines excellence in sales, service and account administration into cross functional teams that are knowledgeable about their clients and responsive to their needs.

Globally, the renowned tradition of Reuter "scoops" has continued. From being first with news of the building of the Berlin Wall in 1961 and first again in 1989 with news it was to come down, to being first with news of the Soviet coup and its subsequent collapse in 1991, Reuters was there providing on-the-spot coverage.

Ten years ago Reuters was a news and information group of modest size. The company now employs over 12,600 people in 83 countries around the world — a global business with a central role in major segments of the world's financial markets.

At a local and at an international level Reuters continues to innovate and to inform, but its underlying values remain unchanged — accurate information, rapidly distributed and without bias.

1. *The Reuters Terminal, based on a personal computer, is the standard keystation for access to Reuter information products. It offers an expanding range of information, graphics, analytical applications and dealing facilities directly to the offices of the global business community.*
2. *Reuters supplies traders, brokers, dealers, analysts, investors and corporate clients with a wide range of real time financial information on currencies, stocks, bonds, futures, options and more.*

2

Roots Canada Ltd.

Millions of people worldwide have become members of an exclusive group, an assemblage of individuals from all walks of life, all willing to purchase products that allow them to proudly display their membership in this highly successful Canadian corporate enterprise known as Roots Canada Ltd. Founded in 1973, it has been dedicated from the beginning to "packaging the wilderness" — selling the ideology of conservation through its products that reflect the company's values. Outdoors, family, recreation, kids, education, working hard at the right time, success and surrounding oneself with friends and good people are but some of the many integral elements that make up the Roots Canada culture, and in whole are part of the explanation as to the company's phenomenal growth and prosperity.

The history of Roots Canada is much the real life story of two friends, Don Green and Michael Budman, and their dedication to the company. Both were originally from Detroit, Michigan, but did not meet until 1962 when they were under the enduring influence of Camp Tamakwa. Located on the idyllic shores of Tea Lake in Algonquin Provincial Park in Ontario, the summer camp proved to be a pivotal apogee — far from home during a formative period in the individual lives of each.

Becoming fast friends, they began to travel until coming together once again in Toronto in 1973. Looking to earn a living, they came across a product known as the negative heel shoe, in which the toes are elevated above the heels.

After approaching a large shoe manufacturer, who promptly turned them down, they approached tiny Boa Shoes and its owner, Jan Kowalewski, who agreed to begin production. Looking for a name, they came upon the idea of Roots — "just as one's feet are connected to the ground." Thus, the two young entrepreneurs, using as their logo the beaver, opened the doors to their rented storefront on Yonge Street in Toronto on August 15, 1973, selling seven pairs of shoes the first day.

Sales quickly increased to the point where lines began to form on the sidewalk, and soon the demand was greater than Kowalewski could supply. By the end of the year, the two partners had purchased Boa Shoes and moved into larger premises, increasing production from 30 pairs daily to 2,000. Within a year and a half, Roots shoe stores were located from coast to coast and the company was well underway to becoming a cultural icon.

During the mid 1970s Roots shifted its production to more conventional shoes, manufacturing rubber-soled versions of loafers, ox-

fords, desert boots and brogues. Portending the future, the company also began to branch into a new line of leather jackets and handbags, all displaying the already famous Roots logo.

In the early 1980s, Roots began to set its sights on the European market, with Budman temporarily moving to Paris to oversee the new division in 1981. With the birth of Green's first child, Roots initiated a new line of baby and kids wear, the design being directed by the two spouses.

Always adept at foreseeing new trends in the popular fashion industry, the two founders successfully piloted the company to ride the crest of the popular sweatshirt wave. The Roots sweatshirt began appearing everywhere, firmly establishing the apparel manufacturer in the consumer's mind.

Today, there are three very successful components to Roots Canada: its retail stores, the wholesale department, and the manufacturing facilities. There are now approximately 95 stores across Canada, a number growing at the rate of one new store opening per month. The

1. *Michael Budman (l.) and Don Green (r.), who founded Roots Canada Ltd. in 1973 and today continue to oversee its successful development.*
2. *Other key members of the management nucleus include (from left to right) Richard, Jan, Karl and Henry Kowalewski.*

1

2

vast majority of these stores are corporate locations, with the franchise locations numbering about 15. Demand is also growing in the United States, where there are six corporate locations. Internationally, sales continue to flourish. Reflecting the high popularity of Roots products in the Asian marketplace, in Japan there are seven franchise locations, all known as Beaver Roots, as well as stores in Taiwan and Korea.

Retail products now include a vast array of items, including sweaters, sweatshirts, sweatpants, jackets, T-shirts, shorts, belts, caps, bags, briefcases, luggage, binders, wallets, blankets, key chains, shirts, jeans, vests, skin cleaners, body creams and bath gels, and of course, shoes and boots.

The wholesale division of Roots Canada involves the production of items for the entertainment and sports industry. An important portion of the work is the manufacture of products for a litany of stars, including Janet Jackson, David Bowie, Goldie Hawn, Michael J. Fox, Paul McCartney, Keith Richards, and more. The company also engages in providing all associated retail items for certain productions, such as the recent *Miss Saigon* musical in Toronto.

The manufacturing segment of Roots Canada is located in a 50,000 square foot factory adjacent to the company's head offices on Caledonia Road in Toronto. In addition, a 65,000 square foot warehouse is situated nearby. The method of manufacturing remains a basic, hands-on process, with each product created by a combination of old-world craftsmanship with efficient high-technology production. Machinery utilized, such as the embroidery machines — able to produce the needed intricate details — are all state-of-the-art.

Richard Kowalewski introduced a 'rink' production system, adapted from its use by other successful manufacturers. Production of products, from the cutting stage right through to packaging, is han-

1

dled by a team of up to ten people. Each member of the team is given the opportunity to learn each stage in the process, as the different tasks are rotated among the members of a team over a period of time. This has the effect of reducing boredom among employees as they are challenged to learn new skills, develop understanding of the entire manufacturing process, and even compete in a friendly way against other teams. The improved morale and motivation among team members and their greater involvement in the production process results in early identification of problems, a high level of pride of craftsmanship and an overall improvement in efficiency and product quality.

Everything sold by Roots Canada, including items sold in the international stores, is manufactured by the company, with quality raw materials sourced from around the globe. Vertically integrated, the company has control over the entire production process, starting at Roots Canada masterful in-house design department.

Every one of the approximately 1,000 employees at Roots Canada is devoted to the success of the company, from the hands-on management team to the sales people at the individual stores. Committed to an open office atmosphere, Green and

Budman shared one office for the first 20 years, accessible to all employees. Other key members of the management group, including the Kowalewski brothers — Richard, Henry and Karl — oversee the production and Leather design departments, remaining in direct contact with everyone in the Roots family.

Looking at the now famous success of the company, which has even spawned a motion picture, *Indian Summer*, Green and Budman attribute it to a sound foundation. From the beginning, there was a dedication to quality products without exception, by capable employees. It is from this solid basis that the company has thrived, propelling itself forward into the future, as more and more eager people become willing customers of and participants in the Roots Canada culture.

1. *Roots Canada currently has 95 retail outlets located across Canada, including this store on Yonge Street in Toronto.*
2., 3. *At the company's 50,000 square foot manufacturing facilities in Toronto, old-world craftsmanship combine with efficient high-technology production.*

2

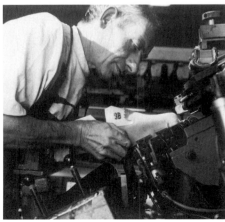

3

Royal Bank of Canada

In 1869, only two years after Confederation, a small group of Nova Scotia businessmen received a federal charter to establish the Merchants' Bank of Halifax. Almost from day one, the bank struck out boldly, sometimes at great risk, to beat the competition along the arteries of developing trade.

By 1901, the Merchants' Bank of Halifax had become a national institution, counting branches from coast to coast, many of which were in frontier towns. It had also expanded across the Atlantic and deep into the Caribbean. That year the Merchants' Bank of Halifax was renamed The Royal Bank of Canada.

In 1907, the bank moved its head office from Halifax to Montreal, then Canada's undisputed financial capital. Royal Bank continues to be headquartered in Montreal, with selected head office functions located in Toronto and Winnipeg.

Through a series of mergers, including the Union Bank of Canada in 1925, Royal Bank became the country's largest bank, which it remains today.

Royal Bank is North America's 6th largest provider of integrated financial services, with more than eight million personal and business clients. Its domestic operations include some 1,600 branches and special business units, some 4,000 banking machines, more than 300 self-serve account updaters and in excess of 40,000 point-of-sale merchant terminals.

Building on the strong international footing established before the turn of the century, the Royal Bank Group operates today in 33 countries through more than 90 business units, which deliver corporate banking, investment banking, treasury and capital market products to institutional clients, and private banking services to high net worth individuals. The bank continues to operate a well-estab-

1

lished retail banking franchise in the Caribbean. Correspondent banking relationships with more than 3,500 of the world's leading financial institutions extend the bank's reach to some 180 countries.

The acquisitions of RBC Dominion Securities Inc. — Canada's leading investment dealer — and Royal Trust — a leader in personal and institutional trust and investment services — have added enormous strength to the Royal Bank Group by expanding and diversifying its reach and revenue at home and abroad.

Other subsidiaries include discount brokerage services and a credit, travel and health-related insurance business.

Royal Bank has long been committed to investing in the vitality and quality of life of the communities in which it operates, as a corporation and in encouraging the giving of time and money by its employees. In 1993, the bank's pledge to donate at least one per cent of its average pre-tax profits resulted in charitable donations of $14 million, the largest corporate donation program in the country.

As Royal Bank celebrates its 125th anniversary, it maintains that success is best achieved through quality people delivering quality service to its customers. To this end the bank continues to focus on the training and development of its people, believing that businesses that are responsive and innovative, with the necessary skills and knowledge and the highest standards of ethics and social responsibility, will be well positioned for the 21st century.

2

1. *The "upstart" unincorporated Merchants Bank opened its doors in 1864 on Bedford Row in Halifax, Nova Scotia.*
2. *"The bank that grew up with the country . . ." Today, Royal Bank of Canada has 1,600 operating units across Canada, including the Royal Bank Plaza in Toronto, with its twin towers of gilded glass, which opened in 1976.*

St. John's Rehabilitation Hospital

A pioneer in convalescent and rehabilitative care, St. John's Rehabilitation Hospital provides orthopaedic, amputee, trauma and neurological rehabilitation. Since its opening in 1937, St. John's has provided quality care for the physical, emotional, social and spiritual needs of its patients, returning each to their greatest possible level of independence in their own community.

The origins of the Hospital trace to the founding of the Sisterhood of St. John the Divine in 1884, an order active in the care of the sick. After travelling to Saskatchewan to manage a hospital during the Riel Rebellion of 1885, they returned to Toronto and opened the city's first Women's Surgical Hospital. Further activities included the opening of a school of nursing in the early 1900s.

In 1933, again responding to community need, the Sisterhood refocussed its vision and organized a Board of Trustees with the mandate of building a convalescent hospital. It was not easy to convince the government and general hospitals that this was a necessary health service, yet the Sisters persisted, and received the first grants in Ontario for convalescent care. They succeeded in having St. John's Convalescent Hospital incorporated by the Province of Ontario in 1936.

Land was purchased in what now is North York, a 64-bed facility was erected, and St. John's opened — to provide convalescent care for patients recovering from surgery, acute illness, or accidents. The care could be summarized by the phrase, "rest, fresh air and sunshine." But this is not to underestimate the sound medicinal practices at St. John's, where physical and occupational therapy completed the medical and surgical treatment begun in general hospitals. Sister Beatrice, St. John's first Administrator,

1

said in 1938 that "The recovering patient must be set in an environment that will send him back to his life and citizenship vigorous and wholesome in body, mind and spirit." St. John's strives to fulfil this task.

The original Hospital soon filled to capacity and within ten years expanded. As demand for convalescent services grew, the present capacity of 210 beds was reached in 1957. At the same time new attitudes about convalescent care were evolving, emphasizing greater activity and vigorous therapy treatments to develop the independence of each patient to their potential. The benefit of active rehabilitation was being recognized by the medical community. To reflect this shift in thinking, the Hospital changed its name to St. John's Rehabilitation Hospital in 1987.

The 1990s brought new economic realities to the healthcare system. In this environment of cost restraint, St. John's continues to be-

1. *Twenty-five acres of former farm land and golf course were transformed into beautiful grounds and wooded areas for St. John's, newly incorporated as a convalescent hospital in 1936.*

2. *St. John's Rehabilitation Hospital today still stands in spectacular surroundings.*

lieve that rehabilitation is a fundamental component of the system. Through early active therapy, costly readmissions and the need for follow-up care can be reduced. And increasingly, St. John's is working with other hospitals and community-based agencies in establishing coordinated, efficient rehabilitation and ambulatory care programs.

St. John's is ready to step into the future — not only with new approaches for the delivery of rehabilitation care but also by continuing to help each of its patients to step into their own future with confidence that is developed through their therapy. In this way, St. John's Rehabilitation Hospital is successfully fulfilling its vision to address the needs of its patients in a caring, professional and effective manner, and to be the foremost among Ontario rehabilitation facilities in achieving this.

2

The Salvation Army Scarborough Grace Hospital

In 1993 The Salvation Army Scarborough Grace Hospital became the first community hospital in Canada to receive a "four year accreditation award" from the Canadian Council on Health Facilities Accreditation. This award reflects the quality of care and service to the community that has been a hallmark of Scarborough Grace since its inception.

The outstanding record of quality at Scarborough Grace is, in part, a reflection of the legacy of The Salvation Army, which has a proven track record of meeting human needs in co-operation with community resources. The Salvation Army, a branch of the Christian Church, is at work in over 100 countries, where its ministries of healing have touched hundreds of thousands of people.

Since it first became a part of the life of Canadians in 1882, The Salvation Army has established a network of health and social facilities that respond to community needs. These facilities include public general hospitals such as Scarborough Grace, specialized hospitals including maternity, convalescent and continuing care, homes for children, unmarried mothers and senior citizens, and other centres which provide shelter and specialized care.

At Church and Bloor Streets in Toronto, The Salvation Army opened a hospital, later known as the Toronto Grace Hospital, in 1905. For over half a century this institution provided valuable service as a women's hospital. In 1963, the Ontario Hospital Services Commission gave approval in principle to increase the hospital's rated bed capacity by adding 120 medical and surgical beds.

However, it became apparent that this expansion was not needed in downtown Toronto and The Salvation Army was asked to relocate the hospital to the L'Amoreaux Community in Scarborough, in recognition of a demand for additional health services in this rapidly growing suburb.

As the plans for relocation matured, a substantial need was identified for chronic and palliative health care in the core of the city, and The Salvation Army agreed to retain its Church Street Grace Hospital with this new focus. This, however, did not alter the plans to build the Scarborough Grace Hospital.

By 1967, Scarborough already had two community hospitals, but due to its rapid growth it was determined that the population would soon require a third general hospital providing inpatient beds for acute and chronic care, 24-hour emergency service and a full range of outpatient services. In co-operation with the Provincial Government, the new 302 bed Scarborough Grace Hospital opened its doors in November 1985. Reflecting the philosophy and religious orientation of The Salvation Army, the patients at Scarborough Grace are treated with consideration for their mental, emotional, social and spiritual, as well as their physical needs. This concern for the whole person extends throughout the hospital, but it also reaches outside the walls through community outreach and health education. Taking seriously the commitment to being "a caring partner in health," Scarborough Grace realizes that it is important to assist members of the community to take

1. *Some of the notables who were on hand for the laying of the Hospital's cornerstone (from left to right): Commissioner Arthur R. Pitcher, Premier William Davis, and M.P.P. Tom Wells. Included inside the stone was a time capsule for which three school children submitted the contents.*
2. *Scarborough Grace Hospital today: a 302 bed community hospital.*

1

2

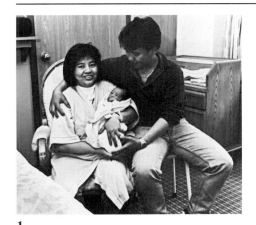

1

responsibility for their health and maintain a healthy lifestyle.

One way in which the hospital achieves this goal is through a program of "community talks." These talks take place four times a year and are free to the public. The subjects for each session vary, and have included information on a variety of topics including migraine headaches, back care, caring for the caregiver, child discipline, menopause, weight control, healthy hearts, stress and sleep disorders. Input is sought from the community for topics of interest and this information is used to plan future programs. Attendance at the talks has grown as word of them has spread.

Caring for the whole person also means continued care as we mature. To this end Scarborough Grace established its "Seniors Day Hospital" in 1988, the only one of its kind in Scarborough. One former patient of the Day Hospital reports, "We owe the quality of our life today to the staff and services of the Day Hospital." This outcome is exactly what the Day Hospital aims to accomplish: to improve the patients' level of functioning so that they can continue to live at home with as much independence as possible. The program removes or delays the need for admission to a care centre and provides relief and support for the caregiver at home.

Scarborough Grace Hospital, with over 3,200 births annually, provides superb care to mothers and newborns. In keeping with the tradition of family-centred health care, one birthing option that the Hospital

provides for low-risk pregnancies is its "Birthing Centre." The Birthing Centre, one of the first to be established in the Greater Metropolitan Toronto area, provides a program that begins early in a woman's pregnancy and continues through the first few months after the birth. The Centre includes four birthing suites that allow for a comfortable atmosphere in which the mother labours, delivers and rests for a few hours after the baby is born. All mothers are at home in less than 24 hours. Family and support persons are welcome in the birthing rooms at the mother's discretion. The program includes antenatal teaching and counselling, follow-up by phone calls and visits by the nurse midwives. The Birthing Centre has the added comfort that if complications should occur, equipment and expertise for any needed intervention are available, adjacent to the Birthing Centre. As a testimony to its success, a full 98 per cent of the Centre's clients say they would return to the Birthing Centre for future births.

Another uniquely specialized service at Scarborough Grace is provided through its Sexual Assault Care Centre. Opened in 1987 as the second such facility in Ontario, it is a 24-hour treatment centre for people who have been sexually assaulted. The treatment centre provides comprehensive care, including, if desired, emergency services such as examinations and assistance with legal action, as well as crisis and follow-up counselling.

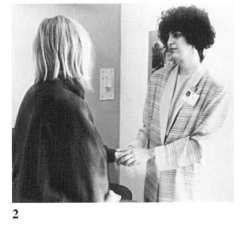

2

This counselling includes ongoing support and information to help the survivor through the healing and recovery process, and optional meetings with family members or friends affected by the assault. In addition, the treatment centre provides information and public education concerning sexual assault. The treatment centre has recently expanded to include a special program for young people from 12 to 15 years of age.

The Sexual Assault Care Centre at The Salvation Army Scarborough Grace Hospital, and the many other health care and community service programs provided by this modern, high quality institution, express the Hospital's commitment to helping those in need while providing high quality professional care; and together reflect the broader mission of The Salvation Army Health Services "to provide a Christian ministry which will involve a broad spectrum of services aimed at the treatment and elimination of disease, relief of suffering and the promotion of health and wholeness."

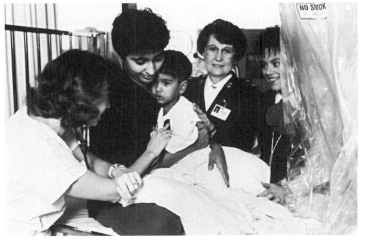

3

1., 2., 3. Scarborough Grace is well known for its many innovative programs and departments, including its Birthing Centre program (1), the Sexual Assault Care Centre (2), and the family-centred Paediatric Care Unit (3).

Samuel, Son & Co., Limited

Samuel, Son & Co., Limited has grown from a small warehouse operation to a large steel, stainless steel and aluminum service centre of North American scope. Spanning five generations as a family owned and operated business, the company and its principals have enjoyed a close relationship with the province of Ontario and the Dominion of Canada.

Known as M. & L. Samuel, the company was founded by Mark and Lewis Samuel in 1855. After selling gas chandeliers in Toronto for a brief while, the company soon developed into commission and wholesale merchants in metal and hardware, with offices in Toronto and Liverpool, England. Mark Samuel settled in Liverpool and sent most of the products to Canada where there were very few metal plants. There was also some eastward trade as some Canadian customers were able to pay only with non-perishables such as hides, tallow and beeswax, which could be shipped to and sold in England. It was good arrangement, resulting in low prices and good, fast, and efficient service for the customer, while building a reputation for honesty, service and quality.

The growth of the company parallels the growth of industry in Canada in many ways. It grew from the distribution of hardware and metals, imported from Europe and principally England, to the distribution of Canadian-made products, with the growth of steel mills here in Canada. When the need for manufacturing arose later, the company started manufacturing also.

As the company continued to grow, it took on Alfred Benjamin as a partner in 1880, and the firm became known as M. & L. Samuel, Benjamin & Company. Lewis Samuel passed away in 1888, but his son Sigmund, born in 1867, was available to carry the company forward. In 1899 the company did away with shelf hardware, which allowed them to concentrate better on metals and heavy hardware. Some of the pig iron and steel that they imported was for such early Canadian companies as the Masseys and Sam McLaughlin's. The company also introduced the first broad flange beams into Canada, which were able to withstand much greater loads.

By 1912 Sigmund Samuel was a fifty per cent partner, while the other fifty per cent belonged to the Benjamins. Moving back and forth between England and Toronto, he managed the company quite successfully, as well as being involved in other endeavours. During the First World War he bought a collection of almost four hundred pieces of Greek and Italian vases for the Royal Ontario Museum, giving it one of the finest collections of ancient Greek and Italian art in North America.

In 1929 the company was ready to change locations in Toronto again, moving to the corner of Spadina and Fleet Streets. This was the company's third home. After originally renting at Front and Wellington St., a location known then and still today as the "Coffin Block," they had built a new brick warehouse and office building at King and Spadina which they also outgrew. When Frank Benjamin decided to retire in 1931, Sigmund Samuel became the sole proprietor of the firm, and immediately changed its name to Samuel, Son & Company. The company soon closed

The changing faces of Samuel, Son & Co., Limited.
1. *Lewis Samuel, who helped found the company in 1855.*
2. *Sigmund Samuel, who continued to manage and develop the company.*
3. *Ernest Samuel, who continues today to direct and expand the company.*

1

2

3

down the London office, becoming more and more a service centre in metals produced in North America.

As the company became more involved domestically, Sigmund Samuel also became more involved in Toronto. He helped acquire a Chinese library for the Royal Ontario Museum. Later, he also donated his lifetime collection of Canadiana, and then helped to construct the building where it eventually was to be located, the Canadiana Gallery. He was also involved in the Toronto Western Hospital and the University of Toronto, which named one of its libraries in his honour. For his involvement in the affairs of Toronto, he received the City's Award of Merit medal in 1958. Continuing in this same tradition, the family also recently made possible the opening of the Samuel European Galleries, the new Canadiana Gallery, and the Heritage Gallery of Canada's Peoples, all at the Royal Ontario Museum.

When the city of Toronto expropriated the Fleet St. location in the late 1950s to build a ramp for the Gardener Expressway, the company moved to its present location on Dixie Rd. in Mississauga. Ernest L. Samuel, a grandson of Sigmund, designed the Mississauga facility, and then became President of the company in May, 1962. As the company continues to expand, the 365,000 square feet Mississauga facility remains as its flagship location, with the corporate head office and administrative central offices situated there.

In 1985 three of its manufacturing divisions were combined to form Samuel Manu-Tech Inc., a public company on the Toronto Stock Exchange which focuses on manufacturing. Samuel, Son & Co., Limited, continues as the majority shareholder in Samuel Manu-Tech Inc. The company develops and sells its technology and products worldwide, such as its metal pickling technology and stainless steel pipe and tubing.

The distribution side, Samuel, Son & Co., Limited, continues to be a private company. Its computer system allows it to have one of the most sophisticated costing and operating systems in the industry, with instant access to inventory, costing, order status, and customer profiles on a national basis for all its divisions. Just-in-time deliveries are not a problem with its massive warehousing capabilities throughout Canada and the U.S. and a huge truck fleet.

The company positions itself as the middle man between the mills and manufacturers. Its state-of-the-art equipment allows it to produce almost any size, gauge, grade or type of metal product needed, ranging from aluminum aircraft alloys, galvanized sheet, stainless plate and rolled bars to virtually any carbon steel, aluminum or stainless steel product.

Beginning as a family business that was customer orientated, the company continues to be family owned and operated, dedicated to its customers, and involved in community affairs. Mark C. Samuel, son of Ernest Samuel, and President of Samuel Manu-Tech Inc., points out that this is a company that has demonstrated throughout its history that people truly are the strength of the firm. This commitment to its personnel has fostered a strong loyalty among its employees, and encourages long-term employment with the company.

Finally, no review of the Samuel Group would be complete without some mention of their highly successful Sam-Son Farms operations. Their champions have included Queen's Plate winner Regal Intention, the brilliant Sky Classic, and possibly the greatest racing filly of all time, Dance Smartly, whose undefeated 1991 campaign included the Queen's Plate and Breeders' Cup Distaff.

Samuel, Son & Co., Limited, today a large steel, stainless steel, and aluminum service centre of international scope, continues to be committed to the best products, equipment, systems and people in the industry. It has a history it can be proud of and a strong future to look forward to.

1. An early location in Toronto, Ontario for a company that continued to grow.
2. The present head offices of Samuel, Son & Co., Limited in Mississauga, Ontario.

1

2

Scarborough General Hospital

Scarborough General Hospital (SGH) is one of Canada's leading community hospitals, with a proud history of serving the needs of an ever-growing urban centre. The hospital was founded by a community organization — the Sisters of Misericorde — in direct response to the needs of the emerging City of Scarborough.

As Scarborough's first hospital, Scarborough General Hospital has expanded services as the population shifted from a rural base of 70,000 people in the early 1950s, to an urban centre of 525,000 residents in 1994. The hospital has maintained the highest quality standards in its health care delivery by attracting dynamic, highly-respected specialists who keep SGH in the forefront of health care in Ontario and Canada.

The many new medical and surgical techniques pioneered at Scarborough General, combined with a record of highly efficient, cost-effective service delivery have SGH consistently ranked as a high performance hospital. SGH has served and continues to serve its community well.

The Founders of Scarborough General Hospital were the Sisters of Misericorde, who had established and were operating another hospital in downtown Toronto in the early 1950s. The Sisters were looking to expand their efforts by establishing a new hospital in an outlying area of Toronto. Oliver E. Crockford, Reeve of Scarborough at the time, was primarily responsible for having the Sisters choose Scarborough as their next hospital site.

In 1952, the Sisters purchased land for the current site at McCowan Road and Lawrence Avenue. Additional funds were obtained from municipal, provincial and federal governments, permitting construction to begin in 1954. Scarborough General Hospital officially opened on May 12, 1956 with

1

1. At the sod-turning ceremony of Scarborough General Hospital in 1954, Metropolitan Toronto chairman Fred Gardiner operated the bulldozer.
2. When it first opened in 1956, Scarborough General Hospital employed 320 people, compared to almost 2,000 today.

185 beds. Within several months, the hospital's emergency department was one of the busiest in the country.

The need for expansion to serve the rapidly growing community soon became self-evident, and the first addition was completed in 1961. Adding many vital aspects to the hospital, it included a children's ward and an intensive care unit, expanding the hospital to 340 beds.

With that expansion barely com-

plete, more room was needed again, and in May 1968, capacity was nearly doubled to 640 beds. This huge increase was accomplished by adding a circular, 10-storey tower — the distinctive landmark for which the hospital building is known. The innovative design put patients' rooms on the perimeter, giving each a window overlooking the community. Equipment, services and staff work areas were located in the centre.

2

1. *Scarborough General Hospital's most distinctive landmark, "the tower," opened in 1968 and became home to Canada's first Burn Unit. Today, the Burn Unit continues to be one of the most advanced facilities of its kind in the country.*
2. *Scarborough General Hospital as it appears today.*

1

During the 1960s, the role of the Sisters of Misericorde at the hospital was gradually diminishing. In May, 1972, the Sisters turned over control, giving full responsibility for running the hospital to the Scarborough General Hospital Board of Governors and ownership to the Government of Ontario.

In the early 1970s, the University of Toronto approached the hospital to become involved in the postgraduate training of its graduating doctors — what was known as the Rotating Internship Program. Since then, each intern has spent a full year at the hospital, obtaining valuable practical clinical experience, before establishing an independent practice. A wide range of other health care professionals now receive similar practical experience through placements at the hospital. In 1991, the University again approached the hospital, this time to become one of three new sites for their Family Practice Residency Program. In just three years, the program has become one of the most sought after training locations in Metropolitan Toronto.

In 1974, one of the first inpatient programs for long-term care at a community hospital in Metropolitan Toronto was developed with the addition of the Crockford Pavilion. This allowed patients with long-term or chronic illnesses to be treated in a more home-like environment and freed acute care beds. Long-term care facilities now include programs for stroke rehabilitation, orthopaedic rehabilitation, palliative care and an amputee unit.

Concurrent with the expansion of the hospital's physical facilities was the continual growth in innovative clinical programs. Scarborough General opened the first Burn Unit in Canada in 1968 and, five years later, pioneered the use of porcine dressings for burn victims. The first hospital sports medicine clinic in Toronto was opened at the hospital in 1972. Also in the early 1970s, the hospital, under the leadership of Dr. Harold Stein, former Chief of Ophthalmology, pioneered the use of intra-ocular lens implants for cataract patients.

More recently, in 1991, Scarborough General became the first hospital in Scarborough to use laparoscopic cholecystectomy techniques. In that same year the Burn Unit moved into new facilities, becoming one of the most advanced and best equipped burn units in the country. In 1993, SGH became the first hospital in Metropolitan Toronto, and only the fourth in all of Canada, to perform prostate reduction laser surgery using the latest in laser technology. Visual Laser Ablation of the Prostate (VLAP) became a ground-breaking surgical procedure and revolutionized prostate surgery. Scarborough General is also a leading hospital for eye donations and is the second busiest hospital in Ontario for corneal transplants, performing approximately 150 operations each year. The hospital has also become renowned for its cataract, implant and refractive surgery.

In 1994, the hospital received a three year accreditation award from the Canadian Council on Health Facilities Accreditation, which explicitly recognized the hospital's commitment to quality improvement and the resulting benefits to patient care. As one of the six "alpha" (test) sites across Canada, the hospital was able to help shape new standards that will guide health care facilities across the country.

As a community hospital, Scarborough General undertakes a multidisciplinary approach, providing a broad range of inpatient, ambulatory and community services in order to meet the community's needs for both acute and continuing health care. In 1993, the hospital registered 23,000 admissions, 2,600

2

births and close to 140,000 visits to its outpatient clinics. The hospital's emergency department, renovated and enlarged in 1982 and again in 1991, continues to be one of the busiest in Canada, with over 63,000 visits annually.

In 1992, Scarborough General launched the "Caring Together" campaign with a fund-raising goal of $8.5 million over a five-year period. The first capital campaign since the original building campaign in 1953, "Caring Together" has been well received with a groundswell of support, both internally from the hospital's doctors, employees, Board members and Auxiliary, and externally from business, service clubs and the general community. The funds will be used for much needed renovations and equipment upgrades to improve the hospital's patient care facilities, including urology, orthopaedics, maternal and children's services, mental health services, chemotherapy and continuing care; critical care areas, such as the Coronary Care Unit and Recovery Room; and diagnostics, including imaging and laboratory services.

In fact, at the time of publication, two patient care areas had directly benefited from the "Caring Together" campaign. In September 1993, a new oncology (chemotherapy) unit was opened, while in April 1994, the hospital became home to a new state-of-the-art

1

angiography suite.

The "Caring Together" campaign will also help Scarborough General Hospital achieve its goal of continuing to be a leader in providing outstanding health care by further developing its innovative care delivery and clinical practices.

Scarborough General Hospital has a proud heritage of serving the people of Scarborough. Through almost 40 years of leadership in providing quality acute and general

1. "Patients are our Priority" is the slogan of Scarborough General Hospital. The hospital is committed to excellent community health care.
2. Arthroscopic surgery of the knee is just one of the many state-of-the-art surgical procedures that keeps Scarborough General Hospital at the forefront of quality health care.
3. Scarborough General Hospital works hard to keep pace with scientific and technological advances. One example is the new spiral CT Scanner that greatly enhances the hospital's diagnostic capability and allows it to serve more patients and provide more precise detection of abnormalities.

health care services to an ever-expanding urban centre, Scarborough General Hospital has proven to be more a community resource than an institution.

The proud history of Scarborough General Hospital provides the foundation for its dynamic future as one of Canada's leading community hospitals.

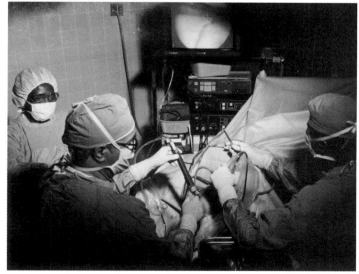

2

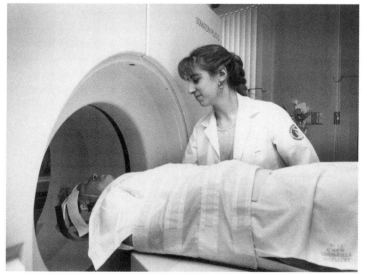

3

Spar Aerospace Limited

Spar Aerospace Limited has an extensive and exciting history as Canada's leading space company. Canadian shareholder-owned, Spar is known throughout the world as the company which developed Canadarm — the space shuttle arm which has performed flawlessly for over 10 years deploying and rescuing numerous satellites. In fact, in late 1993, it was Canadarm that dramatically plucked the giant Hubble Space Telescope from the sky and drew it into the airborne space shuttle, where the defective lens was successfully corrected.

Over 25 years ago, Spar evolved from the Special Products & Applied Research (SPAR) division of de Havilland Aircraft of Canada Limited into Canada's pre-eminent aerospace company. Major aerospace contracts, satellites, Canadarm, the Mobile Servicing System — and acquisitions — have fostered Spar's growth. Today, Spar adds specialization in commercial end-to-end communications, informatics and software systems to its overall portfolio. This new focus is reflected by Spar's re-organization into four strategic business units which include Communications, Informatics, Aviation and Defence, and Space.

Spar's Space business unit continues to be the prime contractor for the Mobile Servicing System (MSS), Canada's contribution to the international space station. The MSS will be more advanced than the Canadarm and will be able to "see" with the aid of a machine vision system, and "feel" using a tactile feedback system. The international space station project is expected to cost about $1.2 billion through the year 2000, of which more than $800 million will go towards the design and construction of the MSS.

Spar is bringing this technology down to earth with new and exciting applications for the remediation and clean-up of hazardous waste sites. Recent work in Hanford, Washington, and an opportunity for applications at the Chernobyl nuclear reactor site, involved Spar's remote handling capabilities.

Spar has a long history of involvement in the design, development, installation and management of satellite and ground system communication networks for customers in more than 30 countries around the world. Spar has contributed to the design and manufacture of over 80 satellites and subsystems, including the sophisticated MSat satellites. These satellites will establish an integrated North American mobile communications system. In the area of remote sensing, Spar is building RADAR-SAT, the world's first commercial observation satellite, which can record data day and night, through clear or cloudy skies.

Spar continues to be a major force in the development of defence systems. The Aviation and Defence business unit provides integrated communication systems and services for customers in the naval communications, aviation and electro-optics markets. It is also a competitive and innovative leader specializing in the repair and overhaul of military and commercial aircraft.

Recent acquisitions and alliances have contributed to Spar's capability of providing total systems solutions in the communications and informatics marketplace. In 1992, Spar acquired ComStream Corporation, a high technology company serving the international telecommunications market, placing it within Spar's Communications business unit.

The emerging "multimedia" revolution in global communications is creating significant opportunities for Spar's leading digital compression technology. This revolution involves the convergence of three technologies — telephone, television and computer. ComStream specializes in the design and development of digital products and systems and this unique technology is used in Spar ground station equipment for satellite-based telecommunications systems. Other ComStream capabilities include audio broadcast terminals and data broadcast products which allow businesses to supply data or audio services from a central location to subsidiaries across the nation or worldwide.

Today, Spar Aerospace Limited employs nearly 3,000 people at locations in Canada, the United States, the People's Republic of China, Indonesia, the United Kingdom, Thailand, and Mexico. Spar is positioned for a new and exciting future that embodies the same qualities of vision and drive that have characterized the company since its inception.

"Spar: Where space is just the beginning."

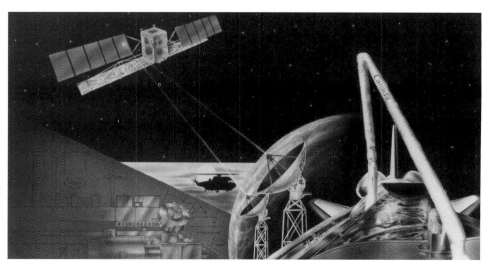

Sears Canada Inc.

For over 40 years, Sears Canada has been delivering quality, value, service and trust, while growing to become the largest single retailer in the country. Its general merchandise catalogues, published in English and French annually since the company's founding, have become an important part of the fabric of the Canadian way of life. Sears has touched the lives of most Canadians in one way or another, yet few people are aware of the extraordinary growth that it has enjoyed or the scope of its current operations.

On September 18, 1952, a partnership agreement was signed between Simpsons, Limited of Toronto and Sears, Roebuck and Co. of Chicago — both giant mail order and retailing emporiums in their own rights — for the formation of a new Canadian catalogue order and retail company. Simpsons-Sears Limited, as it came to be known, emerged as a new contender on the Canadian retail scene, in a time of peace and prosperity in Canada. Under the agreement, Simpsons-Sears Limited agreed not to open, without the consent of Simpsons, Limited, any retail store within a radius of 25 miles of the five stores operated at that time by Simpsons, Limited. In turn, Simpsons, Limited agreed not to establish any stores outside of its Toronto, Montreal, Halifax, Regina and London areas.

In 1953, the company's first full year of operation, it already achieved sales of approximately $100 million, while employing 5,000 people at its 300 catalogue outlets and one retail store. Over 12 million copies of its catalogues were issued, offering approximately 20,000 different items and services. In addition to the common merchandise, it also included such items as car insurance and live baby chicks.

By 1956, Simpsons-Sears Limited was firmly established in Can-

1

ada, having grown to 29 retail stores, 301 company-owned mail order sales offices and agencies, and four mail order distribution centres. The 1960s marked the company's entrance into the mall scene, when new shopping malls began appearing in the suburban areas of Canadian cities, with Simpsons-Sears in the forefront as a strong supporter of this innovative retailing concept.

The company was also becoming a leader in focusing attention on other than the traditional types of department store merchandise. For example, in 1966, the newly opened St. Catharines, Ontario store empha-

1. The company's first Fall and Winter catalogue offered over 20,000 items to Canadians coast to coast.
2. The Toronto, Ontario Catalogue Distribution Centre on Mutual Street played an integral part in the development of the catalogue order business at Simpsons-Sears. Its history stemmed as far back as 1916 when it was built to handle the mail order business of the Robert Simpson Company.

sized the automotive accessory part of its operations, and also provided a wider and better selection of sports equipment, a garden shop with barbecues, patio furniture and swimming pools; the store also offered added on-the-site services such as a travel bureau, an insurance office, a beauty salon, an optical and hearing aid department, a watch repair service, and a key shop.

As telephones became more commonplace in the Canadian home, more customers were able to shop by telephone from their homes, and by the mid 1960s only one order in ten arrived through the mail. As a result, the mail order business was renamed the "catalogue" business.

In 1972 Simpsons, Limited and Simpsons-Sears Limited adopted an approach to store locations under which, by mutual consent, any city

2

in Canada could be served by either Simpsons-Sears or a Simpsons store, or both. Under this approach, Simpsons, Limited approved the opening of Simpsons-Sears stores in the Toronto and Montreal areas (markets previously held by Simpsons). Simpsons-Sears consented to the opening of Simpsons, Limited stores in Ottawa, Windsor and Kitchener (markets previously held by Simpsons-Sears).

To avoid confusion in the minds of the public because of the similarity of names (especially in retail markets where both companies were located in the same shopping centre), Simpson-Sears adopted a modified logo for all advertising and store signing, in which only the single name "Sears" appeared.

Sears Travel was introduced in 1973 with one office in Ottawa, and has since grown to be one of Canada's leading travel agencies with 80 locations coast to coast.

In 1978 Hudson's Bay Company succeeded in frustrating a proposed merger between Simpsons, Limited and Simpsons-Sears Limited. In so doing, the Bay acquired control of Simpsons, Limited. As a result of this acquisition, the federal government required that Simpsons-Sears Limited and Simpsons, Limited operate as two completely separate and distinct companies, and that all shared facilities and services between them be discontinued. To complete the transition toward a distinctive corporate identity, the company's corporate name was changed in 1984 to Sears Canada Inc.

Responding to both internal and wider market needs, SLH Transport Inc. was formed in 1985 with 1,500 trailers, to consolidate Sears Canada's line-haul trucking operations. SLH, a wholly-owned subsidiary of Sears Canada Inc., provides transportation services to Sears Canada as well as other Canadian and United States shippers.

In 1991 Sears Canada acquired five Simpsons and two Hudson's Bay retail store locations in the Toronto market. The completion of this transaction finally brought to fruition the merger of locations into Sears Canada which had been frustrated in 1978. This expansion doubled the presence of Sears in the greater Toronto area, further strengthening its market share in one of Canada's largest retail markets.

Today, Sears Canada Inc. is the largest single retailer of general merchandise in Canada. The company has approximately 110 department stores, 12 outlet stores for merchandise liquidations, and over 1,350 catalogue stores. This giant retailer services all 10 provinces and both territories. Its two core businesses, retail and catalogue shopping, together employ approximately 39,000 regular and part-time employees across Canada. Central administration for both operations continues to be located at the Sears Headquarters Building in Toronto.

The Sears Canada credit card now has more cardholders than any other single retail credit card issuer in Canada, and almost half the

households in Canada have one or more major appliances displaying the Sears Kenmore brand name. In 1992 Sears Canada issued 47.5 million copies of its catalogue.

The success of Sears Canada Inc. has been inextricably linked to the success of the communities in which it operates, and how positively it is perceived by that community. A leader in corporate citizenship, Sears Canada has played an active role in supporting community programs and charitable organizations that contribute to the quality of life in its communities — from the 48 year-old Sears Ontario Drama Festival to its annual Christmas Wish Book programs which generate a donation of more than $500,000 to hospitals across Canada.

Over the years, Sears Canada has had a clear goal — leadership in retailing. That leadership has been based on quality, value, service and trust, and has been achieved through the efforts of the whole organization, making the company what it is today. But Sears Canada Inc. is not resting on its record; rather, it intends to build on it, and to continue delivering more to all Canadians.

1. The new Sears Headquarters building on Jarvis Street in Toronto was opened in 1971, centralizing administrative, merchandising, and the operating functions of the company.
2. Today, Sears Canada is the largest single retailer of general merchandise in Canada, offering Canadians two great ways to shop . . . through its catalogues or at its retail stores.

1

2

Sulzer Canada Inc.

As a partner for advanced technology, Sulzer Canada Inc. has, for more than 30 years, provided the Canadian marketplace with high quality and energy efficient industrial equipment. Being part of a global corporation with subsidiaries and sales offices throughout the world, Sulzer Canada has access to the most advanced facilities, allowing it to deepen its commitment to quality and reliability, its dedication to community service, and its forward-looking view to renewal and innovation.

With its headquarters in Quebec, offices in Ontario and a representative agency in B.C., Sulzer Canada is an autonomous corporate unit, a subsidiary of Sulzer Limited of Winterthur, Switzerland. Employing a total of 30,000 personnel worldwide, the Sulzer Corporation has an acknowledged tradition of quality and caring for the customers' true needs — prime reasons why Sulzer products and services hold leading positions in their fields.

Sulzer Limited was founded in 1834 in Switzerland as a small, family firm specializing in metal castings. As the company grew and expanded, so did its list of industrial firsts. From the first steam central heating installation in Switzerland in 1841 to the world's first marine diesel engine in 1904, Sulzer Ltd. has been on the forefront of industrial technology.

Sulzer Canada Inc. was constituted in 1961 to market the Swiss-made products of Sulzer. As primarily a sales company — with service for many of its products added later — its early business activities were related to marine diesel engines, compressors, textile machinery, and nuclear components and systems. In 1970, Sulzer Canada extended its activities into the pulp and paper and chemical processing industries.

1

1. Jean-Claude Godel, President, Sulzer Canada Inc.
2. A typical 65 MW propeller turbine — one of the 12 units being rehabilitated in the Sulzer Hydro shop in Lachine, Quebec.
3. The amalgamation of two leaders in the Thermal Spray Industry created Sulzer Metco, a worldwide organization.

The excellence of Sulzer's technology, coupled with a strong growth in Canada in the magnitude and diversity of energy-related projects, gave Sulzer Canada an unusual opportunity for further expansion. In response, the company began to subcontract the manufacture of components to local companies, and in 1974 undertook contract management of its first major projects.

Today, Sulzer Canada, with Jean-Claude Godel serving as President since 1984, is active in a number of market segments, including nuclear power, process engineering, chemical engineering, hydroelectricity, compressors, natural gas refuelling equipment, medical technology, marine equipment, textile machinery, diesel power plants, and

2

3

1

2

thermal spray coating materials and equipment. Sulzer Canada's prime market is Canada, but more and more, products or equipment are being exported, mainly to the U.S.A. but also to Latin America and to the Far East.

Sulzer Canada's nuclear process engineering activities began in 1970 to serve the needs of the growing nuclear industry by supplying the technology for heavy water upgrading and tritium removal. Most of the Canadian built nuclear power plants are now equipped with heavy water upgraders from Sulzer — the only company to engage in this activity in Canada — and several tritium removal facilities, such as at the Darlington Nuclear Facility of Ontario Hydro, were supplied by Sulzer Canada.

The expertise proven in the nuclear engineering field led to diversification into other areas, and in 1990 Sulzer Chemtech, North American Operations, was established to serve the dynamic North American market with advanced chemical engineering technology.

Corporate-wide process engineering activities already had begun towards the end of the nineteenth century, with the world's first vacuum evaporating plant for manufacturing condensed milk. Later, activities expanded into the areas of water and wastewater purification, separation and mixing processes, plant construction, and low temperature and fluid bed technologies.

Sulzer Canada has been active since 1969 in designing and building distillation plants in North America in its areas of specialty of chemicals, flavours and fragrances. For example, all Canadian soya bean processors now have Sulzer systems in their mills, producing a better product with considerable energy savings.

Sulzer Canada has also clearly established its position as a leader in advanced hydro technology. As part of the world renowned Escher Wyss Hydraulic group with close to two centuries of experience, Sulzer Hydro is an innovator offering the very latest technology and quality products. Since 1980, the company has been a designer and builder of hydraulic turbines and related products in Canada. It rehabilitates and upgrades existing power stations, and specializes in supplying a package of complete electromechanical supply systems for new stations. Among the many Canadian firsts in this field is the renowned Annapolis Tidal Power turbine in Nova Scotia in 1982, the world's largest.

Sulzer turbo and reciprocating compressors have been marketed in Canada for many years, with some units being more than half a century old. These machines, in excess of 500 units, represent the raison d'être and the challenge for a customer-oriented after-sales organization, which encompasses, amongst others, the most modern valve repair facility. The applications are

1. *Darlington Nuclear Power Plant: a detail of a liquid hydrogen cryogenic unit used in the tritium distillation process.*
2. *Sulzer turbocompressor during factory testing. This process unit is operating in an MTBE facility in Edmonton, Alberta.*
3. *Natural gas refuelling station for a transit bus fleet in Ontario. Sulzer compressors can be seen in the background.*

manifold and cover such diversified activities as industrial gas plants, chemical, refining and mining industries, natural gas distribution, paper and steel mills, sewage treatment and power generation.

Based on this successful business, Sulzer Canada entered the field of natural gas vehicle refuelling as this new market emerged in Canada in the early 1980s. Assembling complete refuelling systems and dispensers, which incorporate Sulzer compressors, Sulzer Canada is now the leading supplier of natural gas vehicle refuelling equipment to the Canadian market. Currently,

3

more than half of the production at Sulzer's Toronto plant is destined for export.

Sulzermedica, as one of the Sulzer product groups, focuses on the development of implantable medical devices and biomaterials for the orthopaedic, cardiovascular and dental-implant markets. Sulzer pacemakers have revolutionized the industry with small, lightweight devices and the company is the world's most fully integrated source of advanced heart-valve technology. Sulzer is a leader in the application of new biomaterials and surface coatings, which help to increase the wear capability and thereby the longevity of implants, giving patients a better quality of life. Serving the orthopaedic community with state-of-the-art products, Sulzer Canada markets reconstructive implants, such as hips, knees, shoulders and elbows.

In the area of marine equipment, since 1960 over 90 per cent of the ships built in Canadian shipyards using low-speed engines have been powered by Sulzer. Its diesel engines are world renowned for their high performance, dependability and fuel efficiency. For example, the company's medium-speed engines are in use in icebreaking duty in the Canadian Arctic. Similar diesel engines are also being utilized in diesel power plants such as Iles de la Madeleine. Other marine equipment includes controllable pitch propellers which allow for optimal maneuverability and efficiency in the propulsion of sophisticated ships. Sulzer is a technical

1

leader for such propellers in naval applications, and Sulzer Canada recently supplied controllable pitch propellers and shaftlines for 12 new highly sophisticated patrol frigates for the Canadian navy.

Sulzer Canada also has a leading market position in the weaving machine industry in Canada. The company offers the textile industry the three major insertion systems, such as projectile weaving machines, rapier weaving machines, and air jet weaving machines, with all types having been installed from coast to coast by Sulzer Canada. Sulzer's air jet technology provides the industry with the fastest and most reliable textile machines in the world. Furthermore, Sulzer Canada offers many complementary services, such as weft insertion tests, weaving trials, economic analysis, comparative cost calculations and installation layouts.

Reflecting Sulzer Canada's emphasis on complete satisfaction, customer support is performed by factory-trained field experts in all the

1. Typical 16ZAV40S Diesel engine for a generating power station producing base load electricity. The Iles de la Madeleine thermal power station has six of these engines.
2., 3., 4. Examples of orthopaedic implants: natural knee (2), hip (3) and shoulder (4).

industries served by the company.

Sulzer Metco is the latest addition to Sulzer's Canadian activities. In 1994, the Sulzer Corporation acquired Metco and integrated it with its Surface Technology group, creating a worldwide organization recognized as the leader in the thermal spray industry. The Sulzer Metco division of Sulzer Canada Inc. serves the thermal spray market across Canada with a wide range of equipment and materials, and local representation in key market areas.

As a scientific and technological leading corporation, coupled with its international character and extensive resources committed to tomorrow, Sulzer Canada has established a set of basic criteria to provide the standards by which the company measures itself, and the framework for future development. These criteria are: to be recognized by its customers as a knowledgeable, leading and future-oriented partner; to be technically excellent; to be profitable; and to be growing with respect to its markets.

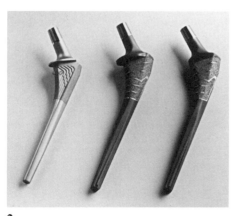

2

3

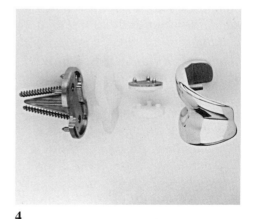

4

The Stewart Group Ltd.

Manufacturing quality products and providing outstanding service, The Stewart Group Ltd. is dedicated to progressive technologies and an unwavering commitment to its customers. Celebrating its 100th anniversary in 1996, the company was founded as a sales consultancy and agency for the textile industry. Early on it acquired manufacturing facilities, and built a tradition of developing new technologies and products in response to international requirements and opportunities.

The Stewart Group began in 1896 when William B. Stewart, the grandfather of the current Chairman and great-grandfather of the Chief Executive Officer, founded Wm. B. Stewart & Sons Ltd. Commencing business as a manufacturer's agent for the Hamilton Cotton Company of Hamilton, Ontario, the elder Stewart was joined by his three sons, Dunlop, Harold and Alan.

Deciding to expand their base of operations, more companies were added to a growing list of manufacturers for whom they could act as sales agents in Canada. In 1940, Wm B. Stewart & Sons became the majority shareholder of one of these firms, Dominion Silk Mills Ltd.

Involved in the conversion of cellophane and other plastic films, Dominion housed the largest film converting facility in Canada. Expanding into new areas, Fabricushon was founded in 1954 to bond latex foam rubber to a variety of fabrics, to produce shoe insoles and carpet undercushion.

By 1974, Wm. B. Stewart & Sons Ltd. and its subsidiaries, having outgrown the original plant in east Toronto, relocated to new premises at its current site in Markham, Ontario, along with a third manufacturing subsidiary, Engineered Yarns of Canada, which was formed at this time.

In 1980 The Stewart Group Ltd. was incorporated as an amalgamation of Wm. B. Stewart and its subsidiaries. In 1989, the company acquired an interest in Engineered Yarns America Inc., with its manufacturing plant located in Fall River, Massachusetts.

On a management level, Ian C. Stewart, the son of Alan Stewart and currently the Group's Chairman, entered the firm as a salesperson in 1946 and became President in 1964. William O. Morris, the grandson of Dunlop Stewart, joined the company in 1983 and became President in 1989 when Ian C. Stewart assumed the Chairmanship.

Today, The Stewart Group is an international business, with associated facilities in Canada, the United States and Italy, including three manufacturing divisions.

The Yarn Coating Division produces "SGL" impregnated fiberglass yarns which are employed as flexible strength members for telephone drop wire and fiber optic cables. Coated yarns are also used in a wide variety of other industrial applications.

In the Pultrusion Division, Glassline™ pultruded composite rods are employed as central strength members for fiber optic cables and many other advanced engineered products. Both Glassline™ and SGL strength members combine the high-performance properties of fiberglass and proprietary polymer formulations to produce a cost-efficient replacement for steel and aramid fiber.

The Fabricushon™ Division is engaged in the coating of a wide variety of fabrics with various foams and other compounds, offering a comprehensive assortment of fabric finishing services for contract seating, transportation, healthcare and other industrial applications. Treatments include fire retardants, water and stain repellants, anti-statics and anti-bacterial applications. Other principal products include the Enviro-Cushion™ line of carpet cushion (made with recycled tire crumb with a biodegradable jute backing), shoe foams and insoles for footwear.

The tradition will continue. The Stewart Group Ltd. acquired ISO 9002 registration in 1994 for the Yarn Coating and Pultrusion Divisions, a clear indication of its capability and commitment to offer ever-improving technologies, products and service to customers around the world.

Some of the head office staff on the occasion of the company's manufacturing facilities receiving their ISO 9002 accreditation.

Sunbeam Corporation (Canada) Limited

From blenders to toasters, bath scales to barbecues, the well-recognized Sunbeam name signifies quality. Built on a heritage of strength, Sunbeam Corporation has established for itself an unsurpassed reputation for a wide range of products and appliances.

Established in Canada in 1920, the Sunbeam Corporation itself traces its first roots to 1893 and its two founders, John K. Stewart and Thomas J. Clark. Involved in the manufacture and selling of a commercial horse clipping machine in Chicago, Illinois, the company was incorporated in 1897 as Chicago Flexible Shaft Company. It products included non-electric sheep shearing machines and hand clippers, along with flexible shafts for other equipment.

In 1910, to offset the seasonal nature of the clipping and shearing lines, the company made a revolutionary departure and entered the electric appliance field with "The Princess" electric iron to "help take the drudgery out of ironing." Its success encouraged the company to add other domestic appliances to its list of products, and thus began the company's foray into electric appliances.

In 1920 the company entered the outdoor products area with the introduction of its Rain King Lawn Sprinkler. That same year, a wholly owned subsidiary opened in Canada with five employees in a 2,000 square foot facility. The growth and success of the Canadian enterprise largely paralleled that of its parent company, with concurrent introduction of many of its new and pioneering products. The following year the name Sunbeam first appeared in national advertising as the company gradually shifted more emphasis to electric appliances.

In 1930 the world was introduced to the famous Sunbeam Mixmaster mixer, followed by the Sunbeam Automatic Toaster in 1935 and the entirely automatic and attractive Sunbeam Coffeemaster Coffee-

1

maker in 1938. Indeed, early Sunbeam products are a litany of today's common household appliances and products, including, among many others, electric blankets, electric frying pans, electric clocks, electric mowers, and electric snow blowers. Reflecting its well-known product label, in 1946 the company officially changed its name to Sunbeam Corporation.

In 1955 a new 225,000 square foot manufacturing and distribution facility in Toronto was completed, employing approximately 550 people. The company's famous slogan, "Built with Integrity — Backed by Service," was adopted in 1965, encapsulating the company's high standards of quality throughout the production of its products.

Today, Sunbeam Corporation (Canada) Limited sits on the northern tier of an overall North American strategy. This strategy includes increasing expenditures for manufacturing in the North American Continent.

1. Some of the many products that Sunbeam offered in 1948.
2. Opened in 1955, this 225,000 square foot manufacturing and distribution facility was the home of Sunbeam Corporation (Canada) Limited until 1995.

Sunbeam (Canada) serves today with totally efficient distribution, sales, marketing and light manufacturing. The Sunbeam, Oster, Counselor Bath Scales and Solaray brands lead the way for countless home use products such as blenders, stand mixers, electric warming blankets, heating pads, bath scales, human and pet hair clippers, temperature gauges and clocks. The outdoor products group includes barbecues, furniture, and other outdoor accessories. Many specialty items are also offered, such as professional hair care products, professional animal shearing equipment, and commercial food preparation equipment.

Reflecting the company's strong Canadian presence and commitment to efficient distribution of quality products, a state-of-the-art automated distribution centre, head office and factory outlet store opened in 1995 in Mississauga, Ontario, with a view to supporting the future growth and successes of the Sunbeam Corporation.

2

Swiss Reinsurance Company Canada

The leading professional reinsurer in Canada, Swiss Reinsurance Company Canada has served its market for more than 40 years as the Canadian arm of the world-wide Swiss Reinsurance Group. From its inception until June 1995 the company was known as Canadian Reinsurance Company. Swiss Re Canada supports many of the country's primary insurers, with participation in products such as property and casualty reinsurance, as well as surety, marine, fidelity and engineered risk covers.

Through the avenue of reinsurance, primary insurance companies are able to spread portions of their portfolio of risk to others, under contracts with reinsurers such as Swiss Re Canada. Just as insurance is the transfer of risk from one party to another, reinsurance is the transfer of risk from the insurer to the reinsurer. This relieves the original insurance company from a burden which may be too heavy at times. This spreading of risk is done under contract with reinsurers through the signing of a treaty or a facultative certificate. A treaty is an agreement to take a specific share in an insurance company's portfolio of risks while the facultative method involves placement on a risk-by-risk basis.

Prior to 1950, this transfer of risk was done primarily outside the country. Based in Zurich, Switzerland and one of the world's largest reinsurers, Swiss Re decided that the time had come to start a Canadian incorporated company. On March 31, 1953, under the leadership of then President Robert F. Clark, Royal Assent was given to a Special Act of Parliament incorporating Canadian Reinsurance Company.

Canadian Re began rather modestly with a staff of two in offices located on Melinda Street in Toronto, Ontario, but soon moved to larger facilities on University Avenue. Expanding operations dictated several other moves to bigger and better locations, and in 1987 Canadian Re moved to its current location on Yorkville Avenue in downtown Toronto, a uniquely open and modern office for employees and clients.

Since the beginning, the company has emphasized care and service for its clients and employees alike; financial strength, service and stability have become the hallmarks of the company's success. Its mission calls for dynamic leadership, aggressively providing solutions to clients' needs. This pursuit is accomplished through traditional and innovative forms of reinsurance and by the unified effort and special skills of the approximately 80 employees located in Toronto, Montreal and Vancouver.

Paul Graham, President and Chief Executive Officer since 1989, has ensured that the company maintains a high degree of corporate citizenship with strong support to the industry and the community through functions such as the annual *Casino Nite* to raise funds for charities; an annual breakfast presentation of the industry's latest statistics with a prominent guest speaker; and the annual *Blood Donor Challenge*.

Although the basic concept has not changed, reinsurance has become very diverse in order to meet the complexity of evolving issues. In response, Swiss Re Canada is continually seeking new solutions for its clients' needs with the long view to maintaining its position as the leading professional reinsurer in Canada.

1. *Paul Graham, President and Chief Executive Officer of Swiss Reinsurance Company Canada.*
2. *The company's new name and logo were introduced in June, 1995.*

1

Swiss Re Canada

2

Telxon Canada Corp, Ltd.

Telxon Canada Corp, Ltd. is the Canadian arm of the world's leading designer, developer, manufacturer, integrator and marketer of wireless and Portable Tele-Transaction Computers (PTCs), networks and systems. Telxon's advanced research focuses on hardware and software solutions for the retail market; industrial applications; warehousing and distribution; logistics and transportation; healthcare; insurance, field service and other mobile workforce applications.

Telxon Corporation was founded as Electronic Laboratories, Inc. in Houston, Texas. Expanding into international markets, in 1969 Telxon established an office in Markham, Ontario. Telxon Canada soon expanded across the country, opening sales and support sites in Montreal in 1974, Vancouver in 1991, and Calgary in 1993. With its head offices remaining in Markham, Telxon Canada now has approximately 65 employees, and is the leading supplier of PTC systems in their fields. Included in its customer base are some of the largest and most successful companies, such as Eatons, Sears, Canadian Tire, Oshawa Group, National Grocers Group, Purolator Courier, Bell Canada and IBM.

In addition to its Canadian subsidiary, Telxon Corporation has operations in Australia, Belgium, France, Germany, Italy, Japan, Spain and the United Kingdom, with additional distributors in Africa, Asia, Europe, Mexico, the Middle East, and South America.

Telxon has concentrated on developing specific technologies to service a variety of strategic market segments. For the retail market, Telxon is a leading provider of in-store, portable automation systems which include shelf price audit, direct store delivery and portable point-of-sale systems. In the industrial arena, Telxon's pioneering applications include PTCs for shipping, receiving, inventory management, work-in-process and quality control and monitoring in logistics and transportation. Telxon integrates its wireless pen-based, and other PTC technologies to automate package tracking, fleet and payload management, inspection, and work order processing. In the healthcare sector, Telxon provides systems for admitting, billing, charting, electronic patient record updating and point-of-care services through its ability to integrate its pen-based computers and wireless communication technology. In the insurance field, Telxon is actively pioneering pen-based com-

puting solutions to audit inspection, property valuation and paperless claims adjusting.

According to A.M. (Tony) Ribeiro, Managing Director of Telxon Canada, a major reason for the company's success in penetrating selected vertical markets is its ability to offer value-added, industry specific services and products to its customers. Ribeiro also states that, "By taking advantage of proprietary technology developed by Telxon internationally, applications and solutions are developed specifically for each Canadian customer, to meet their unique demands."

As Telxon continues to pioneer innovative applications for Portable Tele-Transaction Computer technology and wireless data communication networks, its vision is clear — to meet the ever-changing needs of its markets: both the customers it serves today and those it is prepared to serve in the future.

1. A world leader in wireless computing technology, Telxon's handheld pen-based workstations are pioneering portable solutions for the insurance and healthcare industries.
2. For the retail and industrial markets, Telxon offers a wide range of advanced microcomputer and barcode scanning units.

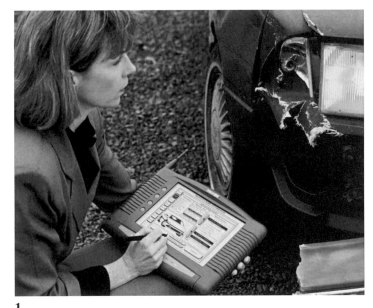

1

2

The Toronto Stock Exchange

Since its founding a few years before Confederation, The Toronto Stock Exchange has been the marketplace where people invest in the future of Canada. Growing with the nation through the years, the Exchange has helped build the Canadian economy by providing a link between people who have savings to invest and companies that need money to expand.

In the early days of the TSE, fewer than two dozen companies were listed for trading, and some days only two or three transactions occurred. Trading took place through a method known as "calling the stocks." Twice each weekday and Saturdays at noon, member brokers sat in a room at the Exchange. After ringing a bell, the TSE's only full-time employee called off the list of stocks in alphabetical order, and recorded matching buy and sell signals. To keep order during trading, members who spoke out of turn could be fined anywhere from 25 cents to five dollars.

More than 130 years later, the TSE still brings together orders to buy and sell stocks. But as Canada's economy has developed, the Exchange has kept pace with dramatic changes in all aspects of trading — from investment products to trading methods to regulations.

Today, the TSE is home to about 1,200 listed companies representing the best of Canadian business. As Canada's leading stock market, the TSE accounts for more than 75 per cent of the value traded on Canadian exchanges, and is the second largest stock exchange in North America. In 1993, the Exchange traded nearly 15 billion shares, worth $147 billion.

Over the years, the Exchange has diversified the financial products it offers. The TSE lists about 35 equity options, enabling investors to profit from and protect themselves against price fluctuations in the underlying stocks. Another extremely popular TSE product is Toronto 35 Index Participation Units (TIPs). TIPs represent an investment in all 35 stocks in the Toronto 35 Index, which includes a cross-section of Canada's largest corporations.

In addition to developing innovative financial products, the Exchange has earned a reputation as a leader in trading technology. In the 1970s, the TSE was the first exchange in the world to develop a computerized system to trade some of its stocks. The TSE is now developing a new fully-automated, remote entry trading system. When the system goes live the Exchange's equity trading floor will close, and traders will enter orders for stock through workstations located in brokerage firm offices. The new equity trading environment will position the TSE to compete successfully in the emerging world of electronic information and trading networks.

The Exchange's technological prowess carries over to areas besides trading. For example, the TSE offers investors a variety of market data in both traditional and computerized formats. Its flagship product, Market-By-Price, shows investors and traders an unprecedented level of detailed, real-time market data.

The TSE also has developed market surveillance workstations that are among the most sophisticated in the world. Using artificial intelligence to suggest a reason for the change, the Intelligent Market Monitor alerts staff to unusual price or volume changes in TSE-listed stocks.

From modest beginnings in the last century, The Toronto Stock Exchange has grown to be a leader among the world's exchanges. The Exchange lists innovative financial products; develops cutting-edge trading systems to enhance efficiency; distributes in-depth market information; and protects investors by regulating the Toronto market. Through a commitment to excellence in all of its services, the TSE has earned its place as the market of choice for the trading of Canadian securities.

1

2

1. *The original Toronto Stock Exchange building at 234 Bay Street was built in 1913 and served as the home for the Exchange until 1934, when it was replaced by another, state-of-the-art facility.*
2. *In 1983 the Exchange moved to its current location at First Canadian Place in Toronto.*

Underwriters' Laboratories of Canada

A safety, certification, testing and standards development organization dedicated entirely to the protection of life and property of Canadians, Underwriters' Laboratories of Canada (ULC) is a not-for-profit organization headquartered in Scarborough, Ontario. With modern and fully equipped testing laboratories, it exists solely for the purpose of investigating devices and materials as to their relation to life, fire or accident hazards, or their value in crime prevention, and to providing authoritative information to inspection authorities.

From 1893 to 1920, Underwriters Laboratories Inc. of the United States had made its testing and inspection services available to manufacturers in Canada who wished to have their products rated, classified or approved. The benefits of that service soon found much utility among the insurance fraternity and the governmental inspection authorities in Canada, which led to the formation of Underwriters' Laboratories of Canada in 1920, operating as an affiliate and under the aegis of Underwriters Laboratories Inc.

The Canadian office was located in Montreal, but no attempt was made at that time to establish testing facilities in Canada because of the limited manufacturing volume involved. All laboratory tests on devices or materials were there-

1

fore conducted in the United States, although an on-site inspection service at Canadian factories was provided.

Following World War II, the volume of test work in Canada grew rapidly. Because of developing differences in standards and agreements between the two countries, difficulties in shipping samples across the border due to customs regulations, and the desire to have a wholly Canadian organization, the need for testing facilities located in Canada was brought to the fore. Therefore, in 1949 Underwriters' Laboratories of Canada as a completely Canadian organization came under the sponsorship, at that time, of the Dominion Board of Insurance Underwriters, whose membership was comprised of leading joint stock fire and casualty insurance companies operating in

Canada.

That same year, steps were initiated to set up a properly equipped and adequately staffed testing facility of its own. The Canadian testing facility officially opened on January 1, 1950, located at 340 Richmond Street West in Toronto, and the first listing cards covering Canadian-made products were published.

Thus, notwithstanding the similarity in names and although their early histories were closely entwined, Underwriters' Laboratories of Canada is a completely separate entity from its counterpart in the United States, Underwriters Laboratories Inc., without any financial or legal connection between the two. However, some technical liaison on matters of mutual interest is maintained.

In order to broaden the acceptance of the ULC label in Canada, a Fire Council was organized in 1952 to assist laboratory staff in properly evaluating the merits of the various products submitted for listing, composed of specially qualified individuals representing federal, provincial,

1. The first testing facilities of Underwriters' Laboratories of Canada were opened in 1950, located at 340 Richmond Street West in Toronto.
2. Construction for new headquarters and laboratories in Scarborough, Ontario began with a formal "Sod Turning Ceremony" on November 3, 1953.
3. A labelling programme for fire department pumpers was established in 1968.

2

3

municipal and insurance inspection authorities from all parts of the country and possessing broad field experience in fire protection and other related safety measures.

Called upon to undertake an ever increasing number of a wide variety of test projects, the need for new facilities became quite clear. In 1953 Underwriters' Laboratories of Canada purchased a four acre site in Scarborough with adequate space for testing and head offices. Opened in 1954, the facilities have since undergone a continual series of expansions and renovations.

ULC was instrumental in the development of the National Standards System which is coordinated by the Standards Council of Canada, and in recognition for its important work in 1973 the organization was accredited by the federal Standards Council of Canada as a Standards Development Organization under the National Standards System of Canada. Subsequent to that time ULC has been accredited as a Certification Organization, a Testing Organization and a Quality Registration Organization by the Standards Council of Canada.

As an accredited Standards Development Organization, ULC provides the secretariat and administrative support for the development of National Standards of Canada in areas related to fire safety, fire protection, burglary protection and flammable liquid storage.

Today, Underwriters' Laboratories of Canada continues to expand in order to maintain and operate its laboratories and certification service for

the examination, testing and classification of devices, construction materials and construction systems to determine their relation to life, fire and property hazards. In addition, it also develops and publishes standards, classifications and specifications for the products and materials. The listings, widely recognized across Canada by federal, provincial and municipal authorities and insurance inspection agencies, are shown in the *ULC List of Equipment and Materials*, published in three volumes: General, Building Materials, and Fire Resistance Ratings.

A completely self-supporting organization, the revenue for its operations are derived from engineering, listing, and labelling fees billed to a wide range of clients and others who submit products for examining, testing and listing, and from the sale of Lists and Standards.

In addition to its Scarborough location, where the majority of the staff and testing are located, Underwriters' Laboratories of Canada also is represented in other locations across Canada, as well as in the United States and 27 other countries around the world.

In order to be capable of undertaking proper testing of products and materials, Underwriters' Laboratories of Canada has assembled an extensive range of varied testing equipment. The laboratory facilities in Scarborough include a building for full scale classification tests on fire extinguishers and fire detection equipment; two 7600 mm tunnel furnaces for establishing the surface burning

characteristics of building materials; a tower room for tests on factory-built chimneys, fireplaces and gas vents; an electrical laboratory; a chemical laboratory; a fully equipped fire service hydraulic laboratory; and full scale facilities for fire testing wall, ceiling, floor and roof assemblies, fire doors, frames, hardware and record protection equipment. In addition, ULC uses facilities at the Canadian Forces Base Borden, Ontario, for the outdoor testing of fire extinguishing equipment.

Underwriters' Laboratories of Canada emphasizes that an important aspect of its work involves the participation of every Canadian in the never-ending crusade against destructive fires by assuring oneself that the ULC label or certification mark appears on fire extinguishers, fire and burglar alarm systems, building materials, and on a wide variety of other devices and materials.

Looking to the future, Underwriters' Laboratories of Canada sees further growth both in the size and scope of its vital work so that the value of its services to federal, provincial and municipal inspection authorities, to the Canadian insurance industry, to the inspection authorities, to the manufacturers, and to the Canadian public in general can continue to increase.

1. *In 1986 ULC commissioned a new floor furnace, the first of its kind in North America.*
2. *The headquarters and testing facilities of Underwriters' Laboratories of Canada today.*

1

2

UNICEF Canada

Improving the plight of children around the world, UNICEF will celebrate its 50th anniversary in 1996. As the organization's Canadian arm, UNICEF Canada has a dual role — heightening the awareness among Canadians of UNICEF's important work with children while rasing funds to support UNICEF efforts in over 130 developing countries.

Founded on December 10, 1946 in the wake of World War II, the United Nations International Children's Emergency Fund (UNICEF) was initially established to provide emergency relief to destitute children in war-ravaged Europe and China. Its mandate was expanded in 1953 to address the needs of the world's most vulnerable children and, in 1965, UNICEF was awarded the Nobel Peace Prize "for the promotion of brotherhood among nations" in recognition of its humanitarian work for children.

More recently, in 1989 UNICEF proposed a World Summit for Children, which was undertaken the following year and co-chaired by Prime Minister Brian Mulroney. In 1991 UNICEF was able to announce that the long-term goal of immunizing 80% of the world's children against six diseases had been achieved; the new target is 90% by the year 2000.

Today, while continuing to meet emergency needs, the principal emphasis of UNICEF has shifted to programs of long-range benefit. Emergency assistance is designed to alleviate the immediate predicament of children and mothers while laying a foundation for long-range rehabilitation operations with lasting impact. Long-term programs include such goals as the eradication of childhood diseases, the ratification and implementation of the United Nations Convention on the Rights of the Child, and programs to meet the basic human needs.

UNICEF initiatives include funding child health programs, water supply and sanitation projects, child nutrition, and community and family-based services for children and education. As an advocate of the world's children, UNICEF works to focus global attention on improving the quality of life and increasing opportunities for children in developing and industrialized countries alike.

Representing the organization in Canada and celebrating its own 40th anniversary in 1995, UNICEF Canada has three objectives: to raise funds for UNICEF's international programs, to promote the needs of children and the work of UNICEF, and to cooperate with other groups to further the goals of UNICEF.

Nationwide, UNICEF Canada boasts of a strong volunteer network of over 40,000 volunteers who donate their time and expertise to UNICEF, including the two million children who "trick-or-treat for UNICEF" and, in 1994 alone, raised more than $3.4 million on Halloween. Voluntary contributions such as these are further augmented by donations from the federal and some provincial governments. Furthermore, UNICEF greeting cards and gifts campaigns are an important revenue generating program, with the proceeds designated for the support of UNICEF projects.

An important aspect of UNICEF Canada's work is education for development. In addition to writing curriculum and educational materials for schools, UNICEF Canada provides volunteer speakers to go to schools and make presentations concerning UNICEF's programs and the situation of children worldwide.

After 50 years of dedicated effort and outstanding achievements, UNICEF's exemplary work is now as important as ever, as it continues to afford the world's children the opportunity to realize fuller, richer and healthier futures.

In 1996 UNICEF celebrates 50 years of dedicated efforts to improve the plight of children around the globe.

University of Toronto

"*May it grow as a tree through the ages.***"** Canada's largest university, and one of the largest in the world, the University of Toronto continues to fulfill the promise implicit in its motto. While maintaining strong roots in a rich tradition, U of T, as the University is commonly known, has flourished remarkably in its 165-year history, keeping pace with the dynamic nation that it has in many ways influenced.

The seeds of this extraordinary growth were planted in 1827 when John Strachan, a leading member of Upper Canada's Anglican elite, obtained a royal charter for Upper Canada's first institution of higher learning, King's College. Six years after the first courses were offered in 1843, the Provincial Government renamed King's College as the University of Toronto and declared it non-denominational.

Once a small cluster of buildings in downtown Toronto, U of T today comprises more than 200 facilities on three campuses, covering 2.5 square kilometres in the Metropolitan Toronto area. Originally providing courses primarily in theology and the liberal arts, the University now offers hundreds of courses and programs embracing almost every aspect of human knowledge and endeavour.

Just as diverse are the 53,000 students and 11,000 faculty and staff of U of T's community. They come from all over Canada and the world, and from a host of ethnic, racial and cultural backgrounds. Indeed, U of T can be seen as a vibrant microcosm of our multicultural society. But the University's international reputation rests on more than size and variety. It is equally a product of the high quality of the University's academic, scholarly and research enterprises.

U of T faculty past and present include author Robertson Davies

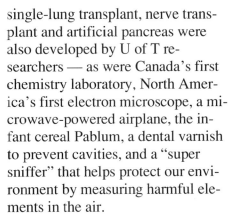

1

and literary critic Northrop Frye, communications guru Marshall McLuhan, and Nobel Prize-winning research scientists Sir Frederick Banting, J.J.R. Macleod and John Polanyi. Former U of T students include Canadian prime ministers and provincial premiers; writers Stephen Leacock, Farley Mowat and Margaret Atwood; actor Donald Sutherland and film director Norman Jewison; media personalities Adrienne Clarkson and Don Harron; musicians Maureen Forrester, Glenn Gould and Lois Marshall; and Roberta Bondar, Canada's first female astronaut.

Many U of T research achievements are as well known as these names — for example, the discoveries of how insulin controls diabetes and the genetic cause for cystic fibrosis. The world's first electronic heart pacemaker, artificial larynx,

2

single-lung transplant, nerve transplant and artificial pancreas were also developed by U of T researchers — as were Canada's first chemistry laboratory, North America's first electron microscope, a microwave-powered airplane, the infant cereal Pablum, a dental varnish to prevent cavities, and a "super sniffer" that helps protect our environment by measuring harmful elements in the air.

Some of the most impressive recent examples of U of T scholarship, such as the *Historical Atlas of Canada* and *Dictionary of Canadian Biography,* are concerned with preserving and promoting Canada's heritage. At the same time, U of T continues to expand its international connections — and impact. Research and training programs in China, forestry projects in Peru, mining ventures in Zimbabwe, education initiatives in Africa, India and Latin America . . . these are only a few of the University's global efforts in economic development, health, technology, trade and urban issues.

Amid these and many other innovations, the University of Toronto's mission remains constant: to continue to serve as an internationally significant research university, and a perennial example of education excellence.

1. *Strachan Hall, the dining room of Trinity College, is named after Bishop John Strachan, who helped found King's College, the forerunner of the University of Toronto.*
2. *The Convocation Procession, 1923. Today, there are more than 53,000 students from across Canada and around the world studying at the University of Toronto.*

Warner-Lambert Canada Inc.

Warner-Lambert Canada Inc. develops, manufactures, markets and distributes a wide range of quality health care and consumer products for the enjoyment, health and well-being of Canadians across the country.

A major international affiliate of the New Jersey based Warner-Lambert Company, Warner-Lambert Canada's innovative and quality products are marketed under four divisions. Adams Brands produces confectionary items such as Trident, Chiclets, Halls, Dentyne and Certs. Razors and blades are recognized under the names of Wilkinson Sword and Schick. Listerine, Lubriderm, Benylin and Sudafed are some of the brand names of the Warner Wellcome Health Care Products Division. Parke-Davis, the pharmaceutical division, is responsible for such drugs as Neurontin, a treatment for epilepsy, and Lopid and Accupril which help address cardiovascular disease.

The earliest roots of today's multi-faceted organization began in 1856 when William R. Warner, a Philadelphia pharmacist, pioneered modern pharmaceutical manufacturing in the United States with a sugar-coated pill to counter the ill taste of the medicinal remedies of the day. The Canadian branch of the Warner Company was inaugurated in 1922 and began with 50 employees in Toronto, Ontario.

In 1881 pharmacist Jordan W. Lambert founded The Lambert Company to market Listerine Antiseptic. In 1955 Warner-Hudnut Incorporated, as the U.S. parent company was then known, made the critical decision to merge with The Lambert Company, forming The Warner-Lambert Pharmaceutical Company.

In 1962 Warner-Lambert obtained the American Chicle Company and its Canadian based opera-

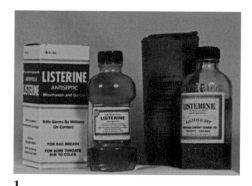

1

tions, Adams Brands Limited. Adams Brands is now the number one gum and confectionery marketer in Canada. In 1970 Warner-Lambert acquired Parke-Davis — a world leader in producing innovative and progressive medical products and supplies.

In 1970 Schick Safety Razor Company was also acquired. 1993 saw the acquisition of Wilkinson Sword shaving products in the United States, Canada and Europe which elevated Warner-Lambert to the world's number two producer of wet-shave products. Warner-Lambert's over-the-counter business was strengthened when it formed separate alliances in 1993 with Wellcome plc and Glaxo Holdings plc.

As a responsible corporate citizen, Warner-Lambert Canada actively initiates and supports efforts concerning the betterment of society and the stewardship of the environment. Working to improve the vitality of the communities in which it is located, the company and its colleagues also sponsor and participate in many local community

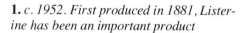

2

events, charitable organizations, educational sponsorships and cultural activities.

Reviewing the many accomplishments achieved throughout the course of Warner-Lambert's notable history, and with a clear vision of the future, the Warner-Lambert Canada Executive Committee concludes, "To be the best — that is the compelling vision of Warner-Lambert... and customers form the cornerstone of all we do. To anticipate their needs, we must demonstrate a restless discontent with the way things are today, constantly pursuing better ways to serve our customers tomorrow, giving us the strength to reach for new opportunity, and enabling us to build a company for the next century of growth and service."

1. *c. 1952. First produced in 1881, Listerine has been an important product throughout the company's history.* **2.** *Old-style packaging for another well-known product, Chiclets chewing gum.* **3.** *Warner-Lambert Canada's head office, located in Scarborough, Ontario.*

3

W.G. McKay Limited
Customs Brokers

1

When he was twenty-six years of age, Winfield George McKay was "Chief Clerk" for the customs brokerage firm of C.W. Irwin in downtown Toronto. Recently passed over for promotion he was about to depart for the customs house when he overheard a senior executive chastising a young lad for attempting to sell raffle tickets at the counter for a charitable cause. Feeling sorry for the boy, he bought a ticket outside on the sidewalk. That ticket, of course, won the prize, a Gray Dort automobile.

The car was presented to him on the steps of what is now the Old City Hall by the mayor of Toronto and Theresa Small, the wife of Ambrose J. Small, the theatre magnate and mysteriously disappeared millionaire, in one of her rare public appearances. W.G. McKay, unable to drive, had his brother James drive the car to the family home. He immediately sold it which provided the needed capital for him to open his own customs brokerage business in 1914.

The new firm was first located at 37 Yonge Street, where it remained until 1924 when it moved to the new (now demolished) Commerce and Transportation Building at Bay and Front Streets. Expansion forced a move to University Avenue in 1977, and again in 1981 to 40 University Avenue, the company's current Head Office address.

W.G. McKay led the company until his death in 1953, but it has continued to flourish under the guidance of his son, Winfield Cleland McKay, the current President. Although Win McKay, as he is best known, did not become President until 1965, he was very involved with the company before his father passed away. His wife Noreen, a Western graduate and former Canadian junior golf champion, works in the accounting department. The third generation, Winfield Laing McKay, chose Queen's for his degree before joining the company in January 1984. He is currently one of three Vice Presidents.

W.C. McKay has also been active in a civic role. In 1968 he was a federal P.C. candidate for Toronto's High Park Riding, finishing a strong second to a Liberal in the Trudeau landslide. From 1972 to 1982 he was a Metropolitan Toronto Police Commissioner, and from 1985 to 1988, an Ontario Police Commission member. He has served as Chairman of the Ontario Chapter of the Young Presidents' Organization and is a past President of the Downtown Kiwanis Club. W.C. McKay still serves on a number of boards and committees, and, in addition, takes particular pride as a champion of heavily taxed automobile drivers in his capacity as a director for many years of the Canadian Automobile Association.

Today, W.G. McKay Limited, which operates ten branch offices across Ontario, deals with customs brokerage, customs and traffic consulting, international freight forwarding, airfreight, pooled freight and containers. The company was among the first to engage in electronic release of goods from customs and the first broker in Canada to effect payment of duties and taxes to the government totally by EDI. Their accounts range from large national Canadian companies to little shops around the corner.

Win McKay points out that it is because of good management and personal attention to its customers that the company has continued to grow. The company "did not outgrow itself, was financed carefully, and only took business it could handle." For eighty years, W.G. McKay Limited has prospered by providing consistent, dependable services to Canadian importers and exporters.

1. *The founder of W.G. McKay Limited, Winfield George McKay, 1888-1953.*
2. *Current President and son of the Founder, Winfield Cleland McKay.*

2

World Wildlife Fund Canada

Canada is losing its wilderness at the alarming rate of over one acre every 15 seconds; the list of endangered animals now numbers 255; and globally, at least three species of wildlife become extinct every day. In response, World Wildlife Fund Canada (WWF), in its more than 25 years of existence, has raised $40 million to support more than 1,000 conservation projects at home and abroad as steps along the road to fulfilling its mission to preserve nature and its ecological processes.

The Canadian organization is one of 28 affiliate organizations of the World Wide Fund for Nature. As the world's largest independent conservation organization with over six million regular supporters, WWF has financed more than 10,000 projects totalling almost $1 billion in 130 countries since its inception in 1961. The international network was founded as World Wildlife Fund when the future for many species and habitats became uncertain. Its mission was to raise money and garner public support for conservation, as defined by the world's leading experts, and its structure was planned around national organizations.

The Canadian branch of World Wildlife Fund was organized in 1967 under the impetus of Senator Alan Macnaughton. A former Speaker of the House of Commons, Macnaughton brought together several

1

Canadian business executives and other prominent Canadians who collectively founded World Wildlife Fund Canada in Montreal. Macnaughton became WWF Canada's first Chairman, and has since dedicated much of his time to WWF activities. To this day, he is actively involved in raising much-needed monies for scientific research and bringing the WWF cause to the forefront of the Canadian public conscience.

Realizing that for WWF to play a significant role an endowment fund should be established, the founding members set out to find Canadian associates in the international network's 1001 Nature Trust, in which 1,001 participants donated $10,000 each. By 1972, when the 1001 Trust's membership was filled, Can-

ada had become the third leading national organization, with 47 members. With endowment funds providing for the operating budget, all raised support could be channelled towards WWF's targeted conservation activities, a principle which continues today.

Growing in scope and public recognition, the Canadian offices were moved to Toronto in 1970. The following year the organization's influential Scientific Advisory Committee was formed. The role of the Committee, composed of leading individuals in their field, has been to analyze incoming research proposals for their scientific merit, thereby also raising the credibility of the WWF in the scientific field.

Throughout the years, World Wildlife Fund Canada has provided, in whole or in part, the financing for a wide range of projects and many activities that have been carried out, often in conjunction with universi-

1. *Senator Alan Macnaughton, a former Speaker of the House of Commons, was instrumental in the formation of the Canadian branch of World Wildlife Fund.*
2. *Walique Lake, Jasper National Park. Through its Endangered Spaces program, WWF works toward the establishment of a network of protected representative wilderness areas across Canada by the year 2000.*
3. *Humpback Whale. WWF's Endangered Species program encompasses WWF's actions in protecting wildlife.*

2

3

ties, government agencies and other groups. During the 1970s, some of the numerous projects included the three year "Polar Bear and Man" investigation, participation on the Committee on the Status of Endangered Wildlife in Canada, raptor conservation research, and studies concerning a wide range of species such as the Atlantic salmon, gyrfalcon, wood bison, Arctic fox, wolves, and the peregrine falcon.

In the early 1980s, the "200 Canadians for Wildlife," a national capital campaign modeled after the earlier international 1001 Nature Trust, was commenced. Highly successful, it too has reached its stated limit and has provided further important endowment funds. These funds have allowed World Wildlife Fund Canada to increase the scale of its conservation activities.

During the early 1980s, along with funding for such species as the mountain caribou, wolves, burrowing owls, Arctic harp seals, polar bears, and the re-introduction of the previously extirpated swift fox to the Canadian prairies, major resources were devoted to the three year "Whales Beneath the Arctic Ice" program.

In 1985, to honour the international organization's 25th anniversary, WWF Canada provided $300,000 for panda conservation in China. Other projects of the mid-80s included a three year project to save significant Carolinian forests in Southern Ontario to protect endangered wildlife and their habitat.

The mid 1980s also marked an important financial plateau. For the first time, in 1984, more than $1,000,000 in funds were raised. This public support, from both individual and corporate donors, has been critical in helping to achieve WWF's conservation goals. The annual revenue has since grown to reach $8 million annually by 1994.

With a philosophy that saving endangered species requires saving the living space they inhabit, World Wildlife Fund Canada launched the Endangered Spaces campaign in 1989. This is one of Canada's most

1

important conservation programs ever. The ambitious goal of the campaign is to ensure that representative portions of all 434 natural regions in Canada are protected as wilderness areas free from industrial activity by the year 2000. All of Canada's federal, provincial and territorial governments have now endorsed the goal of the campaign. Moreover, almost 600,000 Canadians have signed the Canadian Wilderness Charter — the mission statement of the campaign.

WWF seeks to accomplish its mission of the conservation of nature through a three-pronged focus: preserving biological diversity, ensuring the sustainable use of natural resources, and encouraging individuals to reduce the wasteful consumption of the earth's resources.

To this end, WWF Canada's ac-

2

tivities are pursued through four main program areas. The Endangered Species program encompasses WWF's actions in helping to prevent species from ever becoming listed as endangered, as well as fighting to save those which are threatened with extinction. Endangered Spaces has as its goal the establishment of a network of protected representative wilderness areas across Canada by the year 2000. The Wildlife Toxicology program was begun to protect wildlife and ecosystems from harm caused by toxic chemicals. The International Program is predominately aimed at stemming the loss of tropical rainforest, primarily in Latin America. In addition, WWF's education program reaches 200,000 Canadian school children directly with materials designed to build young people's awareness of and active support for conservation.

Measuring its results by the conservation victories it is helping to achieve, World Wildlife Fund Canada can proudly point to a number of successful achievements, including the removal of the white pelican in 1987 and the wood bison in 1988 from the Endangered Species List; the improved status for a number of other species such as the Arctic peregrine falcon and the prairie long-tailed weasel; the creation of a number of new protected areas across Canada; and, internationally, the protection of hundreds of thousands of acres of tropical rainforests in Costa Rica and other parts of Latin American and the establishment of the world's only Jaguar Conservation Area in Belize.

As it looks to the future, World Wildlife Fund Canada can point to these pivotal results as important success stories it helped to achieve. It is precisely such decisive attainments that will ensure WWF's continuing vital role in the conservation of nature, in Canada and around the world.

1. *Monte Hummel, President, WWF Canada.*
2. *WWF measures its success in the improved status of species, such as the peregrine falcon.*

Whitby General Hospital

1

Standing as a beacon for growth in one of Canada's fastest growing communities, Whitby General Hospital recently celebrated its 25th anniversary of providing high quality and compassionate health care to the residents of Whitby, Ontario and surrounding area. Firmly rooted in its community, Whitby General's role has been as an acute care and continuing care hospital; its future, reflecting today's focus on regional planning and cost containment, also includes the realm of rehabilitation services. The Hospital is emerging as a regional centre of excellence for rehabilitation services, ensuring that it will continue as a place of healing for generations to come.

The establishment of Whitby General Hospital began in 1962, when a charter was granted to the Whitby Hospital Association. By 1966, funds had been raised by the community to build the Hospital and architects Craig, Zeidler and Strong began designing the building. Three years later construction was completed on what was hailed as an architectural marvel worldwide, and the first patients were admitted to a modern 97-bed health care facility.

The Whitby General Hospital Auxiliary, formed in 1967, has been instrumental in the growth of the Hospital, raising much needed funds and providing important contact with the community. In 1993 alone, the Auxiliary donated over 20,000 hours of volunteer work and raised a considerable amount of money for patient care equipment.

A community-focused, acute care Hospital, Whitby General provides a wide range of inpatient and outpatient services supported by family practitioners and a range of medical and surgical specialists.

An able Board and a dedicated management group, which includes such persons as Ed Buffet, Past Chairman, Jim Souch, Chairman, Elizabeth Woodbury, Chief Executive Officer, and Dr. Brian Reed, Chief of Staff, have provided important leadership making Whitby General a highly cost-effective facility. Ongoing quality improvement has ensured the highest calibre of patient care. In fact, the Hospital has been nationally recognized in 1995 with a Four Year Accreditation Award With Distinction by the Canadian Council on Health Services Accreditation. "This is national public recognition of the excellence of patient care, management and governance of Whitby General," said Elizabeth Woodbury. "My goal as CEO was to help turn this facility around, and this is acknowledgement that my administration, the Board, physicians, volunteers and staff at Whitby General have all been part of this effort — I'm very pleased with our performance."

In 1993, the Durham Region District Health Council began a regional hospital restructuring project to plan health care services in the Region's six hospitals over the next 15 years. Determining how each hospital can best contribute toward meeting the needs of the region, the Health Council's report, released in early 1995, recommended that Whitby General take on the role of a regional centre of specialization in rehabilitation services. This expansion and enhancement of rehabilitation services will allow many residents who now obtain their services outside the Region to receive them closer to home. The recommendations are testimony to the achievements of the Hospital over its twenty-five years, its value to the community, and its potential for the future.

Having faced many challenges, Whitby General Hospital is poised for what lies ahead. With a new, expanded regional role unfolding, Whitby General looks forward to the future with enthusiasm at playing an ever increasing role in addressing the needs of the community and incorporating and applying new concepts in service delivery.

1. *Elizabeth Woodbury, providing leadership as Chief Executive Officer and President since 1992.*
2. *Whitby General Hospital recently celebrated its 25th anniversary in 1994.*

2

Xerox Canada Ltd.

Its name synonymous with photocopies, Xerox Canada Ltd. is a well established leader in the Canadian document industry. While it still offers the best copiers in the business, its market reach has expanded to also include an innovative array of new digital systems, unique services and broad support for its customers.

Xerox is committed to breaking the barriers that separate paper documents from electronic documents. Providing its customers with unparalleled efficiency, Xerox technology takes information from wherever it resides — on a piece of paper, in a computer, on a desktop — shapes it into new forms, and sends it across the hall or around the world with unsurpassed speed and quality.

The need to produce black-and-white plain paper copies is still a very important part of its business, but the wide spectrum of document management technology Xerox Canada now provides has grown to include digital scanners, workflow management software, fax machines, electronic plotters, workstations, digital colour laser printers and copiers, digital print-on-demand systems, and all the supplies its customers need to run Xerox equipment.

The history of Xerox Canada began in 1953 when Xerox Corporation opened its first Canadian office with 118 employees. The first Xerox Canadian production facility was established in 1967 with the opening of a toner plant in Oakville, Ontario, which was subsequently converted to colour toner production in 1991.

Since 1974, Xerox Canada has competed with other Xerox companies worldwide for global product mandates which create Canadian content for its productions through specialized manufacturing, procurement, research and export activities. The Xerox Research Centre of Can-

1

ada, home to 110 scientists and technologists in Mississauga, Ontario and one of only six Xerox research and development centres around the world, has the world mandate for original and long-range scientific investigation of advanced materials that affect the xerographic process. The worldwide mandate to produce colour toner for Xerox colour printers and copiers is held by the Oakville colour toner plant. Furthermore, the Canadian Manufacturing Centre, a 197,000 square foot facility, also in Mississauga, has the world product mandate to manufacture and export copier document handlers.

Xerox Canada also believes it has a deep responsibility to contribute to the community. Its corporate

1. *Employing 4,300 people across the country, Xerox Canada Ltd. is a leader in both the digital and traditional paper-based document markets.*
2. *The Xerox Research Centre of Canada (XRCC) in Mississauga, Ontario was established in 1974.*

contribution program emphasizes support for "Information Technology Literacy", employee community involvement, and the United Way. In addition, environmental initiatives include Xerox' ambitious waste reduction and energy conservation programs, its cartridge recycling programs, and supplies that are environmentally friendly and free from ozone-depleting chemicals.

Today, Xerox products continue to be distinguished by their hallmarks of quality, dependability, ease of use, and improved productivity. As it draws its strength from past successes, Xerox Canada is facing the future by renewing its ongoing commitment to forging new frontiers in document services.

2

Photo Credits

Chapter 1

1 NAC / C-33320
6 This map is based on information taken from map sheet number SATCAN © Her Majesty the Queen in Right of Canada with permission of Energy, Mines and Resources Canada.
8 NAC / PA-127498
9 From NAC / NMC-131821
10 a. Ontario Ministry of Natural Resources; b. Ontario Ministry of Natural Resources; c. Ontario Ministry of Natural Resources; d. Ontario Ministry of Natural Resources; e. Ontario Ministry of Natural Resources
11 a. Ontario Ministry of Natural Resources; b. Ontario Ministry of Natural Resources; c. Ontario Ministry of Natural Resources; d. Wilhelm Schimdt / Masterfile; e. Janet Foster / Masterfile; f. Gary Black / Masterfile; g. Ontario Ministry of Natural Resources
12 a. After A. Ruger / NAC / C-6557; b. NAC / C-31001
13 a. A. Croke / NAC / C-116871; b. Mary G. Hall / NAC / C-8744; c. W.G.R. Hind / NAC / C-103003; d. William Eagar / NAC / C-13365; e. NAC / C-26597 (detail)
14 a. D. Northall-Laurie / NAC / PA-29181; b. After William H. Bartlett / NAC / C-2400
15 a. NAC / C-10345; b. W.H. Bartlett / NAC / C-2361; c. After James Pattison Cockburn / NAC / C-95618; d. W.S. Hatton / NAC / C-40148; e. Erskine / NAC / C-11209; f. Philip John Bainbrigge / NAC / C-11811
16 a. Edwin Whitefield / NAC / C-46109; b. NAC / C-40810; d. Attr. to Daniel Wilson / NAC / C-40150; e. Ontario Ministry of Natural Resources
17 a. Alfred Ernest Boultbee / NAC / C-46658; b. William Armstrong / NAC / C-40358; c. Philip John Bainbrigge / NAC / C-11883
18 a. NAC / PA-110809; b. NAC / PA-17231; c. A.P. Low / NAC / PA-146680; d. A.P. Low / NAC / PA-146681
19 a. Jenny Russell Simpson / NAC / C-11246; b. Walter Joseph Phillips / NAC / C-110919; c. Walter Joseph Phillips / NAC / C-110923; d. Peter Rindisbacher / NAC / C-1925; e. W.F. Butler / NAC / C-97263; f. NAC / C-8212
20 O'Brien / NAC / C-97667
21 a. Edward Roper / NAC / C-11024; b. NAC / C-58699; c. Walter Joseph Phillips / NAC / C-110922; d. NAC / PA-31772
22 a. NAC / PA-40959; b. Edouard Deville / NAC / PA-62214; c. E.A. Hegg / NAC / C-13384
23 a. E.S. Glover / NAC / C-107375; b. NAC / PA-51347; c. NAC / C-9373
24 a. John Ross / NAC / C-101984; b. Albertype Company / NAC / PA-31683; c. John Mailer / NAC / PA-145355
25 a. Thomas Mitchell / NAC / C-27829; b. NAC / PA-121428; c. NAC / PA-48029; d. George Francis Lyon / NAC / C-1044
26 a. NAC / C-10457; b. George Back / NAC / C-110045; c. Dennis Gale / NAC / C-40180
27 Walter J. Coucill, R.C.A. / NAC / C-113068
28 NAC / PA-48718
29 NAC / PA-84921

Chapter 2

30 Joanna Simpson Wilson / NAC / C-74694
32 a. This map is based on information taken from map sheet number MCR 4001 © 1980. Her majesty the Queen in Right of Canada with permission of Energy, Mines and Resources Canada; c. William George Richardson Hind / NAC / C-33682; d. Richard George Augustus Levinge / NAC / C-30873; e. After Cornelius Krieghoff / NAC / C-13470
33 a. NAC / C-36647; b. NAC / C-38862
34 a. William Armstrong / NAC / C-114501; b. NAC / C-27001
35 a. AO / AO-373; b. NAC / C-36345; c. NAC / C-47435
36 a. NAC / C-113066; b. NAC / C-26182
37 a. Paul Kane / NAC / C-114374; b. George Catlin / NAC / C-119982; c. NAC / PA-44566
38 a. Alfred J. Miller / NAC / C-403; b. 19 NAC / PA-29120; c. Frederick Dally / NAC / C-65097
39 a. Gallo Gallina / NAC / C-33614; b. NAC / PA-11214; c. NAC / C-33512
40 a. B.W. Leeson / NAC / PA-68277; b. Joanna Simpson Wilson / NAC / C-74714
41 a. John Richardson / NAC / C-2263; b. NAC / PA-17946
42 a. NAC / C-1912; b. Richard Harrington / NAC / PA-114701
43 a. Richard Harrington / NAC / PA-129589; b. NAC / C-35376; c. NFB / NAC / C-55253
45 a. Bassot / NAC / C-7694; b. Dennis Gale / NAC / C-40198; c. NAC / C-1959; d. NAC / C-65531; e. NAC / C-3053
46 a. W.W. Wrathall / NAC / PA-95509; b. William George Richardson Hind / NAC / C-33688; c. George Seton / NAC / C-1071
47 a. NAC / C-26043; b. NAC / C-3104; c. Edward S. Curtis / NAC / C-20861
48 NAC / PA-12820
49 NAC / C-3805 & C-3806
50 a. Richard Harrington / NAC / PA-114713; b. NAC / C-37125; c. NAC / POS-855 / with permission of CPC
51 Parks Canada / NF District Office
52 a. Parks Canada / NF District Office; b. NAC / NMC-1867; c. NAC / POS-1759 / with permission of CPC; d. After Carlo Barrera Pezzi / NAC / C-5136
53 NAC / C-3686
54 NAC / C-8856
55 NAC / NMC-84671 / with permission of Maurice Saint-Yves
56 a. NAC / C-17338; b. Walter Baker / NAC / C-11510; c. NAC / C-118314
57 a. Henri Julien / NAC / C-3278; b. NAC / NMC-6322
58 From original in Centre for Newfoundland Studies, Memorial University of Newfoundland
60 NAC / C-114189
61 AO / AO-378
62 Samuel de Champlain / NAC / C-5750
63 NAC / C-36647
64 a. NAC / C-28332; b. After Jan Van Vianen / NAC / C-118401; c. MTRL / T-15468; d. NAC / C-29485
67 a. After W. Décary / NAC / C-7885; b. After Henri Julien / NAC / C-13548

Chapter 3

68 After Claude Étienne Verrier / NAC / C-23082
71 a. After P.L. Morin / NAC / C-6031; b. NAC / NMC-17224

72 © Her Majesty the Queen in Right of Canada with permission of Energy, Mines and Resources Canada.
74 a. Frank Craig / NAC / C-10621; b. After Théophile Hamel / NAC / C-8519; c. NAC / C-6325
75 a. Claude Duflos / NAC / C-89380; b. Arthur E. Elias / NAC / C-29486
76 Paul Caron / NAC / C-18567
77 a. P. Gandon / NAC / C-5066; b. After Louis Philipp Hébert / NAC / C-7183
78 a. NAC / POS-465 / with permission of CPC; b. After John Collier / NAC / C-2061; c. AO / S-18118
79 NAC / C-16833
80 Frederic Remington / NAC / C-747
81 NAC / C-16431
82 a. NAC / C-99251; b. NAC / C-26026; c. Bombléd / NAC / C-7696; d. NAC / C-1854
84 NAC / NMC-24909
86 NAC / POS-430 / with permission of CPC
87 Alf. Sandham / NAC / C-16415
88 a. Confederation Life Association / after Rex Woods / NAC / C-10089; b. NAC / C-19962
89 John Lambert / NAC / C-113669
90 a. NAC / C-17875; b. Cornelius Krieghoff / NAC / C-57
91 H.S. Murrell / NAC / C-122862
92 GOAC / Tom Moore Photography / G. Harlaw White / *Quebec Market Place* / 2388-5
94 NAC / C-34786
95 a. A. Russel / NAC / C-6292; b. NAC / C-8070; c. Sophia Louisa Elliott / NAC / C-3202
96 a. Bohuslav Kroupa / NAC / C-113654; b. After J. Duncan / NAC / C-13343(mid)
97 a. NAC / C-13396; b. Joseph Bouchette Jr. / NAC / C-4356
98 a. John Lambert / NAC / C-113742; b. After Richard Short / NAC / C-354
99 Richard Short / NAC / C-358
100 NAC / C-1090
101 a. Louis Philip Boitard / NAC / C-15594; b. After C. Schuessele / NAC / C-2644
102 a. NAC / C-5197; b. NAC / NMC-228
103 Charles Walter Simpson / NAC / C-13956
104 a. Moses Harris / NAC / C-17598; b. NAC / C-10888
105 a. Capt. John Hamilton / NAC / C-2706; b. J. Gambardella / NAC / C-11070
106 NAC / C-24549
107 NAC / C-16561
108 a. NAC / C-11243; b. AO / S-790; c. W. Hoare / NAC / C-11235; d. Attr. to Joseph Highmore / NAC / C-3916
109 Captain Charles Ince / NAC / C-5907
110 a. Pyle / NAC / C-8991; b. NAC / C-6017
111 a. Hervey Smyth & Frances Swaine / NAC / C-788; b. NAC / C-140387
112 a. R. Caton-Woodville / NAC / C-1086; b. A.H. Hider / NAC / C-21457; c. NAC / C-2834; d. Bombléd / NAC / C-7700
115 a. Thomas Davies / NAC / C-577; b. NAC / C-7224

Chapter 4

116 Hervey Smyth / NAC / C-784
118 a. James Peachey / NAC / C-45559; b. James Peachey / NAC / C-2020
119 NAC / C-140172
120 NAC / NMC-84686; b. Alfred Bobbet / NAC / C-11250
121 a. NAC / C-9418; b. J.S. Meres / NAC / C-2545; c. J.S. Meres / NAC / C-2539
122 Richard Short / NAC / C-4294

123 Lieut. Col. Edward Hicks / NAC / C-11213
124 Richard Short / NAC / C-2482
125 a. NAC / C-31062; b. NAC / POS-660 / with permission of CPC; c. NAC / NMC-88359
126 a. Charles Walter Simpson / NAC / C-13957; b. Charles Randle / NAC / C-277
127 NAC / C-11043
128 a. NAC / C-103612; b. Louis Dulongpré / *Portrait of Joseph Frobisher* / Oil on Canvas / McCord Museum of Canadian History, Montreal / M-393
129 J.R.C. Smyth / NAC / C-1022
130 a. Hudson's Bay Company Archives / Provincial Archives of Manitoba / HBCA 1923/1/3 / N-11374; b. Archives Nationales du Québec, Québec / P600-6 / N-474-20; c. Archives Nationales du Québec, Québec / P600-6 / N-1076-254; d. MTRL / T-16567
132 NAC / C-38989
133 James Peachey / NAC / C-2029
134 Charles Randle / NAC / C-13203
135 a. After Alonzo Chappel / NAC / C-12139; b. NAC / C-21121
137 NAC / C-50087
138 NAC / C-6047
139 a. George Heriot / NAC / C-12744; b. After Wendell Lawson / NAC / C-3493
140 NAC / C-3835
141 a. S.B. Farish / NAC / C-1588; b. George Isham Parkyns / NAC / C-984; c. Le Barbier / NAC / C-7448
142 NAC / C-108129
143 NAC / C-20053
144 Sidney Clark Ells / NAC / C-18665
145 NAC / POS-2521 / with permission of CPC
146 a. Howard M. Pyle / NAC / C-17509; b. NAC / C-17511
147 NAC / C-168
148 a. Robert Petley / NAC / C-115424; b. Mary G. Hall / NAC / C-30959
149 a. NAC / NMC-117639 / By permission of the British Library / K. Top. CXIX.59.2b; b. William Booth / NAC / C-10548; c. W. Booth / NAC / C-40162
150 a. Mabel B. Messer / NAC / C-11230; b. AO / S-2109
151 a. NAC / POS-267 / with permission of CPC; b. J. Ross Robertson Collection / MTRL / T-15717; c. Elizabeth Posthuma Simcoe / NAC / C-20006
152 a. J. Ross Robertson Collection / MTRL / T-15499; b. New York State Parks Commission; c. McIntyre / NAC / C-1529; d. J.E. Laughlin / NAC / C-2481; e. P.J. Bainbrigge / NAC / C-11818
153 P.J. Bainbrigge / NAC / C-11811
154 P.J. Bainbrigge / NAC / C-11878
155 John Hames / NAC / C-24939

Chapter 5

156 GOAC / Tom Moore Photography / Frederick Challener / *The First Legislature of Upper Canada, 1792*
158 NAC / C-44633
159 William Notman / NAC / PA-124296
160 NAC / C-137346
162 a. MTRL / T-30854; b. AO / AO-384; c. AO / S-1072
164 NAC / C-140726
165 a. Sempronius Stretton / NAC / C-14905; b. Elizabeth Frances Hale / NAC / C-40137
166 a. AO / Acc.2624 #8; b. NAC / C-12632
167 NAC / C-2710
168 Sempronius Stretton / NAC / C-18775

169 a. Sepronius Stretton / NAC / C-14818; b. Sepronius Stretton / NAC / C-18826
170 NAC / POS-2879 / with permission of CPC
171 a. Molson Collection / NAC / PA-125228; b. W.H. Bartlett / NAC / C-2349
172 a. NAC / C-11056; b. Daniel Wadsworth / NAC / C-55617
173 a. NAC / PA-116168; b. AO / Acc.11778-4 / S-16944
174 a. Stevens / NAC / C-96612; b. Archives Nationales du Québec, Québec / P600-6 / GH-272-63
175 Rare Book Collection. National Library of Canada / Collection des livres rares. Bibliothèque Nationale du Canada. / NL-18299
176 a. Archives Nationales du Québec, Québec / P600-6 / N-87-0007; b. Samuel William Reynolds / NAC / C-6152
177 a. Burland Lith., Co. / NAC / C-44625; b. NAC / C-83143
178 a. NAC / C-10347; b. After Ralph Stennett / NAC / C-14143
179 J.C. Webster / NAC / C-27421
180 a. William P. Kay / NAC / C-40791; b. Public Archives of Nova Scotia / N-1292
181 a. John Elliott Woolford / NAC / C-3559; b. George Isham Parkyns / NAC / C-982; c. Lieutenant Robert Petley / NAC / C-11208
182 William Eager / NAC / C-21
183 Sir William Beechey / NAC / C-4297
184 William Colbey / NAC / C-40352
185 NAC / NMC-17953
186 a. Ontario Legislative Library; b. NAC / C-102149
188 a. NAC / NMC-6018 / with permission of the Harvard Map Collection, Harvard University; b. J. Ross Robertson Collection / MTRL / T-15268
190 a. After J. Hudson / NAC / C-11222; b. NAC / C-25014; c. Felix O.C. Darley / NAC / C-8982; d. NAC / C-23304; e. MTRL / T-14987
192 MTRL
193 NAC / C-21304
194 a. Henri Julien / NAC / C-3297; b. Anson Dickson / NAC / C-9226; c. Alfred Sandham / NAC / C-93560
195 a. NAC / C-6240; b. NAC / C-140805
196 a. After Thomas Lawrence / NAC / C-1348; b. George Back / NAC / C-15251; c. John Webber / NAC / C-3676
197 NAC / NMC-15652
198 GOAC / Tom Moore Photography / A.H. Heming / *Mackenzie Crossing the Rockies*
200 a. NAC / PA-61873; b. After John Webber / NAC / C-88489; c. NAC / POS-424 / with permission of CPC
201 Gilbert Stuart Newton / NAC / C-8984
202 a. Hudson's Bay Company Archives / Provincial Archives of Manitoba / J.E. Schaflein / HBCA Picture Collection, P-388 / N-11312; b. William James Linton / NAC / C-6615; c. NAC / POS-449 / with permission of CPC
203 a. NAC / C-624; b. Peter Rindisbacher / NAC / C-1937; c. Martin Archer Shee / NAC / C-167; d. H. Jones / NAC / C-1941

Chapter 6

204 Attr. to James Pattison Cockburn / NAC / C-40046
206 NAC / C-41067
207 a. W.P. Kay / NAC / C-17; b. J. Gray / NAC / C-2042; c. John Greeves / NAC / C-122928
208 a. Basil Hall / NAC / C-10000; b. William Robert Best / NAC / C-5578; c. MacKinnon / NAC / C-5795; d. NAC / C-23620; e. Philip Harry / NAC / C-3552; f. Robert Auchmaty Sproule / NAC / C-18887
209 Robert Auchmaty Sproule / NAC / C-16492

210 a. Robert Shore Milnes Bouchette / NAC / C-23387; b. H. Church / NAC / C-45481; c. NAC / C-67365
211 a. James Pattison Cockburn / NAC / C-40346; b. Philip John Bainbrigge / NAC / C-11838; c. After William Henry Bartlett / NAC / C-2384
212 a. AO / Acc. 2579 / S-17696; b. Charles Beauclerk / NAC / C-392
213 NAC / C-138352
214 a. James Pattison Cockburn / NAC / C-12699; b. Henry Byam Martin / NAC / C-115040; c. NAC / C-114547
215 a. James Pattison Cockburn / NAC / C-12649; b. AO / S-657; c. Henry Francis Ainslie / NAC / C-518; d. Attr. to John Elliot Woolford / NAC / C-99574
216 a. L.Z. Tregear / NAC / C-4987; b. William Eagar / NAC / C-13360
217 Public Archives of Nova Scotia / N-7670
218 a. William James Topley / NAC / PA-25465; b. William P. Kay / NAC / C-4060; c. Rare Book Collection. National Library of Canada / Collection des livres rares. Bibliothèque nationale du Canada. / NL-18302
219 a. J. Duncan / NAC / C-13331; b. NAC / C-5414
220 a. Jarvis Hankes / NAC / C-95138; b. NAC / C-115157
221 a. H. Crawford; b. AO / S-2148; c. MTRL / T-31797
222 a. NAC / C-5493; b. AO / AO-68; c. AO / Acc. 264-17; d. AO / S-159; e. AO / S-2123
224 a. MTRL / T-11121; b. AO / S-78; c. AO / S-235
225 a. NAC / C-11322; b. H.H. / NAC / C-17246
226 a. Henry William Pickersgill / NAC / C-4809; b. After T. Phillips / NAC / C-5463; c. Jean-Joseph Girouard / NAC / C-133484; d. NAC / C-108292
227 a. Henri Julien / NAC / C-18294; b. Charles Beauclerk / NAC / C-394
228 a. Charles Beauclerk / NAC / C-395; b. Charles Beauclerk / NAC / C-392
229 a. After Dr. McCallum / NAC / C-161; b. Godfrey Charles Mundy / NAC / C-115855; c. NAC / C-11316
230 a. William Henry Bartlett / NAC / C-40323; b. NAC / C-20976
231 a. AO / S-13289; b. After H.B. / NAC / C-17253
232 a. Sir Thomas Lawrence / NAC / C-5456; b. AO / AO-407
233 NAC / C-140807
234 NAC / C-26743
235 a. Philip John Bainbrigge / NAC / C-11880; b. 73 AO / S-155
238 Brian Romagnoli

Chapter 7

244 Rex Woods / NAC / PA-164727 / with permission of Confederation Life Association
246 a. William James Topley / NAC / PA-25466; b. NAC / C-5961
247 a. NAC / NMC-118145; b. NAC / NMC-26165
248 a. NAC / C-101649; b. H.W. Pickersgill / NAC / C-5655; c. AO / S-2128
249 a. AO / S-167; b. NAC / C-20297
250 a. NAC / C-6737; b. E. Hides / NAC / C-10721
251 MTRL / with permision of the *Globe and Mail*
252 A.C. Mercier / NAC / C-35934
253 a. NAC / C-7399; b. NAC / C-11589
254 a. NAC / POS-33 / with permission of CPC; b. Attr. to A.E. Edmonds / NAC / C-44626
255 a. Amelia Frederica Dyneley / NAC / C-40269
256 a. AO / S-2150; b. Alexander Gaviller / NAC / C-35885; b. C. Williams / NAC / C-13287
257 a. NAC / C-140556; b. William Eagar / NAC / C-13362; c. John H. Walker / NAC / C-117844; d. AO / S-1388; e. NAC / C-8640

258 a. NAC / C-140801; b. John Wilson Bengough / NAC / C-30259
259 a. J. Ross Robertson Collection / MTRL / T-30898; b. NAC / C-140801; c. NAC / C-140800
260 a. AO / S-1622; b. NAC / PA-165997
261 a. Alexander Henderson / NAC / PA-149695; b. NAC / C-46984
262 a. AO / Acc.13281-200; b. NAC / NMC-7043
263 NAC / C-140815
264 J. Ross Robertson Collection / MTRL / T-15382
265 a. James Lockhart / NAC / C-105625; b. NAC / PA-61689; c. NAC / C-4530
266 a. Stephen Pearce / NAC / C-23580; b. Samuel Gurney Cresswell / NAC / C-16105
267 Rare Book Collection. National Library of Canada / Collection des livres rares. Bibliothèque nationale du Canada. / NL-18300
268 a. Sir Henry James Warre / NAC / C-41437; b. P.M. O'Leary / NAC / C-4562
269 a. Edward D. Panter-Downes / NAC / C-9561; b. Savannah / NAC / PA-61930; c. From a photo in the B.C. Provincial Archives / NAC / C-36107
270 Rare Book Collection. National Library of Canada / Collection des livres rares. Bibliothèque nationale du Canada. / NL-18301
271 NAC / C-46672
272 NAC / NMC-22515 / with permission of the Map Society of B.C.
274 a. AO / S-2124; b. George Henry Andrews & C. Williams / NAC / C-13289
275 a. E.J. Palmer / Ralph Greenhill Collection / 20912; b. AO / Acc.6326 / S-8512; c. 58 AO / S-201; d. AO / Acc.9436 / S-15072; e. NAC / C-2162
276 a. William James Topley / NAC / PA-13008; b. NAC / PA-25265; c. Ellisson & Co. / NAC / C-21541
278 a. AO; b. NAC / C-46677
280 a. AO / Acc.1750 / S-264; b. AO / S-227
281 a. AO / AO-363
282 NAC / C-140730
283 Bowron & Cox / NAC / C-9632
284 NAC / C-18737
285 a. NAC / C-21242; c. J. Mullaly / NAC / C-7501; b. 76 NAC / MG24 B115 p59
287 NAC / C-21873
288 AO / Acc.63551 / S-9456

Chapter 8

291 NAC / PA-37487
292 b. W.J. / NAC / C-118610
293 a. NAC / C-140811; b. NAC / C-3892
294 a. J.W. Bengough / NAC / C-4918; b. NAC / C-72110; c. Richard Maynard / NAC / C-9694
295 AO / Acc. 14394-45
296 a. NAC / C-7683; b. Sergt. Grundy / NAC / C-2424
297 a. NAC / C-11789; b. NAC / C-6536
298 a. NAC / PA-27743; b. AO / S-9043
299 a. 17 NAC / C-63487; b. NAC / PA-20506
300 NAC / C-30620
301 a. NAC / PA-127155; b. NAC / PA-30820; c. NAC / C-30143
302 a. AO / S-1338; b. NAC / C-38454
303 City of Toronto Archives / James 342
304 a. F.A. Swaine / NAC / C-3939; b. John Woodruff / NAC / PA-20914
305 a. City of Toronto Archives / James 1151A
306 a. NAC / C-31054; b. NAC / PA-44464
307 a. NAC / C-24059; b. NAC / C-37275; c. Livernois / NAC / C-691
308 a. NAC / C-9062; b. NAC / PA-127561
309 a. NAC / C-36148; b. Kelsy Studio / NAC / C-6908
310 RCAF / NAC / PA-149844
311 a. NAC / PA-139645; b. NAC / PA-35641; c. NAC / C-29461; d. NAC / C-687
312 a. Jac-Guy / NAC / PA-112533; b. NAC / C-31017

313 a. NAC / C-9446; b. NAC / C-32412; c. NAC / C-57365
314 a. Canadian Army Overseas Photo / DND / NAC / PA-143940; b. Canadian Army Overseas Photo / DND / NAC / PA-175773; c. Claude P. Dettloff / NAC / PA-108051; d. George Hunter / NAC / PA-143182
315 Jack Long / NFB / NAC / PA-112908
316 a. NAC / C-18732; b. Paul Tomelin / DND / NAC / PA-128848
317 NAC / C-140178
318 Jack Long / NFB / NAC / C-49481
319 a. John Mailer / NFB / NAC / PA-166282; b. NAC / PA-142920; c. NAC / PA-15867; d. AO / AO-514
320 a. NAC / C-53532; b. NAC / PA-165211
321 a. Don McKague / NAC / PA-117612; b. Dennis Robinson / *Globe & Mail*; c. Arthur Roy / NAC / PA-46989
322 a. Dominion Wide / NAC / PA-147472; b. Alberta Government Photograph / NAC / C-87204; c. Duncan Cameron / NAC / PA-115138
323 Sunday's Photos / NAC / C-87199
324 NAC / PA-168602
325 a. Robert Cooper / NAC / PA-142648; b. NAC / PA-117481; c. NAC / PA-440705
326 c. Albert B. Koene
329 Public Relations / GM of Canada, Oshawa
330 Public Relations / West Edmonton Mall

Chapter 9

338 a. Bob Streeter's Photography
371 Richard Bell
374 a. Sakulensky-Frost Photography
375 a. Sakulensky-Frost Photography; b. Sakulensky-Frost Photography
382 c. Panda Associates Photography and Art Services
383 a. Panda Associates Photography and Art Services
391 b. Gary Gellert; c. Gary Gellert
392 a. Hudson's Bay Company Archives/Provincial Archives of Manitoba
393 c. Hudson's Bay Company Archives/Provincial Archives of Manitoba
419 a. Rancy Bulmer; b. IMS Mount Sinai; c. Rancy Bulmer
452 b. Panda Photography
460 Zehethofer Design/Ajay Photographics
464 a. Eugene Gmitrowicz C.P.P. Photography

***

CPC — Canada Post Corporation
NAC — National Archives of Canada
AO — Archives of Ontario
MTRL — Metropolitan Toronto Reference Library
GOAC — Government of Ontario Art Collection

All reproductions from archival sources are based on originals supplied, with no alterations made on actual images other than cropping as required.

Index